PE
1128
.A2
S37
1986

W9-CFF-945

SELECTED ARTICLES

from

the

WITHDRAWN

Teachers of English to Speakers of Other Languages

1966-1983

WITHDRAWN

Edited by John F. Haskell

GOSHEN COLLEGE LIBRARY
GOSHEN, INDIANA

Copyright © by the
Teachers of English to Speakers of Other Languages
Washington, D.C., U.S.A.

Copying or further publication of the contents of this
work is not permitted without permission of TESOL,
except for limited "fair use" for educational, scholarly and
similar purposes as authorized by the U.S. Copyright
Law, in which case appropriate notice of the source of the
work should be given.

Printed in the United States of America

Library of Congress Catalog No. 86—050889

TESOL Publications Manager, Julia Frank-McNeil
Publications Assistant, Christopher R. Byrne

Printing by Pantagraph Printing, Bloomington, Illinois

DEDICATION

This volume is dedicated to Donna Ilyin who pushed and prodded for this publication long before anyone else; to Lars LaBounty who has worked long and hard in helping to put together this volume both in its original form, the *TESOL Newsletter*, and the present collection; to those past editors of the *TESOL Newsletter* from whose body of effort this volume stems—Harold Allen, Alfred C. Aarons, Richard Light, Ruth Wineberg, and Alice Osman; to Carol LeClair who, in the Central Office, made all their jobs easier; to those Editorial Board and staff members who have over the years contributed to the success of the *TESOL Newsletter*—Charles Blatchford, John and Mary Ann Boyd, Thomas Buckingham, Pat Byrd, Cathy Day, James Davis, Mary Hines, Darlene Larson, Jean McConochie, Richard Allwright, Mary Ann Christison, Irene Dutra, Ronald Eckard, Winifred Falcon, Douglas Flahive, Sergio Gaitan, Roseanne Harrison, Carol Kreidler, Carmen Judith Nine-Curt, Robert Oprandy, Howard Sage, Lise Winer; and last, but not least, Aaron Berman.

INTRODUCTION

This volume is the dream of Donna Ilyin. I have always thought it a good idea too, and have only recently, staring at some 17 volumes of some 75 issues and some 1000 articles, thought differently. It has been an interesting labor, one which puts a reader back in touch with TESOL, its growing joys (not pains) and its personality. From the very first pre-volume I issue, put together in June 1966 by Harold Allen, the newly elected president, and Jim Alatis, soon to be the executive director, one can feel the excitement of individuals coming together to stake their claim on the world. This volume, we hope, reflects that excitement and growth too.

The first set of articles for this volume numbered around 300 items. Ah, if wishes were horses . . ., eh? Slowly, but surely, with much prodding by the TESOL Publications Committee, it has been reduced to around 140 articles (at this writing, anyway). Lars LaBounty of Pantagraph Printing, the company which prints most of the TESOL publications, and I have talked about how to do this volume—how to do it quickly, cheaply and as big (all inclusive) as we could get it. We decided on the present format which would save time and money (no resetting articles), and which would at the same time preserve some of the flavor of what the *TESOL Newsletter* (*TN*) actually has been. Therefore, you will see the articles selected, printed, for the most part, in their original typesetting (and unfortunately this means, with original typos). We did add a word or two to a couple of articles at the author's request. The titles have all been made uniform for this volume and the column arrangements have been redone to fit the pages as much as possible. In the process we hope we made the titles easier to read. We did correct the spelling errors or omissions in a couple of titles. There was, in this regard, the additional problem of the editorial "cuteness" which resulted in titles that could not be deciphered by the casual reader. For example, "Cattle Crossing" by Karen Czarnecki was really about the teaching of road signs in an ESL class—but who would have known by the title? And Larry Cisar's article entitled "Hot Rods" was not about cars, but about the cuisinaire rods used in the Silent Way. "Let's Strip" by Carol Lemelin was not the use of strip poker as a classroom game, nor a new "touchy-feely" natural method of teaching, but simply one more article using Bob Gibson's strip story technique. And there were others, of course. Many an *It Works* column used titles that made little sense by themselves or were missing titles altogether. We have, in the distribution of articles into some 14 categories (sections) and in the introductory remarks to each section, tried to eliminate this vagueness as much as possible.

The choice of which article to select and which to omit was not based entirely on the quality of the writing nor even the value of the content alone. While these were certainly the basic criteria used, articles were sometimes chosen because they filled a gap or otherwise complemented the other choices in the section. The selections included are, we hope, the best available given the limitations of space and the added criteria of up-to-date usefulness. We have not forgotten the articles which were not included. In the introduction to each section many other related articles which have, over the years, appeared in the *TN* are mentioned. A bibliography of *TN* articles has been included at the end of this volume and most articles, from 1966 through 1981 at least, are also available on microfiche through the ERIC system. The ERIC document (ED) numbers are included in the bibliography found in appendix B. (Note that *TN* volumes I through X are included under a single ERIC document number.) Many articles have, over the years, been reprinted in other publications, also.

Some articles, which might otherwise have been included, were left out of this volume for specific reasons. Two articles eliminated because they are reprinted in the *TESOL Leadership Handbook*, as well as elsewhere, are Gina Harvey's excellent article "Establishing Certification in Your State: A Step-by-Step Guide" from an 8/80* issue of the *TN* and the "Statement of Qualifications and Guidelines for the Preparation of Teachers of English to Speakers of Other Languages" first prepared by Albert Marckwardt and revised by William Norris, from the 11-12/70 issue of the *TN*. This latter document is also available in a separate monograph and may be obtained by writing the TESOL Central Office.

There were plenty of other things that filled the *TN* pages. Reports by presidents, reports on conventions and other professional meetings filled much of the space of any given issue. As you look at the *TN* issue by issue in the bibliography at the end of this volume, you will note that some issues were entirely and others almost completely devoted to convention reportage. As the *TN* got older, groups of members within TESOL asked for specific space in the *TN*. The *Affiliate and SIG* (now *Interest Section*) *News* grew out of just this kind of need. While

*Note: Throughout this publication articles mentioned are followed by the month and year of publication, generally in parentheses. These dates are also found at the end of each article or review included in this volume.

most affiliates and Interest Sections today have their own newsletters, the dissemination of information through the *TN* is still widely used. Often, certain types of items occurred with such frequency that columns just naturally formed. The *Standard Bearer* column of the TESOL Professional Standards Committee grew out of the interest in employment concerns and has developed into a forum for TESOL professional concerns. *On Line* grew out of the computer assisted instruction/computer assisted language learning (CAI/CALL) interests before they became an interest section. *It Works* is the most widely copied column in the *TN* and grew out of an idea developed during my editorships of the New York State TESOL affiliate's newsletter, *Idiom*, and Puerto Rico TESOL's newsletter, the *TESOL-Gram*.

When I became the editor of the *TN* in 1975, following my terms as editor of *Idiom* and of the *TESOL-Gram*, I asked Mary Hines, Alice Osman and Darlene Larson to act as readers and evaluators of articles which were being submitted to the *TN*. By June 1977 this group had become formalized as an Editorial Staff and Advisory Board and had been expanded to include Charley Blatchford, Tom Buckingham and Carol LeClair (who had already been a key component in putting out the *TN* for a number of years). By 1978 this group included Jean McConochie and in 1979 Cathy Day was added. John Boyd, Mary Ann Boyd and Pat Byrd were added in 1980 and 1981. I mention these people, not only because what follows in this volume is in large part due to them, but because it is important for the reader to understand the number of people who have been instrumental in putting together such a publication as the *TN*. A look at any issue will tell you the names of just some of the TESOL members who volunteer their time to get those six issues of the *TN* out each year. This volume is dedicated to them.

And certainly the *TN* has changed with each year of its existence. It was seen from the very beginning as a publication which was to serve all TESOL members. Even the first issues, edited by Alfred C. Aarons (volumes I-IV, 1966-1970), contained not only news and reportage, but substantial articles of interest to the teacher and the professional. This practice was carried forward by all the subsequent editors: Richard Light (volumes IV-V, 1970-1971); Ruth Wineberg (volumes VI-VIII, 1972-1975); John Haskell (volumes IX-XVI, 1975-1982); and Alice Osman, the current editor. There has been a hue and cry for many years for a publication devoted to articles for ESL

teachers—"between the news of the *TN* and the research of the *Quarterly*." I believe that the *TESOL Newsletter is* that publication. I think that the *TESOL Newsletter does* bridge the gap, even cover the spectrum, between news and research. With the addition of the topical inserts begun last year under Alice Osman's editorship, it seems to me it has become even more such a publication. It has been, after all, all that the editors and the readers have wanted it to be. I think this volume attests to that fact. This volume reflects the professional and international diversity of our organization. Included in this volume are articles or reviews by authors writing in Kuwait (3), Japan (7), Korea (2), England (10), Scotland (2), Israel (2), Ireland (1), Thailand (1), Puerto Rico (6), Spain (2), Canada (14), Germany (6), China (2), Samoa (1), Saudi Arabia (2), Mexico (2), Italy (1) and Singapore (1). The *TN* has grown and changed and thrived on the demands and needs of the TESOL membership. My guess is that it will do so for a long time to come.

I hope that the selections here offered suit your fancy and your needs. As with any such volume, it has strengths and limitations. It is a fair view of what we have been and what we are. I hope you find your favorite article among those we have included. (If not, tell us. We may do this again.)

This introduction ends with a special thank you to Lars LaBounty, who has been instrumental in getting this volume together; to Elliot Judd, Carol LeClair, Diane Larsen-Freeman and Cathy Day who took the time to read over the manuscripts; and to Michael Tolentino, who edited the bibliography.[2] This volume begins with a poem or part of it by Michael Skupin from a 6/81 issue of the *TN*. It is titled "A Dialogue in Verse Concerning English Teaching." I hope you enjoy it and what follows.

John F. Haskell
Chicago, Illinois
June 1984

[2]Note: Special thanks are also due to my students in the Temple University Japan M.A. in TEFL program in Tokyo and Osaka who used a draft version of this volume this past year—1984-85. In addition to using this book many of them took the time, some anonymously, to rate the articles in this and a companion volume I used which contained a number of TN articles not included here. Thanks to their ratings two additional articles were added to this present version. And so, many thanks to Akira Hagiwara, Philip Kinley, Jeff Cady, Margaret Pine-Otaki, Coleen Bauman, Peter Castagnaro, Cathy and Peter Duppenthaler, Kumiko Kato, Misako Kawaski, Gary Buck, Akiko Kekehata, Richard Monroe, Leonard Lundmark, Randi Donnis, Rich Heimbach, Robert Witmer, Jack Barrow, Peter Grant, Richard Shaepe, Linda Viswat, Naoko Imachi, Joe Geenholtz, Dwight Atkinson, William Black and those many anonymous evaluators.

Tokyo, Japan
May 1985

A DIALOG IN VERSE CONCERNING ENGLISH TEACHING

(an excerpt)

by Michael Skupin
University of Houston

Prof. Malleus accosteth Prof. Forceps

Malleus.

My students writhe and squirm; at times
   they doze.
Beneath the Spartan mask their boredom
   shows.
They doodle, sigh and daydream while I
   sing
Of prepositions, and the joy they bring.
They die a thousand deaths, they say,
   before
The hour's up; they fidget, sleep some
   more.
They curse the clock, and hate the class
   like Hell;
Some file their nails, all strain to hear
   the bell.
I rant, cajole and brandish charts and
   books;
They scowl there sullen-faced with
   martyrs' looks.
Nor clash of rods, projector's blinding
   ray,
Nor chalkboard true commands them as
   they stray.
The choicest fruits of yon ditto machine
I spread t'inflame them, still they sit
   serene.
When old Ulysses to the mast was bound,
At least his ears were teased by Siren
   sound;
But my disciples, like his wax-eared
   crew,
Glide off I know not where and dream
   anew.
While yet my farewell echoes on the
   breeze,
Their books are gathered, and they
   clutch their keys.
And lo! the zombie throng that shuffled
   in
Goes frisking forth to dally, loaf and sin.
I hear a varied babble as they go,
Of heathen tongues; the Bard's they do
   forgo.
Now lordly coaches bear the gang away,
And I bewail another wasted day.
Like Jeremiah now I roam the hall,
Lamenting that I even tried at all.

And yet, as I, distracted, pause to grieve,
I see *your* class, my colleague, will not
   leave.
Still, still they press with questions, still
   they yearn
For words and phrases: they are wild to
   learn.
Behold, Juan leaps and pushes back his
   chair.
His eyes are wide, his hand is in the air.
Stalwart Mohammed scribbles what you
   say,
And Helmut goes not answerless away,
Nor Yakov keen will let you go, until
You bless him, and his ears have had
   their fill.
Like Gideon's squadrons drinking at the
   shore,
They lay their books not down while
   heark'ning more:
Their dictionaries proud are yet to hand.
No TOEFL-terrors fright this doughty
   band.
Reluctantly they part. They warble clear
The new-discovered tongue they're
   learning here.
A Delphi-pilgrim, humble I beseech,
Oh, spurn me not, but teach me how to
   teach!

Forceps.

You rate yourself too low and me too
   high.
You want t'improve your style, and so
   do I.
Let's take a walk; I'll catch a later bus.
We'll have a drink, and then we can
   discuss
The status quo of English as a trade:
The breakthroughs, fads and theories
   that have made
This language-teaching business so in-
   volved.
We'll pick through them until your prob-
   lem's solved.

Malleus.

But soft! I hear a colleague's charges
   roar.
It is no riot; he expounds his lore.

Now see, before a rainbow chart he
   stands.
He opens not his mouth, but waves his
   hands.
He smites the colors with his wand, as
   when
Good Moses struck the rock for thirsty
   men.
Now shrieks and cries of students fill the
   air.
Their brains are puzzled and their hearts
   despair.
The glowering Sphinx now beckons,
   now doth quell
The moans that from their fevered
   throats do swell.
In vain they clamor, still he spurs them
   on,
Breaks silence only when he sees a yawn.
The color-blind, abandoned on the way,
Do pant and squint, but cannot join the
   fray.
Survivors, though, who master every
   hue,
Like Siegfried, full of Fafnir's blood,
   construe
Exotic meanings in the world around:
Some see a striped sweater, they, a
   sound.
Whole volumes writ on neckties, socks
   and skirts,
And mystic runes inscribed on tie-dyed
   shirts;
The sunset's richness and the bower's
   shade
Will keep them well-read when their
   idioms fade.
We leave you, druids, to your language
   bright,
Beyond our reach, but not beyond our
   sight.

Forceps.

In vino veritas, I say. Let's have a beer
And talk about the tricks of our career. □

TN 12/81

SELECTED ARTICLES FROM THE TESOL NEWSLETTER
1966-1983

PART I.   GENERAL INFORMATION

*Names in parentheses are reviewers.

PART II. CLASSROOM PRACTICES

PART I. GENERAL INFORMATION
Section 1. The State of the Art

It seems appropriate to begin a volume devoted primarily to ideas and information for the classroom teacher with a few overviews on the art of teaching ESL. Few could do so better than the late Ruth Crymes who was president of TESOL in 1979. The article which begins this volume is from a speech which Crymes gave at a number of affiliate meetings that year and sets the stage for the changes of which we now find ourselves so much a part. Like everything about Ruth Crymes, her article (8/80) looks forward with a positive statement for the future.

The two articles following it, by Joanna Escobar and Jeffrey Bright (8/79) and by Richard Orem (4/81), directly complement the Crymes article and provide a fairly broad look at current ESL practices. The article by Ramon Santiago (6/82), then president of the National Association of Bilingual Education, is a look at ESL from the other side. His report offers support for and concern about the role of ESL in bilingual education. The article by Richard Light (12/79) is a thought-provoking statement about the art of teaching, a "Note on Teaching English and Making Sense."

There are three book reviews included in this section. They are reviews of volumes which themselves reflect the present state of the art. The volume by Earl Stevick, *Memory, Meaning and Method*, has already become a classic for ESL teacher trainers; H. Douglas Brown's *Principles of Language Learning and Teaching* puts together under a single pen the diversity and dynamism of second language research today in clear and readable terms; and *Viewpoints on English as a Second Language* by Marina Burt, Heidi Dulay and Mary Finocchiaro, is a collection of articles by many of the leaders in the field of ESL teaching and teacher training.

You might also wish to look at articles in other sections of the volume which reflect the present state of the art—in particular, those articles in sections 5 and 9. Cathy Day's article from section 4 on "Career Education"[3] and the "Collective Bargaining" article by Linda Tobash which appears in section 6 will also add to a discussion of where we are today. In section 14, the *On Line* article by David Wyatt "Computer Assisted Instruction Comes of Age" seems to be a statement of things to come.

Other articles which will add to any discussion of the state of the art have appeared in the *TN* in large numbers. From the very beginning, the *TN* seems to have been a forum for introspection, evaluation and prognostication. Its first issue in 1967 included articles on the state of the art of teaching ESL by Harold Allen, Mary Finocchiaro, J. Donald Bowen and Paul Bell. These were followed in successive issues by similar articles by Edward Cervenka and Edward Anthony (1-3/68), Harold Howe III and Paul Bell (5/68), Paul Bell (11/68), Ronald Wardhaugh (2/70), David Harris, Bernard Spolsky and Robert Kaplan (9-12/70), Betty Wallace Robinett (3/74), Mary Galvan (3/75) and Francisco Gomes de Matos (6/82). In February 1976 the *TN* printed statements by many past TESOL presidents on their views of the future of TESOL. Presidents Harold Allen, Mary Finocchiaro, Russell Campbell, Alfonso Ramirez and Betty Wallace Robinett looked at where TESOL had been and where it was going.

In addition the on-going discussion of the appropriateness of ESL as a method of teaching English in bilingual settings began with the first issue of the *TN*. In 1975 and 1976 there was a series of articles which touched directly on this issue beginning with a reprint of an editorial from the *Linguistic Reporter* "ESL is not Appropriate" (6/75). In June 1976 Thomas Buckingham and John Haskell wrote "Is ESL Appropriate?—the Continuing Case of Miscommunication" and this was followed in the 11-12/76 issue by yet another *Linguistic Reporter* editorial, "Warning—ESL (Traditional) May be Hazardous to Children." This was printed, side-by-side, with a response by Robert Kaplan and Bernard Spolsky titled "Warning—CAL [the Center for Applied Linguistics] May be Hazardous to the Profession." You might also find interesting the "Position Paper on the Role of ESL in Bilingual Education" passed by the TESOL Legislative Assembly (9/76). It is to be hoped that we have moved beyond the rhetoric of the 1970's, as reflected in these articles, to a common ground for the 1980's.

In addition to these historical views of our profession, another important article to read is Donna Ilyin's report on the "Limited Legal Victory for Limited Speakers of English" (6/78) which discusses the problems of the limited speaker of English in the U.S. court system. And one cannot overlook the two-part article by James E. Alatis "On Acronyms" (those ubiquitous letters in our profession) which appeared in the 12/75 and 2/76 issues. Part I (2/76) of this article includes Alatis' famous TEFLON acronym—for language that doesn't stick. Part II provides a background on the history and development of the TESOL organization and what it stands for.

A number of issues of the *TN* report on TESOL conventions, from selections of abstracts of convention presentations to reportage. This has been equally true for TESOL Summer Meetings and not occasionally the meetings of other professional organizations. Two such reports of particular interest are Marjorie Morray's report on Henry Widdowson's San Francisco plenary "The Curse of Caliban" (6/80) and the report of the New Mexico Summer Meeting (10/80) which summarizes presentations by Jack Richards, Dennis Preston, Mary Galvan and H. Douglas Brown.

---

[3]Note that titles used in section introductions are often an abbreviated form of the complete title as they appear in the table of contents.

CURRENT TRENDS IN ESL INSTRUCTION

by Ruth Crymes
University of Hawaii

So much is going on these days in ESL instruction that, as a friend of mine once said, it foggles the mind. I am going to try to characterize the current trends in ESL instruction by discussing three anecdotes, three processes, and three instructional tasks. This is, however, no magical incantation. I just happen to have three anecdotes at hand. I have selected three processes to talk about partly because of time constraints and partly because these particular three, at this stage of our knowledge, seem to me to be ones that we can immediately take account of in our instructional tasks. I take the three instructional tasks from pedagogical tradition. All this will clear up, I trust, as I go along.

The anecdotes are actually anecdotal self-reports of second language learners. The first I will summarize. It is the self-report of an American who, in the course of his work, which includes travel to foreign countries, tries to learn enough of the language of each country, before he arrives there, to be understood and to understand what is said if it is said slowly.

Before a trip, his strategy is to spend 40 hours, an hour a day, by himself with a phrase book, studying primarily vocabulary, his aim being to master a basic vocabulary of about 500 words. He concentrates on those words that he will need to use in hotels and restaurants, words like *soap* and *towel* but not words like *closet* and *wall* and *floor*, words like *glass, knife, wine,* and *check,* but not the names of flowers or animals. He does not recommend his word choices to others—he only recommends that each learner make choices in terms of his or her particular communication needs.

He has a particular approach to learning verbs. He learns most of the ones that he learns only in their infinitive form. Of these, he learns to conjugate only six or seven of the most common, and one of these is always the word for *want.* Then he can say "I want to buy . . . ," "I want to order . . . ," "He wants to go . . ." and the only verb he has to conjugate is *want.* I should point out that his examples of languages that he has learned are Romance languages.

After 40 hours of such self-study he hires a foreign student as a tutor and spends a couple of hours a week with the tutor in simple conversation. He doesn't spend time with the tutor on drill. He does that later on his own time. The evening before he leaves on a trip he spends three hours with his tutor speaking only the tutor's language, and often departs for abroad with recom-

mendations for restaurants that are off the tourist track.

He reports considerable success with his method. He uses whatever resources that he has available to him for communication. If he doesn't know how to say something one way he tries another that will get his meaning across. If he doesn't know how to say "I'm finished" he says "Enough" or "No more." (See Tarone 1977 for discussion of conscious communication strategies.) And though he sometimes gets himself into embarrassing situations, that doesn't bother him.

This language learner is Leonard Bernstein. He wrote about his method in an article which appeared in *House Beautiful* in 1974.

You will have noted the strong, integrative motivation, the specificity of the communication goal, the self-drill on the learner's own time and at his own pace, the attention to vocabulary, the deliberate strategy for simplifying the grammar, the willingness to try to use the language.

Let me present the report of the second language learner verbatim. This is what Margaret Mead said in 1964 in a discussion that followed the presentation of a paper at a conference on semiotics (189):

I am not a good mimic and I have worked now in many different cultures. I am a very poor speaker of any language, but I always know whose pig is dead, and when I work in a native society, I know what people are talking about and I treat it seriously and I respect them, and this in itself establishes a great deal more rapport, very often, than the correct accent. I have worked with other field workers who were far, far better linguists than I, and the natives kept on saying they couldn't speak the language, although they said I could! Now, if you had a recording it would be proof positive I couldn't, but nobody knew it! You see, we don't need to teach people to speak like natives, you need to make the other people believe they can, so they can talk to them, and then they learn.

The particular points that I would call attention to here are, first, the way that Margaret Mead perceives successful communication as prior to "learning the language," in one sense of learning a language, and, second, the importance of shared knowledge and experience to the interpretation of meaning.

The last self-report I will also present verbatim. This is a Russian reporting on learning English as a second language. Unlike the first two learners, who report on adult language learning experience, he reports on his classroom experience as a child. He writes as follows:

I learned to read English before I could read Russian. My first English friends were four simple souls in my grammar—Ben, Dan, Sam, and Ned. There used to be a great deal of fuss about their identities and whereabouts—"Who is Ben?" "He is Dan," "Sam is in bed," and so on. Although it all remained rather stiff and patchy (the compiler was handicapped by having to employ —for the initial lessons at least—words of not more than three letters), my imagination somehow managed to obtain the necessary data. Wan-faced, big-limbed, silent nitwits, proud in the possession of certain tools ("Ben has an axe"), they now drift with a slow-motioned slouch across the remotest backdrop of memory; and, akin to the mad alphabet of an optician's chart, the grammar book lettering looms again before me.

The writer is Vladimir Nabokov and the quotation is from his book *Speak Memory* (79-80).

Here I would call your attention to the human propensity, indeed the human craving, to make sense of language as communication, to assume context, to guess what it is if it is lacking. Language is a vehicle for conveying meaning and feelings. Language learners know that. Participants in communicative events interpret the sense of the language being used by drawing on their knowledge of how the language works in communication situations and on their knowledge of the world and their own life experiences. The young Nabokov had skimpy clues, but he had the imagination and the desire to infuse life into the textbook sentences. A bit later he goes on to say:

On later pages longer words appeared; and at the very end of the brown ink-stained volume, a real, sensible story unfolded its adult sentences ("One day Ted said to Ann: Let us—"), the little reader's ultimate triumph and reward. I was thrilled by the thought that someday I might attain such proficiency. The magic has endured, and whenever a grammar book comes my way, I instantly turn to the last page to enjoy a forbidden glimpse of the laborious student's future, of that promised land where words are meant to mean what they mean. (80-81)

I will return to these three language learners as we go along. For now, let me turn to the three processes. These are: first, the natural process of second language acquisition; second, the processes of intervention, whereby a second language learner consciously promotes language acquisition by employing learning strategies, to use Bialystok's distinguishing label (1978:76-80); and, third, the process of interpretation, which participants apply to all communication.

My purpose here is not to review the research on these processes in any detailed or critical way but to characterize the major outlines of our current stances regarding them in order to provide a framework for assessing our instructional tasks. I think the chief current trend in ESL instruction is attention to processes, especially these three.

These three processes are of different types.

Let me turn first to the natural process of second language acquisition. I will devote a disproportionate amount of time to it because it has been the area of most concentrated research in recent years. Second language acquisition is an unconscious process. In recent years, error analysis has contributed to our understanding of the way that it proceeds by approximative stages, called interlanguages, each stage having its own grammar which represents the learner's hypotheses about how the target language works at that particular point in his or her development. In other words, errors, in contrast to mistakes, to use Pit Corder's distinction, are systematic (1967:166-67). But these stages of interlanguage are not sharply divided from each other. One stage merges into the next along an irregular and fluctuating boundary, like the ocean laps at the shore. (See Adjemian 1976.)

Currently, as I have indicated, research into the interlanguages of ESL learners is very active. Many researchers have investigated the order of acquisition of certain morphemes. (See brief history in Krashen 1978.) A few have investigated the order of acquisition of more complex structures (for example, d'Anglejan and Tucker 1975 and Ioup and Kruse 1977). Most of these researchers present evidence for a similar order of acquisition across learners from different first language backgrounds; that is, they argue for a natural order of acquisition.

Most recently, some researchers are arguing that studies of order of acquisition do not reveal how mastery has developed; that is, though these studies may reveal the order of mastery of a form, they do not reveal the process of acquiring that form, a process which involves the association of meaning with form. These researchers are investigating the ways that a second language learner uses a morpheme before mastery of it. It appears that there is system and sense to these pre-mastery uses. The learner uses a morpheme at pre-mastery level in a systematic way to express a meaning he or she feels the need to express, perhaps because of the influence of the first language, and the learner's progress toward the English use of that form follows a chartable path. (See Huebner 1979.)

These studies of second language acquisition have all looked at the acquisition of linguistic competence. It is not clear how the acquisition of the other elements of communicative competence relates to the acquisition of linguistic competence, though of course there must be language intake before linguistic competence can develop and the other elements of communicative competence may encourage intake. Margaret Mead communicated first and let the linguistic competence come later.

What is clear is that we have a great deal to learn about the natural processes of second language acquisition. About all we seem to know for sure is that these are processes of great complexity which are reflected in the developmental and approximative stages of interlanguage. These stages are marked by varying degrees and types of reformulations and simplifications of the target language. Leonard Bernstein's deliberate efforts to simplify the grammar would appear to be a reflex of a natural process.

At this point in our knowledge about the only way that we can take account of these natural processes in our instruction is through our understanding of their general nature and our recognition that these are processes located in the learner. But that *is* one way of taking account of them. It is premature to develop "natural" syllabuses for language instruction as Tarone, Swain, and Fathman (1976) have cautioned.

Researchers are, however, beginning to suggest that we can help learners learn how to consciously intervene in the natural process of second language acquisition. Let me turn now, and briefly, since there hasn't been a great deal of research, to the second kind of process, the processes of intervention—the learning strategies.

It is only fairly recently that researchers have begun to identify and investigate the strategies used by successful second language learners. Rubin (1974: 45-48), for example, identifies such strategies as being a good guesser, having a strong drive to communicate, being uninhibited, practicing, monitoring one's own speech and that of others, attending both to meaning and to form. Leonard Bernstein's method exemplifies a number of these. Certainly he has a strong drive to communicate, is uninhibited, and practices.

We need, as Rubin (48-49) points out, to know more about the nature of these strategies and to find out which ones are helpful for which learners for which learning tasks at which point in their development. We need to understand the many constraints on these strategies having to do with motivation, personality, attitudes, and individual learning styles as well as with opportunity.

The third kind of process, the process of interpretation, is a type of guessing based on conventional clues. It is the kind of problem-solving that we engage in when we use language. Though how we arrive at interpretations of what is being communicated is often out-of-awareness, we know in specific instances what our interpretation is, and we sometimes talk about it or argue about it. It is in the nature of communication that the sense, the import, of what is being communicated is always subject to interpretation, and people differ in their interpretations as well as in their ability to interpret, phenomena we are all familiar with.

Sociolinguists and linguists are identifying the elements that contribute to meaning, and discourse analysts are investigating the ways that these elements interact to provide clues to meaning. There are clues to the propositional meanings—what language says—and to the illocutionary meanings—what language does. Among the clues, in addition to the linguistic structure, there are the explicit ways of linking sentences together, the system of cohesion, which Halliday and Hasan (1976) have explored in great detail for English, and there are the Hymesian components (Hymes 1967) of setting, the relationships between participants, their knowledge and experience, the topics, and so forth.

Think of the task for the second language learner! It is not enough for him or her to attend to linguistic structure alone. Indeed, interpretation of the linguistic structures will sometimes be dependent on perception of their illocutionary meaning which, in turn, may be dependent on interpreting clues located in the non-linguistic context.

What, then, of instruction? It would seem that we should work from the outside in instead of from the inside out, from the world to the sentence, rather than from the sentence to the world.

Traditionally, the methodological tasks of ESL teachers, materials writers, and curriculum developers have been selection, gradation, and presentation. (See, for example, Mackey 1965.)

Selection has been defined as the choice of items to be taught. In the audio-lingual method, for example, these items were linguistic structures and features; i.e., items from the grammatical system, the sound system, and the lexicon. For that particular method, the distinctive criterion for selection of items was evidence of difference between the native and target languages as determined by contrastive analysis.

Gradation is the overall ordering, the sequencing, of those items. Instruction occurs over time, over so many hours in a week and so many weeks in a school term. Gradation is the distribution of the selected items over time. A course syllabus displays a particular gradation. Justifications for particular orderings of linguistic features have appealed to such criteria as moving from easier to harder to learn, linguistically simple to linguistically complex, more to less frequent—contrasts which have not always been reliably measurable.

Presentation is how the textbook or other teaching materials along with the teacher tries to get that which has been selected and ordered across to the learner.

These tasks of selection, gradation, and presentation are still the methodological tasks of ESL teachers, materials writers, and curriculum developers, but we are approaching them very differently from the way we used to.

First, selection. We have come, I think, to general agreement that the domain from which we select that which we teach is not the linguistic system of the target language but the communication needs of the learners. This does not mean that there is not attention to linguistic competency; it means that linguistic competency is viewed as only one of the inter-related elements supporting the learner's communication needs.

Currently, the communication needs of learners are identified along a continuum from specific at one end to global at the other. The specific end is illustrated by some of the work going on in ESP—English for specific purposes—which is at least sometimes marked by attention to the process of interpretation of discourse (cf. Candlin: 1976b:253). That is, it is these processes that are selected for teaching, not linguistic items or speech acts treated as items. The global end is usually discussed in terms of the functional-notional syllabus, which is sometimes perceived as a listing of speech acts with their linguistic manifestations.

It is perhaps natural that English for specific purposes has moved in the direction of attention to discourse and the process of interpretation, since the communication events in which the students will participate are identifiable. In courses with a global purpose, where the communicative events in which students will ultimately participate are not specifically identifiable, there appears to be some tendency to deal with the functions of language as items rather than as processes, a tendency which both Candlin (e.g. 1976b:x-xi) and Coulthard (e.g. 1975:75) have warned against as simply replacing one set of isolates with another, speech acts as items replacing linguistic structures as items. And though of course it is recognized that language functions are realized through discourse, it is not so easy to give attention to the process of interpretation in courses with a more global orientation. The reason, it seems to me, is largely because no shared segment of real world knowledge and experience is automatically there in a more

global course, as it is in ESP, to provide a sustained framework for discourse.

For this reason, part of the task of selection, then, becomes the selection of segments of real world knowledge and experience, which themselves are essential clues to the interpretation of meaning. Remember that Margaret Mead always made it a point to know what people were talking about. She had real world knowledge which she shared with the people she was talking with to assist her in her efforts at communication. And Vladimir Nabokov as a child presumably brought his knowledge of what stories should be to bear on his language textbook and somehow managed to read the textbook sentences as a story with characters, albeit a very thin setting and plot. And although I didn't include it in the summary earlier, Leonard Bernstein also reported on his experience of understanding almost everything that a monk told him, in Italian, about some Italian frescoes. I would suspect that a large part of his understanding came from his knowledge of the subject.

It is not just that language is learned for an end beyond itself. It is these ends beyond language that provide many of the clues that make interpretation, and hence language learning, possible. Selection of the process of interpretation as that which we teach implies selection also of the segments of knowledge and experience that will provide a framework —and a sustained framework—for language use. English for specific purposes has this built in. How can we incorporate it into instruction for other learners?

Segments might be drawn from the subject matter courses of a school curriculum. Or they might consist of stories that create a world that the learners can share—and we need to identify appropriate stories for all age levels. For the adult immigrants the segments might be areas of life like practical economics or practical politics or sociocultural patterns. For children, one is reminded of the Organic Vocabulary that Sylvia Ashton-Warner drew out of Maori children, which helped her identify their common world of feelings and experiences, as she reported in *Teacher*. Anything will do that establishes for the learners a world of shared knowledge experience that has real meaning for them.

What then of gradation? There has not been much attention to gradation in recent professional literature. Perhaps the two overriding points relating to gradation are, first, as far as the communicative aspects are concerned, each syllabus must be developed for its target learners and their particular needs—the question of what the single best sequencing is simply does not arise as it did in the development of linguistic syllabuses; and, second, as far as the linguistic aspects are

concerned, the learners operate on their own timetables, and there are presumably similar processes of mastery and perhaps the same order of mastery for all learners but at individual rates. The existence of a natural process of second language acquisition implies that the learner is the one who does the grading, taking in from the input that which he or she is ready to take in.

For syllabuses, Wilkins (1976:58-69) has suggested an overall cyclic approach to gradation, returning to the same language functions but each time dealing with them in terms of different contexts of situation. He suggests that within each cycle there may be no intrinsic ordering. Candlin (1976b:xi) has suggested what he calls encounter syllabuses, where learners might be given progressive experiences with the Hymesian components in the interpretation of discourse. He has also suggested (1976b: xiii) that grading might be a process of "gradually increasing the questionability of meaning."

Widdowson (1978:91-93), who also argues for the teaching of processes, not items, has suggested grading by establishing meaning first and then moving from simple through complex verbal expression of that meaning. In reading scientific discourse, for example, he would establish meaning through the use of charts and diagrams, first accompanied by simple sentences, and then by discourse, with exercises requiring the learner to draw on the framework of meaning that has been established.

Again, it needs to be emphasized that attention to the process of interpretation of meaning does not mean that attention is not given to speech acts and linguistic features. Indeed, they operate within a discoursal framework. And information about them can certainly be systematized and presented to the learner as appropriate. Such systematization from time to time of portions of the system after the fact of use is probably more meaningful to the learner than it is before the fact of use.

Finally, presentation. Presentation can be roughly divided into two areas. First is the language data that is presented to the learners as input. Second is the procedures for setting up interaction between the learners and the language data to encourage intake and output. The former is the domain of materials and the latter of methods.

In materials, a major issue currently is the use of unsimplified vs. simplified texts, simplified meaning texts prepared specifically for the consumption of a second language learner. In cases where discourse analysts have described the discourse structure of specific communicative events, then we have the information to prepare simplified materials that approximate the real and which provide controlled practice in interpreting the clues to meaning. Where we don't have this information we need to explore how to choose and use unsimplified materials. Controlling the language input requires knowledge of what it is that we are controlling, and if we don't know, we had better err in the direction of exposing the student to too much, rather than to too little data, though of course we need to use judgment and not overwhelm the learner. The use of unsimplified materials is an area that needs a lot of exploration and research.

In methods, we are currently working on ways to bring learners into meaningful contact with the data. Not all our learners will be as highly motivated or uninhibited as Leonard Bernstein. We need to find out more about learning strategies so that we can help the learner help himself or herself. Note that it was in the real world that Margaret Mead and Leonard Bernstein successfully learned second languages, and that although Vladimir Nabokov successfully learned English in the classroom, he had to overcome the impediments that instruction put between him and the language in order to do so. We need to learn how not to interfere with language learning, to use a title from a 1966 paper by Leonard Newmark. We need to learn how to transfer the methods of successful language learners into the classroom.

But I want to reiterate once more that linguistic form—the code—of course needs attention. Let me give one example of how attention to a linguistic feature can be built in to a communication exercise. The example is an adaptation of Dick Via's talk and listen technique which he discusses in his book *English in Three Acts* (1976). It illustrates some of things that I have been talking about.

Let's assume a class of post-adolescent learners who are perhaps at intermediate level. Let's take the overall segment of experience and knowledge to be hobbies and leisure time activities. Let's say that the linguistic feature selected for practice is the use of the articles *a* for first mention, *the* for second mention or shared knowledge, and *one* as a pro-form sometimes for *a* plus noun and sometimes for just a noun.

The example consists of two three-line dialogues with two speakers. Speaker A is given two "first" utterances, Speaker B, two "second" utterances, and Speaker A

two "third" utterances. Each speaker has only his or her own utterances in written read silently and then look up at their partner as they speak.

Speaker A selects one of the "first" utterances. That will determine which one of the "second" utterances that B chooses for a response, which in turn will determine which one of the "third" utterances A chooses.

A. I'd like a book on running. OR
Do you have the latest reference book on antiques?

B. Here's one everyone is reading. OR
Is this the one you mean?

A. Yes. I think that's the one my grandmother told me about.

B. Oh, yes, that's the one they mentioned at the marathon clinic.

Note that B has to understand A to decide whether he must use a definite article in his response. B can also bring real world knowledge to bear. If A has used the utterance about a reference book, it is not likely that it would be a book that "everyone is reading." Note also that there are two forms of request in the first utterance: "I'd like . . ." and "Do you have . . ."; also, that *Yes* is an answer to a question and *Oh, yes* is simply an expression of recognition; also that *talked about* and *mentioned* have different connotations; also, that the reference to "my grandmother" is like talking to oneself. A teacher can talk with the students about these various kinds of meanings and the clues used to interpret them to the depth that seems appropriate for the particular group of students.

The current focus on processes, then, is offering us many insights into the role of instruction in second language learning. I would conclude by pointing out that language instruction, too, is a process. The teacher is a facilitator, and being a facilitator is a very active and demanding role. To be a facilitator requires that the teacher, on the basis of wide professional knowledge and experience, be constantly interpreting the many clues in the learning environment and charting learning activities based on those clues.

REFERENCES

Adjemian, Christian. 1976. On the nature of interlanguage systems. *Language Learning* 26, 2, 297-320.

Ashton-Warner, Sylvia. 1963. *Teacher*. New York, Simon and Schuster.

Bernstein, Leonard. 1974. Visit as a friend—learn their language before you go. *House Beautiful* 116, 3, 123-124.

Bialystok, Ellen. 1978. A theoretical model of second language learning. *Language Learning* 28, 1, 69-83.

Candlin, Christopher. 1976a. Communicative language teaching and the debt to pragmatics. In *Semantics Theory and application*, ed. Clea Rameh, Georgetown Roundtable on Languages and Linguistics. Washington, D. C., Georgetown University. Pp. 237-256.

Candlin, Christopher. 1976b. Preface. In *An introduction to discourse analysis*, by Malcolm Coulthard. London, Longman.

Corder, Pit. 1967. The significance of learner's errors. *International Review of Applied Linguistics 5*, 4, 161-170.

Coulthard, Malcolm. 1975. Discourse analysis in English—a short review of the literature. *Language Teaching and Linguistics Abstracts 8*, 2, 73-89.

d'Anglejan, Alison and G. Richard Tucker. 1975. The acquisition of complex English structures by adult learners. *Language Learning 25*, 2, 281-293.

Halliday, M. A. K. and Ruqaiya Hasan. 1976. *Cohesion in English*. London, Longman.

Huebner, Thom. 1979. Order-of-acquisition vs. dynamic paradigm: A comparison of method in interlanguage research. *TESOL Quarterly 13*, 1, 21-28.

Hymes, Dell. 1967. Models of the interaction of language and social setting. *The Journal of Social Issues 23*, 12, 8-28.

Ioup, Georgette and Anna Kruse. 1977. Interference versus structural complexity as a predictor of second language relative clause acquisition. *Proceedings of the Los Angeles Second Language Research Forum*, ed. Carol Alice Henning, UCLA, 48-60.

Krashen, Stephen. 1978. The monitor model for second-language acquisition. In *Second-language acquisition and foreign language teaching*, ed. Rosario C. Gingras, Arlington, Va. Center for Applied Linguistics. Pp. 1-26.

Mackey, William Francis. 1965. *Language teaching analysis*. London: Longmans, Green and Co.

Mead, Margaret. 1964. Discussion session on language teaching. In *Approaches to semiotics*, ed. Thomas A. Sebeok, Alfred S. Hayes, and Mary Catherine Bateson. The Hague, Mouton.

Nabokov, Vladimir. 1966. *Speak memory*, rev. ed. New York, G. P. Putnam's Sons.

Newmark, Leonard. 1966. How not to interfere with language learning. In *Language learning: The individual and the process*, ed. Edward W. Najam. Part II, *International Journal of American Linguistics 32*, 1, Publication 40.

Rubin, Joan. 1975. What the 'good language learner' can teach us. *TESOL Quarterly 9*, 1, 41-51.

Tarone, Elaine. 1977. Conscious communication strategies in interlanguage: A progress report. In *On TESOL 77* ed. H. Douglas Brown *et al.* Washington, D. C., TESOL. Pp. 194-203.

Tarone, Elaine, Merrill Swain, and Ann Fathman. 1976. Some limitations to classroom applications of current second language research. *TESOL Quarterly 10*, 1, 19-32.

Via, Richard A. 1976. *English in three acts*. Honolulu: The University Press of Hawaii.

Widdowson, Henry G. 1978. *Teaching language as communication*. London: Oxford University Press.

Wilkins, D. A. 1976. *Notional syllabuses*. London: Oxford University Press.

TN 8/80

Editor's note: Ruth Crymes presented this paper at Indiana TESOL's 1st Convention in October, just before her death on a trip to Mexico, October 31st, 1979.

CURRENT TRENDS IN ESL MATERIALS AND METHODOLOGIES: WHERE WE ARE AND WHERE WE ARE HEADED

Joanna Escobar and
Jeffrey P. Bright
Statewide ESL/Adult Education
Service Center-Illinois

It is 1979. What is the place of English as a second language instruction in American Education today? What niche does ESL occupy in bilingual education since Title VII was funded fourteen years ago? What is the nature of ESL after thirteen years of funding under the Federal Adult Education Act? How are the developments in bilingual vocational education influencing what ESL is today? Most importantly, what makes teaching English as a Second Language unique from teaching English per se or teaching life-skills or teaching other foreign languages?

Introduction

ESL has gained a place as an essential element of educational programs of all levels, serving hundreds of thousands of children, youth and adults who want or need to learn English in addition to their native languages. Four major types of programs incorporate instruction in English as a second language as a vital component:

—Academic programs, in bilingual education in elementary and secondary schools (K-12) and in colleges and universities;

—Pre-academic programs, in special institutes for foreign university students and in adult basic education/high school equivalency programs;

—General purpose programs (non-academic), in community centers, churches, community colleges, business and industry and child-care facilities; and

—Special purpose programs (i.e. vocational training) in high schools, technical institutions, junior colleges, industry, labor unions and community centers.

English as a Second Language has a place in these programs because it meets special human needs in a unique way. The characteristic features of ESL instruction are employed with an immense variety of language content. Of course, one goal of ESL is to teach the significant features of the English language, i.e. English sounds, words and arrangements of words in sentences. However, modern ESL instruction is much more than the study of the parts of the language. Language study must be subordinated to the instruction in the uses of English in its socio-cultural context. The skills of reading, writing, listening and speaking must be practiced in realistic situations, with appropriate body language, using culturally-acceptable messages and for specified communication functions.

Furthermore, the English of ESL is language *about something*. The language content may be the problem of mass transportation, the vocabulary of objects of the classroom, the difficulties of finding a good doctor, the ins and outs of asking someone out on a date, or the proof of a geometric theorem or any other real-life communication. Thus, the goal of ESL is to help form competent learners, consumers, workers and society members.

We have organized our discussion of recent trends in ESL around two general areas which continue to be of greatest interest and concern to most classroom teachers. The first of these two categories is materials, that is *what* is selected for study. The second is methodology or *how* what is selected is presented. We recognize that these categories are simplifications. We recognize too that they are not mutually exclusive and that some overlap is inevitable. Nevertheless, we believe these two distinctions are justifiable and provide a useful framework for viewing those trends which are and will be affecting what happens in our ESL classes everyday.

Materials

1. *The Notional/Functional Syllabus.* Probably the major influence on materials today is the development of the Notional/Functional syllabus. The essence of this concept is the priority assigned to the semantic content. The aim is to predict what types of meaning in what precise contexts the learner will need to communicate. The ultimate objective being that learners will know not only *how* to express different meanings (i.e. grammatically) but *when* and *where* such meanings are appropriate. The development of materials is inextricably tied to learner needs arising from identified precise communication contexts.

Perhaps the concept is best viewed in contrast to the dominant influence upon ESL materials for the past twenty-five years, the structural syllabus. Let's look at how a typical structural syllabus is developed. Materials are based upon a linguistically ordered series of sentence patterns in which all of the teaching points are defined in grammatical terms and each new point follows logically from the one before. The major question for the materials developer is the linguistic selection and gradation of structural items. This selection and gradation is the same regardless of learner groups or learning situations. More than three-quarters of the ESL materials presently available are structurally developed.

Now let's look at a materials developer working on a notional/functional syllabus. First, the writer must decide specifically who is the target learner. Once this is determined at least six additional questions must be answered:

1. What *topics* will the learner need to discuss: entertainment and free time, life at home, personal identification?

2. What acts of *communication* will be encountered: information seeking, socializing, expressing emotion?

3. What *roles* will the learner have to play: student, spouse, employee?

4. What *concepts* will the learner require: temporal, spatial, evaluative?

5. What *setting* will affect learner use of the language: classroom, office, factory?

6. What *linguistic activities* will the learner engage in: listening, speaking, reading, writing?

Only when these questions are answered can materials be developed.

It is important to note that developers of structural materials have, on the whole, not found it necessary to define the target learner group except in terms of rather general factors—age, mother tongue, previous educational background. Thus, organized as they are "internally" in terms of abstract linguistic/grammatical logic most structure based materials tend to be much the same.

Notional/functional materials, on the other hand, deriving their learning units from the contextual use of language, must define the learners group in very special detail. Who the intended students are and in what precise circumstances their English will be used are basic considerations. It follows then that notional/functional syllabuses will differ markedly one from another, designed as they are to serve different groups, with different needs resulting in different selections from the language code.

Perhaps the most substantial effort at implementation of the N-F approach has been *Systems Development in Adult Language Learning* by J. Van Eck in 1976. Two additional discussions of this approach are available, *Notional Syllabuses* by D. A. Wilkins and *Teaching Language as Communication* by H. G. Widdowson.

2. *English for Special Purposes.* In a way, the second trend we want to look at may be considered an extension of the above. English for Special Purposes has had a major effect on ESL materials. Of all the trends we will discuss in this article, ESP has resulted in the greatest number of actual texts available for classroom use. Acquiring a total language system is a long term process. However, it is often not necessary to have control of the total language in order to function within a specific context. The language of science and technology, business and industry has distinctive features. These features can be identified, isolated and taught without the need for the learner to master the complete language. Such language learning materials do not take mastery of the language as their goal. They will not equip the learner to function in any context, although they will certainly contribute to the ultimate achievement of both goals. What ESP materials will do is give the learner the language competencies needed to function within the rather narrow limits of a specialized field such as accounting, engineering, banking, welding or firefighting.

Within a special field, materials will emphasize vocabulary structures and whatever language performance modes are principally needed to perform the specific skill. Materials for waiters and pilots, for example, might emphasize reading.

Within the broad area of ESP three major subgroupings emerge. The first, English for Science and Technology or EST has by far the largest corpus of materials available. EST materials for chemists, biologists, doctors, dentists, nurses, even for petroleum engineers, abound. The second large subgroup is English for Business. Available are special second language materials for training secretaries, bookkeepers, accountants, bankers and travel agents. Lastly, the subgroup which has the least availability of materials, but the greatest probability of future growth, vocational ESL or VESL. There are some few syllabuses developed, most not commercially available, coming as they do from special non-commercial educational projects. Among the existing titles are *ESL/Machine Tool Operation, ESL/Maid Service Training, ESL/Custodial Assistant* and *ESL/Automotive Mechanic.* All were developed by Gateway Technical Institute, Kenosha, Wisconsin, in cooperation with the Wisconsin Board of Vocational, Technical and Adult Education. Modules for a prototype *Food Services-Syllabus* have been developed by the Center for Applied Linguistics, Arlington, Virginia. It is expected that these materials will soon be commercially available.

3. *Competency-Based ESL.* Competency based education is the third area having impact on our materials. Alternately referred to as life-coping or performance skills, the original impact was in adult education. Since then the influence has widened. Functional competency has become a factor across all of education. CBE materials are organized around content and skill areas. The content areas usually include consumer affairs, health, government and law, occupational knowledge and community resources. The skill areas are listening, speaking, reading, writing, computation, problem solving and interpersonal relations.

In CB-ESL materials language per se is secondary to the successful completion of life-relevant competencies. Thus, what language forms you use are not critical as long as the desired result is accomplished. For example, you must be able to explain why you went through that red light to the policeman who has just stopped you. So long as you are able to do this, correct language form is *not* the *measure of success.* Language acquisition is not neglected, merely relegated to a less critical place.

CBE materials are based on the premise that the end of learning is performance, is measureable and that successful learning is directly related to the individual's ability to function in society at large.

Thus each learning unit in a CB-ESL module includes stated measureable performance objectives, pre-assessment of learner competencies in content and skill areas, alternate teaching/learning resources and strategies and post-assessment stated in terms of performance objectives.

Examples of CB-ESL materials are *Label (Library of Adult Basic Education LAPS)*, developed under a grant for the United States Office of Education, Department of Health, Education and Welfare by Mary Mulvey, Adult Education Department, Providence Public Schools, Providence, Rhode Island, published by PAR Incorporated and *English for Living*, the State University of New York (SUNY), Albany, New York.

4. *Exposure to Uncontrolled Language.* Finally, a trend which has been growing in importance for the last ten years has been strengthened by the advent of N/F syllabuses and CB-ESL. In the ESL class, use of materials specially written for limited English speakers continues. However, there is greatly increased use of a variety of materials produced for and by native speakers of English. More and more, newspapers, magazines, films, video tapes intended for the native speaker are finding their way into the ESL classroom. This trend, the most widespread and exciting we

have yet looked at, is also perhaps the one which makes the greatest demands upon the training and competency of the ESL teacher.

Methodologies

Accompanying these trends in ESL curriculum materials are developments (in various stages of completion) in the methodologies of English as a Second Language. In the first place, ESL is eclectic methodology. Having encountered such a variety of learners and learning styles, all competent ESL teachers know that no single method of teaching—such as audio-lingual or grammar-translation—is adequate for real-life teaching and learning to take place. In addition to this experientially-based eclecticism in ESL teaching, there are certain new directions in methodology which could be linked to trends both new and old in humanistic psychology, communication and the rest of education.

Two major methodological currents are discernable:

1. *Active student participation and group dynamics.* Any ESL teacher must provide students with samplings of natural language, rules and hints about the language, adequate practice and feedback on their performance. But the teacher must also maximize the opportunity that students have to actively utilize their English. No longer does it suffice that students sit and learn. Language learning demands active involvement by the learner. ESL is no exception to this trend. Certain activities (such as games, puzzles, contests, role plays and dramatizations) and classroom procedures (such as individualization) have been incorporated into modern ESL instruction at all levels and for all ages to facilitate greater individual student participation and more efficient learning.

Furthermore, more and more ESL teachers manipulate the classroom setting itself in order to take advantage of the dynamics of group interaction in the class. The teacher who can arrange for small groups of students to work together for part of the class time without teacher supervision possesses a basic classroom management skill (and a necessary one for multilevel classes!). That teacher also has the ability to create a classroom climate conducive to greater cooperation among students and subsequently, greater learning. It has been found, for example, that peer-correction of student errors is often more effective than teacher correction. Moreover, group interaction, such as that which goes on during simulation gaming and role plays in the classroom, fosters the transfer of skills practiced in class to situations outside the ESL classroom.

2. *Going deeper, and the whole learner.* Critics of traditional ESL (and education in general) have pointed out that most school teaching and learning is ineffective because it only deals with the "surface." Even the most "active" classroom activity involves the student's ears, eyes, vocal apparatus, hands and little else. This realization has prompted a second major trend in ESL, to the end that teaching be more affective and that learning occupy a significant place in the psychology of the learner than before. Some questions and answers along these lines are:

—What about involving the student's whole body? Students act out commands such as "Walk to the door and pretend that you are locked in," in the Total Physical Response method. Vocational ESL includes basic hands-on contact with the tools of trade to be acquired.

—What about the student's goals, hopes and values? Values clarification techniques have become a part of many ESL classes in secondary and adult education. Personal subjects of conversation are encouraged in the late Charles Curran's Community Language Learning mode. Simulation gaming demands learner decisions on questions of right and wrong, better and worse.

—What about the student's insecurity? Community Language Learning seeks to guide the student from "infancy" to "adulthood" in his "new language

self." Tutorial approaches to composition in ESL are based on student-initiated lists of topics to write about.

—What about the student's subconscious resistance? The power of suggestion and a relaxed atmosphere assist the student in the Suggestopedia method.

—What about the student's self-concept? Students in Silent Way lessons feel that they have learned something through their own power.

The popularity of these specialized methods for teaching ESL demonstrates a broad, general trend: the concern for the student as a person with emotions, thoughts, problems and potentialities. The "whole learner" methodology, most clearly articulated by Earl W. Stevick of the Foreign Service Institute, has become manifest in changes in classroom climate, where the ESL teacher's role has become more and more like that of a facilitator, helper or counselor. Depending on the classroom, students are encouraged (allowed in some cases) to select the topic and content of discussion, the actual sentences of drills and dialogs, the type of activity they want to use to practice the lesson content, the seating arrangement or whether the teacher should provide a model or correct the student's utterances. Indeed, the teacher is in the position of being a learner in every classroom at some time or another. This realization has been increasingly translated into classroom practice.

These major trends in ESL method-

ologies have occasionally been accompanied by specifically developed materials. For example, for use with a Counseling-Learning approach, David Blot and Phyllis Berman Sher have written *Getting Into It . . . An Unfinished Book,* a collection of passages focusing on the typical feelings and situations encountered by adult immigrants learning ESL. The increase in publication of games, simulations and audio-visuals bears further witness to certain trends in methods. However, the new ways of teaching do not necessarily demand new materials. Suggestopedia, for instance, can use existing curriculum materials (dialogs, drills, readings, vocabulary-lists) in its unique method. Indeed, the introduction of materials for native speakers and specially written competency-based curricula in ESL has had, in and of itself, a profound effect on methodology.

Summary

The developments in ESL that we have outlined here demonstrate the vitality that exists in the field of ESL today. The interplay of methods and materials, the interaction between students and teacher, the incorporation of life and language study and the relations between teaching and learning: all of these elements of instruction for the limited English speaking are complex and pose a challenge to practitioners. By the evidence of the growth of these trends, teachers *are* attempting to meet this challenge.

TN 8/79

ENTERING THE 80'S — SOME PROFESSIONAL PERSPECTIVES

by Richard Orem
Northern Illinois University

What is the future of language teaching, teacher-training, and the status of the profession in the eyes of the public at large? I'd like to touch upon several issues with the purpose not of making any rash predictions about where we might be in 1990, but to at least pique your interest and concern about where you may be as an individual within the profession and to encourage you to think of where the professional organization serving your interests should be going in the next decade. You may or may not agree with my assertions, conclusions, descriptions, or predictions, but perhaps they can serve as a starting point for future discussion.

TEACHING THE LANGUAGE LEARNER

Perhaps there is no other area of interest equal to this first one—teaching the language learner—to the profession at large. After all, isn't our business that

of teaching, and aren't our students those who are learning English as a second language? The literature is filled with research concerned with improving the instruction of the limited English speaker.

The 1970's witnessed a great surge in concern for teaching methodology and innovations in the development of classroom materials, consumable and nonconsumable. We were deluged with acronyms—ALM, CLL, ABE, ESL, EST, EAP, VESL, CBE, CBTE, CAI, LEA, NABE, LEP, SIG, APL, ESEA, BESC, etc. Perhaps we can characterize the '70's as the decade of the acronym (DOTA).

Behaviorism was thrashed about, but not completely discarded, and cognitivism and humanism became everyone's favorite schools of psychology. The developments in teaching methodology in the 70's have been referred to as the "gentle revolution" by at least one

teacher trainer for several reasons: we have moved from a basically teacher-centered mode to a more student-centered mode—from a mechanistic view of the language learner to a more organismic view—from a notion of the teacher as responsible for all learning, to a notion that the student should assume that responsibility. These changes can indeed identify the 70's as a period of "revolution." Seen in the larger political-cultural context, the decade of the 70's was a period of great instability and flux in this country, in education in general and in language education in particular. The elimination of foreign language requirements in colleges and universities resulted in serious reductions in language education in the public schools. The cry for "accountability" of teacher and student has not left the language teacher and language learner unscathed. Vestiges of behaviorist thinking can be seen in the movement toward competency-based education and teacher training, behavioral objectives, and minimum performance levels. The key to these trends has been "accountability." These trends are bound to continue into the 80's although there has been a noticeable disenchantment with several of these trends in the past few years. Tighter budgets, smaller enrollments at the elementary and secondary levels, and an older, more highly paid teaching force will all put pressures on the system to provide more and faster results. We are a results-oriented society. The ends often justify the means. Materials will become more expensive with increased production costs. Teachers will be expected to spend more of their own time on materials development. Yet, as Joan Morley pointed out at the 1979 TESOL Convention in Boston, very few currently employed ESL teachers, only 30%, have had any training at all in ESL, and very few who have received training have received it in the area of materials development. The bulk of teachers entering the field, therefore, will continue to depend for the most part on commercial materials which will only accelerate the rush of publishers to invest resources in this area and encourage innovation on a nation-wide scale.

I hope I haven't painted too bleak a picture at this point. Let me reveal what I see as some promising positive trends in methodology and materials development for the 80's. The trend toward more humanistic education will undoubtedly gather momentum in the 80's led by educators who will have enough courage to defy the back-to-basics mentality of the late 70's. We are witnessing this humanistic trend in materials development with increasing focus on the learner's communication needs, as identified by the learner, not solely by textbook writers. We are beginning to see a growing awareness of the problem of illiteracy among our adolescent and adult population, both native English and non-native English speaking. Our country has failed in any attempt to this day to reverse the trend toward a more and more illiterate society. The pressure placed on our public school systems by growing numbers of illiterate and even preliterate refugee populations is more than simply an educational problem. It is also a political, social and economic problem.

To slow this trend toward illiteracy we must look to methodologies which can be better suited for these new student populations. Audiolingual methodology was fine for a basically well educated student group who already had developed basic skills in inductive thinking and were literate in their language. But what of the new ESL student who is essentially illiterate and unschooled? To deal with these students we will see

greater movement toward bilingual programs at all levels, elementary through adult, to the use of the student's native language in developing first and second language skills. To accomplish this, we will have to see an increased interest in foreign language education of native English speaking TESOL teachers.

In adult literacy education we are seeing more attention paid to language experience, survival English, and a recognition of certain psycholinguistic principles—namely that the individual brings to each lesson a set of experiences, attitudes, values, feelings, which affect his perceptions of reality and the world around him.

An approach which has received much international attention, especially in developing countries, and one which is being looked at in this country by a small cadre of adult educators in particular for its application in literacy education, was developed by a Brazilian educator, Paolo Freire, an intellectual, Christian Marxist, exiled from his native Brazil, and from Chile, currently working for the World Council of Churches out of Geneva, Switzerland. His radical approach to literacy education is embodied by the realization that education is not a neutral force, that it is a social and political force, the absence of which has effectively disenfranchised the poor and disadvantaged. Although I see little chance of a wide-scale adoption of the Freirian philosophy in education circles in this country (it is extremely threatening to those who hold power), I see a growing movement in the 80's toward a realization that in order for our country to remain viable as a political and economic force, we must adopt a policy of commitment to reducing the absolute and relative levels of illiteracy in this country. In order for this to be accomplished, we will need to make a national commitment.

Another trend in materials and methods which I see advancing into the 80's concerns the technological advances in computers and Computer-Assisted-Instruction (CAI). Advances in computor technology with decreases in costs will make it possible for even smaller school systems to invest more heavily in this area of instruction. By 1990 a criterion of literacy in this country may be one's ability to successfully program and operate a small home computer. The advent of computer games and their popularity among youngsters as well as adults is a portent of things to come in language teaching.

TEACHING THE LANGUAGE TEACHER

My second area of concern is teaching the language teacher. Here I would like to speak to issues related to the growth of professionalism in our field, what the

future of professionalism may be in the 80's, and the state of the art in teacher training in the United States.

The growth of International TESOL and its affiliates in the 70's is a sign of the increased professionalism of the field. Yet this growth in the professional organization has scarcely affected the policies and procedures by which many ESL teachers and bilingual educators are hired and fired. The status of ESL and bilingual education as marginal in the general field of public education— from elementary to adult levels—is evident wherever you turn. Part-time or auxiliary status often characterizes the ESL/bilingual educator in most programs. Evidence of this second class status was vividly illustrated several weeks ago in Chicago when the Chicago Board of Education shifted elementary teachers into adult programs and adult teachers into elementary programs in order to even out some imbalances in instructional loads brought about by student population shifts and budget cuts. The basic principle followed in these shifts was seniority and tenure, not necessarily qualification and training. There is a growing push in Illinois, for example, and elsewhere in the United States for certification of ESL teachers which would hopefully end such practices. (Bilingual educators already possess certification in Illinois.) To many, ESL and bilingual education certification offers a panacea, a cure-all for what ails the profession. With certification would come increased job status, more job security, a recognition of professional worth, perhaps even a raise in pay. Yet certification does not guarantee any of these.

In adult education, the issue of certification has been discussed, ad nauseum, for several years. In many states legislative and professional bodies have required certification of a number of professional groups—pharmacists, nurses, veterinarians, teachers, engineers, and many others. Just as interesting, in several states which were leaders of professional certification in the 60's and 70's, we are witnessing a backlash against certification and actual repealing of laws requiring certification. The reason? It is generally agreed that you can't legislate competence.

Certification is not a cure-all. What may happen in the 1980's is that this single issue of certification will push the professional organization toward a stance more akin to unionism, not professionalism. At that point we may find ourselves as a group more interested in the language teacher than the language learner.

This movement toward certification is also in part a reaction to the attacks from both inside and outside the profession on the whole process of teacher education. Here in Illinois, for example, the present or potential language teacher has available over a dozen institutions of higher education which offer programs of study leading to bachelor's, master's, and doctorate degrees in bilingual/bicultural education, linguistics, TESOL, and related fields.

In addition, a number of federally and state funded agencies provide an abundant array of inservice workshops for specific needs of teachers, administrators, counselors, and para-professionals. Most of these programs of teacher education in institutions of higher education are built on traditional models of teacher education—they are theory based rather than field based. Potential teachers spend 95 to 100% of their training program in the classroom as students rather than teachers. When they receive their degree, they have some competence in literature and language, but little experience in application. Teacher trainers may encourage these new teachers to experiment, to find what works, to pick and choose, to be *eclectic*. Yet perhaps this advice to be eclectic is really a copout, an admission on our part that we really don't know what works, that in reality, every method so far known to ESL and bilingual education is inadequate. Doesn't all the research of teaching effectiveness point to the teacher not the method, as the one crucial variable determining success in the classroom? Perhaps we have overlooked in most teacher training programs a very fundamental point which should be emphasized in the next decade. Materials and methods all reflect this basic deficiency in our training programs. We may be very good in training teachers in the use of specific techniques, gadgets, in a cookbook approach to the classroom, but we have been very lax in developing a cadre of teachers who know why they do what they do, and who have bothered to develop a philosophy of language teaching. In other words, to tell a teacher that it is OK to pick and choose materials and techniques from a variety of methodologies can be interpreted as an admission of a lack of understanding on our own part as to why we are doing what we are doing. Teachers too often lack a basic philosophy of language teaching which can provide them with a general framework within which to design their daily activities. This philosophy can provide a consistent approach to language teaching and bring the teacher to an increased awareness that teaching cannot, should not, be conducted on a day to day basis. The what-can-I-do-tomorrow-morning syndrome runs rampant among all teachers today. Unfortunately, I see little to indicate any change in that direction for the 80's. As teacher trainers we must stress self-evaluation and the development of personal philosophies of language teaching, to overcome this deficiency in the 80's.

TEACHING THE NONPROFESSIONAL PUBLIC

The third issue I would like to discuss is that of teaching the nonprofessional public. This is where TESOL and affiliates as professional organizations can and must be more influential in the 80's. I see the decade of the 80's as a new decade of growth for TESOL and a decade of greater maturity. With added maturity will come greater responsibility and a greater involvement in an advocacy position for its membership. Attempts at this in the recent past include such examples as the recent testimony provided by Illinois TESOL/BE organization at the Lau hearings in Chicago last September. The existence of our jobs is dependent for the most part on legislation at the state and federal levels. Many of us lack job security because of local program priorities, again dictated by funding levels. The name of the game for progress in the 1980's will be advocacy of professional goals whether it be obtaining certification, higher salaries, greater recognition of importance of our jobs among the general public, or whatever. This professional organization will find the opportunities presented to it more numerous in the 80's than at any time in the previous 10 years.

We're talking about the public image of second language instruction and bilingual education, of convincing the general public, and in particular state legislators of the value of this work. By the way, there is a good chance that for at least the next four years, if not eight, that funding for bilingual education and ESL will increasingly depend on state resources, rather than federal, or state determination of funding levels, not federal. So, it's time to begin courting our state representatives.

The image currently held by the general public of our profession, or at least of our professional goals, is not the best. I was recently traveling by car through central Illinois and happened to tune into a Paul Harvey news broadcast. Now Paul Harvey has never been known for liberal thinking, and could be considered a serious spokesman for the majority of Americans who voted in November's general election. The topic was bilingual education and his position was why do we need it? We should be teaching all children and adults in this country how to speak, read and write English immediately, that bilingual education actually promoted diversity, which so often leads to friction and clashes among minority groups in a pluralistic society. He cited the cases of Canada, Belgium and India as bilingual societies where there have been threats to the status quo of those nations as a result of language

policies. Bilingual education does face an image problem in this country. Organizations such as TESOL must take the lead in trying to improve this image.

One way of overcoming an image problem and improve our skills at lobbying is by developing linkages with other state organizations with similar interests; FLTA (Foreign Language Teachers Association) and ACEA (The National Adult and Continuing Education Association) and their affiliate organizations of educators whose futures also depend a great deal on their ability to present their cases to funding agencies and local education agencies.

A final issue I would like to talk about with potential for TESOL has been identified with the term "global education." This concept was treated at length in the 1979 Report of the Illinois Task Force on Foreign Language and International Studies. To quote: Educators and the general public must accept the challenge to develop a global education that will prepare our citizens to cope with a diverse world with its many ethnic and cultural systems. The need is for a broader humanistic approach toward education, which requires new competencies and new broader perspectives of citizenship. It is becoming increasingly clear that the world is demanding new attitudes from all of us. According to Robert Leetsma, USOE Associate Commissioner, among other competencies and sensitivities, each individual needs to develop:

1) Some basic cross-cultural understanding, empathy, and ability to communicate with people from different cultures.

2) A sense of why and how humanity shares a common future—global issues and dynamics and the calculus of interdependence

3) A sense of stewardship in use of the earth and acceptance of the ethic of intergenerational responsibility for the well-being or fair chance of those who come after us.

Later in this same report, Global Education is defined in terms of five dimensions:

1) Perspective Consciousness—a recognition on the part of the individual that his or her view of the world is not universally shared

2) State of the Planet Awareness—awareness of prevailing world conditions and developments

3) Cross-cultural Awareness

4) Knowledge of global dynamics

5) Awareness of human choices—some awareness of the problems of choice confronting individuals, nations, and the human species as consciousness and knowledge of the global system expands.

The implications of this trend for our

professional organization are profound. We must as a profession recognize in wholistic terms the interdependence of all of us, in a continually shrinking yet more complex world society. Unfortunately, unless this concern is shared by our political leadership in this country the concept of global education will not flourish. The actions of the new national administration in the next two to three years could very well set the stage for or against this trend in education for the entire decade.

SUMMARY

To summarize, I've tried to share with you a number of issues which will face our membership individually and collectively in the 80's from my professional perspective. We will see greater use of new humanistic methodologies and at the same time greater exploration of the use of technology in the form of computers and computor-assisted instruction. Our country will continue to face the continuing problems of massive immigration and our membership will confront the education of these new Americans in the classroom.

Certification of ESL teachers in the public schools will likely be resolved in the next decade. In order for us to be involved in the process, we should start the process within our own organization of identifying those standards, behaviors, characteristics, competencies or whatever you wish to call them, which a trained ESL instructor at whatever level should possess. Whether or not you support certification, everyone involved in teacher training in ESL or Bilingual Education must impress upon teacher trainees the importance of continuing their professional education through membership and active involvement in professional organizations, and by continuing participation in various inservice activities.

And finally, this professional association, in collaboration with other education associations serving similar clientele must link organizational arms in the 80's to convince the public of the worth of our efforts and the need to promote the concept of global education, undoubtedly a concept which, if we agree with it, will need our support in the next decade. □

TN 4/81

"THE FUTURE OF ESL AND BILINGUAL EDUCATION IN THE NEXT DECADE"*

by Ramón L. Santiago,
President, NABE

Regardless of our political affiliation, we educators must be concerned about the various postures assumed by the present administration regarding expenditures for educational and social programs, especially those aimed at the poor. Critics point to the administration's reiterated promise to dismantle the Department of Education, dilute the Voting Rights Act, emasculate the Lau Regulations and defund the Legal Services Corporation. While millions of dollars are earmarked for costly and sometimes unnecessary armaments (which we are told some of the conscripts cannot operate properly because of an inadequate education), the Department of Education continues to suffer devastating cuts: from $15 billion in 1982 to $11.4 billion in 1983 to $6.9 billion in 1987. The administration would have us believe that its proposal to replace the present Department of Education with a "Foundation for Educational Assistance" (FEA —which in Spanish means "ugly") does not signal a lack of support for education at the federal level. Educators disagree; they feel that "the foundation is not just a tidying up of the bureaucracy to make it more efficient—it's a full scale attempt by the administration to abolish the federal role in education." They see the foundation as a first step toward the total elimination of federal dollars to support the national role in education.

Moreover, educators worry about the priorities of the new administration. As a recent *Time* magazine article put it: "The problem is that in setting his priorities, the President tends to behave in a way that makes him seem insensitive to minorities on civil rights questions, to the poor where social welfare is concerned, and to women on feminist issues." All this leaves us little cause for rejoicing.

In addition, right now in Washington, D.C. there are several legislative and administrative initiatives afoot designed to seriously curtail the funding for Title VII, as I am sure is happening to Title I and other programs that directly affect not only bilingual education but English as a second language programs. The present level of $157 million for Title VII is slated to be reduced to $134 million for '82, and the administration is asking for only $94 million for 1983, or slightly over half the present funds. The cost of one helicopter not sent to El Salvador would educate a lot of our children in the United States.

The "new federalism" concept, which attempts to shift more responsibility to the local level, might be seen to benefit ESL programs, which have no national source of special funds comparable to those emanating from Title VII. But many state officials and educators worry that the money that would trickle down to the states either won't be enough to meet all the needs or will be utilized at the discretion of local authorities for purposes other than education.

Proposed changes in the language of the Title VII Act are also cause for concern for both our professions. Attempts to totally defund Title VII are not likely to succeed because even the most radical opponents of special programs for linguistic minority children recognize that the educational needs of these children must be met by one mechanism or another. But other suggested alterations to Title VII can be just as damaging. There are proposed provisions to reduce the number of children eligible to receive Title VII services down to one million by aiming these services at the "most needy." "Most needy" would be equated with the lowest level of English proficiency—that is, priority would be given to NEP (non-English proficient) children over LEP (limited-English proficient) children, under the assumption that NEP children have greater educational needs than LEP children. It is a cardinal mistake of the reformers to assume that the main goal of schools is just to teach English, rather than to educate, or that education can be imparted only in English. Research evidence and experience indicate that academic skills obtained through any native language can be transferred to any other language through adequate educational programs. In other words, limited English proficiency by itself cannot be the sole criterion for predicting success or failure in the acquisition of academic skills in the classroom.

The second proposed change in the language of the Act would allow other approaches besides bilingual education to be employed to meet the needs of LEP/NEP children. Presently a district which seeks Title VII funds must offer an instructional program which is bilingual—i.e., which includes a native language component in addition to ESL instruction. Under the new provisions, a district could submit a proposal to carry out autonomous ESL programs or other approved types of English–only approaches (such as immersion).

I am sure that these proposals will

11

generate a variety of responses in different quarters. It is unrealistic to expect everybody to support either the present language of Title VII or the revised versions being proposed. But whatever position we bilingual educators favor, we must not allow ourselves to say that we oppose English-only options under Title VII because bilingual programs constitute the *only* way to serve LEP or NEP children. The evidence simply is not on our side. (I recommend to you Jim Cummins' latest article, "The Effectiveness of Bilingual Education," which addresses this point in detail.) We believe that bilingual education has numerous advantages beyond contributing to the acquisition of English by LEP children, but if we are to be professionally honest, we cannot claim that it is the *only* method or the *best* method in *all* circumstances. We have to admit (and we *do* admit) that under certain circumstances non-bilingual approaches may be more feasible and cost-effective than bilingual programs. Thus we can support or oppose the changes in the language of Title VII, but let us be sure to give the right reasons—reasons that can be empirically supported by research, reasons that take into consideration the best interests of the children we serve and not merely those of our own professions.

With respect to immersion programs as viable alternatives for the U.S., much needs to be clarified. We don't know whether Canadian-style immersion programs or the "structured immersion" variants favored by some will be suitable for U.S. populations who do *not* constitute the majority, who are *not* learning a prestige foreign language in a supportive setting, who do *not* come from high socioeconomic backgrounds. Researchers tell us to proceed with caution in this respect and we should heed their advice.

One final comment in this area. Some people may question the use of Title VII funds, which are so scarce, for other than bilingual education approaches—not because these other approaches are not valid but because other sources of funding such as Title I are available for those purposes. This is another, legitimate argument, which has nothing to do with the validity of the approach itself, but only with the utilization of fiscal resources for particular purposes. Once again, let us keep our positions clear.

Turning to the state and local levels, we need to be concerned with what I call issues of the profession. For too long ESL and bilingual teachers have been treated as outsiders in the educational establishment, whether at the school or college level. We are coming to be known as "LIFO'S"—"last *in*, first *out*." We hear all sorts of horror stories pertaining to employment matters: no

job security, no tenure or permanence, no promotional benefits, no certification, assignment to substitute duties—in short, a less than exalted status for capable professionals. At times bilingual and ESL educators are pitted against each other unnecessarily because state and/or federal regulations allow schools to pay the salary of bilingual teachers but not of ESL teachers, or vice versa. Some states have ESL certification/endorsement but not bilingual, or vice versa. The groups fortunate enough to gain certification or employment become the target of the excluded ones, and I believe that this result is both unfortunate and avoidable. How can we justify benefits for ourselves—such as certification—and yet deny them to our fellow teachers? If certification is so good, then it should be available to *all* our colleagues who meet the established criteria.

In this respect it's ironic that some teachers pay dues to teacher unions who then utilize that money to lobby against their own best interests. It is imperative that we keep our unions and our organizations honest and consonant with our principles. Also, when dealing with matters pertaining to employment, we should analyze the issues from the point of view of the whole profession of language teachers, and not from that of small special interest groups. In every state ESL and bilingual teachers should band together, and whoever has achieved certification or other benefits should support the efforts (financially and legislatively) of other groups trying to obtain the same benefits. The cooperative efforts of COTESOL AND CABBE in Colorado last year are illustrative of what can be done in this respect.

Another issue of moment is the increased politicization of educational policy-making. I think I am not naive enough to believe that education can ever be free from politics, but this year the players have gotten the art of mixing politics with education down to a science (if you'll forgive the mixed metaphor.) A perfect example is the Baker-de Kanter report that came out of the Office of Planning and Evaluation of the Department of Education. This document began as a perfectly legitimate effort to gather supporting evidence for the then Secretary of Education Shirley Hufstedler to use in promulgating the ill-fated 1980 proposed Lau Regulations. It was to be a review of existing Title VII program evaluations—not empirical or action research. Midway through the project (started under the Carter Administration) Secretary Bell and the new Administration withdrew the proposed regulations, and the document should have become moot. But by then the project had acquired a life of its own, fueled by the personal desire of various Department of Education officials to dis-

credit the bilingual program. Even the writers of the document must have been surprised at the way their work was prefaced by a five-page summary with policy implications that were difficult to support on the basis of the main document.

The report, which by then had become an "internal" paper—having been neither commissioned nor approved by the current Secretary—was leaked to the press, and the "trial by newspaper" of bilingual education began. The upshot of all this is that the contents of the report (which incidentally takes potshots at ESL programs) have been quoted as gospel truth despite the methodological shortcomings pointed out by responsible researchers of many persuasions and the obvious self-serving political bias of the Department of Education officials who instigated it.

It is important for *all* of us to realize that more and more the government is resorting to such tactics as circulating damaging reports of dubious authenticity and quality, and passing them off as legitimate "research." In the ensuing hue and cry about the affected programs, public opinion is molded and some accommodating legislator can always be found to introduce a bill radically altering the program in question (cf. Rep. Stauton's and Sen. Huddleston's bills of recent vintage). We have to be on the alert for this type of unethical utilization of research results to formulate educational policy.

I have discussed at some length developments occurring at the national, state and local levels which could affect the future of bilingual education and ESL in the next decade. I have discussed the philosophy of the new administration regarding social and educational programs, budgetary changes (particularly as they apply to Title VII), proposed changes in the Title VII Act, and issues related to employment of the professions. What is the outlook for the future? And what should be our plan of action?

I feel optimistic about the future of ESL and bilingual education, but we have a lot of work to do. First, there must be increased cooperation between collateral organizations like TESOL and NABE at the national and affiliate levels. As I said before, both our organizations have a good record of cooperative ventures. For example, Colorado TESOL helped Colorado NABE fight against the repeal of the state bilingual law, and even though the effort was unsuccessful it resulted in closer ties between the two affiliates. Florida TESOL, in turn, carried out joint fundraising activities with Florida NABE and worked together to develop a national language policy statement. Also, many of you are aware that some local affiliates, notably NJTESOL/NJBE and Alaska TESOL/

BE, are associated with both NABE and TESOL.

In addition NABE participates with TESOL in the Joint National Committee for Languages (JNCL) in the belief that the language teaching profession is and should be one family. Jim Alatis has testified on various occasions on behalf of bilingual education, and recently we both found ourselves as witnesses before the National Advisory Council for Bilingual Education in Washington, DC. In turn, NABE has supported Representative Simon's HR 3231 bill promoting foreign languages. Both organizations strive to have representation from sister groups at their national conventions to maintain contact with each other.

More importantly, TESOL has issued a position paper on "The Role of ESL in Bilingual Education" (I was fortunate to participate in the drafting of the document) which unequivocably supports good bilingual programs with good ESL components. The document makes some telling assertions that we should keep in mind when we are threatened with dissension among the ranks:

"Bilingual teachers and teachers of ESOL must accept a partnership relationship in bilingual education"

"Of the three educational approaches listed above (bilingual instruction with ESL, monolingual instruction with ESL, monolingual instruction with no ESL), TESOL recommends the first, bilingual instruction including an ESL component, as the preferred model, for instructing students of limited English proficiency, whenever feasible."

Under strategies for cooperation the position paper pledges that "TESOL will maintain and enhance the reciprocal liaison which has been established with NABE." Finally the document reaffirms that "International TESOL endorses and supports the bilingual approach to edu-cation, recognizing that it provides students of limited English proficiency with equal educational opportunities. ESL is an integral and essential component of bilingual-bicultural programs in the United States."

For its part, NABE has been very active fighting for the survival of Title VII and joining with local groups in promoting certification of ESL and bilingual teachers in various states. NABE is also cooperating with AACTE to develop standards for accrediting multicultural teacher education programs. Also, our sociopolitical concerns committee is in the process of drafting a new Title VII bill for consideration by Congress, and we continue to work very closely with Jim Alatis in Georgetown. Personally this is my third visit this year to a TESOL affiliate,* and I and other NABE Executive Board members will continue to share with you all for a long time to come. More importantly, NABE feels strongly that we should have an ESL SIG in the same way that TESOL has a Bilingual Education SIG. I am thus issuing a challenge to any of you who are NABE members to assist me in setting up such a SIG in NABE before the year is out.

The existing cooperation between TESOL and NABE is a good first step, but more must be done. There is a need for all of us to become more politically active. It is irresponsible to attempt to avoid political activism by hiding under the label of "educators" and leaving the politicking to lobbyists. *All* of us are lobbyists—we'd better be, if we care what happens to education. This doesn't mean that all of us have to run for office, or that we have to run around the halls of Congress or of state capitols. There are many ways to become involved, and I recommend to the leaders of TESOL affiliates that they obtain a copy of the JNCL manual on political involvement, which lists in cookbook fashion all that can be done to influence the actions of federal, state and local governments in educational matters.

We must also learn to respond to calls for action and not fall back on the "I'm too busy" reply or "I'll do it next time." We should look upon participation in the day-to-day political process as we do upon participation in the affairs of our children's schools. The consequences of the New Federalism may not all be positive, but it may force us to become participants at the local level. We *can* make a difference, but only if we *choose* to get involved.

Above all, it is esssential that we assist the United States in developing a national and rational language policy which, rather than restrict and mandate, liberates the nation and its citizens to be all that they can be. Whatever our philosophy of education or of life might be, knowing more *can't* be worth less. Any policy in any country which endorses monolingualism as a desired outcome of the educational process can't be very enlightened. Whatever our approach or methodology for getting there, all of us as educators and people of good will should be able to support the notion that bilingualism is in the national interest (really in the international interest). Let us agree in principle that bilingualism (multilingualism) and biculturalism (multiculturalism) are good things. Then let us agree to explore all possibilities for a bilingual America and a bilingual, peace-loving world.

¡Que Dios les bendiga! □

* *Address Presented at the Tenth Annual State Convention of the Illinois Teachers of English to Speakers of Other Languages and Bilingual Education Association, Americana-Congress Hotel, Chicago, Illinois, February 27, 1982.*

TN 6/82

A NOTE ON TEACHING ENGLISH AND MAKING SENSE

By Richard L. Light
SUNY at Albany

As teachers of English to speakers of other languages, we seem, perhaps more than others, to be constantly exploring new ways of viewing the teaching and learning of our subject. Competing beliefs and assumptions about the nature of language and the nature of learning are exchanged with enthusiasm in our journals and at our meetings. In turn, the language teaching activities that follow from these beliefs and assumptions are incredibly diverse and under constant scrutiny. A glance at the programs for our meetings reveals some of the exciting diversity in the field of ESL. This enthusiastic exchange of ideas and willingness to examine new options in second language teaching is bound to be healthy; it is certainly exciting.

In the process of keeping abreast of these developments we are continually examining this diversity of ideas and activities in second language teaching. And as everyone must, we attempt to bring our own organization to the diversity. At one point in our discussions at SUNY at Albany recently, we decided to make a list of some of the ideas and activities we had been reading about and to try to organize, interrelate, and make sense of the list. The list went like this: *audiolingual, strip story, counseling learning, pattern practice, visual aids, transformational-cognitive, silent way, conversation circle, space puzzle, community language learning, language experience approach* and *values clarification.* And of course we could have gone on.

So we had this nice interesting, messy list and we wanted to bring to it some organization in terms of our students' English language needs and our own language teaching activities. We wanted to make better "sense" of it. And since we all during the course of our teaching have heard about most of what is on this list. I thought it would be helpful to share some aspects of our discussion. Of course, we can't do justice here to Frank Smith's elegant description of the term "making sense" from his book *Comprehension and Learning*, but we will use the term in a way that is not inconsistent with his description. That is, we use it here as a term for relating new experience to what is known, and for organizing knowledge.

One of the sets of concepts with which we attempted to bring some organization to our messy list was one developed by Edward Anthony back in 1963. He suggested that we look at language teaching activities and the beliefs underlying them in terms of a hierarchical framework involving the categories *approach*, *method* and *technique*. *Approach*, he suggested, is axiomatic, representing a set of beliefs about the nature of learning and the nature of language. Approach states a point of view, a philosophy—something which one believes but cannot necessarily prove. Applying this to our list above we suggested that counseling-learning, transformational-cognitive, and audiolingual are approaches, rooted respectively in beliefs regarding the relative importance of humanism, cognitivism, and behaviorism in explaining facts about learning. While approach is axiomatic, the next concept in Anthony's hierarchy—*method*—is procedural and it is consistent with an approach; it is an overall plan for teaching that is based on a selected approach. Within this framework, community language learning is a method consistent with the counseling learning approach. The use of the dialog/pattern practice combination on the other hand is a method generally associated with an audiolingual approach and behavioral views of learning. Following *method* in Anthony's scheme of analysis is the most specific category, that of *technique*. A *technique* is implementational and is consistent with method. It is what actually takes place in the classroom in terms of actions and technologies to accomplish immediate objectives. From our list then we would include under technique the

strip story, use of specific visual aids to get meaning across, the conversation circle usually associated with community language learning, and the use of cuisinaire rods in the silent way. Also included under technique would be the exotic-sounding space puzzle on our list—actually a technique for teaching listening comprehension. So the concepts of approach, method and technique did provide us with one very useful set of lenses through which to view and begin to organize aspects of our list.

Another set of concepts, perhaps somewhat less clearly definable, is that of *learner-centered* activities and *teacher-centered* activities in the language classroom. It is a commonplace for us now to discuss learner-centered instruction, but Louis Kelly in his comprehensive book *Twenty Five Centuries of Language Teaching* does not discuss the distinction at all. One is tempted to draw the conclusion that for 2,500 years from 500 BC to 1969 (the date of Kelly's book) teacher-centered activities dominated the second language classrooms of the world. And this may still be a true picture of most classrooms in the world, yet in ESL at any rate, the learner-centered classroom is receiving more attention, especially in approaches such as counseling-learning and its application in community language learning. So the notions of learner-centered and teacher-centered classes (though necessarily somewhat loosely defined) nonetheless were useful in helping us sort out characteristics of the items on our list. They proved helpful, for example, in attempting to answer questions such as which of the approaches, methods, and techniques on our list allowed for one or the other emphasis in the classroom.

Another set of concepts that we found useful in applying to our list was that of *skill-getting* and *skill-using*, two terms that have most recently been explicated by Rivers and Temperley in their 1978 ESL methods text. Skill-getting has traditionally involved teacher-directed activities such as repetition drills, pattern drills, and dialog recitation. Skill-using on the other hand involved student-initiated

language exchanges for real communicative purposes. These concepts did help in making sense of our list, but like the others they had limitations. For example, one might assume that the skill-getting takes place primarily in a *teacher*-centered atmosphere, while skill-using happens some time later, mainly in a *student*-centered atmosphere with student-initiated language use. However, this is a somewhat oversimplified view, as we discovered when we examined our list through these two lenses. For example, in the conversation circle technique, which involves student-initiated but teacher-assisted language use, skill-getting and skill-using are closely intertwined. In this technique the student *uses* the target language immediately for real communication, but skill-getting takes place almost simultaneously as the teacher assists by modeling the language the student has chosen. Thus this student-centered conversation circle technique allows for both skill-getting and skill-using to proceed hand in hand.

So in our discussions we have found these categories of *approach/method/technique*, of *teacher-centered* and *student-centered* activity, and of *skill-getting* and *skill-using* to be helpful in trying to interrelate the ideas on our list. Of course a set of categories for making sense of teaching English is presumably open-ended and categories are likely to be added as one continues to study. Stevick (*Adapting & Writing Language Lessons*, 1971) for example has enumerated his own rather extensive set of some 15 categories for analyzing language teaching lessons, including such items as usability, organization, and "responsiveness" (or relevance). And our set of categories is open-ended in another quite obvious sense. As we participate in teaching English to speakers of other languages, we all bring our own categories to bear on what we see and hear. And organizing and understanding the wealth of ideas and activities available for doing our job is what teaching English and making sense is all about.

TN 12/79

BOOK REVIEWS

VIEWPOINT ON ENGLISH AS A SECOND LANGUAGE

Edited by Marina Burt, Heidi Dulay, and Mary Finocchiaro (Regents, New York, 1977).

Reviewed by Audrey Reynolds (Northeastern Illinois University, Chicago)

Viewpoints on English as a Second Language, an anthology of 21 essays serving as a *Festschrift* in honor of James E. Alatis, has two additional goals: "(1) to stimulate those who have been in the English as a Second Language (ESL) field and know it well, and (2) to inform those who are new to the profession about basic concepts and issues in ESL today" (p. xi).

To accomplish these two goals, the editors, Marina Burt, Heidi Dulay and Mary Finocchiaro, have collected a variety of articles from leading scholars and then organized the book by dividing the articles into three categories of variables which affect the teaching and/or learning process: Instructional Perspectives—what occurs in the classroom; Psycholinguistic Insights—what happens inside the learner's head; and Socio-Political Dimensions—events outside the classroom which may impinge on the Teaching of English as a Second Language.

The specific articles included present a diversity of subjects at whose scope one can only hint. The topics range from reflections on characteristics of successful learners and effective teachers to discussion of concrete problems encountered when teaching various language skills; from current research on second language acquisition to historical perspectives on theories of motivation; from the social and educational plight of immigrants to a consideration of the implications of the *Lau-Nichols* decision. Thus, the editors have attempted to cover a wide spectrum of current issues in ESL and, as a result, the collection does reflect the diversity and complexity of the profession as it exists today.

Readers who are novices will be introduced to the wide range of variables which affect the teaching and learning process; moreover, they will discover some cogent summaries of contemporary issues, although some of the articles may seem esoteric or opaque; e.g., the descriptions of elaborate techniques an observing teacher can use to measure teacher-student interaction in the classroom. Readers who are experienced in ESL will find some articles which summarize things already known; other articles may prove to be not only stimulating but also provocative; e.g., Postovsky's suggestion that "speaking" should be delayed; Hernandez-Chavez's discovery that, for at least one child, neither syntactic nor semantic categories already acquired in the first language had an impact on second language acquisition.

In conclusion, the editors have met their goals of providing something for everyone. Not all articles will appeal to all readers, but most readers will find a number of stimulating articles on subjects which interest them—no small accomplishment in a *Festschrift*.

TN 11/77

MEMORY, MEANING & METHOD

(Earl Stevick, Newbury House Publishers, Inc., Rowley, Mass., bibliography and index. xi + 177 p.; 1976.)

Reviewed by Jean McConochie, TESL Centre, Concordia Univ., Montreal, Quebec

Earl Stevick is a teacher—most frequently in the U.S. State Departments Foreign Service Institute, School of Language Studies, of which he is also the director. This book is Professor Stevick's scholarly and personal exploration of the post-Cognitive terrain, a development of his previously-stated (1971) conviction that "language study is a 'total human experience,' and not just an oral-aural

or a cognitive one." (p. xi)

As the title suggests, the book has three sections. The first, "Memory," reviews experimental and clinical studies of the biological bases for memory in general and for verbal memory in particular. The summaries are brief, lucid, clearly documented, and tied directly to aspects of learning and teaching. The concluding chapter of the section, titled "Memory and the Whole Person," emphasizes the central importance of "depth" (a key term in the book)—the degree of personal involvement, including both conscious and unconscious physical reactions—in memory, and thus in the entire learning process.

In Part 2, Stevick explores "Meaning" in its psychological sense, defining it as the "difference participation in a given activity . . . makes to an individual relative to his or her entire range of drives and needs." (p. 47) Here, then, is a further exploration of the concept of "depth," and a foreshadowing of the book's concluding statement that "Memory is a by-product of Meaning. . . ." (p. 160).

To illustrate the relationship between "depth" and "meaning," Stevick turns his attention to two homely aspects of language teaching: pronunciation and drills and exercises. Again citing an impressive range of research studies, he examines adult problems in mastering the sounds of a foreign language, concluding that the critical factor is "the power of deep emotional attitudes to facilitate or inhibit pronunciation" (p. 56) and that "intelligent awareness of [these attitudes] will do more to improve the teaching of pronunciation than all the charts, diagrams, and mechanical devices that we have often depended on in the past." (p. 56)

In the following chapter, "The Meaning of Drills and Exercises," Stevick examines classroom interaction, using the insights of Transactional Analysis, e.g. the classroom version of Eric Berne's "Why Don't You—Yes But" game (p. 72). As in other sections, very practical pedagogical suggestions are included as illustrations of the "direction to take." But the emphasis is never on technique; it is, rather, on the insights which can be gained from a wide variety of sources (the bibliography has some 200 entries) and on the importance of deep personal security and investment before real learning can take place.

The final section, "Method," begins with the "riddle" of why methodologies that are in direct psychological contradiction (e.g. audiolingualism and cognitive code) may both yield excellent results; or, stated another way, why a given method sometimes works and sometimes doesn't. Stevick offers two beliefs to account for that phenomenon, and in them presents the heart of his book:

the *"deeper" the source* of a sentence within the student's personality, *the more lasting value* it has for learning the language (p. 109) . . . [and] this same "depth" fac-

15

tor, far from being an additional, minor consideration to be taken into account only when weightier factors are equal, is in fact *more to be reckoned with than technique, or format, or underlying linguistic analysis.* (p. 110)

Stevick then explores his crucial distinction between "defensive" and "receptive" (the book's other key term) learning, the latter being that which allows for greater "depth." While "receptive learning" is related to Lambert's "integrative motivation," Stevick intends a larger frame of reference for his term, explaining it through an extended agricultural metaphor: "It is . . . what happens to seed that has been sown in good soil." (p. 111) This, clearly, is the sort of learning which he is encouraging in us, his readers—the book itself being structured as a teaching device—and which he hopes we will encourage in our students.

The book's most original contribution to language teaching methodology lies in the analysis of the *psychodynamic* (Greek for "what goes on inside and between folks," the author explains on p. 119) of the language classroom by means of five deceptively simple principles (pp. 120–123):

Ia: Language is one kind of purposeful behavior between people.

Ib: And language behavior is intertwined with other kinds of purposive behavior between people

IIa: The human mind learns new behavior rapidly at any age.

IIb: But (many kinds of) learning will be slowed down when the learner is busy defending himself from from someone else.

III: Help the student to stay in contact with the language.

IV: Help the student to maintain wholesome attitudes.

V: In preparing materials, make it easy for teachers and students to follow Principles I–IV.

"Principle IV sounds a lot like a People's Revolutionary Committee slogan," you say? Well, yes. But now consider its three corollaries (p. 122):

1. *Reduce "reflectivity."* [Where the student merely repeats a previously-given model.]

2. *Increase "productivity."* [Where the student exercises a choice in what (s)he will say.]

3. *Teach, then test, then get out of the way.* [Give the student time to integrate what has been learned. How many of us take that third step?]

To further clarify these principles, Stevick uses them to examine six contemporary approaches to language learning—Community Language Learning, the Silent Way, the St. Cloud (Audio-Visual) Method, language teaching as a branch of applied linguistics, Audiolingualism, and Suggestology. Given the obvious ties of Stevick's approach to that of Community Language Learning, it is not surprising that he finds it the most compatible with his model. However, the principles also clarify the strengths of the other approaches, and there is no suggestion that any one methodology holds the key to successful language learning. It is the principles which are important, in whatever framework they are applied. Stevick makes this clear in his summary statement of "What I Hope for in a Classroom".

May I suggest that this is a book to read first for the delight of stimulating "shoptalk" with Stevick, an exceptionally gifted teacher/colleague who has a very pleasant sense of humor. Then you many want to look it over once more to internalize the challenge of the book's final sentence: "Memory is a by-product of Meaning, and Method should be the servant of Meaning, and Meaning is what happens inside and between people."

TN 11/77

PRINCIPLES OF LANGUAGE LEARNING AND TEACHING

(H. Douglas Brown, Englewood Cliffs, New Jersey: Prentice-Hall, Inc., 1980. 276 pp.)

Reviewed by Anthony F. Lewis
The University of Michigan

Designed as a text "to provide teachers and teacher trainees with a comprehensive and up-to-date grasp of the theoretical foundations of foreign language teaching" (preface, p. vii), *Principles of Language Learning and Teaching* easily fulfills this objective. As a textbook, it can be used in any language methodology course preparing future language teachers. *PLL* also contains material which lends itself to a wider audience. Psychologists, anthropologists, or sociologists may find the information in chapters six and seven treating sociocultural and personality variables of second language learning particularly valuable. Since the average reader of this text is more than likely to be a modern language teacher, I will limit my discussion accordingly.

PLL consists of twelve chapters, an excellent bibliography, and an index. Each chapter of the text is followed by *suggested readings* and *topics and questions for study and discussion*. I find the latter section most helpful as it allows students/teachers the opportunity to seriously consider the practicality of major theoretical points presented in the chapter. Also, the questions in themselves highlight important concepts or key words which the reader unknowingly may have missed. In a word, this section provides an excellent review of the major issues of the chapter as a *point de départ*.

This text presents all the deep issues which have surfaced in the realm of first and second language learning in the last ten years. It is a must for those of us who may need an in-depth survey of the literature pertaining to these fields. Chapter 2 is devoted to first language acquisition. Chapter 3 takes a new look at the old issue of second language learning versus first language acquisition. Within both chapters, we are presented with the major schools of thought (behaviorism, critical period, cognitive, and affective theory) as well as a host of names representative of such schools of thought (Skinner, E. Lenneberg, T. Scovel, D. Ausubel, A. Guiora). Chapter 4 presents a more thorough analysis of human learning via an examination of the behavioral/ cognitive and affective domains. This chapter is *exemplum* of Brown's 'spiraling approach' (cf. p. viii, preface) as a textual linking strategy. Terms and key concepts are constantly reintroduced throughout the text which provide a more meaningful approach for the reader. Chapter 5 is of special interest to educators/educational psychologists. Via Gagné's learning model, we see the importance of many cognitive variables active in the second language learning process. The chapter also examines some of the learning strategies employed by adult learners in a second language setting.

I find chapters 6 and 7 most interesting. Herein Brown discusses such affective variables as empathy, introversion, extroversion, self-esteem and their influence on language learning. Chapter 7 considers such factors as social distance between two cultures to explain the ease or difficulty in second language learning (cf. John Schumann, 1976, "Social Distance as a Factor in Second Language Acquisition," *Language Learning* 26: 135-143). Brown also enumerates four states which second language learners experience in learning a language in a foreign culture; namely, acculturation, anomie, social distance, and perceived social distance (cf. Douglas Brown, 1980, "The Optimal Distance Model of Second Language Acquisition," *TESOL Quarterly* 14:157-164). Chapters 8 and 9 survey the major issues of the Contrastive Analysis and Error Analysis schools of thought. For me the reading here is a little dry, simply because it follows such thought provoking material in chapters six and seven. Perhaps, these chapters could have been placed earlier in the text. Chapter 10 is devoted to discourse analysis while chapter 11 covers the intricacies of language testing. Chapter 12 overviews some of the major schools of language teaching methodology within the American scene (i.e., Direct Method, Grammar-Translation, and Audiolingual methods) as well as surveys some current models which exemplify the language learning/teaching process (Strevens and Bialystok, pp. 250 and 251).

All in all, *PLL* is a must for any library, especially one's personal professional library. Mr. Brown does not espouse any particular L₂ theory nor does his text force anyone of them upon us. Instead, *PLL* presents an array of theorists and theories and lets us judge for ourselves which one(s) may best serve our interests. Douglas Brown is to be commended for putting together such a plethora of concepts in such a fresh way. I highly recommend the book. *TN 12/81*

Section 2. Language and Culture

This section begins with a fine short history of bilingual education by the late Gerald D. Kanoon (4/78), "The Four Phases of Bilingual Education in the United States," and an article by Allan Weiner in which he poses the problem of bilingual education for a "Melting Pot, or a New American Pluralism" (2/76). Ann Carlovich and Ernestine Hazuka attempt to come to terms with bilingual education and ESL in an early article (12/75), "What is Bilingual Education and What Makes Bilingual Programs Work?" It is interesting to compare this article with Ramon Santiago's article which appears in section 1.

The fourth article in this section is a history of U.S. language policy in Puerto Rico—how and why this policy has changed over the years. The article is by Paquita Viñas de Vasquez (4/73), who was then with the Puerto Rican Department of Education. It is followed by one of the most charming first person accounts of language and culture in contact the *TN* has ever received: the account of Wang Nianmei in her letter we titled "My Visit to the USA" (2/81).

The Sharron Bassano article, "ESL and the Cultural Transitioning of Non-Academic Adults" (8/79), and the Douglas Magrath article, "Cultures in Conflict" (12/81), provide input to the cross-cultural problems of the ESL/EFL classroom. Bill Gay shows us how to resolve these problems in his (2/80) *It Works* column "A One-day Intercultural Workshop." Trish Delamere's "Linking Notional-Functional Syllabi and Cross-cultural Awareness" (8/83) and Delamere and Frederick Jenks' "Topics and Techniques for Developing Cross-cultural Community Learning Environment" (12/81) attempt to link cross-cultural learning techniques with two currently popular trends in language teaching: Curran's Community-Language Learning and Notional-Functionalism. The last article in this section is Lois Cuçulla's discussion of the problems of teaching English in a "foreign environment" which she titles "Cultural Accommodation in the Foreign University Classroom."

A book review of Dearld Wing Sue's *Counselling the Culturally Different* is included in this section. In her review, Janet Constantinides discusses the skillful cross-cultural counselor, techniques for specific minority populations and critical incidents in cross-cultural counseling.

In section 4 of this volume you will find two additional articles dealing with language and culture, "Cultural Aspects of Pre-Vocational ESL" (10/73) by Barbara Humak and "Understanding on the Job," an *It Works* column from 10/83 by Carol Svedsen. These articles deal with the cultural conflicts which occur in the workplace.

Many other articles have appeared in the *TN* dealing with bilingual education or language and culture. In the 4/79 issue Jean Romano wrote about "The Cultural Revolution" in which she discussed the changing attitudes towards acculturation. One of the earliest articles about the problems of teaching culture to appear in the *TN* was Serafina Krear's "Thinking and Feeling in Two Cultures" (5/72). Other interesting articles to look at are: "Treating Mental Illness in the Ethnic Community" by Sara Henry (10/80); "Anecdotes for Crosscultural Insights" (9/78) and "Intercultural Appreciation in an ESL Class" (6/79) by Judy E. Winn-Bell Olsen; Margo Jang's "Intercultural Communication" (4/80); and James Brown's "Teaching Cultural Awareness with *The Graduate*" (4/80).

The only articles to appear in the *TN* on the teaching of English to Native Americans were a report by Gina Harvey (11/68) on "TESL Classes on the Navajo Reservation" and an article by June Sark Heinrich on "Native Americans: What Not to Teach About Them" (8/79). One *It Works* column, George Hepworth's "It's a Duck . . ." came from work with Native American Children.

Since 1980 a number of articles about experiences in China have appeared in the *TN*. The first was by Virginia French Allen on her return from China. She wrote for the *TN* "The Challenge of Teaching in China" (6/80). This was followed by Charles T. Scott's "First Impressions of English as a Foreign Language Teaching in China" (12/80); Wang Nianmei's article mentioned above; "A Survey of Language Teaching in the People's Republic of China" by Yang Su Ying (8/81); "So You're Going to Teach in China" by Martha Bean (12/81) in which she offers a number of insightful thoughts on how to prepare for a teaching job in China and which she followed up with "English Materials in China and For China" (4/82). "Employment Conditions in China" were discussed by Carol Kreidler, Gail Gray, Helena Hensley and Patricia Sullivan (4/83).

THE FOUR PHASES OF BILINGUAL EDUCATION IN THE UNITED STATES

By Gerald D. Kanoon

The following information is a historical overview of significant events concerning the bilingual education in the United States. It records its humble beginnings since 1839 and the different phases it has undergone until the present. And then it narrows down to the specifics with regard to its status in the State of Illinois.

Phase I (1839-1923)

Empirical evidence from the study of people's languages and cultures in the United States strongly suggests that America's melting pot concept is not universally verifiable. Ethnic groups comprising the U.S.A. have had linguistic-cultural education in their native origin. For example, as early as 1839 there already existed some form of bilingual education in a Cincinnati community wherein a large majority of the population was German-speaking. To their dismay, the first-generation German-settlers considered America's common schools inferior to those they had known in Germany. As a result, private parochial German schools were established in order to inculcate that superior brand of education from the mother country and also to preserve their ethnic culture, language and tradition for their off-springs. Such schools competed successfully with the public schools for almost a decade despite the fact that parents of such students had to pay both tuition fees and school taxes.

However, in 1840 Ohio passed a law providing tax monies to attract German children into the public schools wherein the German culture and language were also taught. This law made it "the duty of the Board of Trustees and Visitors of Common Schools to provide a number of German schools under duly qualified teachers for the instruction of those youths who desire to learn the German language or the German and English languages together." That same year the city of Cincinnati was mandated by law to introduce German instruction in the grade schools as an optional subject and thus may be credited with having formally initiated the bilingual education program in the U.S.A. This program lasted until 1917.

Other cities like Dayton (1844), Baltimore (1874), and Indianapolis (1882) created programs modeled after the Cincinnati project. In fact, there exists some fragmentary data that suggests that bilingual education benefited at least a million American children who received part of their education in German and part of it in English.

Other states that welcomed bilingual education into their schools were Missouri and Colorado in 1887. The state of Oregon passed a law as early as 1872 permitting German public schools. The German-Americans lobbied for the support of their bilingual education programs and tremendously benefitted from them.

However, some years later Louisville, St. Louis, and St. Paul created a storm among America's German population by dropping their bilingual programs, thus weakening German-American life. This was followed by restricting the teaching of German only to the upper grades in the public schools. This trend marked the anti-German movement in education that broadened itself into an anti-foreign sentimentalism. This motivated legislation geared towards the prohibition of teaching languages other than English in all schools, public or non-public, day schools or supplementary, to pupils below grades eight and nine.

However, a 1923 Supreme Court decision in Meyer v. Nebraska case declared such legislation as unconstitutional. This proved to be a historic decision in favor of all minority groups on American soil that endeavored to uphold the language of their forefathers.

Phase II (1920-1958)

The bilingual education program, often only a language program, was rarely integrated into either the philosophy or the practice of the school or of society. Its fate, therefore, was contingent upon political pressure. For example, the program during this period depended on the German members of a community, instead of reflecting a shared conviction by English-speaking and German-speaking alike that all children stood to benefit from an instruction in two languages.

Consequently, bilingual education (as defined above) disappeared from the American scene by 1920. Ironically, World War II (1941) revived it. The Armed Forces developed techniques of teaching foreign languages in a bilingual setting. This brought about a training program that paved the way towards the creation of the 1958 National Defense Education Act, a precursor to the modern bilingual education.

Phase III (1963-1971)

The first bilingual program in modern times was piloted in the Coral Way School in Dade County, Miami, Florida in September 1963. Counting on public and private foundation funds, this program successfully responded to the needs of children from newly-arrived Cuban parents who were refugees from the Castro takeover. The state of New Mexico launched also in this period an interdisciplinary bilingual education program. This was followed by the United Consolidated Independent School District in Webb County, Laredo, Texas, by the San Antonio School District in Austin, Texas, and a dozen others who replicated the program in 1964. By 1967, 21 states had bilingual education programs concerned with Spanish, French, and Portuguese languages.

Realizing the necessity for such an education, Senator Yarborough from Texas introduced a bill on January 17, 1967 putting such programs on an official basis. He chaired a Special Sub-Committee on Bilingual Education to hold hearings during May, June, July 1967 in various parts of the Country. With President Johnson's backing, the Office of Education established the Mexican-American Affairs Unit on July 1, 1967 to lobby in support of the bill. Congressman Scheuer of New York amended it to include all non-English speaking children from the different ethnic groups, placing emphasis on teacher training, development of materials, and pilot projects. This bill was signed into law on January 1968 and is now known as Title VII, the Bilingual Education Act.

In 1968-1970 the Migrant Program of the Michigan Department of Education created a bilingual education program with both interdisciplinary and linguistic development activities.

It was also in 1968 that Mabel Wilson Richardson reported that a bilingual education program was effective for both English and Spanish-speaking subjects in achieving progress in the language arts and arithmetic in the regular curriculum.

Following the Yarborough program, Massachusetts became the first state, in December 1971, to offer mandatory bilingual education programs for non-English speaking pupils.

The intent of the Title VII law is to use bilingual education as an approach that brings together three distinct elements, namely, bilingualism, bicultural education, and curriculum.

Phase IV (1970-1976)

As an example of how states implemented bilingual programs, under the state of Illinois Bilingual Education Act, bilingual centers were funded in 1970 to provide such an education for the state's non-English speaking pupils. State funds to expand this program are presently provided through Senate Bill 1157.

In June 1973 the Spanish-Speaking People's Study Commission initiated the introduction of House Bill 1223. This established a Department of Transitional Bilingual Education in the Office of the Superintendent of Public Instruction. It further established that every child in the state of Illinois be provided with an educational program relevant to his developmental level and cultural heritage.

In September 1973 this bill was signed into law for implementation in 1974. Academic years 1974-75 and 1975-76 were to be transitional years to close the gap between voluntary programs involving a minority of needy students and mandated programs enrolling most of them. Beginning in July 1976 bilingual education is mandated by this law for all attendance centers enrolling 20 or more limited—or non-English speaking students of the same language background.

Conclusion

The point about the American melting pot is that it did not happen. The fact is that in every generation, throughout the history of the American Republic, the merging of the varying streams of population, differentiated from one another by origin, religion, and outlook, has seemed to lie just ahead, a generation perhaps in the future. This continual deferral of the final "integration" of different ethnic ingredients suggests that we must now search for some systematic and general course of action for the American pattern of sub-nationalities. It is time that the diversity of American cultures was recognized and channeled more conscientiously into a creative force. Bilingual education is moving towards that direction.

Its expansion is slow for it is a reflection of the economic recession in which we find ourselves; although we must also remember the limitations represented by

signed "to meet the special educational needs of children of limited English-the Bilingual Education Act. It is despeaking ability in school districts having a high concentration of such children from families with income below $3,000." In view of these limitations the U.S. Office of Education has tried especially to encourage exemplary demonstration programs, but so far without much success.

The obstacles to success are indeed formidable. Perhaps the greatest of these is the doubt in many communities that the maintenance of non-English languages is desirable. It has not yet been demonstrated that a Latino child can become literate in English best by first learning or becoming literate in Spanish. To resolve this doubt in the public mind we shall need to mobilize all available resources behind a few really convincing demonstrations.

Still another massive obstacle is the education of bilingual teachers. Teacher-preparing institutions are only beginning to become aware that new and better programs are urgently needed to educate qualified teachers in the numbers required.

The achievement of truly exemplary bilingual programs will not be easy. As we have seen, many communities are by no means convinced of the desirability of linguistic and cultural pluralism. Even those that are, are handicapped by the lack of adequately qualified teachers

and other personnel, by the shortage of adequate materials, by inadequate evaluation methods and instruments, and by a lack of collaboration between school and community. Most important of all is the gathering of social data in the planning of such programs.

Finally, to predict that a bilingual education program in the United States will succeed would depend on its quality of teacher training and commitment to its philosophy. For it is a source of pride, a focus of initial loyalties and integrations from which broader loyalties and wider integrations can proceed. If the proponents of this program fail to achieve a newer and higher level of workmanship, we may expect this exciting trend in our schools to languish and fade away as have so many other hopeful educational ideas in the past.

References:

Fishman, Joshua: "Language Loyalty in the United States: the maintenance and perpetuation of non-English mother tongues by American ethnic and religious groups." The Hague. Mouton (1966), p. 377.

Fishman, Joshua: "The Status and Prospects of Bilingualism in the United States." The Modern Language Journal, Vol. XLIX, No. 4 (April 1965), pp. 143-155.

Haugen, Einar: "Bilingualism, Language Contact, and Immigrant Languages in the United States: A Research Report, 1956-70." in Thomas Seboek, ed., Current Trends in Linguistics. The Hague, Mouton & Co. (in press) p. 139.

Yarborough, Ralph W.: "Bilingual Education" in Hearings before the Special Subcommittee on Bilingual Education of the Committee on Labor and Public Welfare. United States Senate, 90th Congress, First Session; U.S. Government Printing Office, (1967). p. 1.

4/78

BILINGUAL EDUCATION: FOR THE MELTING POT OR FOR A NEW AMERICAN PLURALISM

by Allan Weiner
National Puerto Rican Forum

Bilingual education has existed since the founding of this nation. However, as a formal recognized response to a perceived educational need, it is recent. The recent proliferation of Bilingual Programs has been spurred by Title VII, of the ESEA, which for the first time provides funds for the implementation of such programs.

This legislation came into being based on two major observations; that there were certain groups in this country that were not performing in school as they should have been, and the dissemination of information based on linguistics, specifically, that reading and writing in elementary stages were extensions of already internalized structures in a students' vernacular. The humaneness and economy of providing instruction in certain areas such as mathematics in the students' vernacular was also apparent.

Before we proceed into the two main thrusts of what bilingual education is or could be, it might be wise to discuss what bilingual education is not. Bilingual Education is not ESL. Though a strong ESL program

is part of any bilingual program, it is, but one of its constituents. Another myth that should be laid to rest is that bilingual staff does not automatically guarantee the existance of bilingual program. What is most important is that teachers involved perceive of themselves in their bilingual roles and subscribe to the philosophy of what a bilingual program is.

Most current bilingual programs appear to subscribe to the traditional goals of American education. That is, the domination of the various curricular areas and skills, ultimately in English. What is not apparent in this is that Bilingual Education is looked upon in these programs as a technique to achieve ultimate English dominance over the students' vernacular. There is a planned phasing out of the students' native language until, if its study is pursued, it is phased into the area of Foreign language instruction. This is a narrow and ultimately a self-defeating approach to bilingualism.

There is a more ample approach to bilingual education, one which perceives of pluralism as a positive aspect of American society and views

bilingualism and multilingualism as a great national resource. The awareness that occurred with the outbreak of WW II should have taught the Educational Community that we were in the wrong direction when we interpreted Americanization, in a narrow sense, as a goal of our system. We are now, though grudgingly, being given the opportunity to develop the linguistic and cultural resources of this nation. If we continue to interpret our bilingual mandate of just a technique to provide ultimate English dominance, we once again will have missed our opportunity. If, on the other hand, we attempt to develop bilingual capacities in all areas, we will have done our nation a tremendous service.

At this stage of American Education, when so many of the goals that we have struggled so long for are again being threatened, it would indeed be ironic to find out that much we saw as change was not change at all. This is a good time to take a look at what bilingual education should be.

TN 2/76

WHAT IS BILINGUAL EDUCATION AND
WHAT MAKES BILINGUAL PROGRAMS WORK

by Ann Carlovich
and Ernestine Hazuka
West N.Y. Learning Center in N.J.

The NJTESOL/NJBE and the Lakewood Bilingual Consortium (Lakewood, Paterson and Elizabeth) sponsored a Spring Conference at Jersey City State College on April 30, 1975.

The keynote speaker was Dr. Joshua Fishman of Yeshiva University, the well-known sociologist, sociolinguist and author. Some of his writings include: "The Language of Nationalism," "The Sociology of Language" and "Socio-Linguistics: A Brief Introduction."

Through an extensive HEW research grant, Fishman has visited and surveyed over 50,000 educational units in over 100 countries. He has found that although bilingual education is comparatively new to the United States, it is a well-established form of education throughout the world. He further found that bilingual education varies considerably from one country to another and even from one school within a country to another. Fishman categorized bilingual education into three types on the basis of his investigations:

1. *Transitional bilingual education.* The aim of this form of bilingual education is to ease the transition of the students who speak one language into the school system which is based on the speaking of a second, different language. Fishman defines the languages as *marked* (the language which would not ordinarily be used in the school if there were no bilingual education program) and *unmarked* (the language normally used by the majority of the society or normally used in the schools). Words often heard in connection with transitional bilingual education are words like: disadvantaged, adjust to school, join the mainstream. The social goal for this type of program is to serve as an "antidote" to prepare disadvantaged groups to learn the unmarked language so that they may more easily join the mainstream of society or of the school. The United States has many transitional bilingual education programs.

2. *Song and dance bilingual education.* The aim of this form of bilingual education is to maintain one language (usually the marked language) which has an oral history of song, dance, and story-telling. The unmarked language is usually the one in which business is carried on and in which material is written. This form of bilingual education is often associated with nationalistic movements; the marked language is promoted as a way of solidifying the culture, dignifying the historical past, and elevating the status of the common man. This form of education was found by Fishman among American Indian groups and in African countries.

3. *Biliterate bilingual education.* The aim of this form of bilingual education is to have the students learn and maintain two languages. Both of the languages usually have equal status within the country or the school system. An example of this form of education is in Canada with English and French. Fishman has noticed two forms of biliterate bilingual education: one in which there is a functional allocation of which subjects are to be taught in which language in the classroom and this corresponds to the way the languages are used in the society. (In Canada, French-speaking children are taught courses which deal with interpersonal relations, home, family in French while math is taught in English because this is the way in which the children will probably use their languages.) The other form of biliterate bilingual education is more haphazard: classes are taught in one language or in the other because teachers, texts or other materials happen to be available in that language.

Fishman stated that, in general, bilingual education is usually intended to be compensatory education or it is instituted as a response to ethnic or nationalistic movements of minority groups who wish to preserve a dying language or a dying culture. Bilingual education is seldom instituted with its goal being a better education for all.

In his investigations, Fishman has attempted to find out what factors make a bilingual program successful from several points of view: the whole educational community's point of view, a comparison of the bilingual school with other schools in the community, and from the student's point of view.

Several factors were found to be essential. In measuring absolute and relative academic success, the most important factors (there was over a 90% correlation) were: community support (those programs which had most community support were the most successful) and equal balance of students (those programs which had a balance of students whose language was the unmarked language)— less successful were those bilingual programs which were only intended for the minority group or the disadvantaged group. Programs which taught subjects in the language which would be appropriate in society were more successful than programs which taught subjects in any language that they happened to have textbooks in or which taught a course in whichever language the teacher who was assigned to that class happened to speak. Students were most satisfied with programs in which they were allowed a period of grace in which they were free to choose whether to answer a question in their native language or the new language (immersion programs were much less popular).

His closing remarks were directed not only to ESL teachers but to all language teachers. Fishman stated that educators do not usually question the importance of teaching other subjects, but when they do, the other subjects can state a rationale for their importance by stating needs which the society has for their existence. However, when languages are challenged, the rationale which is most often given is: "It's good to know another language." History teachers would never justify their classes by saying: "It's good to know another history." Fishman urged language teachers to justify their courses in societal terms. He feels that bilingual education offers a legitimate base for language for, perhaps, the first time.

He concluded by saying that one of the most serious problems we, as language teachers, have in the area of methodology and content in the classroom is that students usually learn nothing in language classes except the language. When students learn to read, they are also able to learn information at the same time. Language is a vehicle through which that which is unknown is made known to another person or persons. "The book is on the table" is not something which ordinarily needs to be communicated. Bilingual education is designed to teach subject matter and the language at the same time. Through bilingual education, the students thus have a need to understand and communicate in the target language because they are truly involved in a communicating situation.

THE TEACHING OF ENGLISH IN PUERTO RICO

Paquita Viñas de Vasquez
General Supervisor of English
Department of Education, Hato Rey, Puerto Rico

Puerto Rico, a small island in the Caribbean, 1,000 miles southeast of Florida, U.S.A. was discovered by Christopher Columbus on his second voyage in 1493. The island was inhabited by peaceful Taino Indians. Spanish colonization of Puerto Rico started soon thereafter and the Taino population gradually disappeared, not without first leaving the imprints of its culture on the *colonos*.

The Spaniards made Puerto Rico an agricultural colony, once they had disposed of the existing gold, and then imported African slaves to work on the sugar cane plantations.

After almost 500 years of Spanish domination, Puerto Rico, with few resources and a population in which the pride of the Taino Indian, the ambition of the Spanish *conquiatador*, and the sturdiness of the African slave had skillfully blended, was ceded by Spain to the United States at the close of the Spanish-American War in 1898. Puerto Rico was a U.S. territory until 1952 when it became a Commonwealth.

Today, Puerto Rico faces problems common to modern societies: overpopulation (2.8 million people on 3,500 square miles of land), unemployment (12%), low per capita income as compared to the U.S. ($3,000 a year per family), and even rush hour *tapones*[1] (1 car per 5 persons). Yet, it is one of the few places in which different races and religions co-exist, except for occasional demonstrations by dissenting groups, with as great a measure of harmony as can be expected in today's world.

English Language Policies
1898-1947

Up until 1898 Spanish had been the official language and the only language in Puerto Rico. That year marked the beginning of the teaching and learning of English in Puerto Rico. It also marked the beginning of the blending of two cultures, a situation which has met with considerable passive resistance, the majority of the Puerto Ricans being strongly traditional and resistant to change.

Six major changes in language policy in Puerto Rico occurred between 1898 and 1947. The first change was introduced by Dr. Martin Brumbaugh who became Commissioner of Education in 1900. The Brumbaugh policy provided for the teaching of English and Spanish as subjects beginning in the first grade. Spanish was to be used also as the medium of instruction in the elementary grades 1-8 while English was to be the medium of instruction in the secondary grades 9-12. Spanish was to be taught as a special subject in the secondary grades.

Commissioner Roland Faulkner introduced the second major change in 1905.

He aimed at the use of English as the medium of instruction in all the grades of the public school system.

Commissioner Paul Miller introduced the third major change in 1916. Spanish became the language of instruction in grades 1-4, both English and Spanish in grade 5, English in the remaining grades, 6-12. The study of English and Spanish as subjects continued in both the elementary and the high school.

Dr. José Padín introduced the fourth major change in 1934. He made Spanish the language of instruction in the elementary level (grades 1-8) and doubled the time devoted to English as a subject from forty-five to ninety minutes in the seventh and eighth grades.

Dr. José Gallardo introduced the fifth major change in 1937. It involved a series of policies evolving from an effort to use both English and Spanish as media of instruction. Some subjects were taught in Spanish and others were taught in English. The final development was instruction in the vernacular in the elementary school.

Commissioner Mariano Villaronga introduced the sixth major change in 1947. He made Spanish the medium of instruction at all levels of the public school system. In 1948 he initiated the English Program which is in effect today.

Ralph Robinett, director of the English Program in Puerto Rico from 1960 to 1963 wrote in *The Teaching of English as a Second Language in Puerto Rico*: "The Villaronga policy is the culmination of a long struggle between those who were most interested in the general education of Puerto Rican youth and those who were most interested in the general education of Puerto Rican youth and those who were most interested in the ability of Puerto Ricans to speak English. Those who were in favor of Spanish as the medium of instruction realized that Puerto Rico must first be interested in ensuring an adequate education for its coming generations. Those who were in favor of English as the medium of instruction were generally either politically motivated or lacked insight into the role of Spanish in the social-cultural life of Puerto Rico."

The matter which caused Puerto Rican education so many setbacks was settled for good. The policy since 1947 has been the teaching of English as a subject and the use of Spanish as the medium of instruction in all the grades of the public school system beginning in the first grade.

Premises Underlying
the English Program

Underlying the formal English curri-

culum in Puerto Rico are two broad objectives: (1) to develop in the pupils the ability to understand, speak, read, and write English, and (2) to develop in the pupils habits of using English as a vehicle of communication. Also underlying the English curriculum are a series of premises[2] which serve as the basis for the selection and preparation of the material to be taught and how it is to be taught. These premises are:

• The essential elements of a language may be identified through an analysis of the language as it functions in actual usage and as it contrasts in actual usage in the vernacular of the learner.

• The essential elements to be learned by all students are the elements with the greatest recurrence, which are the points of contrast in the sound system and structure; the vocabulary needed for the communication process will vary with the learner's interest and experiences.

• For productive use the student needs a minimum of language forms to cover a maximum number of situations; for receptive use the student must learn to respond to a wide variety of language forms, as he has no control over the linguistic habits of others.

• There are three basic stages in the language learning process: the initial stage is one of simple imitation on the part of the learner; the second stage is one in which the learner consciously selects a particular form in his attempt to communicate; the third stage is one in which the learner demonstrates a degree of automatic control over an item by using it more or less spontaneously.

• The essential elements of a language are most efficiently and economically learned if they are organized and presented in a systematic sequence.

• Language learning occurs best in practice where the focus of attention is consistently on meaningful communication.

• An oral approach with the reinforcements of reading and writing is the most practical approach to teaching English to the large majority of children in the public schools of Puerto Rico:

The basis of language is sound; therefore in the early stages reading must stem from, rather than precede, oral practice.

The graphic representation of English does not provide for many features of the sound system which constitute an integral part of the material to be mastered.

The graphic system does not consistently represent the sound segments; many sounds have multiple spellings and vice versa.

In the early stages the learner is confused by the interference of the spelling system of his vernacular if reading precedes oral practice.

In the early stages, guided oral practice affords an opportunity for faster habit formation than would occur in the extensive use of reading materials as a basic approach.

In the early stages, the natural order of listening, speaking, reading, and writing is the most efficient order to achieve four-fold mastery of language forms.

As would be expected we teach English orally in the first and second grades to give pupils a background in oral English before they start reading in the second language and to allow them a couple of years in which to learn to read and write in the vernacular (Spanish). For the teaching of oral English in the first and second grades, we have prepared interest-centered language units, picture books, and picture cards.

Reading is initiated in the third grade and for that purpose, we have prepared a pre-primer, *Our Animal Friends*, based on the major spelling patterns of English; a teacher's guide and sets of the 70 most outstanding pictures in the pre-primer, to be used for teacher training purposes and to give the children the opportunity of listening to the voices of native speakers of the language, in the event the teacher in charge is not a native speaker as is usually the case.

From the fourth through the twelfth grade we have two parallel programs: a language program in which English structures and vocabulary are presented orally and reinforced by reading and writing, and a reading program which stresses the development of reading skills and the acquisition of vocabulary on both productive and receptive levels.

For grades 4-7 we have prepared a language series, the *American English Series*, Books I, II, III, and a reader series, *The English Reader Series*, which consists of four readers: *New Friends, Fun, Fancy and Adventure, Heroes in Fact and Fable,* and *Tales from Life and Legend.* The *American English Series* is actually a revision of the first three books of the *Fries American English Series*, a pioneer effort produced under the direction of Dr. Pauline Rojas, former director of the English Program, and under the consultantship of the late Dr. Charles Fries. Teachers' guides and tapes accompany the *American English Series.* Teachers' manuals and children's workbooks[3] accompany the *English Reader Series*. A tape of *New Friends* was also prepared and is being used by fourth grade teachers and pupils.

The *Fries American English Series* was used for language instruction for many years and is still being used to some extent. However, realizing that motivation is vitally important in language learning and that both teachers and pupils (especially secondary level pupils) were becoming dissatisfied with the same materials and the same approach, we have decided to try out new materials such as the *Lado English Series*, published by Regents Publishing Co.; the *English for Today* series, prepared by the National Council of Teachers of English and published by McGraw-Hill; and the *Let's Learn English* series published by the American Book Co. At the time the *Fries American English Series* was prepared there were practically no materials scientifically prepared for teaching English as a second language. Today there is an abundance of materials to choose from.

New materials for the teaching of reading skills at the junior and senior high levels are being tried out. For both language and reading instruction, the time devoted to English in each grade, and the attitudes, skills and concepts the pupils are expected to acquire at each level, we have prepared the *Outline Summary of the English Curriculum in the Elementary School* and the *Outline Summary of the English Curriculum in the Secondary School*.[4]

Also, for the purpose of revamping the teaching of English at the secondary level, we are implementing several federally funded projects. Some of these are the Pronunciation Course for the Seventh Grade, Proposal for the Development of Reading Skills at the Intermediate Level, and the Right to Read proposal.[5]

We are also offering elective courses at the twelfth grade level: Conversational English, Drama, American Literature, Composition, and Advanced Placement. The Conversational English course is geared to those students who are not college-bound, and who will perhaps move to the continental United States in search of better opportunities for work. The remaining elective courses aim to strengthen college-bound students in the aforementioned areas.

To supplement the basic curriculum we have language and reading laboratories, TV programs, classroom listening centers, reading corners, school libraries, a Curriculum Center, etc. As Professor Ralph B. Long of the University of Puerto Rico states in *The Puerto Rican Experience in English as a Second Language* (1964), "A great deal of experience has been accumulated, and materials of many kinds have been developed. I do not know where else, in this hemisphere, so great an accumulation of experience can be found, or so much interest in pertinent developments in the field. Both teaching and research in English as a second language can be done in Puerto Rico under uniquely favorable conditions. Puerto Rico would seem to be without equal in this hemisphere in its potentialities as a place to train teachers of English as a second language, especially for Spanish-speaking areas."

Main Problems

In spite of almost 75 years of experience with the teaching of English as a second language in Puerto Rico we still have many problems. Many educators feel that the lack of teacher preparation is our biggest problem; others feel that the lack of motivation, especially at the secondary level, is the greater problem. There is an enthusiasm for English at the elementary level that gradually but steadily melts away beginning in the seventh grade. At the junior high school level the student is old enough to begin questioning the importance and the need for learning some of the things that the school curriculum forces him to learn. English is not the language of everyday life in Puerto Rico; there is no immediate need for the student to learn the language. The promise that some day he will get a better-paying job if he knows English or that he will do better work at the university (if he belongs in the 10% who go to college) does not make the sacrifice of learning a second language seem worthwhile. The young adolescent is not interested in the future; he is interested in the here and now. Conversely, the Puerto Rican child who moves to the United States will need English to succeed in school and also for everyday life. He will have the built-in motivation to learn English that his counterpart in Puerto Rico definitely lacks.

At the senior high level, students begin to show interest in politics and some are deeply influenced by the opinion of some political groups: "Learning English will gradually adulterate the mother tongue, Spanish, and will undermine the Spanish culture."

Fortunately, there is still a tremendous interest in obtaining high grades, especially since each year it becomes increasingly difficult to be admitted to the universities. The present enrollment at the University of Puerto Rico is over 25,000, and only those students with a B+ average who make a high grade on the college entrance examination have the chance to gain admittance to the Río Piedras university. (One-third of the examination, 800 points, is on English.) Therefore, the secondary school teacher of English has to make use of all his resources to get his students properly motivated.

Studies such as those conducted by Dr. Wallace Lambert and described in his

Psychological Approaches to Second Language Learning and Bilingualism indicate that motivation plays an extremely important role in second language learning. Describing the results of studies carried out in Montreal he writes: ". . .two independent factors underlie the development of skill in learning a second language: an intellectual capacity and an appropriate attitudinal orientation toward the other language group, coupled with a determined motivation to learn the language." Of the two kinds of motivation he discusses—instrumental and integrative—the latter is apparently the most effective. A student's motivation to learn a second language is determined by his attitudes toward speakers of that language and by his orientation toward learning that language. Students with an integrative orientation do better than those instrumentally oriented. Because of the geographical distance between Puerto Rico and the United States, our limited contact with native speakers of English, as well as the lack of opportunities to use the language, it is extremely difficult to give students this type of integrative motivation.

Surprisingly, on the other hand, the findings of the 1970 U.S. census, as reported in the January 7, 1973 *San Juan Star*, indicate that Puerto Rico is becoming a bilingual society perhaps even more rapidly than is realized. The Census Bureau reported that more the 38 percent of Puerto Rico's population could speak English; that only about one third of the 1.6 million people 10 years and older who either did not or had not yet finished high school were able to speak English; and yet that of 470,000 high school graduates, more than 403,000 spoke English.

These findings are, in the opinion of this writer, a credit to the English Program of Puerto Rico's public school system. It must be pointed out that private institutions on the island too contribute substantially to education and to the teaching of English.

The second largest problem is, of course, the shortage of well-prepared teachers of English. It has been said that all that is needed for a successful language program are good materials and a good model to imitate. Puerto Rico has adequate materials for the teaching of English as a second language, but good models in the classroom are quite often not available. Many teachers are non-native speakers of English who lack, especially at the primary and elementary levels, the necessary skills and academic preparation. Although there are several teacher training colleges and universities (University of Puerto Rico with the main campus in Río Piedras and six branches, Interamerican University with the main campus in San German and nine branches, Catholic University in Ponce, College of the Sacred Heart in San Juan,

World University and Junior College in Río Piedras, and Central University in Bayamon), the number of teachers prepared is always smaller than the number required. In addition, teachers are taking positions in private industry where the incentives of high salaries and fringe benefits outweigh dedication to the teaching profession.

In order to alleviate the teacher shortage the government offers provisional appointments to candidates who have not fulfilled the following requirements: a Bachelor of Arts degree in elementary education, or a normal diploma plus 24 credits in English and a course on the teaching of English as a second language for teaching in elementary schools, and a Bachelor of Arts degree in education with a major in English for teaching in secondary schools.

Fortunately, in 1968, under the auspices of a sympathetic administration and with the help of U.S. government funds, the English Program started several teacher-training projects, many of which are underway, several with excellent results.

One project which deserves mention and which could be implemented in other parts of the world where bilingual programs suffer from inadequately trained teachers is the Bilingual Teachers Program. The objective of this Title V Law 90-35 and Title I Law 89-10 program is to prepare 2,000 teachers of English in a period of five years or less by training Puerto Rican high school graduates or first- or second-year college students who (1) received their education on the mainland (U.S.A.), (2) are native speakers of English, (3) were unable to pursue further studies because of economic conditions, (4) enjoy working with small children, and (5) would like to make teaching their profession. As a result of this work-study program which started in 1969, more than one thousand provisional teachers are teaching English in grades 1-3. What was once thought of as a never-to-be-realized dream of departmentalizing the primary level, now appears to be an attainable goal.

Even though about one-third of the government's budget is for education, an ever-increasing population makes for ever-increasing problems such as too few adequate schools and well-trained teachers, overcrowded classrooms, double enrollment and interlocking, lack of textbooks and materials, etc. Additionally, a high dropout rate, especially in rural areas, is of current concern.

Teacher and Supervisory Staff

Puerto Rico has a highly centralized public school system which is directed by the Department of Education. The head of this department is the Secretary of Education[6] and a member of the governor's cabinet. The Department of Education formulates the educational policies which are then relayed to the six

educational regions: San Juan, Ponce, Mayaguez, Arecibo, Humacao, and Caguas.

The educational regions work in conjunction with Puerto Rico's 80 school districts in the implementation of the educational policies formulated by the Department of Education.

The Assistant Secretary of Education for academic programs which include English, Spanish, social studies, science, and mathematics, and the program directors are responsible for the preparation and implementation of the school curriculum.

The director of the English Program[7] is also the head of the English Section located in the Department of Education in Hato Rey. The director and her staff composed of seven general supervisors and eight curriculum technicians are responsible for the preparation and acquisition of materials for the teaching of English as a second language and for the orientation of regional and zone supervisors in the use of materials and on teaching techniques.

At present there are about 6,500 teachers teaching English in the public schools from the first to the twelfth grade. Working directly on the local level with the teachers and principals in providing in-service training and orientation on materials and teaching technique are 100 zone supervisors assigned to the offices of the superintendents of schools. In addition to having considerable experience teaching English, these professionals also have graduate degrees in linguistics, applied linguistics, English as a second language, supervision, etc.

Coordinating the work of the zone supervisors, providing consultant services to the local school organizations, and channeling new materials to the zone supervisors and teachers are fourteen regional supervisors. Two supervisors each are assigned to the regional offices of Arecibo, Ponce, Mayaguez, Caguas, and Humacao, and four to San Juan.

English for Adults

The Adult Education Program of the Department of Education started its English Program for Adults in 1953. Since then about 120,000 adults including secretaries, sales clerks, hotel employees, farm laborers, industrial workers, policemen, cab drivers, etc. have profited from the English courses offered by this program.

Courses include a five-month conversational English course, the teaching of English through TV, the teaching of English to farm laborers at their place of employment, and a course on North American culture.

The conversational English course is offered in August and January each year. The Adult Program is planning to offer a similar course to groups of professionals and industrial workers who are not proficient in English. This and the other

English courses for adults listed above are offered anywhere on the island when twenty of more persons are interested in taking them.

The Future of English in Puerto Rico

The success of the English Program in Puerto Rico depends to a large extent on the interest of the political party in power. Every change of administration influences the teaching and learning of English to no small degree. Unquestionably, parents do, in general strongly favor having their children learn English. Thus, there is good reason to believe that English will be a part of the curriculum for many years to come.

In spite of this positive attitude, complete bilingualism will perhaps never be attained because of the general conditions and circumstances cited earlier. Functional bilingualism is a more realistic objective. It represents different things for different students: for students in general, the ability to meet their communication needs in Puerto Rico; for students who move to the continental United States, the basis for a rapid linguistic assimilation in an English-speaking environment; and for college-bound students, the skills and habits necessary to successfully pursue studies with textbooks and instruction in English.

The present government of Puerto Rico has publicly expressed its views toward English in our schools—more and better English for all Puerto Ricans. We welcome this policy and extend our cooperation and professional support in its implementation.

Footnotes
1. Traffic jams.
2. These premises were listed by Ralph Robinett in The Teaching of English in the Public Schools of Puerto Rico *and are still considered valid.*
3. Two workbooks are in preparation.
4. Available upon request.
5. Information on these projects will be available at the 1973 TESOL Convention.
6. Mrs. Celeste Benitez de Rexach, former professor at the University of Puerto Rico, is the Secretary of Education.
7. Dr. Adela M. Mendez, former professor at the University of Puerto Rico, is director of the English Program.

TN 4/73

MY VISIT TO THE USA

Wang Nianmei
Lanzhou University

It is already six months since I came back to Lanzhou, but I am still often haunted by the vivid recollections of the days spent in the U.S.A. So I'd like to take this opportunity to say something about my visit to the U.S.A.

1. Before Starting Off

To tell the truth, I had never thought that I would have a chance to visit the United States until the beginning of this year. So when I was informed that I would be sent to attend the 14th International TESOL Convention, I simply couldn't believe my ears. You can hardly imagine how excited I was in those days. I felt very lucky that I would have such a rare chance to visit the USA. I was especially happy to have Prof. Blatchford as my good teacher and friend whom I could rely upon for help throughout my journey. But at the same time I was still worried very much about my English proficiency. I was afraid that I would not be able to live up to the expectations of my colleagues. It was with such mixed feelings that I went on board the plane bound for Beijing.

2. What Impressed Me Most During My Stay in the U.S.A.

I was a little nervous about how I would get along with Americans as the wide-bodied 747 was landing at San Francisco. But the smiling faces, warm greetings of Americans I met and their willingness to offer me help soon made me relax and feel at ease. I found that they were more friendly to me than I had expected.

Prof. Blatchford did everything he could to make me feel comfortable. He introduced me to a lot of his friends. They went with me to workshops, colloquia or mini-courses for company. I was also kindly invited to his close friends' homes and to have dinner with them. Wherever I went, I was given a cordial welcome.

It happened that a team sent by the Foreign Experts Bureau also came to attend the TESOL Convention. It was at Prof. Blatchford's insistence that I gained the chance to join them in visiting different institutions in Washington and New York and make the acquaintance of many prominent persons in the field of TESOL. With his help I felt very happy and at home, though I was more than ten thousand miles from my motherland.

Dr. Alatis, the Executive Secretary of TESOL and Dean of the School of Languages and Linguistics of Georgetown University, spared no efforts to take good care of us. It was very thoughtful of him to make the necessary arrangements for us. We were several times accorded cordial receptions and invited to dinner by him. I owe a great deal to him for his friendliness and generous help.

At the opening session of the TESOL Convention Dr. Alatis warmly welcomed us Chinese in his formal speech. All the participants of the Convention greeted us with warm applause. A group of dancers were invited to the ballroom to perform a traditional Chinese lion dance before the opening session. The cheers of the jubilant crowds mingled with the beating of drums and gongs. The hall was immersed in a friendly festival atmosphere. I will never forget this exciting moment. At the banquet given in the Empress Restaurant in Chinatown in San Francisco our team leader, the Vice-Director of the Foreign Experts Bureau and Prof. Deng from the Beijing Foreign Languages Institute were honoured by having their seats at the head table and all the other members of the team, including me, were also treated as distinguished guests.

I was also very happy to see that the American people were very much interested in China. There were so many applicants who wanted to come to China to help upgrade our teachers of English that sometimes they lined up outside the recruiting office room waiting for interviews with the team. Everywhere people stretched out their hands of friendship to me and expressed their desire to make friends with me. I was greatly moved by their friendly feeling to us Chinese.

All I experienced in the U.S.A. makes me convinced that the tree of friendship between our two peoples has already deeply taken root in their hearts. What we should do is to take good care of it and water it to make it put forth beautiful blossoms.

3. What We Should Learn From The American People

(1) Efficiency and enthusiasm for work

The thirty-story Hilton Hotel in San Francisco was very much like a huge hive. Thousands of participants of the TESOL Convention were as busy as bees from early in the morning till late at night. They hurried here and there and tried to attend as many lectures as possible. About thirty workshops, colloquia and mini-courses were going on in different ballrooms and parlors at the same time. Lively conversations and heated arguments could be heard everywhere during coffee breaks—in the corridors, on the escalators or in front of the lifts. People kept pouring into the Franciscan Room and Hilton Plaza, attracted by numerous interesting books on display. Newsletters were published every day. Obviously the participants in the Convention loved their own work. They were interested in every new development in the field of TESOL and keen to draw inspiration from others' experience. At the same time, they were also glad to share their own views and thoughts with others.

We were told that about four thousand people attended the Convention. You can easily imagine what an arduous task it was to organize all the activities for the convention. Everything was carried on methodically, in a planned way. So I was greatly surprised when I learned that most people who made all the arrangements for the Convention worked on a volunteer basis. I could not help admiring their enthusiasm and efficiency in work.

This effective way of working could be seen everywhere. Let me take Mrs. Johanson for example. As a secretary of Dr. Alatis, she organized interviews, answered telephone calls, handled day-to-day work, typed letters and documents, made all kinds of helpful suggestions, worked as a tour guide for us and even gave a dinner for us in her home. She was full of energy and dealt with her work ably. She always offered Dr. Alatis timely help when necessary.

I never saw people idling about in their work hours. Waiters in restaurants, shop assistants in department stores or attendants in hotels all seemed to have a good knowledge about their jobs. They served customers well and were warm and polite towards them. Why shouldn't we learn from the American people their enthusiasm and efficiency in work and good attitude in attending to customers?

(2) Initiative and dynamic spirit

I was deeply impressed by the large number of papers with substantial content present at the TESOL Convention. But the active response of the audience to each talk made a still deeper and indelible impression on me. I was amazed to find that they were quite different from us. They were never content with just listening. They were always asking questions, making comments, and airing their different points of view. So the presentation of each paper was followed by a free and lively discussion. In our country the audience at any meeting usually confines its role to just listening. We don't like or sometimes dare not express different opinions in public. I believe we should learn from the American people their frankness and enterprising spirit.

(3) A country full of variety

The U.S.A. is a country full of variety. Ancestors of the American people came from different countries. And even now people from all parts of the world are still coming here continuously. So you can easily see people with different complexions on the street. This variety finds its full expression in San Francisco. Not only did I have the chance to eat Beijing duck in Chinatown, but I could also taste spaghetti in a Spanish cafeteria and Italian pizza at a friend's home. I went to a Mexican restaurant too, where I had a hot burrito for my lunch. Once I was very much puzzled by the names of French dishes. Only with the help of Prof. Deng did I make out the menu and succeed in ordering my food. I was glad to find that typical American dishes such as beefsteak and fried prawns also agreed with me.

The American people like festivities. They have a bright and cheerful disposition. It seemed to me that there were many more festivals in the U.S.A. than in our country. While I was in San Francisco, Chinese Americans happened to celebrate their Spring Festival. One night, there was a mammoth parade in Chinatown. The dragon dances and beautiful Chinese national costumes exerted a strong fascination on all the spectators. It was said that the streets in Chinatown were crowded with about 300,000 curious citizens and tourists that night.

When I was in New York, I saw Irishmen celebrating their St. Patrick's Day. Wearing green clothes and holding green balloons in their hands, they marched along the streets. Lots of pedestrians stopped walking, attracted by the colourful sight of the parade. When I went to LaGuardia Community College, the American host gave me a lovely green flower as a St. Patrick's Day gift.

The day before I left the U.S.A. I went sightseeing with a group of Chinese electronic experts. It was a nice sunny day. The sky was very clear and spring breezes were blowing. We were surprised to see that there were so many people around the Washington Monument. I was especially fascinated at watching lovely children on the grass. They were all flying kites. All the kites were very beautiful. Some of them looked like butterflies, others like eagles, dragons and so on. Light music was being sent out through loudspeakers. That day turned out to be Kite Day in Washington. We were told that the kites which were most beautiful and flew the highest would be awarded a prize.

I couldn't help thinking that the great number of festivals was probably another reflection of the variety of American society. Why don't we diversify our life and make it richer and more colourful?

(4) Independent and industrious

Once I was invited to an American friend's home. Their house was located in the suburbs of Washington. This was a well-to-do middle-class family. The father was a professor at a university. The mother was an activist in the local American-Chinese Friendship Association. What struck me most was their way of educating their children. Two elder sons study at two private universities. Their youngest son studies at a high school. To my great surprise, he gets up at three o'clock every morning and drives a car to deliver newspapers. He earns $400 each month by working as a newsboy. Can't the parents afford their youngest son? No, not at all. The father told me that the fuel the boy used cost much more than $400. Then what were the parents up to? They tried this way to train their son to be independent and industrious. They also told me that both their elder sons work during the summer vacations to earn some money to support themselves. In fact, most American students work their way through college. In a competitive society like the U.S.A. how can a young man expect to achieve success without extreme diligence and tenacious struggle? In our country quite a few young people are spoiled by their parents of position. I don't believe that those who are accustomed to depend on their parents' power and influence will be able to keep pace with the rapid development of our society. Can't we learn something from these American parents?

4. Machine Age

The U.S.A. is a highly developed rich country. This was no longer an abstract concept for me as soon as I set foot on the soil of the country. I saw with my own eyes what profound changes the progress of science and technology had brought to the daily life of the American people.

Telephones are available everywhere. You can make telephone calls either on the streets or at your home. People use them to order their seats at a restaurant, make reservations for their journey, and make appointments with their friends. In a word, the telephone has become a very helpful companion of every common American.

I was also amazed at the popularity and efficiency of copy machines. Electronic computers have come into wide use at airports, in libraries and offices. I was especially interested in the self-service machines which provide people with different drinks. And I felt as happy as a child when I got a can of orange juice by putting thirty cents into the machine.

What struck me most were the long streams of cars on the streets. It seems to me that cars are as indispensable to the Americans as bicycles are to us Chinese. As most Americans live far away from where they work and public transportation is not as developed as in China, they rarely, if ever, go to their offices or go shopping on foot. I can hardly imagine how an American is able to manage if he has no car at all.

The housing conditions of the American people are much better than ours. Not only do they have larger living space, but their houses are also provided with lots of modern conveniences. I had a good chance to visit some American friends' homes. Most of them live in two-story houses with garages and small gardens. Usually each child has his own bedroom with a bathroom and a closet attached, no matter how little he may be. All rooms, whether they are a sitting room, dining room, family room or study, are well furnished and air-conditioned. Whichever family I visited, the hostess would show me with pride her kitchen. There are so many machines in the kitchen: electric stove, microwave oven, dishwasher, refrigerator, garbage compressor and so on. What a great change has taken place in the daily life of an American family. When I thought of the time I have to spend doing housework, I couldn't help envying my American hostesses for their modern conveniences.

I liked the subway in San Francisco, which is called BART. BART—the Bay Area Rapid Transit—as a matter of fact, is composed of one-third subway, one-third elevated, and one-third ground-level track. It is not only quick, but it is also very cheap. What's more, I felt it much safer to travel by BART. I was sure I wouldn't get lost on BART. There is a map at the entrance of each station. And the destination of each train lights up when any train comes into the station. So it is impossible for a passenger to get the direction wrong. Anybody, so long as he can read English, may get anywhere he wants to go under his own steam.

BART is operated completely by electronic computers. There is neither ticket-collector at the station nor conductor on the train. When you deposit some coins in a machine, you will receive a ticket. Then you insert the ticket in an entrance turnstile, and the door opens to let you in. But don't forget to get the ticket from another slot, because you have to put the ticket in an exit turnstile when you get to the destination station. Otherwise you will not be allowed to get out. The electric train goes smoothly. Doors open and close automatically. When the train reaches the bay, it plunges into a four-mile-long tube, which snakes under the bay. At that time you'll feel that air pushes against your ear membrane, the same feeling a passenger usually experiences when an airplane is taking off or landing. But it is still much more comfortable and faster to travel by BART than to crawl along in bumper-to-bumper traffic on the toll-bridge.

In a word, machines are an indispensable part of every American's life. He would find it hard to imagine what life could be like without machines.

5. What The Americans Worry About

The U.S.A. is a beautiful country richly endowed by nature. I was often fascinated by various woods and green meadows there. The American people benefit from good weather conditions and rich natural resources of the country. The U.S.A. is also a highly-developed power with modern industry and agriculture. The American people enjoy all the conveniences provided by their advanced science and technology. So generally speaking, they live a more comfortable life than we do.

But apart from all these advantages, I found that there was still some things Americans are worried about.

(1) Energy crisis

As oil has been in rather short supply recently due to the tense situation in the Middle East and the price of oil has been going up rapidly, the American people are very much worried about the energy crisis. The automobile industry is especially seriously affected by the energy crisis. So everybody is concerned about the way to economize the consumption of oil and the development of new sources of energy.

(2) Two-digit inflation is another problem that troubles the American people. It makes some of them feel uncertain about their future. It is not easy for a woman to be a good homemaker in the U.S.A. She must do careful calculation and strict budgeting to avoid overdrawing her account. Though a middle-class American earns about $20,000-$25,000 a year, one-third of the money is spent on housing. Nearly another third, or at least a quarter of his income, goes in taxes. Tuition fees for private schools are very high and medical care is unbelievably expensive. So everyone has to spend his money very carefully.

(3) Problems of old people

Though people in the U.S.A. get pensions when they retire and there are some organizations which try to help aged people, it still seems to me that old people have a hard time. They are lonely and pitiful. Their own children usually don't live with them and can't take care of them when they are sick.

(4) The automobile—a mixed blessing

While cars have brought better and more convenient transportation, they have also brought new and unforeseen problems. Traffic accidents are increasing steadily and large cities are plagued by traffic congestion, especially at rush hour. Worst of all is the air pollution caused by the internal-combustion engine. Another trouble is that there isn't enough space for parking cars in big cities. Let me give you an example. One day Prof. Choseed invited me to a dinner at the Georgetown University dining-room. But when we got there, he couldn't find a place to park his car. Afraid of being fined by a policeman, he had to drive his car slowly round and round the campus until he heaved a sigh of relief when he saw a car that was going to leave a parking meter. I can still remember clearly the regretful expression on an American lady's face when she told me that she had got a parking ticket the day before and a fine of fifty dollars had been imposed on her. So it turns out, progress has more than one face.

6. Culture Shock

You might be interested in whether I met some difficulties during my stay in the United States. Now let me tell you something about culture shock.

(1) Fast pace of life and fast speed of speech

My schedule was so crowded that it seemed to me that everything went very fast. I usually worked from morning till night. No naps, no rest. It was not easy for me to get used to the fast pace of life in the U.S.A.

I worried very much about my communicative competence before I left China. I was glad to find that I could make myself understood and also make out what Americans said to me in most cases. But I had to admit at the same time there's still a long, long way to go to improve my language proficiency.

Most participants at the TESOL Convention were Americans and the time for each report was limited. So all the speakers spoke very fast. I found it was very hard for me to adapt myself to such a fast speed of speech. Besides, my limited vocabulary and unfamiliarity with certain subjects and background also prevented me from comprehending some of the reports adequately. Once I went to a play at the invitation of Prof. Blatchford. I felt frustrated because I often couldn't figure out what the actors' jokes meant while others all laughed till the tears came.

Abbreviations are widely used, which are another hard nut for me to crack. I don't think my memory is very poor. But I frequently had to apologize for failing to learn the names of a large number of American friends.

(2) Troubles caused by machines

When I arrived in San Francisco, the telephone saved me. It was with the help of the telephone that I made contact with the consulate of our country and learned the way to the Saint Francis Hotel. But it was also the telephone that brought me the first trouble.

It was very easy to find the telephone booths at the airport. But it took me more than half an hour to get through. Why? First, without coins one can't make a telephone call. And I had no coins and no idea about where to get change. Secondly, I didn't know how much a telephone call from the airport to the Saint Francis Hotel cost. So I couldn't decide how many and which coins I should put in the telephone. Thirdly, I didn't know how to use an automatic telephone. Finally, I didn't know what to do when I heard the warning buzzing. So I tried twice but failed to get through. I was racked with anxiety. I was completely at a loss. What to do? Luckily a kind middle-aged lady come to me and helped me out. But I was already wet with sweat.

The next day Prof. Blatchford showed me how to get change from a change machine. I was very happy because I always like to try something new. One day later, I came to BART. "Let me have a try," I thought. In a hurry I inserted a five-dollar bill into a machine. But to my disappointment, no coins came out. What's more, the bill was stuck in the machine and I couldn't get it back. I was upset and tried to find someone to help me. But since BART is operated by electronic computers, there were no clerks at the station at all. I didn't know whom to ask for help. Fortunately, an electrical engineer happened to be passing by. Seeing that I was caught in a dilemma, he gave me a hand and I got the bill back. He explained to me that the machine I had put the bill in was a ticket machine. What a blunder I had made! "I must be very careful with all the machines from now on," I said to myself.

(3) Tipping and taxes

We never tip anybody in our country. But it is very impolite if you forget to tip a taxi-driver or a waitress in a restaurant. I found it hard to get used to the tipping system. I am not good at mental arithmetic. So sometimes it seemed to me a heavy burden to figure out within a few seconds how much I had to pay for a tip.

Tax is another problem. Once I went to a supermarket. A price tag showed that two cassette tapes cost $2.99. "That's not too expensive," I thought. "I'll take them." But when I came to the check-out stand, the clerk told me that they cost $3.17. I got confused. It turned out that in addition to the price of the tapes I had to pay 6% tax.

Anyway, in spite of the culture shock I came across, my trip to the United States was successful. It has made a lasting and exciting impression on me. I have learned a lot about the teaching of English in the U.S.A., about the American people, about the American culture, which cannot possibly be learned in our country. But I still feel sorry that my stay in the United States was too short. I would have learned more if the time of 25 days had been longer. I hope that more comrades among us will have the chance to visit the U.S.A. and stay there longer.

TN 2/81

ESL AND THE CULTURAL TRANSITION OF NON-ACADEMIC ADULTS

By Sharron Bassano
Santa Cruz Adult School

What is the role of an ESL teacher in the process of cultural transition? How do we, as teachers, best assist the immigrant from a Third World nation to succeed at the confusing and sometimes painful task of becoming an active participant in American society? I would like to share with you some thoughts on these two questions.

We realize that the powerlessness pervading the personality and lifestyle of many Third World immigrants can hinder their success in the cultural climate of the United States. Their formal education is minimal; their background is poverty. They carry with them an all-encompassing feeling of inadequacy as a result of never having had any significant control over their lives and destinies. They come from a rural setting with a psychological make-up that poorly equips them to deal with the urban environment they encounter in the United States.

Successful cultural transition for our immigrants is dependent upon their acquisition of specific linguistic skills as well as skills related to survival—the management of day-to-day transactions and tasks concerning such things as work, family, law, consumerism, and health care. Because their ability to acquire these essential skills has a direct bearing on the personal and social adaptation they must make, our classes may help them to maintain more stable self-identities in the face of "culture shock."

The role of an ESL teacher is threefold. We first must transmit certain cognitive skills—listening comprehension, speaking, reading, writing, and spelling—all the aspects of communication that one needs to function in contemporary society. The emphasis on language learning is, obviously, the most explicit in our job description.

Our second role, less clearly defined, is the assistance we can offer our students that is related to re-socialization. In some form or another, we help gather and sort and snap together all the unfamiliar jig-saw pieces of a new and strange cultural milieu. We are cohorts in the frustration of change and the joys of discovery. This phenomenon in an ESL teacher-student relationship has always seemed to me a perfect example of Fritz Perl's philosophy, "Teaching is merely showing someone that something is possible. Learning is nothing more than discovering that something is possible."

Our third role, and the least recognized, is that of facilitator of the psycho-social adjustment of our students in their new environment. And this, I feel, is an area that calls for more clarification and acknowledgement. Before immigrants can experience success in adaptation to the way of life in the United States, they must have a re-affirmation of the validity of their own ideas, needs, and feelings. They must be aware of a sense of security and place. They must know the uplifting quality of group identity and the power that comes from self-confidence and achievement. (Charnofsky)

We, in our ESL classes, can promote the adjustment of our students and heighten their motivation if we carefully attend to five specific factors as we develop our curricula.

Relevance: The language learning process should focus on immediate and relevant topics of mutual interest and concern and be conversational and interactional in nature.

Security: Our classrooms must become islands of security and support, because we know that those who are afraid of embarrassment, ridicule, or failure will not try.

Personal Esteem: To become involved and to want to participate, a person must first value himself enough to believe that what he experiences, feels, and thinks about is worth sharing.

Group Trust: The student must value and trust other class members enough to think that they are worth sharing with.

Success: To achieve a free and motivated atmosphere in our classrooms, we must give our students a feeling of satisfaction in attainment during each class hour.

I would like to explore each of these five points in program and curricula development, and show their importance and impact on the process of cultural change.

1.) A *relevant* ESL curriculum must reach out to the perceptual world of the student. It relates directly to his family, his work, his past experience and his aspirations. In order to stimulate a student's desire to learn, he must feel that the material presented is worth knowing and of use to his future life beyond the immediate learning situation. As Bruner has pointed out, too often a second language has been taught as "an explicit set of rules for generating well-formed strings of utterances out of context." The traditional classroom approach of focusing on grammar and the structural properties of the target language seldom proves to be a successful enterprise—especially not with non-academic adult learners. Our students should be given the opportunity to indicate what it is they wish to learn and discuss. They must be allowed and encouraged to express their personal values.

When we invite our students to talk about something they feel strongly about or something they know a lot about, they tend to forget their shyness. They don't have to be concerned about content—they only need to look for the words to express themselves. Rather than being concerned with, "What can I possibly talk about?" their consideration is only, "Now, how can I say this?"

2. To help our students develop a feeling of *security* and independence, we can create an environment that is non-judgmental, that promotes assertiveness and creativity. We can provide an atmosphere that encourages experimentation and play—free from tension. Lozanov stresses the importance of making our classroom atmosphere "Pleasurable and relaxed, so that psychological interferences cannot distract the students from their task." Something as simple as inviting your class to bring cushions for their hard folding chairs or playing recorded music during writing practice can effect a change in the feeling of the space you create. We have learned that adult learners of non-academic background should be allowed to progress through developmental stages, to make mistakes and experiment with the language much as children learning their native language. They are able to gain confidence through low risk, non-threatening group exercises that ensure success. (Asher) We show them that they are able to understand and be understood even in the earliest stages of the learning process. We try to maximize the opportunities for freedom to be spontaneous and to use their creativity and intuition. Teachers who can draw out these child-like qualities in their students provide the best environment for productive language learning.

3. Given a feeling of adequacy and encouragement about their personal expressive abilities, students will attain *higher self-concepts* and will gain commitment to the pursuit of other learning experiences. People who are consistently encouraged to perceive themselves as real communicators with something valid to say will ultimately educate themselves in new skills. In the past we may have unwittingly set our students up for failure with negative programming through low expectations or, conversely, through setting unrealisticly high goals for them. Now we have become more aware of our power to counteract the fears and conditioning of self-image that the students may have met in their previous environments by sincere expressions of confidence in each one's capabilities. (Finocchiaro)

Students who realize that we have a deep, honest caring respect for each individual, that we find each one unique and valuable to the class family, soon begin to believe in their own desire to know and understand. And this experience lasts much longer than the actual classroom experience.

4. Unless students feel comfortable with the teacher and with each other, they will not be able to achieve the freedom necessary for learning. We can encourage them to work and learn cooperatively—to study in dyads or small groups rather than alone and competitively. They learn that the highs and lows of their reality are a shared experience. A good class pulls together into a cooperative community where all students find their place and their own particular way to contribute. In such a class, although differentiated activities may be prepared for individuals with special interests or needs, the main emphasis is *integrative*. It is not only to our advantage, but to the students' as well, to develop and plan activities that keep our whole class working together, mixing all linguistic strengths, age levels, ethnic backgrounds and sexes. Isn't this setting a more realistic mirror of society at large and better preparation for our immigrants?

We must provide the surroundings that help our students retain pride in their own native languages and traditions. As we encourage them to continue to *identify* with their own co-nationals and to feel strength in their ethnicity, they gradually move toward acceptance of English and its speakers. Cultural differences are noted and lauded as positive factors, just as the universality of human experience is reinforced. With the concept of unity in diversity, feelings of prejudice and defensiveness are minimized. Perhaps more than any other, this dimension of personal and social integration, should take precedence in the ESL classroom.

5. Mary Finocchiaro has taught us that each class hour should give the students conviction that what they are learning is valuable and that they are *moving forward*. This doesn't mean that they must learn a new body of material each day to feel successful. It may mean that they are acquiring a little more fluency in saying a familiar sentence. They may take home three or four new and essential pieces of vocabulary or a new insight as to what is "going on" in this country! It may simply mean that they are arriving at a little more self-confidence or finding a more comfortable framework in which to expand and grow. In order for each student to experience the consistent good feelings of progress, they are given tasks in which they are sure to succeed, goals that they are sure

to reach, while maintaining a sense of challenge. We can accomplish this only by being fine-tuned to each student's capabilities and by maintaining a day-to-day sensitivity to each one's level of performance.

ESL for non-academic adults is best facilitated by structuring our linguistic input in a way that parents structure input for their children. The initial goal should be one of "uninhibited communication"; correcting should be done sparingly in the early phase of acquisition. (Asher) Initially, students should not receive formal instruction in grammatical transformations of their new language; this would merely hinder the learning process. As students progress through developmental stages, they initially experience comprehension through the use of simplified teacher speech, through physical/kinesthetic methods, through visual sequencing (cards, pictures, posters, etc.), through manipulation of real objects, and through rhythmic or musical linguistic practice such as Carolyn Graham's Jazz Chants. Students with no academic background respond best to the visual and kinesthetic approaches rather than through texts, workbooks and drills. The use of tapes, films, pictures, drama, body movement, music and puppets help them to find success and self-confidence early on through viewing, touching, and listening.

To summarize, each day, more and more Third World emigrants are finding their way to the United States in search of better opportunities to provide for their families with dignity. The skills and cultural patterns they bring with them may be poor preparation for finding a comfortable place within our society and for succeeding in their quest for adequate work and living conditions. Sensitive, well-trained teachers can not only assist them to attain essential communication and survival skills, but also offer them a valuable space in which to begin to solve their psychological reacculturation dilemmas in the company of empathetic supportive companions.

Bibliography

Asher, James, *Learning Another Language through Actions*, Sky Oaks Publications, Los Gatos, Calif., 1977.

Bruner, Jerome, *The Process of Education*, Harvard University Press, Cambridge, Mass., 1960.

Charnofsky, Stanly, *Educating the Powerless*, Wadsworth Publishing Co., Belmont, California, 1971.

Finocchiaro, Mary, *The Foreign Language Learner, A Teacher's Guide*, Regents Publishing Co., New York, 1973.

Graham, Carolyn, *Jazz Chants*, Oxford University Press, New York, 1978.

Lozanoff, Georgi, *The Technique of Suggestopedia in Second Language Learning*, Second Language Learning and Maintenance, ATESOL, Dublin.

TN 8/79

CULTURES IN CONFLICT

by Douglas Magrath
University of South Florida

ESL teachers need an insight into the problems of acculturation faced by their students because the students' attitudes and feelings directly affect their classroom performance. Their initial excitement starts to wear off as culture stress begins to affect their lives during the study period. Teachers need to be sensitive to these problems of culture conflict in order to help the students ease the transition into a new culture with a minimum of stress. Here at the English Language Center at the University of South Florida the problems of Middle Eastern students have concerned us especially because many of our students have come from that region. My years of study and residence in two Middle Eastern countries have given me an insight into the cultural background of the students and the potential for cultural conflicts that may occur. I hope that all ESL teachers will benefit from these experiences and observations that I wish to share. I will cite some specific examples and make some general statements based on my experience and research in the areas of Middle East Studies and ESL methods.

At first, most of our students are excited about their new surroundings when they arrive in Tampa to begin intensive English study. In general they adjust well to their new environment. Some, however, have returned home because of homesickness, while others have adopted western ways and neglected their former culture. In fact, they enjoy their newly found pleasures to the detriment of their studies. Culture shock can cause students to withdraw as they go through a period of orientation to the values of the United States in the light of their own cultural system. Conversely, cultural conflict can lead to a rapid attempt to assimilate our culture, both the good and the bad.

This cultural conflict has been going on in the Middle East for some time now. Modernization has already exposed the students to some aspects of western culture, particularly science and technology. Modernist writers and thinkers in the Middle East consider western science to be a necessity for their countries, and the students come to the U.S. seeking this knowledge. However, contrary to the current of westernization and reform in the students' home countries, there is a resurgence of traditional Islamic values. Many leaders now call for a return to the basic faith and value system of Islam. The students bring this conflict in values with them when they come here for ESL. They feel obligated to hold on to some aspects of their religious ritual. For example, our students asked for and got a free period

for group prayer on Friday. This small concession improved student morale because they realized that we cared about their culture and value system. Islam definitely encourages education. For this reason we are not overly concerned if our Middle Eastern students miss a few minutes for prayer. The Koran, the holy book of Islam says, "For God does not change whatever is in a people until they change what is within themselves." (Koran 13:10) If students seem to lose motivation, one can always remind them of what their own religious tradition has to say about gaining knowledge and improving oneself. Even the most conservative Muslims who come here to study are eager to learn. A basic understanding of some of the specific points of cultural interference will help these students avoid potential problems and get the most out of their experience.

Muslims are forbidden to eat pork. This strict dietary law may cause problems for newly arrived students who cannot recognize pork—never having seen it. Pork and pigs should not be mentioned in conversation or lessons, and pork should never be offered to Middle Eastern students. Students may wish to know which food terms refer to pork. When our students asked about this subject, an Arabic speaking faculty member introduced the students to various food service facilities and stores and explained the meanings of the various food terms.

Many Muslims fast during the daylight hours for one month each year—the holy month of Ramadan. They cannot eat, drink any liquids, or smoke during the daytime. Only those who are sick or who are traveling can claim exemption. Students will appear tired and irritable during this period because they usually stay up all night in order to eat and pray. Ramadan gives the students a chance to reaffirm their own cultural values. Our students put great emphasis on their special activities during Ramadan. It is their defense against "anomie," a feeling of not comfortably belonging in one social group or the other." (Lambert, p. 179) The daily fast and nightly feast help the students maintain important links to their home culture. Teachers need an extra measure of patience during this time because students may regress.

The status of women is another concern for those dealing with Middle Eastern students. Islamic reformers have done much to liberate women; however, traditional attitudes linger on, and in some cases the rising tide of conservatism and Islamic nationalism have eroded these gains. The result is that

male students may have difficulty following orders from female teachers and administrators. Female teachers and administrators should establish authority from the first day of contact, remaining firm at all times. One must avoid the temptation to shout at the students. Once I observed a teacher trainee shouting at a group of Saudi men; the result was that she lost control of the group, which had begun to make fun of her. Teachers need to realize that the students may never have been exposed to a female authority figure before.

The American custom of dating is a mystery to newly arrived students from the Middle East. A few will catch on quickly, and their command of spoken English will improve dramatically as a result. Others will remain aloof and will feel offended by the apparent aggressiveness of U.S. women.

Cleanliness is very important to Muslims. They are required to wash before reciting the daily prayers; however, because of the scarcity of water in their home countries, they tend to shower and bathe less often than Americans do. Also, they are not familiar with deodorant; in its place they wash their hands and face with cologne. This measure does not work very well in Florida. Apparently the dry climate of the Middle East prevents any problems from occurring before the students arrive here. My own experience has indicated that a discrete word to one or two individuals is the best way for a teacher to handle the situation. One should never address a large group on this subject.

Differences in proxemics and body language have the potential to cause conflict. Middle Easterners stand closer to one another than Westerners do, and members of the same sex often hold hands or walk arm-in-arm. Such behavior is normal and does not imply anything irregular.

Punctuality is a problem for students and their teachers. A student may come to an eight o'clock appointment or class at eight-fifteen or eight-thirty. Also, any business scheduled for today can be left for tomorrow if not completed.

Most ESL students undergo a period of disorientation as they reevaluate the cultures of the host country and their own country. Properly informed teachers can forestall potential problems if they are aware of cultural differences and areas of conflict while remaining sensitive to the ethnic values of the students in their classes. □

REFERENCES   *TN 12/81*

Lakoff, Robin. "Language and Society" in R. Wardhaugh and D. Brown, *A Survey of Applied Linguistics*. Ann Arbor.
Lambert, Wallace. 1972. *Language, Psychology, and Culture*. Stanford.

A ONE-DAY INTERCULTURAL COMMUNICATION WORKSHOP IN AN ESL PROGRAM

by William C. Gay

Division of International Programs
University of Southern California
and President, NAFSA

At the American Language Institute at the University of Southern California, as in most ESL programs, we try to provide special activities outside the classroom for our students. These activities take many forms, but a recent experiment turned out to be very special. On a beautiful Saturday in November a class in cultural geography from Cerritos Community College visited our campus for a one-day Intercultural Communication Workshop (ICW). There were approximately seventy students—thirty-five Americans from Cerritos College and thirty-five foreign students from USC, give or take a few. Each group had its own cohesiveness, since all the Americans were from a specific class and all the foreign students were from one ESL program. It was not difficult, therefore, to make some preparation for the ICW. The instructor from Cerritos College talked to her students about the different cultures that would be represented, and we talked to our ALI students about community colleges and community college students. All of this preliminary discussion was general; none of the students really knew specifically what to expect in an ICW.

In the preliminary meetings both groups of students were asked what their expectations were. By far the overwhelming idea was that we would get together and talk about our different cultures, traditions, and life styles. Most of the students figured that the day would be spent in classroom-type sessions. Nevertheless, they were interested; some were excited. Since many of the foreign students do not have close American friends, they felt that this would be an opportunity to begin some friendships and at least get acquainted. Since Cerritos College has very few foreign students, the Americans were excited about meeting our students and about visiting the USC campus. All in all, then, it was an exciting prospect. The following detailed outline of one workshop might be a source of ideas for activities that could be repeated in other ESL programs.

8:30-9:30 Donuts and coffee and informal introductions. The students from Cerritos College arrived together in a bus at USC's Student Activities Center. Most of the USC students had already appeared and were waiting when the bus arrived. After some hesitation at first, the students began talking to each other, and before long some lively getting acquainted was taking place. Six teachers from ALI who had volunteered

to assist with the day's events were a big help getting the initial conversation going and helping with the activities during the rest of the day.

Just before 9:30 I announced that it was time to get started and asked that everyone take a seat on the floor. I began by telling everyone that we were there for an Intercultural Communication Workshop and asked them to comment on the meaning of those three words. In the few minutes which followed there were comments on attitudes toward other cultures, on the meaning of communication, and on expectations for the rest of the day. I had decided not to spend much time talking that day because I wanted it to be a day of activity for the participants, so I merely mentioned in passing that we were not there to study other cultures but to meet people and make friends. (I won't go into the purposes for intercultural communication workshops here. Those of you who are interested might read Samovar and Porter, as well as other publications now available concerning intercultural communication theory and practice.) My statement that we were here to meet people and make friends was a gross understatement, of course, because I thought much more than that would result by the end of the day, as indeed it did. However, delineating all the goals of the day seemed unnecessary at the beginning and superfluous at the end.

9:30-11:00 In order to get the students to relax and mingle, we began by playing some theater games. They seem rather trite when described on paper, but they accomplished their purpose. First, everybody lined up alphabetically by the first letter of his or her first name. Since most of our ESL students were at the intensive level in ALI, this was an interesting experience. But it was all in good humor and turned out to be a real ice breaker.

Second, they were asked to line up by the length of their hair. Those of you who know me will understand when I say I was first in line. But a Japanese student was a close second.

The ALI instructors had met with me over dinner several nights before and decided on some of the day's tactics. One of the decisions was that we would divide into six groups for most of the day's activities so that the people in each group would get to know each other fairly well. We formed these groups by asking one American and one foreign student to pair up and stand together. Next, they got together with

two other couples; in other words, three couples as a unit. Last, each group of six was to choose and stand with another group of six. Since we didn't have quite seventy-two students, a couple of the groups had fewer than twelve, but that didn't matter. This process of grouping took a few minutes and was good for getting people to move around and talk to each other.

Once the groups were formed, we began activities that kept these groups in tact for most of the rest of the day. I asked each group to spend five minutes deciding how to build a people machine. At the end of the five minutes, each group in turn built a people machine for the edification of the other groups. The actual building had to be done in complete silence. The most imaginative of all was the group which manufactured a windmill, but a close second was a human typewriter.

The participants were asked to form a circle within their respective groups and sit down on the carpet. Each person, one by one, was then asked to give his first name and tell a lie about his reason for coming to the ICW. For example, Hiroshi said, "My name is Hiroshi. I came here to get married." Then number two was to introduce Hiroshi, tell why he came, and then give his/her name and tell why s/he came. So, for example, Jane said, "This is Hiroshi; he came here to get married. My name is Jane; I came here to play tennis." Number three would then have to introduce Hiroshi and Jane and then him or herself. By the time number twelve had his turn, you can imagine the challenge. It's a good way to get better acquainted.

11:00-11:45 Up to this point the activities might be classified under the "intercultural" part of an Intercultural Communication Workshop. The next exercise would be classified under the "communication" part. All the foreign students in each group were asked to carry on a conversation in their native language, and the Americans and other foreign students were asked to try to guess what the conversation was about. It was all right to use gestures, but no English was permitted. The purpose of this activity, of course, was to point out how language can be a means of exclusion. The foreign students thought that the Americans were really learning a lesson until I asked the Americans to get together for a few minutes to think of a topic and then to talk about it in gibberish. The exercise was fun, and by the end of it, everyone realized a lot about communication.

Next the members of each group were asked to form pairs, sit on the floor facing each other with hands on the floor touching fingers, and look into each other's eyes in complete silence. I knew this would be awkward but I didn't know just how awkward. Most people could not hold out. There was much squirming and looking away. I think it became almost unbearable for some, so I didn't let it go on very long. I asked them to talk about themselves for several minutes, and then they reformed into groups to tell the rest of the group what they had learned about their partners.

It was time to move around a bit, so two activities followed which allowed a lot of movement. I asked everyone to close his eyes and mill around silently, occasionally touching someone else's face at the same time he touched his own face. Touching was brand new to some.

We then spent twenty minutes square dancing. One of our teachers had brought a record player and square dance record. She gave directions and called the dances. This turned out to be a lot of fun with no object whatsoever.

By the end of the square dancing it was time for lunch. Everyone had been asked to prepare a lunch, preferably one which contained some typical food of the home country. We then went outside, sat around in groups, and shared our lunches. This was a time to get into some informal discussion about anything, and that's exactly what happened. In addition, a real estate company provided a hundred frisbees, twenty of which are still atop the Student Activities Center and eighty of which were taken home.

1:00-2:00 After lunch we returned to the meeting room. I talked a little bit about trust and friendship and about what had happened so far during the day. I then asked each group to talk about what friendship and trust meant to them as individuals. Apparently, enough ice had been broken during the morning and they had gotten to know each other well enough to feel at ease, because the discussions got underway immediately, and everyone seemed interested.

2:00-2:30 We again went outside the building, this time in pairs, for a trust walk. One partner was blindfolded and the other led the way. Once outside, the partner who could see guided the other around so that he touched things and other people. After ten or fifteen minutes I announced that they should change roles so that everyone could get a feeling of the trust walk.

2:30-3:00 We went back into the large meeting room and sat down, this time not in groups but anywhere. It was time to wind things up. We talked about the day and what it had meant.

The responses were entirely positive, and those of us who had planned the day were happy. For the very last activity we formed a very large circle and clasped the hands of the persons on either side of us. Then one of the Americans led us in a very effective chant:

Listen, listen to my heart song,
Listen, listen to my heart song,
I will never forget you; I will never forsake you,
I will never forget you; I will never forsake you.

At the end of about five minutes of chanting, I said "goodbye," and the planned activities were over. The goodbyes took longer than we had imagined because people were making plans to get together again and were exchanging phone numbers. I heard one foreign student say to an American, "Do you live lonely?" meaning, of course, "Do you live alone?" The American caught on to the mistake immediately, but smiled and said, "Yes, wouldn't you like to visit me sometime; I am often lonely." And indeed, many of the students really did get together again. There was, for example, a follow-up party at the home of one of the American students from Cerritos College. I'm sure I'll never know exactly how many are still getting together. Most of our students have told us that the ICW meant more to them than anything they have experienced in this country so far.   *TN 2/80*

REFERENCE
Samovar, L. A., & Porter, R. E. *Intercultural Communication: A Reader*. Wadsworth, 1972.

TOPICS AND TECHNIQUES FOR DEVELOPING A CROSS-CULTURAL COMMUNITY LEARNING ENVIRONMENT

by Trish Delamere and
Frederick L. Jenks
Florida State University

The communication-oriented ESL class for adult learners dictates that the teacher provide for a balanced interchange by assuming the role of a "language activity ringmaster" rather than that of a lecturer or prima donna. By creating an open environment for language interchange and by establishing the premises and order of the activities' stages, the instructor leads students to a point where interpersonal communication is absolutely necessary without the continued direct involvement of (or interruption by) him.

By combining the basic procedure for community language learning with the topics selected for cross-cultural discussion, a student-centered learning environment can be achieved. As Stevick writes, ". . . CLL has two main steps: *investment* and *reflection*. In the investment phase, the learner commits himself, as much as he is able and willing, as he engages in a conversation with other members of the learning community. In the reflection phase, the learner stands back and looks at what he, as a part of the community, has done in the investment phase. As he does so, he remains a member of the community." (Stevick: p. 126).

Over a period of several years of directing cross-cultural communication classes for adult students in intensive English programs, we have determined that the following topics meet the test of importance, communicative potential, and reliability in the English-speaking environment:

Specific Course Objective: To provide in-depth exposure to American behavior patterns, values, social relations, customs, and institutions; to provide discussion opportunities to compare/contrast the above-mentioned areas with the students' home cultural norms in a rational attempt to build an understanding of and respect for cultural diversity.

TOPICS:

a. Basic premises underlying U.S. Culture. (Hsu: 1969)
b. Understanding consumer rights.
c. The role(s) of women.
d. What makes Americans laugh?
e. Minorities.
f. Politics.
g. Marriage, Family, and Going it Single.
h. Traditional Social Values and the Contemporary Social Scene (living together, divorce, etc.).
i. American educational system.
j. Current Affairs: the American viewpoint versus the non-American viewpoint.
k. Advertising and the Media.
l. Risk-taking in the new culture.
m. Acceptable Social Behavior.

This sample listing excludes a full complement of sub-topics for brevity's sake. However, to provide readers with examples of related sub-topics, some of the components of (m)—Acceptable Social Behavior—are:

1. Table etiquette.
2. Coping with "pressure" salespersons.
3. Excusing yourself from the company of friends, hosts, or others.
4. Ingestion, digestion, and congestion.
5. Making and breaking business or personal dates.
6. Give me my SPACE but take your TIME.

The teacher's preparatory obligation is to develop introductory exercises—cross-cultural gambits—for securing the IN-VESTMENT of each student in a communicative process. The core activity should provide for discussion on the topic from the "American" point of view while providing for equivalent input from the students' home culture. Several suggested activities are summarized below:

1. **Comfort Bits.** Those sights, tastes, sounds, sensations, and items which provide each person with a personal aura of security, pleasure, and selfness. Their role in one's life becomes more evident when a person finds himself without them; for example, familiar sounds, the aroma of a favorite soap, the delivered newspaper, the flowers or shrubbery in the neighborhood, the way the bed feels at night.

The teacher sets the scene by mentioning that each student may feel a cer-

tain lacking—a sensation of sensory anomie—without knowing precisely what is causing it. "Comfort bits" as a concept is then defined. Thereafter, students *invest* in the activity by first making notes on a sheet containing the topics "Where is that color from home?" "A smell that is missing," "What I miss in the morning (afternoon, night)," "How I know that I don't belong here (yet!)," and "Things I should have brought with me but didn't." When the sheet is completed, students present their thoughts on one topic at a time, elaborating and discussing as urged to by others in the group. This leads to the addition of items by each student on the spur of the moment—things forgotten until mentioned by classmates—and brings *reflection* into the communicative arena.

2. **Action Line.** No city is without a newspaper column or radio program in which problems of the consumer or citizen are submitted in the hope that a solution will be provided. These community-service features of the media provide the format for in-class discussions based on the question, "What problems have you had this week in the community?" When a problem is mentioned, the teacher encourages students to suggest solutions (usually based on their prior experience in their own culture). After numerous potential solutions are posited, the teacher and well-informed students suggest solutions within the American context. These, then, are further discussed, leading invariably to

more shared discussion of related and/or similar problems. Frequently, the problem is presented via a specific experience between a student and an American citizen.

3. **Site-Seeing.** An outreach activity, "site-seeing" requires that each student go to an area of community activity (shopping mall, park, etc.) with specific instructions to observe a particular facet of local color: fashion, eating habits, recreational pursuits, or male-female interaction may be the focus of observation. Students need only observe certain phenomena which have been previously selected in class as being worthy of investigation; it isn't necessary that they talk to people when "site-seeing." On a following day, students gather in the classroom to compare notes and discuss what they saw (or thought they saw). Often, the students will be asked to form a group conclusion or opinion regarding American cultural behavior patterns to close discussion on the issue.

These and similar techniques bring into play the essentials of communicative cause, first culture learning, new cultural awareness, group dynamics, and individual responsibility with students playing the dominant parts in all aspects of the community-learning enterprise. □

REFERENCES   TN 12/81

Stevick, D. *Memory, Meaning and Method.* Rowley, Massachusetts, Newbury House. 1976. p. 126.
Hsu, F. *The Study of Literate Civilizations.* New York: Holt, Rinehart, and Winston, 1969.

LINKING NOTIONAL-FUNCTIONAL SYLLABI AND CROSS-CULTURAL AWARENESS

by **Trish Delamere**
Florida State University

Language education is supported and encouraged by current psycholinguistic and anthropological research. Much of this research points to both formal linguistic universals and universals of language acquisition. In addition, cultural universals, represented by underlying psychological and sociological commonalities basic to the human condition, are now of great interest.

Despite this universality, however, the conventions that relate linguistic forms to their actual communicative effect are not universal. For even though it may be possible to say anything in any language by a process of translation or circumlocution, what is permissible in the use of one language may not be in another. "People who speak the same language share not so much a grammatical competence as a communicative competence" (Wilkins, 1976).

Following this premise, language teaching is no longer merely concerned with grammatical competence but also with communicative competence. Concern is with the *appropriateness* of communicative

acts as well as grammaticality (Hymes, 1972). While communicative competence may not necessarily be the goal of foreign language education (Valdman, 1977) due to constraints of reality—general education goals, community and school expectation, specific class goals, time, budget, and so-on (Strevens, 1977)—nonetheless, it is a practical goal for the teaching of English as a second or foreign language within intensive language centers in the U.S.A.

Teaching for communicative competence concerns itself primarily with facets of the language that deal with:

1. the *function* of a message over the form
2. meaningful interaction
3. fluency over accuracy
4. natural discourse

Cross-cultural awareness instruction is concerned primarily with a student's integration and adaptation to a novel communicative environment. Hence, it deals with:

1. natural discourse
2. the functions of the language for initial

survival and coping skills
3. the socio-cultural appropriateness and acceptability of linguistic behavior
4. the precision of 2. and 3. within and according to specific and specialized linguistic and social environments.

Grammatical/structural/behavioral or situational-based syllabi do not meet the above criteria. Notional-functional syllabi offer a communication-oriented alternative.

A notional syllabus is in contrast with either a grammatical or a situational syllabus because it takes the desired communicative capacity as its starting point. Language teaching can then be organized in terms of the *content* rather than the *form* of the language.

Given the intensive and specialized nature of cross-cultural awareness instruction, a learner-based/experiential approach is taken. Notional-functional syllabi facilitate this student-centered approach to language learning and teaching. The process of deciding what to teach is based on a consideration of what the learner most usefully needs to be able to communicate. Then, decisions are made about the appropriate forms for each type of communication. "In short, the linguistic content is planned according to the semantic demands of the student." (Wilkins, 1976)

Notional-functional ordering thus organizes materials not by syntactic labels but by semantic notions: volition, concepts of space and time, futurity, locality; and/or speech acts: opening conversations, requesting information, apologizing, persuading, stating preferences, expressing enthusiasm, disagreeing and so on. Hence, an emphasis is placed on notions within a meaningful or "functional" context, rather than on manipulation of grammatical structures. The primary goal, therefore, is *use* rather than *usage* (Widdowson, 1978); that is, the ability to use linguistic knowledge for effective communication rather than mere knowledge of linguistic rules.

The philosophy behind notional-functional syllabi emphasizes the content and purpose of language communication. This philosophy accords well with the basic premise behind cross-cultural awareness instruction. In much the same way as the linguistic content is planned according to the semantic demands of the student, the cultural content is planned according to the degree of socio-cultural adaptation that the student needs to make. This depends a great deal on the degree of social and psychological distance that exists between the student and the target culture (Schumann, 1978). Some general cultural objectives might be:

1. engagement and participation in contact experiences with various aspects of the new culture,
2. acceptance and tolerance of novel attitudes and unfamiliar values,
3. facilitation of skills needed to deal with conflicts, both intra-personal and inter-personal, brought about by a new environment.

Clearly, these kinds of objectives syn-chronize well with the semantic notions expressed in a notional syllabus. In a cross-cultural awareness curriculum, therefore, semantico-grammatical categories are assessed according to the socio-cultural-functional needs of the students. Lexical items are dependent to an extent on these needs but also on the topics selected for attention. Instructional units are organized around cultural themes (Nostrand, 1973) and topics might include:

1. personal identification
2. relations with other people
3. education
4. food and drink (Van Ek, 1975)
5. marriage and family
6. appropriate social behavior
7. contemporary and controversial topics
8. awareness of the rights and obligations of aliens in the U.S.A.
9. the conventions involved in writing a research paper
10. advertising and media (Delamere, 1981)

Finally, the correct sequencing of instruction and materials is optimum in cross-cultural instruction. Cyclical progression is advocated for notional-functional syllabi (Wilkins, 1976; Valdmam, 1977), as opposed to linear/structural sequencing. Within a cross-cultural awareness training program, cyclical sequencing is preferred, for this allows receptive and repetitive experience for the students, which in turn encourages the integration of categories and concepts by the student.

All of these factors are an integral part of a teaching philosophy which stresses communicative competence. Thus, not only must the instructional syllabus allow for these experiences, so must the methods of instruction. The methodology must be sensitive to the psychological as well as the socio-linguistic needs of the students (Stevick, 1976, 1980). Community Language Learning (Curran, 1972) suggests a learning environment, involving the modification of traditional student-teacher roles, behavior, responsibility, atmosphere, motivation; in short, the entire learning environment, which lends itself well to a semantic-based curriculum. This type of learning/teaching environment secures and allows for both reflection and investment in the learning process by the student. (Stevick, 1976) Similarly, techniques and activities are selected on the basis of their contribution to the communicative cause, to the group dynamic, and to the experiential learning environment.

Cross-cultural awareness instruction, with its emphasis on self-awareness of all facets of the target culture and target language, (Delamere, 1981) necessarily demands this type of syllabus design and teaching/learning environment.

References

Curran, C.A. *Community Language Learning: A Whole Person Model for Education*. New York: Grune and Stratton, 1972.
Delamere, T. *Teaching for Cross-Cultural Awareness*. Gulf Tesol Newsletter, Summer 1981.
Hymes, D. Models of Interactions of Language and Social Life, in (Eds.) Gumperz, J. and Hymes, D. *Directions in Sociolinguistics*. New York: Holt, Rinehart and Winston, 1972.
Nostrand, H.L. *The Emergent Model*: (A structured inventory of a socio-cultural system.) University of Washington, 1973.
Schumann, J. The Acculturation Model, in (Ed.) Gingras, R. C. *Second Language Acquisition and Foreign Language Teaching*, Arlington, Virginia: Center for Applied Linguistics, 1978.
Stevick, E.W. *Memory, Meaning, and Method*, Rowley, Mass.: Newbury House Publishers, 1976.
Stevick, E.W. *Teaching Languages: A Way and Ways*. Rowley, Mass.: Newbury House Publishers, 1980.
Strevens, P. From the Classroom to the World: from Student to Citizen, from Teacher to Educator. *FLA* 1977.
Valdman, A. Communicative Use of Language and Syllabus Design, *FLA* 1977.
Van Ek, *The Threshold Level*. Strasbourg: Council of Europe, 1975.
Widdowson, H.G. *Teaching Language as Communication*. Oxford, England: Oxford University Press. 1978.
Wilkins, D.A. *Notional Syllabuses*. Oxford, England: Oxford University Press. 1976.

(Reprinted from the *Gulf Area TESOL Newsletter*, Vol. 2, No. 1, Winter 1982.)

TN 8/83

CULTURAL ACCOMMODATION IN A FOREIGN UNIVERSITY CLASSROOM

by Lois B. Cuçullu
Seoul, Korea

Teaching English as a second language in a foreign environment requires cultural accommodation by the instructor. Recognizing this, instructors teaching abroad must guard against the one extreme of cultural imperialism and the other of cultural conversion. In essence the teacher must be aware of his own attitudes which might compromise his teaching effectiveness and must be equally conscious of those in the foreign culture which might adversely affect the student's performance. The manner in which the teacher addresses these possible conflicts in many instances determines ultimate success in the classroom. Cultural objectivity—yes; cultural insensitivity—never. Awareness and flexibility are the key terms, for by identifying problem areas, the ESL teacher can tailor techniques to fit classroom reality.

As an American teacher of English composition and conversation courses at two Korean universities over the last three years, I found cultural differences almost immediately. Two in particular affected the classroom setting: the attitudes toward class attendance and copied work. Both were contrary to my own values and those who share my culture, but were not as important within the Korean cultural framework.

To a Western observer Koreans seem to place more emphasis on form than on substance. Thus, while there are rules prohibiting absenteeism and copying, their enforcement is considered less important than their existence. The presence of rules, publicly acknowledged, satisfies the skeletal requirement of a modern institution of higher learning; however, in reality, socialization remains the primary educational goal. Thus Western academic values exist only as a transparent overlay on the Korean educational edifice. Viewed in this social context, college years in Korea represent a relaxation of the stiff regimentation students experience in middle school and high school. The severest test for students academically is passing the college entrance examination with a college admission slip practically equivalent to a diploma.[1] Once admitted, this breed of

33

super achievers experiences again the freedom not enjoyed since childhood.[2] Furthermore the entrance examination process itself fosters a strong sense of group identification among the survivors with two discernible effects: peer pressure is forceful enough to assure compliance with group demands and indulgent enough to forgive individual transgressions.

How does this translate to the classroom and to the problem of attendance in particular? Beneath the veneer of the college student's newly cultivated insouciance lies an irrepressible drive to reaffirm his worth by continually passing exams and making good grades. While graduation may be a certainty, good grades are not. Thus a clear relationship between grades and attendance can affect students' attitudes toward attending class. If roll is called, students feel bound to attend. Where no record is kept, no obligation exists.

At any level the role of truant officer is a disagreeable one, motivation being preferable over regulation. Yet in practical language courses, class attendance is not only vital but crucial. For conversation classes, a method which satisfied both requirements was to make a name card for every student. Handed out at the beginning of class, I not only knew who was present but I soon learned every student's name and face.[3] It was also obvious from the surplus who was not there. With this technique, a well meaning student could not simply reply "present" for an absent friend (something that happened more than once during my first semester) whose name or number had been called. This procedure changed an impersonal, unpleasant chore into one which was privately acceptable and quite effective, with the added bonus of establishing a more personal basis for class activities.

For composition classes I used another method. At the beginning of each term, when I informed students that attendance was required, I further stipulated that late work and make-up work would not be accepted for credit. From then on, in-class writing exercises, usually unannounced, and out-of-class assignments guaranteed a high rate of attendance. The students not motivated by the chal-

lenge of the work were at least motivated by the desire to get credit for their work.

Copied work was another problem. Whether on examinations or routine assignments, it was pervasive and, in the case of examinations, so frenzied that my choices seemed harsh indeed. By turning a Nelson's eye to this activity, I could, as many teachers did, simply ignore its existence; by using Draconian methods, I could prevent it from happening. It was a case where the two cultures were definitely at odds.

The solution for the composition classes was clear. In lieu of examinations, I decided to base my evaluation on the entirety of the student's work. In this way the student had to attempt at consistency and quality of expression, not for one or two testing periods, but for the length of the term. This furthered the goals of ESL teaching and created a personal, supportive class atmosphere rather than an impersonal, adversarial one.

In conversation classes, a similar technique proved useful in discouraging copying. Giving extra weight to active class participation helped eliminate examination frenzy. Administering more than the usual one or two examinations and assigning projects for additional credit also depressurized the situation. Copying assignments, while less innocuous, just as surely undermined the learning process. In some classes, I was told, copied work was almost as mechanical as xerox reproduction with one or two students selected at the term's outset to perform the work while the remainder of students merely transcribed the exercises. One reason this was so blatant was that too often teachers did not read students' work (understandable in classes numbering over 100 students). For me, reading the same paper 35 times dampened my enthusiasm as well. Undaunted I decided to teach my students two English words: masterpiece and master copy. I told them I wanted to read each and every "masterpiece" but only the one "master copy." Additionally I tried to assign exercises which did not lend themselves to patent reproduction. Inevitably I did receive some "master copies," usually in response to those ex-

ercises whose assignment I had tried to avoid. Yet in general my promise to treat the students' work seriously fostered a sense of responsibility, maybe even pride, in the students for their work.

Still I had to applaud the organizational skill and cooperation among students. To let this go untapped or misdirected was wasting a vital resource. As a result, I encouraged students to *work together* on assignments, to talk over the point of a lesson or lecture, and to explore the various ways an idea might be expressed. At times in class before an exercise was collected, I had students swap papers, read their neighbor's, write one or two positive comments about the work, and then discreetly show their classmates if something was missing, mispelled, or unclear. Everyone benefitted from this type of exchange.

The results were at times heartening. In composition class, on one last exercise on coherence which consisted of rearranging sentences within several paragraphs and then rearranging the paragraphs themselves, I was surprised at the variations the students submitted.

What I have been suggesting here is not new, nor is it limited to the ESL field. Managers, administrators, and diplomats as well as educators, are beset with similar problems whose solutions are not always evident in terms of their own past experience. Where cultural borders intersect, such problems have added significance. Awareness, both internal and external, flexibility in dealing with this knowledge, patience in finding solutions, and respect for both sets of cultural imperatives are the true deterrents to continued misunderstandings, be it in an academic or global context. 🏫

[1] At present the Ministry of Education is considering several plans to ease examination pressure students undergo. The plan put into effect for students entering universities for the first time in 1981 had some serious faults which educators are attempting to remedy for next year's applicants.

[2] James Robinson, 1980, "Spare the Rod & Spoil the Culture," *Korean Quarterly*, II, 1, 6-20. This is one of the best analyses of the Korean education system.

[3] While a seating chart would have had the same result, such a procedure would have negated one of the tangible privileges of the university student—to select his own seat.

TN 10/82

BOOK REVIEWS

TEACHING CULTURE: STRATEGIES FOR FOREIGN LANGUAGE EDUCATORS

H. Ned Seelye.
Skokie, Ill.: National Textbook
Company, 1974

Reviewed by Ann Hilferty
Editor, *MATSOL Newsletter*

Foreign language learning as viewed in *Teaching Culture* includes linguistic mastery, familiarity with the tar-

get culture's contextual referents, and knowledge of the culture's social, religious, and economic attitudes. On

a deeper level, language learning is understood to involve comprehending the functionality of culturally conditioned behavior, that is, seeing incidents in other cultures as responses to needs common to all people and as parts of cohesive, logical systems.

The author considers it part of the foreign language teacher's responsibility to teach culture, and by teaching culture he means helping students achieve a problem-solving orientation to learning and gain skills important specifically for cross-cultural communication.

As recommended pedagogy, Seelye offers examples of goal related performance objectives and goal related learning activities designed around seven identified cross cultural skills. He explains in detail the preparation and evaluation of the objectives and activities, acknowledging that adult students appreciate deductive learning experiences but emphasizing the inductive in techniques such as the exotic-sounding: mini-dramas, culture assimilators, culture capsules, culture clusters, and mini-media units. Always aware of context, Seelye comments on the usefulness and limitations of the devices he describes. He encourages teachers, when preparing classroom materials, to use the social sciences for cultural information and literature for examples.

The book is low-keyed: simply written and understated, somewhat repetitive, and almost programmed in format. As I began to read, although I recognized the author's ambitious hopes for foreign language teaching, I did not expect the book to be profound. Seelye seemed to be writing the way that experienced ESL teachers sometimes talk: more slowly and distinctly than the average native speaker, and down to his audience. As I continued to read, however, I found the book cumulatively and subtly admirable. It is uncluttered: sound teaching principles and advice, presented impeccably in a format which reflects many of the espoused principles, and contained within a frame-

work of perceptive, critical comments on teaching/learning processes in general.

I found little to argue with; a few of the model performance objectives seemed weak. I was uncomfortable, for example, with the implication that to invite a foreign student to dinner necessarily demonstrates or teaches empathy. As recommended in *Teaching Culture*, the act seems more an index of achievement orientation falling short of the sense in William Marquardt's definition of empathy quoted earlier by Seelye:

the habit of trying in times of conflict to see things the other person's way." (p. 88)

That I have so few contentions with the book, however, reinforces my feeling that Seelye's ability to instruct with originality and depth in a virtually programmed format is both a paradox and a triumph in pedagogical writing.

I find *Teaching Culture* relevant to my immediate professional interests in teaching ESL to adult students and giving cross-cultural workshops. Ideas for classroom projects and techniques are intriguing and described well enough to be easily picked out and adapted. Additional values are Seelye's parenthetical comments on learning processes, a running commentary on the history and state of the art of culture teaching in this country, references to related scholarship, and a current bibliography. On the whole, I found the book stimulating, useful, and supportive of the teacher as a learning person.

(Reprinted from *MATSOL Newsletter*, Vol. 4, No. 1, Fall 1975.)

TN 6/76

COUNSELING THE CULTURALLY DIFFERENT

by Dearld Wing Sue. 1981. John Wiley and Sons, 1 Wiley Drive, Somerset, New Jersey 08873 (291 pp., $25.95)

Reviewed by Janet C. Constantinides
University of Wyoming

All too often, I fear, ESL teachers know too much about structure and discourse analysis, about drill and exercises, and too little about how to most effectively communicate with their students. I'm not talking about the methods of teaching English; I'm talking about their expertise in cross-cultural communication. ESL teachers, especially beginning ones, realize that their students come from different language backgrounds; but they may be guilty of cultural (as well as linguistic) snobbism. That is, while they are teaching the target language, they may assume that they must also teach the culture of the mainstream society which uses that language. Generally, that assumption is an unconscious one. But that makes it all the more difficult to deal with. I would assert that one component in any ESL teacher's training should be a thorough awareness of the importance and implications of cultural differences. One way of helping to achieve that awareness is by looking at material outside the field of English as a second language.

Counseling the Culturally Different is written for counselors who work with minorities (Asian-Americans, Blacks, Hispanics, and American Indians). But it has relevance for anyone who teaches/tutors culturally different populations. The specifics given in the book deal with the four American minority groups listed; the general principles discussed can be applied to almost any cross-cultural learning, as well as counseling, situation.

Part I, "Issues and Concepts in Cross-cultural Counseling," discusses how counseling is "rooted in and cannot be separated from the broader sociopolitical environment." The same is certainly true of teaching/learning. Thus the counselor/teacher has to be aware of *both* her/his own cultural set and that of the client/student. Equally important is the perception of many clients/students that the counseling/teaching situation represents cultural oppression. The implications of that perception on the part of clients/students are explored in a chapter entitled "Barriers to Cross-cultural Counseling," in

which Sue discusses culture-bound values, class-bound values, and verbal-nonverbal factors, using primarily the four minority groups as examples. But the discussion of certain "generic" characteristics of counseling is also a discussion of some "generic" characteristics of American culture. Anyone working with the culturally different should be aware of these characteristics and also of how the unconscious acceptance of them affects her/his interaction with those from other cultures.

The description of the "Culturally Skilled Counselor" (Chapter 5) should be required reading for all ESL teachers, especially new ones. The assertions Sue makes about the counseling process are immediately applicable to the teaching situation. For example, in the following description of the culturally skilled counselor, substitute the words "teacher" and "teaching" for "counselor" and "counseling."

Cross-cultural counseling effectiveness is most likely to be enhanced when the counselor uses counseling modalities and defines goals consistent with the life experiences/cultural values of the client [student]. . . . The cross-cultural counselor must possess specific knowledge and information about the particular group he/she is working with. . . . The culturally skilled counselor must be able to generate a wide variety of verbal and nonverbal responses. . . [and] be able to send and receive both verbal and nonverbal messages accurately and "appropriately" [according to the cultures of the students] [pp. 106-9]

Part II, "Counseling Specific Populations," focuses on the four minority groups. Each chapter is written by a counselor/ mental health professional who is also thoroughly familiar with the particular minority group. For ESL/ESD teachers whose students are Asian-American, Black, Hispanic, or Native American, this section contains a wealth of information that should be used to increase the effectiveness of the teaching/learning situation. It also contains explanations of why we often experience failure, or at best limited success, in working with some students from these culture groups (i.e., differences in world view, education/career expectations, learning styles, etc.). Each chapter presents both historical and cultural perspectives and then gives specific implications and suggestions for counseling. Again, the carry-over to teaching should be obvious.

The third part, "Critical Incidents in Cross-cultural Counseling," contains a series of fourteen vignettes portraying cross-cultural counseling issues/dilemmas with commentary on each one. Again, the situations involve only the four minority groups. But the suggestions made in the commentaries can be transferred to situations in which the same point of conflict exists between the client/student and mainstream American society (for example, the concept of time/punctuality, aggressive/passive behaviors, "I" vs. "we" decision-making and activity, etc.)

I recommend this book for anyone interested in interacting effectively with the culturally different, whether they be American minorities, foreign students and scholars, or immigrants and refugees. The specific examples deal with the four largest minority groups in the U.S., but the principles apply in all cross-cultural situations and the suggestions for mediating differences have application to many cultural groups. For inexperienced ESL teachers especially, the awareness of mainstream American culture and its implications for cross-cultural interaction in a teaching/learning situation explored in this book could be invaluable.

TN 6/83

Section 3. Standard English as a Second Dialect (SESD)

One area in which the *TN* has been particularly weak has been in the publication of articles by or about Native Americans. Another has been in the discussion of the teaching of standard English as a second dialect. This section begins with a 1971 article by Roger Shuy about social dialects, such as SESD. He argues for the expansion of TESOL as a professional organization to include more than English teaching to speakers of other languages, but to the vast array of U.S. minority groups as well.

Black English and the teaching of SESD are discussed in the other articles in this section. Iona L. Anderson poses the question teachers often hear, "I Hears, I Speaks, I Reads, I Writes, Why I Failin'?" (12/81). This article is excerpted from a longer article which first appeared in the *CUNY Newsletter*. Susan Kulick attempts to make a case for the use of ESL teaching techniques in SESD and developmental writing classrooms in her article "Teaching Standard English to Dialect Speakers—This is ESL, Too" (9/79). In "Green English" (2/79), Donald Maxwell discusses the value of learning standard English from an economic point of view. In the most recent *TN* article in this area (6/83) Sally Mettler talks about recent research in second language acquisition and relates many of the findings such as interlanguage, fossilization and monitoring to standard dialect training. This is followed by a *Letter to the Editor* by James Ford (8/83), "Standardized Testing, Reading and Black English." Ford outlines briefly the linguistic and sociolinguistic definitions of Black English and then discusses the problem of training English teachers who teach SESD.

Other articles to look at from early issues of the *TN* are Jean Malmstrom's article "Dialects USA" (4/67); Ralph W. Fasold's "What Can an English Teacher Do About Non-Standard Dialects?" (9-12/71); and from the same issue, Michael Shugrue's article "The Price of Accountability in English." More recent articles to look at are "Black English: ESL or ESD, Some Similarities and Some Differences" by Carletta Hartsough (6/76); and Lorraine Goldman's "Yesterday's Taboo is Today's Chic" (8/80).

SOCIAL DIALECTS AND SECOND LANGUAGE LEARNING: A CASE OF TERRITORIAL OVERLAP

by Roger W. Shuy

In his presidential report to the membership of TESOL for 1970, David P. Harris observes: "No picture of the history of ESOL in the sixties would be complete without some consideration of the interaction of ESOL and ESD—English as a second dialect—during the decade now past. For the same decade that saw the emphasis in ESOL shift from the international to the domestic scene also witnessed a growing concern...for those many thousands of American children and adults whose academic success and social mobility are severely restricted by the kind of English they use and by their difficulties in dealing with the written word."[1] Harris goes on to note that a great deal remains to be learned about the transferability of ESOL teaching strategies to the instruction of non-standard English speakers and vice-versa.

In the same issue of the TESOL *Newsletter* in which Harris's presidential report appears, there is a position paper by the Committee on Socio-Political concerns of Minority Groups in TESOL in which the committee laments both the lack of impact which TESOL has had on the American educational system and the unfortunate seperation of language acquisition from the social, economic and political lives of the individuals who are doing the learning.[2]

In this one lone issue of the *Newsletter*, there are two prominent signs of impending overhaul and expansion in this young organization. It is in the context of these foreshadowings of change that I would like to address the issues of the problems of territorial overlap brought about by this recent interest in social dialects in this country and the need for developing wings of social responsibility that will carry our academic institutions, whether they be school systems, universities or professional organizations, out of the shells of their comfortable abstraction.

The influence of TESOL expanded greatly in the forties and fifties. While systematic, linguistically-based methodologies were being developed during these decades, specialists in ESOL found their home primarily in the Linguistic Society of America, an organization which then welcomed such aspects of applied linguistics. During sixties, however, while LSA concerns moved more and more toward linguistic theory and away from applied linguistics, ESOL specialists continued to grow in numbers, publications and federal support to the extent that ultimately a separate organization seemed to be the right and natural outgrowth. The result of this split has proved difficult for both organizations. For theoretical linguists, the separation of applied or related fields has removed at least one perspective from their world-view. However necessary and important linguistic theory is, it is unlikely to thrive on its own for very long. Already the walls are beginning to show signs of cracking, for the field has now replaced itself with more practitioners than the job market will require for some time and some recent Ph.D.'s who find themselves teaching freshman composition are wondering what their new degrees were all about anyway. I make this observation not that this changing job-market will suddenly or even gradually produce a rapprochement between theoretical and applied linguistics. I doubt that this will happen. Rather, the current situation seems to bode well for the development of applied linguistics and it is toward this end that the territorial overlap battle involving social dialects and second language learning seems symptomatic and predictive.

Social Dialects and ESL:

As early as 1961, attempts were made to implement ESL-like programs in the teaching of standard English to speakers of a non-standard variety. The early suggestions of San-su Lin, William A. Stewart, William R. Slager, William Carroll and Irwin Feigenbaum all pursue this line in one way or another with varying predictions of success. In his historical overview of the development of the relationship of ESL methodology in the teaching of standard English, Feigenbaum observes that some of the ESL techniques seem to work in second dialect teaching while others do not. His own experience, as well as the experience of other researchers, clearly indicates that repetition and imitation drilling is of limited usefulness but that other ESL techniques such as contrast and minimal pair drills, grammatical manipulation drills and tag-response activities appear to have more certain values.[3] For our purposes here, the end results of this relationship of ESL methodology to second dialect acquisition are not of major concern. It is perhaps unfortunate that the apparent successes of some of these strategies come at a time when the methods are under attack even from inside the TESOL constituency. The point is, however, that the dialect problems of inner-city black children were seen by the ESL profession as within their special province. And, to a certain extent, their case can be justified.

Social Dialects and English Teaching

Meanwhile, teachers of elementary and secondary language arts and English in this country saw things in a somewhat different light. This new focus on second dialect acquisition was nothing new to them. Whereas ESL specialists brought their extant methodology to a new situation, English teachers brought neither a methodology nor a tradition of research. The native speaking disadvantaged child was long overlooked in our public schools. His specific problems were not identified by or for the English teachers, despite the long available data of the Linguistic Atlas and a presumed tradition of usage studies. The focus was often over-generalized to such writing problems as subject-pronoun agreement, run-on sentences and spelling. Speech was not thought of as the province of the English class, unless the specific lesson called for students to distinguish between *witch* and *which*[4] or unless the student said *brang* for *brought* in an oral report of some sort. Reading problems, of course, were to have been handled long before language arts or English instruction was to have begun (although reading instruction is sometimes redefined at this time as literary appreciation). In any case, the language arts and English classes could claim that at least part of their function in the school system was to teach standard English to non-standard speakers. That they were not indeed doing so very effectively—if at all—could be attributed to the fact that:

1. Teachers were not trained to do so.
2. Research had not identified the crucial problems.
3. Teaching strategies had not been developed to accomplish this end.
4. Publishers have not had the data upon which to base any resonable sort of sequencing of language arts instruction, justifying why one aspect of standard English is taught at one level and another aspect is taught later.
5. The concept of acquisitional stages had not been developed. That is, all differences from standard English were thought of as wrong rather than as closer or farther away on some sort of continuum. An "error" was thought of as an error, all errors being alike in their wrongness. Thus, a child who spelled *penny* as *pinney* was thought to be as wrong as one who spelled it *peny* or *pnftl.* Little thought was given the reasons for the errors.

*A paper presented at the TESOL Convention, New Orleans, March 1971. Roger W. Shuy is Professor of Linguistics and Director of the Sociolinguistics Program at Georgetown University.

All of these sources of failure could be amplified with little difficulty, but for the purposes of this presentation let us merely conclude that the language arts and English teachers had clearly had the mandate to tackle the problems of non-standard English users, but that their tunnel vision along with a kind of predisposition for the more elite aspects of the subject (literature in particular) permitted them to fumble the ball. What would be more natural, then, but for ESL specialists to see the problem and announce that their methodology looked like a reasonable solution. At least they *had* a methodology and it was said to have been successful in the past.

Social Dialects and Speech Instruction

The teachers of speech, like English teachers in general, have held to the assumption that the normal or the correct are definable primarily in light of standard English language production. The common measures of speech behavior in this field, the Goldman-Fristoe Articulation Test, the Peabody Picture Vocabulary Test, and the Illinois test of Psycholinguistic Ability, are all based on standard English. Although speech clinicians are continuously engaged in descriptive research in a diagnostic mode, little or no significant research on the form and function of various social dialects is being undertaken by speech specialists. There is a growing awareness, however, that extant training programs for speech clinicians do not prepare these specialists adequately in the differences between socially induced language variation and actual pathologies. The literature now abounds with horror stories of black children who were given speech therapy when their speech was quite acceptable in the black community.

Thus, it can be seen that although speech might also be considered a proper home for the teaching of standard English to non-standard speakers, the general attitudes and performance of the discipline have been almost totally inconsistent toward this end. Speech, like English, has suffered from an insecurity of some sort that has led teachers to stress either such elitist aspects as debate and eloquence or such pathologies as cleft-palate or stuttering. Meanwhile that area of speech which is related directly to socially induced variation has gone unnoticed, despite the fact that it was right under the profession's nose all the time. Again, since speech specialists did not pick up the ball what is more natural than for ESL teachers to do so?

Social Dialects and Medicine

Since both language arts/English and speech were the historical and natural territories for teaching standard English and since both fields were so long in recognizing this responsibility and so

derelict in doing anything about it, one cannot be surprised to see other perhaps less natural territories trying to fill the void. For one thing, one of the characteristics of the early sixties in this country was the rediscovery of a national social conscience. The Title I Program of the U.S.O.E., education for the disadvantaged, is still thought of as one of the crowning achievements of President Johnson's administration. Education, social concerns and politics seemed to lead the way toward this reordered social awareness, with the more elitist disciplines following slowly behind. Psychiatry, for example, is one area which has hardly been touched in the movement even though it is no small accident that the major successes of psychiatrists is with middle class patients whose speech and life-style are similar enough to the psychiatrist to offer no interference. One of the major realizations of educators who work with disadvantaged children has been that we must start with the children *where they are* rather than where *we* are. Of these two modes available in psychiatry, analysts have apparently chosen to let patients adjust to them linguistically rather than to adjust linguistically to the patient.

Medical doctors have not done much better, although a recognition of the need to do so seems to be evident in a recent editorial in *The Annals of Internal Medicine* (the bible of medical research):

The physician speaks a strange and often unintelligible dialect. . .He speaks of mitral commissurotomes, pituitary insufficiency, and reality feed-back. This world is peopled with cirrhotics, green-sticks, and hebrephrenics. The professional dialect creates a communication gap between physician and patient that is generally acknowledged by neither. Not only does the physician speak a strange dialect, but more often than not he fails to recognize the dialects of his patients. [5]

At least one major medical school has realized this gap in intracultural training, particularly as it relates to social dialects, and is jointly developing a program with monolinquists for obtaining medical histories from ghetto residents. [6]

Social Dialects and the Social Sciences

The social sciences have scarcely even begun to realize the potential usefulness of language data to their fields. American sociology, like American linguistics, has been so busy formalizing its field (with considerable justification) that it has tended to move away from its earlier focus on the ethnology of social problems toward sophisticated techniques of quantitative analysis and large-scale social structure. Of this tendency of sociologists to overlook language as a resource,

Joshua A. Fishman observes:

A concern with language has been contraindicated on yet another score; namely language is often considered to be omnipresent and therefore of no significance in differentiating social behavior. The latter view is undoubtedly related to the monoglot and urbanized nature of the societies best known to the founding fathers of American and European sociology. In addition, American sociology has long been primarily non-comparative and American sociologists themselves, overwhelmingly monolingual. [7]

It was only recently that sociologists have become at all interested in this area, largely as a result of their increased interest in small group dynamics, social change in the community, communications networks and the problems of developing nations. At this time, however, very few sociologists are making contributions to this area.

Social Dialects and Reading

As obvious as it might seem for the influence of social dialects to be felt in the teaching of reading, it has been only within the past two or three years that the topic has even been broached. The concept of language interference seems to be new to the reading profession, despite its obviousness to linguists. Very simply, a child comes to school with an oral language system that differs drastically from that of the written material with which he is taught to read. To be sure, the standard English speaking child's language may also differ from the printed page, but not as drastically as that of the non-standard speaker's. This mismatch of the child's language with the printed page has caused some reading specialists to speculate that this is a contributing cause to such a child's failure to learn to read. Since there is no available way to determine how it is that a child does *not* learn how to read, such specialists have relied on hypothesis testing to determine how important this mismatch really is. Among the current hypotheses being tested are the following:

1. First teach the child standard English.
2. Accept the child's dialect reading of material written in standard English.
3. Develop materials in standard English which minimize dialect and cultural differences by avoiding the areas of mismatch.
4. Develop materials which incorporate the grammar of the disadvantaged child.
5. Rely on the experience method of teaching reading. That is, let the teacher write down the child's own words, then let him read them.

The ESL specialist can relate to several of these hypotheses. Whatever ESL methods have been determined are effective in teaching a second dialect will surely come into play if it is determined that the child should be taught standard English before he is taught to read. If the teachers decide to accept the child's dialect reading of material written in standard English such as *she go* for *she goes*, the teacher will have to be alerted to the precise conditions in which such renderings are to be expected. And this sounds a great deal like the contrastive grammar basis which underlies much ESL teaching. If an avoidance strategy is set up to neutralize the mismatch between the written and text and the child's oral language, the materials developers will have to rely on this same delineation of the contrast between standard English and the speech of disadvantaged children. If it should be decided that special reading material should be developed utilizing the grammar of the child's oral language, it will be necessary to know precisely what that grammar is. And if the experience method is used, thousands of reading teachers are going to need specialized ESL-like training to learn to hear accurately what the child is saying and to avoid editing it to what he would have liked for the child to say.

The Results of This Territorial Overlap

In the preceding paragraphs, I have outlined some of the work in social dialects being done by several disciplines today. Linguists have argued, with justification, that the study of realistic (rather than idealistic) language should lead toward the solution of linguistic problems such as the nature of language change. Therefore, social dialects might be thought of in the domain of linguistics. On the other hand, social scientists might make a strong case for such language data as the foundation for solving problems of social stratification. Few social scientists have done this, with the exception of a handful of anthropologists and even fewer sociologists, despite the fact that language variation might prove to be one of their best analytical instruments. And, of course, the study of language attitudes, that subject which lies somewhere in the territorial overlap of psychology, social science and linguistics, may never be properly assigned to only one discipline.

It is unfortunate that the generally held concept of applied linguistics today is that of ESL alone. Just as the linguist may be stereotyped by his acquaintances as a person who speaks a lot of languages, so an applied linguist is frequently stereotyped as a person who teaches English to foreigners, either in this country or abroad. This situation seems to stem partly from the directions of history but also from an inordinate conservatism on the part of applied linguists in viewing their own discipline. Ten years ago ESL was considerably hotter as a field of research and teaching than it is today.

Perhaps this reflected the growing international awareness of our country during the early Kennedy years. But it is not just the stock market which follows the domestic and international moods of the social, political and economic heartbeat of our country. The academic disciplines must also listen for these heartbeats and be ready to plot new courses as the conditions change. David Harris's observations about TESOL's need to adjust itself to other, new conditions such as the rise of interest in the plight of..."American children and adults whose academic success and social mobility are severely restricted by the kind of English they use and by their difficulties in dealing with the written word" is the sort of vitalization that any discipline requires. Compared with others, ESL teachers have never been what might be called an elitist group. By definition, their task has been to provide aid to those of all economics, races, ages and sexes. Today there are rumblings of possible relevance to such people, however, even from elitist groups such as physicians and psychiatrists, both of whom are beginning to realize that they have not been very successful with the people from the lower-end of the economic and educational spectrum.

We must recognize that the intentions of ESL teachers as they relate to social dialects are good ones. The question still remains: are ESL teachers the ones to do this? Is the teaching of standard English to non-standard speakers the territory of ESL? Despite the many papers addressed to this topic at this conference, my answer, quite frankly, is no. The territorial overlap of the study of social dialects in the past five years has been indicated somewhat in this paper. Language arts and English departments, speech teachers, reading specialists, psychologists, linguists, sociologists—even the medical profession—might also claim the field as its own. In each case, an equally good case could be made against it. One further complication is that at the moment, the educational implications of social dialect study appear to dominate, no matter which discipline it is housed in. The general area of social dialects will be seriously impaired unless the linguistic, social science and educational components are fed and developed with somewhat equal rigor. Within the field of language education itself, however, no single organization or discipline has a clear claim on the field. In fact, if one field is to be chosen as the educational home for social dialect study, it will have to be considerably broader than any organization now seems to be.

Who, then, should be responsible for the educational implications of dialect study? The answer seems relatively obvious: we have no such organization in this country. That is, we have no Society for the Study of Language in Education,

or Society for Applied Linguistics, or something like this, and we have no official organ which represents it. We have journals in which such articles or research could appear (*TESOL Quarterly, Language Learning*, the NCTE journals and others), but no place that all types of applied linguists can really call home. It is becoming obvious that there are scholars from many fields who seem to be looking for the same thing. There are reading specialists for example, who are sensitive to the importance of language and would like a forum to discuss their findings among equally language-sensitive, but not necessarily reading research-sensitive, people. There are psychologists and psychiatrists who recognize the importance of language (even social dialect) in the diagnosis and treatment of disturbed people. There are a few sociologists who believe that important clues to group-identity, social stratification, cohesion and mobility can be found in language, particularly through the features which linguists have so far rather grossly correlated with socio-economic status. Some of these scholars have expressed their needs for a forum rather vocally, to the extent, in fact, that it can no longer be ignored. Are we to tell them that they should join with ESL specialists who have not put much attention on investigating the relationship of a child's social dialect to reading problems? Are we to tell sociologists that they are to join forces with ESL people, whose major contribution to sociolinguistics has been a methodology which works in some but not all cases?

It now seems apparent that the break from theoretical linguistics which ESL specialists made a few years ago was narrower than it needed to be. The natural taxonomies are not theoretical linguistics and ESL but theoretical linguistics and applied linguistics. It is unfortunate that so many people consider ESL as synonymous with applied linguistics, for this confusion undoubtedly contributes to problems of territorial overlap as noted in this paper. Perhaps the word, *applied*, is the culprit in all this. Some scholars would make a distinction between *applied* linguistics and *relational* linguistics, the difference being one of single direction versus mutual direction emphasis, respectively. That is, when linguistics and sociology combine, it is not simply a case of one discipline taking its knowledge and applying it to a given situation in the other discipline. Instead, it is a case of both disciplines offering their assumptions, techniques and knowledge base to each other. Psycholinguists, sociolinguists, neurolinguists or ethnolinguists do not handle this intersection of knowlege exclusively from one of the disciplines to another. Psycholinguistics is not merely psychology applied to linguistics, or for that matter, linguistics applied to psychology. Applied linguistics, on the other hand, has been thought of by many people as the single direction application of linguistics to education; more specifically, the application of linguistics to the teaching of English to speakers of other languages. Now, if we wish to address ourselves to the language problems of disadvantaged native English speakers, we must change the public image of ESL or leave the territory to other fields whose claim on it seems equally defensible. The conservatives may argue that the proper study of ESL is ESL. But the position paper of the TESOL's Committee on Socio-Political Concerns of Minority Groups seems to indicate that another direction is preferable. If we are to take seriously the recommendations of this position paper, which urges that the membership take a leading role in cooperating with communities in which it works, the most obvious thing to do is expand the organization to provide a forum for our co-workers in other fields who are equally anxious to provide this service.

Several things can be accomplished by this. For one thing, those whom TESOL aspires to teach, the vast majority of whom are from minority groups (American Indians, Blacks, Chinese-Americans, Japanese-Americans, Mexican-Americans, Portuguese-Americans, Puerto Ricans and others) will be better served if their language problems are given the combined expertise of a number of relevant fields—not just ESL. *At the moment no such mechanism or forum exists for such a combined effort.* This service will have benefits primarily to our clients.

Secondly, the inevitable and terribly important watch-dog function which re-

lational or applied disciplines can have on the theoretical phases of that same discipline can be better served if the entire spectrum of possible applications and relationships is covered. At the moment applied linguistics is being served in a quite imbalanced way. ESL is served very well. Other areas of application are served only in a helter-skelter fashion (if at all) by linguistics. Sociolinguistics is providing some of that service for social dialects but very little concern is systematically evidenced by linguistics for writing and reading theory or for many other areas. The discipline of linguistics would be largely benefited by such broader coverage.

A third advantage of expanding TESOL to a Society for the Study of Language in Education or a Society for Applied Linguistics would be to the membership itself. It is not widely admitted (and outright hostility will undoubtedly follow this observation) but ESL specialists are often said to be narrow and/or cliquish. Whether or not this observation is accurate, the contact with language teachers and applied linguists with broader interests could have a salutory effect on the membership. There are certain advantages to surrounding oneself with people of similar interests, but the disadvantage of tunnel vision is to be assiduously avoided.

It is fortunate that the case of social dialects in relation to ESL has arisen. It has stimulated the thinking of many people both within and without the territory normally thought of as belonging to TESOL. The lack of a home base for the educational implications of second dialect teaching may have been a

distinct blessing, for it has become apparent that we have all benefited from the absence of an inherited orthodoxy. There has been sufficient cross-fertilization of disciplines on an ad-hoc basis to bring this area of research and teaching to the point of at least asking some useful questions, even if answers have not been abundant. It does provide an interesting example, however, of the void which exists in the field of language teaching and applied linguistics. What would be more natural for the Executive Committee of TESOL to do at this time but to consider expanding the organization to provide this much needed service?

1. David P. Harris, "1970 TESOL Presidential Report to the Membership, *TESOL Newsletter*, Vol. 4, No. 2 & 3 (September/December, 1970)

2. "Position Paper by the Committee on Socio-Political Concerns of Minority Groups in TESOL Feb. 1, 1970," *TESOL Newsletter*, Vol. 4, No. 2 & 3 (September/December 1970) p. 8.

3. Irwin Feigenbaum, "Using Foreign Language Methodology to Teach Standard English: Evaluation and Adaptation," *Florida FL Reporter* (Spring/Summer 1969) pp. 116-122; 156.

4. See, for example, chapter 2 in *Better English* (Boston:Ginn and Co., 1952) pp. 24-26.

5. C.P. Kimball, "Medicine and Dialects," *Annals of Internal Medicine* Vol. 74, No. 1, (January, 1971) pp. 137-139.

6. This program, currently in the planning stages, will involve the George Washington University Medical School and the Center for Applied Linguistics.

7. Joshua Fishman, *The Sociology of Language*, The Hague: Mouton, 1968, p. 8.

TN 12/71

I HEARS, I SPEAKS, I READS, I WRITES, WHY I FAILIN?

by Iona L. Anderson
Medgar Evars College

When a student uses syntactic patterns like I hears, I talks, I reads or I writes he is generally labeled uneducated and unintelligent. These negative connotations brand the student as inferior, and he commands no respect. The fact is that Black English is a rule-governed system of language, historically linked to a West African culture that was transported to the New World at the time of slavery. Both students and teachers need to become aware of the contrastive linguistic features that may or may not be appropriate language performance for certain situations. In the exploration of language, one observes a teaching/learning process in action. This is a new concept for teachers who have been traditionally trained.

The classroom ought to be an organic learning environment where active participation and creative teaching/learning experiences take place. But this educational concept is based upon new phil-

osophies and new theories that are in conflict with the way teachers have been trained in the past. Under old philosophies historically observed in Aristotle's "realism" and Plato's "idealism", teachers have been trained to be the only authority in the classroom, to initiate and direct all discussions, to implement a prescribed curriculum, to instill Western European values and morals, and to expect every student to achieve at the same rate and in the same way.

The criticisms launched against these philosophies derive largely from the fact that they ignore the sensorimotor needs of the individual; set unobtainable goals; overlook the possibility of error; cannot deal with failure; and most importantly, deemphasize the cultural and linguistic experiences students bring with them to the classroom.

The history of education and its progress has become an international concern since the formation of the United

Nations. Many authors (Faure et al., 1972) noted economic progress had the most influence on the development of an education system. However, sociopolitical developments are now progressively beginning to influence education. As more skills were needed for technological progress so also were more people trained to perform these skills. Focusing on the social aspects of life, the authors noted that education in a primitive society was family oriented and revolved around learning from parents or listening to tales passed down from older folks. Education remained static until the Industrial Revolution popularized it. However, James (1909) and Dewey (1956), in attempting to bring meaning to education, reviewed the ancient concept of learning in practical social situations where the individual through problem solving is responsible for his own education. Studies like these remained isolated ones and have difficulty in being implemented. As a result of the Civil Rights movement in America in the 1950's and 1960's American education received a jolt. Minorities were demanding equal opportunities to obtain the "good life" of which education is considered the necessary factor. America was unprepared to meet the educational demands of the minority groups who either immigrated or migrated to inner cities especially in the north. The federal, state and local governments started funding research studies to advance democratic principles within necessary educational reform.

Recent studies in child development and growth conducted by Winnecott, Piaget, Maslow and others are gradually influencing educators to look at each child's learning style based upon his maturation level, his interests, his motivation, his sociocultural backgrounds, his verbal and his non-verbal linguistic behavior.

Modern linguists are also making significant contributions to the learning process. There are movements toward the pragmatics of language communication and discourse, toward the process of learning rather than toward the end product, toward social interaction and shared experiences, and toward language as a common core in everyday life. Linguists are bringing an awareness of the how, why, and what of language learning and an appreciation of the intricacies of human language in a regional and geographic context. The socio-linguists in particular have sparked considerable interest in second language learning, bilingual education, and dialectic differences in language. They are pointing up the importance of language on the development of "self" and this linkage between language and self can hardly be overestimated. Teachers have not been required to study the anthropological nature of language development, linguistics or second language teaching methods needed to understand the problems facing the linguistically diverse groups in their midst. Because society is threatened by change and because education is a reflection of society, the problem of miseducation continues. Many young folks become pushouts or dropouts. Many who aspire for higher learning find themselves enrolled in remedial classes in college because they had not been given the fundamental basic skills for continued learning in their previous educational experiences.

The newly instituted ESL/ESD Program is designed to focus attention on those linguistic differences which have become barriers to upward mobility academically, socially, or vocationally for those who are learning English as a Second Language or Standard English as a Second Dialect. The deficiencies these students have do not imply cognitive impoverishment but years of deprived educational opportunity in which they simply were not taught the language of economic survival even though they needed it in order to succeed in the educational world.

The philosophy behind the ESL/ESD program is that given due respect for one's native language or dialect experiences every student can learn standard English. Students become aware that knowing more than one language or dialect has an educational advantage. The key to survival and success is knowing what language is appropriate to use in various life situations.

Because there have been many studies in teaching the bilingual person, there are programs designed to meet this specific need. However, little or no attention was given to second dialect speakers until very recently. The recent 1979 Ann Arbor Decision that mandated the schools to teach standard English will perhaps spark research coming and eventually programs will be developed to meet the needs of students speaking Black English.

Before the ESL/ESD project was written and funded, ESL students had become college dropouts because they lacked the necessary communication skills to function in the classroom. The retention rate for ESD students was equally low. They were constant repeaters of the freshman basic skills classes. College faculty to some degree recognized that language differences played a significant role in the progress of the second language learners, but the language difference between standard English and Black English was obscure. Sociolinguists, namely Stewart, Shuy, Dillard, Labov and others upon observing Black students in their own environments noted that they were communicating adequately within that milieu, and that their inability to achieve in school had nothing to do with cognitive deficits. The problem was considered an attitudinal one as white teachers looked at second dialect students as incapable of learning; or as blacks themselves believed that white society had to accept their new attention to "blackness." As a result of these attitudinal studies mainly conducted by Stanford Center for Research and Development in Teaching (1976), Washington reacted defensively to ignore this sensitive area of human conflict and to stop funding any programs directed to the language needs of Black students. Because of this neglect students are witnessing extreme difficulties in reading and writing in standard English as they move up the grades through high school or attempt to enter the colleges. We, as educators, must take another critical look at what is happening to our youth. We must face the problems of miseducation much earlier in a child's life and move to reduce or remove the extreme remediation experienced in later life.

Although both ESL and ESD students need to become linguistically competent, in the final analysis, the approach to the teaching/learning process is difficult. The ESL students need a longer period of time to practice listening and speaking English to extend their vocabulary within the content materials, to distinguish those comparative linguistic differences creating language interferences with the target language, and to understand the use of idiomatic expressions in English. For the ESD student the emphasis is on contrasting those phonological, syntactical and semantic aspects of standard English that differ from Black English. Attention is given to oral production of language and its relationship to reading and writing in Standard English. Many of these students were never made aware of the difference between the two linguistic systems until they entered these ESD classes in our college. Psychologically, they are motivated to learn these differences, especially since no effort is made to ridicule anyone's language but to respect it. Using students' cultural and linguistic backgrounds, instructors move them to explore all phases of the teaching/learning process in moving towards mastery of a new language or dialect. When students are exposed to tracing the roots of their language and culture, they discover not only the importance of language but also the fun one can have in learning to use language in the context of life's experiences. For example, the instructor extracts those features of language that students use in their everyday discourse and focuses teaching on those features.

The following examples point up the differences between Black English systems and standard English.

1) Verb and noun agreement differences between the two dialects

I talks	He speak
I reads	He read
I writes	He write

2) Omission of the verb to be. (See example 6)

3) The substitution of /N/ for ing.

Bein for Being
Goin for Going

4) Substitution of d for th at the beginning and ending of words

Dey for they   wid for with
Dis for this

5) Substitution of f for th at the ends of words and sometimes in the middle of words

mouf for mouth   brofer for brother
monf for month
teef for teeth

6) Substitution of t for th
   tank for thank
   trough for through
7) Subject noun pronoun redundancy
   My mother she at home
   His friend he like me
8) Prepositions in different places
   She keep hittin' on me
9) The dropping of letters
   "guf" for "gulf"
   "lef" for "left"

The above grammatical and phonological structures are a few of the Black vernacular structures that are contrasted to standard English. By means of the appropriate exercises, minimal pairs, dictation, cloze procedures, pronunciation games or dialogues, students practice standard English usage for short periods of time several days per week.

In summation, teaching students today means changing from old philosophies to new ones, selecting those theoretical concepts that consider the "whole child" or the humanistic approach to learning. It means more attention to selecting interesting, relevant materials, and to training teachers at all levels—early childhood through college—to employ new methodology in new settings based upon new knowledge about language learning. Teacher training institutions need to prepare teachers for the "real world" by requiring courses in the nature of language, cultural linguistics and other disparate disciplines related to language. Instead of the required 6 credits in reading before receiving a license to teach, it should be 6 credits in language. In the integration of all of the language arts skills, reading and writing problems will diminish. □

FOOTNOTES
1 Faure, D., H. Felipe, A. R. Kaddoura, H. Lopes, A. Petrovsky, including reading. Perhaps with concentration M. Rahnema, and F. C. Ward. LEARNING TO BE: THE WORLD OF EDUCATION TODAY AND TOMORROW. London: United Nations, UNESCO, and George Harrup and Co., 1972.
2 Dewey, J. SCHOOL AND SOCIETY. New York: D. C. Heath and Company, 1956.

(Reprinted from CUNY News)

TN 12/81

TEACHING STANDARD ENGLISH TO DIALECT SPEAKERS—THIS IS ESL, TOO

By Susan Kulick
Jane Addams V.H.S., N.Y.C

During the past few years a non-traditional kind of student has been entering the ESL classroom. These young people already speak non-Standard English fluently and imaginatively, but lack a command of the Standard dialect which has been the cause of a great deal of reading and writing interference. On our equally-weighted Spanish and English tests of linguistic dominance (L.A.B.), these students have been scoring below the competence level in both languages.

Such students have no difficulty in communicating with peers in both English and Spanish, yet are having academic problems in both. These problems arise from their dialect's interference with the structure, conceptual framework, grammar and vocabulary of the Standard English and Spanish. Yet, these students are often sophisticated young persons who are neither amused nor motivated by standard ESL texts and approaches. They are often bored by the subject content and generally slower pace of the ESL classroom, and yet often benefit from more time on a particular structure than the traditional student since things must be unlearned before they can be relearned. Also, these students are often belligerent at being placed in the same class as students with an overt non-native command of English.

What to do? Generally speaking, there should be a dual ESL and NLA (Native Language Arts) approach because the student is often speaking both an alternative brand of English and a creolization of his native language as well. However, as an ESL teacher, my suggestions are geared towards the ESL component.

During the past few years I have developed a list of guidelines based, in part, upon error analysis, and, in part, on my own observations. I vary my approach to them and add to them year by year. I place the students involved in the most advanced ESL class so that they don't feel out of place in terms of verbal fluency with the rest of the class. Basically, I've stressed the following:

1. *Consonant-cluster distinguishing*

This includes hearing and distinguishing between such pairs as: guess/guest; tan/tank; car/card; heart/hearts; study/studying; walk/walked; quick/quickly. The surface structure meaning of the sound should be taught as well, i.e., that the sounds of -*ed* signify past tense, or that the word *an* signals that the sound that follows will begin with a vowel sound, or that the *s* signals plural or possessive at the end of a word.

Many of our students systematically slur or don't pronounce the final sounds of words and are unaware of the link between morpheme and meaning. This should be stressed.

2. *Vocabulary expansion*

The language of these students is very generalistic and undifferentiated and it is hard for them to describe specific things, ideas or people with any degree of specificity or concreteness as they lack the vocabulary.

I usually approach a vocabulary lesson by centering it around one idea or place, and teaching very concrete and descriptive vocabulary to fit that one situation. For example, during one lesson we studied words such as: arched eyebrows, cupid's-bow lips, high cheekbones, heart-shaped face, pursed lips, heavy eyelids, etc. Then I passed out pictures from magazines and each student had to write a paragraph specifically describing the picture that she had. Then, each paragraph was read and the class tried to match the description to the collected pictures. The next day we reviewed the vocabulary again and each student used it to describe her neighbor. The next day each student described a "mystery student" in the classroom, and we had to guess who was being described.

3. *Specific syntactic structures*

A. Difference between "would" and "will".

B. Use of past and perfect tenses.

C. Subjunctive.

D. Uses of "was" and "were".

E. Uses of "do", "does", and "did" in statements and questions.

F. Adverbs and adjectives.

G. Differences in usages of words from the same root-i.e., quick, quickly, quickness, quickening, quicken.

H. Meaning-bearing conjunctions—This includes words such as: *since, therefore, because, hence, thus, and, so, unless, although, so,* and *consequently.* It is important that the student realize the meaning constraints that the use of these words place upon sentence meaning: i.e., I will do it *unless* it rains.

4. *Spelling*

I don't use traditional lists. I use the students' spelling errors from their own paragraphs and compositions.

5. *Other concepts to stress*

A. Recognition that you, as the teacher, are trying to provide the students with an alternative dialect to use

42

when it best benefits the situation, and that you are not casting aspersions upon their own speech. Realistically speaking there are times when the use of Standard English would benefit dialect speakers in a generally Standard English speaking country. These circumstances should be discussed, and role-playing techniques used to illustrate the discussion.

B. Geography—concepts of city, state, country and continent should be taught. Also, different religions, outlooks and cultures should be used as subject matter in drills and stories used to teach grammar and writing. Many of the students are very immersed in their own culture and welcome the opportunity to learn about and appreciate others. Much student intolerance comes from fear of the unknown rather than knowledge of it and this is particularly true of dialect speaking students whose contact with other cultural groups in our society may be very limited.

C. Pride of culture—contributions of second-generation French, Chinese, Spanish, German and Hawaiian Americans, etc.

D. The use of local transportation, and the glories of other parts of the city than their own. In New York City I develop many lessons with reading the intracacies of subway and bus maps included in reading paragraphs.

These ideas which I have mentioned are among those which I've tried; they are the methods I had to develop because I could find no texts that specifically helped bilingual dialect speaking high school students and adults. Doing intensive error analysis of written work, listening to students grapple with Standard English and writing down the major difficulties they encountered, and realizing that much student inadequacy to master curriculum is caused by vocabulary limitation were among the contributing methods to my data collection. I hope my suggestions, combined with your experience and student dialect problems (my students are all Hispanic,) will prove of value. *TN 9/78*

GREEN ENGLISH: SPOKEN STANDARD ENGLISH AS A SECOND DIALECT

By Donald Maxwell
Reynolds Community College
Richmond, Virginia

Even after all this time there is still the argument over what constitutes good English, an argument that too often works to the disadvantage of already disadvantaged students.

Most speakers of English insist that there is "correct" English and that there is "bad grammar." Furthermore, most speakers of "correct" English are elitists who equate such speech with good education, background, and in some special way with virtue. To them, "bad grammar" implies defects in all of those traits. They talk about "purity" and "standards," and seem more interested in testing than in teaching.

On the other side of the argument are those who have become enlightened about regional and ethnic dialects of English. They speak about "White English" and "Black English." Some even understand that students have the right to their own language. And in fact most enlightened English teachers, rather than condemning students not fluent in the so-called "standard" dialect, try to teach them to use it.

We succeed by being neither elitist nor idealistic; but pragmatic. Our students need to be able to land and hold the white-collar jobs they are educated for, so whatever their native language or dialect we prepare them to operate in "Green English," the dialect of economic power.

Green English is the language spoken in Wall Street, in IT & T, General Motors, EXXON, Safeway, the Bank of America. It sounds neither white nor black; it sounds like money, and it is the access code to economic power. That may seem obvious to you—or it may not. Just to be sure that we understand each other, let me review in the next paragraph the relationship between language and power, and then I'l go right on to the specific details of a course in spoken "Green English."

In the army I learned that there are three ways of doing things: the right way, the wrong way, and the army way. In a sense, those ways are analogous to the ways people feel about English. In the right way—the ideal—all of us have the right to speak as we wish. In the wrong way—the real situation—the only rights are made by might, by power, and that usually means economic power. It has nearly always been true that people who have economic power make everyone else speak as they do. Or, to say it the other way around, the most likely way to gain economic power is to learn the language of the powerful.

That is what we do for our underpowered students: help them gain access to economic power—because we believe that they have the right to access. And that brings us to the army way of doing things. It might not be subtle, it might not please everyone, but it seems to get results. We call it "Studies in Pronunciation and Dialect." It's a three-credit elective speech course, and the credits count toward graduation in place of the regular required speech course. Most of these students are preparing to be executive secretaries, court reporters, legal secretaries, and the like. They can do everything in their fields, but they can't get jobs—or keep them, or get promoted—because of the way they speak.

One more thing about these students: they all want the course. They have to ask for it in order to get into it. They all can write "standard" English fairly well. Nearly all of them have gone through a developmental writing program and a course in college composition. Because most of the students will come in feeling—in an academic sense —somewhat stupid and inferior, a lot of time is spent on preparing them for the course; demonstrating that there *are* dialects, using recordings, imitations, and native speakers, trying to make the students feel good about their own dialects, encouraging them to teach the instructor and other students to speak as they do, and by spending as much time as necessary in getting acquainted, in making everyone feel comfortable with each other.

One good way to do this is to introduce the concept of "International English," a term less cynical than "Green English." Although in a strict sense there may not really be such a thing as "International English," using the term avoids the awkward problem of local or ethnic dialects seeming to be inferior to the "standard" (white) dialect. At the same time, it keeps the students thinking about gaining access to the business world—which is, after all, international. (*The People's Almanac* identifies several corporations as "countries.")

Have each student take a new identity for the entire course—a new identity that fits the top level of the student's target occupation. With your help if necessary, the student should choose a new name, a new address, a new family, and so on. Being someone else frees the students from the need to defend themselves, and therefore they can learn much more effectively.

Then start to work on the dialect. At

first, we do a lot of drills based on *Keys to American English*, by Constance Gefvert, Richard Raspa, and Amy Richards, which we use in our developmental writing program. Do recognition drills first, so that the students can distinguish between what Gefvert calls "community dialect" and the "standard dialect." Then substitution drills and other pattern drills.

The drills are mainly to point out differences in the dialects—verb forms, plurals, aspect and tense marking, question word order, and constructions like "It isn't any more books left."

As soon as possible, begin role-playing in alternation with more drills. The plays mostly should involve situations that simulate future reality for the students in their new identities. The situations should be outlined by the students, with the teacher trying to stay out of things as much as possible. It is often good to have outsiders—generally from the business world—play parts. Sometimes *all* roles can be played by native speakers of "International English," while the students study their language and behavior. If possible, videotape each play and have the students watch it several times so that they can get over being conscious of themselves and can concentrate on the language and behavior.

Also be sure to work on *unspoken* International English. The teacher introduces this when necessary, but most students become aware of some differences right away—obviously the handshake. Try to work into the plays awareness of differences in eye contact, proxemics, laughter, touching, posture, walk, and also customs dealing with time, regularity, attitudes toward the job, and so on.

Finally, because ours is a credit course, we have to arrive at a final grade. Right from the start, we assure the students that if they get involved in everything and complete everything, they will get at least a C for the course. We give them an oral test about the time we begin drilling and again at the end of the course. If at the end they score as high as a native speaker of "International English" they get an A. A lower score gets them a B. Grading is pretty arbitrary; but most students get B's.

This course in "Green English"—the "International" dialect—does not work wonders. It does not make a black woman as employable as a white man. But it does work. By the end of the course our students can converse a lot better in the "standard" dialect than before, and they are able to operate with more self confidence. They have a substantially better chance for access to green power—which is what they came to college for in the first place.

TN 2/79

EXERCISING LANGUAGE OPTIONS: SPEECH INTO WRITING—AND BACK

by Sally Mettler
Herbert H. Lehman College

In an address at the CUNY Graduate Center in February, 1981, William Labov enunciated what he called the *Principle of Debt Incurred*, by which he meant the debt owed by linguists to the speech communities they study; in other words, the obligation of the researcher to the researched. Nowhere is this principle more widely acknowledged than in the field of English as a second language and standard English as a second dialect, where the findings and insights of linguists have had a profound and demonstrable effect on curriculum structure and instructional design. Stephen Krashen underlined the relationship between laboratory and classroom at TESOL '81, when he said in the course of his presentation, "Theoreticians need practitioners." The theoretician gives form, framework, foundation to what the perceptive practitioner experiences, feels, observes, *knows*. The practitioner uses the energy of theory to generate the teaching that ultimately pays the debt incurred.

Influential researchers in second language acquisition such as Krashen, Selinker, and Schumann, have focused from several angles on the affective domain of the second language/second dialect learner. His chances of success seem to be lodged as firmly in the viscera as in the intellect. He learns, they say, by really interacting with the purveyors of the needed linguistic currency: its speakers. To the degree that what happens in the classroom is real interaction, he can even learn there! Recognizing thus the importance of setting, occasion, and interlocutor to language acquisition, we acknowledge that students are acquiring English in places which are physically and spiritually quite remote from the classroom, and often under pressure: the stressful pressure of survival or the gratifying pressure of affiliation, that is, making purchases, making money, making friends, making love.

Interaction and Interlanguage

Because many of our urban ESL students come from polychronic, group-supported, oral cultures, they bring the strength of a disposition toward interpersonal communication with the corollary that language acquired in the aural/oral mode is likely to prevail in the students' written and oral expression over language learned in formal settings, such as the classroom. In their academic pursuits, students frequently confront conflicts between the native tongue, the acquired language, and standard English, which surface in the new idiolect being formed. The emerging code of the ESL communicator is what Selinker (1972) christened *interlanguage*, the approximative encoding in English of the message the speaker or writer would precisely encode in the native language. Interlanguage is the code that identifies the communicator as proficient or not proficient in terms of the new syntax, lexicon, and phonology.

Taking into account the acknowledged impact of acculturation on the development of interlanguage (Schumann 1979, Wolfram 1970), the interplay of ethnicity, residence pattern, and personal affiliation tendencies may impel the student into the acquisition of a variety of English which the larger community designates as non-standard, even stigmatized. As a cultural outsider, the second language learner often does not make the standard/non-standard distinction until after the fact of language acquisition. In fact, learners may never make this distinction themselves, but may have it thrust upon them by the institutions or representatives of the larger community: teachers, for example. This means that many non-native speakers of English who consider themselves fluent receive a rude awakening in the classroom when their considerable achievement is discredited on the grounds that what they have acquired is an unacceptable, non-standard variety of English. This interaction-based interlanguage, described by Eskey (1983) as fluent but not accurate, is characterized by an array of *fossils*, incorrect or in any case non-standard forms which have resisted formal correction by teachers and may even be reinforced through interpersonal communication outside the classroom.

Fossils: Stigmatized and Stigmatizing

Fossils appear regularly in the student's utterances and writing, and are especially troublesome because they are impervious to random correction. They may be the products of a number of influences: native language interference (as in the case of the carry-over of the double negative from Spanish to English), peer language influence (as in the use of verbal fillers), faulty instruction, idiosyncratic variations in cognitive strategy and learning style, morphophonemic stumbling blocks in the target language itself (as in the numerous final consonant clusters of English which are unrelieved by interposed vowels), or simply the speaker's "negotiation" to achieve the speed of utterance and response which are highly prized among effective oral communicators in New York and other urban centers of the U.S. Native speakers of Puerto Rican and Dominican Spanish inform me that a fast rate of speech is highly valued in their cultures too. The problem facing these and other ESL learners is that the acquisition of speed in a second language often causes learners to violate powerful phonological and syntactical protocols whose importance they have not fully perceived and accepted. The consequences for grammaticality and simple intelligibility are often dire.

To help us understand how students create the interlanguages which they bring into the classroom we have the Monitor Model (Krashen 1978), which claims that adults subconsciously *acquire* and consciously *learn* a second language, and that they do it synchronically. The model posits, plausibly, that the acquisition of language in life is the more powerful mode, and that learning, i.e. instruction, is useful to the communicator primarily as editor, or Monitor, of the language he has acquired. In the light of our conviction that the constructs of theoreticians can be transformed into the infrastructure of practice, we think that the Monitor can be taken down from from its theoretical pedestal and used to increase competence in standard English by focusing on those fossilized forms which are stigmatized in the mainstream culture and discredit the second-language communicator who has incorporated them into his interlanguage. We have designed instruction on this basis.

Making Standard English Manageable

A curriculum which seeks to make English manageable to the student and which aims at equipping him with a number of specific competencies in the language can go far to reduce the communication apprehension or anxiety factor in speaking and help him with his writing as well. As he modifies his spoken language, he is likely to modify the intrapersonal language of the composing process: the language of the mind. This has important implications.

At Herbert H. Lehman College, in the Bronx, New York, a large proportion of our students are native speakers of a language other than English or a dialect other than standard English. Within our student population there is a wide range of levels of proficiency in standard English. Among the ESL students, the majority are experienced in using English, but many have gained a fast rate of speech and readiness of response at the expense of standard grammar and articulation.

Sensitive to the negative feedback their messages receive, our ESL students are not always clear about the reasons for it. Furthermore, they are often troubled about how to cope with the linguistic dichotomy in our culture. Some students resist speech change in the direction of standardization for fear of breaking important personal, family, and community bonds. But the larger number, wanting to succeed in the mainstream, are interested in making those changes which can be undertaken without undermining hard-won self-esteem.

Recognizing the special needs of nonnative speakers of English, Lehman's Department of Speech and Theatre offers special sections of its basic course in the fundamentals of oral communication. In terms of English proficiency, we have multi-level classes which demonstrate that diversity in language skill can provide a useful counterpoint to the diversity in personality and motivation that exists in any group of students in any discipline. In other words, the dynamic of each group produces a kind of balance between the non-fluent but enterprising students at one end, the knowledgeable but reticent at the other, and the variations between.

Keeping in mind that our students are more likely to write what they hear and speak than to speak what they have been taught to write, an apparently useful direction has emerged. Broadly, the aim is to work with the students' interlanguage, expanding and modifying it while developing rhetorical skills appropriate to this culture. We focus on those fossils in his second-language idiolect which are stigmatized and stigmatizing in this culture, as indicated not only by the rules of the standard dialect asserted in textbooks, but also by the unwritten rules made and promulgated by standard speakers which dictate, Orwellian-fashion, that some errors are more erroneous than others because *those* errors mark the one who makes them as a communicator whose messages are not only incorrect, but also unworthy. In the subtle conflict between social justice and sociolinguistic reality, justice loses out to disdain.

Practically, we help the student to identify certain non-standard forms in his speech and writing and become capable of discarding them when he chooses to by substituting their standard English counterparts, forms which he may have overlooked, never learned, or consistently avoided because he perceived them as impediments to the rapid speech he values. In this situation the teacher is not only an instructor but also an *informant* on the sociolinguistic imperatives of the mainstream culture: the teacher, as standard-speaker, knows the unwritten as well as the formalized rules of the language. The informant role of the teacher is often welcomed by the students themselves who have become conscious of the differing values placed on native speech styles in the U.S. In fact, by the time they reach college age students are aware that in their own countries judgments of and by individuals are made on the basis of speech style and language choice.

Image-Breaker: Catchword for Linguistic Stigmas

Our manageable collection of stigmatized forms, fossils which invite opprobrium and diminish the respectability of the communicator's utterances and writing, are called *image-breakers*. They are introduced to the student following a generalized discussion of the process of interpersonal communication in which the point is made that every participant sends out not only the message he desires to transmit, the encoding of his ideas, feelings, etc., but also his *image*, a picture of his *self* which is highly susceptible to evaluation in terms of his language choices. The grouping of image-breakers reflects not only our own experience- and observation-based judgments but also the findings of researchers, notably Wolfram's matrix of cruciality and Krashen's natural order of morpheme acquisition. These and other researchers tell us through their studies that presumably simple grammatical and phonological rules of the standard dialect, usually taught early on in ESL curricula, are in fact internalized late, and often never, by many learners.

Each image-breaker is a catchword for a grammatical or phonological anomaly customarily described in more formal terminology. The group is presented to the students on an introductory worksheet, with examples. As presently constituted, the list includes:

1) *absent –s (the ending –s or –es absent from the plural, the possessive, or the third person singular, e.g.° He like all kind of music)*;

2) *omitted –ed (the ending –ed omitted from the simple past and past participle forms of regular verbs, e.g.° Last night we ask him if the work was finish)*;

3) *faulty operators (mismatched auxiliaries, invariant be, e.g.° He gonna ask was you there)*;

4) *double negatives and ain't (forms unacceptable in standard English)*;

5) *"amputated" words (ø syllable- and word-final single consonant phonemes and consonant clusters, e.g.° Tha' wha' she tol' us instead of That's what she told us)*;

6) *overcorrections ("extra" –s and –ed endings, as in the possessive° mines)*; and

7) *fillers (intrusive or excessive contentless words, e.g. Like, man, I need a job, y'know, because like I'm really broke, y'know.)*

A given list of image-breakers should be fluid, subject to modification in accordance with the needs and speech habits of the students in question and the norms of the milieu; for example, phonemic substitutions and zero copula may be included in some areas.

All of the image-breakers (*absent –s, omitted –ed, faulty operators, double negatives and ain't, overcorrections, "amputated" words*), with the possible exception of *fillers*, occur regularly in both speech and writing. There is good evidence in our experience to show that once the forms are dealt with in the aural/oral mode, proofreading skill, and therefore writing, will improve. Students have said

GOSHEN COLLEGE LIBRARY
GOSHEN, INDIANA

that their increased understanding of the connection between their oral production of English and their written errors in tense-marking, pluralization, negation, etc., has helped them to produce more carefully edited, correct writing.

Activating the Monitor

The way we activate the Monitor is to speak and get speech down on paper, via tape recorder and transcription. Students speak, in monologue or dialogue, with or without advance preparation; what they produce is the material they work with, individually, in groups, as a class. Listening to himself, the student can discern the image-breakers and other errors which he is learning to identify in the speech of others. Looking at a transcription or at a worksheet containing sentences he has heard uttered by himself or other students, he can identify problems visually and manipulate the language to get the standard configuration required.

When the student confronts a sentence like° *When I arrive in New York twelve years ago, I look for a job,* or° *They turn me down becau' I didn't speak no English,* he has the task of locating the error, naming it, correcting it, and reiterating the sentence, orally and/or in writing, using a "hands-on" approach to get to the rules of the language. The technique does not in-volve teaching, or re-teaching, the whole grammar of Standard English; in fact, it is based on the assumption that students have been taught a good deal of that grammar and that what they have *learned* can operate as the Monitor of their *acquired* langage. As they occur in the speech and writing of students, image-breakers are noted, analyzed, labeled, and corrected. The process of objectifying and categorizing frequently-occurring anomalies tends to neutralize the errors and to dissipate the demoralizing effect of incessant, unproductive, random correction, while maintaining the importance of accuracy in standard English.

In line with the need voiced by Schumann and others for teachers to modify materials to meet the needs of students rather than modify instruction to follow the dictates of materials, we use the language of past and present students as teaching material, reinforced by compact textbooks which provide exercises for improving the pronunciation of certain difficult phonemes. Work on pronunciation and articulation is an ongoing activity, since phonology and morphology intersect dramatically in such image-breakers as absent –s, omitted –ed, and "amputated" words. For example, we work through various problems by paying close attention to the articulation of the /s/ /z/ /iz/ variants of –s and the /t/ /d/ /id/ variants of –ed, following voiced/voiceless guidelines and emphasizing the importance of consonants in intelligible oral English.

If there is any single principle which informs the instruction, it is one brought over from the theoretician's lab: John Schumann's suggestion that the learner's inter-language is not a deformity to be corrected by radical surgery, but a stage in his acquisition of a profound and complex new language system. As learners wade forth into the ocean of English that surrounds them, their teachers can perhaps help them to recognize the deceptive sociolinguistic hazards and by avoiding them to keep their prospects afloat and their heads above water. ⊕

REFERENCES

Eskey, David. 1983. Meanwhile, back in the real world...: Accuracy and fluency in second language teaching. *TESOL Quarterly* 17:2, 315-322.

Krashen, S. D. 1982. *Principles and practice in second language acquisition.* Oxford, U.K.: Pergamon Press.

Krashen, S. D. 1978. The Monitor Model for adult second language acquisition in *Viewpoints in English as a second language,* M. Burt, H. Dulay and M. Finocchiaro, eds. New York: Regents.

Schumann, John A. 1978. The acculturation model for second language acquisition in *Second Language Acquisition and Foreign Language Teaching.* R. C. Gingras, ed. Washington, D.C.: Center for Applied Linguistics.

Selinker, Larry. 1972. Interlanguage. *IRAL* X:3, 209-232.

Wolfram, Walt. 1970. Sociolinguistic implications for educational sequencing in *Teaching Standard English in the Inner City,* Washington, D.C.: Center for Applied Linguistics.

TN 6/83

STANDARDIZED TESTING, READING AND BLACK ENGLISH

by James F. Ford
University of Arkansas

The term "black English" is used widely in the sociolinguistic literature to refer to a variety of American English spoken by the majority of blacks in urban ghettos as well as the rural south. Therefore, it is a social rather than a regional dialect that differs phonologically, syntactically, and lexically from "standard English."

Like all varieties of language that are shared by large populations, black English has an underlying system of rules which governs its production. In the view of some linguists, the quite obvious differences which exist between black English and standard American English have come about due to the Creole-based origin of black English; it has evolved from an early pidginization of West African dialects with slave-trade Portuguese and British-based English.

In support of this view, some striking similarities have been found between black English and pidgin languages such as Jamaican Creole and Gullah, spoken in the Georgia and South Carolina sea islands. Years of racial and social isolation have served to preserve this variety of spoken English and to insure its transferral from generation to generation.

The attention given to black English by the linguistic community has been relatively late in coming and unfortunately, little or none of the literature has had any impact on the language-teaching profession in the public schools. The prevailing view has been, and is now, that black English is a sloppy, deficient version of standard English. The "deficient" school of thought has its origins largely in the writings of educational psychologists whose work with non-standard English-speaking children has led to the development of various compensatory programs designed, in part, to eradicate the nonstandard dialect and replace it with standard English.

On the surface, this view may seem educationally sound; however, many linguists have openly attacked this "deficient" argument on the grounds that it is both linguistically and culturally unsound and that it is potentially harmful to the black child. Language and culture are intricately bound; indeed, it can be said that language is the carrier of culture. Therefore, an attack on one's language is an attack on one's culture, i.e., one's family and friends who share those language and cultural patterns.

During recent years a fair number of professional linguists have become interested in the language problems of poverty children and have conducted field studies with public school teachers at the local level. Based on these contacts, the linguists have observed that, for the most part, language teachers are linguistically uninformed and are not capable of dealing effectively with matters of dialect variation.

This linguistic naiveté is seen as being partly responsible for a substantial body of negative attitudes toward black English and its concomitant culture. In turn, it is believed that the combination of these negative attitudes and the lack of knowledge regarding descriptive linguistics are directly related to the black child's low self-concept, and perhaps most importantly, to his failure to learn to read standard English, a skill upon which most of his academic success will depend.

When large samples of black children or adults are given standardized reading tests they consistently score substantially lower than do whites. Based on the evidence as I see it, our public schools fail to teach them to read. They fail because teachers who are charged with the language component of education are not trained to deal effectively with linguistic differences that interfere with the process of learning to read standard English.

Let me hasten to interject that I do not advocate that the schools teach black English. It does not have to be taught; it is learned at home and in the community, and the schools have made little or no progress in attempts to eradicate it.

It is the business of the public schools to teach all children to read and write standard American English regardless of their linguistic and cultural backgrounds. If this is done effectively, the spoken language will take care of itself; that is, black Americans will learn to "code-switch," a linguistic term that implies the ability to switch from one dialect to another as required by the particular social situation. This will not happen, however, without well-trained, empathetic teachers who are capable of dealing with this singular linguistic problem.

What I do advocate is that institutions of higher learning that are in the business of preparing language teachers (language arts, English, foreign languages, speech) for the public schools undertake a very critical re-examination of their curricula. Language teachers would be much more effective, not only with black children, but with the school population in general if their preparation included more substantive courses in descriptive, historical and social linguistics and perhaps fewer courses in "educationese." If this were the case, I feel quite certain that we would witness a dramatic rise in standardized test scores of black Americans.

TN 8/83

Section 4. English for Special Purposes (ESP)

Among the numerous acronyms currently in favor in ESL are EST, English for science and technology; ESP, English for special purposes; EAP, English for academic purposes; and VESL, vocational ESL. English for special purposes is often used as a cover term for all of the above and is considered by some a term which should apply to all ESL classes.

Cathy Day's excellent article on vocational ESL begins this section. She provides an overview of vocational education and discusses "Going Beyond Career Education" (8/82). Barbara Humak offers us a look at cultural problems which occur in "Pre-vocational ESL" (10/83) programs and discusses the skills necessary to seek and secure entry level employment. Carol Svedsen, in an *It Works* column edited by Cathy Day, writes about gaining "Understanding on the Job" (10/83). In her article she discusses techniques for reporting problems, getting clarification, and getting confirmation in on-the-job situations.

Pat Byrd takes a look at English for science and technology programs in "Intensive English Programs in the U.S." (6/79). Byrd and Greg West look at what they found to be the purposes of "Teaching Technical Writing Courses for Foreign Students in U.S. Colleges and Universities" (4/81). They discuss the problems faced by foreign science and technology students in the U.S. university writing programs and suggest a need for ESL programs to focus on the purposes which students have for writing. Byrd's article on the "Agentless Passive" (11/77) examines what is often pointed out as one of the major grammatical differences between scientific writing and literature, and suggests some techniques to help students acquire the use of this form through sample exercises in writing-up chemistry problems. This section closes with three short reviews. Pauline Robinson's *English for Special Purposes*, reviewed by William Lawler (4/82), surveys the history of the field and discusses current theory and practice. Steven Darien reviews (12/82) the intriguing book, *Communication Skills for the Foreign Born Professional* by Gregory Barnes, which provides advanced study problems in such areas as rules of social behavior. Paul Roberts reports (8/82) on the volume *Reading and Writing for Science and Technology* by Karl Drobnic, Sharon Abrams and Marjorie Morray, who provide excellent exercises for teaching reading and writing in a variety of science and technology areas.

In section 12, Donald Adamson discusses the reading strategies of "Prediction and Explanation" (9/77) as techniques he uses in helping students understand technical reading material. Other ESP articles which have appeared in the *TN* are: "An Overseas View of Scientific English" by John Boyd and Mary Ann Boyd (11/78) in which they report on the uses of and attitudes about English in scientific materials as seen by non-U.S. users; "Vocabulary and the Use of Context in Sci-Tech English" by Robert King in which he discusses the teaching of specialized vocabulary with scientific and technological reading material; "Counseling-Learning and EST" by James N. Davis, in which he applies counseling-learning techniques to the teaching of students in an English for science and technology classroom; "Spelling EST" by James Griswold in which he discusses the problems and techniques of teaching the spelling of scientific and technical words; Gregory Thompson's "Learning for the ESP Classroom" (12/81) presents techniques to use in an ESP classroom; and Cathy Tansey reports on an "ESP/EST Teacher Training Institute" (10/79).

GOING BEYOND CAREER EDUCATION

by Cathy Day
Eastern Michigan University

Career education is usually divided into the three phases of awareness, exploration, and preparation. It includes all ages and all levels of education, and is defined by Kenneth Hoyt, director of the Office of Career Education, as follows: "Career education consists of all those activities and experiences through which one learns about work." ("Career Education and the Handicapped Person," in *Career and Vocational Education for the Handicapped*, pg. 19.)

In those schools which have career education programs, the three phases have usually been implemented as follows: awareness of the world of work in the elementary school; exploration in the junior high; and the preparation in the senior high (what we traditionally think of as vocational education). Proponents of career education insist that it serves all ages, but usually graduation from secondary school is the end of any programmatic career education. There is little provision for adults whether through educational assistance in maintaining career competence, changing careers, or moving up within a career path.

Rupert Evans, in the late 1970's, states that "It would be . . . accurate to say that at least 50 percent of high school students are not now prepared for work of any type, and that traditional programs of vocational education which are designed to prepare people for skilled occupations are unlikely to meet this need. Career education programs which emphasize preparation for nonpaid work and preparation which is useful for all types of work . . . offer real promise of meeting some of the needs of this 50 percent." Remember that he was talking about English speaking students—not the LEP (Limited English Proficient) students we work with. ("Career Education and Vocational Education," in *Career and Vocational Education for the Handicapped*, pg. 11.)

Students need to receive first-hand knowledge of actual industry and employment situations. It is vitally important to provide our LEP students with opportunities to observe, meet, and interact with people on the job. At the exploration level, students should have the opportunities to undertake short term job observations in certain businesses, or to "shadow" a person in a selected occupation for a brief period of time. At the preparation level, LEP students should have opportunities to work part-time in either paid or unpaid experiences. Recent studies have shown that actual work experience is more effective in the success of vocational edu-

cation students' post training employment than the number of years in actual vocational training.

Traditionally, at the elementary level, students should develop a broad awareness of careers and an awareness of themselves in relation to potential career choices. Thus career awareness learning activities for LEP students should aid them in becoming aware of various careers, creating positive attitudes toward work, and building positive attitudes about themselves and others in the world of work. They should also have opportunities at the awareness level to identify different types of work and to strengthen attitudes toward work and positive work habits. Since LEP youth often have primary contact with LEP adults fixed in unskilled, entry level occupations due to lack of proficiency in English, it is even more important to emphasize the wide range of career choices that are possible for a trained, language proficient bilingual student. The upward mobility of career paths must also be emphasized. Furthermore, the first culture attitudes towards work may be different from what is acceptable in this country. The teacher needs to help the student understand and work towards acceptable US work behavior.

At the exploration level, usually junior high or middle school, students should begin the process of career planning, making decisions about their likes and dislikes, and identifying with the competencies and behaviors required in a work situation. Volunteer work, in-school work experiences, and shadowing workers on-the-job are all strategies used for exploration activities. It is extremely important to make sure that the LEP student is not discriminated against during these experiences.

Finally, the preparation phase should begin in high school, and continue later if necessary. A broad range of career awareness, orientation, and exploration experiences needs to be provided for the LEP student to be able to make tentative career choices and to pursue the appropriate types of training. Again, it is imperative we make sure that the LEP student is not discriminated against—or channeled into only one area of training.

We, as ESL and bilingual educators, probably are the teachers who have most contact with LEP students. We need to make sure that LEP students have all three phases of career education available to them, regardless of the age or grade level the student has when he or she comes to our school system. Thus we need to be aware of the three

stages and to try to incorporate them into our regular teaching.

I'd like to ask you to think about the following points for your own situation. Is there a career education program in your school? If so, are LEP students included? If they're included, are they channelled into certain aspects of the program? For example, if your school has a cooperative work program, are your LEP students included? If there is a job shadowing program, are LEP students included? Are they only asked to shadow in one area? Or, are they encouraged to have a wide variety of experiences? Are LEP students permitted to enroll in vocational education classes? If so, are they encouraged to take only one area, or are they encouraged to enroll in whatever area they're interested in? For example, are they allowed to take only food service, and not permitted to take auto body classes? If you don't know the answers to all of these questions, let me encourage you to take the time to find out what is happening in your situation. Once you've done that, then you can perhaps begin to work more effectively for the LEP students. You can offer assistance to the career educator or the vocational education teacher. You can work on the United States work ethic, appropriate behavior, or cross-cultural differences in relation to the work world in the ESL or bilingual classroom. What about the teaching materials that are being used in the career education program? What are the underlying assumptions that are probably accurate for students who have grown up in the United States, but may not be for those students who come from another linguistic and cultural background. Review the materials, and you can help your students understand the unstated assumptions.

Another way you can help is to try to make sure that role-models who are from different linguistic and cultural backgrounds are available in different career paths. Your contacts are probably wider and more extensive in terms of adults from other backgrounds than those of the career educator. It is important for LEP students to see that it is possible to "make it" and be from a different background. It is also important to make sure that students who are from non-urban backgrounds or non-technological societies understand what is involved in the world of work in this country. You are probably the best source of understanding cross-cultural differences and problems which may influence the LEP students' success in the world of work. Thus it is crucial that those issues are handled in the ESL or bilingual class.

Finally, what is going on in your school system to prepare students for what the world of work will be like in ten years? What do you know about the actual employment situation right now? This point was brought home to me very dramatically just this past week. I think it exemplifies the problem.

The local newspaper carried an article about new CETA training programs scheduled to start before the current funding is stopped. One of the programs was for robotics. How many of you know what robotics is? I thought to myself what on earth is that? I've been working with voc ed for the past two years—and in an institution that trains teachers, and is considered to have one of the better voc ed departments. I had never heard of robotics. It must have to do with robots, but what? I asked people at EMU, and all they could tell me was that it had to do with robots. I called the U of Illinois, and my friends said well, it must have to do with robots. Finally, I called the local CETA office and was told that it was a training program to learn how to assemble robots (for entry level)—and that even at that the student needed to have a rather extensive background in electronics, and at least a high school education. Two nights later, the local TV news had a program which showed a robotics training program at a local community college—and stated that there was a waiting list of more than 400 people to get into the program. On the train to Chicago, I was talking with one of the un-

employed union workers coming to a meeting in Chicago, and telling him about my experience with robotics— and he said, "Where? I'd like to get into a robotics training program. Ask this guy, he can tell you about robotics." The other guy was an engineer for an auto company, and he described how robots were being used on the assembly line, and that for him, a robotics training program wor'd be one in which students learned to service, repair and maintain the robots used in industry. As if all of this weren't enough, I was reading an article on the train and found this:

> "Smart machines" performing jobs formerly done by humans are proliferating; the field of robotics, made possible and profitable by the microprocessor, is becoming a major element in industry. About 4,000 robots are in use in the US, mostly in the auto industry, and more than 11,000 are at work in Japan as of 1981. Some can be instructed to see, hear, feel, and even make simple decisions. Robots can now beat most humans at chess, they can perform, and they can learn. General Motors is installing 10 "programmable universal machines for assembly" that can screw light bulbs into dashboard panels, spray paint, weld, load and unload parts, follow typed directions, and even respond to simple verbal directions. In handling hot casings, robots such as these have cut the number of rejects by 15% and increased production by 10% while reducing the need for human labor by 70%—all for $4.60 per hour. (Harold G. Shane, "The Silicon Age and Education" in *Phi Delta Kappan*, January 1982.)

My challenge to you then, and to those in vocational education everywhere, is to go beyond vocational and career education. Those of us in education tend to be relatively sheltered, and not particularly up on the real world of work. We think traditionally. Let me encourage you to go beyond what traditional career and vocational education are—to find out about the business and industry world in your area—to ask what businessmen foresee in the next ten years or so. Use that information to guide you in working with LEP students about the United States world of work. Don't depend on the vocational and career educators in your district to do it for you. They may not know and/or they may not have the resources to work with. We need to be extremely honest with our students given the state of the economy, and we need to get them thinking about real possibilities for employment in the future. That means we need to involve the community, and keep up to date ourselves (and that information is not in the educational literature—it's in business magazines, etc.). Yes, get our students to the place where they can get a job and keep it—acknowledging that an entry level skill may not be the end goal, but it will allow the student to have an income in order to pursue a career which will fit in the future. At this stage of the game, our students need to be better than their native speaking counterparts. *Editor's Note: The foregoing is from a talk given at an Illinois TESOL/BE workshop, January 30, 1982.* TN 8/82

CULTURAL ASPECTS OF PREVOCATIONAL ESL

by Barbara Humak
The School Board of Broward County, Florida

Since April 1980 hundreds of thousands of Cuban and Haitian refugees have landed in South Florida. Such a deluge of people has impacted our lifestyle, communities, and educational systems. This impact has been felt in our ESL programs in Broward County's Adult Education classes. Whereas "general" ESL sufficed previously, now four other ESL/language needs have appeared—academic, literacy training, social and prevocational. In the past three years, prevocational ESL has emerged as the single largest English for Specific Purposes (ESP) program in the county. Early in the design stages of the program, it was recognized that there was a cultural aspect that needed to be incorporated, and it is an aspect that continues to evolve.

In order to discuss the cultural aspects of prevocational ESL, one must define both culture and prevocational English. Culture is a secondary man-made environment that directs and guides our role in life situations, provides models from which we learn expected appropriate behavior,

and stresses conformity. Behavior which doesn't conform is labelled "deviant."[1] Conforming, fitting in, and being accepted are three emotionally charged areas for our students. Both caring instructors and anxious students anticipate the students' eventual mainstreaming into American life. Not until newcomers better understand the culture can they successfully and effectively participate in it. Since culture is a learned behavior, it follows that we can teach it; and teach it we must.

Prevocational ESL is the language and culture necessary to seek and secure entry level employment, and it also includes career-awareness activities. Here in Broward County, Adult Education prevocational ESL is the starting point in a refugee's English career. It is not preceded by "general" ESL. Prevocational topics are: personal data, skills and interests, occupations and duties, maps and directories, time and money, the interview/asking questions, work experience, schedules, safety, want ads, and the interview/answering ques-

tions. The foregoing topics are from *English That Works* (Scott, Foresman, and Co.), which is being used in our classes.

The following sample prevocational idioms illustrate our culture: "time is money," "the almighty dollar," "the American way," "every man for himself," "all men are created equal," "stand on your own two feet," "stand up for your rights," "climb the ladder of success," and "last hired, first fired." As a reference tool to help generate idioms, any idiom book on the market can be used. However, it is recommended that the idiom book be used *solely* as teacher reference. This way the instructor will have a repertoire to use *in context* during a class activity. When a situation arises that calls for an idiom, the time will be appropriate, the teacher will be ready, and the students will be receptive.

In Broward County, Vocational Education has asked that Adult Basic Education Program cover these prevocational topics and activities which will *not* be covered in the vocational schools:

1. Student reads, understands and responds to job advertisements (magazines, posters, newspapers).
2. Student understands and utilizes employment agencies.
3. Student reads, understands, and responds appropriately to job applications.
4. Student reads, understands, and responds appropriately to social security applications.
5. Student practices appropriate grooming habits for the interview.
6. Student displays appropriate interview conduct.
7. Student asks and answers appropriate questions during the interview.

When the students enter the vocational level, they will be taught vocational-specific English with the assumption that they have acquired a basic ability in prevocational language in the preceding level.

Listed below are examples of culture found in each item outlined above:

1. Job advertisements suggest classified ads (complete with jargon and abbreviations), labor union notices (protecting "the little guy" and workers' rights) and trade journals.
2. Employment agencies are public and private. Sometimes you pay a fee, sometimes you don't. When do you pay a fee—before or after the job? Are counsellors authoritarian figures or advisors? Counselling is a *very* American phenomenon!
3. Job applications are packed with culture. First, they illustrate a formal system of applying rather than an informal process of friend/family referrals. Second, we're a paper/form oriented society. Other cultural points are the order of a name (which is the first name? the last name? what is "last name first"?); the number of names we have; the order of the date (month, day, year); the months of the Gregorian calendar; capitalizing the months; the order of an address (number, street, city); having a house number vs. a postal box; the definition of "college," marital status (common law? divorced? separated? Do these circumstances exist in other countries?); using ink, not pencil; printing vs. signing; and markings (dash, an "x," circling, crossing out).
4. The social security system reveals our attitude toward the elderly, aging, and retired.
5. Grooming lessons teach appropriate dress (avoid over dressing and—for women—heavy makeup), and mention hygiene.
6. Kinesics and spatiality are part of interview conduct. Do you shake hands? Do you maintain eye contact? How close do you stand to the interviewer? Do you go to the interview alone or with extended family?
7. The actual interview demands individuality, asserting oneself, and most importantly asking for clarification.

A rule of thumb when teaching culture is to assume nothing. American culture is obvious around us and so internalized within us that it is very difficult to objectively identify it. Remember, too, that we did not instinctively "know the ropes," "the rules of the game," "the how-to's," that is, the culture. We have all been taught what is appropriate and expected. We have patterned our behavior after the role models presented before us. So too must ESL instructors model the correct actions and reactions for our job-bound students when presenting the cultural aspects of prevocational ESL. The cultural imperative says that culture must be transmitted, learned, and lasting. It is our job as ESL instructors to transmit the culture to our students.

¹ Dr. Lillian Gaffney, Fairleigh Dickinson University, N.J.

UNDERSTANDING ON THE JOB

by Carol Svendsen
Bilingual Vocational English Training Program
Metropolitan State College, Denver

One of the greatest needs of recent immigrants anywhere is getting a job. Preparing this student for the language and cultural expectations of the workplace is an important priority for the ESL teacher. This job preparation can begin even before the teacher knows the specific jobs the students will be entering. Here are some techniques I have used in vocational ESL classes for beginning and intermediate students to develop skills in one crucial communicative area: reporting problems and getting clarification on the job.

A limited English speaking worker in an entry level job can often learn the routine duties of the job through observation. But when the routine is interrupted, when instructions are given for a new assignment or when a machine breaks down, the worker must be able to find out what is expected of him. In some situations the worker must take responsibility for informing a supervisor about a problem and understand the supervisor's response. Oral instructions about duties are often incomprehensible because of unfamiliar structure and vocabulary, because they are given too fast or contain too much information to absorb at once. Sometimes instructions are incomplete and occasionally instructions are inaccurate.

It is not enough then for workers to listen mutely and follow orders. They have to verify their understanding of what they need to do before making serious mistakes. They have to "teach" their supervisor ways to make an explanation understandable. They have to ask questions about specific parts of the instructions. When something happens they were not prepared for by their training, they have to indicate the nature of the problem. And they have to do all this in a polite way in order to stay on good terms with the supervisor or co-worker. The supervisor wants to be certain that she or he has been understood, and that if and there is a problem or misunderstanding the worker will ask a question.

TECHNIQUES FOR GETTING CLARIFICATION

Classroom techniques can center on developing skills for reporting problems and getting clarification. Vocabulary is specific to the vocational areas students are training for or it can be general classroom vocabulary. The important thing is that students learn the forms necessary for communicating in occupations and that they develop the necessary assertiveness in speaking up when they need clarification.

Imperatives and live action responses on the part of the students are good preparation for on the job instructions. Most imperatives, however, take more polite forms than "clean this up" or "get a wrench". Following are examples of forms used more frequently at the workplace:

● Would you put those tools away?
● Do you want to go ahead and put that cassette in the recorder?
● Why don't you do Room 605 now?

Students need to learn to recognize these forms as commands.

When students carry out commands in the classroom, they should be required to show acknowledgement. Nodding the head and saying "OK" is usually sufficient. Supervisors don't know what to make of the employee who turns wordlessly to carry out the task. If the request is not understood there are several strategies that can be taught to get repetition or clarification. The teacher should intentionally give imperatives that will not be understood to give the students the opportunity to use these strategies. For example, the teacher can:

● Speak quickly, slurring words together.
● Use vocabulary or idiomatic expressions the students don't know.

Students can then say, "Could you please repeat that" or "I'm sorry, could you speak slowly please." If the student understands all but one word of a command (e.g. "Would you close the blind please?") he can say, "I don't understand **blind**." Or he can point to the object that seems logical and say, "This?" with rising intonation. The teacher then will acknowledge, "Yes, that's right" or say, "No, over there" accompanied by pointing. The student's pointing causes the first speaker to respond by pointing. As a final strategy the student can say, "I'm sorry, I don't understand. Can you show me?"

TECHNIQUES FOR GETTING CONFIRMATION

There are techniques for getting confirmation if the student thinks he understands but wants to make sure before carrying out the instructions. As he begins to perform the action he can say to the teacher, "Like this?" the teacher then acknowledges or corrects. Another strategy the student can use is to repeat back to the teacher what he heard. For example:

Teacher: You want to take this projector over to Linda in Room 509?

Student: I take the projector to Linda in Room 509?

Instead of giving back an entire sentence the student can repeat only the important parts of the message. This teaches the student to focus on the crucial information. ("Linda? Room 509?") Where numbers are involved repeating back is especially important. Stock numbers, for example, are used in many work settings. Classroom items can be labelled with numbers so that the following imperative could be used:

Teacher: Would you bring me a 53-402?

Student: 53-4...

Teacher: 53-402.

Student: 53-402?

Teacher: Right.

Dimensions are used in some jobs ("Why don't you cut it 2½" x 3"?"), and here, too, the student needs to repeat to get verification. Using a small notebook to write down numbers is also valuable. It can be used for students as a clarification tool, by asking supervisors or co-workers to write a word or number that is not understood.

Supervisors sometimes give incomplete information in their instructions. They may ask a new worker to get supplies without telling where they are stored or tell him to get an item without differentiating between similar items. In the classroom students can be asked to get items whose locations they don't know.

Teacher: You want to go get the scissors?

Student: Where is it?

Teacher: Top drawer of my desk.

Student: (finds two pairs) Which one?

Teacher: The small one.

If the student is uncertain he can hold it up and say, "This one?"

Students should also realize that information given to them will sometimes be inaccurate and be prepared to question instructions.

Teacher: Could you clean the mirror with that glass cleaner?

Student: Where is the glass cleaner?

Teacher: In the cabinet.

Student: (after looking) I can't find it.

Teacher: We must be out. (or) May be in the supply room.

Another example:

Teacher: Would you put these boxes on that top shelf over there?

Student: The shelf is full.

Teacher: OK. Just put them on the floor in the corner.

These clarification strategies can be taught, roleplayed, and then practiced in all classroom activities. Teachers should structure activities which demand that students take an active role in discovering what is expected of them. Students will then begin to take responsibility for clearing up misunderstandings and for acquiring the information they need to do the job.

TN 10/83

EST IN INTENSIVE ENGLISH PROGRAMS IN THE UNITED STATES

By Patricia Byrd
University of Florida, Gainesville

Current demands for classes in the English of Science and Technology (EST) create special problems for intensive English programs because of the nature of such programs and also because of the continuing uncertainty as to what EST actually means. Some of these problems derive from the mixed backgrounds and needs of the students in such programs. For example, the advanced level of the graduate track at the University of Florida's English Language Institute in the Winter Quarter, 1978, included 18 students who planned to matriculate into M.A. programs and 1 student who planned to work on his Ph.D. Although their English proficiency levels were practically identical, their fields of specialization were widely divergent, including educational psychology, educational media, chemistry, business, accounting, physics, and agriculture. It would be unrealistic to expect an English teacher to have command of the specialized terminology, concepts, formats, and usage of so many professions. It would also be financially prohibitive to hire specialists in the English of physics, the English of educational psychology, the English of chemistry, etc.—even if such specialists existed.

The problem of deciding what to put into an EST course can be solved only through careful reconsideration of the role of the English teacher and of the uses to which foreign students put English. Accusing English teachers of being afraid of—or hostile to—science is not an adequate response to doubts about just what should be required of the English teacher. On the other hand, it would smack of the widest sort of intellectual arrogance and ignorance to think that a specialist in ESL could brush up his physics and start leading his students through physics texts and journals. In addition to examining the demands to be made on teachers in EST courses, curriculum planners who are making EST additions should keep in mind four considerations about the kinds of English needed by foreign students in American colleges and universities:

(1) The native speaker of English who enters a training program—vocational or academic—does not know the technical terminology yet either. One purpose of the scientific or technical training program itself is to teach such terminology.

(2) The non-native speaker of English who comes to the U.S. to take his professional training has to live in an English-speaking environment. He must have a more general kind of preparation in English to be able to survive outside the classroom.

(3) Moreover, the general English serves as a general context for his specialized English. Typically, foreign students are in classes that are primarily for Americans. Thus, the teacher will be explaining new, unknown information in terms that he hopes his American students will understand. When analogy is used—as it frequently will be—the foreign student will have problems because he will not understand the very part of the explanation that the teacher expects to be helpful. In an article on atomic clocks, the functioning of certain electrons is explained in terms of the functioning of a top: "Put simply, certain chemical elements carry near the outer edge of each atom a single electron that spins on its axis, like a tiny, incredibly fast top." It would be stretching things to call "top" technical vocabulary, but it is likely that a foreign student would have as many problems with "top" as with "electron"—and perhaps more.

(4) Teachers of foreign students in a variety of academic programs repeatedly comment that the students have problems not with the technical language or special formats of each profession but rather with the English that holds it all together. For a hypothetical example, take the agriculture student who understands all of the technical names of the chemicals he is studying but is not sure about the difference between "put on" and "take off."

In the *EST Newsletter* for December, 1977, Karl Drobnic quoted H. G. Widdowson's comment that teachers sometimes achieve their goals by indirection rather than by direct attack on the problem:

The best way may not be what appears to be the most direct route, although one is generally inclined to think that it is. . . . It may be that the students could be more effectively prepared by a course which developed more general communicative strategies over a wider range of language use, which concentrated not so much on direct teaching as on favorable set towards language learning. I am not saying, please note, that the direct route is necessarily the wrong one but only that it is not necessarily the right one.

The assumption that teaching EST means teaching only technical content is a good example of such erroneous going-straight-to-the-point. There are many things that the English teacher can do as an English teacher to prepare students for academic training in science and technology. Teaching them English or American literature is probably not one of them. Although it may be difficult for English or American literature majors to accept, literature is of limited use in preparing non-natives for academic programs in American universities, especially for graduate work in a scientific or technical area. Even undergraduates will not be required to take many literature courses, if any—and learning to read poetry will not be of much help in reading the textbooks used in undergraduate courses in art or history or political science. On the other hand, using non-literary materials as the basis for reading or writing eliminates much of the puzzling cultural content that causes problems in understanding the literature of a different language.

The discussion of EST involves a great deal of muddled thinking because of an obsession with the dichotomy between the English of literature and the English of technical writing. In reality, the choice is not between literature on the one hand and technical content on the other, for there is a third possibility: The ESL teacher can help his students with the language that sticks everything together—with "put on" and "take off." Removal of technical vocabulary reveals that what is left could be, for the most part, used in any non-literary paper. This is not to say that EST is just a vocabulary problem but rather that if the strange vocabulary is removed much of what is left will be very familiar to an English teacher.

The difference between the grammar of general English and that of EST has been exaggerated by faulty descriptions of general English. Pedagogical grammars have overgeneralized and oversimplified the grammar of general English by saying that rules are invariable when they are variable and by giving only one use when there are several uses of a form.

For example, all too often students are being taught that *will* is the only future tense marker in English and *will* means only future time. It is more accurate to teach that although English has many ways of referring to future time, it does not have any one form that refers purely to the future. In addition to all modals and semi-modals like *ought to,* ways of referring to the future include simple present tense (*The play opens tomorrow night. The Party is on Saturday.*) and *be going to* (*I am going to eat lunch at 12:30.*) Even past tense forms of the verb can refer to future time in conditional sentences (*If he brought the money tomorrow, I would be very surprised.*).

The meaning of *will* has been described by Madeline Ehrman, *The Meaning of the Modals in Present-Day American English.* The Hague. (1966, as "the occurrence of the predication is guaranteed, either in a concrete (future time function) or a general (neutral time function) context. . . ."

1. He will go to the beach this weekend.
2. Oil will float on water.

In (1) the speaker is guaranteeing a future time occurrence of a particular event while (2) is a generalized statement which does not refer to a specific future time. The following examples of the use of generalized, non-future time

will are taken from various professional journals and reference books selected to represent both science and technology.

1. Certain highly purified and finely divided metals will also react with hydrogen at room temperature.
2. It is generally wise to assume that finely divided samples of any of the alkali hydrides will react vigorously with oxidizing agents and there is some hazard of detonation with powerful oxidants.
3. The adults may be kept in a large aquarium or tank on a diet of Tubifex, earthworms, or beef liver, and will breed again the following year.

Students who are preparing to enter scientific or technical fields must know that *will* has the potential to be used in future time statements or in non-future time generalized statements about characteristics or inherent qualities. Although general truth statements are primarily made with simple present tense forms of the verb (*Oil floats on water*), uses of *will* for that meaning are common enough to cause problems for any student who attempts to interpret them in terms of future time.

However, all of these generalizations about *will* and present tense are true of English not just of technical or scientific usage. Therefore it should not be necessary to teach them—or many other aspects of English—in the context of materials from physics or medicine or diesel engines. Thus it would appear that ESL programs do not need to be quite literal in adding EST preparation to their curriculums, for an informed understanding of English will prepare students to deal with much that they find in their technical and scientific courses.

TN 6/79

THE PURPOSES OF TECHNICAL WRITING COURSES FOR FOREIGN STUDENTS IN U.S. COLLEGES AND UNIVERSITIES

by Patricia Byrd
and Gregory K. West
University of Florida

Technical writing courses in universities in the U.S. take as their main objective the preparation of students to do the writing required of practicing professionals in the "real world" of work outside the university. This purpose suggests that much of what happens in such classes and in materials prepared for such classes will not be relevant to the academic needs of foreign students. We have no idea what kinds of writing are done by a Venezuelan engineer working in Venezuela for a Venezuelan firm. Perhaps in the world of technology, the cultural differences that exist in other areas do not occur. Before advising a foreign national to take such a writing course, however, one would like to see some information that proves the helpfulness of

such writing in his home country.

There is another reason for suggesting that technical writing courses for foreign students need to be quite different from those now offered for natives: the real world in which the foreign technical or scientific student must survive is that of the educational system of the U.S. university. That this experience is a relatively short one does not mean that it is not real. (Indeed the experience is a "real" one for the U.S. student as well, and our investigations show that many students in scientific or technical areas are not receiving the training in writing skills that they need to complete their educations successfully.)

In a TOEFL Research Report entitled *The Performance of Non-Native Speak-*

ers of English on TOEFL and Verbal Aptitude Tests, the results of the performance of foreign students on TOEFL, GRE, SAT, and TSWE (the Test of Standard Written English) are compared. The purpose of the study was to find if and under what circumstances the scores of foreign students on GRE, SAT, and TSWE are meaningful. Included in the report, however, is information that demonstrates that foreign students enter our universities without the writing skills necessary for equal competition with natives. The mean score on TOEFL for the undergraduates tested was 502. The mean score for this same group on the TSWE was 28 compared to the mean of

42.35 (out of a possible 60) for the native speakers of English. Thus foreign students at the admittable level of 500—for most colleges and universities—are far less skilled in writing than the native speakers with whom they will be competing. These numbers give objective support to something that ESL teachers have witnessed for years: few of our students have writing skills as advanced as their other language skills.

Convinced that foreign students need special training, we have begun a series of investigations to document in detail the kinds of writing required by instructors in U.S. technical and scientific programs. In the first step we conducted a survey of engineering faculty at the University of Florida to find out what types of writing they most frequently require of graduate students (all graduate students, not just foreign students) (West and Byrd, 1980). The results of the survey are, in sum, that the most frequently assigned types of writing for graduate students in engineering are examinations, quantitative problems, and reports. The next most frequently assigned are homework and papers (term and publication). The least frequently assigned are progress reports and proposals:

One irony of these findings is that they suggest that the freshman English class is the only place where a student going into graduate work in a scientific or technical area is getting help with the writing skills he needs for success—for knowledge of the essay would provide a basis on which to build term papers and publication papers. Technical writing classes usually include a minimal amount of practice in converting technical reports into papers and articles.

The literature of technical writing is full of denunciations of freshman English as useless and the essay as a waste of time. From the point of view of those who are preparing the student for his professional future that is, perhaps, true. The essay is, however, extremely relevant to the student's survival in the real world of the university. In the years that stretch between the freshman English class and entrance into the marketplace (especially for the student who gets a graduate degree immediately after finishing a bachelor's), the university student will be required to write many essay examinations and term papers (both of which are, after all, extended essays involving specialized rules of evidence).

It would be unrealistic to argue that the university is out-of-step with the "real world" and should immediately change so that more proposals and progress reports are written and the essay abandoned. Whether or not the training given by a university has direct rele-vance for a student's work on a job, the university experience is a necessary rite-of-passage through which young people must go before the modern technological world will certify them as qualified to move on a certain social and economic level. Thus the skills needed to survive in the university are valuable for the future of the student. Without them, the student has to accept a future on a very different level.

Traditional technical writing courses, in focusing on the multiple readers in industry, fail also to help students with the kinds of audiences that the student will write for while still in the university. Stevenson (1978) suggests a matrix to use in judging technical writing courses and programs in terms of their completeness in covering all of the possible types of technical writing. The vertical axis of the matrix lists the four audiences—self, one reader, many readers (homogeneous group), and many readers (diverse group). The horizontal axis uses the three purposes of writing—to inform, to affect, and to effect. Thus an owner's manual for a car would fit in the matrix as an example of writing to instruct a diverse group. The university student most often is writing for an audience of one—the instructor. But for what purpose? Surely the writing of most students in most situations involves all three of the purposes given by Stevenson: although a student will seldom be teaching his teacher anything new, he will be teaching him about himself. That is, one purpose the student should have is to demonstrate to the instructor that he, the student, is intelligent and diligent. The student is, therefore, also trying to affect the instructor—the student is selling himself and his ideas to the teacher. He wants the teacher to feel good about him and his work. Finally, it is a very rare student who is not trying to influence the grade and any other reward in the teacher's power to bestow. And teachers are powerful influences on a student's future—controlling scholarships, fellowships, admission to graduate programs, paper publication, introductions to important people, letters of recommendation, reports to sponsors, etc.

If we accept that the English-of-the U.S.-university (English for Academic Purposes) is a genuine need of foreign students hoping to get U.S. academic degrees, we must find definite answers to a number of questions about the written English of the academic world:

1. What kind of writing is done on examinations by students in scientific and technical programs?

2. What kind of writing is done on homework?

3. What does a graduate professor mean when he says "term paper"?

4. What does an engineering professor mean when he says that foreign students have problems with sentence structure or with grammar or with vocabulary?

5. What differences exist between the writing required of upper division undergraduates (working in their majors) and graduate students?

6. What kinds of writing, if any, go with quantitative problems?

7. What volume of written work is demanded in undergraduate and graduate classes in technical and scientific fields?

8. Are foreign students aware of the importance of written work at a U.S. university?

9. Do professors notice errors more in hand-written papers than in typed papers? (How much influence does bad handwriting have on grades? The questions could be anything but trivial for an Iranian or an Arabic student.)

Special courses in composition for foreign students in technical or scientific fields at U.S. universities are needed for two reasons:

(1) There are significant differences in writing skills between U.S. and foreign students. Not only do foreign students come from different academic training than U.S. students, but foreign students are also considered admissible to U.S. universities on the basis of reading and listening abilities that usually are far more advanced than their writing skills.

(2) The concerns that have been identified as significant by the field of technical writing in the U.S. are not those which are needed for survival in the university, since that field has taken as its purpose the training of technicians and scientists for the U.S. government and industry.

Together, these differences in skills and needs imply that the English of Science and Technology is, for foreign students, more accurately termed the English of Academic Purposes (for Students of Science and Technology).

BIBLIOGRAPHY

Angelis, Paul J., Spencer S. Swinton and William R. Cowell. 1979. *The Performance of Non-native Speakers of English on TOEFL and Verbal Aptitude Tests.* Princeton, N.J.: Educational Testing Service.

Stevenson, Dwight W. 1978. "Mapping the Unexplored Area: Developing New Courses and Coherent Programs in Technical Communication," *Journal of Technical Writing and Communication,* Vol. 8, Number 3, pp. 193-206.

West, Gregory K. and Patricia Byrd. 1980. "Technical Writing Required of Graduate Engineering Students." *Journal of Technical Writing and Communication.* (Forthcoming.) □

CHEMISTRY AND AGENTLESS PASSIVE SENTENCES: AN ESL—EST EXERCISE

by Patricia Byrd
University of Florida

Ideally a grammar exercise should both illustrate the structure being taught by putting it in a realistic context and also provide an image that will help the students recall the structure. For the past two years I have been working with a passive sentence exercise that incorporates both of these features. In this exercise a simple chemistry experiment is done in class. Then the students work together to write up the experiment in a very informal laboratory report.

The formation of passive sentences is not usually much of a problem—in fact it is just the kind of puzzle that students can solve easily. Their problem—and it is a problem for native speakers of English, too—is knowing when this type of sentence is appropriate. The chemical experiment exercise is a good way to show the students where to use the passive, for writing of this sort frequently resorts to the passive since the important information is not who did the work but rather what was done in the experiment. Thus the exercise teaches not just formation but also use of the passive sentence.

This four part lesson begins with an explanation of the formation of the passive sentence in terms of a transformation of the basic sentence. When working with low intermediate or intermediate students, I do this in terms of changes in position of the subject and complement of the basic sentence rather than introduce the term "noun phrase." In addition, I prefer to talk in terms of passive sentences rather than simply passive voice because the change occurs across the whole of the sentence rather than in just the verb phrase. The rule is

---

1. subject + verb + complement + modifier

2. subject + *be* + past participle of verb + modifier + (*by* + 1st subject).

For example,

1. Someone discovered penicillin.

2. Penicillin was discovered (by someone).

I discourage the use of the *by*-phrase since it is rarely used in the reports on research published in professional journals of science or technology. Obviously the statement of the verb phrase is very rough and must be expanded to show the forms of *be*. In this exercise only simple present tense and simple past tense forms are ever necessary. Before turning to the

experiment I get the students to transform several additional sentences. I select examples that illustrate good use of the passive:

1. *Someone invented the wheel. (The subject is unknown.)*
2. *Someone founded the University of Florida in 1853. (The subject is unimportant to the writer.)*
3. *The police arrested the president of the bank. (The subject is unimportant because it is so obvious.)*
4. *Someone tested the brakes on this used car. (The speaker is a used-car salesman who wants to hide the subject.)*

In the second step we actually do an experiment such as this one from Nathan Shalit's *Cup and Saucer Chemistry* (New York: Grosset and Dunlap, 1972, pp. 88–89). This experiment is very effective because of its simplicity and its drama. I start by showing the equipment and getting the students to tell me the names of the various things used. These words are listed at the top of the blackboard along with other necessary vocabulary. When working with lower level students who might have trouble with the instructions, I do the experiment myself. With more advanced students, I select someone to do the experiment for the class. It is also necessary to talk about the purposes of the experiment so that the students have an overview of what is going on—this information will be used in the final step as the basis for a topic sentence for the report. For example, this hydrogen experiment shows (1) one method for making hydrogen and also (2) some of the characteristics of hydrogen. I defined hydrogen by giving the equation Water = H_2O.

Students who did not know the word "hydrogen" seemed to understand that statement.

The following equipment is needed: a tall glass or glass jar, some aluminium foil, a tablespoon, a stirrer, a ball-point pen, matches, washing soda, and hot water. Cut a dozen or so small postage-stamp-size pieces of aluminium foil. Place these in the

glass container. Add 3 or 4 tablespoons of washing soda. Fill the container almost full of very hot water. Stir the solution well. Cover the container with a piece of aluminium foil and smooth the edge to make a tight cover. Make a small hole in the cover with the ball-point pen. Wait 2 or 3 minutes. While waiting, observe the chemical reaction that is taking place in the jar—the bubbling and the rising of the pieces of foil to the top. After the 2- or 3-minute wait, hold a lighted match near the top where the hydrogen is escaping through the hole. There will be a not extremely loud but quite audible pop. If you are lucky—and I have always been—you will also get a steady flame. (It was found that the flame could be made brighter by shaking the jar.) If not so lucky, you will be able to produce several of the small explosions anyway.

The third step in the procedure comes after the experiment when I have the students tell me what was done. As they come up with sentences, I write them on the board. I give the first sentence to set the pattern because these should all be active sentences. For example,

1. *I put 12 small pieces of aluminium foil into the glass jar.*
2. *I added 4 tablespoons of washing soda to the jar.*

After we have completed this recounting of the experiment, I show them that these sentences will not make a very good report because they focus on the experimenter rather than the experiment. I explain that using the passive sentence is a way to avoid repeating over and over again the name of the experimenter—or the first person pronoun. Then I change the first sentence to the passive—not using the by-phrase. I also erase the active sentence after they seem to understand how I got it so that when we finish this stage of the exercise, there are 10 to 12 passive sentences written on the board.

In the final part of the lesson, after all the sentences have been changed to the passive, I ask for a topic sentence that will tie the whole collection of sentences together. Then we rewrite the report using the topic sentence and sequence connectors *(then, next, first, second, finally, etc.)* to make a well-organized laboratory report.

Shalit's book includes a number of experiments that are useful because they are simple without being insulting. Other good books of experiments are available, including Rudolf F. Graf's *Safe and Simple Electrical Experiments* (New York: Dover Publications, Inc., 1964), Ethel Hanauer's *Biology Experiments for Children* (New York: Dover Publications, Inc., 1962), and Muriel Mandell's *Physics Experiments for Children* (New York: Dover Publications, Inc., 1959).

TN 11/77

BOOK REVIEWS

ENGLISH FOR SPECIAL PURPOSES

(Pauline Robinson. New York: Pergamon Press, 1980)

Reviewed by William T. Lawlor
University of Wisconsin-Stevens Point

Pauline Robinson's, *English for Specific Purposes* is a necessary book. Workers in ESP are distant from one another, and the exchange of ideas is slow or non-existent. The body of previous research is notoriously limited, and almost always the research appears in small newsletters or unpublished mimeos that are not easily accessible. Robinson serves the ESP community by defining ESP, surveying current theories, and updating and supplementing the information guide on ESP published by the British Council's English Teaching Information Center: *English for Specific Purposes: Information Guide No. 2.*

Because ESP is an emerging field, Robinson properly takes time to define her subject. In her introduction, Robinson says ESP is "materials produced for use once only by one group of students in one place at one time." This definition, however, is refined as she contrasts ESP with "general, education-for-life, and literature orientated" courses. Usually, though not always, the ESP student is preparing for a job role that requires English, and consequently, students are often adults. The needs of the learner are the principal factors that shape curricula, and the emphasis is usually on communicative competence.

Moving into the realm of current theory and practice, Robinson surveys the history of ESP, and she examines register analysis, discourse analysis, motivation, needs, curriculum, materials, methodology, and the possibility of generalizing materials. The strength in Robinson's study of varying theories is her faithful acknowledgment supplemented by her sharp questioning and evaluation of all ideas.

The final and most important part of Robinson's work is the analysis of publications and the extensive bibliography. Robinson notes what is available, examining books in the various fields calling for ESP. Concluding her chapter on analysis, she cites weaknesses and points the way toward further refinement and investigation. The bibliography at the end of the book is clearly the most complete and useful resource in the field.

Thus, the word necessary is particularly applicable to *English for Specific Purposes* by Pauline Robinson. The book is an indispensable tool for those working in this diverse field that has gained special prominence in the last decade. *TN 4/82*

COMMUNICATION SKILLS FOR THE FOREIGN—BORN PROFESSIONAL

by Gregory Barnes. 1982. Institute for Scientific Information, 3501 Market Street, Philadelphia, Pennsylvania 19104. (198 pages; paperback $13.95; hard cover $18.95.)

Reviewed by Steven Darian
Rutgers University

Communication Skills for the Foreign-Born Professional serves as an excellent outline of communication needs and resources required by the non-native speaker already launched on his career.

A chapter on Rules for Social Behavior coaches the reader on American attitudes toward social time, personal distance, eye contact, grooming. Another—on Oral Presentations—discusses the use of easel graphics, overhead projectors, slides, videotape recorders, while a chapter on Visual Materials offers a handy summary of graphic resources, including: pie charts and bar charts, graphs, and cutaway diagrams. The architect's floorplan seems unnecessary: Presumably, students working with such material will have had design courses that make the present drawing redundant.

The book draws on the latest research in linguistics and discourse analysis, yet presents it in an applicable easy-to-understand manner. This in itself is reason to recommend it.

The section on reading provides an admirable synthesis of major points in reading theory. It stresses an *active* approach to reading, in the use of discourse markers, text notes and marks, summarizing, defining, and retention (Did you know, for example, that immediate recitation is the best technique for retaining information?).

It is an ambitious book, if anything a bit too ambitious for 193 pages, in its attempt to cover the entire gamut of communication activities. As a result, some topics are slighted, such as the six-page chapter on Public Speaking. Yet even in this short compass, Barnes manages to add some solid professional tips on the art (Wherever possible, use examples, quotes, and facts).

The book is written for a native-speaker level of English and thus aims at a specialized segment of students: those who speak English well "and read it very well." As such, its chief value is providing in one place, a broad range of communicative activities needed to succeed in U.S. culture, especially at the professional level.

An appendix includes a set of exercises for each chapter, in addition to short sections on writing mechanics and grammar. The overall format of the book makes it suitable for self-teaching, in an orientation course for foreign-born professionals, or an advanced course in English for Academic Purposes. *TN 12/82*

SCI TECH: READING AND WRITING THE ENGLISH OF SCIENCE AND TECHNOLOGY

(Karl Drobnic, Sharon Abrams and Marjorie Morray. 132 pp. Culver City, CA: ELS Publications, 1981)

Reviewed by Paul D. Roberts
Free University of Berlin

This is a highly useful book for teachers of students about to enter scientific and/or technological studies at the university level. The ESL student who is not yet ready to attempt authentic materials is the primary audience of this book. The authors have done an excellent job of analyzing textbook prose and then developing a format incorporating the major organizational features of textbook writing into their units. The basic format found in many texts has been followed in putting together the units of this book; i.e., introduction, development, focus, implication(s). These four strategems have been labeled overview, history, focus and concerns for today within the five units of this book. The five units deal with the physical sciences, the earth sciences, the life sciences, mathematics and applied science. The individual lessons contain a number of language learning exercises which directly correlate with the readings but have a distinct advantage in being easily expandable to cover any area of difficulty that might arise. The language analysis exercises deal with such crucial elements as vocabulary building, punctuation, classification, definition, chronology, cause and result, reference, etc. The reading comprehension sections include information gathering, interpreting a graph, diagram or map. The exercises then round out with three writing types: controlled, guided and free. These give the student valuable practice in sentence construction (structural), sentence-type construction (notional) and paragraph production. In addition, the fourth lesson of each unit, entitled Concerns for Today, particularly lends itself to discussion and elicitation of student insights, as do the free writing exercises at the end of each lesson.

Several of the advantages of this book will be of special interest to the EFL/ESL teacher. First, the exercises require no expertise beyond that of normal English language teaching. Second, the material is quite suitable for presentation using the standard methodologies of today. The success of the lessons is not dependent on the bringing of vast amounts of realia into the classroom. And finally, units of no particular interest to a certain group of students may be omitted without significant disruption. An answer key for the appropriate exercises is included at the back.

This is a fine book. Material has been provided which is intellectually interesting, valid and oriented toward proven techniques of language teaching. Teachers can expect an enthusiastic student response to these lessons which will lead to a stimulating teaching experience. It is an excellent introductory text for both teachers and students about to enter the fascinating world of English for Special Purposes. □

TN 8/82

Section 5. Teacher Training

This section begins with Gina Harvey's article (6/80) on the "Preparation of Teachers of ESOL" and Victor Mason's lengthy article (2/82) on getting results from teacher training programs. Mason's article responds to some of the ideas and suggestions of the Richard Orem article found in section 1. Mason uses Orem's thoughts on the future direction of TESOL to discuss his ideas on what should be done to improve the training of teachers. Robert Ochsner takes a look at MA programs in TESL in an attempt to determine the effect of the training in those programs on the quality of ESL teachers (10/80). The Hepworth and Krahnke (10/81) article "Role Models for the ESL Teacher" provides us with a discussion of some of the criteria for teachers to use in preparing themselves to be ESL teachers.

Jack Longmate in his article "Turnover in the ESL Profession" asks us to face a growing concern among ESL and EFL professionals: whether we are a profession of temporary and part-time teachers and whether we can afford to enter ESL teaching as a lifetime pursuit. Marilyn Appelson discusses the controversial practice of using "Volunteer Teachers" (8/80) and presents a compelling argument for their continued use. She provides criteria for the selection of volunteers and offers suggestions on how volunteers can best be used. The section closes with a short article by Richard Showstack, "I Resolve . . ." (6/79) in which he offers resolutions any teacher could make. You may wish to look at other articles in this volume with regard to teacher training, especially those which appear in section 6.

Many articles on teacher training have appeared in the *TN* which could not be included in this collection: Marsha Santelli's article on the preparation of ESL elementary teachers (10/82); the TESOL "Statement on the Qualification of ESL Teachers" (9-12/70); in addition, Emilio Cortez (8/81) wrote about support for ESL supervisors in his article "Suggestions for State ESL Supervisors."

Another area related to teacher training is certification. Certification for ESL teachers has been a regular topic for reporting and discussion in the pages of the *TN* since Donald Knapp's report on certification first appeared (11-12/76). You might want to look at the continuing developments in certification in the U.S. through these *TN* articles: beginning with Knapp and followed by Gina Harvey's "ESL and Bilingual Teacher Certification" (6/79) and "An Update on Teacher Certification" (10/79); Appelson's "Certification in TESOL" (4/80); Harvey's "The Preparation of Teachers of English to Speakers of Other Languages" (6/80), "Establishing Certification in Your State: A Step-by-Step Guide" (8/80), "ESL and Bilingual Teacher Certification in Public Schools, Community Colleges" (6/79) and "Basic Adult Education Programs: Some Recent Developments" (4/81).

Another interesting aspect of teacher training to consider is discussed by Joan Rubin and Rosemary Henze in "The Foreign Language Requirement: A Suggestion to Enhance its Educational Role in Teacher Training" (2/81).

In addition to Christine Grosse's "Teacher Burnout" (2/82), which appears in section 6 of this volume, you might also want to look at Valerie Howard's short article "Thinking About Teaching English as a Second Language?" (2/81); "Reflections on the First Week of Class in an ESL Program" by Janet Martinez-Bernal (8/81); and "Teaching ESL in an Outside Location: Or Things They Don't Tell Us in Grad School" by Beverly Lehman West (4/77). One additional article, which might be appropriate here, is "Go East, Go West, But Don't Come Back" by Peter Hill (10/79). Hill addresses a problem seldom discussed in teacher training programs, should I go overseas to teach and what will my reception be when I return?

And finally, do not overlook either Laurie Wellman's "In a Word . . ." (1-2/77) which gives the teacher-to-be a humorous look at what the jargon in the field means, or James Dean Brown's satirical look at the profession in his "An Empirical Analysis of Psychological Constructs Underlying the Desire to Teach ESL/EFL" (6/82).

THE PREPARATION OF TEACHERS OF ENGLISH TO SPEAKERS OF OTHER LANGUAGES

By Gina Cantoni Harvey
Northern Arizona University
Chair, Committee on Schools
& University Coordination

School systems serving students of limited English proficiency must now comply with federal laws by implementing one of several possible models of bilingual instruction in the elementary grades; at the secondary level, however, a school may adopt an ESL program as an acceptable alternative to bilingual education, unless the local state law requires the bilingual approach for both elementary and secondary grades. Since English is an essential component of instruction in both the bilingual and the second-language approach, it is appropriate to ask who will be responsible for teaching it, and what steps can be taken to insure that the task is assigned to an adequately prepared professional.

Usually the bilingual teacher will be expected to teach both in English and in the students' native language. It is hoped, but cannot be taken for granted, that in teaching English the bilingual teacher will follow an appropriate second-language approach instead of relying exclusively on materials and methods suitable for native speakers of the language. However, not all bilingual teachers have had training in second-language pedagogy; not all universities include ESL methodology in their requirements for a degree in bilingual education.

In some schools bilingual classes are taught by a team consisting of a bilingual teacher, responsible for instruction in the students' native language, and an English teacher responsible for instruction in English. This approach provides a viable solution to the need for bilingual education in schools where there is a scarcity of certified bilingual personnel, as it frees the bilingual teacher to provide instruction in the students' native language to more than one class. It is again hoped, but not taken for granted, that the team teacher responsible for instruction in English will not be just a traditional Language Arts or English teacher but a trained teacher of ESL.

Obviously the need for special training in teaching English to non-native speakers applies to persons teaching in secondary schools that comply with federal legislation by means of an ESL program. Some skills in implementing ESL methodology are needed by any teachers, bilingual or monolingual, whose classroom includes even one child unable to function in the language used as the medium of instruction, for example, a language arts teacher in a regular classroom

including a Korean and a Navajo of limited English ability, or a bilingual teacher in a Spanish/English program whose class includes one Chinese student.

Although teachers of both ESL and EFL may be trained in the same program and attend the same linguistic courses, the prospective clientele of each of the two groups is different and can be better served through a differentiation of approaches. As opposed to the learner of English abroad, for whom the teacher and textbook may be the only contacts with English language and culture, the child of limited English proficiency attending a U.S. school is exposed to a variety of sources of reinforcement of his English skills through the mass media, school and social activities, and his English-speaking peers; the effective ESL teacher will know how to take advantage of this valuable input.

Having identified several categories of teachers as responsible for teaching English to non-English speakers, it is appropriate to discuss how they can best be prepared to meet this responsibility. In other words, what concepts, skills and attitudes do they need in addition to those acquired during their professional preparation either as elementary Language Arts teachers or as high school English teachers? Is it possible for a regular classroom teacher to become an effective teacher of the ESL students in his or her class without the expenditure of time, money and effort required to become a specialist? These are complex issues, especially if we consider not only the differences among the teachers to be trained (in terms of background, experience, attitudes, etc.) but the even greater differences among the ESL learners who will ultimately be affected (in terms of age, ethnic origin, expectations, etc.). This brief paper can only touch upon such issues with a few comments, focusing on three points:

The fine distinction between teaching English to native and non-native speakers.

The problems of accountability.

Some insights from recent research on how languages are acquired and learned.

Some English or Language Arts teachers, untrained in ESL, who have suddenly found themselves in charge of students with little or no English proficiency have been known to proceed with the regular curriculum, using textbooks designed for

native speakers of English and probably faulting the students for their inability to keep up. With the current emphasis on individualized instruction such cases are less frequent now than in earlier days, but even today some teachers may attempt to meet the students at their own levels by using materials that are too juvenile and reducing the conceptual—not the linguistic—load. Others may recognize the existence of a linguistic barrier but proceed on the assumption that anyone who is a native speaker of a language can teach it to others in a "natural" way, as parents teach their children. Since the students are not infants, this natural approach is only partially effective part of the time; it is not efficient enough in leading the students to academic success. An understanding of the nature of language and how it is learned and of possible ESL approaches would instead help the teacher in assessing the approximate level of English proficiency (if any) of each ESL learner and in selecting appropriate activities for further developing his or her command of it.

The ESL teacher should emphasize comprehension before expecting production, should approach reading as a language-based activity, should encourage creativity rather than rote learning, should not insist on correctness at the expense of fluency. The teacher should also avoid downgrading the child's own language and culture, presenting English and the mainstream way of life as alternatives available and appropriate in given situations. Most of these recommendations apply to a student-centered approach in a modern classroom, not just to the teaching of English to non-native speakers. Are the recommendations then sufficient to insure that any teacher who follows them can teach ESL? Only to a certain extent; the specific implementation has to do with the language barrier which (along with possible psychological and cultural ones) separates the student from academic success. Effective implementation of an ESL approach requires an understanding of the nature of the barrier and familiarity with proven ways of breaking through. Good intentions are not enough. For example, the teacher should be able to detect discrepancies between the material presented in a textbook and the needs of the ESL learner; an exercise on the proper use of "a" and "an" is premature for a child who does not use articles with any degree of correctness, leaving them out altogether or using the definite instead of the indefinite or vice-versa.

It is clear from the above comments that the proper attitudes of acceptance, respect and patience are not sufficient to insure effective ESL instruction. The public and the school administration demand results; they must be observable and measurable. The emphasis on behaviorally stated objectives has shifted the focus of instruction from the teacher to the learner; after a given lesson will the latter be able to do something that he couldn't do before? Focusing on the learner is not only appropriate but necessary; what the teacher does should produce change and growth in individual students. However, it is difficult to identify the nature and extent of this growth, let alone find isolated small tangible and yet valid bits of evidence to prove it; a "laundry list" of discrete performance items is inadequate to deal with the complexity of language learning. Moreover, the requirement that a properly stated behavioral objective include a precisely defined stimulus (ex: when asked to choose the correct answer from three written alternatives . . . , etc.) gets in the way of a less formal, more global assessment of language used in a creative, spontaneous, meaningful way. At present it is still impossible to determine exactly what students must know, learn and do in order to learn a language; therefore we can only offer tentative suggestions about the competencies and skills that teachers need in order to facilitate the learning. Competency Based Teacher Education does not provide us with the long-awaited treasure map to effective training of language teachers; nor does teacher accountability necessarily result in teacher effectiveness, although most teachers learn to cope with it.

ESL teachers in U.S. elementary and secondary schools acquire their training from a variety of formal and informal pre-service and in-service sources such as workshops, conferences, publications, and university courses and programs. Some training sessions yield to the demand for the practical, "hands-on" approach, leaving the teachers with an eclectic collection of activities but without a framework for using them constructively. On the other hand, the emphasis on theoretical concerns may ignore the issue of classroom applicability. Because of individual differences some teachers will be more receptive to one kind of approach or to the other, or perhaps to a combination of both; feedback from them can provide valuable information for designing more effective training sessions. In general, university degree-oriented programs and courses tend to have a strong linguistic component; their graduates are specialists representing only a fraction of the teachers who work with non-native speakers of English. For the many teachers who simply want some guidelines on how to better reach the ESL learners in their classes an emphasis on linguistics may be a deterrent. They may have other priorities, or they may be disenchanted with the conflicting claims and confusing terminology of various modern grammars and resentful of the faddish changes in textbooks and curricula that capitalize on the word "linguistic."

In view of the limited amount of time available for training ESL teachers it is reasonable to re-examine the question of how much background linguistic information the teacher really needs, and of what kind. Linguistics is a growing discipline in which today's discovery is tomorrow's reject; teachers cannot be expected to keep up with the latest theories and figure out their relevance and applicability. On the other hand most linguists, even applied linguists, know little about what goes on in a classroom, and are seldom willing or able to relate their findings to useful classroom activities.

Perhaps a better balance between theory and practice in the training of ESL teachers may be achieved by returning the focus to the learner (instead of the language or the teacher) but not in a behavioristic sense. A body of recent research (Krashen, Schumann, and others) has provided us with interesting insights on how second languages are learned or acquired. The concept of "intake," a term first used by Corder (1967) is the key to this model. In order to learn a language a learner must be exposed to it and able to make sense of it, at least partially. The conversations or language activities in which the learner participates at a given time constitute the language "input" available to him; the "intake" represents the portion of available "input" which the learner understands and acquires. There is seldom a perfect match between "intake" and "input"; the most useful input is slightly challenging to the learner but not too difficult. The teacher's responsibility consists of preparing an environment that encourages communication and meaningful language activities. The experience should be pleasant, the focus on meaning rather than grammar.

Teachers usually like to do this sort of thing and do it well; it is not too different from oral language activities that facilitate reading comprehension and creative writing in the regular classroom. The training of teachers or teachers-to-be who are already effective in promoting first language development to become facilitators of second-language acquisition would further refine skills already developed, and add others such as the ability to recognize and handle affective factors impeding the acquisition and especially the ability to select interesting language input at the appropriate level of difficult, which is determined by many factors besides linguistic ones. Student-to-student and small-group interaction activities involving English-speaking peers can result in excellent "intake" for the ESL learner in spite of the fact that the peers who provide the "input" have no formal training in estimating levels of difficulty; they can usually develop some "ad hoc" strategies to insure that they are being understood.

The difference between a Language Arts or English teacher and a teacher of English as a Second Language acting as facilitator of second-language acquisition is one of degree, not of kind; the same person can perform both roles in the same classroom. There is still a place in our schools for the highly trained ESL specialist with linguistic background which is not incompatible with an understanding of how languages can be acquired as well as taught. But it seems that in view of the large numbers of students entering our schools with limited English proficiency the training of teachers as facilitators of English acquisition seems a promising and feasible alternative to either setting unrealistic demands for additional specialization or ignoring the needs of students who have to overcome a language barrier.

TN 6/80

GETTING RESULTS FROM ENGLISH LANGUAGE TEACHING PROGRAMS

by Victor Mason
Kuwait University

A. *Professional Competence and Accountability*

It is heartening to see in the *TESOL Newsletters* of April and June 1981 the extent to which our profession, which has grown so rapidly in recent years, is taking stock to consider areas both of demonstrable past progress and of less than unalloyed success. Richard Orem's excellent essay in the April *TN* suggesting a number of worthy goals for TESOL in the '80s had as one of its main points the need to assure greater effectiveness in the average TESOL classroom and program. The thorough minutes of the proceedings at the March TESOL Convention in Detroit (June *TN*) contained much evidence that a good deal of soul-searching is going on these days over the kinds of fundamental issues of professionalism that Orem raised.

The Orem piece provides a useful framework for the discussion of the profession's three key areas of accountability: 1) to language learners, by their teachers; 2) to teacher-trainees, by their training institutions; and 3) to the public at large, by our profession as a whole. It is plain, however, that these three areas of responsibility are not parallel in importance but have a hierarchical relationship that can be diagramed as follows:

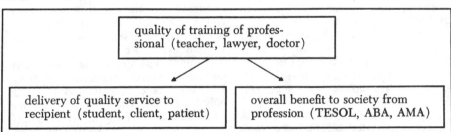

In short, satisfaction of the paying public with results depends ultimately on the quality of the preparation of the professional practitioner (in any field), whose competence and qualifications are attested to by the degree-granting institution.

Further, a professional in any field is being certified only as to basic qualifications at the time of graduation. One of the values that the training institution attempts to inculcate in its graduates is the indispensable need for professional growth, through the wisdom gained both from one's own practical experience in solving professional problems as well as from the experience of others. Thus, the importance of contact with new ideas, in speeches, at meetings and through journals.

Training and experience, however, are not sufficient to assure competence. Professionals with comparable training and seniority may not enjoy equal regard from their peers and publics; some are acknowledged to be demonstrably better or weaker than others. The majority may be considered competent. There will always be some whose performance is only mediocre or even unsatisfactory. Significant differences can generally be attributed to "personal" factors. Our competence diagram should thus be modified as follows:

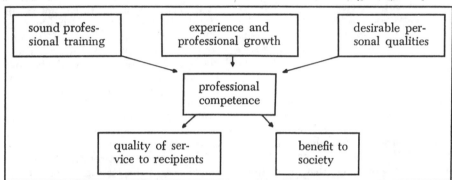

Clearly, the strength of, and public regard for, our profession hinge crucially on the delivery of quality instruction in the TESOL classroom and program. Yet, as Orem (quoting Morley) notes, only about 30 per cent of practicing ESL teachers (in North America?) had had any formal ESL training as late as 1979. Even when they do have it, as former President H. Douglas Brown pointed out (June 1981 *TN*, p. 2), the quality of their preparation may differ greatly from one teacher-training institution to another. Even at many of the best programs, candidates for the M.A. in TEFL or TESL spend all or nearly all of their time absorbing theory and far too little demonstrating that they know how to give that theory practical application (Orem, 2), under the authentic and rigorous pedagogical conditions of the typical English language (EL) classroom.

Perhaps the marginal results of a great many EL classes and programs should not be wondered at. Aside from some exceptional immersion programs (see Imhoof and Murphy, 23) with excellent teaching staffs and better-than-average working conditions, students are not generally expected to make a great deal of progress in the typical TESOL class. One reason may be that, unlike the preparation of aspiring practitioners of most other professions, would-be ESOL teachers are often not taught the "right" or the "best" way to produce optimal results in their profession—in their case, effective learning by their students. As Orem says (2), they are encouraged to be "eclectic" in their choice of teaching approaches, materials, methodologies, and techniques. However, while eclecticism has the virtue of promoting intellectual tolerance, it may, if promoted for inappropriate reasons, also serve to undermine confidence in the specialists, when training in "how to do" does not conclude with a requirement for a convincing demonstration of actually "being able to do."

Yet ours is a business- and results-oriented society, and today EL programs are a huge and growing business worth hundreds of millions of dollars to those delivering services and products to would-be students of EL programs: publishers, course and program organizers, travel agents, universities, teachers, equipment manufacturers and sellers, etc. The growth in demand worldwide for EL courses, especially for educated adults—students, businessmen, diplomats, technicians—has often not been matched by results commensurate with the expectations of the critical paying public. Impatience with the lack of "cost effectiveness" of many ESL programs has undoubtedly provided an important boost to the rapid growth of the ESP movement, which has done much to promote a sense of professional accountability in EL programs, by specifying 1) the relationship between student needs and course or program goals and 2) the responsibility of a program for producing results (i.e., student achievement) in the lessons contracted for.

Specifying student needs, better defining program objectives, and improving course materials, equipment and teaching methodologies have been salutary steps in the right direction for the TESOL profession. The establishment of such requisite conditions for better EL program results, however, does not guarantee student motivation and learning of English; only the effective teacher working under optimum conditions can ultimately do that.

B. Characteristics of the Effective Teacher

Orem notes (2) that the ESL teacher most probably is the single most important variable in the classroom affecting student achievement. Moreover, it is well-known in all fields of learning that without sufficient student interest and motivation, little learning can be expected to take place. The obvious question is: What do effective ESL teachers do to produce results? How do they motivate their students to study hard? To quote from Orem, do they actually "know why they do what they do" and have they "bothered to develop a philosophy of language teaching"?

The answer is certainly yes on both counts. Observation of working ESL teachers makes clear that it is quite possible to state objectively the characteristics of effective ESL instructor (Politzer, Wallace). Effectiveness seems generally to be augmented by possession of an M.A. degree in TEFL or TESL, other things being equal, but may also be independent of it. Just as important are such intangibles (personal factors) as a willingness to work quite hard, a love of teaching, common sense, a good attitude toward the job, good rapport with students, and imagination in trying to solve problems.

Effective ESL teachers are disciplined professionals who follow a strict work routine. They spend a great deal of their time out of class correcting homework, as well as writing and correcting quizzes and tests. They tend, as a result, to be quite strict about good work and about punctuality in attendance and in submission of work due; are meticulous about the materials they produce themselves, for both teaching and testing purposes; and continually feel that they are growing professionally over the years.

Such work habits are an indispensable part of the approach of effective ESL teachers to their jobs. These traits, however, are not sufficient to assure student motivation and satisfactory results. Also important is the strictly personal nature of the teacher-class relationship. Most ESL students want very much to like and respect their teachers, and their regard often hinges importantly on a number of crucial personal factors

seldom discussed in the professional literature. Not least among these, for students from a great many Third World and/or non-Western nations, is neat dress, good grooming and professional bearing—i.e., "looking and acting like a teacher."

Besides needing to work hard and to gain their students' personal respect, successful ESL instructors have probably developed a gradual mastery of three of the most vital "arts" of the classroom for motivating students to study hard enough to produce reasonably satisfactory results. These three teaching skills are too seldom recognized or discussed in the literature, yet lack of proficiency in any one of them may be sufficient to prevent a teacher from producing more than mediocre results in a class. The first of the three, not so obviously, is the ability consistently to be understood in English most of the time by most of the students. Effective teachers begin bolstering their students' often limited confidence in themselves to understand spoken English from the very first day of class, choosing their words carefully but not distorting their speech or making it sound in any way unnatural.

The second requirement is teacher confidence in the instruction of difficult or troublesome language points. The average course syllabus is replete with teaching difficulties in all of the macro-skill areas and components. Serious professionals learn early in their careers that they cannot teach or explain some aspects of the language (e.g., difficult pronunciation and grammar points) as effectively as they can others, and so gear themselves over the years not only to studying the nature of those teaching-learning problems carefully but to developing original strategies to get their teaching points across ever more efficiently.

The third additional "art" of the ESL classroom follows logically from the previous two. If teachers can communicate well with their classes in English and have justifiable confidence in their teaching abilities, it is most probable then that their students will look forward with interest to their English lessons. This happens when students find their English classes challenging, even enjoyable, and never threatening.

C. Administration of EL Programs

ESL teachers may be all that an EL program can expect of them. Yet, if the reverse is not true, serious weaknesses traceable to administrative decisions can undermine student achievement and staff morale as surely as less-than-able instruction. Probably the areas of greatest concern here are 1) the nature and quality of program leadership, 2) admissions and placement pol-

icies, 3) class size and homogeneity, 4) number of contact hours in a course, 5) test development procedures and 6) grading and promotion policies.

As with any other professional field, the most effective leaders of EL programs are, other things being equal, generally those who have "come up through the ranks," acquiring many years of practical experience in making decisions in most major areas of program responsibility. In TESOL, this usually means not only possessing the requisite academic degree(s) but having extensive experience in classroom instruction, materials production, test development and evaluation, and at least some administration. A problem for many ESL instructors, especially in tertiary institutions in Third-World and/or non-Western nations, is that their EL programs are frequently not independent units or departments but rather a part of a department in which EL is subordinate to more traditional and prestigious academic disciplines like literature, linguistics or education. The supervisors or chairpersons of ESL teachers in such programs, therefore, often hold academic degrees in one of these fields and may very well not be conversant with the many theoretical and practical issues relevant to the effective running of an EL program.

Further, qualified English-speaking instructors often have too heavy a work load. They frequently are expected to have a full teaching schedule, as well as to perform burdensome administrative tasks related to TESOL as the resident "experts" in the subject area. The courses they teach, in many TEFL programs, may be described for bureaucratic reasons as "lectures" rather than as skills-development classes and often have no clearly-stated linguistic objectives. ESL teachers commonly find then not only that their courses are much too large and too heterogeneous in ability levels represented to be taught effectively but that there are far too few contact hours each week to do the students much good. Course teaching materials may have been haphazardly selected and be inappropriate for the students. The great majority of students will probably be found to pass through their sequence of English courses with acceptable grades but to graduate unable to communicate properly in the four macro-skill areas of the language.

On the other hand, TESOL professionals running their programs, whether or not they are native speakers of English, tend to avoid most of these serious program weaknesses. They try to hire teachers with suitable degrees, insist on reasonable workloads (in class and out), and press for suitable class size and rational placement decisions, as well as more course contact hours. Texts and other teaching materials tend to be chosen according to professional criteria and excellent program-generated materials are often produced by the teaching staff to meet the special needs of their students. Release time from teaching is given for time-consuming administrative tasks. Major tests are usually prepared with care and are given sufficiently often and made difficult enough to force students to study reasonably hard most of the time.

Despite the obvious superiority of programs which are professionally run over those which are not, administrators at all levels will often find that course and program results (i.e., how much the students are actually learning of the language) are unsatisfactory. One obvious explanation is that there is good reason to doubt the utility and cost effectiveness of any EL program conducted on less than at least a semi-intensive basis, especially in the native land of the students.

A major limitation of too many educational programs is that teachers tend to be too-little supervised. They are rarely observed performing their duties in class on a regular basis, they too often make vital testing and grading decisions on a *laissez faire* basis, and course grades, testifying to student achievement, not only are often based on dissimilar standards for different teachers (even for those teaching the same course at the same time) but tend to be influenced as much by subjective considerations as by "objective" measurement results.

Problems specifically related to the administration of EL programs may also be the consequence of shortcomings in the professional preparation of the administrators and teachers themselves, no matter how conscientiously and ably they may perform most of their duties. Weaknesses of administrators tend to be found in some of the most crucial areas of concern:

a. course evaluation and syllabus design; b. test development: design, writing, review and evaluation; c. program evaluation and integration of courses; d. coordination of policies in placement, promotion and grading matters.

One of the most serious problems of many English for General Academic Purposes courses and programs is that both administrators and teachers may be unable to articulate very clearly the aims of their various courses. Often this is partly a consequence of the fact that such courses were labeled by number (for identification) but either not titled at all or titled too generally as to course aims.

ESL teachers tend to get too little preparation in syllabus and curriculum design and evaluation in their degree programs. An unsurprising consequence is that they often miss the EL "forest" (course and program structure, integration and objectives) for the "trees" (classroom instruction, materials, tests and grades).

In addition, a great many TEFL and TESL degree-holders have little or no training in test design, writing and review. Many who do take courses in testing receive too little opportunity to apply the theory in practice, and so often require extensive on-the-job training before their output starts to become useable, especially in test parts employing an objective format.

Finally, EL program administrators are generally unaware that they bear most of the responsibility for one of the most serious shortcomings of a great many EL programs: excessive heterogeneity of ability levels within courses and classes, which is one of the leading causes of frustration to classroom teachers and students alike.

Thus, for example, it is not unusual in tertiary institutions for new students just out of secondary schools who are placed into a particular course not only to significantly outperform the EL program's "old" students promoted into the same course from a lower (prerequisite) course but to be much more homogeneous as a group as well.

As a result, classes are frequently formed with students whose learning needs may be very different. The first requirement of a rational foreign language program is sufficient similarity of ability levels in a class to make effective instruction possible for all students. In poorly organized classes, a significant number of students will be wasting their time, and may therefore become frustrated—either those who are much better than the majority and will thus quickly feel bored; or those who are much weaker than the majority and may therefore eventually give up; or both. The likelihood of teacher frustration in programs with such classes is then also very high (Malcolm and Mason).

Reduced motivation by a significant number of students in poorly organized classes and programs not uncommonly affects motivation and morale of teachers as well. Unfortunately, dissatisfaction by teachers with their program may well tend to be fixed on their students, as a result—and by students, on their teachers. The irony is that neither teachers nor students in such circumstances realize that their mutual problem —undesirable course enrollment patterns —is almost entirely attributable to decisions (or lack thereof) on policy matters generally falling within the often jealously guarded preserve of their program administration.

D. *Contributions of Teacher-Training Institutions*

The foregoing discussion of various problems of teachers and administrators of EL programs should be suggestive of some of the kinds of contributions that teacher- and administrator-training programs might make in helping to produce more uniformly effective learning of English by ESL students.

An essential requirement of an effective TEFL or TESL program would seem to be a practicum involving responsibility for all aspects of teaching a class of students for the equivalent of no less than an entire course. The practicum should, it seems, conclude with a lengthy report by the degree-candidate covering all important aspects of the course (lesson planning, materials development, testing, proper record-keeping, end-of-course evaluation of self and of each student) and demonstrating to staff advisers that the candidate has been able to combine theory and practice to the advisers' satisfaction.

Similarly, administrator-trainees should be involved in helping their advisors supervise the practica of the teacher-trainees. They, too, should be given extensive responsibility for helping to run the integrated sequence of EL courses being taught by the teacher-trainees, and should likewise have to produce a comprehensive end-of-course paper summarizing problems, procedures and accomplishments.

It is conceivable that the burden on the TEFL and TESL departments might then be increased. A great deal of supervisory work might then be required, especially for staff members specializing in methodology, testing and EL program design and evaluation. Limitations of time and feasibility in most university programs would probably make the sustained observation and evaluation of a group of degree-candidates nearly impossible if not performed throughout a given semester or term on virtually a full-time basis. But any possible added burden on staff from such program requirements to provide an authentic laboratory for training both teachers and administrators would presumably be more compensated for by the concomitant stimulation of useful research on the part of both department staff and trainees alike. Theory and practice could be combined in a great many more theses and dissertations that come to grips with the knottiest language-teaching and -learning problems of the profession. There seems to be no other obvious way of assuring that degree of competence which the public, both at home and abroad, has a right to expect of all those requesting government certification and anticipating its consequent material rewards.

E. *Contributions of the TESOL Organization*

The world of English-language teaching has grown so rapidly in the recent past that it should not be surprising that progress in some areas of professional concern has not kept pace with that in others. The fact that a great many EL programs worldwide hardly produce more than marginal results is no surprise to members of the profession, but should be as much a challenge to do better as it is a source of genuine concern.

EL programs worldwide vary enormously in effectiveness, funding, quality, objectives, policies, etc., according to local circumstances, and it is plainly unrealistic to hope that the assertion of the need for global standards in maintaining quality control of EL programs would be as quickly followed by their implementation on a global scale as would likely be the case in such "life-or-death" fields as medicine, engineering or agriculture. Nevertheless, TESOL, as an organization, could have an even more salutary influence in the spread of reform efforts than it has had in the past, by producing at an early date an official statement of principles setting at least minimum standards of professional performance in the teaching of English to speakers of other languages in the most important problem areas.

Orem says rightly (3) that what is needed is to "start the process within our own organization of identifying those standards, behaviors, characteristics, competencies . . . which a trained ESL instructor at whatever level should possess." It is probable that TESOL should go further, including in its state-

ment of principles references to desirable attributes of EL programs, of the administrators of such programs, and of teacher- and administrator-training institutions as well.

At a minimum, that statement of principles should, in my opinion, include:

a. minimum standards of academic qualifications and professional performance for all ESL classroom instructors, required of organization approval for certification as to on-the-job competence
b. standards for acceptable teaching conditions, without which effective instruction and meaningful learning of English cannot reasonably be expected to take place
c. appropriate criteria for the qualifications needed by EL program administrators
d. a recommendation that a degree in a TESOL-related field constitute a certificate of clearly specified minimal professional skills and knowledge, to which the granting institution testifies by virtue of issuing it.
e. a recommendation for "appropriate" professional recognition and compensation for all qualified degree-holders, under the given local circumstances of their employment as ESL instructors.

It is likely that those guidelines would be equally beneficial in those many institutions worldwide where conscientious and able teachers have to struggle under less-than-satisfactory conditions, often with both heavier workloads and notably less compensation and/or status than their colleagues in other academic fields. The stated official position of TESOL then becomes a useful yardstick of program performance and quality, providing a diplomatic and

completely objective basis upon which practicing ESL professionals can attempt to work within their systems to produce needed administrative change and eventually, it is to be hoped, better language-learning results.

In conclusion, it is worth noting that an important reason why many ESL teachers do not demonstrate that professional growth that Orem rightly calls for (3) is that they are often both greatly overworked and severely underpaid. With better working conditions, many would not only find the time to read more journals but be able to subscribe to more of them and to attend more conferences. Thus, leadership by TESOL in promoting basic professional standards and suggesting feasible performance goals, better working conditions and adequate levels of compensation in the various lands around the world could help lead to even more dramatic growth in the organization in the years to come. □

REFERENCES

Imhoof, Maurice and Mary Murphy. 1980. Language, Communication, and Human Needs: A Look at Second-Language and Rhetoric Programs. *English Teaching Forum:* 18, 3: 22-27.
Malcolm, Donald J. and V. W. Mason. 1980. *Test Development Manual.* Kuwait: Kuwait University Language Center (M-28).
Orem, Richard. 1981. Entering the '80s—Some Professional Perspectives. *TESOL Newsletter:* 15, 2: 1-3.
Politzer, Robert L. 1980. Requesting in Elementary School Classrooms. *TESOL Quarterly:* 14, 2: 165-174.
TESOL Newsletter: 15, 3: pp. 2, 3, 12, 17-18, 21. (June 1981).
Wallace, M. J. 1981. Toward a Skill-Based Analysis of EFL Teaching Skills. *TESOL Quarterly:* 15, 2: 151-157.

TN 2/82

A REVIEW OF ESL COMPREHENSIVE EXAMINATIONS IN M.A. PROGRAMS

by Robert Ochsner
University of Maryland

In the last few years we have become increasingly self-conscious about the TESOL profession. In 1974 the directors of American and British "teacher-preparation programs" were surveyed in order to find what goals and requirements these programs share (Acheson, 1976). At the 1977 and 1978 TESOL National Conventions, special panels were organized to discuss present trends and future developments in the training of English-as-a-Second-Language (ESL) teachers. More recently, Waggoner (1978) has obtained census data regarding the need for ESL courses, and especially the need for better trained ESL teachers. She notes that only three out of ten ESL instructors in this country have taken course work in ESL theory/methods; the other seventy per cent are basically untrained.

If the needs of ESL students are to

be well served, we must as a profession promote adequate training for ESL teachers. But to do this we must first know how ESL teachers are trained and then recognize areas of teacher training which can be improved. Of particular concern then is how teachers are trained in graduate ESL programs. To this end Cooper (1978) has reviewed over 200 ESL theses and dissertations written since 1975. His purpose was to identify "topic areas and methodologies" with the goal to highlight where little or no ESL graduate work is now being done.

In this paper I will review 428 Comprehensive Examination (CE) questions used by fourteen graduate ESL programs that require a CE of their M.A. candidates. Russell Campbell gave a preliminary analysis of these CE's at the 1977 TESOL National Convention. My

final observations can be added to Campbell's remarks and Cooper's review (cited above).

The M.A. programs in our field vary greatly. Some last for one year or less; others extend for two or more years. Given this variety, the evidence from CE's provides only a general indication of teacher training; furthermore, the subject-areas tested may represent only a limited part of the total M.A. program. Certainly practice-teaching must be considered as an important feature of an M.A. program that cannot be easily inferred from CE questions.

But taken as a whole, the CE's do provide a broad sample of what "well-trained" ESL teachers are expected to know. Thus, the CE's tell us a great deal about what our profession considers to be fundamental training. Equally important, the CE's show areas of possible neglect in our M.A. programs, a point emphasized by Cooper in his review of theses and dissertations.

METHOD

During 1976-1977 I contacted twenty-four schools offering an M.A. in ESL and asked them to forward copies of their CE questions. To assure confidentiality, each school was asked to send "sample" CE questions or old copies. Of the twenty-four programs contacted, sixteen replied. I decided to analyze only the 1975 and 1976 CE's; questions from previous years had not changed significantly during the first half of this decade.

Most CE's had ten or more questions, of which the students were required to answer five. The average time allowed for each question was thirty minutes, and the entire CE lasted approximately four hours. These points should be kept in mind when I discuss the CE's content below.

CLASSIFICATION OF THE COMPREHENSIVE EXAMS

My basic principle in analyzing the CE's was to isolate "question clusters," that is, questions eliciting the students' knowledge of the same basic ESL subject areas. From a total of 428 CE questions, I identified thirteen general

subject-areas in ESL (see Chart A). Several schools distinguished first and second language acquisition as different from psycholinguistics, and nearly all schools asked questions that involved both contrastive and error analysis. It is possible to collapse or separate these and other categories on Chart A, but I chose to represent the categories as the schools have listed them.

Of course, not all the questions addressed a single subject-area in ESL. These "Integrative Questions" combine more than two from Chart A. For example, one CE question reads:

We in the teaching profession are actually doing our students a disservice with the policies of bilingualism and bidialectalism. Furthermore, attempts to make teachers aware of the complex issues in socio- and psycholinguistics vis-à-vis ESL serve only to cause confusion and unnecessarily complicate the ESL teacher's job. Our job is to teach English, not to motivate our students to learn. We simply cannot control factors outside the classroom.

Discuss this statement, making sure to show where you stand. (50 minutes)

I have also included under this heading those questions which allow students to combine in their answers different categories:

Describe the history of ESL over the last 40 years. (One hour)

As Chart A shows, 13 of 14 schools ask questions about Language Analysis (pure and applied linguistics) and about Pedagogy (theory, methods, and materials of teaching). To suggest the range of these CE subject areas, I have listed in Charts B and C (below) the sub-topics that comprise Language Analysis and Pedagogy:

CHART B: Language Analysis

CE SUB-TOPICS:	Language theory	Classroom application	Syntax	Phonetics	Phonology	Morphology	Semantics
SCHOOLS: 1	√		√	√	√		√
2	√*	√					
3	√	√	√		√	√*	
4							
5	√*		√*		√*		
6	√*		√*	√	√	√	
7	√	√	√*	√		√	√
8	√	√	√*				
9	√*		√				
10	√	√	√*	√	√*	√	
11	√*		√*				
12	√		√*		√*		
13	√*	√	√				
14		√	√	√*			
TOTAL:	12	12	12	11	10	3	2

Key: Asterisk (°) designates theory that is applied to classroom

For Language Analysis (Chart B) there are three main sub-topics: General language theory (12 or 14 schools ask a CE question under this heading); Syntax (12 of 14 schools); and Phonetics/Phonology (11 of 14 for phonetics and 10 of 14 for phonology). Examples of these sub-topics follow:

General language theory: (30 minutes)

In concise form, describe the *method* and *goal(s)* of linguistic analysis. Include in your answer a comparison of the *American structuralist* (e.g., Bloomfield, Gleason, Hockett, Bolinger) and transformational-generative (e.g., Chomsky, Langacker, Fromkin-Rodman) points of view.

Syntax: (30 minutes)

Show how to argue for an underlying *do* in all the following sentences. There should be at least four independent pieces of data.

a) Chomsky wrote *Syntactic Structures*.
b) Nixon resigned over a year ago.
c) Richard swears a lot.
d) Jimmy and George hate each other.
e) Tom kidnapped the heiress.

Phonetics/phonology: (30 minutes)

The *basic* and *most common* method used

CHART A: Comprehensive Exam Questions (1975-76)

CE QUESTIONS:	Integrative Questions	Language Analysis	Pedagogy	L₁ and L₂ Acquisition	Culture	CA/EA	Testing	Socio-linguistics	Psycho-linguistics	English as 2nd Dialect	Language lab	Bi-lingualism	History of English language
SCHOOLS: 1	√	√	√*	√		√*		√	√				√
2	√*	√*	√*	√		√*							
3		√*	√*		√	√*							
4			√*	√		√*							
5	√	√*	√	√	√							(√)	
6	√*	√*	√*	√*	√*		√*		√				√
7	√	√*				√		√					
8		√*	√								√		
9	√	√*	√						√				
10		√*	√*	√	√			√		√	√	√	
11	√*	√*	√*	√*		√	√*			√		(√)	
12	√	√*	√		√		√						
13		√*	√*	√	√					√			
14		√*	√		√	√		√		√			√
TOTAL:	8	13	13	8	6	6	5	4	3	3	3	2(4)	2

Key: Asterisk (°) designates theory that is applied to classroom

for "classifying and describing vowels" is said to be not completely adequate. What is this "basic method" (i.e., briefly, how does it work), what is the problem with it, and what solution has been proposed?

In addition to the remaining two sub-topics of Chart B (4 or fewer questions per 14 schools), I have included under Language Analysis this item: General classroom application (12 of 14 schools). The reason for including this pedagogical item under Language Analysis is to clearly show the schools which make a connection between the study of language and its application to the classroom. For example:

Student X has been trained only in structural linguistics. Student Y has been trained only in transformational linguistics. Both students have been asked to prepare materials to teach English sentence structure to speakers of other languages.

1) In what ways do you predict their materials will differ from each other?

2) What differences in theory regarding how languages are learned would their materials reveal? (40 minutes)

However, Chart B does not show the relative emphasis each school places on language study versus pedagogical considerations. As a rough generalization, about half the schools emphasize linguistics, while the other half are more concerned with the teacher. A few schools concentrate almost entirely on one or the other extreme. In order to partially display the teacher-oriented schools and those with a linguistic emphasis, I have marked those subjects which co-occur with applications to the classroom. Thus, an asterisk next to a checked item indicates some type of classroom application.

CHART C: Pedagogy

CE SUB-TOPICS: SCHOOLS:	(Read, write, speak, hear)	Classroom application	Teaching theory	Vocabulary	Curriculum	Lesson plans	Sequencing	Teacher training	Visual aids
1	✓	✓	✓						
2	✓	✓			✓			✓	
3		✓			✓	✓			
4		✓						✓	
5	✓		✓	✓		✓			
6	✓	✓			✓				
7									
8			✓						
9	✓								
10	✓	✓	✓				✓		
11	✓	✓	✓	✓			✓		
12	✓			✓					✓
13	✓	✓	✓						
14			✓						
TOTAL:	9	8	7	3	3	2	2	2	1

The Pedagogy sub-topics listed in Chart C obviously overlap. "Sequencing of lessons/courses" and "Curriculum and materials development" is one example. This redundancy cannot be avoided: I have listed these sub-topics, as I have listed all the other categories in this paper, in a manner that is consistent with the schools' CE wording. This redundant listing does, however, provide an important insight.

The most remarkable feature of Chart C is that these pedagogical topics deal more with theory than with classroom application. For example:

Compare and contrast *any* 2 of the following four approaches to language teaching: (a) Grammar-Translation, (b) Direct Method, (c) Audiolingual Method, and (d) Cognitive-Code Learning. (30 minutes)

Only eight of the fourteen schools (or slightly more than one/half) ask students to "apply" theory:

There is currently considerable emphasis on what is known as "communicative competence." First, describe what is meant by "communicative competence." Mention the names of any persons whom you associate with this concept. Next, in a brief essay, describe exercises, class activities, and assignments that could be used to help students achieve communicative competence. (30 minutes)

This theoretical emphasis can be partially explained by noting that many CE questions assume, but do not explicitly cite, a classroom setting. Also, for some M.A. programs, perhaps the more applied aspects of pedagogy are handled in a practice-teaching requirement. It is also possible that only "experienced" teachers are admitted to some programs. But there remains a possibility that teaching theory is not "applied" in several ESL teacher-training M.A. programs.

About half of the schools ask questions about Contrastive Analysis (CA) and Error Analysis (EA), Testing, and Culture (see Chart A above and Chart D below). It is important to note that Culture is really five separate items: American culture, literature, stylistics, proxemics, and philosophy of language. Considering these items separately, we find that four schools have questions about American culture, while only two have literature questions and only single schools ask questions about either stylistics, proxemics, or the philosophy of language. Moreover, the American culture and literature sub-topics often involve classroom applications.

This same point can be made about CA/EA, although the proportion of "applied" questions is somewhat smaller (i.e., 3 of 6 schools ask pedagogically related questions):

Discuss briefly how a second language teacher might use "contrastive analysis" and "error analysis" to advantage in his materials and his teaching. (30 minutes)

Testing is perhaps the most applied of all the subject-areas (4 of 5 schools make this connection):

Discuss the pedagogical implications of testing in EFL classes. (One hour)

CONCLUSION

Chart D below summarizes the number of CE questions per subject area, their relative frequency, and the approximate length of CE questions. This last measure is indicated by the number of typed (8½" X 11") pages that the collected questions add up to.

As Cooper noted in his review of graduate theses and dissertations, there is in ESL teacher training a very strong emphasis on pedagogy (Cooper's "methods, techniques and materials"), but very little emphasis on bilingualism, English as a Second Dialect (ESD), testing, or the use of language laboratories. My review of CE's, especially the figures of Chart D, bears out Cooper's observations.

In addition to Cooper's remarks, I can add that we largely ignore these subject areas: history of the English language, proxemics (kinesics), socio-linguistics (including ESD), and culture. Also, there were no CE questions about English for Specific Purposes, and very few questions about linguistics

CHART D:

Summary of Comprehensive Exams

CE Topic:	# of CE Questions	Frequency	# of Pages
Language Analysis	160	37%	35
Pedagogy	130	30%	25
CA/EA	38	9%	4
Culture:	24	6%	4
American culture	(10)	(2%)	(1)
Proxemics	(8)	(2%)	(2)
Stylistics	(3)	(1%)	(½)
Literature	(2)	(½%)	(½)
Philosophy of language	(1)	(¼%)	(¼)
L₁ and L₂ Acquisition	19	4%	2
Integrative Questions	16	4%	1½
Sociolinguistics	10	2%	3
Testing	10	2%	1½
Psycholinguistics	7	2%	1
Bilingualism	4	1%	½
History of English language	4	1%	½
English-as-a-Second-Dialect	3	1%	¼
Language Labs	3	1%	¼
TOTALS:	428		78½

that covered "new" trends (i.e., generative semantics, pragmatics, daughter-dependency grammar, etc.). Of course, after four years it is easy to overuse hindsight.

However, this review of CE's does make clear two points. Although Cooper found rather few theses and dissertations that dealt with linguistics, my review of CE's shows that linguistics comprises an apparently large part of the ESL teacher-training programs. Furthermore, these schools' programs are, in most cases, rather evenly divided between language analysis and pedagogy.

But some schools obviously emphasize certain subject areas in their CE questions, and schools differ markedly in how they apply linguistic and teaching theory. Having noted these differences we can now ask what kind of preparation best serves ESL teachers. Much worthwhile research can be directed towards answering that question.

BIBLIOGRAPHY

Acheson, Palmer. 1976. English for speakers of other languages: a survey of teacher preparation programs in American and British colleges and universities. Paper presented at the Colloquium on the Preparation and Certification of Language Teachers, 10th Annual TESOL Convention, New York City, March 2, 1976.

Campbell, Russell N. 1977. Presentation made at the round table discussion: ESL degree programs around the country. 11th Annual TESOL Convention, Miami Beach, Florida, April 26-May 1, 1977.

Cooper, Stephen. 1978. The thesis and dissertation in graduate ESL programs. TESOL Quarterly, 12, 2, 131-138.

Waggoner, Dorothy. 1978. Non-English language background persons: three U.S. surveys. TESOL Quarterly, 12, 3, 247-262.

TN 10/80

WHAT DO YOU WANT TO BE?: ROLE MODELS FOR THE ESL TEACHER

by George R. Hepworth
University of Washington

and

by Karl J. Krahnke
Colorado State University

We have been employed as teachers and administrators for the past several years in a variety of programs and we have become increasingly concerned that a major source of dissatisfaction with working conditions in the field is an absence of agreement as to what professional ESL teachers are or what they should be doing. In short, there is a lack of a role model for ESL teachers both generally and in specific employment settings. Our question is not one of qualifications or standards, but of what qualified teachers expect to do and are expected to do as part of their jobs, and what is excluded from such expectations.

Confusion on this point has seriously impaired relations between employers and teachers in a number of cases we have observed. Such confusion has diminished the effectiveness of the teaching programs and undermined morale, sometimes resulting in disillusioned teachers who have just one more reason to consider leaving the field.

In an attempt to alleviate this stand-off somewhat, we have developed three operational role models. Our intent is not to promote or recommend any particular employer-employee relationship, but to allow both participants in the relationship to better articulate their conception of what it is ESL teachers are to do in a given position. We begin by defining two extreme types, both derived from elements found in actual practice, and add a third, ideal, intermediate type. There are probably other dimensions to the modelling. They would be welcome additions to a continuing discussion of this matter.

On the one hand are the teachers generally found in highly managed teaching programs with well-defined curricula and little need for originality or innovation. They are *teachers-as-technicians*. In general, technicians are viewed by management as interchangeable with any other teachers who meet the same minimal set of qualifications. More specifically, the employer may

view technicians as: a) not expected to develop materials or approaches but to implement existing ones, usually following a highly structured syllabus based on some comprehensive instructional theory; b) expected to teach a large number of hours; c) expected to adhere to program management policies such as record keeping, hours on the job, preparation and submission of lesson plans, etc.; d) hireable and fireable at will, i.e., the relationship requires no long-term commitment.

From the point of view of technicians, the role of teacher involves: a) low personal involvement in shaping the instructional process; one merely does what one is required to do, b) practical concerns only, i.e., "teaching a good class". Theoretical matters are beyond the scope of the job; c) teaching towards easily quantifiable objectives—lessons taught, scores increased, performance objectives met. The relationship of these outcomes to more realistic or individual needs is not a matter of concern for teachers themselves, d) concern with students only in the classroom; e) heavy reliance on published materials and materials in general, especially comprehensive packages or those that reflect an identifiable "approach"; f) voluntary compliance with employment and program management policies.

In summary, technicians are materials-oriented teachers who are interested in the practical, not the theoretical, are systematic, organized, and interested in minimizing the individual differences between students and between teachers. Technicians believe that program management is the responsibility of the management and that teachers' concerns are peripheral or subordinate.

At the other extreme are the *teachers-as-artists*. Teachers exhibiting similarities to this type are probably far more numerous than those approximating the technician. Artists view themselves as working in a classroom-studio where

From the point of view of an employer, artists are preferred when: a) control of classroom content and procedure is believed to be the responsibility their creativity and individuality are highly-valued. They believe that: a) teaching is an individual act which is heavily dependent on personality and experience. Many believe that "teachers are born, not made", and while training can be useful, personal classroom experience is the key to development of good teachers; b) no existing approaches or materials are really adequate to the task, so successful teaching *requires* a great deal of personal innovation and creativeness, c) because "approaches" are inadequate, individual "techniques" are more important in the success of teaching, especially techniques that are created by individual teachers; d) determine whether a technique or activity is successful, whether it works or not. If something seems successful according to a teacher's private criteria, that is enough reason to prefer it over something that a book or theorist has recommended; e) each *student* is an individual also, and good teachers determine individual needs and teach to them. Students' needs cannot and should not be predetermined; f) external and objective measures of student success and failure such as standardized tests and evaluations done by persons unfamiliar with the student and his or her instructional experience are not valid. Such measures do not take into account the teachers' contributions, which exceed the curriculum as defined by objectives, and they do not measure the affective value of teachers' contributions; g) the employment situation must include substantial time for teachers to prepare their lessons (cf. *b* and *c*, above). Teaching more than 10 or 15 hours a week reduces necessary creativity and leads to exhaustion and a deterioration of teacher-effectiveness; h) good teachers can only operate in skill areas and at ability levels where their interests and strengths apply.

of individual teachers; b) program management is restricted to the formalities of class size, room assignments, scheduling, etc.; c) coordination among teachers is either not necessary or is sufficient when conducted on an *ad hoc* basis; d) program goals, curriculum matters, policies regarding classroom procedure (attendance, lesson plans, etc.), and presence on the job site are matters for individual teacher discretion or democratic determination. Management's role is either advisory or limited to enforcing the decisions of individuals or the group.

In summary, teachers-as-artists are characterized by a need to be free of program constraints which they perceive to interfere with creativity or with the teachers' freedom to adapt to their perception of students' real needs. Artists claim to be able to achieve a high degree of student involvement in their classes because of their own commitment and skill at maximizing appropriateness. Artists and their students often report a high degree of satisfaction with a class, although this may not correlate with success measured objectively.

It would be possible and useful to come up with additional attributes of both extremes (and we would be interested in your suggestions). What concerns us here, however, is not the specification of the extremes but: a) the extent to which they are or should be matched in practice; b) the degree to which they differ from extreme to extreme; and c) the degree to which employers' and employees' views of teacher-roles differ. The first two concerns should be better addressed by teacher education programs and by professional journals and organizations. Certification and other efforts towards professional standardization are relevant here. The third concern should be addressed to employers, either by individuals in the process of job-hunting, or again, by professional organizations. Too often we have seen employers hire under an unspoken understanding of one or the other role-type and get the opposite, to the dissatisfaction of both parties. There is an obligation on employers to articulate their conditions and on teachers to seek and accept only what they regard as professionally responsible.

But many teachers and employers reject both role-types and claim something else which is often an impossibly inconsistent mixture of both. We believe that there is an intermediate ideal, an ideal which defines teachers who are responsive to both the established goals of a coordinated teaching program and to the theoretical and practical state-of-the-art. Ideal teachers actively and continually try to achieve a balance between individual students' needs and the concerns of the broader program. Not surprisingly, we label our ideal *teachers-as-craftsmen*.

In our definition of craftsmen we join in a rejection of both extreme models. Technicians are convenient for management and several well-known ESL programs seem to be characterized by something approaching this type. It is unjust to characterize the whole profession with this model, however. There is no theory, approach, or set of materials which can adequately determine classroom practice or program design in ESL today. Inadequacy and inappropriateness require a significant amount of teacher interpretation and contribution. Performance objectives can be instrumental in defining and standardizing a curriculum but no set of objectives adequately characterizes communicative competence in any domain. Objective measures are useful in determining some aspects of performance, but many of the major critical variables remain resistant to measurement.

On the other hand, the artist's highly personal view of teaching precludes meaningful efforts toward program continuity and coordination. Cooperation between colleagues is difficult for artists since one teacher's goals and techniques may not be compatible with another's. The degree to which artists restrict themselves to certain skill areas or ability levels limits their ability to articulate their classes with others in other areas or levels because they are likely to be unfamiliar with what is taught elsewhere and quite likely to be distrustful of others' techniques.

Finally, there is a disturbing attitude toward the teaching act which is common to both many artists and technicians, that is, that the *subject matter* being taught is subordinate to the *manner* in which it is taught. Extreme technicians believe that they can teach anything, given the right techniques, materials and approach. Extreme artists also believe that their approaches are so original and distinctive that they will work for almost anything or can be adapted to almost anything. We reject these extremes because neither recognizes the importance of the most salient quality found in craftsmen: to begin with knowledge and principles and to modify them to the degree that individual cases require but program concerns allow.

ESL craftsmen are students (not finished knowers) of the subject matter first, and principled and disciplined communicators of it second. Craftsmen know the language, what is known about it and what is not. Craftsmen also know how languages can and cannot be taught, and how they may be taught under what circumstances. All of this is based on critical review of the body of knowledge that constitutes the profession, not on hearsay or personal speculation. Having prepared themselves, craftsmen approach the classroom with a set of principled assumptions which they attempt to apply in a controlled and consistent manner to the reality of the given class.

Because they are students of the subject they are able to teach over a broad range of skill areas and ability levels, modifying approaches accordingly. Their knowledge, both theoretical and practical, is not bounded by personal experience nor embodied in whatever set of materials is being used. They are able to articulate their classes with others at different levels and in different skill areas because they know what is, or should be, taught elsewhere in a coordinated program. Craftsmen are acutely aware of the need for ongoing self-education. They are aware that the teacher who does not seek out and share knowledge is doomed to continually reinventing the wheel.

The profession of teaching ESL contains a healthy variety of teacher-types, but, in practice, we lack a definition. This may be what leads so many employers to insist on "experience" as the single most important criterion in judging teachers, potential or practicing. We are suggesting that there are more specific criteria than that, that experience can be evaluated in terms of the teacher role it has prepared a candidate for. And the all-too-frequent conflict between individual teacher goals and program or employer goals might be avoided if more attention were paid to the role that the teacher, experienced or not, is expected to play in the overall instructional process. □

TN 10/81

"TURN OVER" IN THE ESL PROFESSION

by Jack Longmate
Seattle Pacific University

Many things about the TESL field happily suggest growth and stability. For one thing, the TESOL organization experienced a 12% growth in membership last year, indicating that more and more people are employed in ESL and consider themselves ESL professionals.

But the brillant growth has to be viewed in terms of the numbers of trained and experienced ESL teachers who give up the field because of the instability they see for themselves by staying in TESL: the low pay and low status, infrequent cost of living adjustments, etc. Is there any reason to rejoice when twenty new people come into the field if ten or fifteen have just given it up?

This apparent "turn over" might seem to be advantageous for some; more trainees imply more university teacher trainer positions. But such "advantages" are far outweighed by the deleterious effects on all, including the teacher trainer, of having a field that is in practice transitory to other fields. Training individuals for short-term careers is as futile as training people for jobs soon to

be taken over by machines. The security of everyone at every level is threatened when a field's fundamental personnel are being forced out. To quote an astute colleague: "Every time another colleague leaves, the profession takes a step backwards. Training ESL teachers for 5- to 10- year careers is not cost effective and no profession can afford to continually lose proven, competent members." (Bogotch, 1979)

Is the dead-endedness of TESL and the attrition of TESL people inevitable? Some might say yes. There is not much hold on the market teaching English in an English speaking country. And, after all, teaching itself is a field notorious for low pay. But the low status is more the result of a lack of uniform standards and bargaining organizations. Of course, the field is represented by TESOL, a thriving organization. But only as of the San Francisco Convention, with the Resolution dealing with health and life insurance for uninsured members and the excellent 8-point Resolution on employment issues, has TESOL begun to address these issues that are indeed as primary as academic

ones.

Making TESL a true career would benefit not simply those employed in TESL. Our country would be served since the field is an important instrument for confronting social issues. What is the future of the Indochinese refugee, the Hispanic groups, and other non-native speaking immigrant or resident populations in the United States? If being on welfare is their calling, then learning English takes on the importance of a mere pastime or hobby. It is entirely appropriate, then, for ESL instructors to be acknowledged as hobbiests. If, however, we are sincere in assisting these groups to lead productive lives in our country, and to achieve self-sufficiency and adaptation, then the ESL teacher must be allowed to relate to the field as much more than just a hobby. He must be allowed to have security in his profession.

REFERENCES

Bogotch, Ira. "Before You Quit . . ." Reprinted in the TESOL Newsletter, December 1979.

TN 6/80

AN ESL INSTRUCTIONAL SUPPLEMENT: THE VOLUNTEER

by Marilyn Appelson
Oakton Community College, Illinois

According to national statistics, there are 70 million people willing to give free time and talent for the satisfaction of helping others. Recently, the prospect of using a portion of this vast group in English as a Second Language Programs has produced some anxiety. Based primarily on misinformation, a patchwork of prejudices and predispositions have emerged. It would be unfortunate indeed for dedicated ESL professionals to prematurely and arbitrarily foreclose volunteers from participation in the field of TESOL. This descriptive review is intended to help resolve some of the anxiety over volunteers in TESOL.

The impact of an increased population of non-native speakers of English, coupled with limitations of instructional time and budget, result in ESL classes that cannot always answer all students' needs. The policy of open entry enrollment brings new students into each class session and an unanticipated increase in student/teacher ratio for many classes. Non-compulsory attendance and cost free instruction result in some irregular class attenders.

Incoming students cannot always be placed appropriately. Speaking abilities, literacy levels and even grade levels do not generally coincide. Within an ESL classroom, teachers contend with students

with varying speaking and reading levels; students who can speak, but can't read or write; students who can read and write English, but are reluctant speakers and perhaps students who have learning disabilities or physical impairments. The list can go on and on. The demand to expand the opportunities for language acquisition and the necessity to provide an increased variety of communication skills to newly arrived foreign students, while still maintaining quality instructional situations, are challenges with which every classroom ESL teacher can identify.

Accountability is also a reality of Adult Education ESL programs. A measure of a teacher's success is often the retention rate of the students and the documented progress made in learning. Therefore, in ESL tuition free classes which consist of voluntary attenders, teachers must seek out knowledge, methods, techniques and resources from many fields to insure quality performance.

Instruction which will provide students with "communicative competence" is the goal toward which every professional ESL teacher strives. ESL literature and academicians advocate that an instructional approach to adult ESL teaching be governed primarily by students' goals. Based on the identified needs and goals

of the students, the professional ESL instructor makes judgements and choices concerning appropriate strategies, methods and materials which will assist students in reaching their goals. Materials and selected human resources are all "teachers" if they help the students learn. Several forms of "teachers", both human and non-human, both professional and non-professional should be employed, if the ESL teacher is to truly facilitate the learning of language skills. A volunteer can be categorized as still another learning aid in the instructional environment. Since the professional teacher makes the choices and judgements in the classroom, it follows that, as with techniques and materials, the decision to use volunteers be governed by the appropriateness for both the students' needs and the teacher's instructional techniques.

Community volunteers are scattered throughout the United States. Men and women with expertise in many fields are willing and eager to assist with their time and energy to help students. As professional ESL teachers search for appropriate teaching devices, attention should be given to this skilled group of dedicated individuals. They have helped with many of society's problems, why not with TESOL? The question, however, is how can the efforts and talents of volunteers be constructively utilized to help students learn. To be a functional component of an instructional ESL program it is imperative that volunteers be *adequately screened, oriented, effectively trained, assigned specific tasks and properly supervised.* The concept that volunteers can be selected indiscriminately and summarily assigned the task of tutoring non-native speakers is counter productive to all concerned.

The training of a volunteer begins with the initial contact made by the interested volunteer candidate. Similar to the process through which paid employees are selected, volunteers respond to advertisements, articles in newspapers, flyers or to word-of-mouth publicity. A new volunteer fills out an application and is scheduled for a one-to-one interview and orientation with a program staff member. The mission of the program, the types of volunteer opportunities, the availability, the commitment and the special skills or talents of the volunteer candidate are discussed. The interview has important training aspects. In this learning environment, both parties are seeking information. The prospective volunteer is given an opportunity to understand the specific program and to decide if the volunteer services sought are of interest. Determining the ability, suitability and talents of the new volunteer are the concerns of the program interviewer. Since the initial interview serves as a learning process for the new volunteer, the interviewer must be an integral part of the program, knowledgeable in the unique components of the particular program, the population it serves, its organization,

its rules and policies, its requirements and, above all, the expectations which the volunteer may anticipate from the program. The interview is an orientation process, a time to evaluate the volunteer's potential and an opportunity for the volunteer to make a commitment to the program.

In adult ESL programs, the professional ESL teacher is more often than not a part time employee and hence unavailable to provide in-depth, in-service training for the volunteer. Therefore, structured workshop sessions conducted by program specialists are required for all volunteers prior to their specific assignments. Individuals, concurrently involved and familiar with the program, the materials, and the student and teacher needs, train and prepare the volunteers for possible tasks identified by the ESL teachers. After the volunteers are oriented, trained and assigned, staff members provide supervision, support and evaluation. The entire training process is continually evaluated to insure responsiveness to students, teachers and program.

Students in ESL classes can generally benefit from additional help and practice. Volunteers recruited, selected, effectively trained and supported, provide an additional resource to help meet the needs and concerns of ESL students; assist with beginning students needing individualized attention; provide additional conversational opportunities for reluctant speakers; provide literacy instruction to limited English speakers, illiterate or semi-illiterate in their native language, or literate in a

language with a non-Roman alphabet; give individualized attention to students whose goals tend toward individual instructional approaches; supplement and help expand the students' use of English; provide "catch up" tutoring for late registrants and "make-up" tutoring for irregular attenders; supply an additional personal touch and concern for the students' needs which will encourage adult students to keep regular attendance; augment language production through a casual and informal format not always available in the classroom setting; provide home instruction to non-native physically impaired students unable to attend regularly scheduled ESL classes; provide the ESL teacher with another native speaker as a role model and someone who can monitor small group activities.

ESL volunteers and professional ESL teachers can mutually benefit each other and jointly provide a unique educational atmosphere for learning. The professional teacher is still the "best teacher" to select appropriate materials and an instructional plan which will help students achieve communicative competency. The volunteer, however, can contribute to the humanistic trend in teaching which stresses the whole student. In addition, the volunteer will enrich good instruction and assist the classroom teacher in responding to open entry registration, diverse levels and irregular student attendance. Volunteers are a talented force which can expand the innovative and creative aspects of teaching English to speakers of other languages.

TN 8/80

"I RESOLVE . . ."

By Richard Showstack
Chofu, Japan

Often in job announcements for T.E.F.L. positions the words "overseas teaching experience preferred" appear. When seeing such advertisements, I can never figure out why teaching *overseas* would make a person a better teacher than teaching foreign students in the U.S. (especially since, in many cases, it is much easier to get a job teaching English overseas than to get an equivalent job in the States).

One kind of experience that I think *would* make a person a better teacher of English to foreign students, however, is the experience of *studying* a foreign language overseas.

This experience has been a tremendous one in opening my eyes to the way language learning looks from the students' point of view.

To be more specific, below are listed some thoughts I plan to post in a prominent place when I return to the States so that I can read them each day before entering the classroom to face my students.

I RESOLVE:

1) Not to get angry when my students occasionally come late to class; or if they occasionally prefer to speak to each other in their native language instead of speaking to me in English; or if a student asks me a question the answer to which I have just finished giving; or if they occasionally decide to take a day off to explore the city instead of coming to class.

2) To be more careful to make sure they understand exactly what they are supposed to do when I give them an assignment.

3) Not to accept the fact that they've understood something (even if they say they have understood it) unless they can use it correctly.

4) To trust them more to work on their own without my interference.

5) To be more tolerant of different students' learning styles.

6) To listen more carefully to students' complaints and criticisms and suggestions and problems.

7) To be more sensitive to what level the students are on and what they need to learn.

8) To be more understanding of the problems of memorizing new vocabulary; of the problems of using newly-learned structures; and the problems of trying to practice the language outside of class.

9) To realize that there are times when it is very difficult to think or speak on cue in a foreign language; and also to realize that when living in a foreign country there are often many other important things on the students' minds besides studying the language.

10) Lastly, I resolve to try even harder as a teacher; to care even more for my students and to try to see what happens in the language class from their point of view so that I can provide them with the kinds of language-learning experiences they need.

TN 6/79

Section 6. Other Areas of Professional Interest

This could be considered the catch-all section of the volume given the diversity of the articles selected. Unlike section 5, which discusses ideas on teacher training and preparation, this section looks at teacher problems and practices, ranging from identity crises to assigning homework.

The first three articles, Elinor Gregor's "Promoting Good Relations with Classroom Teachers" (2/81), John Haskell's "Out of the Closet and Into the Classroom" (4/78) and Emilio Cortez' "The Elementary School Curriculum: Let's Try for Relevance" (8/79), deal with the need of ESL teachers to become a part of the academic community. The development of special curricula is discussed by Joyce Gilmour Zuck in "The LES Child in the Elementary Science Class" (12/79) and by Dennis Terdy in "Transitioning from ESL at the Secondary Level" (8/80).

Marc E. Helgesen (8/82) presents us with the kinds of activities that can be used in "Coping with Multi-Level ESL Classes" and Caroline Dobbs discusses the use of behavioral objective in "Planning Lessons Around Competencies" (4/79). In his article on homework, Richard Jenks (8/79) addresses a problem confronting many ESL teachers—whether and how to assign homework. He offers some reasonable and practical suggestions on how to implement practical out-of-class exercises. Another current area of teacher interest is classroom-centered research. Kathleen M. Bailey (8/83) discusses the problems she encountered in attempting such research and offers a practical accounting of how "Murphy's Laws" seem to apply even in well-planned research. You might also want to look at Dick Allwright's article, "What Researchers Read and Recommend" (8/83). This section also includes one of the most often requested articles for reprint which has appeared in the *TN*, Larry Anger's checklist entitled "Some Priorities for a Good ESL Class" (5/75). A major decision confronting all ESL teachers is discussed by John Daugherty in "But How Can You Teach Them English If You Don't Speak Their Language?" (6/78). Daugherty provides an interesting set of pros and cons on the issue of using translation in the ESL class. David Liston discusses the "Adult Language Variables That Affect Efficient Instruction" (9/78) and Christine Grosse's article on "Teacher Burnout" (2/82) was one of the articles which most prompted readers to write to the *TN*. A special language learning situation is discussed in "Second Language Acquisition of English by the Deaf" by Gerald P. Berent (4/83).

Another set of topics which has been of continuing interest in our profession is employment practices: full-time versus part-time; tenure versus non-tenure; pay scales; benefits; para-professionals; tutors; and volunteers. The article by Carol Kreidler from her *Standard Bearer* column defines the terms, "Standards, Accreditation, Certification" (8/83) for the ESL professional. Linda Tobash discusses the importance of "Collective Bargaining for ESL Teachers" (6/83), and provides information on where and how to begin organizing professionally.

Phyllis Ryan and Brigitte Chavez' review (10/83) of *The Third Language* by Alan Duff discusses the problems of translating, a process which results in a third language according to Duff. This is an interesting lesson for those teachers who insist upon using the student's native language as the medium of instruction in the second language classroom.

There were a number of articles which might have been included in this section; the selection of articles for each section was difficult. For example, the discussion of content area instruction in ESL classes presented in the first set of articles in this section was first addressed in an article by Emilio Cortez "Content Area Instruction in Elementary School" (2/78). David Liston presented, at great length, problems of program development in adult education in his article "Adult ESL Programs: Student in Focus" (8/82) and Norman Coe presented his views on using translation in the EFL classroom in "The Use of the Mother Tongue in ESL'" (8/79).

The Tobash article on collective bargaining reflects the growing recognition in our profession of the need to become active on such issues as certification, employment and professional standards. The *Standard Bearer* column edited by Carol Kreidler addresses just these issues. You might want to look further at some of these columns. The first article on employment issues, pre-dating the column, was a report on "Employment Conditions" (10/79) by Linda Moussouris and Daphne Mackey. In many ways it set the stage for TESOL to move forward on the issues of employment and standards. Notable articles include "Employment Issues Forum" by Carol Kreidler and Ira Bogotch (10/81); "Employment Issues in ESOL: Answers and Questions" by George Bozzini (2/82); "Collective Bargaining in Higher Education" discussed in the *Standard Bearer* (10/82 and 12/82); "ESL Employment Survey" (2/83) by Carol Kreidler and Philip Edmondson; and "Collective Bargaining: An Update" by Kreidler and Tobash (6/83).

Three interesting articles, dealing with program problems teachers often face, are discussed in Joyce Winchel Namde's article, "How to Gain Support For Your Program" (4/83), Emilio Cortez' "Suggestions for ESL Supervisors" (2/78), and Martha Pennington's "ESL

Administrators and Teachers—Getting Together on Curriculum" (6/83). Another excellent article is Robert Mullins' "Choosing Your Job Overseas" (9-11/74); the information is dated but the strategies are still sound. You might also look at two very good articles on elementary school teaching situations which complement the Zuck article in this section and the Cortez article of 2/78; "On the Care and Nurturing of the Elementary Bilingual Teachers" by Marsha Santelli, and Fay Pallen's "In Defense of Pullout Programs in Elementary Schools" (12/80). Other excellent articles are Carol Frazer's "The Modular Learning Lab: An Experiment in Individualization" (1-2/77); and the *It Works* column by Linda Zinn and Judy E. Winn-Bell Olsen "Going to a Convention?—Make a Lesson of It" (2/78). An interesting teaching situation is described in "English the Family Way" by Thomas Rafferty (6/76) in which he discusses the practice of teaching ESL in the home.

PROMOTING GOOD RELATIONS WITH CLASSROOM TEACHERS

by Elinor Gregor
Eakin Elementary School, Nashville

The relationship of the ESL teacher and the classroom teacher is an unfortunately neglected area in ESL education. Communication between the two teachers generally awaits the first appearance of the foreign child, report card time and crisis situations. All too often the classroom teacher is unprepared for non-English speaking students. My intention in this brief paper is to offer some practical suggestions for establishing good relations with classroom teachers prior to their contact with foreign children. If we can enlist the classroom teacher as a strong supporter of non-English speakers in the classroom we will construct a solid basis for enhancing the educational experience of both native and non-native English speakers.

One of the more potentially difficult situations faced by ESL instructors is to encounter classroom teachers who have never had non-English speakers in their classes. Realistically, such children can be a considerable burden for teachers untrained in working with them. A classroom teacher who is understandably apprehensive and concerned about this new experience represents a special challenge and opportunity for the ESL instructor.

One device that I have found effective in facilitating a collegial, working relationship is to spend a few minutes with each classroom teacher prior to the opening of school. Since much of the information about new programs is based on hearsay and rumor, the first topic discussed is the nature of the ESL program. Many teachers welcome a brief description of the rationale behind the program and its role in continuing the American tradition of providing a haven for immigrants fleeing repressive regimes and seeking improved educational opportunities. Although it seems obvious to teachers of ESL, it is well to point out that in the United States there can be no equal oportunity without fluency in English. I have found it especially helpful to assure the classroom teacher that the ESL program is designed to provide non-English speaking children with the shortest and smoothest route to English language competence.

After giving a general overview of the program, ESL teachers should define the special role they play in the child's acquisition of English. ESL teachers are, above all, language teachers trained in specific methodology and equipped with special materials created for non-English speakers. Each ESL activity, whether songs, games, art projects or stories, is selected to facilitate the child's language competency. It is helpful to explain briefly the teaching methods employed and to demonstrate how the specific activities selected can improve comprehension, strengthen vocabulary or increase control of grammatical structures.

In addition to discussing the school's program and the role of the ESL teacher in the program, ESL teachers must also encourage the classroom teacher to continue the process of language education within the homeroom. Beneficial proposals are those that are specific and serve to incorporate the foreign child into the regular classroom.

A good starting place for practical suggestions is the classroom seating arrangement. I regularly advise my classroom colleagues to seat the foreign child next to a sociable, outgoing student who can assist both the new student and the teacher. This role should be rotated among all the students in the class so that each child has the opportunity to become involved in the teaching situation. Tempting as it is, I do not believe that children who speak the same language should be seat mates. On occasion a bilingual child can be a helpful interpreter, but this assistance should be kept to a minimum. It happens all too frequently that new English learners become so dependent on another speaker of the same language that they wait for translation rather than put forth the effort to understand the English directly.

The duties assigned to the seat mate include explaining the assignments of the day and assisting in the child's adaptation to the new American classroom through friendship and support. Peer teaching starts the non-English speaker into the school year with a network of special tutors who are his friends and helpers. The American children who serve as seat mates receive first hand experience with foreign children and develop qualities of patience and understanding as they help the child solve problems and deal with unfamiliar situations. Being spared the drudgery of constant repetition and demonstration for one individual student, the classroom teacher more easily accepts the foreign child into the classroom.

Once the initial seating problem is resolved and the general student-teaching-student plan is discussed, the ESL teacher can address what is, in all likelihood, the overwhelming concern of the classroom teacher: how to keep the non-English speaker occupied during the day. I have approached this problem by bringing my language learning materials to my first meeting with the classroom teacher. Familiarity with the text books, language learning games, workbooks and art activities is an essential part of the classroom teacher's understanding and appreciation of the ESL program. In discussing curriculum materials, I emphasize those activities that can be done by the foreign students in the regular classroom. This assistance is appreciated by the classroom teacher and is beneficial for the student since it maintains continuity between the ESL and regular classroom programs.

A simple picture dictionary is a particularly helpful example of the type of material that can be used in the classroom. The peer teachers can utilize the book to drill vocabulary, reviewing spelling, reproduce pictures of the dictionary entries as art work as well as many other applications the students will devise themselves.

In addition to the picture dictionary, classroom teachers should be encouraged to use other ESL materials for their non-English speaking children. Language materials, workbooks, cue cards, bingo picture games, and other devices that are part of the ESL teacher's standard repertoire can be shared with the classroom teacher for extra practice, review and enrichment.

Another way in which ESL teachers can extend the impact of their instructional efforts is to act as liaisons between non-English speakers and American children. Some of the material shared with the classroom teacher, for example, should focus on the ESL child's country of origin. A good first project is a booklet on the native country. Pictures and descriptions of maps, flags, types of houses, principal products, foods and samples of the written language are a few of the items that can be included. At the same time, the entire class (or the seat mate) can put together a parallel booklet on the United States, thereby participating in a social studies unit based on the comparative study of both cultures.

In conclusion, ESL teachers do well to reach out to their classroom colleagues. The time spent with classroom teachers gives the ESL teacher a better understanding of their viewpoint and an opportunity to present the school's ESL program in a positive light. Simple, practical suggestions encourage a positive attitude towards non-native English speakers and prepare the classroom teacher to work with them effectively. Above all, personal contact with the classroom teacher creates an atmosphere of mutual respect that provides the foundation for future growth and development.

TN 2/81

"OUT OF THE CLOSET" AND INTO THE SCHOOL

By John F. Haskell
Northeastern Illinois University

Mary Galvan, in a recent speech before the 6th annual Illinois TESOL Convention, made the comment that it was time for ESL teachers to "come out of the closet". She was referring to the fact that ESL/TESOL must get itself involved in a number of educational ventures that are truly language (therefore, ESL) related such as bilingual education, adult education, vocational education, "Right to Read" programs, and migrant education, and her use of the term 'out of the closet' referred specifically to the prevalent condition of many of our ESL classes—held in hallways, corners, and storage closets.

For everyone in the audience she hit some nerve, triggered some kind of response or reaction; an "I've been saying that for years" or "It's about time", or "Right on, Mary!" Hearing Mary Galvan speak is always a joy, but listening to her is even better. And I was excited to hear her speak of a workshop that she had been part of, with Virginia French Allen, at Temple University. The topic the class dealt with was "ESL in a greater school context." And I believe, that if ESL is to thrive, grow, perhaps even survive, it must prove itself to be the viable and important, necessary part of the educational curriculum that it is (a fact which though apparent to you and me, is still not accepted or acknowledged in any real way by 'other' teachers nor by school systems as large as that of the city of Chicago). I think our public relations efforts, to date, stink. As ESL teachers, we must not only set an example of good teaching but become missionaries. Our efforts must touch, in a personal way, the other teachers and administrators in our school. It is not enough that there are "pull-out" classes in a school—places where one "gets rid" of that student who can't speak English. A closet, even though it contains an effective program, implies lack of importance, support, acceptance.

In the past, when I have suggested to teachers that ESL classes need to move their content away from English literature to other academic (and non-academic) school areas, most teachers reply on the order of "I tried talking to the other teachers but their response was 'get that kid out of my class until he can speak English!'" I concede that the already overburdened math and social studies teachers may not have the time nor the expertise to deal with the limited English speaking student whose problems seem totally unrelated to the subject matter at hand; that the teacher already perceives of the ESL teacher, if there is one, as having been hired to handle the problem, but we cannot survive, we cannot serve our students by retreating into a self-righteous closet, "doing our job". Despite the subjective reaction to "special" teachers and programs that most teachers (administrators and communities) have; negative in terms of jobs and millage and space and equipment and time, and positive only because it "gets that problem kid out of my class", it is time the ESL teacher, the ESL profession, did something positive, 'up front', it is time to come "out of the closet". It will require tact and skill, and confidence, and not a little dedication to the profession. ESL is not a "special" program. It is, for many schools and communities an integral and necessary component of the curriculum. ESL teachers, even those that show up in any one school for half a day once a week, need to become part of the school, of the faculty, of the curriculum making process, to be seen as a member of the school community and not as an outsider. The visiting school nurse, though not determining curriculum, still is eagerly accepted and thought of positively by the more permanent members of the school.

The immediate classroom ESL teacher's job, it seems to me, is twofold—first, to make oneself recognized and recognizable, and indispensable, and second, to take a good look at the content of the ESL class, in terms of the needs of the student in the rest of the school program—rather than solely as an adjunct to the English (literature) class. Tooting the ESL horn, the sweet sounds of Goodman or the more raucous of "Kiss," will depend on the individual teacher's style, and more importantly that of the school (colleagues and community). One of my students, Sr. Mary Melady, used the "shock" technique on her colleagues. She brought to a teacher's meeting an Iranian student, who spoke (lectured) for ten minutes to the faculty—in Farsi. Sr. Mary then handed around a mimeographed "test" in Farsi (Arabic script) for the teachers to "do." But hers was essentially a sympathetic audience of people who needed, perhaps, only to be made aware of the problem, albeit in a very real and personal way. And Sr. Mary was already a part, an accepted member of the school community.

Certainly more subtle and individualized approaches are necessary in those schools where the teacher is not yet a well integrated and recognized member of the school community. In these cases, it seems to me, a direct attack by the ESL teacher, on each faculty member, separately, may be in order. Asking the content area teachers' what problems s/he is having with individual foreign students might be the first order of business. Thy to find out what specific language problems the student might be having or what skills he needs to be able to handle (e.g. special vocabulary, specific classroom skills such as panel work or oral reports, special types of content organization such as chronology, or mathematical theorems, taxonomies, formulae, etc.) Find out what things the teacher knows (and conversely needs to know) about the limited English speaking students (whether language knowledge or culture). Try to find a way of helping the teachers become aware of the special knowledge the student brings to the class, knowledge that might be tapped and used by the teacher. It may mean that the ESL teacher will have to become a "jack of all trades,"—with all that that implies. It means the ESL teacher will have to make a special effort to learn a new language, a number of new languages. Not the languages of the students but the languages of the various content areas that the students need. The ESL teacher will have to become sensitive to the problems of the other teachers. But promise of help, both for the student and the teacher, will, hopefully, make the content area colleague aware of the student in a positive way, and provide that ego involvement that will make further help possible. The administration, too, can be positively influenced if the ESL teacher will follow up on individual students, outside of class, and act as a liaison between student and school and family.

The second major area of attack is in the ESL classroom itself. The ESL teacher must begin to move the student, not only into the English speaking milieu of the English class, but also into a geography class, a history class, a science class, a math class, etc. This means that the teacher must avoid, what Virginia Allen calls "empty lessons", those ESL lessons that focus on grammar and ignore content, in favor of "full" lessons that deal with language, not incidentally, but as part of a larger context, in this case an area of study important to the student. This means obtaining vocabulary, and content, and content specific skills, around which lessons can be built. It means becoming familiar with "special" English vocabularies and a wide variety of texts, materials, and testing devices that students need to deal with in other classes. It means that the ESL teacher may have some language learning to do, to teach language they are unfamiliar with, to deal with school skills not directly related to literature or grammar. Why not a writing exercise dealing with geographical description? Why not a grammar or structure lesson centered around a historical period? Why not a reading selection related to a science topic being encountered in the science class. Mary Hines (TESOL Newsletter, "It Works", Sept. 76) suggests the use of math hypotheses as tools for teaching paragraph organization. There are a million ideas for lessons in every 'other' class in the school and their immediate relevance is the often immediate but always ultimate

need of the student. And wonder of wonders, the content of the lesson can be expanded or simplified—used modularly—to fit the level of any student, just as easily, perhaps more so, than the 'usual' grammar lesson. And those sterile patterns and structures and pronunciation exercises can be dealt with, learned, in a medium that is transferable to another class.

Mary Galvan closed her speech with a thought that also struck me anew and which seems relevant here. She said, "One Vietnamese student in the classroom puts that teacher in an ESL situation." We ESL teachers can capitalize on that fact by serving not only as the school ESL specialist, the person who

is called on to teach the "foreign" student, but also as the missionary, the visionary, the evangelist, the proselytizer who can show the other teachers the joys of being able to help a "foreign" student, of seeing the growth of the limited English speaker, right in their very own classes. I see no hope for certification, or even a "mandate" as they are about to call it in Chicago: no hope for full time positions in teaching ESL, until we, who are, however reluctantly, now admitted into the schools, become welcome faculty members—welcome and accepted as part of the total educational community. We won't get out of the closet until someone knows we are there.   4/78

THE ELEMENTARY-SCHOOL E.S.L. CURRICULUM: LET'S TRY FOR RELEVANCE!

by Emilo G. Cortez
Philadelphia Public Schools

This article supports the position that a need exists for a re-evaluation of the elementary-school E.S.L. curriculum. Practical suggestions and considerations for devising a more relevant curriculum are presented.

Prominent educators are expressing their dissatisfaction with the existing E.S.L. curriculum in the elementary-school setting and recognizing the need for the inclusion of content-area concerns. Virginia F. Allen et al. elaborate further:

Carefully selected content from several of the subject-matter fields can be used by the E.S.L. teacher as content for language instruction. In the E.S.L. class, pupils can learn basic elements of the social studies . . . science . . . and mathematical processes. . . .[1]

John F. Haskell reflects similar sentiments.

The E.S.L. teacher *must* [emphasis mine] begin to move the student, not only into the English speaking milieu of the English class, but also into a geography class, a history class, a science class, a math class, etc.[2]

If the non-English-speaking child is ultimately to function satisfactorily in the monolingual English classroom and to compete academically with his/her English-speaking peers, a major portion of the E.S.L. curriculum should include the English expressions, vocabulary, grammatical structures, and concepts most frequently encountered in the monolingual English classroom. Unfortunately, many of the commercially-prepared E.S.L. programs neglect such considerations.

For a discerning evaluation of commercially-prepared E.S.L. materials, in addition to linguistic, cultural, and pedagogic factors, teachers, supervisors, and program directors should consider the question:

Do these materials realistically reflect the language and curricular concerns of the elementary-school classroom?

The teaching of reading comprises a major component of the elementary-school curriculum. Consequently, the E.S.L. curriculum should reflect similar reading-related concerns.

To begin devising relevant E.S.L. materials that reinforce or complement the school's reading program, we might ask ourselves the following questions:

1. Which reading program is being used by the pupil's classroom teacher?
2. Is the pupil's classroom teacher stressing specific reading skills? Is it possible to introduce and/or reinforce these skills in my second-language teaching? (Which aspects of the E.S.L. program might the classroom teacher reinforce in his/her teaching?)
3. Which district-wide tests are used for assessing children's reading levels? What testing expressions might be culled from such tests and taught in the E.S.L. class? (Such expressions might include: "Circle the correct answer"; "Underline the correct response"; etc.)

Many schools utilize commercially-prepared reading programs that include colorful posters and flashcards. A familiarity with the words depicted in such visual aids can be a valuable asset to the E.S.L. pupil since such reading-related vocabulary is crucial for reading comprehension. Furthermore, words featured in reading materials that reflect specific pronunciation difficulties for the non-English-speaking child can be compiled and utilized for pronunciation practice. Consequently, pupils are afforded pronunciation practice in a more meaningful way.

An appropriate sequential presentation of reading-related vocabulary is important. Many advantages result when the young second-language learner is

taught English vocabulary from stories which classmates *will be* reading. A look of self-satisfaction and confidence is often observed when an E.S.L. student successfully decodes a familiar, yet difficult, English word. On occasion, the child will receive favorable peer recognition for having unraveled a word that his or her English-speaking classmates are finding difficult.

In addition to using reading-words that pose pronunciation difficulties for students, English numbers can also be used in brief pronunciation drills. For example, for pronunciation practice involving voiceless *th*, the numbers *three*, *thirteen*, and *thirty-three* can be used effectively. Thus, the auditory exposure and oral repetition of the simple equations below can help students overcome one aspect of linguistic interference while reinforcing mathematical concepts.

$3 \times 1 = 3$	$3 + 10 = 13$
$3 \times 10 = 30$	$13 + 0 = 13$
$3 \times 11 = 33$	$3 + 3 + 7 = 13$

Pedagogic dialogues are an integral part of many commercially-prepared E.S.L. programs—and rightfully so. Few language teachers would disagree with Frederick Veidt when he says:

One of the cogent and enduring manifestations of the evolved emphasis on oral activity in foreign language learning in the last decade has been the utilization of the dialogue technique.[3]

Although the dialogue is widely utilized and often featured in E.S.L. texts, few teaching dialogues realistically reflect the language of the English-speaking classroom or its curricular concerns. Nevertheless, short teaching dialogues can be devised to include content-area concerns. Consider the dialogues below that subtly reinforce mathematical concepts.

A. I bought seven cookies for lunch and I ate three.
B. How many do you have left?
A. Just four.
B. Can I have one?
A. Sure.

A. Sandy, you don't look happy.
B. I had fifteen cents, and I lost a nickel at recess.
A. How much money do you have left?
B. Just a dime.
A. Maybe Deanna found your nickel. Let's ask her.

A. I had five pieces of candy, but now there's only three.
B. Maybe you lost them.
A. Now I remember; I ate two at recess.

In the dialogues presented, the students are exposed to simple subtraction in an incidental way as well as exposure to key phrases such as: "How many . . . ?" "How much . . . ?" Furthermore, many young children can identify with the situations depicted—which fosters interest and ultimately facilitates learning.

Science facts are featured in the two dialogues below.

A. Did you know that Mars has two moons?
B. Yes, I did.
A. Who told you?
B. Nobody—I read it.

A. Is Jupiter bigger than earth?
B. Yes, it is.

A. Are you sure?
B. Yes, I am. But let's look it up anyway.

The expenditure of effort required to write relevant dialogues will have been well spent. For there can be little doubt that the pedagogic dialogue is a potent teaching tool whose full potential has yet to be determined.

The following schema has proven helpful in appropriately adapting content-area lessons for inclusion in the E.S.L. curriculum.

1. Identify the key words in the lesson. (Many teacher's editions include the key words in the behavioral objectives.)
2. Summarize the key concepts.
3. Prepare several relevant sentences in keeping with the students' level of English proficiency.
4. Prepare and/or adapt appropriate comprehension questions concerning the gist of the lesson.

The descriptive terms: "strength," "lightness," and "transparency," as explained by Earl Stevick in *Adapting and Writing Language Lessons*, are useful concepts for preparing and/or adapting E.S.L. materials. Stevick comments on "strength":

Concern about strength will lead to questions such as:
Is the content relevant to the present and likely future needs of the trainees?
Does the textbook provide for the tools, both in vocabulary and in structure, that students will need in order to reach whatever goal has been set?

Are the materials authentic both linguistically and culturally?[4]

The quality of "lightness" is a measure of the ease with which a lesson can be learned. In other words, light materials are not excessively difficult, long, or frustrating.

"Transparency" refers to a lesson's clarity; i.e., Does the student readily perceive the teaching point and its relationship to other items previously learned?

In closing, it is suggested that whenever possible, the E.S.L. teacher and the classroom teacher should apprise one another as to the salient specifics of their respective curicula. In this way, both instructional programs may truly complement one another. For without a relevant and effectively implemented elementary-school E.S.L. curriculum, the non-English-speaking child has little chance of attaining academic success in the mainstream culture.

[1] Virginia F. Allen et al., "A Memo: Educating Children with Limited English," *Educating Personnel for Bilingual Settings: Present and Future* (Philadelphia, Pa.: M.E.R.I.T. Center, Temple University, 1979), pp. 81-82.
[2] John F. Haskell, " 'Out of the Closet' and Into the School," *TESOL Newsletter* (April, 1978), p. 3.
[3] Frederick P. Veidt, "The Dialogue: An Aid to Oral Production in Beginning Language Study," *Modern Language Journal* (January-February, 1973), p. 3.
[4] Earl W. Stevick, *Adapting and Writing Language Lessons* (Washington, D.C.: Foreign Service Institute, 1971), p. 46.

TN 8/79

THE LES CHILD IN ELEMENTARY SCHOOL SCIENCE CLASS SUGGESTIONS FOR THE TEACHER

Joyce Gilmour Zuck
E.L.I., Univ. of Michigan

The probability that a classroom teacher will have one or two limited English speaking children in his classes continues to increase. When there are small numbers of children of any one language background, supplementary materials are not provided. Recently a group of elementary school science teachers asked me to make general suggestions for the teacher or volunteer tutor in such a situation. I was given the school district's curriculum packet on LIGHT as an example of the available materials. Based on the Ann Arbor Public School's science program, my suggestions fell into two major points.

I. Minor modification resulted in very appropriate lessons for the limited English student.

II. Many problems were the result of divergent cultural expectations rather than deficiencies in English.

Modification of existing materials

The following suggestions can be easily implemented on the spot by the classroom teacher, a volunteer tutor or even a peer from the class.

1. Put important ideas in writing. The student can look at the written ideas at a later time. Often students who understand the explanation in class are unable to remember the important facts because of their limited second language memory. Also, the written ideas can often be translated by an older child, tutor, or parent to check comprehension. The child should be encouraged to make a bilingual dictionary of the important terms he encounters in class.

2. Provide an outline of the structure of the lesson, reading or film. The learner can organize his expectations if the structure is made explicit to him in advance. The structure can be made by writing a sentence outline of the passage using exact sentences from the text whenever possible. Key vocabulary words appear to be best presented in the order in which they appear rather than as alphabetical lists of nouns, verbs, adjectives and the like.

3. Multi-media materials. Non-native readers have been shown to benefit from the redundancy provided by visual images in the form of pictures, charts, films, etc. Film strips and non-verbal films are usually self-sufficient without any sound-track. Bilingual tutors could be asked to make a cassette in the student's native language to accompany a film strip related to a specific content lesson. The student should be provided with questions to answer when he works with visual material so that he knows when he has understood well enough.

4. Modify existing activity sheets. Many activity sheets provided in curriculum packets can be made available to the limited English speaking student by providing additional clues and information. In the LIGHT packet which I examined, the majority of exercises could be modified by simply adding a list of words to be used for each of the fill-in-the-blanks, word finds, and crossword puzzles. By narrowing down the choices, the teacher puts less of a load on the second language memory and allows the student to practice the same material in the same way as his classmates. Classes

which utilize a modified buddy system could have a peer make the word list; rotated peer teaching usually not only increases learning but also increases interaction and understanding among the students.

5. Start a sharing file. It is useful to keep a file in the school library or in the curriculum office for each major unit that you modify. This file should contain simplified exercises, readings at different proficiency levels, and references to visual materials. Once such a file is started, it is amazing how often you discover materials to add to it.

The major point to be made in the first part of this list of suggestions is that much of the material that is already available is appropriate to use for the occasional ESL student who has been immersed in an English speaking educational system. However, teachers should be aware that many of the problems created in the science classroom are not the result of inadequate language but rather the result of different educational expectations.

Recognition of educational differences.

As I examined the LIGHT packet with its emphasis on activities, games and ditto materials, I realized that the biggest problem for the science teacher is the approach to education which appears to differ significantly from many other approaches throughout the world. Obviously, teachers cannot be aware of the educational practices of all the countries from which they may have students; however, they should be aware that different practices may be a greater cause of confusion to the student than his language ability. This type of problem increases with the number of years of education a child may have had in his own cultural environment but it exists to some degree for all students. Some potential problem areas are listed below.

1. Emphasis on memorization. In many countries of the world, education is heavily reliant on book learning and the student is expected to memorize the material provided in his book. Students who are accustomed to the use of a single book find it very difficult to synthesize material from books, lab manuals, handouts, etc.

2. Education as serious work. Students are often puzzled by the use of films, games, and other activities which do not seem to them to be the proper way to learn in school.

3. Authoritarian education. If the teacher asks a question, there is expected to be a single right answer. Students are often upset when they are asked to hypothesize or speculate; they think that the teacher is withholding information when he asks, "What do you think will happen?"

4. Non-experimental education. The emphasis on the experimental process is often confusing to students who have been taught that the information is more important than how it was discovered. They have come to expect that they cannot perform an experiment as well as the scientist in his laboratory and they do not understand why they are asked to try.

Supplementary material

Some sources of useful information for elementary school science teachers are listed below.

a. *National Geographic World*

b. *Reader's Digest Science Readings*

c. Hauptman, Philip and Jack Upshur *Fun with English.* (New York: Collier McMillan, 1975.) Good examples exercises for word games.

d. Thelen, Judith. *Improving Reading in Science.* (Newark, Delaware: International Reading Association, 1976)

(Reprinted from the *BESC Newsletter*, Vol. VI, No. 5, May-June 1979)

TN 12/79

TRANSITIONING FROM ESL AT THE SECONDARY LEVEL

by Dennis Terdy
*Illinois Resource Center
BESC, Arlington Hts., Ill.*

Thousands of secondary school districts throughout the U.S. are being confronted with significant numbers of Limited English Proficient (LEP) students. The first step in providing English instruction is to establish an ESL class. However, the establishment of a TESL program is clearly not the only necessity. Experienced ESL teachers will readily concur that there is a need for a continuation of the ESL curriculum to include a transitional course. This would serve as the link between ESL and the regular English curriculum. Obviously, the struggles, politics, committees etc. for just the establishment of an ESL program often do not allow for the focus on an additional class. Nevertheless, justification for the need is present.

ESL texts at the secondary level often consist of a series of six levels. Besides tiring of the format, ESL students, especially at the intermediate or advanced levels, often require additional supplementary work in the development of reading and writing skills. A "transition" ESL class which considers the LEP student's additional needs and combines them with the traditional freshman-sophomore or junior English curriculum is a wiser choice. The components of this curriculum often consist of an introduction to composition and a general survey of literature and literary types.

The implementation of such a curriculum may be on a semester by semester basis beginning with either literature or composition. On the other hand, it may be an integration of both areas throughout the school year. Either way, elements of both curricula, ESL and regular English, are being combined.

In the literature component of such a course, work in one of the previously mentioned weak areas of ESL texts, reading, should be included. This reading, reading/literature component should include the following:

1) Reading skills development
2) Vocabulary enrichment
3) Reading techniques/content area
4) Survey of literary types—structured or adapted reading if preferred—i.e. poetry, novel, short story, etc.

A focus on reading skills development in conjunction with the literature survey content may include the following: developing individual reading skills in sequencing getting the main idea, and reading from content. Continuing work on vocabulary development is also recommended. This should include not only vocabulary enrichment but also elements of word study (i.e. word origins and prefixes suffixes) (Paulston, 1976, p. 181-2.)

An additional component of the reading skills development is the teaching of reading techniques for study purposes.

They include the SQRRR approach (Robinson, 1961) and speed reading techniques which deal with many pre-reading skills, i.e. noting purpose of reading, content, format, subtitles etc.

The literature survey component should include elements of the short story, poetry, the novel and myths and fables. Many structured readers and adapted versions of classics, if desired, are available for this area of study. Myths and fables are not only very interesting to LEP students but also can lead to discussion topics of cultural issues.

The writing component must focus on the skills the regular English classroom teacher minimally expects of all students. To teach these skills, the writing component of this transition course should contain the additional following elements:

1) controlled composition—on a paragraph level
2) sentence combining activities

3) elements of a traditional grammar program (to know the right words to describe the right things)
4) paragraph development (topic, sentence, etc.)
5) outlining
6) spelling activities (not generated from the study of rules, but from general errors committed on composition)
7) expository writing
8) a survey of the research paper (not necessarily writing a term paper)

Although quite obvious, eliminating simple errors of format in composition writing, simple spelling errors, elementary errors of writing mechanics, (i.e. paragraph indentation) and even the cosmetic appearance of the paper are essential improvements to meet the minimum expectations of the regular English teacher receiving LEP students. These are often included in controlled composition texts. Sentence combining activities, which are also sometimes included, are ones which are proving to be more related to growth in writing proficiency than any others. (Zamel, 1980.) The further adaptation of the writing curriculum should include the elements offered in the regular English curriculum as elements of grammar study, paragraph development, outlining, and procedures of term paper writing. The decision as to whether or not to include a term paper assignment is optional. A possible approach might be to discuss the process of writing the research paper rather than the actual product.

If the implementation of the mentioned reading and writing programs are not a possibility given fiscal constraints within districts, consider including elements of each within the final level of the presently offered ESL classes.

Often because of parallel regular English and ESL curricula at the secondary level, rarely are elements of either integrated into the other. Therefore, it is clearly an educationally desirable approach to include a "transitional" ESL component.

The suggested content of a transitional class will provide not only a more gradual joining of the two curricula, minimize the trauma of that first non-ESL class for the LEP students, but also provide competitive skills which will better insure successful performance of the limited English proficient student outside the ESL curriculum.

BIBLIOGRAPHY
Paulston, Christina Bratt. *Teaching English as a Second Language Techniques and Procedures,* Cambridge, Mass., 1976.
Robinson, Francis P. *Effective Study,* New York: Harper Row, 1961.
Zamel, Vivian. "Re-evaluating Sentence Combining Practice", *TESOL Quarterly*, Vol. 14, March, 1980, p. 81.

TN 8/80

PLANNING LESSONS AROUND COMPETENCIES

By Caroline Dobbs
Harper College

As a result of the Northcutt Adult Performance Level study (APL), the current thrust in competency-based education (CBE) is its application to Adult Basic Education. The extension of competency-based adult education (CBAE) into the ESL classroom is a natural one and, consequently, it would seem timely to look at the terminology used in CBAE.

Functional competency in adults (originally called *literacy* in the APL study) as defined by the Northcutt summary[1] consists of the ability to use skills and knowledge for the purpose of coping with the requirements of adult living. Underlying this is the assumption that more functionally competent adults are more successful in society. Therefore, functional competency is considered to be culture-bound, i.e., geared to the society in which the individual is living. Consequently, CBAE is a 2-dimensional model consisting of a series of skills applied to a series of general knowledge areas. The skills involved are listening/speaking, reading, writing, computation, problem-solving, and interpersonal relations. The general knowledge areas in the APL model are consumer economics, occupational knowledge, health, community resources, and government and law. (The knowledge areas have been expanded, or at least re-defined, by other groups.)

Since CBAE is performance-based, it aims not just at cognitive development but at producing demonstrated mastery of skills and knowledge in areas important to adults with respect to their ability to cope with the societal demands of every-day life. This seems very familiar to the ESL teacher of adults. TESL has long been concerned with teaching such things under the heading of survival skills. Furthermore, many of the concepts being utilized in the CBAE construct are basic tenets of TESL—the knowledge that listening and speaking are separate skills, the need to focus the learners' attention on what it is that they are going to learn in a given lesson, the understanding that learning is not a passive activity, and the use of role-playing, among others. However, the CBAE module does present a new and consistent method of tying these things together.

In support of this view, let us consider the format of a CBAE lesson module as applied to ESL. Each module is set up to include the *purpose,* the *outcomes, evaluation,* and *instructional activities,* in that order.

The *purpose* of the module is clearly stated at the beginning—e.g., in a module on finding an apartment, the purpose might read *To prepare the learner for apartment-hunting.* A statement of the purpose of the module focuses the learners' attention.

The *outcomes* (goals of the lesson) state, in terms of observable behavior, what the student will be able to *do* when s/he has mastered the module. One outcome might be as follows: *Reading:* The learner will be able to read the classified ads for apartments. In other words, mastery of the module will be demonstrated by performance in class of certain pre-set activities in each of the skill areas listed in the second paragraph of this article. As Roueche et al.[2] state it, "Foreknowledge of objectives directs the student to relative subject matter and gives him a structure for organizing diverse information."

The *evaluation* section lists the ways in which the instructor will be able to determine whether or not the learner has achieved mastery of the module within a stated degree. (An example of degree of mastery is that at one time the Illinois driver's test required the applicant to identify signs on the test with 100% accuracy, but allowed him/her to miss a small number of multiple choice questions. Consequently, the stated degree of mastery for knowledge of the signs was 100%, whereas for the information necessary for the multiple choice test it was somewhat less than 100%.) The evaluation includes role-playing and worksheets. The former, in the apartment-hunting module, could require the learner to role-play a dialog, with the instructor acting the part of a landlady/lord, in which the learner asks pertinent questions about the size of the apartment, the rent, the lease, utilities, etc. The worksheets would be concerned with the reading of want ads, choosing an appropriate apartment for the learner's needs, and computing expenses. The evaluation is totally based on the outcomes. Nothing that is not clearly stated in the outcomes may be included in the evaluation.

A primary consideration for ESL modules in the *instructional activities* should be the linguistic level of the learner. Dialogs and worksheets must be geared to the learners' level, and a note must be made of new vocabulary and structures used in the module so that the instructor may teach these before going further. Material for the worksheets can be taken from local sources—local newspaper classified ads, Yellow Pages from local phone books, local bus schedules, etc. Thus the skill the learner is acquiring can be directly applicable to the learner's functioning in his/her community.

A last factor of CBAE, but one of concern to all teachers, is the fact that the goal is *mastery* of the module being studied. Time is not a factor. A learner has completed the unit when, and only when, s/he has demonstrated this mastery in accordance with the evaluation. In this way, different rates of learning are catered to. The learners' attention is focused on a definable goal and instruction is more easily individualized.

Adult functional competency was defined at the beginning of this article. CBAE has been defined elsewhere as a performance-based process leading to demonstrated mastery of basic life skills necessary for the individual to function proficiently in society. It now seems possible to define competency-based adult education in ESL as a perform- ance-based process leading to demonstrated mastery of identified goals in the basic life skills necessary to function as an adult in an English-speaking society.

[1] Northcutt, et al. Adult Functional Competency: A Summary. University of Texas at Austin, Division of Extension. March 1975.

[2] Roueche, John E., Herrsher, Barton R., and Baker, George A. III. "Time as the Variable, Achievement as the Constant: Competency-based instruction in the community college." "Horizons Issues" Monograph Series. American Association of Community and Junior Colleges. 1976

TN 4/79

COPING WITH THE MULTI-LEVEL CLASSROOM: HOW TO MODIFY MATERIALS AND METHODS FOR INDIVIDUALIZATION

by Marc E. Helgesen
Illinois Department of Corrections

The usefulness of individualizing ESL instruction is well established in the literature and recognized by nearly every teacher who has tried it. Ganserhoff (1979) pointed out that individualization is a valid approach to any group of students with varied linguistic, social and/or educational backgrounds, and differing learning rates and goals, as well as to any program situation with open-entry enrollment policies or irregular student attendance due to illness, job conflicts, etc. Most adult ESL classrooms face some or all of these problems. Further, the current political climate often means less money for programs. This lack of funds regularly translates into larger, multi-level classes. At this point, individualizing is more than a good idea . . . it may be the only way to cope!

By individualizing, I'm not suggesting that each student should work alone a great percentage of the time. Certainly communication training doesn't lend itself to such an approach. Nor am I suggesting a return to the days when each student spent hours listening to taped audio-lingual drills. While A-L activities can be useful at the practice phase of learning, individualization goes far beyond that stage.

The key to effective individualized instruction is the creative use of grouping methods that allow students to work on a variety of tasks in a variety of contexts. The purpose of this article is to discuss these grouping methods and to suggest ways that the materials and activities you are currently using, as well as new ones, may lend themselves to use in an individualized setting.

The grouping strategies I find most effective are "small groups," "duets," and "solos." "Small groups," identified by Sawkins (1978), usually consist of three to six students. The specific ac- tivity determines whether those groups are skill-level homogeneous or heterogeneous. "Duets" and "solos" have each been discussed by Ganserhoff (1979). "Duets" are pairs of students working on a single activity. "Solos" are activities engaged in by a lone student. As a sub-classification of "solo," one can include "solo-automated" activities, which involve a single student working on a task that requires the use of some electronic medium (e.g. tape player, video player, Language-Master, etc.).

One should consider the phase of instruction for which each of these grouping modes is most appropriate. Escobar and McKeon (1979) have identified the four phases of learning any element of language, and therefore the logical blueprint for any ESL lesson, as follows:

Phase I. Establishing Meaning.
Phase II. Practice (including structural manipulation).
Phase III. Purposeful Student Communication (student using language for his/her own needs).
Phase IV. Review, recombination, or reteaching.

In the course of this discussion of the modes of grouping, the particular phases in which each method is most likely to be effective will be noted.

Small Groups

According to Olmstead (cited in Sawkins, 1978), effective small group instruction is predicated on the acceptance of three premises:

1. Groups of "reasonably capable" adults are able to learn independently, given the cooperation of the teacher.
2. Teacher control of all discussion input is unnecessary for the creation of a valid learning experience. 3. Maximum learning is contingent upon groups accepting responsibility for their own progress, thus becoming less dependent on the teacher.

The primary advantage of small group instruction is a dramatic increase in student interaction and communication. This increase is both quantitative due to the increase in the time each student is speaking, and qualitative arising from the necessity of being understood by peers. This shift from a teacher-centered interaction to a student-centered model also leads to students becoming comfortable offering ideas and suggestions without feeling that they are being disrespectful to the teacher.

The optimal size of a small group is determined by the nature of the educational task in which the group will be engaged. For example, Verschelden and Harbers (1976) suggested that when students are grouped to provide skill-level homogeneity, beginning level students should rarely work in groups larger than three.

In addition to skill-level, several other criteria may be used in determining the makeup of a group for a particular task. Among these factors are sex, cultural background, and individual personality conflicts/friendships. Sawkins (1978) noted that a teacher with several students who tend to monopolize discussions may wish to place those students in one group, thereby requiring them to share the available time. This will also allow the less verbal students more opportunity to participate. The nature of the group task may well determine the selection criteria. The characters in a roleplay, for example, may determine the age and sex makeup of the group. Discussion of issues and values are frequently more exciting if group members come from a variety of cultural backgrounds. Long (1977) pointed out that many groups form naturally due to respect, friendships, and dislikes among the members.

Since most teachers have their classes engage in various large group activities, implementing a small group task often requires only the identification of a way to make the teacher less essential in some or all parts of the activity. For example, you may wish to introduce an element of language to the whole class prior to dividing the students into small groups. In breaking up the large group, the students may be assigned to groups according to their skill level and then given a task that requires competency at their present level. A student who has mastered the skill may be assigned to function as the group leader. This allows you to circulate among the groups offering suggestions and evaluating progress. In tasks calling for specific correct results, write out basic instructions and answer keys and give these to the group leaders, who take responsibility for group self-correction.

While the variety of activities available make any grouping strategy possible for any phase of instruction, the interactive nature of small groups makes (II) Practice and (III) Purposeful Student Communication the most relevant phases of learning for this grouping mode.

While students are working in small groups, the teacher should remember that the objective is the process as much as the end product. You won't catch all the errors, but the vast increase in student "talk-time" seems more than a fair trade-off.

Duets

"Duets" are activities in which two students work together on a specific task. As with small groups, a variety of considerations are involved in duet grouping. Byers (cited in Olsen, 1980:9) encouraged frequent regrouping of duets stating that:

The frequent changing of partners is based on the idea that it is better to be able to communicate effectively with many different partners than with only a few partners who are close friends. The frequent changing of partners produces useful results. Some learners catch on . . . very quickly; others are less quick to catch on to directions. With changing partners, the quicker learners soon teach the slower learners how to play the game.

Nabokov and Ramirez (1979) identified four modes of peer-mediated (duet) instruction:

1. Tutorial. In this mode, a higher level student helps a lower level one. This strategy serves to solidify the knowledge of the tutor while the lower level learner

gains the educational benefits of personalized instruction.
2. Instructional. In this mode, the teacher identifies a series of skills that the students need to learn. One student is assigned the task of providing instruction in a skill which s/he has mastered. Students work through this series of peer-instructors (i.e., tutors) until they are qualified to function in that role.
3. Mechanical. A student monitors the responses of another student on predetermined questions. The monitoring student simply identifies the responses as correct or incorrect and does not engage in instruction.
4. Transactional. Two students at equal skill levels engage in a problem-solving activity requiring them to pool their knowledge. This mode facilitates the use of spontaneous, original language.

Implementing the tutorial, instructional, and mechanical modes simply requires that the teacher gives one student the teacher's guide or an answer key for an activity. Transactional duet activities are often most successful when students are given tasks that are open-ended and do not have a specific correct or incorrect response (e.g., the task of identifying the pros and cons of a given social issue). Such activities often encourage fiery discussions involving a great deal of communication.

One of the most exciting and useful types of transactional duet activity is the "dyad." Identified by Olsen (1980), a dyad is "any group of two students working on a specified task in which one student has different information than the other." Two roles exist within any dyad. These roles are referred to as "monitor" and "performer." Throughout the dyadic experience, the members exchange roles. Many classroom activities may be adapted for use in a dyadic setting. Olsen went on to suggest the following procedure for adapting materials to the dyadic mode:

1. Make the exercise twice as long as usual.
2. Provide at least two items (or a

multiple of two) for each skill covered.
3. Divide the exercises into two parts, one for each member of the dyad.
4. Alternate the cues and answers to facilitate the shift between the monitor and performer roles.

Because the tutorial and instructional types of duet activity feature a student who has mastered a specific skill working with a student who has yet to achieve competency on that skill, these structures for interaction lend themselves to use at the (I) Establishing Meaning phase of instruction. The mechanical mode is most likely to be helpful for evaluation, a key in the (IV) Review phase. Finally, transactional instruction, especially through dyads, is an excellent way to provide (II) Practice and (III) Purposeful Student Communication.

Solos

"Solo" activities are those in which a student may engage alone. When an electronic medium such as an audio or video tape or other teaching media is added, the activity is referred to as "solo-automated."

Solo activities are not necessarily in-class activities. Finocchiaro (1974) suggests, for example, that little or no writing practice should take place in class. Solo activities are, by definition, those which may be completed without the constant assistance of the teacher or another student. Such lessons make effective homework assignments, thereby freeing class time for communicative activities which students cannot do alone.

The simplest method of transforming existing material for use in a solo context was suggested by Ganserhoff (1979). She urged teachers to cut lessons from textbooks, to rearrange and supplement them as necessary, and to place them in folders for individual student use.

Some solo activities involve giving the student incomplete data. For example, the student may receive a dialogue with one speaker's part completely or partially deleted (Taylor, 1976), a

Grouping strategies appropriate for various learning phases

	Small Group	Duet			Solo	
		tutorial, instructional	mechanical	transactional	solo	automated
I. Establishing Meaning		X				X
II. Practice	X			X	X	X
III. Purposeful Student Communication	X			X		
IV. Review, Recombination or Reteaching			X		X	X

cloze procedure story, or a cartoon with the characters' conversation eliminated (Rigg, 1976). The student's task is to fill in the missing words or lines, based on the information given, so as to create a complete, meaningful story or dialogue.

Other solo activities give the student a complete set of information such as a paragraph or a story. The student is required to respond based on this data. The response may involve multiple-choice or short-answer comprehension questions or the writing of a particular type of question (Bright, 1978).

Solo activities are not limited to paper and pencil lessons. Fitzgibbons (1980) suggested that teachers make cards with variant spellings of the same sound (e.g., /aɪ/ as in "night," "eye," and "fly."). Students match the sounds and check the answers on the back of each card. The strip story (Gibson, 1975) may be converted into a solo reading/sequencing activity by pasting a picture to the back of a reading passage. The passage is then cut into strips. When the sentences are placed in the correct sequence, the strips are turned over to reveal the complete picture. Multiple choice activities become self-correcting when each item is placed on an index card and a pencil-sized hole is punched next to each possible answer. The student puts a pencil through the hole representing the answer s/he chooses and reverses the card to reveal a circle drawn around the correct choice.

As has been noted, solo-automated activities are not limited to audio-lingual practice, although they certainly are useful for that. To move beyond A-L and thus avoid the boredom so often resulting from an excess of this approach, you can design the activities so they don't allow the student to remain passive. By including a reading and/or writing activity in a listening/speaking exercise, the student is encouraged to become involved with the lesson. This effective element (i.e., learning by doing) increases the probability of a successful learning experience. In addition, the use

of tapes containing varied voices, "real" English (e.g., "gonna" rather than "going to"), and instructions for the student to stop the tape to do the writing component serve to keep the student actively participating.

A great deal of existing print material may be modified for solo-automated use by taping the instructions that would normally be given by the teacher. Stern (1972) suggested rerecording existing tapes in three versions. For the students who learn new material very quickly, much of the repetition can be deleted. Average students can use an unmodified version. Students who require a great deal of repetition and practice receive a version of the tape in which the practice section is repeated.

A wide variety of realia may be incorporated into solo-automated activities. Television and radio commercials certainly constitute a stimulus which students regularly meet outside the classroom (Hafernik and Surguine, 1979). Taped class lectures can be excellent for helping students involved in academia learn to take notes (Coltharp, 1969). A series of sound effects can form the basis of vocabulary identification lessons for beginning students or writing lessons for intermediate and advanced students (Hares, 1978). The possibilities are limited only by the teacher's imagination and energy.

Solo activities are most likely to be useful at the (II) Practice and (IV) Review phases of learning. The addition of an automated component adds (I) Establishing Meaning to the list of phases for this mode.

Conclusions

In this article, I've suggested ways that you can modify the materials and methods you are currently using in order to individualize your ESL class. The step will help transform your classroom into a more active, student-centered learning environment. While the effort expended, particularly in the initial stages can be immense (i.e., teaching as an aerobic activity), the payoffs are more than commensurate. Increased stu-

dent skill acquisition is, of course, the primary function of individualization. However, I think you'll also find an equally valid, though less tangible result: By virtue of placing more responsibility on the student, the individualized classroom becomes a context for sharing and personal growth. And as a teacher, it's great fun. □

References

Bright, J. P. What to consider in individualized reading programs for adult students of English as a second language, Arlington Heights, IL: Statewide ESL/Adult Education Service Center, 1978.

Coltharp, L. H. Expanding the use of the laboratory. TESOL Quarterly, 1969, 3(3), 211-214.

Escobar, J. S. & McKeon, D. Four phases of the teaching and learning of a second language. In D. E. Bartley (ed.), The adult basic education TESOL handbook. New York: Collier Macmillan, 1979.

Finocchiaro, M. English as a second language: From theory to practice. New York: Regents, 1974.

Fitzgibbons, B. Working with vowel sounds using minimal pairs. Paper presented at meeting of Illinois Teachers of English to Speakers of Other Languages, Chicago, March 1980.

Ganserhoff, K. A. The why, who and how of individualized instruction for adults. In D. E. Bartley (ed.), The adult basic education TESOL handbook, New York: Collier Macmillan, 1979.

Gibson, R. E. The strip story: A catalyst for communication. TESOL Quarterly, 1975, 9(2), 149-154.

Hafernik, J. J. & Surguine, H. Using radio commercials as supplementary materials in ESL listening class. TESOL Quarterly, 1979 13(3), 341-345.

Hares, R. J. Sound effects as an aid in the teaching of English as a foreign language. Audio-Visual Language Journal, 1978, 16(2), 95-99.

Long, M. H. Group work in the teaching and learning of English as a foreign language: Problems and potential. English Language Teaching Journal, 1977, 31(4), 285-292.

Nabokov, P. & Ramirez, R. Mutual instruction handbook: A guide for the use of peer-tutoring in ABE/ESL classrooms. San Diego: San Diego Community College District, 1979.

Olsen, J. W. B. Using dyads for maximum communication practice. Paper presented at meeting of Statewide ESL Service Center-IL, Springfield, IL, October 1980.

Rigg, P. Choosing and using dialogues. TESOL Quarterly, 1976, 10(3), 291-298.

Sawkins, M. Small groups in the adult ESL classroom. TESL TALK, 1978, 10(4), 29 42.

Stern, R. H. Individualizing instruction in the language laboratory. Foreign Language Annals, 1972, 6(3), 284-289.

Taylor, B. P. Teaching composition to low level ESL students. TESOL Quarterly, 1976, 10(3), 209-219.

Verscheiden, R. J. & Harbers, E. Practical considerations in organizing and maintaining a viable ESL program. Adult Leadership, 1976, 24(5), 174-175.

TN 8/82

HOMEWORK ASSIGNMENTS IN THE ESL CLASS THAT WORK

By Frederick L. Jenks
Florida State University

Homework assignments were long viewed as an integral companion to classroom activities. Homework was the means by which (a) classroom learning was "reinforced", (b) work not covered by the teacher in the allotted time was doled out to students for completion on their own, (c) students might preview new material in preparation for upcoming classes, and (d) students were to review for quizzes and exams. Many

are the instances in which homework became a punishment when students did not perform per the teacher's expectations within the class. Homework, frequently assigned and infrequently accomplished, became a major factor in determining the level of teacher popularity as mass media and mass transportation absorbed a greater portion of students' out-of-class attention. Thus, what was (and is) a logical means for

enhancing classroom learning has been virtually eliminated from the curriculum, joining the whipping board and dunce cap as an academic artifact.

When "work in class" is lexically separated from "work outside class", negative reactions appear to escalate. However, just as "extra-curricular" activities of the 1950's evolved into "co-curricular" activities in following decades, so may extra work at home become "co-class" activity. Indeed, in a communicatively active E.S.L. class for adults or high schoolers, co-class work can be—and probably should be—the core of the syllabus. If, as Altman states, "It is the meaningful and realistic application of language in actual communication settings which leads to competence and/or communicative fluency," (1978) it follows that activities which provide meaningful and realistic scenarios for language interchange outside the classroom are critical components in the instructional plan.

How can a teacher plan "homework" activities with communicative requisites? How can "role play" be replaced with *real-play?* The suggestions offered in this article can be broadly characterized as "community-oriented tasks" (Paulston and Bruder: 1976:63), techniques that bring native English speakers and E.S.L. students together in a non-classroom setting.

The Autograph Book. The purpose of this technique is to acquaint learners with the community while simultaneously requiring that they engage in basic conversations (introductions, greetings, departings, etc.) with a native speaker of English.

The major planning responsibility of the instructor is to elicit the cooperation of willing autographers. Experience indicates that the autographers should be accessible, approachable, and willing to participate.

This technique activates no less than fifteen times the inclass lessons on greetings, introductions, requests for permission, and departures. In addition, contact with native speakers of English are made and, in most cases, several minutes of liberated conversation occur.

The imaginative selecting of autographers can introduce students to the doorsteps of campus and community services, to consumer agencies, to civil servants, and to helpful individuals. Some examples of reliable autographers are the athletic trainer, the football team's manager, the director of women's athletics, the editors of the student newspaper and university publications, the director of alumni affairs, an officer of the Junior Chamber of Commerce, the manager of the local shopping mall, a librarian, a registrar's assistant who handles foreign academic transcripts, and an employee of the tourism office.

Intercultural Inquiry List (IIL). The purpose of this activity is to promote real-life oral communication between E.S.L. students and native speakers of English by providing each party with a printed sheet of questions answerable only by the other person. Each IIL has a dual intent: (a) to provide conversation starters in the form of assigned questions to be answered, and (b) to bring to the learner information that

may be of interest and/or importance.

The two groups of students are brought together through the cooperative planning of the E.S.L. instructor and several Foreign Language instructors representing different languages that are being taught to native English speakers. The instructors prepare IIL's for their target language, arrange a timetable for students of E.S.L. and foreign languages to meet, and reserve a site for the meetings. The two groups of language learners will meet, complete the questioning of each other, and leave with completed IIL's.

From the following example of an IIL for an E.S.L. learner, it can be seen that the nature of the questions is informal; questions may deal with common or global topics such as food, entertainment, currency, and holidays. Furthermore, the answers to the questions are not readily available without the aid of a native speaker of the target language. That factor alone seems to be a major key to the enthusiastic participation of the answering party.

Example:

Intercultural Inquiry List

Questioner: E.S.L. student

Answerer: native speaker of English

Directions. Ask your partner the following questions. Write your partner's answer on the IIL. After your partner has answered five questions, you must find another partner. No one native speaker of English may answer more than five of your list's questions. At the bottom of the page, the English speaker will sign his/her name and indicate the questions answered.

1. What is "succotash?"
2. What is Harlem?
3. What instrument does Pete Fountain play?
4. Who is Dumbo?
5. What is a "Baby Ruth?"
6. There are two major leagues in American professional baseball. What are the names of these leagues?
7. How much is "two bits"?
8. What is a corn plaster?
9. Abraham Lincoln is a national hero in the U.S.A. What were two of his occupations prior to becoming President?
10. A young actor captured the attention of teenagers in the 1950's. Two of his most famous movies were "Rebel Without a Cause" and "East of Eden." What was his name and is he alive?
11. What sound does "Rice Krispies" make?
12. Pets are very common in the U.S.A. Who are "Black Beauty", "Mister Ed", "Rin Tin Tin", and "Fred" (on the television program, *Baretta*)?
13. Who is Rip Van Winkle?
14. What would you do with an "Edsel"?
15. Where would you put a "knick-knack"? (pronounced: nick nack)

Questions ____, ____, ____, ____, ____ answered by_____.

Questions ____, ____, ____, ____, ____ answered by_____.

Questions ____, ____, ____, ____, ____ answered by_____.

When I observed E.S.L. students and native speakers of English at work on these assignments, I calculated that approximately twenty percent of the conversation centered on answering the specific questions. Additional explanations, cross-cultural comparisons, related questions and answers, and simple chatting accounted for the remaining eighty percent of language interchange. Also, even though the questioner talks less than the respondent, the fact that both parties will play the inquiring as well as the answering roles brings the quantitative output into balance.

Real-Play. A commonly used and generally successful technique for practicing "real language" usage in typical communicative situations is the role play, an "exercise where the student is assigned a fictitious role from which he has to improvise some kind of behavior toward the other characters" (Paulston and Bruder: 1976:70). After the teacher describes a scenario, assigns roles, provides characterizations, and explains underlying assumptions to the class, the playlet is acted out. Evaluations are generally completed with attention to communicative completeness, naturalness of delivery, and conversational flow. When well designed, well explained to students, and sufficiently controlled, the role play is a stimulating language-to-life exercise. But, there are recurring problems.

A major problem was illustrated at a TESOL 1977 Conference session on role plays (Furey:1977). Videotapes of in-class role plays portrayed, in one instance, a group of five E.S.L. learners discussing a real estate transaction. The roles were well-defined, the hidden agendas were verbalized smoothly, and everyone performed adequately. In spite of these factors, the role play suffered from numerous factual errors delivered by the "real estate agent". His gross misconceptions about mortgages, monthly payments, and down payments were stated in flawless English. The problem is obvious; a role play which permits participants to unwittingly spout misinformation in front of an audience of learners is poor preparation for real communication.

A second common problem is kinesic inaccuracy. For example, a "dead fish" handshake usually accompanies a role play in which participants who are non-Americans greet each other. Since the looser handshake may be customary to them, neither reacts negatively to it. Even when it is seen by the teacher, it is rarely noted in the evaluation as being a negative feature. In "real situations" (Stevick: 1971), gestures and touch signals are major vehicles of messages. As such, they should be explained, performed, and evaluated as vital components of the role play.

The *real play* is a response to the above-mentioned problems. In addition, it employs the positive aspects of the role play. It is a role play performed outside the classroom in the actual setting with a native speaker of English playing one major role. The necessary ingredients, then, are an English speaker who is willing to cooperate, prepare, and participate, advance permission to use an actual setting, and classroom instruction of learners in both the linguistic/kinesic probabilities *and* the factual information supporting the encounter.

A sample real play on "Installment Purchasing" would adhere to the same pre-planning outline as used for a role play. Additional planning steps include the following:

(1) The teacher will secure the active assistance of an English speaker who agrees to participate in the real play during a specific week at selected times of the day. Some potential assistants are used car dealers, managers of furniture or appliance stores, and mobile home dealers. To minimize any "shady" activities, the teacher should rely on friends, cooperative university alumni, and spouses of T.E.S.L. majors.

(2) The teacher will explain and discuss the activity personally with each American participant, and receive assurances that they will make the real play an educational experience rather than an actual selling opportunity.

(3) The teacher distributes for classroom discussion a learning activity packet in which retail terminology, installment buying, methods of payment, etc., are provided. Also included are

typical contracts, brochures describing the products, sales tags, and advertisements.

(4) Sample conversational openers are distributed to students on mimeographed sheets. In-class role plays transpire, based on this sheet and material in the learning activity packets.

(5) E.S.L. students will select the retailer that they wish to visit, sign up on a time sheet to indicate when they will appear at the store, receive directions (a map) to their selected store, and obtain a one-page evaluation sheet.

(6) The teacher will deliver the time sheet to the participating retailers several days in advance of students' visits. He/she is asked to supply a brief comment in writing regarding each student's visit and the conversation.

(7) Classroom discussions and question-answer sessions ensue based on the real-play experiences as post-activity exercises.

In one instance, videotaped recordings of real-plays were made in the retailer's office or store. The participating English speakers portrayed themselves while graduate assistants conducted the filming and played the other roles. Replay of the tapes in E.S.L. classes provided valuable information and an opportunity for students to see their future conversational partner and surroundings. Furthermore, it helped the native English speakers to "loosen up" and practice for the real-play.

Since this technique requires considerable preparation, the assistance of graduate students in T.E.S.L. is of great benefit. Their involvement in the development of packets, in observing the real-plays, and in assisting in the preparatory stages is not only a source of sound

Intern experience but also an aid to learners and the instructor.

As with the *Autograph Book* technique, it is imperative that the teacher have a great deal of confidence in the "outsiders". Their levels of integrity and sincerity are keys to the overall success or failure of the exercises. Furthermore, the teacher must express his/her gratitude and that of the students by sending thank-you notes or by giving token gifts. Among these gratuities may be a "Friend of the Department" scroll, an invitation to a campus event with an international flavor, or a small item from another country. When there has been constant support on the part of an individual, a letter from the teacher to that person's employer is a thoughtful gesture, one that usually brings continuing support.

All of the suggested techniques provide out-of-class practice for students while increasing community involvement. Each technique requires careful preparation and monitoring both in and outside the class. Finally, each activity has proven to enhance students' interest in, and attention to, daily classroom work since the pivotal activity—the "homework"—takes place beyond the protective boundaries of the class.

REFERENCES

Altman, Howard B. "Individualizing, Personalizing, and Humanizing Second Language Education." ACTFL Session, 1978 TESOL Convention, Mexico City.
Furey, Patricia. "Role-play and Interaction Activities in the Classroom." SIG Session, 1977 TESOL Convention, Miami.
Paulston, Christina B. and Bruder, Mary N. 1976. "Teaching English as a Second Language: Techniques and Procedures." (Cambridge, Massachusetts: Winthrop Publishers, Inc.).
Stevick, Earl. 1971. "Adapting and Writing Language Lessons." (Washington, D.C., Foreign Service Institute).

TN 8/79

ILLUSTRATIONS OF MURPHY'S LAW ABOUND IN CLASSROOM RESEARCH ON LANUGAGE USE

by Kathleen M. Bailey
Monterey Institute of International Studies

These are three laws attributed to Murphy although no one seems to be quite certain of who he is. No. 1: Nothing is ever as easy as it seems. No. 2: Everything will take longer than expected. No. 3: If anything can go wrong, it will.

This paper is neither a report of research nor a methodological treatise. It's not a report of "work in progress" since it does not discuss any progress. It does not theorize (or at least not much) and it is not a "how-to" paper. Rather it might be characterized as a "how-NOT-to" paper on classroom-centered research.

If we accept Long's definition of the field (and I do), this is not even a paper about classroom-centered research on language teaching or learning:

. . . Investigation of classroom language learning may be defined as research on second language learning and teaching, all or part of whose data are derived from the observation or measurement of the classroom performance of teachers and students (Long, 1980, p. 3).

Instead, this paper reports on some facets of the data collection procedures in a study of (second) language use in classrooms. This paper is also somewhat of a departure from previous classroom-centered research of interest to ESL teachers, since the study was not conducted in language classrooms. Rather, it reports on an

investigation of the language used by university teaching assistants (TAs) in physics and mathematics courses as they interacted with their undergraduate students in laboratories and discussion sections. The potential appeal of this study to ESL teachers and language researchers is that half the subjects were non-native speakers of English. This particular paper was written for anyone who has tried (or will try) to collect data in classrooms.

Some background information on the study is necessary before turning to the data collection issues that are the focus of this article. This research, which was part of a larger project involving both quantitative and qualitative research techniques, centered on the following question:

What are the classroom communication problems of non-native speaking teaching assistants, as perceived by the TAs themselves, their students, and an outside observer?

In order to answer this question, an observational study was designed which compared native speaking and non-native speaking TAs.

Two main data collection techniques were used in this portion of the study: audio tape recording and intensive note-taking. In Long's terms, this part of the study may be described as "unstructured observation" in the "anthropological approach" to classroom research (Long, 1980, p. 21). As the researcher I assumed the role of a "non-participant observer," which means, in this case, that I took notes as the classroom events occurred, but did not personally try to participate in the physics experiments or the discussions of math or physics. In non-participant observation, as Long has pointed out:

Data are mostly in the form of written notes, analyzed subsequently but . . . generally recorded openly, during the events observed, for in non-participant observation, the observer does not take part in the activities being studied or pretend to be a participant in them. . . . There is no question of being covert (in nonlaboratory settings, at least) or, as a result, of the researcher's witnessing truly natural, i.e., "unobserved," behavior in the way undisclosed participants can. While the principal means of gathering data may . . . be note-taking, the non-participant observer will have the option of supplementing this through the use of other techniques (ibid., p. 24).

Thus during a classroom observation, I took notes at the same time I tape recorded the lesson. The tape recorder was in full view of the teacher and students. Each TA in the sample (n = 24) had given his permission for me to observe and tape record his classes.

One last issue to be mentioned before turning to the problems in the data collection process involves time sampling. The duration of this study was ten weeks, which coincided with the academic quarter. Ten weeks is a relatively short time for conducting ethnographic research, but it is the total period in which these particular people—TAs and students—interacted together. Unless the subjects became friends or happened to continue in the student/teacher relationship in subsequent classes, the ten-week academic quarter was the sum-total of their common experience.

In a pilot study, which also lasted ten weeks, I found that the attitude of the students toward the TAs seemed to change over time. As the students and TAs became more familiar with one another, the inter-

action patterns changed, whether for better or worse. In addition, the relationships seemed to vary somewhat in response to outside pressures (e.g., impending mid-terms or final examinations) or other course-related factors not under the TAs' control (for instance, the students' attitudes toward the professors or the grades they received from the "readers" who scored their homework assignments). For this reason, I decided to observe the subjects at the beginning, middle and end of the academic quarter, three observations for each subject.

The issue of the time sampling is a key question in naturalistic research, by which I mean research in which the investigator does not control or arrange the stimuli or purposefully influence the response behavior of the subjects. (See Guba, 1978, for a discussion of the various ways that "naturalistic research" has been defined.) For example, in this study I did not try to control either what the teachers said or how the students reacted to them. Instead, the researcher's aim in naturalistic research is to describe, document and analyze events that occur naturally, without exerting rigid control over time, setting, participants, etc.

Much of the classroom-centered research on language teaching and learning (see Bailey, in press) falls within this broad description of naturalistic research, although some researchers have introduced a particular curriculum as a measure of control (e.g., Fanselow, 1977; Long, Adams, McLean and Castaños, 1976; the Essex team under the direction of Allwright, 1975). The salient point to be made here is that if a researcher does not arrange the lesson to be observed, but sets out to observe naturally occurring events, then he or she must be prepared to generate data as the events occur. That can be a very tricky business.

My intent is to describe some of the difficulties encountered in this study of classroom language use, in hopes of saving other classroom researchers some time and a lot of trouble. This might even be considered a data-based paper, since I have gathered some examples from my work to illustrate these problems. "What could go wrong?" you ask. "It's a simple observational study. All she does is take notes and tape record." But I maintain that classroom-centered research, like playing the guitar, is something that is easy to do, but very hard to do well.

One sort of problem that can arise has to do with the researcher's actual physical preparation for collecting data. During the pilot study I developed a system of note-taking, which included some mapping conventions borrowed from Melbin (1960) and some techniques described by Knapp (1972) for recording nonverbal behavior. I was prepared to generate "rich" data. What could possibly go wrong? Well, to begin, it helps to be able to see what it is you're

observing and to have the proper tools for recording. The following excerpt is from the fieldnotes in the pilot study. I had been invited to a departmental meeting of faculty and TAs. The meeting was held in a large lecture hall with about ninety people present. Through a series of manipulations by the people in charge, I was moved from my original vantage point to a seat in the front row. The fieldnotes state:

I am sitting in the front row and feel I am at quite a disadvantage in terms of judging the audience reaction among the TAs. Also, like a d—————d fool, I forgot my clipboard, so I don't have any paper for fieldnotes. I quickly look through some folders in my brief-case and decide which papers I don't need and can sacrifice to fieldnotes. Next time I must be better prepared.

A foolish mistake, you say, and after all, that's what pilot studies are for: making all the foolish mistakes. **Lesson Number 1** If you're going to take notes, *always* carry paper and pens or pencils and something firm to write on, like a clipboard.

Lesson Number 2 is related. If you're going to tape record, make sure you have access to a good tape recorder and that you know how to operate it correctly. "That's so obvious!" you say. "Anyone can use a tape recorder. What could possibly go wrong?" The following excerpt is from the fieldnotes on the first observation of a math TA.

I got to school in plenty of time to check out the tape recorder and get to the classroom. I chose a seat near the back, then decided to move to sit next to a plug. This is an old lab room of some kind, and there was an auxiliary line of [electrical] plugs running around the side and back of the classroom. I chose a seat near the window and plugged in the tape recorder. . . . I turned it on. Nothing happened. I tried again. Nothing happened. My palms began to sweat and I thought to myself, "Don't panic. It's only a machine. You can deal with this." I tried another plug on the auxiliary line: nothing.

The TA had started writing on the blackboard, but he hadn't started to talk yet. I got up and walked over to the door and turned the lights on, thinking that the power in the auxiliary line might depend on juice in the main line. As I returned to my desk, the TA thanked me for turning the lights on. I just smiled—rather weakly, I imagine.

I sat down and tried to record something—anything! Still no power. Then I began to think I didn't know how to use the tape recorder. I thought you had to depress both the "play" key and the "record" key to record. I tried pressing just the "play" key: still no power. I had a vision of a bleeding ulcer starting to develop in my gut somewhere, and I considered running back to the department for another tape recorder: there was clearly something wrong with this one. But the TA had started to talk, so I decided to sit still, forget about the tape recorder and try to take notes. I felt pretty sick . . . through the entire class.

I had scheduled another observation immediately after this one, but I decided to scrap it and make it up later, rather than getting only a partial set of data (i.e., the fieldnotes without the corresponding tape recording). The field notes state, "I returned to the office to get another tape recorder. I plugged the tape recorder in . . . just to try it one more time and it worked. The power must have been off in that auxiliary line."

I suppose it's obvious that if you're going to tape record, you should always carry batteries, even if you plan to use the wall socket. But perhaps less obvious is the real message of **Lesson Number 3:** *Always* investigate the classroom where you'll be observing before the actual observation begins. This safeguard can make the observation easier as well as protecting your data.

These experiences led me to anticipate further possible realizations of Murphy's Law. What else could go wrong? A tape might break. Solution: always carry extra cassettes. I might accidentally re-record a cassette that contained observational data. Solution: label all the cassettes prior to recording on them and immediately remove the tabs to prevent the tapes from being erased. There might be a time when I would not be able to use the departmental tape recorder. Solution: buy a good tape recorder. I might not be able to identify the various voices on the tape and the sound might be muffled. Solution: buy a high quality omnidirectional stereo microphone and cross your fingers that these expenses will be tax deductible.

By now you are saying, "My gosh! She is really paranoid!" Call it neurotic if you like. I have simply come to believe that in classroom-centered research anything can go wrong—and a lot will. This maxim is especially true when one is dealing with naturally occurring lessons, with students and teachers who are going on about the business of learning, with or without the researcher and all the investigative accoutrements. I now firmly believe that it pays to anticipate problems that might make the data either less valid or less reliable—or just plain worthless.

There are other threats to the usefulness of classroom-generated data, particularly in research where the subjects are not a "captive audience." One such potential problem is related to the threat of mortality. In experimental research, the term "mortality" refers to the "differential loss of respondents from the comparison group" (Campbell and Stanley, 1963, p. 5). But the effects of mortality are not limited to comparison groups. They can influence the data even in research on a single classroom and even when the researcher is not measuring post-treatment performance. For example, one result of the disappearance of subjects in classroom-centered research with repeated observations is that types and patterns of group interaction change as the numbers of participants change (see Schmuck and Schmuck, 1975).

The fieldnotes in my study provide a drastic example of subject disappearance. The scene is the hallway outside the classroom where I was to observe a non-native speaking math TA. I arrived early but

The professor and the last few students [from the previous class] were leaving the room. It was noon. There were no [math] students. I couldn't figure out what had gone wrong. Then I saw the TA and another Asian student come walking down the hall toward me. I said hello to him and told him I had thought I was in the wrong place since there were no students waiting. His friend slapped him on the back and kidded him that he was such a lousy teacher that he didn't have any students. The TA smiled weakly. I was horrified to realize that it could be true—there might not be any students at his class. His friend left and I stood in the hall outside the classroom with [the TA]. He looked at the clock on the wall. It was 12:05. . . . He said that the students had had a test on Friday in the professor's class, so maybe they wouldn't come to his class today. He looked rather sad as he said this and I felt awful for him. I asked how many students usually attend the section and he said seven. Then I made the mistake of asking how many are enrolled. He said there are about thirty students enrolled (in his section).

We waited in the hall for another fifteen minutes. No students came. As I left the TA waiting alone in his classroom, I thought of the haunting question of the 'sixties: "What if they gave a war and nobody came?"

This experience led to **Lesson Number 4,** which involves strategic flexibility: if you are observing regularly scheduled classes *always* leave room in your plan to reschedule an observation as needed, in case a class is cancelled, or the teacher gets sick, or you miss your bus—or all the students simultaneously and unwittingly commit temporary group mortality. Having the flexibility to reschedule an observation can be problematic, given the time constraints of the academic quarter. As a footnote to this episode, I was able to return to this TA's class the following week. There were three students present for half of the discussion, at which point one of them left.

One final problem I wish to discuss here is "reactivity." In naturalistic research, this refers to the effects of the researcher's presence on the behavior to be observed— what Labov has called "the observer's paradox" (Labov, 1972). This issue is particularly relevant, as Long has pointed out, if the observations are not covert—if the observer is not truly a participant and is not masquerading as a participant in the classroom. Possible reactive effects of the observer's presence in the classroom could involve changes in the teacher's behavior, as in Fanselow's (1980) description of language teachers bringing carloads of pictures and realia to class on the day of the inspector's visit.

An example of such reactivity occurred in my pilot study when I observed a non-native speaking TA in a physics lab for the first time. The experiment that day had to do with measuring light and observing the spectrum. The fieldnotes state:

I entered the room intending to sit near the windows where I could see [the TA], the students, and the blackboard. However, as I walked in, the TA said, "Oh-oh, here comes the spy." Some of the students looked at me. I quickly sat in the first chair by the door. . . . I smiled at the TA, hoping he was joking. I just sat at the desk and did not begin to write or do anything that anyone would notice. I just sat still for a few minutes as the TA began to talk again. He stopped in mid-sentence and said, "Oh-oh, you are making me nervous." I smiled again and said, "Just pretend I'm not here, please." He laughed (a bit nervously) and went on with his explanation. I sat still for a few more minutes and when it seemed that he was, in fact, ignoring me, I began to write some notes.

As it turned out, the TA got back at me a few minutes later by insisting that I try to do the experiment. I was more than slightly nervous about that arrangement since he had told the students at the beginning of the experiment, "This is a killer machine. It has quite high voltage so be careful." Of course, while I was looking at the spectrum with the killer machine, my note-taking was inhibited more than just a little. This didn't matter too much though, because after explaining the experimental procedure to the class, the TA had closed the door and turned out the lights so the students could make the necessary measurements without any stray light in the room.

This experience led me to two more caveats. **Lesson Number 5:** *Always* plan free time immediately after an observation so you can write your fieldnotes if you aren't able to record them during the actual observation for any reason (e.g., the lights go out, your pen runs out of ink, your chronic writer's cramp suddenly becomes acute, etc.). Even if you do take notes during the events, the human hand can't write as fast as life happens in classrooms. Scheduling a free hour immediately after an observation will enable you to "enrich" your notes—to add to them and clarify them while the memory of the experience is still fresh in your mind. This post-observation period will also allow time to talk with the subjects.

Lesson Number 6 bring us back to the issues of reactivity and sampling: *always* arrange a big enough subject pool that you can re-sample from among the possible subjects if your presence seems to affect someone's behavior noticeably and *always* allow enough time for your subjects to become comfortable with your presence before you try to collect data on their behavior. In the example cited above, I had introduced myself to the TA only a few hours before this ill-fated observation.

Of course, teachers are not the only ones who are likely to react to an observer's presence in a classroom-centered research project. Depending on what the students have been told about the research, how they feel toward the teacher and the course, their level of confidence, etc., they may or may not be disturbed by an outsider in the classroom. Although note-taking is fairly unobtrusive in most classrooms, nonparticipant observers (especially those with tape recorders) are usually recognizable, and the presence of such an observer may engender in students reactions ranging from curiosity to open hostility.

The following illustration is taken from the tape recording and the fieldnotes of my first observation of a math course on differential equations. I sat in the back of the room taking notes and holding the microphone on my desk, with the tape recorder on the floor beside me. A young man entered the room after the lesson had begun and sat two seats to my right. He glanced over and saw that I was tape recording, so he moved one seat closer, bent over and said, "Hi!" directly into the microphone. He asked me what I was doing and I whispered that it was my dissertation research. I continued to take notes on what the TA was saying. The student said, "Must be 'sosh'!" (i.e., sociology). I whispered, "Applied Linguistics," and kept taking notes. I didn't look at the student. I wished he would go away or at least leave me alone. I had already modified my note-taking behavior somewhat because he was reading what I was writing. A few minutes later as I rubbed my wrist for a moment the student asked me, "What's the matter?" Oh, the power of the interrogative! The proper response would have been to say "Nothing" or to say nothing or to shake my head with a bored expression. Instead I whispered that I had writer's cramp. He said, "Poor baby—aww!" I began to dislike this person intensely—not exactly an objective attitude for a researcher to take.

More wisecracks followed, even though the student managed to keep up with the lesson and interact appropriately with the TA. At one point the student took the microphone out of my hand to look at it. He said, "Your hands are cold," and began to rub my hand. I thought maybe I had managed to sit next to an unstable young man who had spent too many lonely nights in the Computer Center, so I tactfully pointed out that he was making it rather difficult for me to concentrate.

The student paid attention to the lesson for a while and I took notes frantically, trying to make up for what I'd missed while reacting to his reactivity. But then he offered to hold the microphone for me and started to take it out of my hand. I said, "No thanks," as firmly as I could, but he began to rub my hand again. I considered moving, but the room was small and the desks were bolted together, and I though the movement would be disruptive. I told the student he was distracting me and to please leave me alone so I could do my research. He left off temporarily, but then he began to rub my back. I was startled so I resorted to an absolutely useless feminine ploy: "My husband would be very unhappy if he could see us now. Please, I can't concentrate!" I think he saw that I was mad, because he left me alone for a while.

About ten minutes later he apologized for having annoyed me, but he pointed out that at least I was getting it all on tape. I looked down at my brand new tape recorder with its new stereo microphone, somewhat comforted by the thought that technology would succeed where the human recorder had failed. I felt sick: the spindles weren't turning and the cassette wasn't moving. The machine had stopped working a few minutes into the second side. I thought for a moment I would cry right there in the middle of differential equations, but femininity had availed me not at all during this crisis, so I resorted to rational steps. I took the cassette out of the tape recorder and looked at it. The tape was not broken. Perhaps it had just not been inserted properly when I turned it over. I reinserted the cassette and started the record mechanism. The spindles turned for a moment and then slowed to a stop. The batteries were dead. Oh, Murphy, you were right!

After the observation, I played back the tape on another machine. The first twenty minutes were fine (except for the clipped conversations with the student), but after a while the teacher's voice began to go through puberty in reverse. As the batteries had run down, the tape had moved slower and slower. Playback at normal speeds created a "Munchkin Effect." After twenty-five minutes of tape I had a terrific recording of Alvin the chipmunk discussing delta and epsilon. This strange experience led to **Lessons 7 and 8**, respectively: *always* carry extra batteries (preferably the nickel

cadmium rechargeable type—and preferably with the recharging apparatus) and *never* allow yourself to be entrapped in an unwanted discourse act with a subject during an observation.

Reflecting on these events should also lead us to **Lesson Number 9**: *always* use, or consider using, multiple data collection procedures. (See Bailey and Lazar-Morrison, 1981; Denzin, 1978; Patton, 1980.) Of course, the data collection techniques in any study must be determined by the research questions and the desired outcomes, and different settings impose different limitations on the types of recording that can be done. But, if it is true, as Birdwhistell maintains (1970) that about seventy percent of communication is nonverbal, and if we are investigating communication in the broad sense, then audio tape tape recordings alone will miss much. By the same token, videotape recordings, while potentially capturing the visual channels of communication, may be more obtrusive at the same time they are limited by the camera's "tunnel vision." Likewise, the human recorder—even equipped with the best note-taking or coding system and the fastest short-hand—cannot capture life at the speed and depth with which it occurs in classrooms. In addition, on those awful occasions when Murphy's Law is realized, multiple data collection procedures at least provide some safeguards against the types of data loss experiences described above.

The final caveat about conducting observational research is **Lesson Number 10**: *always* do a pilot study. In this paper I have tried to illustrate how many different and unusual things can go wrong in classroom-centered research. Unfortunately, some of these blunders occurred during the data collection phase of my dissertation research. Mercifully, some occurred during what turned out to be a pilot study. Because I made those mistakes, and lost time and data as a result, I now go fully prepared to every observation. (At least, I *think* I do.) This does not mean I have stopped making mistakes, but I have been able to anticipate and thereby avoid a number of pitfalls.

Perhaps by now you are saying, "Boy, those were funny experiences!" Or, if I have failed to amuse you, you may be saying, "What a fool! She calls that research?" But I do have a point to make and I hope it will be considered seriously by people who are interested in classroom-centered research on language teaching and learning (and use). My message is this: classroom-centered research is not easy. People who make a distinction between "hard data" and "soft data" are sometimes prone to think that so-called "soft data" (which usually means unquantified data) are the result of "soft" research, and that observational research is "simple" and the data "anecdotal." (See Hymes, 1980, for an interesting discussion of the role of narratives and anecdotal evidence in American education.) This is not the case, although there have been many problems in our classroom-centered research to date. (See Gaies, 1980, for a discussion of some "consumer guidelines" on classroom-centered research.)

You may feel that this paper has been nothing but story-telling. I would say instead that I am working toward an epistemology of classroom-centered research by examining what Denzin has called "the research act" (1978).

I do not claim that these ten "rules" for conducting classroom-centered research are inviolable or that following them will produce fool-proof data. Nor do I claim that this list is exhaustive. There are probably a thousand potential rules to follow in conducting an observational study, and it might be worthwhile for every incipient researcher to memorize them all before entering a classroom to collect data. However, I do believe that attending to these lessons and others, which will surely emerge as we scrutinize our methods of classroom-centered research, will help us to clean up our collective research act.

Finally, I wish to propose Bailey's Corollary to Murphy's Law:

It's likely that if anything can go wrong, it will. But if we anticipate what might go wrong, it may not. ⊛

REFERENCES

Allwright, R. L., Ed. 1975. Working papers: language teaching classroom research. Colchester: University of Essex, Department of Languages and Linguistics.
Bailey, K. M., in press. Classroom-centered research on language teaching and learning. In M. Celce-Murcia (Ed.), Essays for language teachers. Rowley, Mass.: Newbury House, Inc.
Bailey, K. M. and Lazar-Morrison, C. 1981. A multi-method investigation of the communicative competence of non-native speaking teaching assistants. Paper presented at the Second Annual Ethnography in Education Research Forum, University of Pennsylvania, Philadelphia.
Birdwhistell, R. 1970. Kinesics and context: essays on body motion communications. Philadelphia: University of Pennsylvania Press.
Campbell, D. T. and Stanley, J. C. 1963. Experimental and quasi-experimental designs for research. Chicago: Rand McNally.
Denzin, N. K. 1978. The research act. New York: McGraw Hill.
Faneselow, J. F. 1977. The treatment of error in oral work. Foreign Language Annals. 10, 5, 583-593.
Fanselow, J. F. 1980. What kind of flower is that?—A contrasting model for critiquing lessons. Paper presented at the Goethe Institute, British Council.
Gaies, S. J. 1980. Classroom-centered research: some consumer guidelines. Paper presented at the Second Annual TESOL Summer Meeting, University of New Mexico, Albuquerque.
Guba, E. G. 1978. Toward a methodology of naturalistic inquiry in educational evaluation. Los Angeles: Center for the Study of Evaluation, UCLA, CSE Monograph Series in Evaluation, No. 8.
Hymes, D. 1980. Narrative thinking and story-telling rights: a folklorist's clue to a critique of education. In Language in education: ethnolinguistic essays. Washington, D.C.: Center for Applied Linguistics.
Knapp, M. L. 1972. Observing and recording nonverbal behavior. In Nonverbal communication in human interaction. New York: Holt, Rinehart and Winston.
Labov, W. 1972. Some principles of linguistic methodology. Language in Society. 1, 97-120.
Long, M. 1980. Inside the "black box": methodological issues in classroom research on language learning. Language Learning. 30, 1, 1-42.
Long, M., Adams, L., McLean, M. and Castaños, F. 1976. Doing things with words: verbal interaction in lockstep and small group classroom situations. In J. F. Fanselow and R. H. Crymes (Eds.), On TESOL '76. Washington, D.C.: TESOL.
Melbin, M. 1960. Mapping uses and methods. In R. N. Adams and J. J. Preiss (Eds.), Human organization research: field relations and techniques. Homewood, Ill.: Dorsey.
Patton, M. Q. 1980. Qualitative evaluation methods. Beverly Hills, Sage Publications.
Schmuck, R. A. and Schmuck, P. A. 1975. Group processes in the classroom. (Second Edition) Dubuque, Iowa: William C. Brown Company.

TN 8/83

SOME PRIORITIES FOR A GOOD ESL CLASS

by Larry Anger,
LaGuardia Community College

The more I observe classes, the more excited I become about the sometimes surprising, yet always impressive, techniques and strategies currently being applied in ESL classrooms. To say the least, I have seen variety, innovation and eclecticism — many approaches that effectively get the message across. This is not to say that I have gone so far as to encourage methodological anarchy for I do have certain specific guidelines that are necessary to follow regardless of the approach an instructor chooses to help his or her students learn and use English.

Of course, I have visited some very bad classes at different times, too — bad to the point that it amazes me that an instructor can be so unaware, so out of touch with what is happening in his or her classroom, that he or she does not realize that the students are not learning and that they are very often bored to death. How can an instructor not put himself or herself in the place of his or her students to determine whether the lesson in progress is successful or not?

The above is only one of the questions that an instructor must ask himself or herself to maintain an excellent class during which learning is maximized. I have assembled a list of questions which are, in fact, priorities indicative of a good class. Although the topics of these questions are teacher centered, their focus is on student learning. Rather than group the questions into categories such as "teacher preparation," "teacher awareness," or "student interaction," I will leave them in the form of a checklist:

YES NO 1. Do you demonstrate adequate planning and sequencing?

YES NO 2. Do you use material that is relevant to the students' world and at an appropriate level for the students?

YES NO 3. Is the aim of your lesson clear to your students, i.e., is the target structure or activity clearly delineated and reflected in your preparation?

YES NO 4. Do you have a clear understanding of the structure so that you will not be "surprised" by irregular items?

YES NO 5. Are your directions clear and to the point?

YES NO 6. Do you keep rules, diagrams and explanations to a minimum?

YES NO 7. Are your handouts well prepared and legible and NOT poor duplications characterized by light print or minute type which students, already struggling in a second language, must struggle to read?

YES NO 8. Do you speak naturally, at normal speed?

YES NO 9. Do you maintain an appropriate pace to keep the class alert and interested?

YES NO 10. Do you have good rapport with your class, respecting the students' time as well as exhibiting sensitivity to the students (as adults or children) and offering positive reinforcement?

YES NO 11. Do you listen to your students and are you aware of student errors, limiting correction to what is necessary and relevant?

YES NO 12. Do you promote student self-editing?

YES NO 13. Do you utilize peer correction?

YES NO 14. Do you respect students' abilities to use their own grey matter to come up with new items and do you invite them to use their own powers of analogy or analysis to make "educated guesses?"

YES NO 15. Do you promote student participation and activity?

YES NO 16. Are you aware of the ratio of student and teacher talk, keeping teacher talk to a minimum rather than dominating the class?

YES NO 17. Do your students have an opportunity to communicate with each other in real language activities so that the emphasis is not on pattern practice?

YES NO 18. Is your class arranged for successful communication between students and easy accessibility to the teacher?

YES NO 19. Can your students to something new linguistically after the class?

YES NO 20. Would you, as a student, enjoy your own class?

TN 5/75, 2/76

"BUT HOW CAN YOU TEACH THEM ENGLISH IF YOU DON'T SPEAK THEIR LANGUAGE..."

by John Daugherty
Illinois Adult and Bilingual Services Center

As a teacher of ESL to adults, have you ever heard this question from people at a party, from your family, from other ESL teachers? Along the same line, the following questions are often heard: "What materials do you have for Chinese speakers, for Polish speakers, for Spanish speakers?" "Do you have any bilingual materials?" "Do you have anything that will help me learn some Chinese, some Polish, some Spanish?"

Under certain circumstances, these might be valid questions and concerns while under others, these types of questions should be of least concern. All this is really linked to the question of the use of translation and/or the students' native language in ESL class, a controversial topic in our field. In fact, if you're giving a presentation or workshop and want blood pressures to rise, eyes to widen or close, and teeth to grit, just say something like, "Translation has no place in an adult ESL class". You'll surely get a mixed reaction but you *will* get a reaction.

Let's address the issue in terms of local adult ESL classes, i.e., classes composed of limited or non-English speaking adults whose primary need is the development of listening and speaking skills in English, adults living in an English dominant environment where if you want to 'play the game'; get, keep and progress in a job commensurate with your skills and abilities; and assure yourself of mobility, then you've got to do it in English. This isn't the English as a foreign language situation, i.e., foreign students in an American college who intend to return to their country (or so they tell the INS), or the overseas EFL setting, usually with a homogeneous group who aren't living or working in an English speaking environment and whose primary goal isn't mastery of spoken English.

Before looking at the pros and cons of translation, it should be strongly emphasized that there is one situation in which translation or the use of the student's first language is definitely out— a class composed of students who speak different languages, e.g., two Chinese speakers, three French speakers, two Polish speakers, and 15 Spanish speakers. Unless you are able to translate for *everyone*, it should not be done at all. The mere existence of a majority of speakers of one particular language gives no one the right to cater to one group and discriminate against those whose native language the teacher doesn't speak. Not only is this pedagogically unsound, it is simply rude. If it seems preposterous that this type of teaching exists, be assured that it does.

Now, you say, "But I have a bilingual aide who is a great help. What now?" If the bilingual aide is working only with the group whose first language s/he speaks, then the use of translation would be acceptable in that small individualized group setting, but not if the aide were working with the entire class.

Having discussed translation in the heterogeneous class, here are some of the advantages and disadvantages of using translation in a homogeneous class of adult ESL students. The list is by no means complete.

Some Advantages: Translation:

—can save time in explaining concepts like "lucky" and idioms like "I can't take it anymore."
—can help build rapport between teacher and class, especially if your foreign language isn't the greatest.
—can help students who enter the course late to catch up with the others, especially in vocabulary and grammatical explanations.
—makes teacher preparation easier, especially for Mondays.
—can clarify grammatical explanations for those who have a grasp of grammar in their first language.
—can help to clarify differences in similar words, e.g., chubby, fat.
—can be an immediate and quick test of students comprehension.
—gives the *teacher* practice in using the students' first language (especially good for teachers planning a vacation abroad or those who majored in a foreign language but never learned to speak it).
—can reassure those students who feel the need to understand everything.
—can make some students more comfortable because that's the way they studied English in their country.

Some Disadvantages: Translation:

—is impossible for some words.
—can cause students to become involved in too much contrastive analysis, thereby delaying the ability to *think* in English and sometimes focusing on the differences between the two languages.
—affords some students the opportunity to ask too many inappropriate questions about grammar.
—can shift the focus of the class from English to the correctness of teachers performance in their language.
—can foster discussion of correctness of the native language and even animosity in cases of dialectal differences.
—encourages some teachers to teach the book and nothing else (the best ESL materials are seldom in a bilingual format; they're appropriate for all students).
—may encourage teachers to prepare for class by making sure they can translate every word and structure if necessary. A more valuable use of time would be experimenting with and perfecting ESL techniques.
—can become a crutch, even a roadblock, in learning English. Many will expect it of you all the time.
—means they really don't have to *listen* to your English because a translation is expected. If it doesn't come, they'll be put out with *you*.
—often means that the class ends up talking ABOUT the language and not IN the language.
—can assure you that the students understand a word but in no way guarantees that they can use it when they need it in context.
—takes away from the time that *students* should be speaking in English. For some, the ESL class may be the only time they really have an opportunity to speak it in a protected environment.
—may discourage and frustrate some students who know that they haven't come to hear their native language spoken, that they desparately need to be able to understand and speak English, and need all the help and practice they can get.

Obviously, there are valid advantages and disadvantages in using translation just as there are pros and cons in every approach and method. However, putting aside teacher conveniences and time savers, what is it your students need most? Do they need to understand every vocabulary item and structure and to be able to recite rules or do they need to be able to protect and defend themselves and market their skills in English in order to upgrade employment and become more productive members of society?   *TN 6/78*

(Excerpted from the *Illinois ESL Vessel*, Jan/Feb 1978)

ADULT LANGUAGE LEARNING VARIABLES THAT AFFECT EFFICIENT INSTRUCTION

By David Liston
Smithsonian Institute

With the coming of "cultural pluralism", shifts of educational perspective, and the larger age span of adult education, the need for adult language teaching has grown rapidly in this country. We teach adults in high school and college, in English and foreign language classes. We teach language to foreigners and immigrants, military people, people in government programs, businessmen, public clerks, scientists, doctors and nurses, shopkeepers, and government representatives. The adult language teacher is reaching out to borrow from many disciplines to teach adults a language more effectively.

Language teaching is traditionally based on a child-learning model because most people learn their language in their early years, before puberty. The adult, it is commonly believed, learns similarly. But child and adult differ greatly, and the traditional methodology for teaching children is not appropriate for adults. The adult, for example, usually learns a second language as an adult, with greater difficulty and conscious effort. An adult teaching/learning strategy needs to identify particular adult language learning factors that operate specifically for adults. With such a set of factors the adult language teacher could deal with adult learner needs and identify characteristics in those factors which would aid in finding appropriate methodology for successful adult language teaching.

Over the last ten years contributors to language learning journals have identified a number of adult language learning variables that influence the speed and success of second language learning in adults. These variables are listed below. Teachers can use these variables by evaluating their particular teaching needs, finding strengths and weaknesses of their present methodology, and planning approaches that might bring more effectiveness to the teaching/learning situation. A good flexibility of methods, then, is a great asset for the teacher if the needs of the learners are to be adequately dealt with.

About half of the variables identified are fixed characteristics of the learner present in varying degrees in the learning situation. As significant variables for language learning, the teacher should be interested in applying them to determine to what degree the learning situation is affected. The teacher can reinforce these learner-determined variables through the use of confidence, counselling, and praising in the classroom.

The other half of these variables are attitudinal and situational according to the learning circumstance. As such, the teacher has more ability to determine them and can manipulate them more easily to effect a successful teaching/learning situation. It must be clear that the teaching/learning situation is more dependent on the learning portion, and the teaching portion is more adaptive for successful instruction.

The personality variables of the learner are the most widely-ranging and probably the most influential to the teaching situation, especially when there are negative aspects present. The more prominently displayed the need for learning a new language is in the classroom, for example, the more conscientious and efficient becomes the teaching/learning experience. Even minor changes in confidence and self-assurance greatly alter performance in a second language. Underlying these, the will to learn (and change), and persevere to succeed, are variables that, when low, disrupt the situation simply by having little desire to continue learning be a negative influence.

All these variables have been found to be relevant to successful teaching of languages to adults in one circumstance or another. Some or all may apply to another circumstance. Also, these variables are subject to further definition, extension, and investigation. The pursuit of effective teaching begins with perceptive, critical analysis of need and circumstances. To reach the learner, a judicious use of flexibility to match need and method that fulfills that need is effective. By reviewing the adult language learning variables below, the teacher should have better success and control in evaluating the adult language learner's needs and selecting an appropriate method of instruction.

Student-genetic-biologic

a specific intelligence and learning capacity
brain patterns using logic, categorization and analogy
maturation and fixation of first-language usage
a maturing self concept
a need for meaningfulness
a need to communicate

Experiential

a maturing adult perspective and feeling of responsibility
a functional first-language ability
a need for the practical and the timely

Educationally-experiential

a preference for formal approaches
first/second language (and usually cultural) educational experiences and preferences
situational/sequential preference for ordering materials
deductive/inductive preference for learning

Situational-language-specific

first/second language (and usually cultural) differences and degree of difference
positive and negative language and culture transfer
prestige, acceptability, pressure, and demand on first and second language and dialects used
academic first-language proficiency
America monolingually, monoculturally oriented by tradition

Educational-specific

class format
class composition and size
teacher's role in class

Attitudinal-personality variables

motivation and need for learning
self-assurance and confidence
perseverance and will to continue
functional learning/memory/study skills

TN 9/78

BURNOUT IN TEACHERS OF SECOND LANGUAGES

By Christine Grosse
Eastern Michigan University

The problem of burnout has been well documented as it relates to the helping professions—social work, nursing, teaching, but the relationship of burnout to the language teacher in particular has not been studied or reported. Burnout is defined as the exhaustion that results from excessive drain on a person's energy and resources because of overwhelming problems. Victims of burnout feel frustrated and cynical about their work and gradually lose their effectiveness on the job. Consequently, burnout seriously affects the productivity of many professionals under stress, including foreign language teachers (Foster 1980: 24).

Burnout is a relatively new term for an old problem. The introduction of the word is attributed to Dr. Herbert Freudenberger, a New York psychologist who first used it about ten years ago to describe the condition of emotionally, physically and mentally drained social workers who worked for extended periods of time with drug addicts (1975:3). The term then spread to other helping professions and eventually to all professions where people work under pressure.

No one knows how many language teachers suffer from burnout, or how many eventually leave the profession because of it. Most foreign language teachers, however, have seen the effects of burnout on colleagues, if not on themselves. For a variety of reasons, which will be described below, they are especially susceptible to burnout.

Cherniss (1978) found burnout to be related to a negative change in job-related attitudes and behavior (Pagel and Price 1980:85). Burnout among foreign language teachers can, I think, be reduced through the development of positive attitudes about subject, students, colleagues, and self which alleviate many causes of stress.

Why Stress is High on Foreign Language Teachers: 1) Parents, administrators, and students may have unrealistic expectations for results; 2) Teachers may set unrealistic goals for classes to achieve; 3) Communication is a problem in language classes because of students' limited proficiency; 4) Second language programs traditionally are afforded low status and priority by parents and administrators; 5) There are many qualified teachers for a limited number of jobs; 6) Many professionals suffer from job insecurity, holding temporary positions with low pay and no benefits.

The stress on language teachers is acute for several reasons. First, parents, students, administrators, and even teachers may have unrealistic expectations for progress of the students. Many people are unaware that language skills take years to acquire and are disappointed if students do not achieve near fluency in months. Teachers may be anxious to see evidence of progress in their students and consequently are frustrated when students do not achieve the desired results.

Another source of frustration for the language teacher is the problem of communication in the language class. Because of the students' limited proficiency in the target language, teachers expend considerable energy trying to understand the students' attempts at communication. It is also difficult for the teachers to make themselves understood by the students; indeed the teacher must often resort to pantomime, facial expression, or other quickly invented alternative means of communication. In the sense that elementary and intermediate students are handicapped by a limited knowledge of the second language, the language teacher faces a situation similar to that of a special education teacher. Both teachers need patience, flexibility, and realistic expectations in order to minimize frustration on the job.

The low status and priority given to a school's foreign language program are other problems that language teachers frequently face. Despite Presidential recognition of the importance of foreign language study, many administrators continue to eliminate foreign language requirements from the curriculum and trim budgetary allocations for foreign language departments. The attitudes of administrators toward second language classes are sometimes unfavorable because of certain misconceptions. A dean in the College of Arts and Science from a state university declared his belief that foreign languages were easier to teach than other subjects such as chemistry or economics. This attitude sounded irrational until he explained the basis for his opinion. He had once taken a Spanish-for-Faculty course that gave no tests and no homework, apparently catering to the time limitations of faculty members. He assumed all language courses were similar to the one he had taken and justified budgetary decisions unfavorable to the language department on the basis of his one atypical experience. Language teachers should be aware of possible bias in administrators in order to face and correct possible misconceptions about the profession.

Another factor that contributes to the relatively low status of language teachers is the excess supply of qualified teachers and scarcity of jobs. As a result of supply exceeding demand, schools and universities can hire language teachers at low salaries and on a part-time rather than full-time basis. Part-time contracts may be renewable from term to term, or from year to year, and often do not provide any fringe benefits to the teacher. Because of low salaries, language teachers may work at several different schools—teaching mornings, afternoons, and evenings to support themselves. After years of working at various schools on a part-time, no benefit basis, language teachers may feel discouraged and lose self-esteem. Yet they know if they quit, there will be others who will gladly take their place. Long hours, low pay, and job insecurity contribute to the hazard of burnout among language teachers.

Clearly a number of complex factors are responsible for burnout in language teachers. Various techniques can be used to develop positive attitudes toward subject, students, colleagues, and self. Not all techniques will be suitable for every teacher; the teacher should choose those of most value and interest to the individual.

How to Develop a Positive Attitude Toward Your Subject: 1) Maintain your interest in the subject by varying materials, techniques, and course levels; 2) Exchange ideas with colleagues; 3) Set realistic goals to achieve in class; 4) Stimulate your interest in a subject by learning more about it.

One of the signs of burnout is loss of interest and enthusiasm for the subject. Any teacher can go stale for a variety of reasons including frequent repetition of level, subject, and materials. It is not easy to stay fresh and enthusiastic for the 27th rendition of Dialog 6. Yet it is essential for language teachers to stay excited about their subject to be effective teachers.

Variety in texts, materials, approaches and class levels can help a teacher stay interested and challenged by a particular subject. If it is not feasible to vary the texts or levels taught, it is always possible to use new techniques which can be drawn from one's colleagues. Colleagues can provide a rich source of new ideas to be shared for mutual inspiration and classroom innovation.

Setting short-term goals to achieve in the classroom is another way teachers can maintain their interest in their subject. The goals can be scheduled on a daily, weekly, and/or monthly basis. The teacher works to achieve a specific goal, such as mastery of the past tenses of five irregular verbs by 90% of the class and enlists the students' interest and competitive spirit to achieve the goal within the specified time period.

At times teachers are faced with the problem of teaching an area within a subject that simply does not interest them; yet they must teach it. In this case, the language teacher should read more about the subject, or talk about it with a colleague who likes the subject. By learning more about a disliked subject you can stimulate your interest, or at least enhance your tolerance for it.

How to Develop a Positive Attitude Toward Students: 1) Get to know your students as individuals; 2) Show interest and concern for the students; 3) Be sensitive to students' needs and goals.

The best way to develop positive attitudes toward students is to get to know them as individuals. In this respect, language teachers have a distinct advantage over other teachers. Since the very essence of the language classroom is communication, opportunities for personal communication between student and teacher are many. At the beginning of each class, the teacher can take a few minutes to ask the students about their activities, interests, and backgrounds. Throughout the class the teacher can insert personal questions and references in dialogs, drills, homework, and quizzes to add interest and life to the class, and to obtain further information about the students. Eventually the students become individuals to the teacher and to each other.

The need for a teacher to take an interest in students does not imply the need for friendship between student and teacher (Abinum 1977:297). The student-teacher relationship can function effectively on many levels and should not be restricted by a narrow definition such as friendship. As Hendley observes, to limit teacher-student roles by strictly defining them "limits the possibility for mutual learning" (1979:73). However, a teacher's concern and interest in the student is important both as a source of renewal and an inspiration for the teacher and as a source of motivation and confidence for the student.

How to Develop a Positive Attitude Toward Colleagues and Program: 1) Be supportive of colleagues; 2) Keep lines of communication open to make constructive suggestions; 3) Be proud of colleagues and the language program.

In the interest of avoiding burnout, language teachers should be mutually supportive. That is, they should recognize each other's achievements and praise them, rather than look for weak points to criticize. If a colleague has a problem to discuss, fellow teachers should listen and offer possible solutions. The work atmosphere is much more enjoyable and conducive to productivity when colleagues respect one another. The language program also benefits from the teachers' positive attitudes toward one another, gaining a sense of unity, harmony, and pride.

It is important to keep lines of communication open between colleagues and administrators in order to quickly clear up misunderstandings before they lead to frustration. Teachers should feel they can offer constructive suggestions to the administration with the confidence their suggestions will be heard and weighed. Administrators should ask for teacher input into decisions affecting the language program. Thus, language teachers feel they can contribute in a positive way to their work environment and that their suggestions can make a difference. Such participation in the decision-making process helps language teachers develop positive attitudes toward themselves and the language program.

How to Develop a Positive Attitude Toward Yourself: 1) Have confidence in your abilities; 2) Keep a proper perspective on your problems; 3) Face problems realistically, assess them, and seek a viable solution.

Ultimately to avoid burnout language teachers must believe in their own competence. If teachers think positively about their own capabilities, they will likely be capable provided they are also realistic in their thinking. When problems do occur, teachers should keep them in perspective and face them objectively. After an assessment of the problem is made, the teacher should search for possible solutions. Often it is helpful to talk over a problem with colleagues and/or administrators who may be able to help find a solution. Thus a teacher of languages can work confidently toward resolution of a problem before it leads to burnout.

Burnout is not an inevitable hazard of language teaching. The negative effects of burnout can be reduced substantially with the cultivation of positive attitudes toward subject, students, colleagues and self. Hopefully increased awareness of the problem of burnout and ways to overcome it will lead to the reduction of burnout in the language teaching profession.   *TN 2/82*

REFERENCES

Abinum, Joseph. 1977. "Teaching and personal relationships." *Educational Theory* 27, 3: 297-303.
Cherniss, C. 1978. "Recent research and theory on job stress and burnout in the helping professions." Mimeographed paper. Ann Arbor: University of Michigan, Department of Psychology.
Freudenberger, Herbert J. 1975. *The staff burnout syndrome*. Washington, D.C.: Drug Abuse Council.
Hendley, Brian P. 1979. "Teaching and personal relationships: a response to Joseph Abinum." *Educational Theory* 29, 1: 73-75.
Pagel, Susan and Joseph Price. 1980. "Strategies to alleviate teacher stress." *The Pointer* 24, 2: 88-94.

SECOND LANGUAGE ACQUISITION AND ACQUISITION OF ENGLISH BY THE DEAF

by Gerald P. Berent
National Technical Institute for the Deaf
Rochester Institute of Technology

Many linguists, psychologists, teachers of English, and others concerned with language remain unaware of the similarities between second language acquisition and the acquisition of language by prelingually deaf individuals. Deafness and the language deprivation which results lead to language problems which are not unlike those of other hearing language learners. Because of the similarities ESL methodology is often employed in teaching English to the deaf (see for example Goldberg and Bordman 1974), and ESL proficiency exams have been advocated for use with the deaf (Bochner 1977). There are accordingly career opportunities in deaf education for people with ESL training and experience, and there are vast unexplored areas for research into language and deafness.

Albertini (1981) provides an overview of English language teaching and the deaf, addressing similarities and differences between teaching English to the deaf and the field of ESL. He discusses the characteristics of those hearing-impaired individuals in the U.S. who are generally in need of special language instruction. Included in this group are many of the college-level students who attend the National Technical Institute for the Deaf (NTID) at Rochester Institute of Technology. Albertini describes this type of student and reports on some of the innovative language research taking place at NTID. Crandall (1978) gives an assessment of the reading and writing skills of deaf students and proposes a model of English instruction, currently followed at NTID, based on five levels of proficiency.

Quigley and King (1980) report on research into the syntactic abilities of deaf individuals. They provide a description of the distinctive syntactic constructions found in the language of deaf students and conclude, on the basis of a review of the acquisition literature, that the same distinctive structures occur also among other language learners, primarily individuals learning English as a second language. An important difference between deaf learners and other learners of English that Quigley and King note is that the deaf learners' syntactic errors often occur in profusion and persist into adulthood. Indeed, in my experience with both types of learners, I have found that prelingually deaf adults often do not improve in their language proficiency as rapidly as adult speakers of other languages. Nevertheless, they do make significant gains.

Free writing samples provide a clear picture of the kinds of syntactic errors made by deaf individuals who are in need of further language instruction. NTID administers a written language test as part of its English placement procedure. The test is scored following guidelines set forth in Crandall (1980). Students watch a five-minute nonverbal cartoon after which they are instructed to write a composition about what they have just seen. Errors are scored on a ten-point scale roughly as follows: 10 (no errors), 9 (spelling and punctuation errors), 8 (inflectional and article errors), 7 (derivational errors), 6 (function word errors), 5 (content word errors), 4 (word order and major constituent omission errors, 3 (multiple type-4 errors), 2 (listing of single words), 1 (listing of unrecognizable words). Each sentence receives the score of the most serious (lowest number) error in that sentence. The entire composition receives as its score the average of the scores of the first ten sentences.

The following anonymous writing sample, which received a score of 10, is one student's interpretation of one of the cartoons.

> I saw a cartoon about a man who seemed to have problems because he always had a black cloud hanging over him. This man's name was Mr. Koumal. At the beginning of the cartoon Mr. Koumal was writing a suicide note; next he attempted to blow his brains out. However, he failed, because the gun jammed up and he managed to shoot his whiskey bottle instead. Koumal keeps fouling up on his suicide attempts, trying harder and harder each successive time. The reason he stopped trying to kill himself is indeed a strange one. It happened that a thief holds him up and threatens him with his life. After that incident Mr. Koumal is happy. I thought it was a strange film, but it had a moral. The moral is, in my opinion, some people do not value life until someone else tries to take it away.

The next sample received a score in the range of 7. Note some of the derivational errors: **depression** for **depressed, robbery** for **robber, peace** for **peaceful**, etc.

> The man name is Mr. Koumal, was very depression after what he had done with himself. He tried to suicide by jumped in the deep water and drank alot of whiskey and smoking the cigarettes. It never happened to cause him to die. He had tried to think of anything that would kill him. He walked with depression among dark place. The robbery man appeared and had a gun to him. Mr. Koumal scared when he saw the gun pointing to him. So he gave the bad guy alot of money, value of watch, and anything what the had in his pants; after he dead then went to heaven and felt so peace. He is happy now in peace forever. The butterflies fly around him to cheer him up.

The final anonymous sample received a score in the range of 5. Note some of the more serious structural errors.

> The film was about "Mr. Kaumal death face." Mr. Kaumal tried to kill by himself, He took his gun on his head. At this time was he thinked, "Should I die" but happened he was mistake shot to the glass was broken. Later, he tried think of the other ways to death, finally, he put the rope, nail and hammer on his wall to died be a hang up but, other his negihbor heard that what he did, the negihbor were broken the wall prevent him, then Mr. Kaumal was other try jump off the bridge, he jumped but were to boat came, he were at boat. Mr. Kaumal still can't be death. One man who is robber tried him got money, Mr. Kaumal gave him everything body off. Mr. Kaumal was happy because, he have not nothing at all.

The foregoing samples reveal syntactic (and other) errors not unlike those produced by second language learners. But there are likewise similarities among deaf and hearing learners in the comprehension of syntactic structures. Because of such similar comprehension errors, Quigley and King (1980) conclude that deaf learners are probably employing the same strategies as other language learners in the processing of syntax.

This assumption is supported in Berent (1983), where I analyzed the judgements of adult second language learners and prelingually deaf adults on infinitive complement structures. I found that, in assigning a logical subject to an infinitive, both the deaf and hearing learners made the same kinds of errors in roughly the same order of difficulty. In a sentence such as the following, the logical subject is the noun closer to the infinitive: **John told Bill to leave.** Some main verbs exhibit an exception to this nearness principle: **John promised Bill to leave. John asked Bill what to do.** And passive reverses the normal tendency of regular verbs: **Bill was told by John to leave.** Both groups were using the same strategy — an overextension of the nearness principle — when they interpreted infinitive complement structures incorrectly.

The same relative order of difficulty was explained in terms of relative degrees of complexity as predicted by markedness theory in linguistics. For example, both groups had more trouble with sentences containing **ask** than with sentences containing **promise**. The reason for this is that **ask** is not consistent in its behavior. When it occurs with a **wh**-word as in the example above, it violates the nearness principle; but when **ask** occurs without a **wh**-word, it follows the nearness principle: **John asked Bill to leave.** The verb **promise** is consistent in its violation of the nearness principle and is accordingly easier (acquired earlier) than **ask**, which is inconsistent.

Interestingly, first language studies report the same relative order of difficulty with verbs like **promise** and **ask** and explain the difficulty also in terms of markedness and an overextension of the nearness principle. Thus three groups — children, hearing adult speakers of other languages, and deaf adults — are applying the same comprehension strategy in the acquisition of infinitive complement structures.

Despite differences in degree or persistence, the language problems of prelingually deaf learners of English resemble those of second language learners in many respects. In other respects deaf learners resemble first language learners (cf. Bochner 1978) and, as has been shown in Berent (1983), the three groups behave similarly relative to certain phenomena. For those involved in English language teaching or in language acquisition research, language and deafness remains fertile ground for exploration and experimentation. ⊕

References

Albertini, J.A. 1981. "English Language Teaching and the Deaf: Questions We Are Asking at NTID." *The Linguistic Reporter* 23.5.
Berent, G. P. 1983. "Control Judgements by Deaf Adults and by Second Language Learners." To appear in *Language Learning* 33.1.
Bochner, J. 1977. "Assessing the Language Proficiency of Young Deaf Adults." *Teaching English to the Deaf* 4.2.
———. 1978. "Error, Anomaly, and Variation in the English of Deaf Individuals." *Language and Speech* 21.
Crandall, K. E. 1978. "Reading and Writing Skills and the Deaf Adolescent." *Volta Review* 80.5.
———. 1980. "Written Language Scoring Procedures for Grammatical Correctness According to Reader Intelligibility." Experimental Edition, NTID.
Goldberg, J. P., and M. B. Bordman. 1974. "English Language Instruction for the Hearing-Impaired: An adaptation of ESL Methodology." *TESOL Quarterly* 8.3.
Quigley, S. P. and C. M. King. 1980. "An Invited Article: Syntactic Performance of Hearing Impaired and Normal Hearing Individuals." *Applied Psycholinguistics* 1.4.

TN 4/83

STANDARDS, ACCREDITATION, CERTIFICATION: DEFINING TERMS

by Carol J. Kreidler
Georgetown University

The words *standards, accreditation, certification, license, endorsement,* and *program approval* have been circulating in the ESOL field in the United States for a number of years now. They come up in discussions of teachers and their need for training to deal with the limited English proficiency students in their classrooms and in discussions of whether an ESL program meets what we think is a standard of good practice, whether it lives up to its advertising, whether the program is fair in its employment practices, or how the ESL program ranks compared with ESL programs at other institutions. The purpose of this *Standard Bearer* column is

to discuss these terms as they are used in the United States and their relationship to each other, as well as to describe TESOL's work in these areas. If people who are working in other parts of the world find it useful to have definitions of similar terms as they apply to their educational systems, I invite you to write to me. I am planning a column on the British system to appear soon.

To begin with, the words *standards, accreditation* and *program approval* all apply to programs while *certification, license* or *endorsement* apply to individual teachers. Programs are accredited; teachers are certified. Let us

begin with individuals and move to programs.

Certification. Certification requirements are set by the states. For public school certification, requirements usually consist of a specified number of college credits in general subjects and in general education, materials and methodology along with a specified number of credits in the field(s) of specialization. Often successful completion of a course of study at a college or university leads to the initial certification of a teacher. Some states mandate the number of credit hours in college subjects, while others use tests such as the National Teacher Examination. In some states there is free-standing certification granted on the basis of classes taken (including ESL or bilingual education) in the college certification program. More frequently there is an add-on *endorsement* or add-on *license* which usually requires courses in linguistics, ESL methodology, cross cultural studies and another language. At present at least 16 states and the District of Columbia have both ESL and bilingual education certificates or endorsements. At least 17 plus D.C. have ESL certificates or endorsements and at least 26 plus D.C. have bilingual education certificates or endorsements.

Dorothy Waggoner, in a draft paper distributed at Toronto TESOL, reports that one-half of all public school teachers in the United States in 1980-81 had immediate or previous experience teaching young people whose home language is other than English and who had limited English proficiency. However, only a quarter of the teachers who had limited English proficiency students in their classes were teaching English as a second language in 1980-81. About 40 percent of those teachers had taken a university course or inservice training to prepare them to teach English as a second language.[1] From statistics like these the need for certification, or at least endorsement, is obvious.

Some states with recently-developed certificates or endorsements have limited the effectiveness of certification with "grandfathering." This is the practice of permitting "unqualified" (according to the standards set by the new certificate) ESL teachers to continue in their jobs, usually for a specific amount of time, after new certification requirements are put into effect. During this time they may be encouraged to complete courses for certification. This protects the teacher who has been teaching ESL, whether or not he or she is qualified.

TESOL has worked with affiliates that want to establish certification in their states for at least eight years. Most recently Gina Cantoni-Harvey, former chair of TESOL's Schools and Universities Coordination Committee, published *Nine Steps to Establishing Certification for English as a Second Language in Your State* (available from the TESOL office). This is a booklet of materials which includes resources and names of resource persons, background materials, and, most important, specific things to do to begin to initiate certification in a state. The process of getting ESL certification in a state which does not have it is a long one. TESOL is ready to help.

Certificates. Having a certificate is different from having certification. There are many places offering professional preparation courses which grant certificates for completion of a specified number of courses or hours. The hours spent in obtaining such a certificate can be from six in a summer session on up to twenty-four. The value of a certificate thus obtained depends entirely on what an employer wants to make it.

Accreditation. In his book *Self-Study Processes: A Guide for Postsecondary Institutions* H. R. Kells defines accreditation as "a voluntary, non-governmental process conducted by postsecondary institutions to accomplish at least two things—to attempt to hold one another accountable on a periodic basis to live up to stated, appropriate institutional or program goals; and to assess the extent to which the institution or program meets established standards. The major purposes of the process are to foster improvement and to identify institutions and programs that seem to be achieving stated goals and that seem to meet the agreed upon standards."[2]

Kells divides accreditation into institutional and specialized accreditation and characterizes them as follows: institutional accreditation deals with the entire institution, focusing somewhat on general, qualitative standards, with heavy emphasis on ascertaining whether an institution appears to be achieving its goals and is functioning in a way that will permit it to continue to do so; specialized accreditation, on the other hand, deals with programs, relying heavily on standards, some of which may be quantitative, while focusing somewhat on goal achievement. Emphasis is more on ascertaining which programs meet standards of good practice.

Program approval. Program approval is basically another term for accreditation. The Ad-Hoc Committee on Employment Issues (TESOL 1981) looked into the accreditation process as did the Committee on Professional Standards. Both groups concluded that accreditation was impractical. Disadvantages include excessive amounts of time and money; problems regarding the legality of issuing or denying accreditation to ESL programs; and difficulties in securing the cooperation of educational institutions to add yet another accrediting organization to what many institutions see as an already burdensome list. For these reasons the accreditation process is becoming more and more a self-study process. TESOL will go the route of program self-evaluation.

Standards. *The Random House Dictionary of the English Language* states, "A standard is an authoritative principle or rule that usually implies a model or pattern for guidance, by comparison with which the quantity, excellence, correctness, etc., of other things may be determined." TESOL already has standards or *Guidelines for the Certification and Preparation of Teachers of English to Speakers of Other Languages in the United States*—one of the sources of information mentioned in *Nine Steps.*

Now TESOL's Committee on Professional Standards is trying to establish standards for programs—not just postsecondary programs—but all ESOL programs. However, because we are one organization with representatives of many kinds of programs, we feel it is necessary to have certain core statements for any program and specific statements that fit each type of program.

There are still those who believe that program self-study alone is not enough and that we need to police our profession and to let everyone know which programs are the best by giving a "seal of approval" to programs which meet our standards. In contrast, there are others who believe that program self-study is for the purpose of program self-improvement, and that granting recognition does not coincide with the goals of self-study. It is still too early to know what TESOL's final decision will be on this.

Regardless, the Committee on Professional Standards will be presenting the TESOL standards to existing accrediting bodies, to local, state and federal education agencies and officials, and to other professional organizations for their endorsement.

We would like to solicit your views on the core standards, and your ideas as to what should be included in the specific standards. For copies of *Draft II of the Core Standards* write to Carol J. Kreidler, School of Languages and Linguistics, Georgetown University, Washington, D.C. 20057. If you feel that there is something we might forget to include, please write to us. Remember that TESOL decided to set standards as a result of work in the area of employment concerns. Let me assure you that the specific standards will include statements on employment issues. *TN 8/83*

Footnotes

[1] The figures are from the 1980-81 Teachers Language Skills Survey conducted by Inter-American Research Associates, Inc., for the Office of Bilingual Education and Minority Languages Affairs, U.S. Department of Education.

[2] H. R. Kells. *Self-Study Processes: A Guide for Postsecondary Institutions.* Washington, D.C.: American Council on Education, 1980, p. 9.

COLLECTIVE BARGAINING: AN UPDATE

by Linda Tobash
The English Language Center
LaGuardia Community College, CUNY

Professionalism. In the field of TESOL that word conjures up images of scholarly endeavors, educational ideals, meeting instructional commitments, fairness in the classroom, and a sensitivity to students' needs. However, where does fairness in terms of economic matters belong when one speaks of professionalism? Likewise, how does one address the areas of job security, salary, benefits, contracts, workloads, and grievance? Recognizing economic concerns as an integral component in any definition of professionalism, WATESOL submitted a resolution to the Legislative Assembly during the 1980 San Francisco TESOL Conference requesting study in the following areas: benefits, contracts, salaries, job security, grievance procedures, bargaining organizations, program approval, management training, job market survey and lobby-

ing. This resolution was subsequently passed.

The passing of this resolution signaled that economic opportunity, along with academic growth and freedom, was an issue which the profession and the organization had to address. TESOL set for itself the task of gathering, compiling and disseminating information. In 1981 *Reports of the Ad Hoc Committee on Employment Issues*, which addressed the above areas, was published. This publication is available from TESOL. The purpose of this article then is to share with you information dealing with collective bargaining and bargaining organizations. This will not be the first time such information has been found in the *TESOL Newsletter.* This column, "The Standard Bearer," was specially created to address employment concerns aiming both to disseminate in-

formation and to provide the membership with a means by which it could react and voice concerns. This article will hopefully add to the information already shared and in some cases summarize it.

The words "union" and "unionization" (the term bargaining organization is a euphemism) cause many people, especially educators, to cringe. Michael Lehmann, President of the Union of the University of San Francisco in his address at the 10th Annual Convention (New York, 1982) for the National Center for the Study of Collective Bargaining in Higher Education and the Professions (NCSCBHEP), stated that faculty prefer to be called professionals, not employees. However, in truth, they can never own the business; they are employees. He further stated that governance vehicles such as the university senate, committees and peer review, which are really advisory in nature, give the impression of shared authority. However, in reality they only give shared responsibility. In light of this growing sentiment, there has been a greater movement in education toward collective bargaining as a viable and sometimes the only means to improve one's job situation. Organizations such as the American Federation of Teachers (AFT), the National Education Association (NEA), American Federation of State, City, and Municipal Employees (AFSCME), and the American Association of University Professors (AAUP) have been primary to this movement.

In short, collective bargaining is the system whereby a third party—a union, professional organization, or a specially appointed mediator—meets with employers to present and negotiate employee concerns, hopefully producing a better working situation. This third party acts as a representative for a "unit," a group of people who share common employment interests and conditions. The National Labor Relations Act (NLRA), which was instituted in 1935 to sanction the right of employees to unite and negotiate, sets guidelines as to what constitutes an "appropriate" bargaining unit and details conditions for bargaining. The National Labor Relations Board (NLRB) determines if a unit is indeed "appropriate." *A Guide to Basic Law and Procedures under the National Labor Relations Act*, published by the U.S. Government Printing Office, describes in laymen's language the Act as it pertains to the rights of employees, collective bargaining and representation, unfair labor practices on the part of employers and labor organizations, decertification procedures (literally, getting rid of an existing union), and enforcement of the Act. Private institutions fall under the NLRA; however, public universities or state systems are subject to state laws which vary from state to state.

In the October and December 1982 issues of the *TESOL Newsletter*, Myra Shulman and Salvatrice DeLuca explain in detail how the English Language Institute of American University, Washington, D.C., went through the NLRB process and successfully became an independent bargaining organization, ELIFA, which could negotiate its own contract. Some of the highlights of the agreement they negotiated include: formal recognition of ELIFA, a procedure for increasing or decreasing full-time positions, a job title of "language specialist," a step table for wages, wage increases averaging 13% for full-time employees and ranging from 40%-65% for part-time, paid sick leave for full and part-time, special leaves of absences with pay for full and part-time, a clearly stated substitution policy where the University provides and compensates substitutes, paternal and maternal leave, seniority scheduling, grievance procedures for full and part-time, and binding arbitration (reported at the Toronto TESOL Conference).

The process of establishing a group as a bargaining unit is actually extremely complex but to outline it briefly:

1. A group must become an "appropriate" bargaining unit as determined by the NLRB or state laws. In the case of educators, one of the criteria is that they be classified as non-managerial.
2. Thirty percent of the employees must sign a petition which is filed with the NLRB or the Public Employees Relations Board.
3. A hearing is held to define who is to be included in a unit, in other words, who

can vote in the election of a representative.
4. Given that the unit has been found "appropriate", a secret ballot is held to determine if a union is desired and if so which one. This "representation election" can take place at any time.
5. If a majority of those voting go for a union, a union is formed.
6. Members are polled to decide collective bargaining demands.
7. Representatives meet with employers to start collective bargaining negotiations for contracts.

This entire process can become quite lengthy as seen by the situation in the California State University College System (CSU). After four years of intense campaigning, 80% of the vote in the secret ballot advocated unionization. However, neither of the competing agents, the University Professors of California/AFT or the Congress of Faculty Associations/NEA/AAUP, secured the necessary number of votes needed to become the bargaining representative. This led to a run-off election where again the votes were too close; thus, no bargaining agent for the entire system was designated.

Probably the most famous case and one which has had the greatest impact on university employees' ability to bargain collectively was the U.S. Supreme Court's decision in *NLRB v. Yeshiva University*, 444 U.S. 672, 1980. The Court held that the entire faculty at Yeshiva was managerial and thus not entitled to bargain collectively under the protection of the National Labor Relations Act. As reported in the August/September 1982 *NCSCBHEP Newsletter* (vol. 10, no. 3), since that time a great number of Yeshiva-like claims have been made. By September of 1982 nearly 50% of private institutions where collective bargaining activity was taking place had made Yeshiva-like claims challenging the right of faculty to organize and bargain collectively under the NLR Act. Indeed, the ramifications of this decision have been felt quite strongly. *The Chronicle of Higher Education*, a weekly newspaper which is a good source for current trends in collective bargaining in higher education across the U.S., reported in its April 28, 1982 issue that although faculty-union membership was at an "all-time high" with more than 157,000 faculty members belonging to certified collective bargaining units, in 1981 only *two* full-time faculty bargaining unions were certified. This is the lowest number in 10 years. The *Yeshiva* decision is without a doubt a contributing factor. The *NCSCBHEP Newsletter* contains updates on the institutions being affected by the *Yeshiva* decision.

Unionization is not the answer to everyone's problems; sometimes it only provides partial solutions. Indeed at times employees are literally stuck with a bargaining representative which does not meet their needs. "A collective bargaining relationship once begun, need not continue forever," say W. Krupman and G. I. Rasin in their pamphlet, *Decertification: Removing the Shroud* (available from Commerce Clearing House, Chicago, Illinois). This pamphlet discusses the extent of current decertification activity, NLRB election procedures, the extent to which employers can lawfully become involved in employee efforts to decertify an incumbent union and when they can do so. The process for decertifying an incumbent union parallels that of certifying one; however, there are some very important time stipulations:

1. Thirty percent of employees must sign a petition stating that they no longer want to be represented by the incumbent

union. This petition should be filed 90 days before but no later than 60 days before the contract ends. If it is filed at other times, it is ineffective.
2. The NLRB holds a hearing to determine who can vote in the election.
3. The election is held.

The employer cannot initiate any decertification procedure; however, the employer can answer questions and once the petition has been filed and accepted by the NLRB, the employer can (but only at this time) legally campaign for a "No Union" vote.

Many issues are not being addressed both at the bargaining table and in the courts. Part-time issues are beginning to be emphasized in negotiations. The Supreme Court of Pennsylvania passed a ruling on the right of adjuncts to organize. The State University of New York has pro-rata part-time employees included in its negotiating unit. Pro-rata part-timers' fees and benefits are pro-rated according to the various functions they perform; they are members of the negotiating unit and are covered by the negotiated agreement. Nonetheless, part-time concerns are generally viewed ambivalently by unions today.

For those of you interested in collective bargaining, the Committee on Professional Standards has a subcommittee on bargaining organizations whose task is to gather and disseminate information. If you have any information to share or if you have any questions, please send them to:

Linda Tobash
The English Language Center
LaGuardia Community College
31-10 Thomson Avenue
Long Island City, NY 11101

I cannot guarantee any answers but can share any information we have.

There are quite a few sources one can refer to regarding collective bargaining. Some additional sources of information broken down by agency follow:

AFT. AFL-CIO: 11 Dupont Circle, N.W., Washington, D.C. 20036:

- *Handbook on the Structure and Function of College Unions*
- *Hard Times, Values, and Academic Unions*
- *How Collective Bargaining Works*
- *Statement on Part-Time Faculty Employment*
- *Statement on Tenure*
- *Tenure, Unionization and Collective Bargaining in American Higher Education: The Recent Experience*

Bureau of National Affairs, Customer Service Division, 910 DeCoverly Road, Rockville, Maryland 20850:

- *How to Bring a Case Before the NLRB*
- *Labor Relations in Higher Education: A Special Report*, 1982

Josey Bass, Inc., 433 California Street, San Francisco, California 94101:

- *Faculty Bargaining and Public Education*, J. Garbariao, et. al, 1977
- *Unions on Campus: A National Study of the Consequences of Faculty Bargaining*, 1972

National Center for the Study of Collective Bargaining in Higher Education and the Professions, Baruch College, 17 Lexington Avenue, New York, NY 10010: This is one of the best sources and has the most up-to-date information.

TESOL is a member of this organization.

- *Bibliography of Collective Bargaining in Higher Education and the Professions*
- *Contract Development in Higher Education: Faculty Collective Bargaining* by J.M. Douglas, 1980.
- *Directory of Faculty Contracts and Bargaining Agents in Public and Private Institutions (issued annually)*
- *Faculty and Administration: Five Issues in*

Academic Collective Bargaining by M.K. Chandler and D. Julius, 1979

University Research Center, 121 Adams, Chicago, Illinois 60603:

- *How to Lose an NLRB Election,* 1974
- *Three Management Errors that Lead to Unionization,* 1971
- *Why Not Decertify Your Union,* 1977

BOOK REVIEW

THE THIRD LANGUAGE

by Alan Duff. 1981. Pergamon Press, Headington Hill Hall, Oxford OX3 OBW, England. Also Maxwell House, Fairview Park, Elmsford, NY 10523 USA. (150 pages; paperback, $11.95)

Reviewed by Phyllis Ryan and Brigitte Chavez
Universidad Nacional Autonoma de Mexico

The main difficulty facing the translator is that of obtaining in the second language an impact similar to that of the original language (Nida, 1974, 22). The product of a translation which does not satisfy this need for equivalence is a "third language." Alan Duff's book, *The Third Language*, is an ambitious endeavor to demonstrate the importance of the equivalence of impact by analyzing the negative aspects of this third language.

The author examines the end product to see if it is acceptable or unacceptable, a faulty or questionable text. He searches for the problems which a translation reveals, without claiming to make his book a manual for correct translation. His aim, as stated, is to focus on recurring translation problems/difficulties, and to indicate means of overcoming them. All of the sources he selects are those with "high editorial" standards, although he fails to define this term clearly.

Chapter One serves to introduce and organize the content of the book and to prepare the reader for the six chapters which follow. It reviews some of the problem areas which exist when the reader cannot go to the "fountain" but has to depend on the "water jar." The third language which can result when the translation is faulty is the cause of Duff's concern. He therefore addresses himself to six general areas: From Thoughts to Words, From Words to Words, Structures and Idioms, Style, From One World to Another, and Cultural Differences. Translation excerpts are introduced in this chapter. Their presence in an introduction, however, is questionable.

In the part entitled "The Word Alone: Lexical Problems," the author examines the problems of appropriateness, meaning, padding, and gutting, as well as the importance of word order. The appropriateness of any lexical item within any text will depend on the consistency existing between the register of the text as a whole and each particular lexical item. What Duff refers to as "register" includes "tone" as well as some words which can be "too emotive and powerful," "informal speech," or "neutral or semi-neutral." The influence of the source language (SL) is again believed to be of some importance since a literal translation may not necessarily convey its "tone" or "register."

The chapter on meaning focuses on the necessity of thinking in the target language (TL). It stresses the difficulties inherent in the use of bilingual dictionaries. Although they propose several translations for a single word, they often do not indicate the context.

It is also important to be aware that the translation should represent the best possible combination of the "dictionary definition, the author's intended meaning, and the translator's own interpretation of the word or phrase" (17). This brings us to the problem of clarity of style and/or meaning in the SL text and of the origins of this lack of clarity. If the lack of clarity is due to the personal style of the author, should the translator respect the author's style or should he attempt to clarify the author's ideas? According to Duff, "consultation with the author is. . . the best solution" (20), but that may not always be possible. If the lack of clarity is caused by a word whose connotation has no absolute equivalent in the TL, this brings up the problems of over- and under-translation. These problems have to be solved according to the rules of the TL.

Clearly, some items could be considered untranslatable; for example, "paprika" and "sauna." Duff proposes a few interesting solutions to this problem on pages 26-30.

Chapter Three is divided into five sections: Punctuation, Choice of Structures, Word Order and Emphasis, Tenses, and Structure and Meaning. Duff begins with a cartoon about the perfect interpreter from Asterix the Legionary (the interpreter who can switch from Gothic to Greek or from Latin to Egyptian at will). Then in his sub-headings, Duff examines problems in translating from the SL to the TL. It is true that the excerpts he considers illustrate problems of structures; however, at times they seem to reflect the translator's own writing skills as well. "Punctuation," which takes up one quarter of this chapter, would seem more appropriate in a guide for good writing, such as Sir Ernest Gowers' *The Complete Plain Words*, which Duff refers to when discussing verbosity in prepositions. It is difficult to agree with Duff when he states in the introduction that this book is "not intended as a guide to good writing or a manual for correct translation" (xi). The opposite would seem to be true.

Under the sub-heading, "Word Order and Emphasis," the author discusses the "foreign ring" of a passage and then proceeds to illustrate the odd choice of words made in a translation of Maurice Nadeau's *The History of Surrealism*. Why Duff interrupts his text with this aside and then continues to discuss the value of word order is not clear. His aside might best have been included in the sub-section of the previous chapter, "Word Order: Reference and Agreement."

The problem of metaphor and that of professional language and jargon are the two areas that form Chapter Four, "Idiom and Meaning." Metaphor can be considered as coloring and is defined as an idiomatic use peculiar to language. Translation of metaphors is difficult because of their uniqueness; it can be made all the more difficult if the SL text includes mixed metaphors. However, one has to be conscious of the difference between metaphor and idiom: the former clinging to the power of imagery, the latter comprising a set expression.

Euphony (defined by Duff as rhyme, rhythm and assonance) is considered an inherent part of many metaphors, folk sayings, advertising catchphrases, or political slogans. The only solution for the translator is, according to Duff, intuition and a "good feeling" for both the SL and the TL.

According to Duff, professional language is a specialized language understood by the members of a profession but not by the general public. It is to be differentiated from "jargon," which is "to professional language what sentimentality is to sentiment: a decadent form" (98). It is thus too obscure for everyone and imprecise, a parasite on professional language. The translator's problem in this particular case is to know the more specialized forms of each language and to think of the reaction of the native reader.

Different languages divide up reality differently. The translator thus has to consider the impact on the reader of the texts (SL and TL). It is easy to fall into the trap of writing in a third language, which would be an intermediate style between the SL and the TL. To avoid taking this risk, the author advocates the use of a dictionary of synonyms. Nevertheless, one can always wonder about who the translator should be.

Chapter Six rather abruptly concludes the text. Duff draws the reader's attention to what may have been uppermost in his mind all along — public opinion. His quotations illustrate the public's attitude, because flaws in translation attract more attention than positive points do. Anticipating a rather negative reaction to his book, he implies that his examples are not intended as bad translation solely, but as examples which can be improved. Assuming that the public believes translation to be inherently defective, Duff appeals to the reader ("Please do not shoot the pianist/He's doing his best.") while offering slight comfort to the translator.

A book based on a string of translation excerpts is a unique book. In a field where theoretical books abound, it is refreshing to find a book which focuses on practical aspects of translation. Nevertheless, the need remains for a textbook with more precise translation techniques.

REFERENCES

Gowers, Sir Ernest. Revised by Sir Bruce Fraser. 1948, reprinted 1978. *The complete plain words.* New York: Penguin Press.
Nida, Eugene and Charles Taber. 1974. *The theory and practice of translation.* vol. III. Leiden: E. J. Brill.

Section 7. Language Assessment

In this section we have included diverse articles under the heading of language assessment. In the first article, "Teaching Immigrants in Open-Enrollment Programs" (11-12/76), Donna Ilyin talks about testing adult ESL students for placement through a variety of teaching-testing techniques. She also provides a resource list of information on testing, tests and test-making for adults in open-enrollment programs. Philip Roth's "Procedures for the Identification and Assessment of Students" (10/80) presents procedures for identifying students to be placed in Lau (bilingual) programs. Joan Tribble writes about "Constructing Diagnostic Tests for Placement and Teaching" (8/83). She offers five maxims to keep in mind when preparing a test and discusses how to use test results. In the next article in this section, Mary Newton Bruder writes about the "Assessment of Reading Skills for Beginning ES/FL Students" (6/82) in higher education programs; she provides a hierarchy of categories of basic reading abilities. Virginia French Allen writes of her experiences and observations in "Adding Insights from Optometry" (8/81) in which she presents a look at testing from another point of view. Also included in this section is the "TESOL Statement on Statewide Programs of Competency Testing" (4/79) approved by the TESOL Executive Board on February 28, 1979. This section concludes with a review by Anthea Babaian (12/76) of J. B. Heaton's very readable volume on language testing titled *Writing English Language Tests*.

Another article on testing in this volume is John Haskell's article on the evaluation and use of cloze deletion and scoring procedures to test readability and to "Select Reading Materials" (2/76), found in section 12. And in section 3, James Ford discusses "Standardized Testing, Reading and Black English" (8/83).

Other articles and reviews which have appeared in the *TN* and which have dealt in some way with testing or language assessment are: "Measuring Interest of Non-Native Speakers with White Noise" by Charlotte Leventhal (2/82); "Improving Interview Tests" by Paul Nicholson (2/81); and *It Works* by Mona Schreiber, "The Mini-play: A New Dimension in Oral Proficiency Testing" (8/80); and Donna Ilyin's article on the importance of and methods for testing LEPs to determine language proficiency, "Limited Legal Victory for Limited Speakers of English" (6/78). Ilyin also reviews "A New Cloze Test for Adult Education" (4/82).

TESTING ADULT IMMIGRANTS IN OPEN ENROLLMENT PROGRAMS

by Donna Ilyin
Alemany Community College Center

Open enrollment classes or any classes where student attendance is erratic or transient pose many specific problems. The teacher is constantly faced with presenting, reviewing, and testing at the same time. Often a teacher may have three or four different levels of proficiency in the same class. In adult ESL classes for immigrants, the teacher may also be responsible for the placement of students and for accountability which in ESL classes means student progress in attaining ESL proficiency. The constant flux of new arrivals all during a class period into these multilevel classes with no common denominator of interest, no common language background, and no common level of education in students' own language or educational system challenges and frustrates the teacher. Both teaching and testing open enrollment classes are difficult.

PLACEMENT AND ACCOUNTABILITY

Short time saving tests are helpful in placing students into classes or in deciding what materials may be suitable for a student. (See ESCOBAR or ROBSON). Tests can show students their ESL level of proficiency and show that they are progressing in general English proficiency.

Teachers can also encourage students to assess their own language growth by giving lists of questions students answer about their own language abilities. (For beginning students, these lists can be translated into students' languages.) Given when students enter a course of instruction and again when the course is completed, the student self diagnostic survey usually reflects language growth and can also show where each student feels more work is needed.

Teacher made tests and other devices such as criterion referenced charts, pre and post test tape cassettes, and cummulative record folders containing class work, text tests, cloze tests and dictations also help show students who attend classes regularly that they are progressing.

TEACHING ONESELF

With the many challenges of open enrollment teaching in adult ESL classes, I would like to provide another challenge. Why not teach ourselves more about ESL assessment and then share what we learn? More and more teachers are adapting EFL and native speaker materials and methods for group work as well as for individualized instruction. With only a little more effort, teachers can learn to make tests and devise ways to add student self checking devices for each unit or objective. (See BESL Reporter; HARRIS; VALETTE; etc. and recent papers on testing).

TEACHING AND TESTING AT THE SAME TIME

What interests me even more than routine testing of units of work, or specific skill areas is collecting ways of teaching and testing at the same time. Dr. Alice C. Pack from Brigham Young University in Hawaii demonstrated such a technique in her presentation at the tenth annual TESOL convention in New York City, 1976: Learning English Prepositions, Pronouns and Verbs through Participation in Peer Dyads.

I have also been working with some ideas of my own and adapting other peoples ideas in order to present, review, practice and test at the same time. In addition to specific skill areas, I find it is even more interesting and easier to present, review, practice and test in contextual situations. I believe students perform better when the material is interesting and follows a theme or story line. I hope that other teachers will join me in discovering, developing, creating and adapting ways to teach and test students at the same time. Guess Tests, Picture Dictation Teaching Tests, Dictation/Reading Tests, Picture Created Cloze Tests and Dictation Cloze Reading Tests are some techniques that have helped me.

Guess Tests—specific skill areas (vocabulary, numbers, time, etc.)

Preparation:

—Make flash cards or use regular drill pictures, want ads, advertisements, tapes, whatever.
—Shuffle or mix each so that the teacher does not know what the student sees or hears.

Number lesson example:
1. Teacher/student technique
—put some numbers on flash cards eg. 6, 60, 16, $.05, $.50, $5, 1, 423; etc. (Use 4 x 6 cards for small classes, and put only one number on each card.)
—shuffle the cards
—show a volunteer student a number that you cannot see. (Numbers are toward students)
—tell the volunteer student to read the number

—repeat what student says and write on board or transparency the students exact words.
—ask the class if the number on the board is the same as on the card. (If not, class corrects)
—repeat above until student fails two or three times or until the volunteer passes the number test successfully.
—record when each student passes your informal test.
(At this point the number lesson is an informal test for the volunteer student, a review for others and a presentation for newly arrived students. It also provides a means to check the volunteer's oral ability since the teacher does not know what is going to be read or said. The student has to really communicate clearly or the result will not be the same on the board as on the card.)

2. Student/student technique
When one or more students are successful with all the cards:
—ask for other volunteers to go to the board to write the numbers.
—shuffle the cards again and show only to students who were successful in step 1 above.
—ask students who demonstrated their success in step 1 to read the numbers to students at the board.
—ask students at the board to write the numbers. (Later those students can assume reader-speaker roles when they feel successful)
—Tell students at their seats to practice writing the numbers the reader-speaker students are saying. (Again be sure to shuffle the cards and show a card only to the reader-speaker students).
—next show the number card just read to the students at the board and ask each to correct his number if it is not the same. (Students in their seats can also correct their numbers.)
—record when students are successful.

Guess Tests—context or situation

Instead of testing numbers in isolation as described above, choose one of the survival content areas necessary for a student here in the United States. For example banking and business are two areas most people need to understand when working or conducting business.

Preparation:

—make a number of checks filling out numbers, names, dates, amounts, etc. (Use blank checks or large flash cards made into checks, or a ditto with a number of checks each designated by

a cue. eg. check x, check xx, check xxx)
—Shuffle the checks. (If using dittos, make flash cards each with a cue designation on each card eg. x, xx, or xxx, etc.)
—make a large replica of a blank check on the board or use a transparency of a blank check.

Teacher/student technique

—tell students to look at the check you are holding, but that you can not see. (If you are using flash card cues, tell the students to find the check your card refers to. eg. If the students see XX on your flash card, they find check XX on the ditto sheet.)
—ask a volunteer student (one ready for testing) to tell you the amount of the check.
—repeat what student says and then write the number in the proper place on your blank check. Write a student's exact words.
—ask the class if the number on the board is the same as on the check referred to. (If not, class corrects). Only the numbers can be written, or both the numbers and the number words on the check.
—erase the amount on your blank check repeat with more cards until student fails two or three times or until the volunteer passes the number test successfully.
—record when a student is successful.

Student/student technique

—ask for volunteer students to go to the board and make replica's of blank checks.
—ask for volunteers to write the amounts they will hear. (If using a tranparency, only one student can be tested at a time).
—distribute a check or a flash card referring to a check on a ditto to students who have successfully completed step 1.
—tell a student at the board to ask one of the students with a check or flash card for the amount of the check he has. eg. "Jose, How much is your check?" or "Chi Wai, What is the amount of the check you have?" (Be sure that students who are writing the numbers do not see the check of the students who are reading the amounts.)
—tell all of the students at the board or those at their seats who are practicing to write what the reader/student says. (More advanced or quicker writers can write the number words too)
—keep a tally for students who answered correctly.
—next tell student/reader to show the check he has read.
—ask writers to correct their answers.
—point to a correct answer at the board.

—continue asking other individual board students to ask another student with a check for the amount of each check. (Always be sure that students writing the numbers do not see the check or cues, copy from other students or get prompting help.)
The check writing technique can be expanded to include questions such as: "Who wrote the check?; When did he/she write it? (a good way to practice common men's and women's names and spellings); Who will get the money?; or (for cancelled checks) Who got the money?, etc.
Very often students help each other with the answers and the teacher walks around answering questions and checking the work of students who are just practicing.
When using this dictation-teaching technique, some students can be formally tested in spite of the bedlam that may seem to have occurred. Have a specific area in the room for testing where volunteers go. The teacher proctors as the questions are asked, the answers given and dictation written. The rule: there is no testing if others are contributing to the effort.

Picture Dictation Teaching Tests

Situational pictures present opportunities to teach, review and test at the same time.

Materials needed:
—a large (preferably colored) story provoking picture in a context of interest and student need. (Transparency can be used)
—a regular deck of playing cards (52)
—blank dittos

Preparation:
—add a clock to a picture.
—tell students to name the people in the picture.
—draw out a story about the picture from the students.
—write the story on the board or ask an advanced student to write the story (The teacher quickly corrects errors after recording students skill at dictation.
—ask another student to copy the story on a ditto. (Teacher corrects errors later and reproduces for a class reading lesson.)
—draw out questions that can be asked about the story just created.
—write those questions on the board or have an advanced student write the questions. (Correct any errors quickly after recording students dictation efforts.)
—number the ten best questions students can ask and answer about the story.
—instruct an advanced student to write the ten best questions on a ditto. (Teacher corrects errors later and re-

produces for a reading comprehension lesson).
—obtain an ordinary deck of cards (52).

1. Teacher/student technique
—shuffle the 52 cards.
—hold the cards with the numbers, or face cards toward the students. Don't look at them.
—tell students that each time an ace appears the students must ask you the 1st of the ten questions they have just chosen about the story they have just created. If a two of any suit appears, they ask question number 2. (They never tell you the number and you do not see the card. Since there are four suits, any number can be asked four times)
—tell students if a face card appears they must ask you a question about yourself. . . or about the class or the room, but not about the story. (Suitable types of questions might be elicited and put on the board before beginning.)
—do a few examples by showing a card to the class. Students ask the question cued. Teacher responds with the answer.

2. Student/student oral technique
—ask for a volunteer to answer questions.
—select about 15 or 20 cards. (be sure to have all 10 questions represented, a few repeats and a few face cards. Do not let volunteer student see the playing card.)
—give a playing card to students who understand the system.
—ask a student with a playing card to ask the volunteer the question cued by his card. (Do not let answering student see cue card.)
—record volunteer student's success in answering the question. Class corrects if answer is wrong.

3. Student/student written technique
—replace repeated numbers with different numbers (eg. If you have two fives, keep one five and add an extra three)
—shuffle cards again.
—ask for volunteers to go to the board to write answers. (Other students practice in their seats)
—give a playing card to students who understand the system.
—ask a student with a playing card to ask the question cued by her card.
—tell writing students (at the board or seats) to write a natural answer to the question. (Those who are faster or more advanced can write a longer more complete answer under the natural answer.
—A natural answer to the question: "Where are Mr. and Mrs. Anderson?" is *in the bank*. A complete sentence

answer is *They are in the bank.* or *They have just gone to the bank to cash Mr. Anderson's check.* etc.)

Dictation Reading Tests. Created stories from a situational picture or stories in class room materials can be used as a dictation test for some and a reading comprehension lesson for others. (1) Give lined paper to students taking the dictation test (group 1). (2) Give typed copies of the story to those desiring to relate sound to symbol (group 2). (3) Give some students the typed copy of the story with comprehension questions to answer (group 3). (4) Instruct students in the first two groups to listen as the story is read. (Students in group three, read the story and answer the questions). (5) Then read the story aloud once. (6) Tell students taking the dictation test (group 1) that the story will be read line by line and that they will write. (7) Instruct those in group two to follow along as the story is read. (8) Read the story a line at a time. Repeat each sentence only two times. Read in a natural conversational manner pausing after phrase groups. (9) At the end, read the story completely one more time. (10) Collect the dictation from students in group 1 using it as a test. Give one point for each correct word. If desired, spelling and punctuation can also be scored, but make separate categories.

Collect reading comprehension answers from group 3.

Picture Created Cloze Tests. Another variation of the created picture story (or for any reading materials) is to use the stories as originally written and make a cloze test for the lesson or a cloze dictation test. (When material has been used before as a reading or dictation lesson, paraphrase the story. Use slightly different structures and vocabulary still keeping in the contraints of the proficiency level . . . and keeping the essential meaning of the original story)

Making the clozes (1) delete every 7th word leaving the 1st and last sentences intact. (2) Number the blanks. Three prefered rules for cloze tests using class created or teacher made stories or when paraphrasing are:

1. Use natural easy flowing sentences within students proficiency level and on a topic students have studied.

2. Select blanks that are different words if for some reason the same pronouns and articles seem to appear as the 7th word. Rewrite the story adding an adjective or a noun phrase or two to avoid this.

3. Avoid using difficult parts of structure elements or words where the context does not make the blank clear. (Before giving students the test, try it out on some native speakers. If they can't fill in the blanks, rewrite the story so that the blanks will be more easily done.)

Directions to students taking the cloze:
1. Read the whole story.
2. Then go back and fill in the blank the word you think is missing. Use a pencil, For example:
    Mr. and Mrs. Anderson went to
    ——1—— a check at the bank.
    They ——2—— going to buy some clothes.
3. Use only one word for each blank.
4. Words like *"don't"*, *"can't"*, *"he's"*, and *"you're"* can be used to fill a blank.
    Their son needs shoes, but he ——3—— need any pants.
5. Try to fill every blank.

Dictation Cloze Reading Test
Alternate directions to students taking the dictation cloze test are the same except for 2. which is changed as follows:
2. Then listen as I read the story. Fill in the blanks with the word, that I read.

Administering the cloze or the cloze dictation:
Many ways of giving and scoring this type of test are possible. One way to give the test to some and yet use it as a practice device for others is to give two copies of the deleted reading pages with a carbon between to those desiring to take it as a test. Instruct them to turn in the original when the test is completed.

Then if using the dictated cloze, get volunteers to read the words that were read for the blanks. If using the picture created cloze, get volunteers to tell the words they selected for each blank. Be certain that students know which words are acceptable or not. Draw out reasons from the students.

Teacher/student sets of tests.

At this point Teacher-student sets of tests (similar to those developed by Alice C. Pack) could be utilized. After the discussion, hand out teacher sets of the cloze with the correct word typed or written in the blank in another color if possible or at least put in a box. Alternate acceptable words could also appear in a vertical line in the box.

Students can correct their work.

Later these sets could be used for review or testing in the peer, dyad technique developed by Dr. Pack.

TESTING RESOURCE LIST
for Adult Open Enrollment Programs

For a quick easy to read report:
—"Focus on Testing." *BESL Reporter* Vol I No. 2, September 1975. Bilingual/E.S.L. Center, 100 Franklin Street, New Holland, Pennsylvania.

Two recent testing bibliographies
—Escobar, Joanna Sculley and John Daugherty—1976. *A Teacher's Planning Handbook for Developing the ESL/ABE Instructional Program.* Illinois ESL/ABE Service Center, 500 S. Dwyer Avenue, Arlington Heights, Illinois 60005.
—Robson, Barbara and Sutherland, Kenton—1975. *Selected Annotated Bibliography for Teaching English to Speakers of Vietnamese.* Arlington, Virginia 22209.

A quick oral placement test:
—Kunz, Linda et al. "The John Test" An oral production test developed in New York City for adults. For free copies write to: Jean Bodman, AERC, Jersey City State College, Jersey City, New Jersey 07305.

Four books helpful to teachers making their own tests:
—Burt, Marina K. and Kirparsky, Carol—1972. *The Gooficon,* a repair manual for English. (Rowley, Massachusetts: Newbury House).
—Harris, David P.—1969. *Testing English as a Second Language.* (New York. McGraw Hill).
—Nilsen, Don L. F. and Nilsen, Alleen Pace—1971. *Pronunciation Contrasts in English* (New York: Regents).
—Valette, Rebecca—1967. *Modern Language Testing, a Handbook.* (New York: Harcourt, Brace & World, Inc.).

Two recent collections of papers on testing:
—Jones, Randall L. and Spolsky, Bernard—1975. *Testing Language Proficiecny.* (Arlington, Virginia, Center for Applied Linguistics).
—Palmer, Leslie and Spolsky, Bernard—1975. *Papers on Language Testing 1967–1974.* Washington, D.C., Teachers of English to Speakers of Other Languages.

Some other testing papers:
—Aitken, Kenneth G.—1976. "Discrete Structure Point Testing Problems and Alternatives." *TESL Reporter,* Vol. 9, No. 4. Laie, Hawaii, Brigham Young University.
—Haskell, John—1975. "Putting Cloze into the Classroom." *English Record,* Vol. 26, No. 2, Spring. Oneonta, NY 13820.
—Herbert, Charles H.—1975. "Language Diagnosis and Assessment Testing Techniques and a Program for Natural Language Development." Paper delivered at TESOL Convention, Los Angeles, California.
—Ilyin, Donna—1975. "What Grade is Dr. Chan in?" *TESL Reporter,* Vol. 8, No. 4. Box 157, Laie, Hawaii; Brigham Young University.
—Jonz, Jon—1976. "Improving on the Basic Egg—the M-C Cloze." For copies write to Jonz at Lancaster-Lebanon Intermediate Unit, 1110 Enterprise Road, East Petersburg, PA 17520.
—Olsen, Judy E. Winn-Bell—1976. "Adapting an Oral Interview to a Mass Listening Test." Paper presented at the tenth annual TESOL Convention. For copies write to: Judy Olsen at Alemany Community College Center, 750 Eddy Street, San Francisco, CA 94109.

TN 11/-12/76

PROCEDURES FOR IDENTIFICATION AND ASSESSMENT OF STUDENTS FOR POSSIBLE INCLUSION IN A COMPREHENSIVE LAU EDUCATION PROGRAM

by Phillip Roth
Indiana Dept. of Public Instruction

The tremendous influx of refugees (Indochinese, Soviet Jews, Cubans, and Haitians) into American communities in the past five years has caused public schools across the nation to look at civil rights legislation more closely than ever before. The reason for such scrutiny is that the Office of Civil Rights (OCR) is reviewing policies and practices of school systems to assure that limited English proficiency (LEP) students are not foreclosed from equal educational opportunities because of a lack of English language skills. Whether they do so voluntarily or in response to court orders or to citations by OCR, school administrators must develop and implement educational programs which are consistent with the requirements of such legislation as Title VI of the Civil Rights Act of 1964; Title IV of that Act (as amended in 1974); Title IX of the Education Amendments of 1972 (sex equity); and Public Law 94-142, which addresses, in part, provisions for LEP students who are handicapped. In addition, school districts which are currently receiving funds under the Emergency School Aid Act, or districts which are applying for such funding, must now submit and implement a comprehensive educational plan for LEP students.

Considering the multitude of legislation and attending regulations with which school administrations must comply, it is little wonder that school systems are confused as to how to satisfy all the requirements beset upon them in one educational program. While an instructional program which meets all of the requirements mandated in the legislation mentioned above is possible to design and implement, it is premature to discuss such a program without first considering two important questions: which students in a school district should be enrolled in the program, and what are the unique needs of those students which such a program would presumably address? This paper, therefore, will discuss a procedure to 1) identify students who have potential limited English language abilities and 2) assess their particular educational needs (i.e., English and/or native language instruction and any possible special education needs). Information gathered as a result of following this procedure will help school personnel to make appropriate decisions about the kind(s) of instructional program(s) to implement and thereby satisfy civil rights requirements and (more importantly) meet the needs

of the identified students by providing them equal educational opportunities.

Before beginning the discussion of the identification and assessment procedure, the reader should be aware of the specific protection of rights, as embodied in Title VI, which is the genesis of this identification and assessment procedure and subsequent educational programs designed as a result of this process. Title VI provides that:

"No person in the United States shall, on the basis of race, color, or *national origin*, be excluded from participation in, be denied the benefits of, or be subjected to discrimination under *any program or activity receiving federal financial assistance.*

(emphasis added)

Substance was given to this protection of rights in a memorandum issued by HEW on May 25, 1970, regarding children of national origin minority groups with limited English language skills. The memorandum was issued in response to findings by OCR that a disproportionate number of students whose primary or home language was other than English were not receiving special assistance in many schools around the country. It requires that:

"1. No student be excluded from effective participation in school because of inability to speak and understand the language of instruction.

2. No student be misassigned to classes for the mentally retarded by reason of his/her lack of English skills.

3. Programs for such a student be designed to meet his/her language skill needs and not operate as a dead-end track.

4. Parents whose English is limited receive notices and other information from the school in a language they can understand."[1]

With this in mind then, the discussion will focus on the identification and assessment procedure. The reader will notice as each step of this process is described that references are frequently made to OCR requirements to assure that the suggestions here are consistent with Title VI and related regulations and guidelines.

Step 1. Identification of the Student's Primary and/or Home Language.

An essential first step for the school district is to accurately identify *all* students whose primary or home language is other than English. The reasons for identifying students in this way are 1) to make certain that *all* national origin minority group students who potentially have limited English language

proficiency have their language proficiency and academic progress assessed and 2) to determine which students are national origin minority group students for the purposes of Lau compliance. Moreover, taking this step as an initial activity in the identification and assessment process assures that the school district will not make the same mistake that other districts have made, as reported by OCR in January, 1975.[2] Among the most common violations cited by OCR was the practice by school districts not accurately identifying all students with a primary or home language other than English. If a school system is unable to accurately identify its students, it necessarily follows that the school district will not be able to assess the language proficiencies of its students.

Identifying a student as having a primary or home language other than English does not mean that the student necessarily has limited English language proficiency, or that (s)he is underachieving. These can only be determined after the student's language proficiency and academic progress are assessed.

A good way to determine the primary or home language of students is to use a home language survey which elicits at least the following information:

1. the language first acquired (learned) by the student;
2. the language most often used in the home; and
3. the language most often spoken by the student.

Results of the survey will produce two groups of students as indicated below:

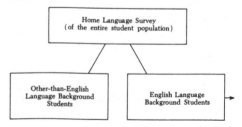

Notice that the diagram above indicates administration of the home language survey to the entire student population. Some school districts rely only on student surnames as a short-cut method to identify students having a primary or home language other than English. Student surnames may give the district some general idea of the numbers of such students, but the surname of an individual will not necessarily indicate what language is most often used in the home. This practice, therefore, is not advised in the identification process.

Notice in the diagram above that those students determined by the home language survey as coming from an English language background are immediately dismissed from further consideration in the identification process. The general education program, it is assumed, is already designed for these students. We are concerned about those students who, because of their lack of English language abilities, cannot progress through the general education program in a manner commensurate with their English proficient peers.

Step 2. English Language Assessment

The assessment of English skills is important here to refine the group of students identified as Other-than-English Language Background Students. Furthermore, making this assessment will help the school district to avoid committing another violation which has been cited by OCR: failure to assess adequately the language proficiency of LEP students.[2] If a school system cannot adequately assess the language skills of these students, it cannot prescribe a program specifically designed to meet their needs and to rectify their English language deficiency.

Various English language tests can be used to determine which students are limited English proficient and which are not. (This paper will not discuss the various English language instruments which can be used; it is concerned only with the identification and assessment procedure.) The figure below indicates the groups of students generated by this assessment:

The determination as to whether a student is Non-English Proficiency (NEP) or Limited-English Proficiency (LEP) can easily be made during this assessment by following the definitions of language categories as described in the Lau Remedies:

"Category A—Monolingual in a language other than English.
Category B—Predominate speaker of the language other than English.
Category C—Bilingual, i.e., has equal facility in English and the other language.
Category D—Predominate speaker of English though knows some of the language other than English.
Category E—Monolingual in English, speaks no other language."[3]

Those students classified in Category A are considered to be NEP students. Those classified B and possibly some in Category C (since they may be equally

dysfunctional in both languages) are considered to be LEP students. The reader is cautioned against assigning students into language categories at this point. That will be done later in the process. The reference to the Lau language categories here is only for the purpose of distinguishing between NEP and LEP students. The reason for this distinction will become apparent later.

Some program planners dismiss the English Proficiency Students at this point. As you will see below, there are some important reasons for continuing to consider these students.

Step 3. Review of Achievement Test Data

When planning an appropriate instructional program which will serve as many qualified students as possible, it is not enough to use English language abilities as the sole criterion. Achievement test data give some insight into problems encountered by students who come from an other-than-English language background but who are proficient in English. Some of these students may be underachieving for reasons other than language differences. The figure below indicates the groups of students defined by this step:

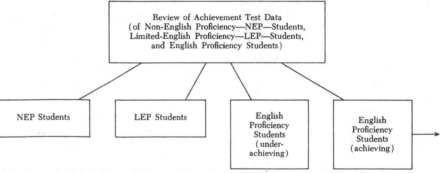

Implementing this step, the school district will avoid committing yet another violation often cited by OCR: improper placement of LEP students into classes for the mentally retarded.[3] Many times this violation occurs because school systems use tests and procedures which rely exclusively on English language abilities to assess and place students. Following the above step helps the school district to comply with the Lau Remedies, which state that:

"Students having a primary or home language other than English who are underachieving must be provided remedial programs, regardless of whether they have

limited English abilities. Underachievement is defined in the Lau Remedies as performing at one or more standard deviations below the mean score for non-minority students."[3]

Referring to the figure above, notice that those students identified as English Proficiency Students who are achieving at grade level are dismissed from further consideration at this point. The process is concerned only with the three groups of students which are underachieving: NEP Students, LEP Students, and the English Proficiency Students who are not working at grade level.

Step 4. Native Language Assessment

This step examines a very critical albeit often neglected area of the identification and assessment process. Information concerning the level of native language development of students identified up to this point as NEP, LEP, or English Proficiency (underachieving) may give some insight—especially when compared with English Language Assessment and achievement data—into such learning problems as speech problems, mental retardation, other learning disorders, and emotional disturbances. When such learning problems are suspected, further diagnosis via appropriate instru-

ments and procedures is necessary to assure proper placement into appropriate programs. The figure below shows the possible groups identified by this assessment:

Notice that for each of the three groups of students identified as underachieving in Step 3 there is a counterpart identified as "special." Making provisions for the appropriate assessment and subsequent placement of students who may need special education services, regardless of their English language proficiency, is consistent with the requirements of Public Law 94-142.

Reasons for considering the NEP and

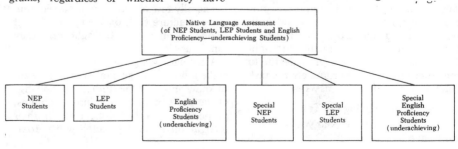

LEP students and all of those students identified as "special" for inclusion in a comprehensive Lau education program are rather clear. What may not be so obvious is the rationale for continuing to consider the English Proficiency (underachieving) students who do not need special education services. In many school systems, these students are underachieving not so much because of language differences, but because of cultural differences. The work of Dr. Jose Cardenas and Dr. Blandina Cardenas suggests that incompatibilities between the student's cultural characteristics and those of the dominant society represented by the school result in the student's low self-concept especially when the school makes unrealistic expectations of him/her.[4] Including these students in a program where there is an understanding of these and other factors which affect learning, provides the students with opportunities to succeed in a manner commensurate with their Anglo peers.

Step 5. Assignment of Students into Lau Categories

The final step of the identification and assessment process involves the assignment of the students identified in the previous four steps into Lau Language Categories. The purpose of these categories is to plan appropriate instructional programs to meet the specific needs of students identified in each group at the inception of a comprehensive Lau program. It should be noted that the groups identified below are not intended to be used for tracking purposes. It is quite feasible that students will move from one group to another as they develop language (English and/or native language) and conceptual skills. The figure below indicates the possible groups of students identified by this step who could (should) be included in a comprehensive Lau education program:

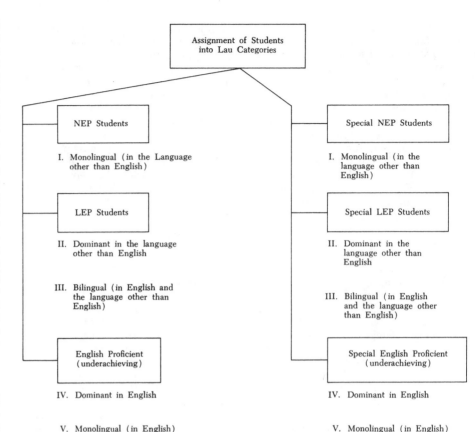

With the administration of Step 5 above the identification and assessment process is complete. The information gathered from the steps described above should provide school administrators with enough data to make educationally sound decisions about the appropriate type(s) of instructional program(s) to implement—one(s) that will effectively meet the needs of students identified through the process just described.

It is not the purpose of this paper to prescribe specific programs for particular populations of students. Such decisions can be made by reviewing the descriptions of program designs in *A Guide to the Selection of Bilingual Education Program Designs* by Ned Seelye and Billie Navarro. Published by the Bilingual Education Service Center, Arlington Heights, Illinois, supported by the Illinois Office of Education, 1977.

REFERENCES
1. Memorandum to "School Districts with More Than Five Percent National Origin—Minority Group Children" from J. Stanley Pottinger, Director of the Office for Civil Rights, May 25, 1970.
2. In January, 1975, OCR identified 334 school districts which, on the basis of information supplied in the HEW 101 and 102 Forms, were found to have disproportionate numbers of students whose primary or home language was other than English and who were not receiving special assistance. These districts were required to complete and return an investigative questionnaire (OS/CR 53-74) intended to assist in the effort to determine whether the districts were in violation of *Lau v. Nichols*.
3. "Remedies Available for Eliminating Past Educational Practices Ruled Unlawful Under *Lau v. Nichols*", Summer, 1975.
4. Cardenas, Jose A. and Blandina Cardenas. *The Theory of Incompatibilities*. San Antonio, Texas: The Intercultural Development Research Association, 1977.

TN 10/80

CONSTRUCTING DIAGNOSTIC TESTS FOR PLACEMENT AND TEACHING

by Joan F. Tribble
Jefferson Community College
University of Kentucky

Diagnostic testing generally facilitates proper placement of students into class and enables the teacher to begin teaching where the students are—not where the book, the syllabus, or the teacher thinks they should be. An equally important purpose of diagnostic testing is to aid individualized language instruction. However, it is sometimes difficult to find the right diagnostic test and so one may decide to construct one's own. Fortunately the task is not as formidable as it may seem.

Constructing the Test

First, determine what skills your students must have to succeed in the course. Each skill requires a different type of test. Also decide whether to test recognition or production, as production—oral or written—requires greater knowledge of the language and is harder to test accurately. Therefore, I generally test recognition of correct sentence structure first, on the theory that, if students cannot select the right form, they cannot use it.

After narrowing the scope of the test, make a list of the general areas you want to know about: 1) the students' knowledge of the parts of speech—nouns, pronouns, prepositions, verb tenses, etc.; 2) their recognition of correct usage—word order, agreement, ellipses, idioms, sentence fragments, etc. However, items like vocabulary, spelling, and punctuation can be easily tested in many ways and do not have to be included in a diagnostic test, but they can be. If you like, you can select items from all of these lists; choose what you want to know about your students' language.

Once you have decided what to test, you should think about how to test. To simplify the analysis, use some form of multiple-choice question. You may give up to five possible answers, but a choice of three is the easiest to write. Ask the student to choose the correct sentence.

1. A. The student will writes with a pen.
   B. The student write with a pen.
   C. The student writes with a pen.

On the other hand, you may prefer to point out the item being tested by presenting one sentence with a blank and a choice of items to make it correct:

2. I will see you _____ six o'clock.
   A. at
   B. on
   C. to

3. These (two books large)
                 A
   (two large books)
                 B
   (large two books) are old.
                 C

You may use more than one type of question in the same test; just be certain that the students understand what they should do and that the same answering system is used for all questions (A, B, C; or a, b, c; or 1, 2, 3).

Writing the sentences takes time, but it is not an impossible task. Keep a few maxims in mind:

1. Use the simplest possible vocabulary. Test knowledge of structure, not meaning.

2. Be sure that each sentence tests only one structure. The possible answers must not introduce problems with number, gender, and/or tense. Test each area separately.

3. Make one answer clearly right and the others clearly wrong; however, the distractors (wrong answers) should include errors the students often make or be very close to the correct answer.

4. Write as many sentences as needed to test each construction you want to analyze. Eliminate some if your test is too long. I use 6, 12, or 18 sentences for each part of a 150-item test.

5. Write each sentence on a 3 x 5 card, and label the area it tests. Keep these areas in separate packs until you have written all the sentences and are ready to assemble the test.

What I have suggested thus far could apply to any test. What converts these items into a diagnostic instrument is their arrangement so that the answers reveal the student's strengths and weaknesses. The answer sheet is the key.

To construct the answer sheet and to arrange the sentences, divide the total number of sentences you have written into a suitable combination of columns and rows to fit on one sheet of paper: 5 columns of 10 rows for 50 questions, 5 columns of 20 for 100 questions, 6 columns of 25 for 150, etc. Then number the paper vertically, down the columns.

Now, working horizontally, divide the rows into groups, according to the area being tested and the number of sentences you have written for each area. For instance, rows 1 and 2 might test nouns; rows 3, 4, and 5, pronouns;

and rows 6 and 7, verbs:
(See **Figure No. 1**.)

Figure No. 1

NOUNS	1	21	41	61	81
	2	22	42	62	82
PRONOUNS	3	23	43	63	83
	4	24	44	64	84
	5	25	45	65	85
VERBS	6	26	46	66	86
	7	27	47	67	87
	etc.	etc.	etc.	etc.	etc.

Then assign a number from the correct group of rows to each sentence, and write that number on the 3 x 5 card.

When you have numbered all the sentences, arrange the cards in numerical order and type the sentences, without the structure labels. With this arrangement of the questions, the students will be less aware of the specific language areas being tested, but you will be able to use the results. You can also make alternate forms of the test by rearranging the sentences in a set of rows and retyping.

To diagnose each student's abilities, provide a numbered answer sheet, arranged in the same columns and rows that you used to number the sentences. You may ask the students to mark their answers in any way you choose: by circling, Xing, or supplying the correct answer. (See **Figure No. 2**.)

Figure No. 2

1. a ⓑ c	21. a b c	41. a b c	61. a b c	81. a b c
2. a b ⓒ	22. a b c	42. a b c	62. a b c	82. a b c
3. ⓐ b c	23. a b c	43. a b c	63. a b c	83. a b c

or

1. _ X _	21. _ _ _	41. _ _ _	61. _ _ _	81. _ _ _
A B C	A B C	A B C	A B C	A B C
2. _ _ X	22. _ _ _	42. _ _ _	62. _ _ _	82. _ _ _
A B C	A B C	A B C	A B C	A B C
3. X _ _	23. _ _ _	43. _ _ _	63. _ _ _	83. _ _ _
A B C	A B C	A B C	A B C	A B C

or

1. 2	21. ___	41. ___	61. ___	81. ___
2. 3	22. ___	42. ___	62. ___	82. ___
3. 1	23. ___	43. ___	63. ___	83. ___

Diagnosing of Test Results

In order to minimize the effects of guessing, calculate the score by subtracting one-half the incorrect answers from the correct ones. Ignore those which were omitted. This will give a general score to compare with the scores of the other students in the class and to help in placement. After you have used your test for several semesters, you will know what score is needed for each level you teach. Then placement will be easier.

To diagnose the problems of each student, you must determine the percent correct in each set of rows, this time including the omitted items as incorrect answers. For example, from the illustration given previously, the percent correct in rows 3,

4, and 5 would show how well the student recognized correct pronoun usage.

After calculating all the percentages, list the areas for each student in ascending order with the lowest percent correct number 1. This ranking of problem areas can then be reported to the student, with or without the exact percent correct. In order to discourage comparison with other students and to encourage concentration on individual problems, I report only the ranking of areas and the approximate percent correct (less than 50%, 51-80%, 81-90%). I never report the overall score.

Using the Test Results

Having diagnosed the language problems of the individuals in your class, you can use the results to design treatment. For instance, if you discover that a number of students have the same problem, you can provide class instruction to correct the deficiency. Or you can assign extra drills or review exercises for the entire class.

For individual students make special laboratory or homework assignments. And if tutors are available, they can use diagnosis as a basis for individualized instruction.

Another important use of the test results is to enable the teacher to evaluate improvement by retesting with the same test or an alternate form at periodic intervals or at the end of the course. Simply subtract the ending score from the beginning score to determine improvement. Then compare the improvement scores of all the members of the class to establish part or all of the grade. By making improvement an important part of the grade, the teacher will encourage the slower student who improves but is still weak.

After you have used a diagnostic test, especially one that tests what you want to know because you wrote it yourself, you will wonder how you ever taught without it. You will soon discover that treatment is much easier if you have first diagnosed the problem.

🌐

ASSESSING READING SKILLS OF BEGINNING ES/FL STUDENTS

by Mary Newton Bruder
English Language Institute
University of Pittsburgh

Until recently it was fairly safe to assume that foreign students studying English in the U.S. prior to entering university knew the rudiments of reading in English: the Roman alphabet and the basic sound-symbol correspondences. The major task of the reading teacher was to present reading material in an orderly fashion, and get the students to read.

In the past few years we have seen a number of students who cannot profit from the normal reading class because they don't know the basics we assumed.[1] Frequently, these students have better than average speaking skills, a fact which masks the reading problem—the students talk a good game, get help with their reading homework, and the teacher is lulled into thinking all is well.

Another problem in assessment is the make-up of standardized tests. The reading section is often at the end of the test and many students, even those who can read, do not finish the test. Thus, little information can be derived—did the student not do well because he couldn't read or simply because he read very slowly and didn't finish the test. In either case reading may be a problem, but we don't know the nature of the problem.

When students in the ELI test into the beginning level (MTELP 0-44) we administer a separate reading test to help us identify students with basic reading problems.

We have discovered that students who cannot read beginning level ESL materials exhibit a wide range of skill possibilities. In all cases the students are literate in their native language, so at least we have that advantage. The major problem areas lie in the code and/or comprehension, and while it may theoretically be possible for someone to comprehend without knowing the code, we have yet to encounter anyone who can. Therefore, we have constructed a hierarchy of skills as follows:

Code Knowledge

1. The student knows nothing about the Roman alphabet, neither the names nor the sounds of the letters. Students in this category are always speakers of languages with writing systems different from the Roman alphabet.

2. Students may know the letter names, in English or his own Romance language, but have no notion of the sound-symbol correspondences of English.

3. The student knows consonant sound-symbol correspondences. Students may know the regular consonant S-S relationships, especially if they are similar to native language (S [s] as in *see*, but maybe not S [š] as in *sugar*). They may not know the troublesome English vowel-sound relationships (for example oo [u]/[v] as in *food/good*.

4. The student recodes with ease. Students know most S-S relationships, can sound out unfamiliar words and sound quite fluent when reading aloud.

Goodman (1970) distinguishes recoding, the ability to transfer language from one modality to another (reading aloud, for example) from decoding, the ability to get the meaning from a piece of language. It is important to remember that people can recode without decoding. Students who have studied English for years some years ago may retain basic recoding skills but may not comprehend what they are reading. I can perform this trick in a number of languages when in fact I don't understand a word. Therefore, it is very important to sort out various levels of comprehension as well.

Comprehension Level

1. Students with 0 knowledge of the written code have always exhibited 0 reading comprehension as well. In fact, we often have to have translators explain the directions for the test in the native language. But we also have students who are quite good oral-aurally and who can recode with ease, but who don't understand what they read. Students from all language backgrounds fall into this category.

2. The students comprehend questions and can find verbatim answers. The students understand direct questions and can find answers if they come from the passage with the same sentence structure and vocabulary.

3. The students comprehend questions and can answer inference questions. These are the basic skills required to read most beginning/ESL materials. English taught as a foreign language in most countries emphasizes the reading skill, just as foreign language programs do in this country. Until recently we did not get university oriented foreign students going abroad with the equivalent of 1 year of high school English or less. But now that students are arriving with so little background in English it is crucial for us to accurately assess their skills in the most critical ability for success in American universities—reading.

We have a short, simple test (approximately five minutes administration time) which sorts students into the categories outlined above. The test material was written by Lionel Menasche, our testing specialist. The administration procedures are my own responsibility.

Step 1. The student is told he is to answer to his best ability, that he shouldn't be nervous, etc. (We do this during orientation week when all the testing is done, so it's "just one more test.")

Step 2. The student is asked his name and is asked to spell it as the tester writes it on the answer paper. The student should look as the name is being written, so he can correct any errors. Here you discover the first bit of information regarding the code. Some students cannot do this at all, even with translation of the directions. If this is the case, you can safely stop the test at this point.

Step 3. The student is asked to read aloud the following passage: Peter wanted to buy a book for his Physics course, so he called the Lazy Fox Book Center to find out if they had it in stock. The person who answered the phone very quickly gave him the necessary information. Peter's friend offered to go to the store to get it for him, because he was going there anyway to buy a book for his English course.

The tester gives a rating from 1-5 (high) for intelligibility. This is the assessment of the student's knowledge of the Sound-Symbol relationships. We listen to see what the students do with words like "physics" if they happen to be unfamiliar ones. If they make some attempt to sound out the word, we know they have certain basic skills. We can also tell by the intonation and pauses they make whether they have some notions of English grammar.

We do not ask comprehension questions on this passage because we have found that most students do not process information when they read aloud and they have to go back and read it again to understand it. So, to avoid letting them think that "reading aloud" is equivalent to reading, we just don't ask them questions.

Step 4. The student reads the following paragraph silently, after which the tester asks the questions:

It was a hot day and Jeanie was feeling thirsty. On the way home she stopped at the cafeteria to have something to drink. To her surprise, she was told that there was only coffee available, so she decided to go home immediately, because she wanted a cold drink.

Questions for Passage II (Student listens to and reads the questions.)
1. Why was Jeanie thirsty?
2. Why did she stop at the cafeteria?
3. Did she drink coffee at the cafeteria?
4. How long did Jeanie stay in the cafe-

teria?

5. Did the cafeteria have many kinds of drinks for its customers?

6. What did Jeanie want to drink?

The student reads the questions along as the tester reads them, and he may look back at the passage for the answers.

We look for a number of things here as well as comprehension. The first is the amount of time it takes the student to read the passage. As a rule, the longer it takes, the poorer the comprehension. We also look for reading strategies—following along with a finger, retracing with the eyes, subvocalizing—all characteristic of slower, less proficient readers.

It is important to let the student read the questions and look back if he wants; we're testing reading comprehension, not memory. Notice that only the first two questions can be answered by reading

---

Hierarchy Categories of Basic Reading Abilities

(Native Language Literacy Assumed)

English Code Knowledge

0
Letter Names
Consonant S-S
Recodes with ease

Comprehension

0
Comprehends Q + can find verbatim answers
Comp. Q but can not find inference answers
Comp. Q and all answers

---

sentences from the passage, and the poorer readers do just that. Better readers answer with one or two words.

If the students sail through our five minute test, we confidently place them in our regular beginning classes. When they do not, we are faced with a whole range of reading problems which we are only beginning to come to grips with. They will need special materials for recoding as well as special attention to the grammar required for reading at the very least. □

1 Teachers of adult immigrants have been faced with the problem for years, but those of us with University bound students have been exempt until now.

REFERENCE

Goodman, Kenneth S. "Reading: A Psycholinguistic Guessing Game." in *Language and Reading*. V. Gunderson, ed. Washington, DC: Center for Applied Linguistics, 1970.   *TN 6/82*

INSIGHTS FROM OPTOMETRY: A SIDE-VIEW OF TESTING

by Virginia French Allen
Temple University

For the test of peripheral vision, the subject peers into a darkened screen on which a point of light sporadically appears. The light, flashed by the technician, advances from one direction or another toward the center of the screen. The subject presses a button whenever the point of light is perceived.

The task is tedious. Even an adult with professional interest in testing loses interest; attention often flags. The performance has little apparent relevance to everyday *seeing*. It is artificial, as paper-and-pencil tests are artificial when used as measures of communication skills. So muses the subject, a language teacher, while dutifully pressing the beeper at each appearance of the lighted dot.

Afterwards, assured of the hoped-for 20/20 score, the Subject quizzes the Technician about the test procedure:
S: I've done some work with *language* testing, so I'm wondering how you feel about this kind of *vision* test. It's so mechanical, so different from real seeing. How can you get a valid picture when you ask someone to sit there press-

ing a button every time a light appears? That's an unfamiliar technique.
T: Right. So I don't even keep score during the first few minutes of the test. I didn't record your responses till I could see you were feeling comfortable with the procedure. I paid attention to your reactions, though.
S: What do you mean?
T: People have different reaction times. Some can do the task faster than others. Some get tired sooner, too. I had to find out how you reacted, so I could evaluate your responses when I finally began to record them.
S: So you would not give this sort of test to several people at the same time?
T: It wouldn't mean anything. You have to notice so many things about the person while the test is going on.
S: You just mentioned the fatigue factor. When you were trained, did they tell you how long a testing period could be, without reaching the point of diminishing returns?
T: Like I said, every person is different. You have to notice how the person is responding. There's no one length of

time that's right for testing everyone. Sometimes, when they're really elderly, I tell the person to come back for another short session after I've been testing for just five minutes. Once I had a man who had played poker till 4 a.m. that morning. I could tell he was falling asleep in front of the screen. I had him come back another day. You have to watch what is happening as the test goes along.
S: Don't you find that *attention* makes a difference? I'm sure I missed some dots because my mind was on something else when you bashed them on the screen.
T: That didn't really matter. You see, the *pattern* is what's important. I look for the pattern of performance, not the occasional missed beep here and there. That's where the art comes in. The test may look mechanical; that's the word you used. But interpreting what happens, what someone is doing with it—that's what counts. And that takes *art*.
[How many applications to language testing does this episode suggest?] □

TN 8/81

TESOL STATEMENT ON STATEWIDE PROGRAMS OF COMPETENCY TESTING

More than 60% of the States of the United States have mandated programs of competency testing in the basic skills during the last few years, and several more are about to do so. Because the insights gained from recent movements of competency-based program design and of individualized instruction have made us increasingly aware of the complex nature of this kind of measurement, we would like to bring to your attention the following considerations to bear in mind

when planning a testing program.

A. The professional organizations and academic departments specializing in the teaching of English to speakers of other languages provide expertise and should be consulted when decisions are made concerning competency testing of students whose home language or dialect is other than standard English.

B. Parents of the groups being tested and the students themselves need to be consulted. Questions about relevance

and appropriateness of topics, the language to be tested, and the purposes of the tests all need student and parent input.

C. The development of effective measurement instruments is time consuming and costly, but we warn against any cost saving shortcuts that might be considered.

1. Translating existing tests from one language to another does not result in a reliable instrument.

2. Tests developed for or normed on native speakers of a language are not valid or reliable indicators of the language knowledge or skills of a person who is not a native speaker of that language.

3. Tests of proficiency in the modern foreign languages designed for English-speaking students in the U.S. are scaled inappropriately to measure the talents and knowledge of students who are native speakers of those languages.

D. No single instrument can adequately measure students' competency in the basic skills. We urge, therefore, that a variety of opportunities be given to students to demonstrate what they know and that decisions regarding competency never be made on the basis of a single test.

E. Sound objectives and precise goals are essential to any effective testing program. Therefore, the starting point must be to reach agreement on the meaning of "basic" in "basic skills." (For example, specialists in the area of reading know that different reading skills are "basic" to different purposes. What is the purpose of the reading test in your state? To assure success in an academic career? To assure success in a vocation? To document that a student can read directions? a manual? a novel? an application form?)

F. Knowledge of language must be separated from knowledge of subject matter. A test of one should not be used to measure competency in the other.

It is particularly important that, as a student is acquiring a second language or dialect and is concurrently adding to this knowledge in subject matter areas, the testing of the latter be conducted in the *first* language.

Further it is of utmost importance that students who are acquiring knowledge of the language and the content areas simultaneously receive the benefit of considerable instruction in both areas before being tested in either.

G. Because students whose home language is other than standard English may enter a curriculum late in its progression, it is imperative that alternative measures be provided for the testing of late-arriving students.

H. We support a program of assessment which periodically measures the progress of each student, a program of assessment which helps ensure educational success for all students by providing a measurement of what the school needs to do to help the student, e.g., offer remediation or programs of career guidance. We oppose an assessment program to weed out students, to end their academic advancement.

TN 4/79

ing measured, and the description of how to prejudge the reliability of a test. *Item*, incidentally, is preferred over the word "question," since many tests include multiple choice, sentence completion and true/false testing types, and these are obviously not "questions" in the true sense. The latter part of the book contain's the would-be tester's "homework . . . sample tests and workouts . . ., and an impressive and extensive bibliography.

Many of the observations made in this volume are very much a matter of common sense; for example, (on the subject of avoiding "traps" for the student):

In the following example, the testee has to select the correct answer (C), but the whole item is constructed so as to trap the testee into making choice B or D.

When I met Tim yesterday it was the first time I _____ his since Christmas.

A. saw   C. had seen
B. have seen   D. have been seeing

When this item actually appeared in a test, it was found that the more proficient students, in fact chose B and D, as they had developed the correct habit of associating the tense forms *have seen* and *have been seeing* with SINCE and FOR. Several of the less proficient students who had not learnt (sic) to associate the perfect tense forms with SINCE and FOR chose the "correct" answer.

The section of the book devoted to testing listening and comprehension skills is especially well-presented, with valuable clues to the successful choice and use of test pictures and charts.

To add to the invaluable information on how to compose valid English Language Tests, there are practical hints on techniques of administering tests, including oral production tests. Again, many of the observations made are a matter of common sense, so that the reader asks himself "Why didn't *I* do/think/see/say that?" In short, this is a practical, no-nonsense guide to language test writing, a highly readable and unpretentious work.

In recent years, ESL (like other fields of academe) has been replete with boring, confusing or inaccurate publications which offer little information or guidance to either teacher or student; *Writing English Language Tests* is the antithesis of all those worst excesses of the "publish or perish" philosophy. Even to one not interested in writing English Language tests it would be refreshing to encounter a work of solid scholarship, lucidly presented in clear, precise English. This volume belongs in every ESL department's library or resource room, not only as a guide to writing tests but as an example of how to present well-founded knowledge in an articulate way.

TN 12/76

BOOK REVIEW

WRITING ENGLISH LANGUAGE TESTS

(J.B. Heaton, published by Longman Group Limited, 1975)

Reviewed by Anthea Babaian
LaGuardia Community College

It would probably be a source of amazement to English Language Testees (and also, unfortunately, to many testers) to discover that teachers require help with the preparation of tests. Nevertheless, it is true that, with rare exceptions, test-writing has been a highly inexact science, marked by a well-developed tradition of "muddling through." Even commercially-produced tests are often extremely deficient in many areas, although the classroom teacher can encounter difficulties knowing exactly where the faults lie.

Writing English Language Tests is one of Longman's *Handbooks for Language Teachers* which enumerates and clarifies the common pitfalls and problems in English Language test composition, and presents practical and multiple solutions. However, not only is the how-to of test-writing covered, the why-to is also discussed, and this in itself is valuable information for ESL teachers. As we all know, formal tests have been in disfavor for some time, so it is interesting to read

some well-balanced arguments in favor of testing, most markedly as a teaching (prescriptive) tool rather than purely a traditional instrument for student assessment. The book contains fair evaluations of every conceivable type of testing procedure, even down to the déclassé and unmentionable DICTATION, which, the author concludes, can be a worthwhile teaching aid but is a faulty testing method.

If one accepts the assertion that some Language Testing is necessary and that teachers have to write and administer tests in order to evaluate student needs in the individual classroom, then it is clear that many teachers could benefit from practical information in five major areas.

This book covers all these points thoroughly and clearly and is, therefore, invaluable to the classroom teacher.

Other topics discussed in the book include the evaluation of several different kinds of test items in relation to the particular language elements or skills which are supposed to be being

Section 8. Sharing the Professional Wealth

This volume is evidence of one of the ways that teaching professionals share their ideas with each other. Included in this volume are articles by teachers and researchers, administrators and teacher trainers telling us what they do that works. A newsletter such as the *TESOL Newsletter* also acts as a forum for ideas and causes which affect the teaching profession. It provides our members with the opportunity to try out an idea. More importantly it provides a forum for feedback on such ideas.

Another way that teachers share is through professional presentations either for their own school community, local professional organization or for wider regional, national and international audiences. What makes our profession as vital as it is today is this sharing. One of our professional obligations is to "keep up" with what's going on by reading professional publications and attending professional meetings. Another is to share our ideas and our concerns. We encourage you to write to and for your local, national and international professional publications. We encourage you to stand up in front of your fellow professionals and share your ideas and your concerns.

In this section we reprint five articles which provide aids to proposing, organizing, presenting and writing papers and other professional presentations. While each workshop or conference establishes what the content and format for presentations should be, the ideas presented here are basic to any professional presentation. "Making Your Abstract Concrete" by Margot C. Kimball and Adrian S. Palmer (6/79) offers examples both of what to do and what not to do in writing your proposal for a professional presentation. Richard Yorkey follows this article with his outline on "How to Prepare and Present a Professional Paper" (2/78).

One of the problems with a conference paper is delivering it; how to present it orally when it is a written document. Fraida Dubin's "The Conference Paper as an Oral Script: Writing to be Heard" (2/80) helps us to come to terms with this problem and Marge Kaplan offers "Conference Paper Presentation: Step-by-Step Procedures" (12/81). Finally, Yorkey offers us some cogent remarks about the problems in producing a presentation which concludes that "A Workshop is Work" (2/79). All presentations and their preparation are work; we hope these views from the experts will make that work easier.

We have included one book review in this section; *Research Writing: A Complete Guide to Research Papers* by Dean Membering, reviewed by Macey McKee (6/83). While it discusses documentation styles, the evaluation of evidence, and the use of the library, it also deals with the organization and development of proposals and papers in a way useful to the researcher or classroom practician.

It might also be useful to the writer/presenter to look again at Kathleen Bailey's article in section 6, which takes up the possibilities and pitfalls of information gathering (whether for research or paper presentation) in her article "Illustrations of Murphy's Law Abound in Classroom Research on Language Use" (8/83).

MAKING YOUR ABSTRACT CONCRETE: HOW TO GET THE MESSAGE ACROSS IN 250 WORDS

Margot C. Kimball and Adrian S. Palmer
Westminster College   University of Utah

For several years now we have been evaluating abstracts of papers submitted for presentation at the TESOL conventions, and we have often felt frustrated by abstracts which were either so vague or so unstructured as to make it nearly impossible for us to judge fairly the content lurking inside. Moreover, in some extreme cases, the author even appeared to be deliberately secretive about his intentions—a strategy which surely does not enhance the abstract's chances for acceptance.

Having wrestled with this problem, we have gradually developed some criteria for a well-written abstract, as well as a procedure for putting an abstract together. We believe that the criteria and the procedure, which are both discussed below, will help writers of abstracts communicate their intentions clearly to readers, though we cannot, of course, guarantee that the content will be interesting or worthwhile.

Criteria of a Good Abstract

The following are the criteria that we, as readers, apply when we evaluate an abstract. They fall into two categories: those criteria which indicate that the paper will be *well* presented and those which indicate that it is *worth* presenting.

1. The abstract should state the author's topic *and* position clearly. It should say what he will talk about and why he feels it is important. For example, it is not enough for the abstract to state that the presentation will demonstrate a given technique; it must also state why the technique is important and to what use it may be put.

2. The abstract should outline the areas or sub-topics which the presentation will cover. It is not enough for the abstract merely to describe the technique being demonstrated; it must also indicate, for example, that the presentation will compare the technique to similar ones, will detail the steps the teacher must follow in using the technique, and will discuss ways of adapting the technique for students at different levels.

3. It should be apparent from the abstract that the amount of material to be included in the presentation can be covered adequately in the allotted time. Trying to cover too much in too little time will leave the audience both confused and, possibly, irritated.

4. The writing in the abstract should be literate. A poorly edited, unproofed abstract gives the impression that the paper or presentation will be equally ill-prepared.

While we use the above to judge how well thought-out the presentation will be, we rely on the following criteria as indications of whether or not it will make a valuable contribution to the field:

5. The topic should be of current significance for the specified audience. "Current significance," of course, does not necessarily imply that only the new and the innovative are worth hearing. A workshop in applied linguistics, for example, may not necessarily present any new applications, yet it may still be of considerable interest to the classroom teacher.

6. The assumptions, premises, or experimental design upon which the presentation is based should be sound. While this is certainly a highly subjective consideration, it is also an important one. Thus, the abstract should give enough information—about the problem which the presentation will attempt to solve, about the premise on which the research is based, about the procedures which have been followed, or about the principles which underlie the application—that an informed reader can feel assured that the presentation is based on solid ground.

7. When it is relevant, the abstract should refer to some recognized authorities in the area. While there are, of course, many kinds of presentations for which it is either not necessary or not possible to refer to the literature, a brief reference to leading authorities does indicate that the author has done his homework and is building on a foundation which has already been laid.

A Procedure for Writing Abstracts

Now, how can all this be organized into a 250-word abstract? We have developed a three-step procedure for writing which is outlined briefly below and then illustrated with four well-written abstracts taken from past TESOL programs.

STEP 1. Give the background to the topic. State what the need or problem is, why there is such a need, and/or refer to others who have addressed this need.

STEP 2. State the thesis: describe the topic *and* the position you will take.

STEP 3. Give the divisions or sub-topics you intend to cover and, if relevant, the steps you will follow in your presentations.

Example 1

(Report on research which had been completed at the time the abstract was written. 1976 TESOL Program, 30 minute presentation.)

TOWARD THE MEASUREMENT OF FUNCTIONAL PROFICIENCY: CONTEXTUALIZATION OF THE 'NOISE' TEST

by Stephen J. Gaies
Harry L. Gradman
Bernard Spolsky

The noise test, as originally designed by a team headed by Bernard Spolsky, is a dictation of fifty discrete English sentences, varying in syntactic complexity, recorded on tape with accompanying background white noise. In terms of both its theoretical rationale (that is, that speakers of natural languages normally communicate under less than ideal conditions with reduced redundancy as the behavioral norm) and its statistical reliability, the noise test has generally been accepted as a useful instrument for evaluating overall English proficiency.

A recent study, however, suggests that "while the noise test brings into undeniably clear focus the nonnative proficiency of a subject, it exaggerates to some degree the difference between a subject's ability to function in a normal, real-life situation of reduced redundancy and that of a native speaker." The study also asserts that further judgements about the usefulness of the noise test can be made only after revision (with a special emphasis on contextualization of the instrument).

The present study describes the process of revising the noise test. The revision was carried out in such a way as to increase the face validity of the test in terms of the situation in which it is most often used: namely, to evaluate the proficiency of EFL/ESL students planning to pursue university degree work. The technical aspects of adding background noise are outlined. In addition, the problem of controlling for syntactic comparability among the test items is discussed, and preliminary data on the performance of revised instrument are given.

(Paragraphs 1 and 2 give the background. The first sentence in paragraph 3 states the thesis, while the rest of the paragraph outlines the sub-topics and the steps the presentation will cover.)

Example 2

(Report on research which was still in progress at the time the abstract was written. 1975 TESOL Program, 30 minute presentation.)

CHILD AND ADULT PERCEPTUAL STRATEGIES IN SECOND LANGUAGE ACQUISITION

by Eileen Nam

Bever and Denton (unpublished paper) showed that Spanish speaking children learning English as a second language go through the same states in the use of NVN=SVO perceptual strategy (taking the first noun as the agent and the second as the object regardless of morphological cues) as do native children, although they do so at a later age because of their later exposure to the language. Ervin-Tripp (*TESOL Quarterly*, June 1974) showed that English speaking children learning French recapitulate the same developmental stages of production as do natives, again at an older age because of later exposure.

Adults learning a second language, however, appear to rely on strategies different from those available to the child. Bever, Nam and Shallo (unpublished paper) showed that Spanish speaking adults learning English as a second language do not go through the stages used by children with respect to the NVN=SVO strategy. Rather, they get better in the comprehension of all sentence types tested as their mastery of English increases.

All of the studies mentioned have dealt with Indo-European speakers learning an Indo-European language. If we are to begin to replicate the universal validity to such results, it is necessary to replicate the experiments with speakers of languages from other families. I propose to begin this needed research by comparing speakers of Korean and speakers of Spanish learning English as a second language.

My proposal is to use the same comprehension tests used by Bever and Denton, and Bever, Nam, and Shallo on adult and child native speakers of Spanish and Korean who are learning English as a second language, either through instruction or through exposure. Similar tests in the native language will also be given. The tests in English will be scored according to correctness, as will the tests given to the children in their native language. The tests given to adults in their native language will be scored according to reaction time, as few if any errors are expected. Each of the four groups will be divided into quartiles, as will both groups of adults and both groups of children; this will be done according to native English speaker raters' judgment of their mastery of English based on a taped oral interview.

The data will be analyzed in several ways. It will be determined whether the children, irrespective of native language, go through the same stages as Bever and Denton's subjects with respect to the NVN-SVO strategy. If not, it will be determined whether native language is a factor. The adults' data will be analyzed to see if the results of Bever, Nam, and Shallo are replicated and again to see if native language is a factor.

In addition for the adults (and possible for the children) it will be determined whether there are individual perceptual strategies. This will be done by comparing subjects' responses on the native language tests with their responses on the English test.

(Paragraphs 1 and 2 give the background. The thesis and position are stated in paragraph 3. Paragraphs 4, 5, and 6 outline the sub-topics and the steps the presentation will cover.)

Example 3

(Report on a teaching technique. 1978 TESOL Program, 30 minute presentation.)

A TECHNIQUE FOR AIDING SECOND LANGUAGE READING COMPREHENSION

by Howard R. Selekman
Howard H. Kleinmann

The participation of second language learners in communicative interaction activities has been recognized as a necessary step in developing learner communicative

or sociolinguistic competence in speaking a second language (Hymes, 1972; Paulston, 1974). Few suggestions, however, have been offered as to how second language learners can effectively deal with the socio-cultural content of reading material, which often times is the source and cause of misunderstanding and misinterpretation.

The present paper describes a technique for facilitating reading comprehension in a second language at the intermediate and advanced levels. Rooted in the theoretical framework of Goodman (1972) and Smith (1971), who emphasize the importance of categorical organization and prior experience in reading comprehension, the present paper suggests the inclusion of a communicative interaction/problem solving activity in which the crucial underlying socio-cultural pattern(s) of the reading passage are actively experienced by students prior to the reading activity. The paper also reports on the application of this technique in an ESL class comprised of native speakers of Russian.

(Paragraph 1 gives the background. The thesis is stated in the first sentence of paragraph 2, and the rest of the paragraph outlines the sub-topics and the steps the presentation will cover.)

Example 4

(Workshop in materials development. 2½ hour presentation.)

WORKSHOP IN CRITERION-BASED COMPOSITION GRADING

by Adrian S. Palmer
Margot C. Kimball

When the language teacher grades student compositions, he faces two major problems. First, he must decide what his criteria for grading are and how heavily to weight each one. While there are already a number of grading scales for compositions by native speakers (Diederich 1974, Braddock 1963, Cohen 1974), they are not properly weighted for evaluating non-native speakers' compositions because they emphasize style and editing over communicativity.

The presenters have developed a criterion-based and quantified composition grading kit which includes a set of grading scales, graded and annotated compositions at various levels, and a grading grid for the student. The system was developed specifically for the non-native speaker of English and has the following features: (1) It equates to the most widely-used composition grading scale, that of the Michigan Test Composition; (2) it not only establishes criteria, but quantifies the grading; and (3) it is easy to learn, and grading with it takes no more time than grading on a more wholistic basis.

The workshop will cover the following: (1) a discussion of problems of grading compositions; (2) a presentation of grading scales and the criteria for each area; (3) an analysis of graded student compositions; and (4) practice in grading sample compositions.

(Paragraph 1 gives the background. The first sentence of paragraph 2 states the thesis. The rest of paragraph 2 and all of paragraph 2 outline the sub-topics and the steps the presentation will cover.)

The Three Cardinal Sins

While the above abstracts illustrate what the writer of a good abstract *should* do, perhaps a word of warning about what *not* to do is in order here.

In the course of reading abstracts, we have identified the Three Cardinal Sins of writing abstracts. To highlight these sins—and otherwise exhort the Prudent to avoid them—we have trumped up some representatives of their breed, which we herewith offer, albeit diffidently, as Bad Examples.

The first says rather too much—and promises to exhaust the audience by doing so in a mere 20 minutes. The second, on the other hand, is a study in secrecy! it reveals nothing three different ways—and tritely, at that. The last one, however, is our favorite. We are offering a prize to the reader who can make sense of all that jargon. Moreover, while a restrained and careful reference to the literature sheds a glow of credibility to any abstract, citing 10 sources clearly constitutes a snow job.

Bad example 1

(The "All Your Eggs in One Basket Approach." 20 minute paper.)

THE BI-DIALECTAL PARADOX: IS BI-DIALECTALISM REALLY POSSIBLE?

With the current emphasis in the United States on programs which contribute to students' positive self image, the question of bi-dialectalism has assumed considerable importance. In this presentation, theoretical issues concerning the value of bi-dialectalism to the individual, the degree and amount of code switching involved, and the question of proficiency in not one but two dialects are explored. The problems of implementing, developing materials for, and staffing such a program will be discussed. The considerations of the feasibility of such a program will include a survey of the phonological and socio-linguistic issues involved; and a brief run-down on bidialectal programs currently operating in the U.S.A., Canada, and India. Time permitting, a case history of the five year program instituted at Panguitch, Utah in 1973 will be presented.

Bad example 2

(The "Don't Go Near the Water" approach.)

HOW THE OTHER HALF LIVES: AN ATTEMPT AT LETTING THE LEFT HAND KNOW WHAT THE RIGHT HAND IS DOING

Most ESL programs operate for and by themselves. As a result they are isolated from the innovative approaches and techniques of other programs—approaches and techniques which could be of great use to them.

The authors will attempt in their presentation to "let the left hand know what the right hand is doing" by surveying the innovative approaches and techniques used in Thailand. It is the thesis of this paper that "what's sauce for the goose is sauce for the gander," and that an exploration of cross-insemination of ideas in Thailand will prove useful in any country where ESL programs operate in isolation.

Bad example 3

(The "This'll Kill 'em in Carson City" approach.)

A THEORY OF INTERPERSONAL SYLLABI: 60/20/20, THE GOLDEN MEAN

This paper proposes a way of organizing materials for language didactics which the authors call the "interpersonal syllabus." Based upon Lewin's Field Theory, an off-shoot of the Berlin Gestalt Group, the goal of such a syllabus is to create the optimum environment for three types of native-non-native feedback in dyadic interaction. Turescheva and Comaneci (1976) have identified three types of corrections: "negative plus" protocols, "positive minus" protocols, and "negative minus" protocols.

A survey of the literature reveals that a 60/20/20 ratio is optimum. This is in line with the findings of Anusvara (400 B.C.), Grimm and Grimm (1893), Grmzwski and Hsiu (1964), Jarvik (1912, 1932, 1962, 1978), Neilson, Schilling, and Jennings (1883), Ntsantsa (personal communication), Richelieu (1758), Sakamoto (1977, 1978), and Smith (in press).

Next, the authors describe several popular approaches to sequencing to see whether or not they incorporate this optimum balance of correctional heuristics. They conclude that most existing syllabi emphasize "positive minus" correction—with the result that the classroom ambiance is either disfavorable, affectively speaking, or unconstrained (in the usual "laissez-faire" sense).

As a way around this problem, the authors propose the Interpersonal Syllabus (technical term) in which the syllabus developer begins, not by selecting structures, but by providing a climate for self-selecting affectivo-correctional routines. It is believed that these routines limit the verbal content of the interpersonal transactions in such a way that the cognitive load does not exceed the limitations of short term memory.

A Proposed Rating Chart for Abstracts

In order to quantify the evaluation of abstracts, we have constructed a rating chart which provides a weighted scale for each of the criteria mentioned above.

A. *Indications that the paper will be well presented*

	High	Medium	Low
1. Author's topic and position are clear	(6)	(3)	(0)
2. Abstract gives a list of areas or subtopics the presentation will cover	(6)	(3)	(0)
3. The amount of material outlined can be covered adequately in the time allotted	(6)	(3)	(0)
4. The writing is literate	(6)	(3)	(0)

B. *Indications that the paper is worth presenting*

	Yes	No
5. The topic is of current significance for the specified audience	(6)	(3) (0)
6. The assumptions, premises, or experimental design upon which the presentation is based is sound	(0)	(−12)
7. IF APPLICABLE: The abstract refers to some recognized authorities in the area	(0)	(−6)

TN 6/79

HOW TO PREPARE AND PRESENT A PROFESSIONAL PAPER*

By Richard Yorkey
Concordia University, Montreal

It may seem presumptuous to write a "how to" article of this kind for teachers. However, at almost every recent professinoal conference, I have heard numerous comments about the disappointing way in which papers are delivered. This seems to be a polite way of saying that many are read badly. It is surprising—and discouraging—to realize that many ESL teachers do not know how, or do not take the trouble, to prepare and present a professional paper effectively.

1. How to prepare a paper.

A. By "paper" is meant a report on some theoretical aspect in the field, on research results of some kind, or on some particular method or materials that are worth sharing with colleagues.

B. Papers of this kind are usually assigned about twenty minutes at a conference. (The longer, one-hour papers are reserved for keynote addresses and plenary sessions. Many of the following suggestions apply to these longer papers as well, but attention is directed here to the shorter papers as defined above.)

C. Whatever your topic may be, remember that it should be written with your expected audience in mind. Admittedly it is often difficult to gauge the knowledge and interests of the audience; there is always the danger of appearing to speak either down to them or over their heads.

1. This problem can be partly resolved by choosing a title that, though perhaps less catchy, accurately describes the content of your paper, one that implies the kind of audience who

would likely be interested and prepared to understand. At some conferences an abstract of the papers is published in the program. Here also might be a statement that defines the intended audience.

2. The problem can also be partly resolved by announcing at the outset the kind of audience you expect. (This need not be quite as blunt as Chomsky was at McGill University several years ago when he announced that he expected no more than five per cent of the audience to understand what he intended to say about his trace theory; on the other hand, there was therefore no excuse for one of the few remaining members of the audience to protest at the end that he had said nothing about his political philosophy.) Particularly if your topic is esoteric or highly theoretical, you can anticipate complaints of irrelevance by clearly stating your understanding of the interests and needs of the audience. Those who do not fit into this category should feel free to leave quietly; their time could probably be spent more profitably elsewhere.

D. From this listener's point of view, it is also useful to be told such things as (1) what, in brief, is going to be said; (2) whether a synopsis or outline (including a bibliography) will be distributed; and (3) when and where the paper might be published or if a copy can be obtained before publication.

E. The most common problem in the presentation of papers seems to be the pressure of time. At least half the papers I have attended are rushed, extemporaneously edited, or actually not completed because of the failure to plan the time carefully. (In one well-known case in which the chairman tried but failed to stop a presentation after more than the allotted

time, the next speaker actually was not able to present his paper at all!) Remember: your topic should be narrowed down to the time available. Using a twenty-minute paper as an example, here are some suggestions that may help:

1. Outline and organize your paper. Do this well before the date of your presentation.

2. Write the paper. Do this well enough in advance to put it aside for a while, or to circulate it among colleagues for critical comments. Then revise it. A paper that is to be delivered orally should be written in a somewhat different style from a paper that is to be read silently. This is a matter of individual preference and judgment. Generally speaking, however the style may be less formal, with shorter sentences and with parenthetical comments. Acknowledgements that usually appear in footnotes should be worked into the text itself.

3. You are a speaker, not a reader. Time the paper by reading it aloud at the speed and with the phrasing and pauses you expect to use during the actual presentation. (The average page of double-spaced type takes between 1½-2 minutes to read at an appropriate speed, but it is best to time yourself by actually reading the paper aloud.) Include the approximate time that may be necessary for any visuals you use, such as overhead transparencies, or for the distribution of or reference to handouts.

4. If the paper comes out to exactly twenty minutes, go back over the paper and cut four or five minutes. During the presentation before an audience, you will generally find that you take more time than you planned. (A rule of thumb might be: for a twenty-minute paper, plan a practiced fifteen minutes; for a thirty-minute paper, plan a practiced twenty-two minutes;

*I am pleased to acknowledge the critical comments of my colleague, Prof. Gwen Newsham, and my graduate student, Jeffrey Barlow, in the preparation of this article.

for a sixty-minute paper, plan a practiced fifty minutes.) It is much better to say less than to read faster! By giving yourself a leeway of a few minutes, you avoid the pressure and the need to rush, to read or speak faster, to cut out examples, or to have the chairman interrupt you in mid-paragraph.

F. Giving a paper is giving a performance. no professional performer would presume to appear on stage without adequate rehearsal; neither should a professional speaker. Once your paper is written and timed, have it typed double- or even triple- spaced. The typing should be so neat and legible that, whatever the lighting problems, it can be read without hesitation or difficulty. Practice reading the paper aloud. Mark the pauses, underline key words and phrases that should be emphasized. There is no need to feel rushed; you have already timed your presentation. At this point concentrate on delivery. Sufficient practice will make you familiar with the sequence and the sentence structure; thus you will develop confidence:

1. to speak rather than merely read the paper aloud, even if this means occasionally departing from the exact words or phrases of the paper;

2. to look up at your audience (eye contact establishes rapport and creates interest and attention; remember to include everyone in the audience: the front, back, left, right, and center);

3. to feel free to extemporize. By looking at the audience, you may sometimes recognize the signs of doubt, confusion, or misunderstanding. You may want to briefly digress from your text to elaborate, explain, or clarify a point.

II. How to present a paper.

A. Before your presentation, it is a good idea to check the room where you will give the paper. Is there a lectern on which to place your paper? Is the lighting adequate? Is there a microphone? Is it necessary? If you are going to use audio-visual aids (e.g., a tape recorder or overhead projector), is there a convenient outlet? How large is the room? What is the arrangement of chairs? What is a convenient way to distribute handouts? When should they be distributed?

B. Be on time. In some convention hotels, conference rooms are difficult to find. If you have not already been to the room (as in A above), allow enough time to locate the room, to meet the chairman and possibly other speakers at the session.

C. You may be asked to sit on stage or at the table with other speakers. During the presentation of preceding papers, relax and show interest. It is too late to do any more preparation for your own paper. Furthermore, papers are often grouped according to similar areas or interest; you may hear something in one of the papers that you may want to refer to during your own presentation.

D. After you are introduced, it is useful to have some spontaneous comment to make before launching into your paper. A formal greeting is not necessary, but you may want to introduce your paper by some relevant reference to an incident or idea that has occurred during the conference or preceding papers. In any case, try to avoid standing up, fiddling with your watch, and then head down, starting to read with no information introduction whatsoever. Some kind of personal comment at the beginning establishes rapport with the audience.

E. Do not be intimidated by a microphone. If one is available and necessary, adjust it so that you can speak audibly and so that it doesn't get in the way of your paper. If a lectern is available, it is probably best to use it. The pages of your paper should be loose so that each page can be easily slid to the side or placed under the others.

F. Keep an unobtrusive watch on the time.

The chairman of the session may give you a five- or two-minute warning. This should not rattle you if you have carefully planned and timed your presentation. you should, in any case, be near enough to the end so that you don't have to rush.

G. Adjust the volume and modulation of your voice to the room and the size of your audience. Avoid a droning monotone. Try to enliven your voice with appropriate pace, pauses, meaningful emphasis, and animation. These points of diction and elocution are what you have already praticed numerous times.

H. After the presentation of papers, there is usually time for questions. These may be immediately after each paper or after all of the papers during the session. in either case, if a question is directed to you:

1. Listen! Be sure you understand the question.

2. It is helpful and courteous to repeat the question if you feel it has not been heard by everyone in the audience.

3. State your answer as completely but as concisely as possible. Some questions are frequently preceded by anecdotes or lengthy statements of doubt or disagreement. Professional courtesy demands patience, but listen carefully for the possibility of red herrings or traps of various kinds. You may want to ignore, or use wit to respond to , thinly-veiled professional attacks. Simply identify what you feel is the basic question and answer only that.

I. You may be asked to submit your paper for publication in a journal or the proceedings of the conference. On the basis of your presentation and the feedback acquired, make whatever revisions will improve your paper. Revise it to be read silently. it is best to do this immediately while the ideas are still fresh in your mind and before other obligations crowd your life.

THE CONFERENCE PAPER AS AN ORAL SCRIPT: WRITING-TO-BE-HEARD

by Fraida Dubin
University of Southern California

Two years ago *TESOL Newsletter* (February 1978) published an article by Richard Yorkey on 'How to Prepare and Present a Professional Paper.' As TESOL participants get ready for the 1980 Convention in San Francisco, that article is still an invaluable reference. In one section, the part in which the author comments on the stylistic characteristics of a paper that is written-to-be-heard— Yorkey, I believe, has moved over the heart of the matter too lightly. Particularly since it is the matter that is most pertinent to specialists in language.

In the article Yorkey stated: "A paper that is to be delivered orally should be written in a somewhat different style from a paper that is to be read silently. This is a matter of individual preference and judgment. Generally speaking, however, the style may be less formal, with shorter sentences and with parenthetical comments. Acknowledgements that usually appear in footnotes should be worked into the text itself."

Then, in the final part on revision, he said: "Revise it to be read silently."

There is nothing in these statements with which one would want to take issue. But do these brief suggestions about the "somewhat different" styles of oral vs. written language tell the whole story? I believe they overlook many interesting characteristics of writing intended for a listening audience. Few people, in fact, consider the paper to be delivered orally as a distinct type of writing, indoctrinated as we are with the conventions of expository prose. My purpose is to delve further into a type of writing I call the oral script, to point out how it is distinct from writing intended to be read.

The separate domains of spoken vs. written language have been well described. While written form requires polish and refinement, spoken language is characterized by spontaneity. In writing one seeks clarity, but more often in spoken discourse the aim is rapport. Written language presupposes distance between an author and audience, while spoken language only flourishes when

there is reciprocity. On the other hand, in preparing a paper for oral presentation the writer strives for the tone of spoken language, knowing all the time that it will not be a successful performance if the script sounds too natural.

For the talk prepared for a listening audience is neither purely spoken nor written language. Rather, it lies somewhere on a continuum between these two poles, containing features of each along with special characteristics of its own. In many respects, it is a rare species in a culture such as our own in which the printed word holds authority. Apart from the conference paper and its sub-types, only a specialized few come to mind: the sermon, the political address, the comic monologue. Not many of us have had to learn the craft of producing any of these forms.

Suggestions on how to write a conference paper for oral presentation may be beside the point for some. One colleague pointed out to me that for conferences he prepares "a paper for publication" and then simply makes a few notes on a 3 × 5 card from which to talk. This procedure may suffice for those seasoned to standing at a podium and speaking without a script, or for professional talk-givers who, more likely than not, replay the same material before different audiences. But many of us at TESOL Conventions have not had this kind of experience. Or we prefer the security a fully worked out script in-hand provides before approaching the microphone and a room full of strange faces.

In developing Yorkey's suggestions, I have looked at the following materials: 1) Comments on giving oral talks in representative English handbooks—prescriptive beliefs. 2) Assorted published work for radio, together with examples of conference papers in which both an oral and a written version had been prepared by the authors—descriptive data. 3) Characteristics I have noted while listening to effective talks at conference sessions—participant observations. These various sources offer provocative ideas concerning the phonological, lexical, syntactic and organizational features of writing-to-be-heard.

Prescriptive beliefs

The following suggestions are from two authorities, Barzun and Wood:

1. Phonological characteristics: "Watch the sound of your prose. You will have to *speak* these sentences, so you must assemble words that your tongue can wrap itself around. Avoid the noun plague in your compound sentences, or you will be giving out -*tion*, -*tions*, -*sion*, -*sions* like a steam engine; and remember that *s*, *ce*, *sh* coming in a row are disagreeable as well as a possible danger to your delivery ('she sells seashells by the seashore'). (Barzun, pg. 74).
2. Lexical characteristics: "More personal pronouns (*I*, *you*, *us*, *we*) are used in an oral report than in a written report because the listening audience is there, immediately present." (Wood, pg. 176).

"Use as few technical terms as possible, not because they may not be understood but because they may not be heard aright; they are not common words and many are alike in sound." (Barzun, pg. 74).
3. Syntactic characteristics: "No listener, however sharp or intent, can perform the feat of following by ear and retaining by memory the turns and twists and factual contents of a long complex sentence . . . The paper that is to be read must be written in simple and compound sentences and—to prevent monotony—in complex sentences of the shortest kind. The heavy work of exposition must be done by the main clause. Short and long, simple and short-complex must be mixed, not only for variety but for additional

emphasis, a short simple sentence serving to clinch a point or, again, to introduce a new topic." (Barzun, pg. 76).
4. Organizational characteristics: "Oral reports have fewer main ideas than written reports . . . they contain more supportive material . . . they have more transitional material . . . to show when a speaker or writer is leaving one idea and introducing the next." (Wood, pgs. 175-176).

". . . there is more occasion than in writing to indicate changes of subject in so many words: 'Now I want to turn to' . . . (or 'take up' or 'remind you'). Everything that helps the audience know where they are or what they should be thinking of will be gratefully received. You must therefore observe more than you usually do the principle of matching parts, the exact tethering of pronouns and anglers, and the close linking of modifiers." (Barzun, pg. 74).

Descriptive data

1. Radio writing: In an earlier era, writing for the listening ear was produced as a distinct form by radio writers. Although it no longer flourishes, there are a few extant examples such as the Columbia Broadcasting System series, 'The Odyssey File,' literally radio editorials. From this corpus, which included the non-dramatic work of Norman Corwin and the CBS editorials, these characteristics have implications for oral presentations:

—*Word repetition*: While expository writing frowns on repeating the same word in a paragraph, Corwin frequently does just the opposite:

"How *would* you like to get up before an audience of five million people and introduce yourself? *Would* you rap on the edge of a glass with a spoon to get attention, like this? (Rapping on glass) Do you think that *would* quiet such an audience? *Would* you clear your throat like this? (clears throat). Or *would* you try to ride over their noise by shouting through a public address system the traditional salutation . . . And assuming you got the five million to quiet down, how *would* you then proceed to introduce yourself?" ('Anatomy of Sound,' in Corwin, 1944. p. 233).
—*Aliteration*: Frequently, words close to each other begin or end with the same sound, despite Barzun's warning about sibilants: ". . . as though you were a night *base*ball game, only *big*ger" (ibid.)

"Good *z*enith to you, in all *z*ones, in all island*s*, in all continent*s*." ('Program To Be Opened in a Hundred Years,' in Corwin, 1944. p. 395.)

"They *w*on it by the *w*eight and the pers*ua*sion of steel and flame and by the *blood* of their *bodies*, and by a *vio*lence ne*ver* seen be*fore* that time; nor, *thanks* to *them*, since *that* time." (ibid.)

—*Title expansions*: In the radio editorials, titles consist of a catchy phrase (for example, 'We're All Plugged Into the Same Socket,' 'Dying Standards,' 'Just Plain Kids.') Then the introductory sentences identify and explain the phrase. The idea contained in the title is sustained over two minutes of air-time with only supporting illustrations but no new ideas introduced.
—*Short sentences*: One reads/listens to numerous air editorials without ever seeing/hearing an introductory clause. Sentences are simple or compound, frequently quite brief.
—*Sentence connectors*: The *and's* and *but's* are repeated over and over with very few examples of other connecting material.
—*Paragraph length*: The numerous examples of the two, three, or even one sentence paragraph probably indicate that paragraph development has little relevance for the oral script.
2. Oral/written versions: Writers are apt to labor painstakingly over one or the other version, oblivious to the special requirements of each. However, I was able to look at two versions in which the authors had consciously aimed at first a listening and then a reading audience:
—*Intensifiers*: For publication purposes, the adverbials that add extra emphasis are frequently crossed out, but the oral version is filled with words such as: *really, quite, particularly, too, very, nearly, pretty, awfully, terribly, simply, solely*, etc.
—*Pronominal reference*: Oral versions have repetition of titles, proper names, and place names rather than pronouns referring to previously mentioned items.
—*Traffic signals*: Oral versions tend to have many more expressions that signal what has just been stated and what will follow: ('I've just listed,' 'Now, I'm going to explain,' 'What comes next is . . .')
—*Appeal to senses*: At times, vivid vocabulary in the oral version becomes subdued in the version for print: For example, 'cuts, clips, and pastes' changed to 'manages the intricacies of classroom management.'

Participant observaions

The familiar formula offered for a successful oral talk is, "begin with a funny story." But a humorous beginning in which the presenter catches the audience's attention needs to be followed with a listenable script. From my own observations, I suggest that speakers consider these points:

1. Latecomers and early leavers: Since latecomers and early leavers are more the rule than the exception, a good oral script should take the occurrence into account. The conventional outline type of organization does not fit an audience

made up of many who will not be present for the entire presentation. Building up to an ending in which the main points are only summarized in the closing minutes may be lost on one-third of the audience, just as announcing only at the beginning what will be said during the talk loses another third. I prefer a modified cyclical plan in which the same point is made three or four times in the script but in each cycle it appears in slightly different language and from an altered point of view. So, instead of an outline of main points (plus supporting details) such as A, B, C, D, one uses a plan of A^1, A^2, A^3, A^4. A possible cyclical plan is the type where a main point is illustrated by three or four long, narrative-style examples.

2. The handout: An effective accompaniment for an oral script gives a quick, visual cue to the presenter's plan. Some listen better when they write, so make the handout sparse, allowing space for people to take notes if they wish. In addition, the handout can provide bibliographical references that will be useful after the conference; tell the audience that the piece of paper is a "take-home." Providing too much detail often draws people's attention from the speaker. If the handout must contain technical information, statistics, graphs, etc. try distributing it at the end of the session.

3. The wind-up: If you want questions and comments, guide the audience's participation by seeking their responses to *your* questions. This technique tends to ward off attention seekers who may try to dominate the session with long-winded comments or even hostile questions.

Finally, try monitoring the sessions you attend at TESOL/San Francisco for good oral script writing. It is likely that the effective presentations will contain most of the features cited in this article.

REFERENCES

Barzun, Jacques. 1975. Simple & Direct: A Rhetoric for Writers. New York: Harper & Row.
Columbia Broadcasting System. (no date) 'The Odyssey File.' (audio-tapes).
Corwin, Norman. 1942. Thirteen By Corwin. New York: Henry Holt & Co.
———. 1944. More By Corwin. New York: Henry Holt & Co.
Wood, Nancy V. 1978. Reading & Study Skills. New York: Holt, Rinehart.
Yorkey, Richard. 'How To Prepare And Present a Professional Paper.' *TESOL Newsletter.* XII:2 (Feb. 1978). pgs. 3-4.

TN 2/80

CONFERENCE PAPER PRESENTATION: STEP-BY-STEP PROCEDURES

by **Marge Kaplan**
Roseville Minnesota Public Schools

Your paper has been accepted for conference presentation. Initially you have a burst of pride and self-satisfaction that your work has been considered valuable. But, subsequently, you realize there are several issues about the presentation to be considered. Will you plan to read the paper as you have written it? Or, will you adapt the written form to an oral presentation: If the latter is your choice, how is this done?

Although there are some presenters who literally stand in front of an audience and read what they have researched and organized, the success of this approach is questionable. Possibly, if you are well-known in your field, an audience will allow you this type of latitude. However, most people who take part in such a session go away feeling they could have read the paper themselves and at their own convenience. The nature of conference attendance allows the professional several concurrent options. Since sessions are chosen on the basis of interest, need, and application for the classroom, it is not uncommon for people to walk in and out until they find something they consider valuable. The technique of reading a paper can be deadly. One must always be aware that people consider their time a precious asset and few will tolerate being bored.

How then can a writer be faithful to his conference topic and, at the same time, keep his audience informed and involved? Prior to the actual presentation, there are several options which can be investigated. Basic to all these approaches is the premise that the written word must be supplemented. Supplements can include: input and critiquing from other professionals, audiovisual aids, and audience participation.

No matter how thoroughly a topic has been researched, people in the field have both practical suggestions and additional literary resources. Other professionals are flattered when asked to critique another person's work. Even though it might take them considerable time to give either verbal or written input, it is rare to find a person who would refuse this opportunity.

At the most basic level, a critique of the clarity of the paper can be very helpful. Rewriting, no matter how frustrating and time-consuming, should be an inherent part of paper presentation. In fact, subsequent to the conference, requests for papers to be published in the conference journal are common. Written revision, at this point, is time well spent.

Once the writer has revised his paper, he should re-outline its contents. This can be used in two ways: first, as a skeletal framework for the verbal presentation, and, second, as a guide for creating an abstract—the written summary which will appear in the conference program.

Unlike the written paper, in your "talking" paper audiovisual aids should be plentiful. Initially, with the use of an overhead projector, the presenter can flash an outline of what he will be discussing. The audience is then able to get a quick overview of the presentation and is better prepared to ask questions. This is also an excellent way to help people remember what you have said. A knowledgeable presenter must be sensitive to the conference-goer who attends several sessions in a brief period of time. After the second or third presentation, the person watching starts to confuse one paper or presentation with another and can experience conference "burnout." Audiovisuals will help minimize this problem. If you must read parts of your paper, follow the reading with visual examples.

Another inclusion, often considered essential to conference presentations, is the use of the handout. Conference-goers like to walk away with something they can take home. Many people have been sent by their schools or universities and they are expected to share their experiences. When the handout should be distributed varies with the topic presented. Some feel that a handout is distracting and should therefore be given at the end of the session. In this way, people have a written record of what has been said, can refer to it for ready recall, and, at the same time, have given their full attention to the oral presentation. Another approach is to distribute handouts as people walk in. This worked well in a group where suggestions for encouraging verbal interactions were given. Since transparencies were also included in this presentation, the participants could quickly copy the information from the visuals and put it beside the suggestions on the handout. In this way, if the observer wanted to summarize the paper for his colleagues at home, the data was already correlated.

How you handle audience involvement is another area to be considered. Decide what your comfort index is in dealing with on-the-spot discussions, controversy or problem-solving. If you don't want to involve other professionals, discourage questions or don't allow time for this to take place. However, this aspect of a presentation can be very exciting and can provide the discussion leader and his audience with supplemental information.

One part of paper presentation that is rarely discussed is the financial cost. Transparencies and handouts are expensive. Who is expected to finance these extras? Several resources are available and should be investigated. In some instances, your conference program chairperson may have funds for this purpose. Or, your school or university may allow use of their facilities. If these are not options, the presenter must consider financing the expenses himself and submitting the bill as a deductible professional expense.

Now that you have intellectually digested your solicited professional critiques, revised your written paper, decided on audiovisuals and prepared them, and structured the type of audience participation you feel comfortable with, it is professionally obligatory to practice and time your "talking paper". Using your skeletal outline, coordinate when and where you want to include your audiovisuals and then rehearse ex-

actly what will be presented. Although presenters have often had considerable experience talking to groups, the fluidity and coherence of your presentation will be improved by practice and will free you to deal with your live audience.

At this point, you are ready. However, don't forget one important detail—how you look, or in more sophisticated terms, your professional demeanor. Although there will be many people at the conference who will be wearing informal clothing, you may be surprised to find that presenters are often wearing suits and dresses. Being dressed more formally adds a dimension of specialness to how you think of yourself and how your audience perceives you. Never underestimate how valuable this is.

Although anxieties and nervousness may precede your presentation, once you

begin an air of confidence is important. You are a professional. You have something valuable to offer and the tone you set should corroborate this.

After all your preparations, you stand before your audience and give your paper. Afterwards, be critical and analyze what went well and what needs improvement. Many times you are asked to present the same paper again. So, keep all your notes, you master copies for handouts and your transparencies. After having gone through this experience, you should feel a sense of professional growth and achievement. You have added a new dimension to your skills and have shared information that you have researched and synthesized with other professionals. You are to be congratulated! □

TN 12/81

A WORKSHOP IS WORK

by Richard Yorkey
Concordia University, Montreal

Workshops are a common feature of many ESL conferences and in-service training programs. They can be an exciting experience and a valuable way of upgrading professional skills, provided the participants are satisfied that they have had the chance to learn. In the case of workshops, *learning most definitely means doing!* That is the expectation of most of the teachers who sign up to attend; they expect to participate, to learn by doing. Unfortunately, judging from the many murmurs of discontent at conferences, it seems that some workshops do not live up to the participants' expectations.

Some workshops probably disappoint participants because of the presenter's failure to understand what a workshop is—or what it should be. By definition, a workshop involves application, involvement, active participation and practice—in short, work! Participants do not expect to sit passively and listen to a theoretical paper being read or a topic being discussed by a panel. A workshop is a kind of "hands on" opportunity to learn by doing.

The key to conducting a successful workshop is probably divided among (1) choosing an appropriate topic and defining it in practical terms, (2) avoiding a teacher-centered, lecture-like presentation, and (3) carefully planning a sequence of activities in which participants have the chance to actually apply and practice the ideas that have first been described and demonstrated.

Certain areas in the field of ESL lend themselves more readily to workshops than others. A session entitled "What is Applied Linguistics?" is more suitable for a paper, seminar or round-table discussion. "English for Occupational Pur-

poses" is likely to be more a presentation and discussion with occasional examples than a workshop in which participants actually get practice in preparing special materials for special purposes. Even "Jazz Chanting" is no more than an interesting demonstration unless participants have the opportunity not only to observe the technique but also to practice it, not as students but as teachers, and perhaps to prepare their own jazz chants for practice and criticism.

The Workshop Topic

All important is the selection of your topic. You may be asked by conference organizers or a school committee to present a workshop or some particular topic or you may make the choice yourself. In either case, consider the selection from the viewpoint of skills rather than of knowledge. Certainly there may be need to introduce some background information, some brief explanation of the theoretical basis for your topic, but the main emphasis should be on the application of theory to a practical situation, usually as a classroom activity. Obviously your topic should be one with which you are personally familiar and have sufficient practical experience, and which you want to share with other teachers.

The Participants

Specify the participants you have in mind and the number you can handle in the workshop. For example, is your workshop intended for teachers of elementary, secondary, or adult students?, untrained teachers, experienced administrators? So that participants can make an informed choice of workshops they

wish to attend, this kind of information is usually published in the conference program or clearly announced in advance. Even so, it is wise to expect a fairly wide range of interests and expectations.

If possible, before the workshop try to get from the conference organizers some idea of the background and needs of the participants. What kind of education and training can you expect? What schools or programs do they teach in? What books and materials are used? In national conferences, answers to questions like these will vary considerably. In local school systems, the needs, interests, and expectations can be more accurately identified and the participants are likely to be more homogeneous.

The Presentation

Narrow your topic down to the amount of time available, and divide your time between (1) background information, (2) explanation and demonstration, (3) participants' practice, and (4) final questions and discussion. This division and the proportionate amount of time will, of course, vary depending on the topic, but as a general rule of thumb, the following comments may be useful.

Background information should be presented as cogently as possible. Your purpose is not to impress the participants with the extent of your knowledge, the range of your reading, or the brilliance of your teaching. Your purpose is to provide only the theoretical or empirical basis of the activity you intend to present and practice. This may be best done by handouts, overhead transparencies, or by simple explanation. It should not take more than 10-15% of your time.

Explanation and demonstration may follow directly from the background information. Your purpose here is to show *what* and *how* and it's also a good idea to explain *when*. A workshop focuses on only one of the many aspects of ESL, and the presenter is naturally enthusiastic and convincing about this narrowly defined topic. Participants may misunderstand the proportionate amount of time or emphasis that should be given to the activity during their regular teaching. For example, "How to Make and Use Puppets" may be an interesting, worthwhile workshop, but it should not be assumed that puppets are the best or the only way to teach ESL to elementary students. "Jazz Chanting" may be an immensely popular workshop, but the technique should be interpreted only as a novel way to teach the rhythms of English and should not be overused. Or "The Silent Way" may be an innovative approach but its appropriateness or potential success must be viewed from the perspective of your own particular situation; is it completely applicable, or if it is adapted in any way, will it still be successful or better than some other approach?

Practice. The proportion of time allotted to explanation and demonstration depends on your topic. A rule of thumb might be to devote 50% of the workshop time for practice. The kind of practical work that participants do depends, of course, on the topic of the workshop. While planning practice activities, however, ask yourself the following questions:

In order to benefit from your ideas, what must the participants *do?* What kinds of activities will give them insight into the pedagogical value of the ideas and help them understand the procedures of the activity?

Can they do what they need to do in large groups, small groups, or individually?

What kind of space and room arrangements are necessary?

What special equipment and materials will be necessary? What can the conference or school authorities provide, and what must you yourself provide?

Can you handle the participation activities yourself, or will you need some assistance? If so, who? ·

Questions and Discussion. Allow time at the end for questions and discussion. By the very nature of a workshop, questions and comments are likely to occur throughout. Handle them as they arise, since they are the most meaningful at that moment. But also keep track of the time so that there can be a general summing up at the end. Although for the purpose of demonstration and practice you may have considered the participants as students, *remember that they are actually your professional colleagues with varying kinds and amounts of experience.* The chance for their personal reactions and professional feedback is an important feature of a workshop—for yourself and the participants.

Miscellaneous Suggestions

It is difficult to plan your time as closely as you can for reading a paper, but you can probably arrive at an approximate distribution of time. It is better to plan more than you may have time to do. Otherwise, the workshop may flounder and drift as you extemporize. On the other hand, do not plan so much that the work is hurried, unfocused, and undeveloped.

Check the room carefully before the workshop begins and ask yourself these questions: Are the chairs and/or tables arranged as you want? Is the equipment you need in place and in working order? Is the lighting, ventilation, etc. acceptable? If not, can anything be done about it? Will there be any distractions from a competing workshop next door or on the other side of a partition? Can anything be done about it?

Try to plan your workshop well in advance. Although workshop presentations are not as highly regarded as scholarly papers, for teachers they are as important as a professionally published paper. Handouts should be neatly and legibly reproduced; transparencies should be clear; and pictures and diagrams should be large and visible from the back of the room.

Keep your plans reasonably flexible, and be willing to adjust them whenever necessary. Careful planning should include possible alternatives (for fewer or more participants than expected, for a late-starting, lightly-attended workshop the morning after the Grand Ball, etc.).

Finally, immediately after your workshop record your impressions. Evaluate the workshop: what went well, what didn't and why? You may be invited to give the same workshop again; how could it be improved? *TN 2/79*

BOOK REVIEW

RESEARCH WRITING: A COMPLETE GUIDE TO RESEARCH PAPERS

by Dean Memering. 1983. Prentice-Hall, Inc.: Englewood Cliffs, N.J. 07632. (218 pp., $5.95).

Reviewed by Macey Blackburn McKee
Western Illinois University

"Excited" may be a little strong as a description of my reaction to this book, but it is the most interesting and useful manual of its type that I have ever seen. I would like to call the attention of ESL teachers to the following features.

First, in addition to a complete and modern treatment of the MLA (Modern Language Association) documentation style, *Research Writing* covers the APA (American Publishers Association) equally thoroughly. Since most foreign students are in fields whose style sheets differ from the APA in trivial ways, I think that it is much more sensible to teach the APA style if one is not up to coping with the particular sheet from each field represented in the class. Use of

the name and date method of documentation will help students with their reading in their major fields as well as with any research writing they do.

Second, the section on evaluating evidence is the best short treatment of this topic that I have seen. The exercise on "Can Apes Talk?" carefully takes the student (and teacher) through the necessary steps in evaluating evidence, including the one most likely to be neglected—the expertise of the person being cited.

The section on the use of the library is a good addition since not all schools provide library training adequate for the needs of the student from an underdeveloped country.

The careful delineation of the difference between student library research, which results in a documented essay, expert library research, and other types of research is a small, but to me important matter. Many foreign students go from a course of this type almost directly to the writing of a thesis. An instructor could build on this section to help such students learn to do the

review of the literature section, which differs substantially from the usual freshman documented essay.

What I like best about this book is the inclusion of a section on fallacies in reasoning and argumentation (see Memering and O'Hare, 1980, for further explication and supplemental exercises), a topic not covered adequately in most writing books although it is common in reading books. The instructor could add *The Propaganda Game* (Greene and Allen) or his own version of such an activity to enliven what is often one of the dullest parts of students' education—as well as to teach them about other types of fallacious argument. *TN 6/83*

REFERENCES

Greene, Lorne and Robert Allen. *The Propaganda Game.* Ann Arbor, Michigan: WFF 'N PROOF Publishers.
Memering, Dean and Frank O'Hare. 1980. *The Writer's Work.* Englewood Cliffs, New Jersey: Prentice-Hall, Inc.

Macey Blackburn McKee is the curriculum director of the WESL Institute at Western Illinois University in Macomb. She also teaches ESL and TESL methodology.

PART II. CLASSROOM PRACTICES
Section 9. Language Learning: Methods and Models

This chapter is, perhaps, as eclectic as ESL methodology today. Despite the Anthonian trichotomy of "Approach, Method, and Technique" (Edward Anthony, *ELT* XVII, pp. 63-67) espoused in most methods texts, many teachers confuse and are confused by these overlapping categories. Further, we tend to look for, ask for and talk more about specific strategies and techniques which we can immediately apply to the classroom, rather than finding a means of implementing those techniques.

The first article, by Haskell (4/78), asks the question what is "An Eclectic Method?" and attempts to present a brief history of what lies behind the present mood of both teaching and theory. The article by Sandra McKay, "Syllabuses: Grammatical, Situational, Notional" (11/78) which follows, is a general overview and offers one of the first straightforward comparisons of those approaches currently applied to syllabus or textbook development. The report of Carlos A. Yorio's speech on "Models of Second Language Acquisition" (9/80) originally from the *TESOL Spain Newsletter* is also a brief outline of current thinking in ESL research and practice. These three articles set the stage for the reader to move from a philosophy of teaching to a brief look at some of the currently popular methodologies.

Articles on most of the current methods are included: two on Suggestopedia, one on the Silent Way, one on Pragmatics, two on Counseling-Learning and one on Total Physical Response.

Suggestopedia is discussed in two articles in this section, one by Myrna Hammerman "Suggestion and Education" (8/79) and the other by Donna Hurst Shkilevich "Suggestopedia: A Theory and a Model" (4/80). The Silent Way article in this section by Haskell (6/76) is one of the first to attempt to describe a Silent Way experience. Also in this section the pragmatics of John Oller and L. G. Alexander are discussed by Ronald Taubitz in "Pragmatics" (4/78).

Carol Weiner provides us, in this section, with a short look at "Total Physical Response" (4/80). Counseling-Learning is discussed in the articles by Jennybelle Rardin (4/76), "A Counseling-Learning Model for Second Language Learning," and by Karen Czarnecki and Joseph Ramos (12/75) in their article "Counseling-Learning: A Wholistic View of the Learner."

One should not overlook the approach to language teaching taken by Paolo Freire. Nina Wallerstein suggests that "Problem Posing Can Help Students Learn" (10/83) and adapts some of Freire's ideas to refugee teaching situations. David Wilkins discusses "Communicative Language Teaching" (2/81) in an excerpt from Johnson and Morrow's book *Communication in the Classroom*. A

review of the Johnson and Morrow book appears at the end of this section. "Reconciling Competing Approaches in TESOL" (12/82) by Dale Otto attempts to bring together an overlay for any approach or method of language teaching.

The reviews in this section are of the most popular methods books available today. The first two are Audrey Reynold's review (9/76) of Kenneth Chastain's *Developing Second Language Skills: Theory to Practice*, which is not only a methodology but a history of ESL teaching, and her review of the wonderful "cookbook," *Teaching ESL: Techniques and Procedure* by Christina Bratt Paulston and Mary Newton Bruder. Reynolds also reviews Wilga Rivers' and Mary Temperly's *A Practical Guide to Teaching English as a Second Language* (11/78). As mentioned above, Samuela Eckstut reviews the Johnson and Morrow volume *Communication in the Classroom*. Greg Stricherz reviews Betty Wallace Robinett's *Teaching ESL: Substance and Technique*, a volume which in addition to its practical information on classroom techniques includes a very useful section on the linguistic information needed by an ESL teacher. Carol Weiner reviews the collection of articles by Marianne Celce-Murcia and Lois McIntosh, *Teaching English as a Second or Foreign Language* (10/79), and Paul Roberts reviews Chris Brumfit's *Problems and Principles in Language Teaching* (10/81). Richard Orem reviews (8/82) the TESOL publication edited by Donna Ilyin and Thomas Tragardh, *Classroom Practices in Adult ESL*, which is a collection of practical articles by adult educators on classroom teaching techniques and strategies. The next review is a look at a collection of newsletter articles from the *Idiom*, edited by Jean McConochie and others, appropriately titled *Idiomatically Speaking*. It is freely reviewed by Gary Gabriel (8/82).

There are a number of articles in other sections which deal with the various methods and approaches discussed in this section. There are two other articles, for example, which talk about the Silent Way. The article by Larry Cisar, "Hot Rods" (11/78), appears in section 14 and in it Cisar deals with the use of cuisinaire rods in a language teaching class. In section 11, Shakti Datta writes "On the Importance of Melody" (4/81)—the teaching of those prosodic features which are a basic element of the Silent Way and of language learning in general. Eugene Hall's situational reinforcement is reflected in Suzanne Griffin's chart which appears in section 10, "Teaching Grammatical Structures in Situational Contexts" (4/76).

A number of other articles in this volume discusses counseling-learning techniques. In section 2, Trish Delamere and Frederick Jenks write about "Topics and

Techniques for Developing a Cross-cultural Community Learning Environment" and in section 13, Jeffra Flaitz uses counseling-learning techniques when she discusses "The Role Play Comes Alive Through a Technological Twist" (12/83). Also in section 13, the article "Community Language and the Teaching of Composition in ESL" by William Myers (6/82) relates CL/CLL techniques to writing strategies for ESL students. Freirian philosophy is discussed in Caroline Dobbs' article "Freire and Literacy" (4/82) which appears in section 12.

You might also want to look at the articles which discuss various teaching approaches. In section 14, we have included an *It Works* column by Helen Fragiadakis called "A Notional Approach to *Frankenstein*" (4/81) and in section 2, Trish Delamere writes about "Linking Notional-Functional Syllabuses with Cross-cultural Awareness" (8/83).

Many other articles on these methods and approaches have appeared in the *TN* over the years. The first article on suggestopedia to appear in the *TN* was a report from the *New York Times* written by Brooks Shearer, "Suggestive Language" (4/78). Other articles on the Silent Way which might be of interest are "Reflections on My Learning Process During a Silent Way Japanese Weekend" by Raymond Maher (8/83) and "Separating the silent way from the Silent Way" by Richard French (6/80). Pragmatics is discussed in "A State of the Art Report on Pragmatics" by Emily Thrush (6/79), and a discussion of

Eugene Hall's situational reinforcement can be found in a 6/78 issue article by that name. Among the articles which have appeared in the *TN* dealing with the topic of counseling-learning are Jim Davis' "Community Language Learning and English for Science and Technology" (4/79), Gregory Thompson's "Roleplay in Community Language Learning for ESP Classrooms" (12/81), and Daniel Trane's "Questioning in Counseling-Learning" (8/80).

Other articles originally intended for this section are Francisco Gomes de Matos' article on "Humo(u)r, a Neglected Feature in Foreign Language Teaching" (5/75), John Boyd and Mary Ann Boyd's "Adding a Notional-Functional Dimension to Listening" (2/80), and, of course, the unforgettable parody of ESL methodologies, "The Timbuktu Method" (4/81) by Clea Shea (which was actually written in a moment of devilment by Maurice Imhoof and Mary Finocchiaro).

Among other interesting articles on teaching are Cathy Tansey's "Fanselow Talks at Fall Conference" (6/76) in which she reports on John Fanselow's presentation about the need for and use of feedback in the classroom; Darlene Larson's "Natural Language," an *It Works* column from 6/78; "The Golden Rules of Second Language Acquisition for Young Children" by Bruce Gaarder (8/79); and Richard Showstacks' excellent insights for all of us in his short article which lists "Ten Things I Have Learned About Learning a Foreign Language" (6/80).

AN ECLECTIC METHOD?

By John F. Haskell
Northeastern Illinois University

Many changes are taking place in language education today—as always—and there are many newcomers to the field who might appreciate a defining of terms. The following is an overview of English language teaching methodology with some general conclusions of a somewhat 'eclectic' nature.

I. Grammar-translation Method

The Grammar-translation method, sometimes called the "traditional" method, consisted of the following basic tenets:

A. Read, then translate (into the student's native language).

B. Learn, (often, "copy into your notebook"), the rules (again, in the student's native language).

C. Memorize (lists of) vocabulary items and their meanings (in the student's native language).

D. Write sentences (in the target language) using the memorized rules and vocabulary.

E. Read 'good' literature (no matter how stylistically or grammatically complex or archaic), history, and other aspects of the target language culture.

Note: Foreign Language (FL) education, using this method did not generally intend to produce "speakers" of the language, only provide the broad liberal arts education necessary to produce a "well educated person" (who could read a foreign language). FL education was usually limited to those entering or in college. ESL (EFL) taught with the grammar-translation method was meant to be for language replacement rather than addition. Students were placed in regular English classes and expected to swim or sink, learn or leave.

Until W.W. I, bilingual education (education in languages other than English) was common in the U.S. Anti-foreign attitudes during the first half of this century were reflected in such diverse ways as the closing of German schools, the placement of Japanese-Americans into camps, and the delay of Hawaiian statehood until 1959.

II. The Direct Method

As an approach to language teaching, the direct method was "ahead of its time." Devised by Gouin at the end of the nineteenth century and all but abandoned in the twentieth century except for a few stalwarts such as Harold Palmer, Otto Jesperson, and Emile de Sauzé, who held on until the thirties. The basic elements of the direct method are:

A. Exclusive use of the target language in the classroom. No translation or use of the students' language.

B. Step by step progression of material—generally from easy to difficult.

C. Meaningful exercises, i.e., meaningful use of the language.

De Sauzé, in the 1920's added:

D. Early use of writing.

E. Student self-correction of errors (mistakes). Students need to understand their errors.

F. Explicit formation of rules.

Note: Interestingly enough, most methodologies or approaches to language teaching that have developed in the twentieth century reflect the basic tenets of the direct method, in whole or in part—as you will see below.

III. The Audio-lingual or Aural-Oral Method

The 1940's saw a growing need for "other" language speakers both in the armed services and in the field of diplomacy, and at the same time there was a growing need to deal with the influx of foreign scholars that thronged into U.S. universities as European universities were closed by the war. Linguists Kenneth Pike, Charles Fries, and others, long experienced in working with American Indian languages and Bible translation, helped to develop an A-L (Audiolingual) approach to language teaching. A-L methodology was the result of a "resurrection" of the direct method and the influence of structural linguistics and behavioral psychology.

Structural linguistics said (1) natural language learning occurs first through listening, then speaking, and then reading and writing. (2) Language is made up of three systems; phonology (sounds), morphology (word formation), and syntax (the arrangement of words in sentences) and these systems work exclusive of meaning. (3) Language appropriateness is determined by usage and *not* by prescription (the rules culled from grammar books and based on principles of written language). (4) All languages are different and unique (contrastive analysis). (5) Language (that is used) is constantly changing.

Behavioral-psychology learning theory (as advanced by B. F. Skinner, among others) said that language was a conditioned habit and that language learning was a mechanical process of stimulus-response strengthened by reinforcement of correct responses (behavior modification).

Sociology (and politics) still championed the "melting pot" theory and pedagogy (education) viewed English language learning by immigrants as language (and culture) replacement.

The resulting methodology consisted of:

A. Exclusive use of the target language.

B. Step-by-step progression of materials based on linguistic sequencing.

C. Use of language comparison (contrastive analysis) to "predict" error.

D. Mim-Mem (mimicry/imitation and memorization).

E. Mastery of language systems (in pronunciation classes, grammar classes, reading classes, conversation classes, and writing/composition classes). Structures and rules learned by example, demonstration not formulation, analogy rather than analysis.

F. Use of mechanical drilling to teach production and discrimination (choral and individual drills, substitution, transformation and completion drills, etc.) Emphasis on question/answer (stimulus-response) type teaching.

G. Vocabulary building deferred until "intermediate" stage. Strict vocabulary control at beginning stages; emphasis on words with regular spelling and pronunciation, and high in frequency, to reduce interference with mastery of structure.

H. Emphasis on speaking.

I. Use of language laboratories to provide practice.

J. Emphasis on language as communication rather than translation.

Note: The "classical" approaches to the A-L method are represented by such 'methods' as (1) the Michigan Method, which came directly from Fries and Lado and the University of Michigan and was developed primarily for college level students. (2) The Army Method, which also come out of the University of Michigan and is now used at the Defense Language Institute and was aimed at intensive language learning for military and diplomatic personnel. (3) And the Berlitz Method, which is the best known of the commercial adaptations of the A-L method, directed at people traveling overseas.

IV. Transition

In the late 1950's and early 1960's structural linguistics came under attack by Noam Chomsky and others (as did behavioral psychology). Developmental learning theory and the growth of the ESL teaching profession (TESOL) with its humanistic approach to teaching/learning produced many changes in second language teaching practices. Support for these changes was based upon research in a variety of fields.

A. In linguistics, Chomsky stated: (1) Language is innate (a product of a thinking brain and not habit formation). (2) Language is rule governed behavior. (3) "Correctness" is determined by the users of the language and is based on understanding (i.e., meaning cannot be separated from language.) (4) All languages have "universals" or similarities (e.g. processes or elements in their basic systems). (5) Surface grammar (what we see, say and hear) is only a manifestation of deep grammar (the meaning, rules, and processes which we use to produce language). (6) Our language competence (*our ability* to use language) is not always accurately reflected in our performance (*how* we use the language).

B. Cognitive-mentalist psychology (as opposed to the behaviorists) states: (1) Language learning is the result of active brain utilization, not passive response to outside stimulus. (2) Child acquisition of language is reflective of, shows parallels to the developmental stages of his physical growth. (3) All children, whatever their language, go through similar stages and apply similar strategies in language acquisition.

C. In sociology: (1) studies in dialectology, particularly "Black English", brought new insights and emphasis on language variety (*non-standard* as opposed to *substandard*). (2) Bilingual education studies indicated the need for affective modes in education (understanding the emotional needs of children).

D. Pedagogy: (1) prompted by the Supreme Court (Lau vs Nichols) finally found a legal (if not moral) justification for at least a 'transitional" bilingual/bicultural language program for non-English speaking students. (2) Studies in second language acquisition showed the use of similar strategies and developmental patterns to those used in first language acquisition. (3) There was a re-emergence of bilingual education with emphasis (as a result of such programs as the Hawaii English Program and Black English studies) on language as an additive process rather than a replacement one. (4) Emphasis on individualization. (5) Growing (but still faint) concern for training, certification, and full-time employment of adult education, ESL, and bilingual teachers.

V. Variations on a Theme

A number of new approaches to second language teaching have come into being as a result, I think, of many teachers feeling that the basic A-L approach (as defined above) is somehow neither as affective or effective as it might be. As research and new thinking have pro-vided new information about language acquisition, language learning, and learning in general, the A-L approach has been modified and often given new names to emphasize the major thrust of the modification (or the name of the author). The best progress has been made thanks to sensitive, thinking, trained teachers whose common sense and experience have provided us with new techniques and approaches. Below are some of the new/old methodologies (and non-methods). They are all basically direct method and audio-lingual in approach (with the exception of Counseling-Learning) and in large part are influenced by the cognitive-affective (humanistic and developmental) psychology and pedagogy of today.

A. **Total Physical Response.** Sometimes the *Asher* method. Utilizes extended periods of listening and following commands before speaking. Students learn by physically performing actions based first on commands of the teacher and then by commands from other students.

B. **Aural Approach.** The aural approach of *Winitz and Reed* asks the beginning language student to first listen to the teacher (or tape recorder). The only overt behavior is selecting pictures indicated in each utterance. Speaking occurs after basic grammar and vocabulary are learned. *Joan Morley* also suggests early and extensive listening but utilizes written response.

C. **St. Cloud.** Sometimes called the *CREDIF* Method or the *Audio-visual* method. Students are encouraged to speak by means of situations as presented by firm and filmstrips.

D. **Suggestopedia.** Also called *Suggestology* or the *Lazanov* method. Uses non-verbal elements (tone of voice, music, facial gestures) as major factors of communication. Learning is in a comfortable 'living-room' type of situation. Students listen to learn.

E. **The Silent Way** or *Gattegno* method. The teacher supplies a minimal amount of oral support and information. Student is required to "work it out" for himself. Visual stimulation by rods and charts and later, reading materials. No mechanical drilling of any kind. Emphasis on a 'feeling' for the language.

F. **Situational Reinforcement.** Lessons using language (patterns, vocabulary) from situations which are reinforced by the reality of the situation itself. Situation dialogues and realia used.

G. **Modular Learning** (or learning modules). Units (or modules) of lessons in some general sequence of difficulty of language, revolving around a single topic or theme, and encouraging a variety of patterns and structures in each lesson, reused and reinforced in succeeding lessons. Emphasis on realistic dialogue and topics of interest to the learner.

H. **Pragmatics.** The suggestion that emphasis in language teaching should be on linguistic forms in situational settings, recognizing that they are inseparable.

I. **Counseling-Learning.** Also called *Community Language Learning.* Student centered approach with the teacher acting as a counselor or mediator at the beginning and gradually becoming a part of the language learning group (community). Language based on what the student wants to say. Translation used in initial stages (student says what he wants to say and the teacher/counselor/mediator shows him how to say it in the target language) until student feels comfortable and capable of initiating or responding by himself.

Note: A number of other terms have been used of late with reference to method, technique or approach to language learning, teaching, or program planning. They are part and parcel of present day language teaching. (1) *Individualization.* An approach to classroom organization which emphasizes individual differences and the need to deal with each student as a separate individual. (2) *Sector Analysis.* A linguistic approach to language that emphasises the manupulation of various elements in a sentence (connectives, nouns, substitute words, X-words Wh-words, etc.) and a recognition of the variety of slots. Stress on student being able to identify elements before being asked to use them. (3) *Error Analysis.* Suggests a variety of causes of error (besides language interference) such as poor teaching and poor learning strategies, and language fossilization. (4) *Cognitive approach.* The acceptance that the student is a thinking human being who brings knowledge about language to his learning situation and also brings human experience and an innate learning ability. (5) *Communicative Competence.* A term, much in vogue of late, from a theory of language learning suggested by Dell Hymes, Perhaps similar in importance, in present language learning/teaching pedagogy, and to the same extent that Chomsky's theory of language (linguistics) is. Although the term is used indiscriminately in almost all new materials and in all discussions and evaluations of materials, most writers and speakers seem to be referring to that manifestation of communication which reflects our interest in the child as a human being, Piagét's developmental levels, Currans' whole learner concept, non-verbal communication, and a renewed interest in culture as a componant of language learning. Perhaps its current popularity reflects our need for a comfortable cover term for the changes occurring in language teaching/learning practice—one that feels more comfortable than, say, eclectic.

VI. An Eclectic Method?

An eclectic *methodology* (or approach) is one which utilizes the best (most appropriate and/or useful) parts of existing *methods*. There is the danger in eclecticism, of creating a Frankenstein monster rather than a Cinderella. The use of the term "an eclectic method" suggests, in one sense, the need for a single, best, method to follow. It also suggests an inability to *be* eclectic.

As in the "pragmatic" approach of Oller and the "ethnomethodology" which Eskey finds appealing, there is a growing awareness among ESL teachers of the need to be concerned with teaching "appropriate" use of language. If not an eclectic *method*, then, perhaps we can come to terms with some general principles or attitudes, some conclusions that can be drawn from current research and thinking in the field.

A. Language learning must be meaningful, real.

B. Translation is a specialized language skill and is inappropriate for the beginning language learner (and most teachers) to rely on as a method of learning. It is a crutch that, though immediately useful, becomes harder and harder to throw away the longer it is used. As used in Counseling-Learning, it may be a useful tool in establishing an initial basis for comfortable communication.

C. Language learning should be done in the target language.

D. Mimicry, memorization, and pattern practice do not "teach" language. They may sometimes be appropriate techniques for a variety of classroom needs but are in general disfavor because of their mechanical (meaningless) nature, their overuse by teachers, and their tendency to be stilted and boring.

E. Reading aloud (oral reading) while useful during the decoding stage (when students, new to the English alphabet, are learning to associate letters and words with already learned language), does not teach reading. It is not useful as a tool for correcting pronunciation, and in fact, inhibits good reading skills acquisition. It promotes word reading (not useful in reading nor accurate for conversational pronunciation) and does not allow for normal regressions in reading; nor facilitate comprehension.

F. Vocabulary acquisition, the use of a large and varied vocabulary, should come early. Vocabulary should be dealt with in meaningful contexts. Retention is not required of all new items; but continuous, appropriate usage is encouraged. Lists of words promote translation and are another crutch that is hard to get rid of, eg., multiplication tables, days of the week.

G. Reading and writing should not be delayed but taught as soon as the student is ready. Spelling interference is not felt to be the problem it once was.

H. Although structure is still generally accepted as being most efficiently taught in some organized way, language acquisition (developmental) strategies should be taken into consideration rather than exclusively linguistic ones. Teachers need not insist upon mastery of one pattern before moving on to another, nor the presentation of one item at a time, but should provide ample opportunity for reinforcement and continuous use of all patterns and structures in meaningful real contexts.

I. Most student errors are not caused by language interference (less than 10 percent according to Burt and Dulay and then, mostly in the area of pronunciation.) Learning strategies, incorrectly applied, are the cause of some 67 percent of student error. Attention should be placed on the regularities and the universals of language rather than on differences.

J. The first step in any class/program should be to determine what the student needs (and perhaps, more importantly, wants) to learn.

K. Second language students bring a great deal of experience and knowledge about language to their learning situation. Language learning is facilitated by helping the student relate to his own experience.

L. Communicative competence suggests that appropriateness and utility are crucial variables in language acquisition (and language learning must consider such things as non-verbal communication, kinesics, culture, stress, rhythm, intonation, and vowel reduction).

M. Language learning will not occur unless the student is able, wants to, makes a personal committment to learn. In whatever way you measure or define motivation, it will be the students choice and decision that determines his language learning success. The expectation of the teacher and the program, and the support of the "community" will greatly influence that decision.

Note: As Larry Anger suggests, language learning can and should be enjoyable. Darlene Larson likes to quote Benjamin Franklin on education and I think it is an appropriate maxim to conclude with. "Tell me and I forget, teach me and I remember, involve me and I learn." 4/78

References:

1. Anger, Larry. "Some Priorities for the Language Teacher," *TESOL Newsletter* (May 75).
2. Bancroft, W. Jane. "The Psychology of Suggestopedia, or Learning Without Fear," *The Educational Courier*.
3. Brown, H. Douglas. "The Next 25 Years: Shaping the Revolution," *On TESOL 75* (1975).
4. Chastain, Kenneth. *Developing Second Language Skills*, Rand McNally (1976).
5. Czarnecki, Karen E. and Joseph A. Ramos. "Counseling-Learning: A Wholistic View of the Learner," *TESOL Newsletter* (Dec. 1975).
6. Diller, Karl C. "Some New Trends for Applied Linguistics and FL Teaching in the U.S.", *TESOL Quarterly*, IX:1 (Mar. 1975).
7. Eskey, David. "A Revolutionary New Idea: The Student and Teacher as Human Being," *Language Learning* (June 1976).
8. Gattegno, Caleb. "Some Remarks and Additions on the 'Silent Way'," *Idiom* (Winter 74).
9. Hall, Eugene. "Situational Reinforcement" *TESOL Newsletter* (Apr. 78)
10. Haskell, John F. "The Silent Way" *TESOL Newsletter* (June 1976).
11. ———. "The Silent Way: A New Look at Language Teaching" *Idiom* (Fall 73).
12. Henrichson, Lynn F. "Sector Analysis and 'Working Sentences'" *TESOL Newsletter* (Sept. 77).
13. Johnson, Frank. *ESL: An Individualized Approach*, Jacaranda Press, 1973.
14. Knapp, Donald. "The Utility of Oral Reading" (speech given at Illinois TESOL Workshop, Nov. 1977).
15. Oller, John. "Transformational Grammar, Pragmatics, and Language Teaching," *English Teaching Forum* (Mar.-Apr. 1971).
16. ——— and Jack Richards (eds.) *Focus on the Learner: Pragmatic Perspectives for the Language Teacher*, Newberry Hse. 1973.
17. Paulston, Christina B. *Teaching ESOL in the U.S.; 1975: A Dipstick Paper*, TESOL, 1971.
18. Rardin, Jennybelle. "A Counseling Learning Model for Second Language Learning," *TESOL Newsletter* (Apr. 1976).
19. Richards, Jack (ed.). *Error Analysis: Perspectives in Second Language Acquisition*, Longmans, 1974.
20. Shearer, Brooks. "Suggestive Learning," *London Sunday Times*, Nov. 19, 1972 *TESOL Newsletter*, (Apr. 1978).
21. Stevick, Earl. *Adapting and Writing Materials*, Foreign Service Institute, 1971.
22. ———. The Modular Mousetrap" (paper presented at TESOL Convention, Apr. 1967).
23. ———. *Memory, Meaning and Method*, Newberry House, 1976.
24. Sutherland, Kenton. "Book Review of 'Learning Another Language Through Actions'," by James Asher *TESOL Quarterly* (June 1978).
25. Taubitz, Ronald. "Pragmatics," *TESOL Newsletter* (Apr. 1978).

SYLLABUSES: STRUCTURAL, SITUATIONAL, NOTIONAL

by Sandra McKay
San Francisco State University

One major decision that all teachers face is which text to use. In order to make a wise decision, it is important to recognize the assumptions that the materials make about what should be taught in an ESL class. Although the selection of materials has implications for the way they are presented, what is studied and how it is presented are separate components of the classroom. Linguistic structures, for example, can be presented either deductively or inductively, with the teacher as model or facilitator.

First of all, what is a syllabus? Clearly, a syllabus is not the same as a method. Anthony and Norris maintain that a method must include the "selection of materials to be taught, the gradation of those materials, their presentation, and pedagogical implementation to induce learning." In my mind, the first two concerns—the selection of materials and the gradation of those materials—provide the foundation for a syllabus. A syllabus provides a focus for what should be studied, along with a rationale for how that content should be selected and ordered. Currently, the literature reflects three major types of syllabuses: structural, situational, and notional.

I. STRUCTURAL SYLLABUSES

The primary focus of structural syllabuses is the grammatical structure of the language. Girard in describing the components of a structural lesson maintains that "the modern language lesson must be first of all a lesson in the *language*, aimed at building up linguistic competence and performance." In view of the focus on linguistic structures, the question of what to include in the syllabus is relatively easy; namely, the full range of grammatical structures in English. The question of how to sequence this content is more difficult to answer. According to Wilkins the standards that are typically applied are: simplicity, regularity, frequency and contrastive difficulty. These criteria, however, may be at odds with one another since a structure with high frequency may not have structural simplicity (e.g. polite request forms, "could you tell me?", "do you happen to know?", etc., while frequently used are not structurally simple).

Structural syllabuses are associated with pattern practices and text translations. There is, however, nothing inherent in a focus on linguistic structures which necessitates this type of classroom presentation. Grammatical structures could be symbolized by charts or objects, with the teacher acting primarily as a facilitator rather than a model. (This, of course, is exactly what occurs in classrooms which use The Silent Way).

II. SITUATIONAL SYLLABUSES

Situational syllabuses focus on language as a social medium by recognizing that language use is affected by such things as the participants, the topic and the setting. The basic assumption of situational syllabuses is clearly reflected in Kitchin's comment: "Structures are dead without the situations which engender them." In discussing situational syllabuses, Kitchin maintains that it should be possible to "devise a learning system based on graded situations rather than graded structures."

In most situational syllabuses the selection of content is based on a prediction of what situations the students will have to deal with. Selecting materials on this basis certainly provides the opportunity for highly relevant content. However, as Wilkins points out, the social situation alone does not determine what will be said. An individual at a bank could have a variety of intentions (opening a savings account, registering a complaint, seeking employment, etc.).

In general situational syllabuses do not demonstrate clearly defined criteria for the sequencing of the material. Some syllabuses are ordered on the basis that the learner will encounter the situations (e.g. a text for a foreign student might proceed as follows: landing at the airport, finding a place to live, registering at the University, etc.). Other situational syllabuses rely on the structural complexity of the dialogues within the situations for the sequencing of the material.

Traditionally the classroom presentation of situational syllabuses involves role playing and dialogues (at times combined with pattern practices). Given the focus on the social dimensions of language, other techniques could be equally effective in promoting the students' awareness of language variation. One technique would be exercises which require students to observe language use outside of the classroom and note how it varies according to the participants and setting.

III. NOTIONAL SYLLABUSES

Wilkins maintains that the essence of a notional syllabus is its priority to the semantic content of language. The aim of such syllabuses is to ensure that the students know how to express different types of meanings (e.g. disagreements, compliments, disbelief, etc.). Like situational syllabuses, the question of the selection of the content is related to the needs of the learners. Wilkins maintains that the first step in designing the syllabus is to predict what types of meaning the learners will need to communicate. In view of the tremendous number of semantic categories (Wilkins himself lists 339) the problem of selection is a formidable one. The question of selection is further complicated by the fact that a variety of linguistic forms can be used to express the same meaning (e.g. asking for permission can be couched in various forms ranging from "Can I use" to "I wonder if I might use"). Wilkins suggests that the selection of which forms to include be based on the stylistic dimension of formality and politeness, the medium (speech or writing) and grammatical simplicity. The syllabus designer needs to predict in which contexts the student will be using the language (spoken or written, formal or informal) and select the forms on that basis.

At present there appears to be little rationale for the sequencing of materials in a notional syllabus. Wilkins recognizes that the designing of a notional syllabus could result in linguistic and thematically disconnected units. He suggests introducing a story line to ensure thematic continuity, but he considers this technique extrinsic to the idea of a notional syllabus.

The method of presentation for notional syllabuses is still largely undefined. Most existing syllabuses involve role playing, and reading and listening to authentic language materials (newspaper articles, broadcasts, journals, impromptu dialogues, etc.) in order to analyze the various intentions that they contain.

Clearly each syllabus has its strengths and its weaknesses. While each one focuses on an important component of language (grammatical form, situational constraints and semantic uses), each presents unique problems in the selecting and sequencing of materials. The teacher alone, who knows the proficiency and needs of the students, can best decide which syllabus to use when.

BIBLIOGRAPHY

Anthony, E. M. and Norris, W. E. "Method in Language Teaching." In Croft, Kenneth. 1972. *Readings in English as a Second Language*. Cambridge: Winthrop Publishers.

Girard, Denis. 1972. *Linguistics and Foreign Language Teaching*. Hong Kong: Longman.

Kitchin, M. V. 1974. "Some Thoughts on Situationalised Teaching." *ELTJ* 28, 4 (292-98).

Wilkins, D. A. 1976. *Notional Syllabuses*. Oxford: Oxford University Press.

"MODELS OF SECOND LANGUAGE ACQUISITION"

Dr. Carlos Yorio, in his speech before TESOL Spain, considered three models of the acquisition process: Krashen's Monitor model (with certain modifications of his own), Selinker's Interlanguage model and a recent model proposed by E. Bialystok.

I. The Monitor Model (Krashen)

A learner acquires what he picks up 'naturally', subconsciously. Immigrants who have picked up a second language without consciously working on rules have *acquired* that language. This is essentially how children learn languages. *Learning*, on the other hand, takes place when the learner is conscious of what he is doing. This may involve studying, but not necessarily. The acquired system is responsible for what comes out automatically, when the learner is not worrying about grammar problem areas like the subject/verb agreement and so on. The learned system, the system of rules that the learner has consciously worked on, monitors or checks the output of the acquired system and produces what Yorio terms "monitored output". It's the acquired system that initiates an utterance for communicative purposes. The Monitor never does. It concentrates on form over communication. The Monitor only functions when there is time to be conscious of rules. It is more likely to be drawn upon in writing than in speech, for example. Learners differ greatly in their use of the Monitor. Monitor over-users are so rule conscious that they can scarcely get anything out. Monitor under-users hardly check anything. Flagrant errors do not necessarily interfere with communication, however. Under-users may be very good communicators. The optimal monitor user *does* monitor, but this doesn't interfere with communication. A very select group of superusers, people who have managed to approach native competence in a second language, communicate well but use the Monitor even more than optimal users. It is interesting that native speakers also monitor such things as can vs. may, as vs. like, and register restrictions.

II. The Bialystok Model

In the Bialystok Model, the learner is exposed to language either consciously (if the teacher gives him a grammar rule) or unconsciously (perhaps seeing several situations where the present perfect is used). To this raw input, he brings not only explicit linguistic knowledge (similar to Krashen's learned system) and implicit linguistic knowledge (similar to Krashen's acquired system) but also "other knowledge". This includes his native language, other languages he knows, knowledge of linguistics and his general experiences of the world. This component helps to account for individual differences in language learning success. Like Krashen, Bialystok believes that acquisition is central to second language learning. As a result of the application of knowledge to language input, different kinds of rules are generalized. Some rules are automatic and spontaneous; others require time, and are used for monitoring. Bialystok's system is interesting because it attempts to account for individual learners' differences. Bialystok suggests that the more different strategies a learner can draw upon, the more successful he will be.

III. The Interlanguage Model (Selinker)

As learners learn a second language, they make systematic errors. They leave off the third person 's', they say "goed" instead of "went", etc. To Larry Selinker, these errors are clues to the learner's learning strategies. They show that learners transfer rules from their native languages and overgeneralize target language rules. The result of the application of these strategies are systems of rules that differ from the learner's native language on the one hand, and from the target language on the other. Selinker calls this "interlanguage". In time, this interlanguage may approximate the target language, though it will probably always remain different in some respects. As a learner becomes more proficient, his use of transfer from the native language decreases, but overgeneralization of target language rules increases. Selinker sees the learner moving from the native language through Interlanguage 1, IL2, IL3 . . . ILn until he reaches his final interlanguage. Learners can backslide, start leaving off final third person 's', etc. *after* having apparently surmounted these errors. Other errors may appear in an early interlanguage and stubbornly refuse to disappear. Such errors are termed as "fossilized" since they persist despite the learner's advancing in other respects.

(Reprinted from the *TESOL Spain Newsletter*, Spring 1980)

TN 9/80

SUGGESTOPEDIA: A THEORY AND A MODEL

by Donna Hurst Shkilevich
University of Colorado, Denver

Current trends in second language learning and teaching include interest particularly in humanism and the humanistic approach. Among the methods that fit beneath the 'humanistic umbrella', various recurrent themes are evident. Many of the basic tenets of Suggestopedia, or the Lozanov Method, are compatible with those of Charles Curran's *Counseling-Learning* and Caleb Gattegno's *The Silent Way*.

It seems obvious that the establishment of a pleasant and trusting environment certainly will both increase learning and make it more enjoyable as well. To promote this environment, there must be warmth, security, and understanding between teacher and learner and among the learners themselves. Once trust has been established, anxieties are resolved and thus more effective learning takes place. Once the learner is relaxed both physically and emotionally, s/he begins to feel more comfortable with making errors and begins to focus on real communication.

One principal theoretical element of Suggestopedia, i.e. the establishment of authority, lies with the learner's perception of the teacher.

We influence their attitudes, affect their motivation, and contribute to their total development as individuals.

The Lozanov Method, or Suggestopedia, is based on the principles of waking state suggestion and how they can be applied to accelerate learning. Much of the theory and many of the philosophies of the method are quite esoteric.

Recent studies conducted show that suggestology, or the science of suggestion, is an effective psychotherapeutic method particularly in the treatment of many illnesses; in reducing pain, curing skin diseases, and even in treating cancer. It has also been shown to affect almost every other communicative process. Suggestopedia has been developed mainly to increase the reserve capacities of the brain (i.e. that 90% unused portion) to improve memory ability. It deals with learning at both conscious and unconscious levels and in activating the brain globally.

There exist four basic truths behind the Lozanov Method; first, the human potential is far greater than we realize and this potential can be tapped right within the classroom. Partly, this can be accomplished by incorporating the v' of both sides of the brain simultaneously to involve the whole person in learning, and involving both mental and emotional activities—a system based on an overall approach. Another factor involved includes harmonizing with existing barriers, or overcoming those negative suggestions and feelings on the part of the learner, while maintaining compliance with them. By giving constant praise and encouragement and fostering a pleasant learning experience, the barriers can be dealt with.

Second, the mind functions within the belief system it considers true. That is to say, teacher expectations play an important role in the learner's behavior. High performance will result from high expectations. Pygmalion experiments show that teacher expectations caused children to gain significantly on IQ tests (Ferguson, 1976 and Claiborn, 1969).

Third, one is subject to suggestion, both direct and indirect, both conscious and unconscious. (Examples of indirect suggestion include the effects of body language and even the clothes that we wear.) Our suggestibility, or how prone we are to suggestion, depends on various factors. Lozanov discusses 'suggestive readiness' which varies from person to person and from moment to moment. Studies show that younger people are more suggestible than adults.

Fourth, one learns best in a positive and relaxed atmosphere. The atmosphere that affords the learner the best is one that fosters enjoyment. Physical and mental relaxation between teacher and learners result in maintaining positive attitudes, which in turn affect the internalization of subject matter. Encouragement and praise, along with proper verbal and non-verbal communication, and the use of classical music (which will be discussed later) with its subconscious effects, will create a pleasant learning experience. Again, we can see that these truths ascribe to basic humanistic principles.

To implement the method, certain theoretical elements must be put into practice. Lozanov emphasizes the importance of establishing authority, by first establishing respect. The teacher's suggestion and unobserved messages which are constantly in play, are first perceived by the learner's unconscious mind and are processed down to the conscious level; the teacher's facial expression, tone of voice, attitude towards the students—all of which constitute signals directed toward the unconscious may be more directly responsible for results achieved by the students than the actual logical presentation of the material taught.

Once authority has been established and maintained, the child-like state, or infantilization, can occur. The process of infantilization involves creatively returning the individual to an earlier time, a time which provokes feelings of trust and security. In terms of the child, there seems to exist greater attention and spontaneity which result in a greater ability to memorize and internalize the material. The learner becomes less concerned about making errors since inhibitions are lowered.

The 'concert pseudopassiveness', or concert state, can now take place. The mechanisms of authority and infantilization come into play. Any barriers can be easily overcome. A state of relaxation occurs. The mind becomes ostensibly inactive. It becomes highly receptive toward learning. Rather than attending to memorization, the learner becomes involved 100% with the music. (The music played is classical in nature, having a 4/4 beat, with no overwhelming rhythm, instrumentation, or words.) The whole brain becomes activated. The musical beat smooths out the transference of information. It is during the concert state that the actual language lessons are presented.

I have experienced success in incorporating a modified version of Suggestopedia in my English as a second language class. (Lozanov has modified the method many times himself, and is continually adapting and changing as a result of further studies.)

A basic tenet of Suggestopedia is belief in its pedagogical value to produce effective achievement, both cognitively and affectively. It has been suggested that we have to start from our own roots and have to develop the Suggestopedic Method in our own style; that we should consider different cultural aspects and different educational systems.

The teaching model presented here is one that I have found to be effective in teaching children English as a second language, using a modified suggestopedic approach.

My first task is to establish an atmosphere which is conducive to learning under relaxed conditions, an atmosphere in which the students feel secure and comfortable with me, and with one another as well. In addition to smiles and touches, every day prior to class activities, we do a series of exercises designed to relax and to make the students more comfortable. Specifically, these involve tensing parts of the body, usually working from the toes on up, then relaxing. I stand in the center of the room and, as the students observe, I demonstrate the tensing and relaxing and verbalize what is taking place. The next activity involves having the students extend their arms over their heads and touch their toes, four or five times. Following that we breathe in, hold until the count of four, and breathe out, again four or five times. The students quickly became familiar with the routine and in a few days are calling out parts of the body themselves and eventually conduct the exercises themselves.

In most other suggestopedic classes, relaxation and reduction of tension is also brought about through 'mind-calming' techniques.

Similarly, techniques such as 'Early Pleasant Learning Restimulation' (remembering pleasant and successful learning experiences) which contribute to the state of infantilization, can be done in the language of the students.

One technique which has been quite effective, contributing to better student involvement and attention, is the 'Fantasy Trip'. Being able to 'take' the child to far-off lands, or become a famous person, frees the mind from the everyday routine. All of the above techniques could effectively be used with students at more proficient language levels, if English is the only language used in the classroom. Otherwise, they can be conducted in the student's native language.

At the initial presentation, or the active concert stage, the students have in front of them a series of pictures (of interest to the students; things from the child's world) with the text written beneath it. The pictures should be graphic enough so as clearly convey the meaning of the written words. Usually the pictures are numbered so that the students are easily able to follow the text. As I read the sentence, the students' attention is focused on the picture, on the words, and on my presentation. The music is played in the background. I usually read each sentence three times and use many facial expressions and gestures, along with variations in the tone of my voice. I read the text in conjunction with the rhythm of the music. Lozanov claims that the use of rhythm affects the physiological processes and facilitates the suggestopedic process. It helps to create a particular attitude and promotes greater memory retention.

Many times the texts are quite lengthy, with as many as 30 pictures and up to 50 new vocabulary words presented in one session.

Also, during the initial presentation, I encourage the students to associate the words presented with something already familiar to them. I accomplish this by providing examples of imagery and association of vocabulary words that are already known to them. For example, 'meat', you *eat meat*, mm—meat, etc. Other associations can be made through gesturing, facial expressions, and through pantomime. Eventually, the students would select their own associations. I can recall on more than one occassion, my students calling out words in their native languages that sounded like or reminded them of the English words. Experiments show that when associations and mental processing occur that performance and memory retention improve.

Throughout this time, for the most part, the students remain quiet (unlike their A-LM counterparts) and attentive.

Following the active segment is the *passive concert stage*. The students are directed not to concentrate on the text or materials, but rather to sit back, relax, and attend only to the music. Calm and soothing music is selected. (Lozanov states that during the active stage the music should be more 'emotional' and during the passive stage more 'philosophical'.) Again they remain quiet as the text is read one more time, and again adapting the rate of speed of the presentation to the existing rhythm of the music.

The next two or three sessions are devoted to practicing the material, the vocabulary and structures, that have been presented during the concert. It is at this point that the teacher can utilize other valid techniques. There are some invaluable techniques which I feel incorporate the total person, may tap the reserve capacities, and involve physical, emotional, and mental processes, and thus stress communicative competence.

Carolyn Gragham has developed a most fascinating tool fr effective language learning called "Jazz Chants". Jazz Chanting is based on the natural rhythm of the spoken language and its relationship with the beat of jazz.

Total Physical Response, or TPR, uses commands which involve physical movement.

Role-playing is a technique advocated by Lozanov. The students act out the dialog or text from the previous day. It is especially during this activity that the students attempt to use the language in seemingly real situations. They begin conversing in the new language. According to Earl Stevick "retelling stories, verbatim or in one's own words, improvising variations of a memorized dialog", contribute to the student's depth of understanding.

How should student errors be dealt with? Lozanov emphasizes that "Mistakes made in conversation should not be corrected immediately, but a situation should be created in which the same words or phrases or similar ones are used by other students or by the teachers themselves. Not only in this phase, but during the whole course the students should never be embarrassed by the mistakes they make. That is why the correc-

tion of mistakes is considered one of the most important things in the art of giving suggestopedic instruction."

To reach an even deeper level of cognition, I have found the use of 'attribute cards' to be a highly effective tool. The cards are designed to elicit from the students various attributes of objects and vocabulary words, attributes such as color, shape, size, function, number, group, place, etc. The cards themelves are simply drawn symbols that represent certain attributes. For example, a rainbow represents color. Squares, circles and triangles represent shape, etc. Questions are asked *about* the word so that the student must further process it. To exemplify this technique, the shape card is held beside an object (or picture) which depicts a particular vocabulary word, like 'table'. The student responds by saying, 'The table is rectangle', etc. Again, the level of difficulty, in terms of the type of attribute requested, may be increased as the proficiency level of the student increases.

Other never-ending and forever popular techniques include games, songs, and art projects. All can be used effectively during the practice stage to reinforce the content of the formal presentation. Of particular value are games which incorporate the whole person and simultaneous use of both hemispheres of the brain.* (* The left hemisphere processes verbal and mathematical reasoning, while the right processes the more creative abilities such as appreciation of art and music.)

There should be an emphasis on sensory experience, i.e. touching, smelling, and tasting, hearing (non-verbal), and seeing, whenever applicable. As the student's proficiency level increases, include drama and expression of 'gut level' feelings, intuiting, imaging, divergent thinking; activities which contribute to whole person learning, activities which allow the students to express themselves and become more creative in the process.

The modifications that I have made in order to make the Method workable in my situation, are not extremely different from some of Lozanov's original ideas.

Lozanov also advocates the use of assigning the student a new and occupation, so that s/he comes to assume the role of that person. It is his contention that the student feels less inhibited in making errors, since s/he recognizes the errors as being made by a 'different person'.

In terms of physical room arrangement, Lozanov's ideal class set up includes 12 students (six boys, six girls),

with the classroom itself containing soft and unobtrusive lighting, open circle chaise lounge chairs, and a separate stage area. Tlthough my classroom was lacking such luxuries, I attempted to keep it as bright and cheery as possible. Setting up a class with the ideal number of students was also difficult for me to arrange. Whenever feasible, I would try and include other students (both non-native and native-English speaking) to participate in game situations and a few other activities so that more interaction could take place.

Some teachers might hesitate in using classical music with children. My students were exposed to it at their first class session and recognized its use as part of the class routine. They actually enjoyed it. I believe the music facilitated in not only relaxing the students and making them receptive to learning, but actually contributed to better memory retention by activating right and left brain hemispheres.

Although the Method contributed not only to improved cognitive skills, it also seemed to have positively affected attitude and motivation. All students enjoyed class and were eager to learn.

The Suggestopedic Approach should be recognized as a viable alternative in second language learning and teaching, especially in teaching children English as a second language. The learner can experience a great sense of personal achievement, thus positively affecting his/her self-esteem. S/He can become more spontaneous and confident in communicating a new language. The learner can experience effects on his/her whole person. S/He can become involved in real communication; actually experience it. The Bulgarian researchers think, and rightly so, that direct immersion in a foreign language through the act of communication is one of the major accomplishments of Suggestopedia.

The teacher can come to know the students not only linguistically, but emotionally as well. In addition, the teacher recognizes the power of the unconscious mind, of body language, and what they convey in the total communication process.

We must be prepared to choose intelligently by making ourselves aware of current research and its pedagogical applications. We must be willing to attempt to use and experiment with a variety of techniques in order to expose our students to as many different learning styles as possible. By doing so, we will be exploring the human potential.

TN 4/80

SUGGESTION AND EDUCATION

By Myrna Lynn Hammerman
Northeastern Ill. Univ., Chicago

In January 1979, two papers were presented on suggestion and education at the TEX-TESOL-IV convention in Houston, Texas. Mary L. Lindeman discussed the historical precedent of Suggestopedia and Valdemar Phoenix investigated the technique. Both Lindeman and Phoenix are affiliated with the Language and Culture Center at the University of Houston. The following is a synopsis of the two presentations and their conclusions.

In her paper, "Suggestion in Education: The Historical Path of Suggestopedia", Mary L. Lindeman points out that it is safe to assume that historically methods of education have used some form of suggestion, be it good or bad. She chooses to explore those pedagogical methods and the research connected with them that specifically utilize the special technique of suggestion.

One of the earliest forms of organized education were the yogic schools that date back 3,000 years and still are in existence today. They produced professional memorizers of sacred Indian literature by means of yoga which was developed as a method of mental enrichment for religious purposes. Western culture has had difficulty understanding Indian mysticism and has not been permitted familiarity with the yogic mental techniques due to their private religious nature. As a result, Western scientists have not been able to establish conclusive evidence for or against the notion that yoga improves intellectual faculties. Nevertheless, super-memory feats have been observed by Westerners in India.

The course of history in Western education over the past two thousand years has been based on the faculties of logic and reason in which education was considered hard work and reason was the tool by which the mind became educated. Suggestion, although always implicitly present, was neglected in historical Western pedagogy. It was by accident that suggestion found its place in official Western history with the introduction of hypnotism to medicine in the eighteenth century by a Viennese doctor named Mesmer.

The medical history of hypnosis in the West is thoroughly outlined by Lindeman in her presentation. It traces a rocky road fraught with lack of understanding, wariness on the part of the public, and fear of the occult. But along the way there have been enlightened scholars who have recognized the value of hypnotic techniques in the educational setting.

The father of modern hypnotism, a French physician named Liébeault who practiced in the last half of the nineteenth century, recognized hypnosis as a valuable educational tool to be used with delinquent children. In 1935, Clark L. Hull of Yale, extended the interest in hypnosis to the study of psychology in which he investigated susceptibility to hypnotism, the posthypnotic suggestion, learning in hypnotism, and hypnotic amnesia. It took Émile Coué, a Frenchman with a working knowledge of hypnotic technique, to discover that light positive suggestion was more effective than a state of deep hypnotic trance. It wasn't until the twentieth century that his intuitive insights were verified by psychological and educational research.

As early as 1890 articles on research relating to suggestibility in children may be found in books and professional journals. Since that time there have appeared numerous studies, scrupulously detailed by Lindeman, to attest to the positive contribution that light hypnotic technique has to offer to education. Most recently Martin Aster and Stanley Krippner have been strong advocates of educational hypnosis. Krippner, at the Kent State University Child Study Center, used hypnosis as an aid to better study habits, increase of concentration, reduction of test anxiety, increase of motivation, and help in special language skills. Ralph Alan Dale (1972) listed nine uses of hypnosis in education. Jampolsky (1970) reported the effective use of hypnosis in special education with learning disabled children. In the 1970's there has materialized in the West a growing acceptance of the principles of suggestion in the classroom and significant research is being conducted at a number of leading universities in the U.S.

In the 1970's Dr. Georgi Lozanov, a Bulgarian psychiatrist and yogi, developed Suggestopedia, a new method of foreign language teaching based on suggestion and subliminal stimuli gleaned from his experience with hypnosis in the West and his observations of a yogi lawyer's ability to perform computer-like memorizations. Lindeman gives a thorough description of the method as she understands it using what information is available to us at this time. (see Bancroft 1976)

Valdemar Phoenix in his presentation, "Suggestion and Creative Potential", discusses the theory of suggestion as it is understood by contemporary philosophy and psychology and the application of suggestion as a teaching/learning tool—both in relation to how Lozanov's method complies with what is known of suggestion.

According to Phoenix there are two minds, the conscious mind that makes decisions, reasons, judges, and analyzes, and the subconscious mind that controls and creates—the synthesizer of all the information fed into it through the conscious mind and through all sensory and non-sensory channels. An important concept to understanding Suggestopedia is the realization that it is not only the thought image that gets passed into the subconscious, but also the emotional state or feeling that the thought evokes, and both of these are stored together in the subconscious memory. Once a person consciously accepts an idea or belief as being logical or true (whether it is true or not) he passes it into the subconscious along with the emotional content that it evokes. All beliefs start out as direct or indirect suggestions that have been accepted by the individual and then become externalized as a reality in the person's life. There is more opposition to direct suggestion than to indirect suggestion. Indirect suggestion is directed towards the subconscious mind and therefore is less subject to conscious interference and resistance. Lozanov uses positive suggestion to overcome previous beliefs. He suggests a new positive idea to replace the old negative belief. He begins training with brief re-suggestion sessions that the teacher himself must experience in order to be able to conduct.

The authority of the teacher is very important to the practice of Suggestopedia. The students must have total respect for the teacher in order to accept the suggestions offered by the teacher at a deep level. This respect comes from the teaching institution as a whole, to the methods employed, to the credentials of the teacher. Suggestology attempts to recapture the learning inquisitiveness and spontaneity of childhood via a process termed "Infantilization" by Lozanov. It is believed that a Parent-Child attitude between teacher and student will foster creativeness thereby enhancing the ability to learn.

Suggestopedia contains a concept entitled double-planeness which refers to ". . . a form of *communication* which accesses both the left hemisphere of the brain, which is generally endowed with what we've been calling the conscious functions of the mind; and the right hemisphere, which generally houses the subconscious." (Phoenix, 1979:13) Phoenix discusses this concept in relation to maintaining the on-going suggestion of a vast, and creative learning potential and presenting actual material in a 'suggestive' manner. He especially notes that all communication is not verbal and that a strong sense of legitimacy (decor of room, teacher's personality, etc.) is a form of non-verbal suggestion that is an important influence on the student's ability to learn. It is essential, according to this method, that the teacher present the material in a controlled, knowledgeable way so as not to inadvertently reinforce a student's learned limitations. Therefore, double-planeness also refers to how the teacher behaves in relation to the student when the student is learning. The teacher must be able to reach both hemispheres of the brain (the conscious and the subconscious) as well as all of the students in the class.

According to Phoenix, students have their own preferred input channel or combination of channels and also a preferred representational system (auditory, visual, and kinesthetic) for learning, as do teachers. It is essential for anyone who uses suggestion as a teaching method to know the specific techniques for determining a person's preferred input channel and representational system and to be able to present material in a manner that is agreeable to the student. In other words, the teacher must train himself to be fluent in communication in all channels (not only in his own preferred channels) in a congruent fashion thereby expanding his own potential as

well as that of the student. Phoenix and Lindeman are at present working on the development of specific techniques for congruent teaching.

Two examples from the techniques of Suggestopedia, intonational-rhythmic readings of material and concert listening are good ways of directly communicating with the subconscious right brain. These techniques when used correctly place the student in a super-suggestive, relaxed state and allow him to subconsciously absorb what is being taught while the logical left hemisphere is being distracted by auditory input (music).

Phoenix concludes by saying that specific methodologies are not as crucial to the learning situation as the rapport established between the teacher and student. It is in the total behavior of the teacher, on a personality level, and on conscious and subconscious planes, wherein lies the value of the suggestive approach.

Both Lindeman and Phoenix point out that the success of the conscious and effective use of suggestion in education depends on the creativity and sensitivity of the individual teacher. Lindeman delineates some of the benefits derived

from this method as relaxation for learning purposes, creating a good mind set for being a student, developing the use of the subconscious to enhance learning, change of student attitude from negative to positive, increased motivation, and overcoming emotional blocks. In conclusion she says that "In education suggestion is a force so powerful, but so basic, that it goes unnoticed. Those educators who are aware of its potential and sensitive to its use will be in a position to enhance every teaching activity, directly and indirectly."

References:

Bancroft, Jane. "Suggestology and Suggestopedia: The Theory of the Lozanov Method." ERIC, ED 132 857, 1976.
Dale, Ralph Alan. "Hypnosis and Education." ERIC, ED 087 710, 1972.
Jampolsky, Gerald. "The Use of Hypnosis and Sensory Motor Stimulation to Aid Children with Learning Problems." Journal of Learning Disabilities, 3, No. 11, November 1970.   TN 8/79

Editor's Note: Both of these articles reported here contain excellent bibliographies. An even more complete bibliography on suggestion and hypnosis can be found in Hammerman's excellent M.A. Thesis "Hypnosis and Language Learning", Northeastern Illinois University, January 1979.

A LOOK AT TOTAL PHYSICAL RESPONSE

by Carol Weiner
Northeastern Illinois University

The Total Physical Response (TPR) is an approach to language learning devised by James Asher, a psychologist at San Jose College, California. The TPR method claims to produce rapid, nonstressful and effective language learning using a strategy that achieves accelerated listening fluency in the target language of the student. This is achieved through the mode of synchronizing language listening with body movements.

TPR is an approach derived from the strategies of children learning their first language. Children acquire a high level of listening ability for English long before they are able to say their first words. They can follow simple and complex commands before these words are spoken. Asher (1972) believes the child's listening comprehension is not only far superior to his speaking, but is also critical to the development of speaking. He believes this is so because the brain and nervous systems are biologically programmed to acquire language in the sequence of listening before speaking. Therefore, in TPR, the first stage of training focuses upon only listening, followed by an action. Of the four language skills: listening, speaking, reading and writing, Asher believes listening has the most positive transfer to the above areas.

The learning strategy is to let the student listen to a command in English and immediately follow with the physical action. For example, the teacher gives the command, "stand up", and along with the

teacher the students stand up. Brief utterances are used at the beginning, but as Asher claims, the "morphological and syntactical complexity" of the command can be increased to:
Stand up and walk to the door.
Stand up and walk to the door and open it.

Many experiments have been conducted (Asher 1964, 1969, 1972, 1974) to examine the questions of whether: 1. all linguistic features of the target language can be achieved with TPR, and 2. will there be a positive transfer from listening to the other 3 language skills areas. The findings were encouraging. Most of the grammatical features of a language can be utilized in the imparative form; also listening has a positive transfer in the areas of reading, writing and speaking.

What accounts for this technique's effectiveness is believed to be the action, which facilitates and accelerates the comprehension of language learning. Asher (1964) found that the action was extremely important in the retention of many complex utterances, even though there was a long interval between the act and the retention test. However, Asher has tested and also found that if the students attempted to learn listening and speaking together, their comprehension decreased.

Many other methods use the imparative drill, but only in TPR is oral produc-

tion delayed until language comprehension has been developed, as responding physically seems to produce long-term memory storage.

For those interested in learning more about this method, Asher has a film called, "Demonstration of a New Strategy in Language Learning", which is available from the film library at the University of California, Berkeley. In this film he shows how three 12 year old boys show their understanding of complex Japanese utterances after only 20 minutes of training. It also shows retention after a delay of one year. Asher also has a book titled, "Learning Another Language through Actions" (1977) Los Gatos CA, Sky Oak Productions.

Asher, James. (1964) "Toward a Neo-Field Theory of Behavior." Journal of Humanistic Psychology 4:85-94.
(1965) "The Strategy of TPR, An Application of Learning Russian". International Review of Applied Linguistics in Language Teaching. 3: 291-300.
(1972) "Children First Language as a Model for Second Language Learning". The Modern Language Journal. 56-133-137.
(1974) "Learning a Second Language through Commands." The Second Field Test. The Modern Language Journal 58: 24:32.

TN 4/80

COUNSELING—LEARNING: A WHOLISTIC VIEW OF THE LEARNER

Karen E. Czarnecki and
Joseph A. Ramos

Counseling-Learning, a new method introduced by Charles A. Curran, seeks to facilitate language learning through a synthesis of the student's affective and cognitive domains.[1] In simplified terms, this means that the student's interests, values and attitudes are utilized (the feeling aspect in a broad sense), and synthesized in the classroom with the more usually employed cognitive or thinking domain. This synthesis brings about a more complete language learning experience. How does this work?

First, the instructor's recognition and acceptance of the whole student requires him to modify his teaching technique. He must take into account the fact that the student is not only a thinking, but also a feeling human being who comes to class with anxieties and insecurities.[2] In so doing, the instructor's emphasis changes from a questioning modality to a listening one. He must therefore abandon the usual teacher-questions, student-answers technique which has the stultifying effect of putting the student on the spot, further creating anxieties related to his fear of not being understood. The instructor should instead act as a reflecting device to the student's utterances by paraphrasing them in correct English. For example, the student might say, "I no feel good today." Whereupon, the instructor, instead of asking why, or saying "No, that's not right, you should say "I don't feel good today," paraphrases the student's response by simply saying "you don't feel well today." Several things will be accomplished: one, the student immediately recognizes the difference between his use of the language and the instructor's (usually instantly correcting himself) and is led to further enlarge upon that point, thus experimenting with and using the language. Two things may be pointed out here: one, the value of self-correction is obvious; second, the student continues in a vein most relevant for him, thereby helping to teach himself. The fact that the instructor reflects back the student's statements without making judgments or affixing diagnostic labels encourages greater self-knowledge and confidence on the student's part, and with it, the increased ability to communicate well and effectively in English.

The success of this approach depends on the instructor's own security with the method which will in turn affect his ability to create an understanding and accepting atmosphere for the learner. Because it is much easier to ask questions or to correct the student than to wait for utterances which may be long in coming, the instructor may feel uncomfortable. However, the successful creation of an accepting atmosphere will help to defuse an *ordinarily and or confrontational experience* for the student. Counseling-Learning then, requires that the instructor retrain himself by restraining from the normal focus-on-instructor to the far more effective focus-on-student. In this way, the student is encouraged to take the greatest responsibility for his own learning. When the student's whole self becomes actively involved in the learning process, not just his committed brain, personal investment takes place and an actual growth process begins. This is analogous to the insemination process, wherein a seed is planted, and through the process of nurtured growth, it is allowed to branch out, taking on new direction for further growth.

Curran's counseling-learning can be used by itself or as a technique in addition to other techniques. Take for example, a lesson being taught on simple prepositions of place. After the instructor has introduced the structures using whatever techniques and methods he is successful with, and the students have been led to achieve some competency, he can then encourage the greater creative use of the structures by utilizing the counseling-learning method. This is easily accomplished by presenting a picture with visual representations of previously learned prepositions (such as a magazine illustration) and by allowing the student to speak freely without teacher (questioning) interference.[3] *The instructor's use in his paraphrasing feedback of the structures taught* will encourage further use of them by the students. The instructor's role is to give understanding feedback in correct English, but he does not otherwise interfere by drawing attention to mistakes or by asking innumerable questions. That students will correct each other becomes particularly evident when this technique is used in a small group.

In every class there will be at least one student who cannot or will not interact with the others in a conversation modality. The non-interactor, then, can be reached on a one-to-one basis using the counseling-learning technique. A casual, non-threatening statement made directly to him by the instructor while passing out papers, for example, but requiring some response from the student, can be the opening wedge. Later, contacts before and after class can be utilized to lessen stress and encourage confidence so that an everwidening circle of intreaction becomes gradually possible. It is important to reiterate here that the instructor resist the desire to ask questions and instead replace this activity with encouragement and acceptance of the student's utterances. This acceptance by the instructor nurtures growth and allows for student involvement, not only with his peers, but also with the learning process itself.

By understanding and utilizing the counseling-learning method the instructor encourages the student's greatest possible use of English because he utilizes the whole person. The student, like any other human, must have a positive self-image, be accepted by and be able to convalidate his experiences with his peers. These feelings and needs which are not normally encouraged inside the classroom, are allowed to surface and are explored in an accepting way. The student is consequently enabled to invest his total self in the learning process. Thus an actual internal growth takes place which augments the more usual external overlay of facts which a student "puts on" much as he would an overcoat. A further bonus is that the student's internal growth, which is a live, dynamic thing, extends far beyond the confines of the classroom, enabling him to more competently utilize his everyday experiences as part of his own learning processes.

In using the counseling-learning method the instructor has the responsibility of requiring the student to utilize his own best langauge learning abilities which are not, as we have seen, only restricted to his cognitive self. By involving the whole person in the learning process, the instructor encourages the student to develop an inner criteria for correct English usage. Therefore, through this method more so than others, the student is enabled to function both correctly and creatively outside the classroom as well as within.

[1] Charles A. Curran, *Counseling-Learning: A Whole-Person Model for Education* (New York: Grune & Stratton, Inc., 1972).
[2] Many of these anxieties and insecurities are of course directly linkable to the language learning experience itself.
[3] As an example, *Progressive Picture Compositions*, Donn Byrne (London: Longman Group Limited, 1967).

TN 12/75

A COUNSELING-LEARNING MODEL FOR SECOND LANGUAGE LEARNING

by Jennybelle Rardin
Counseling-Learning Institute

The Counseling-Learning model for education, developed by Dr. Charles A. Curran of Loyola University, Chicago, and his associates, has been receiving much attention recently from educators and particularly from the language teaching profession. Much of this interest is due to Earl W. Stevick, who reviewed Curran's book in 1973 and Carol and Nobuo Akiyama, who generated interest in the Peace Corps which resulted in several Community Language Learning Teacher Training Programs.

"Community Language Learning" is the name given to the application of this model to language learning since it results in a special kind of learning community.

Original Research

The original research which began in the late fifties, was designed to study the psychological dynamics involved in adult learning, specifically, foreign language learning, rather than to develop a methodology of language teaching. Foreign languages were chosen as the learning task. As a result, students in the research classes—some using four languages simultaneously, some, one at a time—achieved varying levels of confidence and "communicative competence" in one or more foreign languages.

One of the questions that was raised at the outset of the research was whether awarenesses from counseling and psychotherapy could facilitate the learning process by becoming an integral part of that process. Since many of the blockings that language learners expressed were quite similar to those expressed by persons coming for psychotherapy or psychological counseling, it was theorized that if language experts were also trained in counseling sensitivities and skills, this double expertise would bring about significant changes in the quality of the learning relationship between teacher and learners and among learners themselves.

Curran's book, *Counseling-Learning A Whole-Person Model for Education*[1] (1972) presented the findings from over twelve years of research in this model of "creative affiliation between teacher and learners." The findings and model itself are as Earl Stevick puts it, "infinitely rich in subtleties" and a process of study and experience with it in learning situations, re-study and re-experience can yield an increasing grasp of its complexities.

The five following statements while not exhaustive, are basic to an understanding of the Counseling-Learning model. 1) All final human learning is value learning; 2) Resistance is inherent in any adult learning situation; 3) Human learning is whole-person learning; 4) Human learning is persons; 5) Human learning moves through a five-stage process of internalization.

Value Learning

A basic concept underlying the Counseling-Learning model is that all whole-person, human learning is, in fact, value learning. This concept is treated by Curran in his book, *Counseling and Psychotherapy: The Pursuit of Values* (1968).[2] By "values," Curran means conscious or unconscious self investments—that is, such self-investments are either determined by oneself or pre-determined by the cultural, family, religious neighborhood, etc., values one is born into.

In other words, if we as teachers see ourselves as the cause of a learning conflict within the student, simply because we represent a certain body of knowledge which the student wishes to learn, then we will be more understanding about the kind of struggle that we have created in the student. That this struggle is not just intellectual is especially evident in the area of foreign language learning whenever "communicative competence" is stressed. The whole-person of the learner is especially involved if he or she aims at a speaking ability rather than simply grammar, vocabulary and reading.

Many students in a language class at first "get butterflies" just thinking about having to pronounce the foreign language in front of the class, let alone trying to carry on a conversation. This would be one level of struggle. But suppose, for example, the Spanish speaking student is consciously or unconsciously aware that by learning English he/she is in a complicated way alienating himself/herself from the parents who speak no English; it is obvious that we are at another level of struggle.

What the Counseling-Learning model offers therefore, is a means of understanding these personal learning conflicts in such a way that learners as well as teachers may deal constructively with negative as well as positive feelings. As a result, both can make genuine investments in the learning relationship and so experience less discouragment with one another and the material to be internalized or learned. Personal learning conflicts and confrontations then, in this sense, can always have a positive tone because the student's anger, anxiety and similar psychological disturbance—understood and responded to by the teacher's counseling sensitivity—are indicators of deep personal investment. Even indifference, seen this way, proves often to be a form of defense against anxiety and fear of failure rather than resistance to learning.

D. D. Tranel talks about teaching as "not just an intellectual encounter with the student but as a psychological encounter."

Begin, found that in the human learning situation, students are "appraisers." Curran originally treated this under the concept of man's search for meaning and as "Man: The 'Why' Animal." Just as a client seeks to understand himself and his relationship with others in the counseling process so a student is consciously or unconsciously seeking a satisfactory "why" for his/her studies. This is fundamental to and prior to any adequate self-investment. Such evaluation is needed to arrive at value investments and decision making. But misunderstood and misinterpreted it can throw the learning exchange between knower and learner into a "games-we-play" routine of questions and answers which avoid personal engagement in the real learning experience.

The course content in most universities and colleges, is usually described in abstract and impersonal terms. The student, however, at a more personal level or inward direction, is most likely trying to evaluate the "why" in some relation to his own life goals. Curran's contrast of traditional British and European upper-class education for the few, which presumes an established value system, with an American democratic education for all, resulting in a confusion or decrease of accepted values, is helpful here. It helps illuminate why so much of this value confusion and struggle may now be going on in our classrooms—known or unknown to us as teachers.

So, under the surface of the learning that is apparent to us in our classrooms, may be not only the "questing" of "Why am I learning this?" but also "Who am I?" and "How does what I am learning, relate to who I am and where I am going in life?" This makes the teaching/learning relationship immeasureably more complex and challenging but, at the same time, more humanly satisfying. It also suggests the necessity of additional teacher awarenesses and skills beyond good classroom techniques.

Adult Resistance

Another basic concept of the Counseling-Learning model is that in most adolescent or adult learning there is an inherent resistance to the new knowledge being presented. This results from the developmental process that produces self-awareness or self-"consciousness" after twelve or so. The learner's need for personal self-assertion, often begins to show itself against the knower—seemingly impeding the acceptance of and submission to, the learning process. This is an additional cause of "clash" in any learning situation. This resistance is generally not conscious or at least not always made evident to the teacher—particularly as we move into adult learning—but rather is often disguised in the form of "questions" or similar tactics.

Applied to the language learning experience, we have, for example, often seen groups of students who came together for the purpose of speaking a second language, suddenly find themselves asking questions *about* the language, the culture, the country—in their native tongue—rather than personally engaging in the struggle to communicate in the second language. From the point of view of their ego-assertion need, such submission to the handicapped state of a second language is too humiliating.

But, if the learner is to make the second language his own and so make it operational—be able to speak French, say—there must be an acceptance of an initial state of ignorance and, in this sense, "humiliation." This is difficult for adults to do. This does not mean total helplessness but rather a kind of dependency on another with which adolescents and adults are generally not comfortable. This is why, in the Counseling-Learning modality, native experts were trained in counseling sensitivities. This then provided the necessary security at the beginning of the learning process which enabled adolescent or adult learners to regress to a childlike—not childish—trust in the language-counselor-expert. As a result, they could, with less anxiety and resistance, accept and submit to strange language sounds and structures and to the process of learning. This produced too, a growing closeness to and deep sense of supportive community from the other learners—the opposite of our usual classroom competitive individualism.

Whole-Person Learning

Once this trust has been established in the Community Language Learning setting, it becomes clear how human learning is whole-person learning. As adults, we are extremely skilled at masking our feelings. But once we are free to "feel about" the language learning experience and are understood in our feelings, then we are free to "know-feel" the language. It is in proportion as teachers are skilled in an ability both to understand these feelings and to "re-cognize" them—that is, adequately cognize them in their responses—that learners in the Counseling-Learning modality are able to assimilate or internalize the second language in an authentic total-person way. In other words, they can "invest" in it and so make it a personal value goal. Such investment is basic to the growth of a new "language-self."

Current literature is concerned with this when it talks about having "real" communication in the classroom. Real learning, in Counseling-Learning terms, means learning that is brought about by an "interaction between the knower and the learner in which both experience a sense of their own wholeness." In the first stages of the learning process, for example, this can mean that the material to be internalized is generated by the learners in a "childlike" but real conversation, limited only in the extent of words used. Such conversation, however, demands the aid and support of the language expert. Both learner and knower are therefore deeply engaged: the learner willingly accepts his need for help; the knower gives this help in such a way that it can be easily utilized. Such a mutual process gradually frees the learner from his dependency on the knower. The teacher, in this sense, willingly strives for and accepts the final goal of being no longer needed by the learner.

It is this engagement that makes possible a "whole-person" entry into the language.

Learning Is Persons

We come then to the notion of learning as an intensely personal experience. This resulted in Curran's expression, "learning is persons." As students in such research groups came together, for example, their central purpose was to share and communicate as persons, much as they would in an ordinary conversation. The difference, however, was that they did so in a foreign language, through their "other self," which at first was the language-counselor-expert. Each student's natural urge for independence soon produced a slow emergence of a new inner language self as words and phrases were picked up and so internalized. This arrangement also created a strong sense of support, responsibility, and belonging from all members of the group. Such a secure and deeply personal engagement and commitment together, came to be called "community language learning."

Five Stage Process

Learning in this modality moves through a five-stage process from dependency to a basic independence. This five-stage process can be seen from varying points of view such as the gradual growth from dependency on the expert to the learner's independent linguistic competence; the personal learning group process as it moves toward a deep sense of community; the changing functional relationships between knower and learner; and other aspects of the five stages. To go into detail about each is beyond the scope of this article. But the footnotes lead to the original sources where the reader can find extended explanations and illustrations of these stages.

A Multi-Faceted Model

From what has been said of Counseling-Learning, it becomes clear that this is a model rich in subtleties. It has, therefore, a wide variety of applications. These applications involve such areas as the group process in foreign language learning; evaluative and emotional factors in foreign language learning; the process of education in general and its effects at the elementary, high school and university levels; the acquisition of two foreign languages simultaneously and finally, intensive adult learning. Some common conclusions emerge. Through Counseling-Learning, learners begin to understand themselves better as persons while, at the same time, they increasingly make a part of themselves an area of knowledge outside themselves. Such results, as we see, combine aims shared by both counseling therapy and education.

We are treating here, therefore, a multi-faceted model rather than a simple technique. From the underlying concepts of this model various techniques can be developed, depending upon the needs of different learning situations.

Curran has said:

In order to unify and bring together the whole person in the learning process, we have to do more than merely label it whole-person learning. We must basically restructure our approach.

REFERENCES

1. Curran, C. A., New York: Grune and Stratton, Inc., 1972.
2. Curran, C. A., 1st edition, 1968; 2nd edition, 1976, Apple River Press, Apple River, Illinois.

TN 4/76

THE SILENT WAY

by John F. Haskell
University of Puerto Rico, Rio Piedras

(In the last issue of the Newsletter, Jenny Rearden talked about the CL approach to language learning/teaching developed by Dr. Charles Curran. We also mentioned other approaches to language teaching such as that of Lazanov and the "Silent Way" of Dr. Caleb Gattegno, and there was an in-depth article on Robert Allen's "Sector Analysis" especially as it was used in the teaching of writing. In this issue, both Earl Stevick and LINC are quoted as having been greatly influenced by the Silent Way and so it seems appropriate that something be written about it. In 1973 I wrote a short article for the NY TESOL Newsletter (Idiom) to which Dr. Gattegno responded. This article takes note of that response and other more recent remarks about the Silent Way. The Editor.)

Earl Stevick says it has influenced him, Charles Blatchford says his teaching has been changed by it, the LINC people have put much of it into practice, and at the recent TESOL Convention in New York City, teachers thronged to the workshops of Dr. Gattegno as he demonstrated and talked about his Silent Way of teaching.

The Silent Way is not a new idea. The philosophy of the Silent Way, as proposed by Dr. Gattegno, has been around for 22 years, according to Shelley Kuo, the director of the Gattegno Language Schools. Originally, it was used as a math teaching device, but in the past few years it has been "discovered by language teachers, and is now widely touted as a method or approach for the teaching of reading and language." Elements of the Silent Way have always been present in our traditional approaches. For example, teachers and student teachers have been admonished for years to reduce their own speaking time and give more opportunity for the student to speak.

To quote the Silent Way materials, "as a general technique, the Silent Way is a way of teaching that liberates students systematically." It is an attempt to approach language learning by having the learner acquire as a primary step in language learning, a "feeling" for language. It aims at putting the learner into a situation where he is challenged to use his powers of thinking and his ability to analyze and experiment; it demands that students test hypotheses about the languages he is learning, taking advantage of his/her knowledge and experience with language. Dr. Gattegno says, "When I

teach a language, that language remains a secondary preoccupation of mine although it is the prime concern of the students. My function as a teacher is to do all I can to make students find for themselves the powers required to be successful in the new language as they are in their native language. Since one is free to use the mastered language for expression of emotions, feelings, ideas, perceptions and so on, teachers have to aim at a similar freedom in the new language. Clearly there is too much to learn for any student and teachers have to know what comes first and when to move to the next assignment. In my perception of the task, from the start and as soon as sufficient mastery is attained in the utterance of say twenty or so words, the student must prove capable of being on top of the four demands of spoken speech: correct sounds and correct stress in each word, a feel for which words run together in each statement or phrasing, and how intonation generates the melody of the language as natives express it."[2]

The syllabus or lessons of a Silent Way language course, are basically linguistically determined and sequenced. The difference is that the demand on the student to perform is not continuously stimulated by oral models given by the teacher. Instead the stimulus is 'silent'. The teacher manipulates a set of colored rods—rectangular wooden blocks of various lengths and colors (rather like children's building blocks), putting them into different arrangements of color and length which stimulate the learners to make on their own, statements about them: their size, color, shape, and their relationships to each other, in an ever more complex set of patterns and sentences. The only oral model has been given, once, by the teacher as s/he first arranges the rods. Some meaning comes from the learners perceptions of the situations as they are demonstrated by the teacher. This kind of stimulus avoids the need for translation into the learners language. The basic vocabulary has been provided and the students, collectively, may try to ask or describe to the teacher what has been 'arranged' with the rods. Collectively, because often the whole class participates in putting together the correct sentence while the teacher, not speaking, indicates approval or disapproval of form, vocabulary, pronunciation, and melody. Without the oral model supplied for him again and

again, the student is forced to pay attention to any initial utterances by the teacher and those of his fellow learners, to understand the situation or stimulus as presented by the arrangement of the rods, and to respond in a linguistically correct way. The teacher may occasionally point to a "sound chart" (a color-coded chart of letter/symbols or words which reflect the basic vowels and consonants in the language and the basic vocabulary used in the first lessons), to reinforce or to reestablish the correct pronunciation. Since one color represents one sound on the charts, pointing from one letter or combination of letters to another can evoke a string of sounds or words for the learner to work on. The systematic use of colors on the word charts permits the language to be handled phonetically without any modification of the actual orthography. The charts are used in the very first lessons. Miss Kuo states that "it starts by making the students conscious of the amount of linguistic equipment they already have so that they can concentrate on what they do not already know. Many languages require only a few sounds that the students are not familiar with, so the first few lessons focus on these. Having given the students the experience of sounding like native speakers in this very restricted area, the way has been cleared to acquire the elements of a functional vocabulary and, through that, an extended vocabulary."[5]

After the student has attained fluency with the restricted vocabulary used in the first lessons he is then stimulated to oral production by means of the teacher's pointing to words and symbols on the charts and then by writing on paper.

Reading also accompanies the lesson with emphasis on the melody of the language—the stress and intonation patterns. This emphasis, as with the initial lessons on pronunciation, is to promote, first, the "feeling" for the language—to build a confidence in being able to speak it "naturally." And secondly, to allay the fear of "saying it wrong" which is often the reason why students, however successful in class, often stumble and remain silent outside of class.

The techniques used in the Silent Way are basically oral-aural mechanical substitution and stimulus-response drills though the stimulus is visual rather than oral. The sequencing of materials (patterns) is in general linguistically based much as most

ESL texts are today.

So what's new—other than the "special" materials—charts and rods—and the fact that the teacher is silent and the student is forced, allowed, finally, to have the entire lesson time at his command, to speak?

As Dr. Gattegno puts it, the thing which he is striving to do is to build in the student, at the very beginning, a "confidence" that what he is saying is right. "The inner criterion of rightness . . . is the rock bottom on which the future acquisition will stand, increasing the sense of freedom that motivates learners and creates the joy which accompanies good performance."[1]

Blatchford states that his 'romance' with the Silent Way results from his recognition of the humaneness of the approach. He states that it has affected his approach to teacher training, resulting in his desire to provide, along with the methodology, the techniques of language teaching, "encouragement, self-reliance, and support"—the very things potential teachers will need "in the classroom they will be guiding."[1]

After participating in a Silent Way experience, it was apparent that certain basic facts stood out as important for the language teacher. *First,* the student is immediately and almost totally responsible for the language learning situation. That is, his mistakes provide the teacher with direction for the succeeding lessons, his successes determine how quickly he moves on to the next step, and the speaking is entirely his responsibility. *Second,* the language of the classroom is entirely, from the first instant, the target language. The students' language(s) are never used. His intelligence, his desire to learn, his compulsion to "try" the new words, sentences, patterns, language, is drawn upon instead. *Third,* after an initial anxiety, supported by long years of varying successes and failures in classrooms and especially foreign language classrooms, Silent Way students relax in the interaction between themselves as they learn to stimulate, encourage, and reinforce each other—respond to each other in a real, "thinking", meaningful way, rather than merely responding to the teacher. The "feel" for the language becomes part of the learning and with the responsibility for speaking comes not only the challenge to do so but the feeling that one *can.*

1. Charles Blatchford. "My Silent Way Experience—One Model for Training Teachers and Students" (Paper given at TESOL Convention, March 5, 1976, New York City).

2. Caleb Gattegno. "Some Remarks and Additions on 'The Silent Way: A Look at Language Teaching' ", *Idiom,* 4:2, Winter 1974.

3. Caleb Gattegno. *Teaching Foreign Language in Schools the Silent Way.* New York: Educational Solutions, 1963.

4. John Haskell. "The Silent Way: A New Look at Language Teaching", *Idiom,* 4:1, Fall, 1973.

5. Shelley Kuo. "Learning Chinese by the 'Silent Way' " (Mimeographed paper printed by Educational Solutions.)

TN 6/76

PRAGMATICS

By Ronald Taubitz
ACHNA, Madrid, Spain

The purpose of this paper is to show that in both America and Europe emphasis has shifted from concern for language as such to concern for language as manifested in a communicative context in a particular situation. In one sense, then, interest has moved almost full circle from the situational or direct methods of the 1920's and 1930's through audiolingualism and cognitive-code theories to contextualization and realistic communication. Two popular exponents of these latter persuasions are John Oller in the United States and L. G. Alexander in England; both have made the transition from earlier, more narrowly linguistic, positions to broader-based theories. It is important to trace this change in their positions and the reasons which helped bring it about so that language teachers everywhere can begin reexamining their own approaches to TEFL in the light of these developments.

In an article entitled, "Transformational Grammar, Pragmatics and Language Teaching," (*English Teaching Forum,* March-April, 1971) John Oller expressed his dissatisfaction not only with audiolingualism (pattern drills and the mechanical manipulation of language in the classroom) but also with mentalism (transformational theory and its derivative cognitive-code applications). In both cases, the "false assumption that language is a self-contained formal calculus" (Oller:8) underlies the theories and leads to the notion that language is isolated, "unrelated to the communicative contexts" in which it is normally used. Oller summarizes his argument by noting that "transformational theory incorrectly assumes that language is a self-contained system and can be understood by asking the question: 'How do sentences and other units of language relate to each other?' Without a doubt this question is important, but it leaves the following more significant question unasked: 'How are the sentences and other units of language used to convey information?' " (Oller:8)

Oller defines his alternative view of language as "pragmatics," which he defines as "the correspondence of linguistic forms to situational settings," or in question form, "how does linguistic form relate to contexts?" To illustrate his meaning, Oller quotes a humorous anecdote from the book *Pragmatics of Communication* (Watzlawick, Beavin and Jackson, 1967:20): "In a fenced-in grassy field near a rural house, a bearded man is creeping around in figure-eights looking back over his shoulder and 'quacking' without interruption (quack, quack, quack). A curious crowd of passersby begins to form at the fence. One man with a look of horror runs off to a phone booth to call for the men in white. The man engaged in the bizarre quacking behavior is Konrad Lorenz, the famous ethologist. Far from being insane, he is performing an experiment in which he has substituted himself for the mother of the little ducklings who are following him, hidden in the tall grass, out of sight of the curious crowd."

The point of the story should be immediately evident, "if we want to understand the basis of complex behavior, we must consider the context in which it occurs." The language learner, then, must go beyond such purely linguistic considerations as phonology, morphology, syntax and lexicon and consider the situation in which the language act takes place if he is to be able to decode and properly encode information. And the language teacher must be able to present linguistic structures in meaningful contexts "that observe normal sequences of events" and that permit the students to work first from ideas, concepts, or notions that they want to communicate to linguistic forms in the target language.

L. G. Alexander, in an article in the *English Language Teaching Journal* (January, 1976) entitled "Where Do We Go From Here? A Reconsideration of Some Basic Assumptions Affecting Course Design," presented some thoughts of his own on recent developments in language theory which parallel those of Oller in important ways, although Alexander takes as his point of departure the structural syllabus found in most language courses that employ audiolingual and audio-visual techniques. As Alexander sees it, "the framework

130

adopted in virtually every up-to-date language course is a structural one. Structural or linear grading, as it is often called, is the embodiment of the cumulative experience of language teachers. It is based on steps which are ordered in terms of apparent increasing difficulty. For instance, most language courses begin with *be + noun/adjective* combinations, proceeding to *have/have got + noun/adjective* combinations and then on to the present continuous, the simple present, the simple past, and so on."

Alexander finds three main weaknesses to the structural syllabus, which he uses to introduce an alternative approach which is called a functional syllabus. The first weakness is that each lesson is focussed on some particular grammatical point, often without reference to its practical application in a real situation. (Oller would agree completely.) The second weakness is the reliance on both high and low frequency grammatical items, some of which have little or no practical value. (Oller would no doubt agree again.) The third weakness results

in the students' not being made aware of "the stylistic register and the kind of language that is really appropriate to a given situation." (Oller would certainly agree here as well.) At this point Alexander would have language teachers ask themselves "what the student wishes to do through language, that is, which functions he wishes to perform." (Alexander:92) Alexander is prepared to reconcile the structural syllabus with a functional syllabus having six general categories of functions: imparting and seeking factual information, expressing and finding out intellectual attitudes, expressing and finding out emotional relations, expressing and finding out moral attitudes, getting things done, and socializing. The emphasis on this hybrid syllabus would not be on the grammatical items, but rather on the functions represented through the grammar.

Oller defined "pragmatics" as "the correspondence of linguistic forms to situational settings." Alexander noted that "the presentation of language in situational dialogues is as old as formalized language-teaching itself, and

has served as the only effective antidote to the surfeit of tedious mechanistic drilling" (Alexander:95) used by some teachers. But beyond the refinements of audio-visual presentation and grammatical contextualization, "the technique has not been further developed." Oller's pragmatics, then, appears to be a restatement and justification of a well-established approach to language teaching, while Alexander's position appears to pick up where Oller's leaves off and introduce a greater refinement of the practical needs of the students in a variety of real-life situations.

The important point, however, is the emphasis which both Oller and Alexander place on the practical requirements of the language learner and his basic need to communicate and understand ideas, feelings, etc. for a variety of reasons. Language teachers should be aware of this change of emphasis and reexamine their own approaches, incorporating some of the insights described above where needed. *TN 4/78*

COMMUNICATIVE LANGUAGE TEACHING

by David Wilkins
Excerpted from "Approaches to Syllabus Design" in Functional
Materials and the Classroom Teachers *by K. Johnson and K. Morrow*

"Notional", "functional", and "communicative" are terms which have entered the vocabulary of language teachers and applied linguists only within the last three or four years. Yet, as the spate of recently published and promised textbooks shows, they represent ideas which have been eagerly taken up by the language teaching profession. It may not be clear yet whether these developments are merely another manifestation of the transitory fashions which seize the language teaching world from time to time or whether we are witnessing a much more substantial and long-lasting change of orientation.

Whereas the focus in conventional modern language teaching has been on the language itself, it is proposed that the first priority should be given to the purposes that language serves, that is to say, communication. Few would wish to argue nowadays that learning the form of a language is a desirable educational end in itself, but, in practice, most of our language teaching enshrines the principle that a foreign language is best learned through systematic exposure to its formal system. We do this because we hold that a fairly comprehensive (practical) command of the grammatical ("structural") system, supported by an adequate vocabulary, is a necessary precondition for any effective communication in the language. This being the

case, it seems only sensible to organise language teaching in terms of this grammatical system. While it would be foolish to deny that mastery of the grammatical system is important for wide-ranging and effective communication, it can be argued that in concentrating our attention on the forms by which communication is achieved, we have tended to lose sight of the purposes for which language is being learned. If instead, we take the communicative purposes of language learning as our starting point, we are more likely to obtain a proper balance between the ends of language learning and the means. It is this belief that forms the recent developments that concern us here and that enables us to characterize them as *communicative.*

Once we adopt a communicative perspective, we will note that there are a number of ways in which existing language teaching falls short of what we are trying to achieve. Most importantly, what we typically regard as the meaning of a sentence is by no means the same thing as its potential for use. An interrogative sentence may be used for many things other than asking questions, and, indeed, questions may be asked by many other means than the use of an interrogative. It follows that having learned how to construct sentences, one has still not necessarily learned how to use them. A second point is that in conventional

modern approaches we seek to enable the learner to advance by means of the progressive accumulation of grammatical structures. The criteria by which these structures are selected and ordered are of a general linguistic and pedagogic character. They are not selected because they provide the means to meet identifiable social needs. As a result, a good deal of what is learned at the beginner and intermediate levels offers little immediate return for the learners' efforts. It is only when a fairly substantial range of language has been mastered that the learner possesses a linguistic repertoire which he can begin to learn how to exploit. Real communication is, in effect, a deferred objective in much current language teaching.

We will content ourselves with one further point which is of a predominantly methodological nature. Existing language teaching provides the learner with a carefully controlled linguistic environment. With the best of teaching, the learner readily becomes able to recognize the language to which he is exposed in this environment and to produce sentences of the type being taught with some fluency and accuracy. To this extent, it may be said that the learner has a practical mastery of what he has been taught. However, it is worth noting that this is a linguistic experience quite unlike that which is provided by language use outside the classroom. Far from being controlled and limited, natural language use is richly variegated, and the learner will eventually need both to understand language in its full variety and to draw on the whole range of language which constitutes his personal repertoire. If language teaching does not provide adequate opportunity for him to do this, he will not be able to perform outside the classroom with any degree of fluency, accuracy, and appropriateness.

Communicatively oriented language teaching will seek to overcome these weaknesses by taking as the starting-point in the planning of language teaching the communicative potential which is sought for the given group of learners. To put it another way, the first step will be to establish a set of objectives which will have to be expressed not in terms of the grammatical structures and words that should be known, but in terms of the content and purposes of the acts of communication in which the learners can be expected to engage.

Ideally, the objectives will be determined by what is known about the actual needs of the learners. In this case, objectives will be the result of accurate predictions of future language behaviour. Often, however, accurate predictions cannot be made.

It follows from the above that there is no single set of objectives that will suit all kinds of learners. It is a mistake to imagine that "functional" language teaching is exclusively concerned with the everyday use of spoken language. The general argument is often illustrated by reference to spoken language, but it is equally valid for other language skills and other kinds of language situations.

It does not even follow that the "general" language learner should be primarily concerned with the spoken language. This may be a suitable aim, but the case would have to be argued. All in all, then, it is no part of the intention to set up a new, normative syllabus that all language teaching should follow.

In using the term "communicative" to describe the newer approaches to language teaching, we have done little more than indicate in a general way that we are seeking to give a more explicitly semantic orientation to language teaching. We have left open the question of how these communicative objectives are to be defined. A full characterization of the aimed-at language behaviour would draw on many dimensions of description. We would certainly need to know how far both the spoken and written channels would be involved and to what extent the learners would need to be both producers and receivers of language. We would have to establish the domains in which the language activity would take place and in what "styles" it would be

useful for the learner to be able to operate (e.g. colloquial, informal, formal). But in themselves neither these nor a number of other possible factors determines *what* it is that is communicated on a given occasion, however significant they may be in conditioning the form that a particular act of communication may take. It is to meet this need that much use has been made of the concept of "function".

Reference has already been made to the distinction to be drawn between the terms "interrogative" and "question". "Interrogative" is a grammatical term, describing a particular kind of sentence structure. "Question" is a category of use, i.e. a *functional* category. We are much more readily able to understand what someone is doing with language if we say that he is asking a question than if we say he is producing an interrogative. It is possible to see any larger stretch of language, whether produced by one or several speakers, as being made up of a succession of such functions. Analysing the functions to be found in any piece of speech or writing enables us to establish what it is a person intends to communicate to the person or people addressed.

It would probably be impossible to establish a definitive list of the functions to be found in a given language, but, in English for example, it might include such obviously interactive functions as questions, requests, suggestions, invitations, refusals, agreements and denials, the expression of such emotions as pleasure, sorrow, sympathy, anger, surprise and dislike, and functions commonly found in longer stretches of language, such as narrative, comparison, reason, exemplification, description and condition.

A functional approach to language teaching will be one that sees the communicative purposes of language users in terms such as these. It will therefore set out to enable learners to master those functions that are seen as relevant to their needs. The majority of the "communicative" courses that have appeared so far have, in fact, been *functional* in this sense.

The question will now arise as to why it has been thought necessary to introduce the further distinction of a *notional* approach to language syllabus design. If we assume that we are seeking to make our approach to language teaching a wholly communicative one, we have to take account of the fact that functional meaning, in the sense in which this is presented above, is not the only kind of meaning that sentences or utterances convey. Most sentences also contain some kind of proposition which further contributes to the meaning of the sentence. To put it crudely, we do not simply ask a question; we ask a question

about something. This aspect of the meaning of sentences has been variously called propositional, cognitive or ideational. It expresses our actual perceptions of events, states or ideas. As we construct sentences, we are invariably involved in expressing concepts of time, place and quantity, in representing the relations between the persons, things and actions that we are recounting, in relating what we observe to the context in which it occurs. In any language teaching we could not possibly be satisfied unless the learners could handle (i.e. express or recognize) these concepts or, to introduce a further term, *conceptual meaning*. An adequate language competence presupposes the ability to express *both* functional and conceptual meaning. . . .

Much of the conceptual meaning in a language is expressed through the grammatical system. "Time", for example, correlates closely with "tense"; "place" with "adverbials". If learners have already mastered a reasonable proportion of the grammatical system, whether or not this was through a communicative style of teaching, they will probably be able to express a good deal of the conceptual meaning that characterizes the language. In such a case, a functional statement of objectives and a functional organisation for language teaching is not unreasonable, since the other important aspects of meaning can be taken for granted. It is no accident that most purely functional courses are aimed at intermediate learners. In that way, the problems of teaching conceptual meaning are avoided. . . .

It is very important to realize that a functional approach to language teaching does *not* mean teaching people handy phrases for everyday situations. We wish the students to learn *the ways* in which important functions are performed, and we are interested in these in so far as they are conventionalized in the language. In this way, what is learned is applicable to many situations of use. Anything less would be merely an elaborate form of phrase-book learning. This point about generalization is, if anything, even more important in the case of the grammatical system. The grammar of a language remains its heart. There is no serious way in which a person who has not substantially mastered the grammatical system can be said to know a language. The grammar provides the essential mechanism for the individual to construct sentences (utterances) which are appropriate to his communicative intentions. We will have to satisfy ourselves, therefore, that in adopting a broadly communicative approach to language teaching, we are not sacrificing the grammar of the language. *TN 2/81*

A Review from The *JALT Newsletter*, 3:12, December 1, 1979

PROBLEM-POSING CAN HELP STUDENTS LEARN: FROM REFUGEE CAMPS TO RESETTLEMENT COUNTRY CLASSROOMS

by Nina Wallerstein
University of New Mexico

Problem-posing—a curriculum for critical thinking based on students' lives—comes from the writing of Brazilian educator Paulo Freire. This adult educational approach, which I adapted to ESL teaching, is particularly suited for refugees and immigrants. These students often experience social or emotional barriers to learning English: discrimination, cultural conflicts, and lack of self-esteem. Yet curriculum based on these same emotions can involve learners in the ESL classroom and help students gain control over their lives.

In the early 1960s, Freire developed a highly successful native literacy program for disenfranchised slumdwellers and peasants in Brazil. Using socially and emotionally laden ("generative") words and pictures of students' problems, Freire provoked students into discussions on how to improve their lives. With a phonetic recombination of syllables, students learned word literacy, as they learned social literacy, the understanding of their worlds.

Although the phonetic method is not directly applicable to English learning, the basic premises apply to ESL and ABE classrooms. Education is neither neutral nor separate from students' culture and experiences in society. A curriculum based on Freire's method, therefore, reflects students' lives, and, through dialogue, motivates them to examine their world critically and to seek change in their lives. Dialogue, according to Freire, involves a mutual exploration between teachers and students as co-learners of their world.

In the fall of 1982, I brought this Freirian approach to ESL to a refugee camp in Bataan, the Philippines, one of three resettlement centers in Southeast Asia. At these centers, the refugees complete several months of English language classes before flying to their resettlement countries.

Problem-posing is an ideal approach for ESL students, the majority of whom come from low socio-economic backgrounds with limited access to jobs and education in the U.S. They often face conflicts in their new society that leave them feeling vulnerable and inadequate. The curriculum therefore, should encourage students to develop self-confidence and to use their cultural and personal strengths to resolve problems in their lives.

To translate this philosophy into ESL classroom practice, problem-posing involves a three step process: 1) listening (or learning our students' culture and daily concerns); 2) dialogue (or codifying student concerns into lessons for discussion and language learning); and 3) action (or bringing the dialogue to a resolution, i.e., talking about the changes students can make in their personal lives and communities).

At the refugee camp, I thus began my teacher-training sessions with a listening or investigative stage. The first days were spent talking to the American and Filipino ESL teachers (150-200 total), community organization staffs and to the refugees. I wandered for hours through clusters of barracks from the Buddhist temple overlooking the ocean, to the lower entry gate four kilometers away. I saw families—some visiting as they watched passersby, others digging in their flower gardens, or returning from class holding umbrellas to stave off the tropical heat. The smells of food cooking on hot plates or fires mixed with odors that arose from the ditch waters. The population at that time had decreased from a capacity of 17,000 to over 9,000, with 35 percent Cambodian, 60 percent Vietnamese, and 5 percent Laotian living in ten separate ethnic neighborhoods.

I was still ignorant of the problems of everyday camp life. How had the refugees found the strength to survive their ordeals? What were their concerns or the sources of conflicts at camp? What resolutions of conflict were possible within the camp's structure? And, most important, which of these issues were appropriate for the English curriculum?

The existing curriculum was a multi-level competency-based program developed with assistance from the Center for Applied Linguistics. It covered survival language for resettlement countries: i.e., clothing, housing, food, health, transportation, employment, yet little of the refugees' immediate needs. Problem-posing on camp issues could appropriately supplement the competency-areas. For example, the housing could include living conditions at camp.

After a few days, I discovered that camp life was charged with issues: overcrowded billets; insufficient water (the spigots were turned on only two hours in the morning and evening); sanitation problems; long waits at the clinic; ethnic conflicts between groups, including the Filipino merchants who ran a local food market; time strains caused by four hours of English class, two hours of mandatory work brigade, and family demands; and the effects of changing family relationships. Despite these problems, there were avenues at camp for resolving conflicts. Although they were underutilized, small neighborhood associations had been set up by the Filipino social service agency in charge of camp administration.

In addition to camp issues, I learned that many refugees' traumatic escapes were still fresh and often overshadowed their lives. "I'm sad," said one, "I think of my husband under the sea." Everyone lived "on hold," nervously waiting for a new life to begin. These traumas or anxieties had already surfaced in the classroom. Students told teachers about their escapes or inabilities to learn: "I was made to climb a tree and fall down ten times. That's why I can't remember."

In discussions about camp issues, teachers expressed concern that problem-posing would invite inappropriate emotional discharges beyond their ability to counsel. Our discussions clarified the difference between including camp issues in ESL discussions and dwelling on traumatic events from the past. Through discussions of current issues, refugees could for the first time live in the present—and not just wait "on hold" for their next lives. The healing process would begin, enabling refugees to leave behind their painful experiences. As they shared their lives and cultures with others, the refugees would also be less likely to fear the loss of their own culture when they began to live in a new one. Those refugees who needed extra help were fortunate to have a new Mental Health Center at camp.

ISSUE-BASED CODES AS LESSON PLANS

Translating the many camp issues into a curriculum which fit the existing competency areas proved challenging. In the workshops, teachers developed fifty lesson plans or "codes" based on the issues.

A code—or codification in Freire's terminology—is a concrete expression of the issue that can take any form: a picture, photograph, story, role-play, puppet show, tape, song, etc. Because it is concrete and one-step removed from actual experiences, students can project their own emotional and social responses into the code, making for lively discussions. A good code will 1) present a daily problem easily recognized by students, 2) contain the many sides of the problem, and 3) be open-ended, leaving the students to reflect on actions that are possible. Codes are more than visual aides. They are a key to the educational process, for they inspire critical thinking about issues in students' and teachers' lives.

One code developed by the teachers presented the changes in family relations that refugees experience at camp. Because everyone must attend four-hour English classes, husbands take care of the children during their wives' sessions. Cultural changes such as this one begin for refugees long before they reach the U.S. The code below presents the husband's and wife's feelings about the changes, using vocabulary at levels three and four; the problem is codified, but no answers provided.

Once the codes were developed, we

began a five-step inductive questioning strategy, the "tools for dialogue" which aid in decoding the problem. Students start by describing what they see and how the situation applies to them. They then explore why the problem exists and what can be done about it. For this code, the questioning might follow this sequence:

1. Have students describe the content in the code: *"What do you see? Who is the man? What's his name? What is he doing? What is he thinking/saying? Where is he? Who is the woman? What is she doing? What is she thinking? . . ."*

2. Ask students to define the problem(s); use questions about how the different characters in the story feel: *"How does the woman feel about leaving her husband in the billet? How does she feel about studying? Is she happy, sad, worried? How does the husband feel when he's washing clothes? When he's taking care of the baby? When he's cooking? . . ."*

3. Raise similar questions concerning the students' own lives: *"Are you married? Do you have children? Is your husband taking care of them now? Is this the first time he's taken care of them? Did he take care of them in Laos? Is he the same as this man? Is he different? How is he different? How are you like this woman? How are you different? . . ."*

4. Encourage students to fit their personal experiences into the larger historical, social, cultural perspective; ask "why" questions: *"In your culture do men take care of children? Is it difficult for men? Why is it difficult for men? Why is he taking care of them now? Where you come from, do women go to school? Why or why not? Why is she going to school now? Is school important for men and women? . . ."*

5. Encourage students to discuss alternatives and actions to resolve the conflict: *"Can men learn how to take care of children? In other cultures, do men take care of children? Can men learn to to cook? When is it necessary for men to take care of the family? How can you help men to learn? . . ."*

The answers to these and other questions will differ from class to class. Each class may focus on various issues: men's cooking, the role of grandparents, or the importance women's education.

To encourage full participation, teachers should spend enough time on the first two steps so everyone answers a descriptive or feeling question. These simpler questions develop vocabulary and can be answered even by beginning students. The later, projective questions are difficult, but equally important, for they allow students to

An example of an issue-based code

A blackboard drawing (code) depicting Lam's and Nguyen's contrasting morning activities. Hastily drawn stick figures serve quite adequately as visual aides to spark conversation around familiar situations of students' everyday lives.

discover they are not alone in their problems; others in the class may offer new ways to see the problem or their own successes in making changes. Step Five encourages positive steps for action, though solutions may take a long time (even a lifetime). This process is therefore called "problem-posing" and not "problem-solving," recognizing the complexity of solutions for individuals and communities. After each discussion of the code, teachers may evaluate whether to pursue the issue further or choose a related one. The curriculum and language learning is in constant evolution as teachers fashion lessons by listening to their students' response.

For beginning students, full discussions are impossible in English, though bilingual discussions may be feasible. Yet problem-posing can work for beginners. One group of teachers at the camp developed a beginning level code depicting the same situation of changing family relationships. They drew a picture of a wife waving goodbye to her husband who stands in front of the billet holding a baby. The dialogue accompanying the picture was simple:

Wife: "Take care of our baby."

Husband: "Please come home right away."

Wife: "I'll come after class."

Although the discussion would be limited, the lesson still evokes a daily concern, teaches family vocabulary, and provides group support for the issue.

Another code developed at the camp examined the problem of insufficient water. This written dialogue (at levels five and six) enabled students to discover their own actions through the five-step questioning process.

Nguyen: "What time is it?"

Mai: "It's almost one o'clock."

Nguyen: "Is lunch ready? I'm hungry after four hours of English class."

Mai: "I'm sorry, but I haven't cooked the rice yet."

Nguyen: "Why not? You've been here all morning."

Mai: "I know, but there hasn't been any water since 7 a.m."

Nguyen: "Why don't you ask our neighbors for some water?"

Mai: "I did. They don't have any either."

The solution (or actions) for this code are not simple, but will require refugees and teachers to work together, using English outside the classroom, through the neighborhood associations and camp administration. Problem-posing with ESL lessons like this one provides the important link between language learned in the classroom and language used in the outside world.

As these refugees (and other immigrants) reach their resettlement country, problem-posing helps students analyze and overcome difficult situations. By listening to their students, teachers can readily develop codes on unemployment, problems with social service bureaucracies, lack of translators at clinics, miscommunication between groups, etc.

After hearing about this approach in one of my workshops, a teacher confided, "You know, I've always thought of us ESL teachers as sensitive to students, helping them in any way we can. but we've overlooked the importance of bringing their concerns into the classroom. Students get inspired to learn English by helping each other find solutions." ⓣ

REFERENCES

Freire, Paulo. 1973. *Education for Critical Consciousness.* New York: Seabury Press.

Dobbs, Caroline. 1982. Freire and Literacy. *TESOL Newsletter* 17(2):19-20.

RECONCILING COMPETING APPROACHES IN TESOL

by Dale Otto
Central Washington University

One interesting and important problem with the state of TESOL now appears to be our struggling with disparate but important elements in teaching. These elements generate debate and often appear as bi-polar pairs in opposition to each other. They are said to reflect separate schools of thought, of technique and of materials. As identified, these are:

known_____unknown (materials)
boredom_____newness (motivation)
form_____function
drill_____communication
accuracy_____fluency.

Those on the left side are associated primarily with the *audio-lingual/form* school of thought and teaching, while those on the right are associated primarily with the *functionalist/communication* school.

On second and third glance, however, we may be using these useful terms in less than useful ways by creating opposition where none may exist (as with the pair *accuracy-fluency*), or by contrasting competing approaches to teaching in a way which implies mutual exclusion (for example, the teacher either teaches only *form* and never *function*). It may be profitable to look again at these elements to become more sensitive to their relationships to each other and to the teacher; this is what the balance of this paper will attempt.

An Analysis

I. What: *Known–Unknown*

The element of moving the student from the *known* to the *unknown* in language learning is a very useful place to begin, for it forces us to immediately shift to a *student* focus rather than retaining a teacher focus. We ask ourselves, What do my students (or What does each student) already know? What makes sense to move on to next?

Further, adopting a student focus also encourages us to be a little more analytical in determining what the student already knows so as to sensibly move into lesser-knowns and unknowns. Often, the content of what we teach is perhaps more complex than we realize. We tend to concentrate on the lexical side of language, on new words (both of content and function) and their uses and contexts. Because of this, we may not always see clearly that a lesson or activity which seems simple from our (teachers') point of view may in fact put too much that is new in front of the student, new not only of meaning but also of grammatical structure, role and function, and often of pronunciation and paralinguistic features as well.

In addition, attending to the *known–unknown* element also encourages us to consider the *interest* to the student of the content of our lessons and activities, how attentive they are and what applications and uses they see to their own lives, situations and work.

We thus have in the *known–unknown* elements a true bi-polar pair, one which indicates the heart of *content*, of the *what* of the lessons and activities which are taught. It also provides a worthwhile point for the teacher to study and retain currency with the matter of *motivation*: are my students *curious?* Do they seem *engaged* in the content of my lessons? Are my students bored, stimulated or frustrated by the content of my lessons? Figure 1 is intended to illustrate these aspects of the *known–unknown* element.

FIGURE 1
Known - Unknown: The *What* of Language Learning

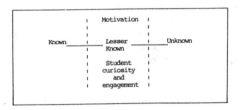

II. How: *Form–Function*, and *Drill–Communication*, with a Note on Redundancy

Here we are presented with two non-bipolar pairs. Rather, we have four elements, all of which relate to decisions in teaching. We are seduced into placing these elements in bipolar opposition in part because they *are* related. Let's take them out of opposition in order to look at how they are related, again with a focus on the student.

Function implies meaning. *Form* suggests the structure of how we both receive and intend/share meaning. To emphasize one or the other is most likely foolish. A portion of meaning is communicated by *form* (syntax) and the heart of meaning (semantics) is provided by the *functions* and contexts in which a linguistic item is used. They are more like plant and blossom—interdependent rather than in opposition.

The student of language is driven by acquiring the ability to understand and communicate more and more in the target language. *Form*, without understanding and communication, ignores the drive for meaning; *function*, without conscientious attention to form, deprives the student of the tools for meaning.

A more fruitful view of these two

elements, then, is to see them as partners. The student needs both function and structure to understand and produce meaning. We can toy with the order and relationship of these two elements for hour after hour, including the interesting debate over what it is that the learner has as competence within himself. However, the more useful questions for the teacher probably are those such as the following: Do my students *show* me and others that they can understand and use the forms I am teaching (i.e. pronunciation, intonation and grammar)? And do they command the meaning (i.e. functions and paralinguistic features) of what I am teaching?

Figure 2 may come closer to what the student needs from the teacher and the content of lessons and activities.

FIGURE 2
Function, Meaning and Form in Learning

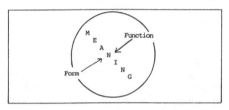

Our second non-pair, *drill* and *communication*, are very similar in relationship to form and function. In language learning, the student will practice (drill) items which he needs to practice; it is very fortunate when these items coincide with what the teacher sets out for practice. The student will also want to understand what is being said, and to use each new language tool as he moves from exposure to proficiency—he wants to communicate. Again, the relationship seems cyclical rather than linear, and interdependent rather than in opposition. Figure 3 represents this relationship, with the use of the term *practice* in place of *drill*, a term which has acquired unfortunate connotations of militaristic absent-mindedness.

FIGURE 3
Proficiency, Communication and Practice in Learning

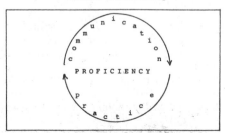

When we view form and function, practice and communication in a cyclical, interdependent manner, we perhaps have a useful clue as to a profitable meaning of the term *redundancy* in language learning. One aspect of redundancy surely has to do with dealing with the student's proficiency in language. We do this by knowingly providing learning situations which cycle the language to be learned through foci on form *and* function, through foci on practice *and* communication. To include either form or practice only, without including meaning and communication, ignores the essence of redundancy in language learning, redundancy based on their inter-relationships.

We may also view redundancy not as repetition, but as enrichment—the taking of what is already known and going farther with it. Redundancy in language learning, then, consists of the student's gaining greater and greater understanding of, and competence in the forms of the new language and the meanings they can embody. Redundancy implies both repetition *and* extension.

III. Pulling *Content* and *How* Together: *Accuracy–Fluency*

Our last non-pair of elements, again a related pair, represents the desired outcome for the student of the *content* and *how* of language teaching. Accuracy and fluency, then, are the goals of language learning.

It may be argued that accuracy precedes fluency, that I must understand that which I am to be able to use with ease and automaticity; it cannot reasonably be argued that fluency precedes accuracy, that I can possess ease and automaticity of performance for that which I don't understand. Surely we aim for our students to be both accurate in the language and to be able to communicate fluently. The relationship here for the student is more profitably seen perhaps as one of both order and interdependence, not one of 'either-or.' Very simply, we may illustrate these two elements as follows.

FIGURE 4
The Goals of Language Learning

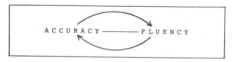

IV. What Else is Missing? *Learning Load*

So far, so good; but something is missing. We have the matter of *student learning load* to consider. Regardless of what we teach or how we teach it, what school of thought we subscribe to or set of materials we use, we still need to recognize the amount of learning we are requiring in any one lesson or the number of objectives we are expecting every student to master.

Those of us in language teaching find it all too easy to forget the matter of

student learning load, or to see it too dimly. We ordinarily don't teach subject matter *content* when we teach language; rather we teach the tool for the student to use in dealing with subjects—language. We therefore often lack information teachers of subject areas get when they organize and sequence the subject's concepts and skills for a given group of students. As teachers of language we know the language we are teaching very well—we use it automatically most of the time and with relative ease when we use it self-consciously. The teacher of math, gardening, welding or surgery, however, must keep learning his subject area if he is to stay on top of it, if he is to remain a competent teacher.

Furthermore, the subject matter teacher is always conscious of the concepts he is presenting to students. He thus has a clearer feedback system available to use when making decisions about *what*, *when* and *how* to teach. We language teachers have no such feedback system because we are teaching what we are already competent in.

Attention to how many objectives we expect our students to learn in each lesson and to their variety also assists us with clarifying aspects of both motivation and redundancy. If the teacher expects student competence in a few, thoughtfully chosen objectives for each lesson or period, she is likely to promote student interest because of a high rate of success—of mastery. Further, such thoughtful attention to the objectives of each language lesson will also furnish

guidance to the teacher regarding when to repeat and extend previously learned material—when to furnish redundancy.

Again, perhaps a small diagram will help illustrate the relationships among student learning load, motivation and redundancy.

FIGURE 5
More Factors for Student Success
and Their Relationships

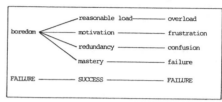

V. Application: *The Lesson or Activity Plan*

By way of overall summary, I would like to suggest a format for language teaching lessons which can emphasize the central column of Figure 5, above. Such a lesson plan finds primary use in the more formal portions of the curriculum; however, portions of it are probably appropriate for all aspects of teaching language, whether in the classroom or in the cafe. In addition, I would guess that this proposed lesson plan format can find applicability to any set of materials and even to any approach to teaching, from the most serious audio-lingual approach to the most zealous Counseling-Learning approach.

TN 12/82

Figure 6: A Lesson Plan Format

Objective(s):	(Here are stated the one, two or possible three objectives of a lesson, in terms which clearly indicate student performance and language.)
Materials:	(All materials needed for the lesson and directions for their preparation are given here.)
PRESENT:	The teacher *models* the performance expected of the students. If the objective requires dialogue, the teacher *shows* the students what is in the dialogue and who are the speakers. The teacher also shows the students any actions which accompany the language to be learned, in ways which accurately present all student actions as well as teacher actions. A teaching partner or puppets which always show student action and language are useful here.
PARTICIPATE:	Volunteer students take the place of the teaching partner or puppet(s) and practice the action(s) and language of the lesson or activity. Correction is done by the teacher re-presenting (re-modeling) the portion of language which contains the error, with the student being given additional opportunity to perform and practice.
EVALUATE:	The teacher calls on students at random to continue the same action and language of PARTICIPATE. Correction continues as in PARTICIPATE. The suggested student performance criterion is that at least 90% will successfully perform the objective(s).
EXTEND:	An optional phase right after the EVALUATE portion ends, during which the materials remain available for student use and free discussion.

BOOK REVIEWS

DEVELOPING SECOND LANGUAGE SKILLS: THEORY TO PRACTICE

Kenneth Chastain
2nd edition (Rand McNally:
Chicago, 1976)

TEACHING ENGLISH AS A SECOND LANGUAGE: TECHNIQUES AND PROCEDURES

Christina Bratt Paulston and
Mary Newton Bruder
(Winthrop Publishers:
Cambridge, Mass., 1976)

Reviewed by Audrey Reynolds
Northeastern Illinois University

Although both of these books are concerned with teaching second language skills, their emphases are quite different. Kenneth Chastain's book can perhaps best be characterized as a survey of theoretical issues which should be confronted by prospective teachers of any second language (not just ESL) in U.S. high schools, and of ways of applying those theories in the classroom. Christina Paulston and Mary Bruder concentrate on classroom techniques and procedures for ESL. Each book has its advantages and its disadvantages.

Because Chastain believes that students must know something about the 'science' of teaching before they can be expected to apply the science, his book is divided into two sections which are approximately equal in length: theory and practice.

In the first section, Chastain gives a reasonably objective description of the various educational issues—both linguistic and nonlinguistic—which have contributed to the current status of second language teaching in the U.S. secondary schools. Audio-lingual method, cognitive code theory, emphasis on the 'affective' in learning, and the impact of individualized instruction are some of the topics which he considers. This partial lists illustrates one of the strengths of the book—that its scope is broad—and suggests one of its weaknesses—that no topic is handled in depth. As a result, students who are receiving their first exposure to learning theories may be slightly overwhelmed. Used judiciously as a text, however, the book does provide useful summaries of the various issues.

The practice section also covers a wide range of topics, with chapters devoted to each of the four language skills: listening, speaking, reading, and writing; and to such topics as 'cultural content,' lesson plans, and 'meeting student needs' (including discipline problems). Undergraduates will find the practice section useful as a general introduction to the problems which they can expect to encounter in the classroom and to some of the techniques which they can use. Graduate students with teaching experience, however, may be frustrated by the amount of time spent on the general mechanics of teaching and by the lack of an extensive list of things to do in the classroom.

Thus, Chastain's book would be quite informative for undergraduates who want to teach a second language and need a survey introduction to the variables which must be taken into account by a successful second-language teacher. As such, it would be a useful component in a TESL methods course for undergraduates.

Paulston and Bruder's book is much more limited in scope. The authors set out to do one thing: to write a 'cookbook' of various classroom techniques and procedures which they and others have found to be successful in developing the language skills of ESL students. Their philosophical orientation is pragmatic and eclectic, so they feel free to use any technique which works.

The book is divided into six chapters: Grammar, Speaking, Pronunciation, Listening Comprehension, Reading, and Writing. Thus, all of the language skills are treated in some detail, and this is one of the strengths of the book.

The specific techniques described are, with a few exceptions, the standard ones in the ESL repertoire. For examples, the chapter on grammar contains an extensive classification and typology of structural pattern drills along with a format for a lesson plan which uses a dialogue and drills to teach a specific grammatical construction; the pronunciation chapter includes information on how to apply knowledge from articulatory phonetics; the chapter on writing has a discussion of controlled and free composition. Among the exceptions is the chapter on reading. The authors have read and assimilated Kenneth Goodman and Frank Smith's work on reading'; consequently, the ideas presented are quite provocative. Sound-symbol correspondences are relegated to a paragraph. Instead, Paulston and Bruder concentrate on 'decoding meaning.' Inasmuch as the vocabulary used in a passage can be an important clue to the meaning, the problem of how to enrich the students' receptive vocabulary is given more attention than it frequently receives.

Because the authors have gleaned information from both standard and not-so-standard sources. the book serves as a useful compendium of current techniques and procedures. Students who need an intensive guide to 'things to do' in an ESL classroom filled with high school students or adults will find it quite useful.

Those who consider using the text in a TESL methods course should be advised that it has certain limitations. For one thing, many of the techniques discussed are specifically designed for foreign students studying in U.S. universities. Although the authors suggest that the techniques can be adapted for use with other kinds of students, it is not always easy to see how the techniques can be modified to meet some of the special needs of children or adults who are semi-literate in the first language. A second difficulty arises from the fact that the authors occasionally assume that the reader is as familiar with a subject as they are. For instance, students with no experience teaching a second languae will find the section on the dialogue lesson plan opaque because there is no illustrative dialogue. Finally, only cursory attention is given to theories of second-language acquisition; so those professors who like to include some theory in a methods course will have to find supplemental material (perhaps of the kind presented in the theory section in Chastain's book).

In-service teachers will find the book especially valuable because it will give them the recipes for which they are looking.

In conclusion, Chastain provides scope; Paulston and Bruder provide detail. Chastain surveys the problems; Paulston and Bruder concentrate on classroom solutions. Either or both of the books could be used in a TESL methods class depending on the professor's inclination and the students' backgrounds.

TN 9/76

COMMUNICATION IN THE CLASSROOM

Edited by Keith Johnson and Keith Morrow.
1981. Longman Group Limited, Harlow, Essex,
England. (152 pages.)

Reviewed by Samuela Eckstut
*Teachers College, Columbia University
and the Hellenic-American Union,
Athens, Greece*

Communication in the Classroom is the newest
in the Longman series of Handbooks for Language Teachers. The book provides a good
survey of major themes, procedures and techniques now current in Britain. In addition to a
number of contributions by the editors, the
book contains papers by fifteen materials developers and teachers well known in Great Britain
for the practical contributions they have made
to EFL/ESL. The book's collection of papers
deals with communicative language teaching
and as the editors state, it "provides a coherent
overview of what a communicative approach
to language teaching might involve."

The book is divided into two main parts. Part
A, Applications, primarily deals with syllabus
and course design and Part B, Methods, with
different aspects of methodology in communicative language teaching. Each part begins with
an introductory paper. Keith Johnson's introductory paper to Part A on defining 'functions,'
'notions' and 'communicative,' terms used more
and more frequently in recent EFL/ESL publications, is especially useful in light of how these
terms are so often confused. Keith Morrow's
introductory paper to Part B discusses what he
considers to be five major principles of communicative methodology.

In Part A writers such as Louis Alexander,
Robert O'Neill and Christopher Brumfit discuss
their considerations when producing communicative materials. The papers are concerned
with how the development of the functional/
notional syllabus has affected these considerations. Such a syllabus is based on the communicative needs of the learners; in view of this
the writers discuss the value of the functional/
notional syllabus for EFL students whose language needs are not clear, e.g. the 'general'
adult beginner. Nicholas Hawks in his paper,
"Primary Children," further examines the development of materials based on the functional/
notional syllabus for children when it is not
possible to determine their future language
needs.

The writers all recognize the validity of the
functional/notional approach to syllabus design.
However, it is clear from the divergent views
expressed in this part that there is no one
approach to course design even though the
writers all take the development of the func-
tional/notional syllabus into account when they
produce materials.

In Part B writers such as Marion Geddes,
Donn Byrne and Alan Maley deal with the four
skills in communicative language teaching and
also various procedures and techniques. The
papers on the four skills provide insights and
useful hints on ensuring that students are involved in true communicative acts when practicing any of the four skills. These papers all
emphasize that in real language acts the skills
are integrated with each other rather than separate and unrelated. Therefore, good classroom
communicative activities should involve students
in practicing more than one skill.

The remaining papers in Part B are devoted
to specific communicative activities such as role
play and role simulation, drama, games and
problem-solving. The paper by Andrew Wright
discusses how to involve students in communicative activities through the use of visual aids.
These papers not only discuss the advantages of
such procedures but also contain actual material
that has been used in the classroom.

The book is especially valuable for those in
the United States not yet fully acquainted with
new developments in Britain. Readers in America who have had little access to British materials
will find all of the papers in this collection of
great value. However, readers up to date with
British trends and procedures will probably
find the papers in Part A more resourceful than
those in Part B because a good many of the ideas
expressed in this part have appeared elsewhere.
The papers in Part A, on the other hand, provide
important insights into questions and problems
that have arisen out of the development of the
functional/notional approach to syllabus design.

Communication in the Classroom is a valuable
addition to the Handbook series. It joins the
fifteen previous handbooks in providing worthwhile information on different aspects of methodology. Because of the practical aspects of the
material, the books are especially important for
practicing teachers, teachers in training and
their trainers. The light writing style makes the
books easy and enjoyable to read. *Communication in the Classroom* like the other books in
the series provides pleasant reading and at the
same time gives readers especially in the United
States the opportunity to share in recent British
developments.

TN 12/82

A PRACTICAL GUIDE TO THE TEACHING OF ENGLISH AS A SECOND OR FOREIGN LANGUAGE

By Wilga Rivers and Mary Temperley
(Oxford University Press, 1978)

Reviewed by Audrey Reynolds
Northeastern Illinois University

When approaching a book designed
for future teachers with a title like *A
Practical Guide to the Teaching of English as a Second or Foreign Language,*
one anticipates that the book will minimize "theoretical" considerations about
language teaching and stress "practical"
considerations which affect the every-

day life of the classroom teacher. And
this book provides exactly what its title
suggests: a little theory and a lot of
practical considerations.

The theoretical position advocated by
Wilga Rivers and Mary Temperley can
perhaps best be summarized in the following way: (1) The goal of language

teaching is to move students to a point
where they can communicate in the
target language. (2) To accomplish this
goal, teachers must provide students
from the very beginning with opportunities for both "skill-getting"
(achieving linguistic competence) and
"skill-using" (achieving communicative
competence) in the target language.
(3) Teachers need to "bridge the gap"
between skill-getting and skill-using by
guaranteeing that skill-getting activities
are *pseudocommunication*; i.e., linguistically meaningful even though not "true"
communication where the students express their personal thoughts and feelings about subjects which are important
to them. (4) There is no one "right
way" of teaching a second language.

Thus, beyond an insistence that ESL
teachers should never forget the communicative aspect of language, the authors show no overt commitment to any
theoretical model for either native-
speaker linguistic competence or second
language teaching and, furthermore,
make an effort to expose the reader to
the broad spectrum of TESOL techniques. For example, in the section of
chapter one called "Supplying the student with a basic corpus," the reader
is introduced to the "object-centered
approach," "the Silent Way," the Gouin
verb-centered approach, and the use of
standard dialogues, all of which are presented as possible answers to the problem of introducing beginning students
to English.

The book itself is divided into two
sections. The first section, which emphasizes spoken language skills, contains
not only chapters on listening comprehension, grammar, and pronunciation,
but also two rather lengthy chapters on
'communication' activities for beginning,
intermediate, and advanced level students. The second section, which emphasizes written language skills, provides two chapters on reading and two
on writing.

Throughout the book, the authors attempt not only to present a variety of
possible teaching techniques but also to
lead the prospective teacher to a more
profound awareness of the task encountered when seeking to learn a second language. For example, in the section on spoken English, they provide
information about real native-speaker
conversations in the hope that second-
language teachers will not expect more
fluency and coherence from ESL/EFL
students than from native speakers. Similarly, in the section on teaching reading,
a reading passage is presented where
"blanks" represent the vocabulary items
which might be unfamiliar to an ESL
student, so that the prospective teachers
will realize how frustrated a student
feels when he or she encounters a reading passage which is much too difficult.

Thus, the book presents a reasonably comprehensive survey of the field of TESOL, with a focus on the everyday concerns of classroom teachers and, as such, should prove quite useful in methods classes for prospective teachers.

There is, however, one potential disadvantage in the book which those who consider using it should keep in mind. For, in the authors' attempt to present a variety of approaches, so much material is presented that students who lack either second language teaching experience or some background in linguistics may feel inundated by a myriad of details which sometimes appear to be unrelated. Such a flaw may be inherent in any book which introduces students to a field which is in ferment; nevertheless, any teacher who uses the book in a methods class will have to do so judiciously depending on the sophistication of the students.

In spite of this reservation, the book is, I suspect, the best survey of current TESOL methods which is now available and, as such, is a valuable addition to the library of those who teach English as a second or foreign language.

TN 11/78

PROBLEMS AND PRINCIPLES IN ENGLISH TEACHING

By Christopher J. Brumfit (Peragmon Press: Oxford, 1980)

Reviewed by Paul D. Roberts
Free University of Berlin

Mr. Brumfit has written a book of primary interest to all teachers of English as a foreign language. Within it, he has collected a number of articles written over the past decade based on his vast experience and expertise in the field of English language teaching methodology.

Part one entitled Specific Situations is subdivided into four sections wherein classroom procedures, teaching syllabuses, teacher training syllabuses, and the language teaching profession are discussed. Some of the topics include correcting written work; intensive reading development; language and literature; the role of methodology in ESOL teacher training; as well as education, ideology, and materials design. Included in these considerations one finds a tremendous amount of useful material of practical value to the classroom teacher. These specific suggestions based on extensive experience are among the most appealing aspects of the book.

Part two entitled General Principles is also subdivided into four parts which include very interesting and highly pertinent discussions on such matters as English, ideology, and international communication; notional syllabuses; English for special purposes; communicative language teaching; language acquisition; the role of research; as well as professionalism and language teachers. For the most part, the ideas presented in this section are quite stimulating, thought provoking, and cogent. They very well demonstrate the author's deep commitment to the concept that language teaching is an integral part of the whole process of education.

Finally, there is a delightful little coda attached called "Ode to the acronym" spoofing the numerous abbreviations we encounter in our profession.

All in all, this is a fine book, most readable, dealing with matters of great interest to all of us concerned with not only the state of the art but also the direction it is taking. □

TN 10/81

TEACHING ENGLISH TO SPEAKERS OF OTHER LANGUAGES—SUBSTANCE AND TECHNIQUE

By Betty Wallace Robinett, U. of Minnesota Press: Minneapolis and McGraw-Hill: New York, 1979).

Reviewed by Greg Stricherz
Tokyo, Japan

"I couldn't put it down" is a blurb found on the back cover of a thriller. This book isn't a thriller, but it is a very interesting and readable book. I literally couldn't put it down.

Teaching English to Speakers of Other Languages—Substance and Technique gives the teacher a wealth of information about the language itself and about how to teach it. The book is divided into two major sections.

The first section is a general description of the grammar system, sound system, and vocabulary system of English.

noon tea"—something frequently neglected by, or more likely unknown to, the teacher.

In the vocabulary section, I was surprised to see the adverbial suffix "-wise" (as in timewise) mentioned. It may be decried in some quarters, but, as the book says, it's quite a productive affix in present-day English. I had never thought of teaching it, but it's definitely something an advanced learner should be aware of. I'm sure that the first section of the book will provide even the most experienced teacher with a few things that can be used in the classroom.

The second section should appeal to almost all readers. It covers a large number of things that a teacher should think about beyond what is presented in the classroom. How does a student learn? What can a teacher do to facilitate learning? What makes a classroom physically conducive to learning, and what can the teacher do to improve a poor classroom? Some of the answers are obvious . . . in fact, so obvious that we might never think of them.

I realize it's pretty hard for regular readers of the *JALT Newsletter* not to be aware of the major teaching methods, past and present. But for anybody who has ever wondered what, for example, the Silent Way is, this book gives a very good overview of the various methods. And it does it in language that is completely understandable.

Another helpful part of the book is the inclusion of cartoons to illustrate a particular point. My favorite (going back to the "-wise" suffix) was from the *New Yorker*: "Did I understand you to say 'hopefullywise'?" And for the native speaker who can't appreciate the difficulty students have in understanding idioms, the "Hi and Lois" strip on page 126 should be enlightening.

As I said in the beginning, this is a very readable book. It presents a great deal of information and does it in straightforward language. Whenever definitions are given, they are clear. There is little that the layman would have trouble with. Terminology is also precise. For instance, we are cautioned against equating "productive" (e.g., speech as a "productive" skill) with "active," and "receptive" with "passive." The author states that "there is just as much activity in the exercise of receptive skills as in that of their productive counterparts." A difference such as this may seem minor, but it's a good example of the kind of sensitivity a teacher has to have if he wants to help his students acquire proficiency the most effective way possible.

Some readers might wish for a more detailed treatment than this book gives. But considering the range of topics, that would be almost an impossibility for one author, or at least take a lifetime of work. This book isn't intended as a

There are also lots of useful hints on teaching these three aspects of English and making usable, realistic practices for them. This section would be invaluable for a teacher who hasn't had a lot of experience. As the book says, "Being an English speaker does not of itself qualify one to be a teacher of English to speakers of other languages." But even for the experienced teacher, there are things to think about. The pronunciation section mentions the difference between stress on words in isolation versus words in a phrase, e.g., "afternoon" versus "after-

scholarly reference. It's a practical guide, meant to be read and reread. It's the kind of book you'd take home with you as a guide for the preparation of the drills or the test you want to use in your next class. Each chapter does have an extensive bibliography though. In fact, there are almost 29 pages of bibliographical material. A person who is interested in more reading on a particular subject can easily make selections from the bibliography. Many of the sources listed are readily available in Japan.

When I finished reading this book, I had two very strong feelings. First, I wished that this text could be used in all training programs for Japanese teachers who are going to be working with students at the secondary-school level. That would make it much easier for those of us who don't see the students until they've had six years of English "education" in the Japanese school system. (The book, by the way, doesn't throw translation—the core of high school English courses—out the window. But it does emphasize that its usefulness is limited and its usage should be too.) Second, this book reminded me of why I became a teacher of English to foreign students in the first place. And it made me happy that I am one.

(Reprinted from the *JALT Newsletter,* III:6, June 1, 1979)

TN 10/79

IDIOMATICALLY SPEAKING

Edited by Jean McConochie, Ellen Block, Gay Brookes, and Barbara Gonzales (NYS ESOL BEA, 1981, Teachers College, Columbia University, New York, NY 10027.)

Reviewed by Gary Gabriel
Hunter College

I hadn't done much ESOL teaching of late. A six-week stint here, a few days of subbing for an ailing colleague there—not the stuff from which professional excellence derives, no matter how extensive one's previous experience. Growth and development only occur, if at all, as a result of continuity of performance.

So it was with trepidation that I stared down at a blank sheet of paper on which I hoped to sketch a first-night lesson plan. It was a Saturday evening, and I was trying to cope with the *What-Do-I-Do-On-Monday?* blues. Or, more accurately, *What-Do-I-Do-On-Tuesday?*—for on the following Tuesday, I was to return to the ESOL classroom in earnest, beginning an eight-week spring course for which I could now come up with no openers. Why this anxiety? Wouldn't the creative juices flow again, once I was back in the classroom? Or had the old well run dry?

I needed contact with the mainstream—ideas, reassurance, perspectives from the field. And so I reached for the book nearest at hand: the New York State English to Speakers of Other Languages and Bilingual Educators Association collection of selected articles from the organization's newsletter *Idiom.* Entitled *Idiomatically Speaking* and edited by Jean McConochie, Ellen Block, Gay Brookes, and Barbara Gonzales, the book is, in a narrow sense, a compilation of articles from ten years of *Idiom*; in the broad sense, it is a celebration of NYS ESOL BEA and a decade of sharing academic convictions, insights, and techniques among its membership via the newsletter.

I was no stranger to the anthology. I was well aware of its pained, painful history; I even had an article in the book myself. But now, in my quest for Instant Inspiration, what did I really expect to gain from a non-stop weekend reading of a series of 1970's articles by mostly New York-based teachers? Well—desperate ills, desperate remedies; and desperate, I was. Besides, I had never read the book all the way through; like chicken soup when you've got pneumonia, it might not help but it couldn't hurt.

So I took an intensive, twenty-four-hour reading course. I was a student body of one; my faculty was the *Idiomatically Speaking* collective authorship. I read almost without interruption; it was a rewarding, if exhausting, experience.

The articles are arranged in eight sections plus appendix. The first section, Our Profession, consists of a single article: an address by Harold B. Allen entitled "What It Means To Be A TESOL Professional." After that article, I was ready to quit the profession! I mean, who could possibly measure up? The preparation, the awareness, the diligence Dr. Allen argues for—well, I thought, press on; we can't all be champions. Then I had second thoughts. We can all aspire; perhaps it is that urging toward the aspiration itself that is Dr. Allen's clarion call.

Section Two: Approaches to Teaching . . . Ah, now we were getting down onto my here-and-now territory. John Haskell's comments on the Silent Way, Iren Dutra's impressions of Community Language Learning and Suggestopedia—I was at once reminded of both how innovative and experimental the 1970's often were, and at the same time how discipular, even apostolic some of us sometimes were about this "way" or that "method." Larry Anger's suggested checklist ("Some Priorities for a Good ESL Class") was a reminder of how essential self-monitoring is, and of the importance of standards by which we can test, measure, even evaluate ourselves professionally. Who, however, is to decide what constitutes a "good" ESOL class? I wondered.

To this one reader, perhaps the most arresting article in this section was the retrospective, by Mary Coit and Arnold Kaltinick, of the classroom devices practiced and perfected by the late Milton McPherson ("Exploiting the Environment: The McPherson Approach"). I had visited Mac's classes myself at New York University, and frankly, I had forgotten how much I had forgotten (*sic*). Here was a teacher doing wondrous things in the classroom, too in-

volved in his work to get out and talk about it but always altogether welcoming to visitors, expected or unexpected—and only he, his students, and a few observers knew what he was doing and why. Yes, there's a certain amount of unsung heroism in the ESOL classroom.

I was rolling now. I enjoyed Section Three (Lessons That Work) not only for the many practical suggestions by Darlene Larson and confreres, but also because of the stimulus effect: I remembered ideas of my own that I could incorporate into my impending classes. Yes, this section set off a chain of recollection and recall—and the utter simplicity of some of the lessons in the section was further inspiration; the artistry seemed to lie in that very simplicity.

The book reviews in Section Four were the least useful to me vis-a-vis my immediate needs, but they very effectively chronicle what was happening in the profession during the 1970's, and how a handful, at least, of professionals felt about those happenings. But are ESOL texts really "reviewed"? Is this very article, for example, a "review" in the true sense? A reviewer, it would seem, should possess appropriate credentials and should be practicing the critical craft consistently, applying uniform standards to all the works that fall under consideration. What *Idiom* published, and still publishes, as "reviews" were actually comments by a teacher about the effectiveness, proven or projected, of a textbook often by another teacher. I'm not sure that this constitutes genuine criticism. Still, it's fair commentary; without it, many worthy texts might well languish in relative obscurity.

Sections Five (Research Reports), Six (Cross-Cultural Insights At Home), Seven (Cross-Cultural Insights Abroad), and Eight (Speaking Out) consist of informative, often provocative articles about a wide range of sociolinguistic and psycholinguistic concerns; the articles ask, collectively, who our students are, what their needs and wants appear to be, and where they seem to be coming from—in both senses of the phrase. My own article, on reexamination, seemed overly formal, compared to the refreshing informality of most of the other contributions. But then, I had just completed a dissertation at the time of the writing; I'm afraid I tended to write even a postcard as if it were going before committee.

Barbara Gonzales' touching little recollection, "The Trouble with Juan," struck this reader as the most meaningful, perhaps even the most disturbing selection. I knew that when I walked into my own classroom that following Tuesday evening, there might well be a Juan or a Juanita on the scene. Would I be perceptive enough to sense the presence? Resourceful enough to deal with the situation? I pondered all this, as I turned to the final section of the book: The Appendix, and its reminiscences of the late Ruth Crymes.

An effective juxtaposition, this. At the beginning of the book, Harold Allen states the qualifications of the real professional; the book ends with an intimate, affectionate personification of that professional—a profile of a human being who was, according to those who knew her, all that we should each aspire to in our continuing quest for professionalism. Small wonder that *Idiomatically Speaking* is dedicated to the memory of Dr. Crymes.

TN 8/82

TEACHING ENGLISH AS A SECOND OR FOREIGN LANGUAGE

Marianne Celce-Murcia, Lois McIntosh (Editors). Newburg House Publishers, Inc. Rowley, Massachusetts, 1979.

Thank goodness TESL has become such a growing industry of informative and useful texts. We as teachers and students of ESL can now pick and choose our area of methodology and techniques from a plethora of written works by various authors in our field.

After reading Celce-Murcia and Lois McIntosh's book I came away with a feeling of "fulfillment and appreciation," that I have not gotten from any other book thus far. In its 300 plus pages, it gives a comprehensive history of teaching ESL, with a balance of the theoretical and practical, research, and technical areas. While this book can be used as an excellent reference by the experienced teacher, it is easy enough to be understood by the beginning ESL teacher as well.

The book is comprised of various articles written by 27 different professional ESL contributors. It is divided into four sections: teaching methods, language skills, students, and teachers.

Part I, teaching methods, provides an outline of five major language teaching approaches used in the United States during the 20th century. This section includes articles which discuss and identify the foundations of ESL methodology, along with its background and growth.

Part II reveals in a very comprehensive manner the language skills of listening, speaking, reading, writing, and a final section which includes grammar and vocabulary development. The listening chapter shows the need of not only teaching the student to listen but the all important good of listening and understanding. There are two excellent articles in this section which deal with different methods, but both agree that the ultimate result is preparing the student to understand the speech of a native speaker.

Reviewed by Carol Weiner
Northeastern Illinois University

The reading section covers such areas as teaching reading to illiterate adults, including intermediate and advanced students and some language and cultural problems the ESL teacher might face when teaching advanced literature.

Writing follows with articles on teaching composition that include such categories as controlled writing, directed composition, guided composition and free writing. Most of the articles in this section include techniques, methods and activities.

Grammar and vocabulary are treated next dealing with methodological issues on the "how to" aspects. It covers teaching grammar to beginning language students and choosing the appropriate vocabulary to teach. Celce-Murcia and Rosenwerys' article is full of excellent examples of teaching syllabuses.

Part III evolves from the differing needs of the ESL student to various choices of teaching practices. I especially found Heaton's article on the adult ESL classroom useful, because it included activities and strategies for the survival of the non-academic student.

The final chapter on teachers deals with various skills, lesson plans, and a very useful section "how to evaluate a textbook". Most important it stresses the idea of keeping up with the current trends in our ESL field.

Last, but not least are the very interesting discussion questions, suggested activities and references, at the end of each article.

I believe that *Teaching English as a Second Language* stands out as a most understandable and useful text for both the new teacher and the experienced teacher. It is a well rounded, thorough volume which finally pulls together articles that reflect current practice and thought. I recommend it highly. *TN 6/80*

CLASSROOM PRACTICES IN ADULT ESL

(Donna Ilyin and Thomas Tragardh (Eds.). Washington, D.C.: TESOL, 1978.

According to the 1981 *TESOL Membership Directory*, roughly 23 percent of the total TESOL membership identified Adult Education ESL as either a primary or secondary interest group, making the Adult Education Special Interest Group (AESIG) the third largest SIG in the organization. Yet, if the size of AESIG is any indication as to the number of teachers in Adult Education ESL relative to the rest of the profession, there is certainly good reason to feel neglected in the literature. Adult education ESL teachers can be characterized as part-timers, without formal training in the theory or practice of ESL at any level, probably certified at another level of education (elementary or secondary). Few have

Reviewed by Richard Orem
Northern Illinois University-DeKalb

had any formal training in methods and materials of ESL, to say nothing about classroom management and the needs and characteristics of the adult second language learner. Many methods texts on the market today speak of the adult in terms of the university-bound or of those already enrolled in intensive English programs in academic settings. These language learners are usually already literate and highly educated in their first language. Their goals are academic and specialized. On the other hand, the "typical" adult education ESL learner has needs which are distinctly different, often of a "survival" nature. More and more frequently they are only semi-literate. In increasing regularity they are illiterate.

In most cases, programs are marginally funded and staffed. Training needs are frequently met through hit-or-miss inservice provided by individual consultants, state agencies, or university programs. Due to limited staff development funding (which is becoming even more limited in this era of Reagonomics), systematic inservice training needs to be supplemented by giving teachers greater access to classroom techniques through professional literature. For this reason, Ilyin and Tragardh's *Classroom Practices in Adult ESL* is a welcomed addition to that literature.

Donna Ilyin and Thomas Tragardh have assembled in one handy and inexpensive volume over 40 articles which have previously appeared mainly in TESOL and TESOL affiliate journals and newsletters, articles which provide teaching hints on topics ranging from classroom organization and management to techniques for specific skill areas. In between are included tips for evaluation, materials, general teaching practices, cultural consideration and techniques for special programs. Altogether, these articles provide a cornucopia of ideas to help both the novice and the experienced ESL classroom teacher meet the challenge of the adult education ESL setting.

The selection of articles has been obviously strengthened by drawing on the experience and creativity of an advisory board representing geographic and professional diversity. These advisory board members are all well known as practitioners and teacher trainers in ESL.

The major weakness of such a collection may be in the possibility that the less experienced teacher may envision a program of instruction based solely on a cookbook approach without the necessary theory of instruction on which to base the total program for the adult learner in nonacademic settings. The editors provide a useful discussion of the characteristics of adult ESL programs in their introduction. Yet, with few exceptions, the articles individually make no mention of the nature of the adult second language learner as distinct from other learners. How are adults in nonacademic settings different in learning style and need from the child learner?

The collection also suffers from a lack of uniformity caused in part by the nature of assembling so many articles written by 47 different individuals and originally published in a variety of formats. For all this inconsistency, there are several selections which merit special attention. Sadae Iwataki's "Bridging the Cultural Gap" provides useful tips for avoiding many embarassing moments with the recently arrived Indochinese and other Asian students. Richard Via describes his technique for enhancing conversation in "Talk and Listen." Finally, Karen Bachelor, Jack Wigfield, and Monica Weiss outline in detail their approach to teaching literacy skills in "ESL Adult Literacy—Some Want to Read."

TESOL should be encouraged to publish more volumes of classroom techniques such as *Classroom Practices*. At $4.50, this volume can be an inexpensive, handy reference guide for the novice adult educator in the ESL classroom as well as for those adult educators who have been teaching for years, but who need a change of pace to enliven their classrooms. They are sure to find something of interest in this collection. □

Section 10. Teaching Communication

This section begins with a shortened version of an excellent article on the topic of moving from the audio-lingual methodology of the 1950's and 1960's to the communication needs of the 1970's and 1980's. Darlene Larson's "From Repetition to Reality" (2/76) was excerpted from a speech which was first printed in the *TESOL-Gram*, the newsletter of Puerto Rico TESOL. Almost as a precursor of *It Works*, this article provides a variety of practical exercises for real classroom activities. From the same issue of the *TN* we find "An Idea That Works" by Sharon Theiss (2/76). It precedes the *It Works* column by one issue and discusses ideas a teacher can develop utilizing the various senses. The next two articles in this section, "Scripted Dialogues" by Eamon Roche (6/77) and John Boyd and Mary Ann Boyd's "Communication Strips" (5/78), are two of the many articles which have used Bob Gibson's "strip story" technique as their starting point. You might want to look first at an early *It Works* column which we have retitled "Bob Gibson's 'Strip Stories'." In this article Larson quotes from the original *TESOL Quarterly* article written by Gibson. (Note also Richard Yorkey's "Shuffled Comics," 10/81.) Jean McConochie's article on "Shopping for Community Contacts" (4/81) is a collection of techniques and ideas which she, Virginia Allen, Donald Knapp and Gary Gabriel devised in summer courses for a Japanese teachers' program. In "The Pocket Calculator" (6/77) Rebecca LeMaitre discusses not only problem solving, but listening techniques that can be enhanced by exercises using the pocket calculator in the ESL classroom.

We have lumped together, to use a word from one of the following selections, a number of the *It Works* columns which have appeared in the *TN* over the past few years. Most of the *It Works* columns from April 1976 until 1982 were edited by Darlene Larson. Since 1982 the column has been edited by Cathy Day. While *It Works* dates from April 1976, Larson had edited a similar column for the *Idiom* and contributed *Lessons That Work* to the 5/75 issue of the *TN*. We should also note that *It Works* articles appear in every section of Part II of this volume.

The first selection for *It Works* is "Use Your Imagination" by Darlene Larson. In it Larson offers two oral activities which students can do in small groups. Some of the *It Works* articles included in this section may need further explanation if their titles are to make any sense to the reader. The *It Works* column, originally untitled, which we have called "Milton McPherson" (11/78), refers to a column which discusses some of the original ideas and classroom techniques of one of the great teachers of New York University.

"Radio News" by Karen O'Neill (2/79) is one of several articles on the use of radio in the classroom. A more recent article is found in the 12/83 *It Works* column by Wilhelmina Juhlin "Using News Broadcasts." In "Soap Opera, Murder Mystery, or Home Town Lore," Larson draws upon ideas from Mary Sarawit and Salvatore Sinatra to give us some suggestions for eliciting classroom conversation. Donald Montalto's "Overcoming the Fear of a Foreign Language Phone Conversation" (12/81) suggests tactics for reducing students telephone anxieties. The Mary Ann Christison and Sharron Bassano *It Works* column "Where Do I Put It?" deals with the arrangement of pictures and the recognition of similarities and differences as a means of developing observational skills.

"Time Out for Classroom Ideas from TESOL 1977" (9/77) and its companion column titled "TESOL 77" (11/77) are selected ideas from a session on "Ideas That Work" which Darlene Larson chaired during the 1977 TESOL Convention in Miami. It includes ideas by Joyce Zuck, Penelope Alatis, Palmer Acheson, John Dumicich and Mary Hines. The Richard Yorkey *It Works* columns, "Shuffled Comics" (10/81) and "Paired Practice" (12/81), are two of the many ideas Yorkey presented in a paper on ideas for classroom teachers. "Shuffled Comics" refers to his use of comic strips as a means of getting students to come to terms with logical and chronological order as a means of helping them write better. "Paired Practice" helps students explain differences and similarities in pairs of pictures. "One Lump or Two" (4/76) by Darlene Larson brings reality to the classroom by presenting activities, such as planning and having a party. "A Lesson That Works" (5/75) is not really an *It Works* column and, like the Sharon Theiss article, precedes the column by a year. In it Larson discusses Christina B. Paulston's notions of role playing and presents some role playing ideas suggested by Mary Hines. Two more recent *It Works* columns are also included in this section: "Getting to Know You Through Questionnaires" by Ruth Shernoff (4/83) which asks students to interview each other as a first step in initiating communication, and Keith Maurice's (8/83) article on a "Fluency Workshop" which offers ideas to help students achieve comfortable and easy communication.

The book reviews included in this section are some of the more unusual and innovative (and even controversial) books published in recent years. Two are the review of *Dangerous English* written by Elizabeth Claire and reviewed very cleverly by Lise Winer (6/82), and *Whaddaya Say!* written by Nina Weinstein and reviewed by Arlene Malinowski (6/83). Both books deal with language which teachers are reluctant to deal with directly. In *Dangerous English*, it is the language that students often learn first and retain longest, but language they also often misunderstand and use inappropriately. In *Whaddaya Say!* the language is that reduced form of rapid speech which teachers often agonize over teaching, but which students need desperately.

No Hot Water Tonight by Jean Bodman and Michael Lanzano provides conversation based on the kinds of problems and situations a typical city dweller might encounter. (See also, the review (8/81) of the sequel to this volume, *No Cold Water, Either*.) David Eskey's review of the *Active English* volume by Patricia Porter and Alan Sharp, *Understand, Practice and Communicate*, is part of a larger language series that provides active communication practice for beginning students of English as a second language. *Listen In and Speak Out* by James, Whitley and Bode, *Getting Into It . . . An Unfinished Book* by Blot and Sher, and *Sounds Intriguing* by Maley and Duff are three examples of innovative approaches which help elicit communication in the classroom. *Connections* by John Boyd and Mary Ann Boyd is a volume which like their book *Alice Blows a Fuse* uses strip dialogues, à la Gibson, as a means of creating communicative conversations. *Shuck Loves Chirley* is a short review of Leonard Olguin's book about techniques for helping Spanish speakers practice English pronunciation. *Dialogues and Drills in Idiomatic English* by William B. White and reviewed by John Boylan is three volumes of natural dialogues packed with idioms. *Gambits* by Eric Keller is also a three volume set, presenting exercises which help the student learn and use conversational tools for introducing information, interrupting conversation and changing the subject. The review was edited somewhat.

There were a great number of other excellent articles in the area of communication which have appeared in the *TN*. Two worth mentioning on the chance that they are your long-searched-for-idea-come-to-print are: "Using Problem Solving Techniques in Advanced ESL Conversation Classes" by Myrna Knepler (9/78) which outlines a number of clever ideas with which to help students develop problem solving skills; "Communication Strategies for ESL" by Mary Ann Christison and Karl Krahnke (4/81) which presents techniques for developing communication in the classroom; "Talking it Up," an *It Works* column by Howard Sage (8/81) and "For Some Sparkling Conversation" by Darlene Larson (6/80), both of which offer tactics for developing communication strategies. A walk through the table of contents of the *TN* (see the bibliography at the end of this volume) might suggest others.

FROM REPETITION TO REALITY: SOME MEASURABLE STEPS

By Darlene Larson
New York University

I want to share with you some of the notions I've been kicking around about how we can chart a more systematic course for our students for moving them from a sketchy knowledge of English to "communicative competence," the word of the day.

I believe that in order to plan courses, write materials, teach and test and assess progress—in order to tell students about what they are going to learn and then discuss with them how they think they are doing—in order to move them one step at a time to free use of the language, we have to re-think, redo, re-write our entire repertoire of classroom procedures. I don't pretend to have come close to such a goal, to have a thorough understanding of what is to be discarded, nor to have identified with certainty all of the elements that should be added. There is much to be discarded—much to be replaced—and much to be devised afresh.

As ESL teachers, we have been listening for years to the anthropologists, the sociologists, the psychologists, the multiculturalists, the cross-culturalists, the self-awareness groups, the group interaction groups, the grammarians, the speech correctionists, the drama coaches and the lady next door. I think TESOL, on the whole, shares its podium with a wider range of specialists than any other group. Not only do we share the podium, but we listen!

We are aware of the fact and we agree that language learning is far more than pronouncing a string of phonemes. We believe that it is risk-taking behavior.

As teachers, we do not address a classroom filled with mechanisms capable of sound production. We are quite conscious of the fact that all of the points and manners of articulation are housed in a human being who brings to class his or her ego, age, upbringing, pride, desires, accomplishments, failures, fears, sex-appeal, quirks, tics, nerves, worry beads and dictionaries—as well as Pavlov's dog's hunger and thirst.

Need for Efficient Instruction

But the pressure is on us. Second language learning is no longer a pastime of the wealthy that can be carried out over decades, nurtured with private specialists and trips to far-away lands where the culture can be assimilated as well as the sounds—all done in relaxation and luxury. No, not at all. Second language learning is more likely a necessity for survival. Efficiency of instruction has never been

more needed than it is now.

The need is felt not only in second language programs, but our entire system of public education is awakening to the fact that it must become more accountable, more precise, more responsive to individual needs, more articulate about what it can do. Program planners long for the day when improved tools of assessment will diagnose a child's needs and improved systems of scheduling will provide immediately, modules of instruction precisely attending to those needs. Students will master these bits of knowledge at their own speed and move on to the next challenge for which they have been properly readied.

There are numerous fears about, flaws in, and arguments against this proposed wave of educational change. Whether in the end the change be miniscule or major, I for one, would like to see such change conceived, proposed, and decided BY CLASSROOM TEACHERS.

Structure Versus Task

Many are accustomed to thinking of language learning as a progression of steps outlined in terms of structures. Until now, somehow, a certain structure has belonged in the advanced course while others are always found on page 1 of book 1.

Yet, when the right conditions are present, every structure is easy! I have become more and more convinced that it is not the structure that determines difficulty as often as it is the task. The language task, the communication task, the classroom task. It is to what teachers have students do with these structures that we must give our attention.

Let us adhere to the old goals of helping students meet success in language learning situations, of avoiding failure situations, and of considering students errors as teacher errors. However, let us demand that an equally careful progression be applied to the kind of language task—rather than to the kind of drill and let us not become ensnared in the linguist's categorization of structural complexities.

The Difficulties

My efforts to outline a progression of difficulty of language tasks seem forever thwarted for any number of reasons. A few of them follow:
A. The difficulty of language tasks doesn't seem to advance in a linear progression.

After utterance 1 in hour 1, there can never again be a single focus.

About five years ago, I scrapped the whole idea of "review." It is never a goal of a teaching segment, and I have tried to remove it from my pedagogical vocabulary. Instead, once I have presented an item, I attempt to incorporate that item continually, or at least regularly, into all future lessons.

By merely attending to meaning, structure, and pronunciation, there is at least a triple focus for any lesson. Usually a teacher has a number of other goals in mind in addition to these three and they are all operating at the same time if the language task has any transferability to reality. In fact, it is precisely when a number of aspects are all alive and operating at the same time that language lessons become real.

A second notion under "never a single focus" is my doubt that we could ever list all of the aspects of a communication task, let alone program them into a progression of difficulty.

B. One cannot separate the language performance expected of students from the amount of assistance given by teachers.

Have you ever participated in a faculty meeting in which the level 5 teacher expresses how well her students are finally doing in writing paragraphs—whereupon the level 2 teacher sniffs that her students have been writing paragraphs for 6 weeks. That's right, the students are performing the same task. But on investigation, the level 2 students are doing it with a complete model from which to write and are merely changing the singular model to a plural form. The level 5 students are producing their paragraphs with only a choice of topics as assistance. That's what I mean when I say that we cannot assess the difficulty of a language task until we know what assistance the students have been given. And this leads to item C.

C. Smaller progressions of difficulty exist within larger ones.

Requiring the performance of the same task, but giving less assistance in smaller amounts can provide a whole series of steps, each one of which contributes to the student's ability to perform a singular task.

D. Some elements of language behavior seem better learned if they are ever-present from hour one, day one and are learned in conditions with transferability to reality.

Classroom Arrangement

Create in the classroom a physical

setting that permits eye contact. Rigid rows make students look at the backs of other students' heads. Even native speakers rarely feel the desire to communicate with the back of the heads in front of them. Why should we expect genuine communication to take place in this situation with speakers of English as a second language?

Pronunciation—Transfer to Reality

I'm talking about normal speed, intonation and pronunciation as opposed to word-by-word production. Word-by-word production, by the way, is an achievement. And, it's our trap. We feel gratified when the student finally gets there. . . as does he. . . and we rejoice in his accomplishment with him. When students who didn't know the structure on entering the class, know what to say at the end of class, it's worth celebrating. But you're celebrating a hit to third. He's not home yet. And if you don't get to home plate, you never score a run. Oh, sure, you pile up statistics: he attended class. He satisfactorily participated in the exercises. But you don't even get one tally towards winning the game. Even when you're not around, he'll be listening for all of those words that he knows so well and can line up like little tin soldiers. And he'll never hear them. Oral language doesn't occur in that form. Your students will feel discouraged and gradually come to believe either that everyone speaks sloppy English but his teacher—or that he just can't learn.

One more step is needed in the classroom. On hearing a student perform with every word correct and in the right place, I often hear myself rejoicing with the student with something like: "Good for you. You've got every word correct. Now, here's the way you say it," and I am convinced more and more here is the place where I teach pronunciation. Never, never in a separate time-slot called, "Pronunciation," but rather, at the end of a communication task with, "Now, here's the way you say it."

Classroom Cues

Instead of attempting to label the kinds of drills one does, I prefer to think in terms of the cue and the expected behavior. And I make a further distinction between an expected behavior being a response to language as opposed to those occasions in which the expected behavior will be an initiation of language.

When I am expecting the students to respond to language, to my way of thinking, the one and only acceptable kind of cue is one that a native speaker would respond to with the same structure that I'm expecting the student

to use. There is, however, one exception to this rule.

The Exception

The one exception is repetition. Repetition does not transfer to reality. Repetition is mechanical and non-communicative. It can be deadly dull or devilishly difficult. If repetition is also the place where, with backward build-up, the student is supported until he can repeat at normal speed, intonation and pronunciation, then it is devilishly difficult and that's when it's worth doing.

That's the starter—and it is the only mechanical cue that I currently allow myself to use. Once I know that the students can produce the utterance, I force myself to elicit it from them subsequently with the same kinds of cues that would elicit it from me.

Which Fit

It's easy to decide which exercises fit this category.

The question to ask is: Would a native speaker ever, on hearing X, respond with Y? If the answer to this question is, "Yes," then this X and Y sequence is worth taking class time to practice.

This criterion eliminates forever any more of the "long answers" expected as responses to yes/no questions.

There is no time for this kind of artificial code manipulation in the classroom. Let's not force any more speakers and writers to make the case against mechanical exercises. It has long been made. We see their point and agree with it. I am all for declaring an end to such a waste of classroom time forever. It prepares the students for no real life situation that I can imagine.

Upon applying my "reality test," I rarely have any trouble deciding whether or not a certain cue is justifiable. And if it doesn't meet this standard, it goes.

Change of Tense

It is true that native speakers do have conversations that do little more than change tenses. What are the cues in these conversations that cause the change of tense to happen? Employ the same ones in the classroom in order to signal students that they need to switch forms.

I have a feeling that all of the "Do you. . . "questions are asked together somewhere in the second unit. All of the "How long've you been doing" questions are asked togther somewhere in the 14th unit, but they are never put together systematically. It is often in the mix of questions that native speakers find the cues that signal a change of tense. Our students need

this kind of practice incorporated systematically into their classroom exercises.

Initiating Language

First, we must remember that this is, after all, an unreal exercise. We are deciding that they should initiate language. One initiates language when one feels the need—not when one is told to say something. Furthermore, on those rare occasions when one is requested to say something, there is often at least a momentary block of all initiating processes, and one wonders if he'll ever be able to utter a sound again, let alone say something. Thus, telling students to ask something, describe something, say something is an unreal command in itself, and, furthermore, a stifling one.

So the teacher attempts to program into the students some reason for them to ask questions. Unreal cues have to be allowed at first. Sometimes they are merely repetition. Sometimes they consist of cue cards or symbols for certain wh-questions. All of this is preparation, one hopes, for giving them the appropriate question forms to put into use when and if they should ever want to. But this is not enough. One can never be sure that students will bridge the gap—on their own—from unreal conditions to real conditions.

Task Oriented Exercises

Thus, one step closer to reality is putting them into some kind of situation in which they will need to seek information or describe something or explain something or discuss something. Task-oriented exercises seem to be the most useful ones of which I know. In order to complete the task, the students will have to employ language—initiate language.

If you send them out of the classroom to get information, the chances are that you will have no real check on whether or not they do, in fact, employ information seeking language forms. Thus, a beneficial follow-up in the classroom would provide a way for the students to ask each other the questions that supposedly it had been necessary for them to address to someone else.

There is no way that students can jump into this kind of language initiation task on the first day. Some unnatural kinds of cues have to be used to prepare them for uttering these questions. Repetition is certainly the first step. The important consideration in the steps that follow is that we *be aware* of the fact that our strategies are still contrived. When one uses a cue that does not transfer to reality, the important thing is to be aware of the implications of that non-transferability.

Changing Cues

And the last thing I have to say regarding cues is that *in all cases,* when expecting the students to switch from one structure to another, there must be an accompanying change in the cues. In fact, it is this change in the real world that should cue the change of the structure in the student. When this criterian isn't met, students are merely mouthing sounds in different patterns.

Eventually one moves away from speaking about observable objects. *Adverbs of time, and time expressions* and *tenses of questions* then become the cues for changing the structure of the response.

Setting the conditions for communication to take place is part of our new job description. I have sometimes felt that as a language teacher, I am, in fact, a conditions engineer. As such, my challenge is to design conditions and manipulate them in such a way that students would recognize the matching of conditions and structures, would learn to change structures as I changed conditions and would eventually recognize analogous changes in conditions in their lives and employ those English structures even when I wasn't there.

So the question was/is: How would I manipulate classroom conditions in order for this transfer to take place? One of my primary concerns has been in assuring the best possible chances for a transfer to reality to occur. Another has been in identifying kinds of language tasks.

Basic Language Tasks

One of the seemingly most basic communication tasks with direct transferability to reality is that of questions and answers. However, questioning and answering can increase in difficulty endlessly. Thus, what are some elements that increase the difficulty of question/answer tasks?

Decrease in assistance. The difficulty of any step can be increased a second time around by removing the former props, rods, realia, pictures, whatever. Change the subject, give a new set of realia and instruct the students to apply the same questions and answers.

Questions and answers, but in more than one structure.

After a structure is presented individually, it is best learned when incorporated systematically into subsequent lessons. At first this combining happens purposefully on the part of the teacher. At times, one even says

to oneself, "I've asked Ben four questions in the present tense. The next time I come to him, I'll have to try a past tense question."

Despite my urging systematic combinations of structures, I must state that *I do not* have in mind the services of an enthusiastic mathematical linguist running to his computer this afternoon to produce a print-out of all the possible combinations of structures. It is neither necessary nor desirable to practice all of the previously acquired structures in every communication task. There is nothing worse than lessons which were designed to "get everything in that we've studied."

Which ones go where and in what combinations can only be determined by employing the standards of judgment and choice of structure that native speakers would use when performing that task.

Next Step

A new step of difficulty is added when conditions are set and language is employed regarding them *without* the conscious effort to alternate structures regularly. This might be referred to as a random integration of taught structures. Forget whether or not Ben has had four opportunities to answer in the present tense. By now he should be familiar enough with it to handle it with success anytime he meets it. If it's been studied in class—at first individually, then in combinations—it should then occur as it would in a conversation with native speakers.

Textbook organization is another trap that we fall into. Authors have to divide the language into some kind of identifiable units and present these units in some organized way. But the students don't meet the language in these units at any other time. We

have to mix the units—integrate the structures to get the language back to reality. Our mistake is that we now and then allow ourselves to think that we have "finished a unit." No unit is ever finished. Once taught, it must be incorporated into future lessons as often as it is meaningfully and naturally possible.

Tasks That We Know of but Haven't Incorporated into a Syllabus:

1. Significant contributions are being made in the identification of gestures, use of space, paralanguage in general which accompanies linguistic features. This paralanguage is being described in kind as well as occurrence. Thus, it can be incorporated into communication tasks systematically—it needs to be, as yet, it hasn't been.
2. A variety of materials need to be developed for each strategy. Teacher-made materials are often the most relevant. But teachers cannot write every lesson. We need new kinds of materials. We don't need whole courses and 100 volume series. We need materials to compliment language tasks instead of materials to compliment linguistic descriptions of structures.
3. Question-answer tasks involving three speakers. Incorporating two speakers and pronoun replacement in the second utterance has led to an interesting kind of tasks.

We've never approached this kind of language instruction in an organized way. We've hoped and prayed and crossed our fingers that somehow, someday, students would "pick it up along the way," but we didn't know how nor when nor where.

I think we do know how. Where, is in the classroom. And when? is just as soon as we decide to "get it together."

TN 2/76

AN IDEA THAT WORKS

Northeastern Illinois University

THE SENSES

Objective: To develop the students descriptive vocabulary through sense activities.

1. *Taste*—blindfold a student, give him an unusual food to taste and ask him to describe it.

2. *Sight*—blindfold a student and have him describe the feeling of an object he's touched.

3. *Smell*—describe the following odors; gasoline, a hospital, stables, cookies baking, a Christmas tree, a gymnasium.

4. *Touch*—put various objects in a closed bag and have them search for one (stone, sponge, clay, etc)

5. *Hearing*—blindfold students, drop objects and ask them to guess what you dropped.

Have students close their eyes and listen, then tell what kinds of sounds they hear (this is a good outside activity)

6. Hold up pictures of objects and have them tell what senses are involved.

7. Have them write a sentence using all the senses.

Purposes: stimulates creative thinking, encourages oral response, familiarize students with common objects, awareness of the role our senses play.

TN 2/76

SCRIPTED DIALOGUES

by Eamon Roche

English Language Institute, Dublin, Ireland

In their article on discussion classes in the *TESOL Quarterly* A. Kaltinick and C. W. Kalinick remind us that "an interesting, productive discussion class, especially with students from diverse cultural backgrounds, remains a highly valued but elusive prize."

The elusiveness stems from the number of pitfalls that must be avoided. To begin with, we have to create some common ground for the discussion. This helps to focus the students' ideas, gives them something to react against and, hopefully, encourages interaction among themselves. The problem is to find topics and areas of discussion which fulfill this need and at the same time spark off and maintain student interest. Awkward silences are just so many nails in the coffin of any discussion class. Once under way, how do we prevent the better, or even more vociferous students from intimidating the weaker or less articulate ones without frustrating either group? *Then we have the problem of the teachers own time-consuming interventions. Teacher-talking, no matter how necessary to keep things moving along at a lively pace, is ultimately one step backward to every step forward in the discussion.* (editor's italics)

The use of a technique, which I have called scripted dialogues can solve these problems and bring added advantages. It could be described as a hybrid form lying somewhere between drilled dialogues practised in the language laboratory and open, non-structured discussion, and can achieve the aims of both these exercises very satisfactorily.

The script is basically a set of instructions. These establish a character for each student and give him a role to play in the dialogue or discussion. They also cover as wide a range as possible of emotions and attitudes from anger through puzzlement to gentle persuasion.

Each student concentrates on bringing his portion of the script to life. He has to express his set of instructions in dialogue form drawing on his fluency in structures, his store idiomatic expressions, exclamations and his range of vocabulary. At the same time he is faced with a challenging opportunity to demonstrate his proficiency in pronunciation, but more especially in intonation and stress.

The instructions are clear but at the same time open-ended in that they allow the student to be creative in choosing the way in which he will express himself according to his role in the dialogue. For example the opening section of a scripted dialogue on a hijacking could take the following form, each of the six students involved having been assigned a number.

1. Threatens passengers—talking about the weapons and explosives he has and at the same time tries to stop them from panicking.

2 and 3 (Passengers) Are frightened, puzzled and almost hysterical.

4. Shows that she is very excited and nervous and explains what they are going to do with the planes.

5. (Over the intercom) Tells everybody, cheerfully, that he is the captain, explains about the height etc. of the plane and wishes everybody the usual things.

6. (has just gone into the cockpit) Threatens the captain and tells him what has happened. He explains what is going to happen to the plane.

1. Tells passengers to do various things so that he can watch them carefully and easily. Gets angry at some of the passengers.

2. Is anxious about what is going to happen and begs the hijackers not to be violent.

Each student receives a copy of a page of the script on various days during the week. This gives him time to study and prepare his role in the dialogue keeping in mind what the others will have to say. Then at the end of the week the situation is acted out, each student having his own copy of the scripted instructions as his only aid.

The performance in class is taped. The students are encouraged not to wait rigidly for cues, but to make the dialogue or discussion as natural as possible. A sprinkling of the usual conversational remarks or interruptions fitting the roles being played by students enhance this naturalness greatly. Bungled cues can even be helpful in this respect, provided they do not make what follows illogical. The fact that a student does not know exactly how the others are going to express their instructions helps to give a natural ring to the dialogue as well. The recording is extremely useful for highlighting good expressions and turns of phrase which can be drilled from the tape if required. It also means that all the students can be involved in the correction of mistakes in grammar, pronunciation intonation and stress when the dialogue is played back. Once they have overcome their shyness about hearing their own voices the recorded version can be very encouraging for the students. It shows them how well they can express themselves as well as making it easier for them to listen for their mistakes.

One of the great advantages of the script is that it supplies a focal point which reduces the risk of flops and long silences to an absolute minimum. With scripted dialogues we make the assumption that topic in a discussion class is only a medium through which language learning takes place to its logical conclusion. All the emphasis is put on fluency and self-expression. Equal participation by all students is also guaranteed by the structure of the script. The usual domination in terms of time by the better students is converted into domination in terms of fluency, from which the others can learn. Once the dialogue is under way teacher talking time of course is reduced to zero because of the script.

The greatest advantage of scripted dialogues is their adaptability. The range of possibilities is infinite. Highly dramatic situations, humourous ones, everyday situations in which the students find themselves, arguments and debates can be given more latitude by using a very short script which merely establishes the topic to be discussed and the roles the students are to play. They then complete the script themselves, supplying their own ideas while keeping in mind the attitudes and characters they have been assigned.

It is obvious that, because of the instructions, this technique works better with students from Intermediate level upwards. With careful preparation, however, it can also be adapted to lower levels. The instructions are simplified and situations are chosen which involve invitations, requests, offers, apologies and various moods. Very useful opportunities can also be given to practice such structures as conditionals, reported speech and commands, and passives. At this, and indeed at all levels, the student is given opportunities to use in a natural way the structures, idioms and so on that he has already learnt. The teacher can then see how much of what is taught is remaining passive knowledge and how much is being used actively.

With this technique we minimise the frustration students often feel at not being able to express themselves. This often shows itself as a reluctance to prepare well for dialogues or discussions. Most important of all we make maximum use of the student's time and he actually talks freely . . . using what we have taught him.   *TN 6/77*

Reprinted from the *ATESOL Newsletter*, Vol. 5, No. 1, May, 1977.

COMMUNICATION STRIPS

by Mary Ann Boyd and John Boyd
Illinois State University

What starts shy, self-conscious adults communicating in the ESL classroom? What process supplies meaningful yet controlled content that gives these students the impetus to participate? For us and for our intermediate level ESL students of several first language backgrounds one answer to these questions has been the strip story.

The idea of using strip stories with our students evolved after we read Robert Gibson's article in the June 1975 *TESOL Quarterly*. The procedure he described consisted of breaking down a story sentence by sentence and typing each sentence on an individual strip of paper. These sentence strips were then to be randomly distributed to the students. The students' task was then to communicate the contents of their strips to the others in the class and in so doing, to orally re-assemble the strips putting the sentences of the story into a logical sequence.

Our first attempts to use this technique in our classes did not meet with much success. After much thought and experimentation however, we made three alterations in the procedure as outlined by Gibson and have since seen the technique flourish with our students.

We had initially thought that it was essential that the students memorize their strips as suggested in the article. But the adult students resisted this and the struggle to memorize their strips became the paramount issue facing them to the detriment of communication. We therefore decided to let them keep their strips in front of them making only the request that they did not show their strips to the others in the room. Being sporty about it all, they carefully kept the written strips to themselves.

Secondly, it was suggested that the students mingle with each other in a manner similar to a cocktail party while communicating their strips. Our students wanted and seemed to profit from more order. Thus they group themselves in a circle and say their sentences one after another around the circle. This allows maximum student input in the problem areas of vocabulary identification, pronunciation assistance and overall comprehension of the sentences. We try to stay with one sentence until all in the room are familiar with the vocabulary items, pronunciation and meaning of the strip.

This does not mean however that we as teachers dominate the proceedings. On the contrary, we become the observers, assisting only when the collective knowledge of the class cannot solve a problem. We feel that it is crucial that the students turn to each other and rely on that collective knowledge to decipher the meanings of the strips rather than to turn automatically to the teacher for answers.

Our third innovation came about because of the difficulty involved in choosing material to be used. We discovered that not many stories lend themselves to this technique without massive rewriting on the part of the teacher. A story too difficult to comprehend will frustrate the students and one without adequate sequence clues will perplex. In neither case will the objective of the lesson be met. After trial and error, we decided to write our own strip stories to tailor them to our specific purposes. To meet the students' needs the stories all revolve around life-coping situations, contain vocabulary and sentence patterns common to oral English and employ clues to sequence as a matter of course.

Depending on the class we follow various procedures with the strip stories. Most commonly we hand each student a strip without explanation of content or technique. (Our students are now quite familiar with the technique although we did explain it at the outset.) They take a minute to read over their strips, look up an unfamiliar word if they like and begin to feel comfortable with their sentences. Then they assemble themselves in a circle and the first round of speaking begins. This first round takes the most time because all of the vocabulary, pronunciation and comprehension problems have to be ironed out to everyone's satisfaction. When this has been accomplished, second and subsequent rounds of oral communication of the strips continue until the students begin to get a feeling for the context of the story. Then, and at this point a leader always seems to emerge, the students start to try different sequences of sentence order until the completed whole seems "right." Discussion and debate ensue with one student defending his rationale for a particular sentence order while others point to the illogic and/or impossibility of such an order. Finally, when the sentences have been arranged to the satisfaction of all and a proper sequence has been obtained, follow-up exercises can be done.

If the story lends itself to one, a role play can occur with student prompting of the actors from individual strips. A pantomime can be used to set the sequence of actions if desired. To make the students more aware of the need to communicate clearly, a dictation can follow with each student dictating his sentence to the others in the class in order until the whole story has been given.

With a less advanced, more inhibited class, the teacher may wish to follow another procedure which we have used successfully; namely, a reversal in the above order. With this procedure the teacher begins by writing potentially unfamiliar vocabulary words on the board and elicits the meanings from the class. When this has been done to everyone's satisfaction, the teacher sets the scene of the story orally or through a picture if possible and briefly introduces the characters. (A danger here is for the teacher to talk too much—this step should be carefully self-monitored by the teacher.)

At this point the sentences are read randomly by the teacher to all of the students as a dictation. When the dictation has been completed and corrected, the teacher distributes copies of the already-dictated strips and the students orally put the story together. This sense of familiarity with the strips and the context can certainly aid a less self-confident class to communicate.

Whatever the procedures followed, the goals and the value of the technique remain essentially the same. Each student is forced to communicate a small slice of information without which the whole cannot be achieved and yet each student is given the exact information to be communicated. The students thus concentrate on communicating without the pressure of sentence constructing as well. This blend of controlled content and communicative responsibility tends to result in a productive, profitable and enjoyable class session each time it is employed. What more could an ESL teacher want?

Editor's Note:

John and Mary Ann Boyd are working at present primarily with Vietnamese students. They have written a set of fifty strip stories which they have found successful in their classes. In their materials they suggest the following 'follow-up' exercises.

Follow-up exercises:

1) Students can role play the story with the other students prompting the "actors" from individual strips.
2) Each student can dictate his strip, in story order, to the rest of the class until the whole story has been given.
3) One student can change the story into reported speech and retell the story to the class.

TN 9/78

SHOPPING FOR COMMUNITY CONTACTS

by Jean McConochie
Pace University

Introducing foreign visitors, or new residents, to varied aspects of American life is a normal component of English language programs in the United States. It is sometimes difficult, however, to devise ways in which students may be led to make their own discoveries, rather than simply accept the word of a teacher. Another program goal which may also be difficult to achieve is to have students use the language they are learning in relatively unstructured situations outside the classroom.

Both of these goals are part of the Japanese Teachers Program (JTP) sponsored by the Council on International Educational Exchange. Since 1968, the Council has offered an eight-week summer program through which a Japanese teacher may come to the United States for four weeks of intensive language study on a university campus, followed by travel and an extended homestay with an American family.

The teachers come, as they say, "to brush up their English." In effect, this means that they want to meet and talk with as many Americans as possible, for in Japan they find few opportunities to use English outside the classroom. Their instructors are equally interested in having the Japanese move beyond the safety of classroom English to less structured "real" language and in having them see more of American life than that represented by the academic community. These interests converge happily in the "errand."

Origin of the Errand

The idea originated with Dr. Virginia French Allen, who suggested it at a JTP planning session in 1969. Gary Gabriel, director of the JTP at Rutgers University that summer, elaborated the framework, developing the "errand assignment," as it came to be known. Staff members, of whom I was one, collaborated in inventing the errand topics and editing the final reports for duplicating.[1] The following summer the errand assignment was used in two Japanese Teachers Programs—one at Fordham University, directed by Mr. Gabriel, and one held in Moorestown, New Jersey, under the sponsorship of Temple University, co-directed by Dr. Allen and Dr. Donald S. Knapp.

Twenty-one errands were devised for the 42 participants in the Rutgers program. The assignments were given to teams of two—an interviewer and a reporter. In each case the more passive member of the team was assigned the more active role. He was responsible for doing all the talking required by the

assignment, though he was allowed to ask the reporter for help during the interview if that became necessary.

The reporter was responsible for taking notes and turning in a written report. The format for these reports was left unspecified beyond the requirement that the Japanese teachers indicate when and where they went and that they describe what happened. Assigned at the end of the first week, the reports were due in written form by the final class meeting; however, teams gave oral reports on their errands as they were completed, since the program participants were eager to share their adventures.

Two "Old Boys" at the Florist's

The more fluent teams were given the more complicated errands, and vice versa—as the teachers themselves realized in at least one case. Two of the older men in the Rutgers program were given the task of going to a local florist to find out what flowers are most popular in the United States, what special meaning different varieties of flowers have, and how much flowers cost. Mr. Watanabe reported on the questions posed and then added,

Mr. Gabriel was kind enough to offer an easy errand of going to a florist's to us two old boys who are are not good at English conversation, but in fact this errand was not so easy for us.

He explained that neither he nor Mr. Tanaka had been interested in flowers in Japan and that neither knew the Japanese names of any flowers except cherry blossoms and chrysanthemums. "But anyway," he concluded—with typical Japanese grace—"we are very glad to have done our duty and acquired some knowledge of flowers."

Going into a florist's to ask questions rather than to make a purchase obviously required that the teachers explain their assignment. This was also the case in several other errands. For example, Mr. Suzuki (No. 1 of the three Suzuki's in the program) was allowed to identify the team's mission when he and Mr. Toda went to a local stockbroker with a hypothetical $1,000 to invest.

When we entered the office, we found several clerks, some of them watching the ticker-tape and others working with the phone in their hands at the desk, which looks like a booth in a language lab. Then we told a young lady at the information desk of our intention and she introduced Mr. Marder, a tall, kind man, to us.
The salesman gave them a list of recommended stocks and "wiregrams" giving figures on individual issues.

For interest we selected Niagara Mohawk

Power out of the list, considering the safety and pursuit of profits. For speculation, we chose Union Oil of California, because a wiregram said that the firm had drilled two wells in Alaska and they are expected to bring about a great profit. We told him of our selections and asked for his opinion. He said we have an expert's eye right at the beginning and recommended both of them with confidence.

The men "purchased" 26 shares of NMP at 17⅞ and 10 shares of UOC at 51⅝. (Union Oil is up a few points at the moment; Niagara Mohawk hovers between 16 and 18. So much for expert eyes.)

Furnishing a Living Room

Another pair were asked to find out the cost of furnishing a Western style living room. When a furniture store owner expressed surprise at their errand, Mr. Yoshida told him, "with a proud look," to quote the reporter, "that it is a most unique way of learning English created by our honorable instructor, Mr. Gabriel." The teachers' pride in their accomplishment was matched by their imaginative pleasure in the task, made vivid by Mr. Murata's use of the historical present.

Next we go into a pottery store, because we want to have a clock in our living room. . . . We think we want to add a TV set in our room, too, so we decide to buy one. In this store, however, we can't find any TV sets except those made in Japan. Besides, the prices of them are all the same—$99.95. Anyway, we buy one.
When we walk along the street, we find a fruit garland and buy one. We think it is good for the decoration of the room. The most expensive prices for the living room furniture total $4,887.95, and the cheapest, $597.75.

Diamond Rings

A final example of an errand that required self-identification is "The Engagement Ring." Mr. Tsuchiya and Mr. Tashiro, both in their 30's and married, drew the assignment of pricing engagement rings and finding out how the cost was determined. Two clerks in a New Brunswick jewelry store graciously showed them many rings and explained the factors of carat, cut, color, and clarity. Mr. Tsuchiya, a born story-teller as it happens, concluded by giving us a rare glimpse of his inner thoughts.

On our way out of the shop, we decided to choose a diamond ring priced at $675 as an engagement ring. The bright summer sun blinded us. I thought to myself, "If only I were 10 years younger!"

Remedy for a Sore Throat

For other errands, the Japanese teachers were specifically instructed *not* to say that they were on an assignment for a class. Rather they had to complete their task in as natural a manner as possible. One such errand was to go to a drug store and buy Kleenex and a cold remedy for an imaginary sick friend. (One of the instructors had agreed to reimburse the shoppers to the extent of $2 and to find a use for the purchases.) Mr. Hazama reported:

Suzuki [No. 3] asked the man behind the counter to give him a packet of medicine for a cold, adding that a friend of his had caught cold and was in bed. The man led us to the stand where various kinds of medicine were displayed. He asked Suzuki about the condition of his friend. At this inquiry Suzuki was a little bewildered, but he contrived to answer that his friend had a sore throat.

American Barbers

Even greater ingenuity was required of Mr. Sano, who was to interview a local barber about his business. He and Mr. Takanami went into a shop, expecting to engage the barber in conversation while having their hair cut. They were relieved to find no other customers in the shop, but relief changed to unease when the barber remained expressionless as he cut their hair. Suddenly inspiration came.

After each of us had a haircut, Sano immediately said, "We have become much more handsome than before." Then the barber smiled. Sano continued to say, "In fact, I have a barber friend in Japan, and he asked me to ask about American barbers." The barber said, "With pleasure," as his reply.

He answered their questions about how one becomes a barber and how long he had been one. However, he demurred when asked about his volume of business, saying only that many Rutgers students have their hair cut in his shop—"We were dodged cleverly," Mr. Takanami admitted. He also noted that while they had heard of the high price of manual labor in the States, they were amazed to pay $2.50 for a 15-minute haircut. For considerably less than that in Japan, Takanami remarked, a man could have the "full course" of shampoo, haircut, shave, and massage. (A haircut alone would cost the equivalent of two cups of coffee.) Discovering the prices and availability of basic services was a useful aspect of the errands, for it gave the Japanese teachers an idea of what their American counterparts' seemingly astronomical salaries mean in purchasing power.

No American-Made Souvenirs

A related feature was introducing our Japanese visitors to the kinds of goods that can be purchased here, and letting them see the ubiquity of Japanese-made goods. Mr. Haruta and Mr. Kanaya were asked to find souvenirs to take back to Japan. They first tried the gift section of a department store, but saw nothing that isn't also available in Japan—except for a $12 coin collection, too expensive an item for their purpose. A policeman who had shown them the way to the store had also pointed out Woolworth's, which they decided to try next.

In this store we found many Japanese-made articles which are all a little more expensive than in the stores of Japan. We again asked the clerks whether they had typical articles of America. They all hesitated and one of them said, "What about hot dogs?" with laughter. One clerk recommended to us American flags and America's oldest model cars. But to our regret, they were also what we might find even in Japan.

The Woolworth's clerk suggested a nearby hardware store, where they found "seal collection—New Jersey, patriotic, Civil War—for 25 cents each." Mr. Haruta's conclusion was perceptive: "On this errand we recognized that America is too young a country for us to find her typical articles without difficulties."

Finding a Store

The conversations involved in locating an appropriate store proved to be a bonus in a number of the errands and suggests that the instructions need not be too explicit. In fact one of the most successful errand assignments of the Fordham University JTP[2] was for two of the women to buy iron-on seam binding. Having no idea of what that item might be, the women tried various stores and were finally referred to the neighborhood sewing machine dealer. However, no one realized that in asking for "an iron-on seam binding," the women didn't know what they were looking for; so when the Singer clerk said that they didn't carry seam binding, Miss Habu and Miss Taguchi were stumped. Imagine their triumphal delight when, stopping in a local drugstore for a Coke one evening after an excursion to Manhattan, they found seam tape in a notions rack. They marveled at the American need for such an item, and each bought several packages as souvenirs for their friends at home!

Even when the site for performing the errand is specified clearly, the participants may have a certain amount of adventure in finding it. A visit to the Rutgers Agricultural Experiment Station, for example, required asking directions of several people and riding on the campus bus. (The errand was to find out the average annual rainfall in New Brunswick; the research data confirmed our suspicions that we were in the midst of an exceptionally wet year.)

At the Police Station

However, perhaps the most exciting errand, in terms of tracking down information, was the seemingly prosaic assignment of inquiring at the local police station about regulations for keeping dogs as pets. Mr. Suzuki (No. 2) questioned four people before he and Mr. Nagashima located the police station. Once there, they chanced on a policeman who had been stationed in Japan after World War II. He spent a long time answering their questions and wrote out "veterinarian" for Mr. Nagashima, who was understandably troubled by the spelling. Then the policeman suggested that they might also want to visit the SPCA—and arranged for his Japanese visitors to be taken there in a patrol car. It was the talk of the program for days.

The "dog" errand was suggested by the number of dogs running loose in New Brunswick and by a suspicion that the American preoccupation with pets would seem strange to a Japanese. Quite a different use of the police station was made by Drs. Allen and Knapp in the Temple University JTP: they sent a team to find out how many crimes had been committed since the Japanese teachers' arrival.

Unexpected Bonus

One Rutgers errand grew out of a genuine need, which suggests another source of errand ideas. Mrs. Kagiya lost the crown of her watch and asked the program director where she could have it replaced. Seizing the opportunity, he changed her errand assignment to one similar to the engagement ring errand—to find the cheapest and most expensive watches at a jewelry store and to find out what determined the cost. Mrs. Kagiya and Miss Kaji went to a local jeweler (not the one with the rings) and asked about having the watch repaired. A 3-day wait and a $3 charge, they were told. When they inquired about new watches, they were turned over to another clerk. After he had shown the women many watches and discussed the differences in price and quality, Mrs. Kagiya explained the assignment behind her questions. The salesman, like the policeman, had been in Japan. He surely had pleasant memories of Japanese hospitality, for he arranged to have Mrs. Kagiya's watch fixed on the spot and for a dollar less than the original quotation. He is undoubtedly still receiving Christmas cards from his two customers.

Not all errands were equally productive, of course. Assignments to find the admission requirements for Rutgers and postage rates to Japan may have occasioned pleasant meetings but resulted in brief and dull reports. The least successful errand of all, through no fault of the team, was that performed by Mr. Sakai and Mr. Shimokawa. Here is their report, in its entirely:

After lessons were over, both of us went straight to the railroad station. At the station three clerks seemed to be very busy. So we had to wait for a couple of minutes, and then Shimokawa asked one of them the first question, "How often does the train go to New York?" The clerk didn't answer the question but handed him a copy of a timetable, and to the next questions, "Is the seat reserved or not?" and "Where is the New York Station?" he just answered, "Not. 33rd Street and 8th Avenue." That's all.

Clearly, these were poorly conceived errands. The assigned questions had simple, straightforward answers which offered no opening for conversation. And there was little possibility for imaginative treatment of the topic. A successful errand assignment need not be complex, but it should have an open-ended solution.

Cooperation From Townspeople

The courtesy of the New Brunswick townspeople in responding to questions that may have struck them as bizarre was gratifying—and perhaps unusual. JTP program directors who used the errand assignment in the summer of 1970 felt it prudent to inform the local merchants about the overall program before the arrival of the Japanese. The Temple program also introduced the idea of two errand assignments, so that each participant could have a turn as questioner and as reporter. Since a week is sufficient for the completion of an errand, it is certainly possible to do two in a 4-week program. For both the Rutgers and Fordham JTPs, the errand reports were du-

plicated for distribution to all the participants at the end of the 4-week session.

What accounts for the success of the errands? First, the assignment is sufficiently structured that students in the intermediate range of language proficiency can succeed. Second, the errands, if cleverly devised, provide an opportunity for independent discovery of some aspect of the host culture. Third, the errands provide an opportunity for meaningful use of language outside the classroom—the ultimate aim of any language program. Finally, as the participants' reports demonstrate, the errands are fun for everyone involved.

Reprinted from The *Idiom* October 1980. *TN 4/81*

THE POCKET CALCULATOR AND LISTENING COMPREHENSION

by Rebecca Lemaitre
Intensive English Language Program (IELP)
Temple University, Philadelphia

Has this ever happened to you? A student comes up after a session in the language lab (where he had listened to a lecture and exercises involving—on your part—at least ten hours of preparation) and says, "Well, yes, it was a nice tape, but not at all amusing. I wasn't interested in the subject."

Sound familiar? As a result of living in this fast-moving electronic world, students tend to have a sense of apathy and disinterest in materials, a "but what have you done for me lately" view. Consequently, to keep student involvement at a peak, a teacher needs to accumulate a bag of tricks for practicing various points of study. Yes! One more duty has been added to a TESOLer's job description: ENTERTAIN!

While it certainly isn't necessary that every bit of instruction be sugar-coated, it is definitely necessary to have variety in one's instructional methods. Students like to have a general schedule, but within that schedule, the teacher should have a variety of ways to approach each activity.

This article offers a specialized type of listening comprehension exercise, specifically aimed at technologically oriented students—engineers, economists, chemists. . . . Many students in intensive programs are interested in this type of material; moreover, they are often enrolled in some type of math review course and frequently have pocket calculators.

At Temple, I have experimented informally with using these calculators in listening comprehension exercises. The experiment has been so well received that I think others involved in teaching groups of this sort may find the idea a useful addition to their "bag of tricks."

I have come up with three general types of activities: (1) low-level problem solving and number recognition; (2) letter/number similarities games; and (3) analytical listening. This article explains and illustrates each type.

Low-Level Problem Solving

For students whose English is at a basic or low intermediate level (or for use with other students as an introduction to this type of exercise), begin by reading numbers aloud. Insist that the students listen while the entire number is read before entering it, for example, "ten thousand, five hundred and ninety-two." Alternatively, the teacher can read the number, have the students repeat it aloud, and then enter it on the calculators. Then have individual students read back the numbers; one student can put the number on the board as a check.

The next step is problem solving. Read a short problem to the students and have them read back the answer. Obviously, the problems can range from elementary to advanced and can work on familiarizing the students with terms describing mathematical usage as well as with recognition of numbers. This is an interesting exercise with immediate feedback because (barring a slip of the finger), a wrong answer indicates a listening comprehension problem. Problems here should involve numbers and operations, rather than word-problems, since the goal is familiarity with numbers and operations.

Letter-Number Similarities Games

This type of game, which is popular with American students, results from the fact that certain numbers on the calculator resemble letters, when

viewed upside-down. On a standard calculator, we can find three vowels and five consonants.

Numbers	Vowels	Consonants
0	O	
1	i	
2	E	
3		
4		h
5		S
6		g
7		L
8		B

The result of this is that we can spell words containing the above vowels and consonants. A game of this type requires students to listen to a story involving numbers and enter the numbers on their calculators, performing operations such as addition, subtraction, multiplication and division which are also indicated in the story. The answer, when viewed upside down on the calculator, will be a word which logically completes the story.

Help the students get the idea of the game by beginning with something very simple, like this one:

"*Directions: Enter each number that you hear: His real name has many letters. But 7718 persons call him_____.*" (*Turn the calculator upside-down and the letters spell BILL.*)

Here is another, slightly more complicated, story of the same type:

"*Directions: Enter each number that you hear: The general had been directing the battle for 77 hours. Sometimes he became so tired that he fell asleep on his horse. Once he managed to sleep for 3 hours and another time for 4. When a newspaper corre-*

spondent asked him, after the battle, for a definition of war, he answered him in one sentence: 'War is_____.'" (HELL)

Notice that in the next game an addition operation is required. If students fail to follow directions appropriately, the result will be a wrong answer.

"Directions: Perform each addition operation you hear: Last week I went to visit a famous mountain. I decided to try to walk to the top, so I walked quickly for 2771 steps. Then I ran for another 2771 steps. Finally I walked very slowly for 2172 more steps. There I was—at the top. I felt very proud of myself for having climbed such a steep _____." (HILL)

Several books with this type of game are on the market, but they tend to have such farcical stories that their value to an ESL class is almost nonexistent. The teacher should work out words that can be made with the vowels and consonants possible on the calculator. Then it's easy to devise a little story that will end with the word.

Analytical Listening

While this is the most difficult of all the games, in my opinion it is probably the most useful for the student, who must not only listen for cue words but also grasp the main idea of the reading. Typical cues that can be worked into this type of practice are signals for addition such as *and, moreover, furthermore, not only . . . but also, in addition to,* etc. Subtraction cues can be such words as *but, however, on the other hand,* etc. Verb tenses can be manipulated so as to provide false cues and increase the difficulty of the game. I feel that it is *very important* to state the question first, to aid students in hypothesizing as they juggle the information they are receiving. Then read the passage

through once while the students listen only. Then read it a second time while they perform the indicated calculations. By approaching the exercise in this way, we accomplish three objectives (aside from letting the students have fun with their calculators): (1) We give practice in listening for main ideas. (2) We give practice in hypothesizing, in trying to anticipate the applications of what they are hearing. (3) We give practice in recognition of cue words and signals.

Let's look at some examples of analytical listening games.

"Directions: Listen as I read the story through once. Then listen again and find the answer to the question: How many people came to the president's dinner?

"The President invited his five best friends to dinner. All but one accepted and said they would come with their wives. Later one called up and said he was sorry but his wife was sick and they couldn't come. Then another friend called and asked permission to bring a house guest."

Notice the cues that the students must pick up in order to arrive at the answer:

1. "invited his five best friends"   (enter 5)
2. "all but one accepted"   (subtract 1)
3. "with wives"   (enter 4)
4. "they couldn't come"   (subtract 2)
5. "another called"   (false cue)
6. "bring a house guest"   (enter 1)

Therefore, we find an operation of $5 - 1 + 4 - 2 + 1 = 7$ guests.

The next example becomes more complex. It contains false cues, such as the son's age and the breakdown

of the cats. This is a good example of a time when the first reading (for the main idea) becomes important.

"Directions: Listen as I read the story through once. Then listen again and find the answer to the question:

"My son, who has been an animal lover since about age ten, has ten large cats of various colors. Three are black, two are yellow, one is white, and the other four are variegated. He likes cats very much; moreover, one of the cats just had four kittens. However, since one died shortly after birth, only three are living at present." (The answer, of course. is only 13 cats.)

Obviously, with more advanced students, the stories can be very long, containing many cues and many calculations. I would like to point out that these exercises can be used in group work, with one student (rather than the teacher) reading the problems while the others listen and calculate. This obviously necessitates care with enunciation and can be of benefit to the reader also. Another variation might be to have the problems ready on dittos so that students may work on them individually. This would then become, of course, a reading exercise (problems given in this way could be more difficult). Using the calculators this way would provide an interesting and useful bit of "busy-work" for a student who has finished early. Since a calculator suitable for this purpose can be obtained for less than $10.00, a program could even invest in a supply for student use in class. Granted, this is not an activity one would wish to use every day. But given a group of students who are interested in math, a teacher who plans interesting exercises to take advantage of the calculator's possibilities in an ESL class, may find that, for a while at least, the students find the relevance of their special interests in their language class.   *TN 6/77*

IT WORKS

USE YOUR IMAGINATION

Edited by Darlene Larson
New York University

Is anyone looking for a lesson idea for oral activities with a minimum of teacher direction? Here are two.

The first idea will make use of those "odds 'n ends" of pictures you've clipped but haven't known how to use. Or, if you're not a picture file enthusiast, you can gather enough pictures for the lesson the night before you want to teach it. The ease involved in getting these materials together comes from

the fact that the only goal in mind is to find a group of pictures that have no obvious relation to each other— neither in grammar nor in subject matter. The task for students is, then, to create a story which incorporates each picture into a unified tale. (Each picture's contribution need not get equal weight in the story segments.)

Since two heads are usually better than one, I have assigned this task to

partners or small groups of three or four each time I've tried it. Prepare manilla envelopes containing five or six unrelated pictures and give an envelope to each group. Tell them that their task is to create a story, imaginary or real, which will contain as many bits of information found in the pictures as is possible to include, and for sure, at least one bit from each picture. I like to add a performance goal, that they should decide their story and get ready to record it on tape, or get ready to tell another group about it. I've often found it difficult to monitor the conversations all around the class because the exchanges taking place in each one are interesting enough that I want to stay and listen. Another teacher who used this idea, after collecting the pictures, assigned as homework that each group member *write* the story he had just helped create orally.

Another technique that sets students' imaginations humming is the following: Write a series of mathematical equations on an index card. The only limitation I've given myself is that the last number of one equation is the first number of the next. For example:

a. $1,000 \div 5 = 200$
b. $200 - 40 = 160$
c. $160 \times 2 = 320$
d. $320 \div 10 = 32$
e. $32 \div 16 = 2$

The cards, all with different sets of equations, can be given to individuals or groups, but I prefer groups. The directions are to make a story that uses these numbers. Another way to word it is that the numbers tell a story—but they have to decide just what the story is.

There is no generalization that can be made about the kinds of language practice which will result. Some groups take a minute to get the English terms (mathematical) that are used in reading an equation. Some proceed directly to matching numbers with nouns—a thousand apples and five stores, or a thousand children in five grades. Recently the above set of equations began as a thousand acres of land divided among five brothers. Each brother had two hundred acres and set forty of them aside for a garden. When two brothers pooled their resources and then divided their 320 acres into ten plots, the students decided to revise the second equation. The minus forty acres had to be waste. Off to their dictionaries they went for the word *swamp*. Back to equation d. to categorize ten different plots of land of thirty-two acres each; an orchard, a pasture, a golf course, a garden, a swimming pool, etc. Involved in their story was a student-initiated vocabulary lesson, the discovery of a set of words which are the names for plots of land. Another equation turned into a story which involved the recipe for wine, including pounds of sugar, pounds of grapes, gallons of water, bottles and people.

After a period of time, I write all of the "stories" (sets of equations) on the blackboard. Once there for all to see, I ask each group to tell us their story. Numerous queries come from other members of the class. Demands for clarity and more explicit transitions are routine, and groups are usually quite willing to come up with more details to support their main ideas. The student-initiated talk generated by these two "starters" is not only plentiful, but usually includes a good bit of humor and a lot of language that is relevant to the students' own experiences. Enjoy.   TN 6/77

MILTON MCPHERSON

By Darlene Larson
New York University

The last few years have seen our profession sharing many ideas about how to get students talking. "Mistakes" may not be nearly as important as we used to think they were. It may very well be that in language acquisition, communication comes first and grammar later. (Widdowson, TESOL '78 plenary) Experience has led a number of classroom teachers to ease their concern for accuracy and get students talking first. But sooner or later, students become aware of the difference between their pronunciation of English and a native speaker's pronunciation, and they often ask for help. Other students are being misunderstood and need to have help offered. What kind of help can we give?

An experienced teacher at NYU, the late Professor Milton McPherson used to tell us, "An explanation has to be simple. A complicated explanation is a description, and it is of little use to students. The useful aids are the simple ones." It is difficult to think of improving on Mac's work, but I think a better word for *explanation* is *direction*. An explanation and a description are often one and the same. And many students can understand the explanation—are, indeed, fascinated with it—but can't translate that understanding into production. What kind of *direction* can we give students once they want to make a change in their oral production?

McPherson's wealth of experience has not yet been put into print but he left notes and we all hope they'll be made available eventually. Among other gems that he shared freely are these:

R = WR. For those students who have some facility with written English but trouble with pronunciation, tell them to "think WR" for R. It works. For those who are not burdened by an orientation to the written form, but, nevertheless, have trouble with R, the key is lip-rounding. We often stress a few tricks with the tongue when aiding students to pronounce the American R, but rarely mention lip-rounding. Try it.

Timing. Many vowels in the accented parts of the American English intonation contour are held far longer than average syllable time in other languages like Spanish or Chinese. The glottal stops in Chinese make unbelievably short syllables. According to McPherson, an instruction to a speaker of Chinese to hold the *ah* in *hot* is far more important than to work on the production of the final t. Vowel length in the stressed words of the English intonation contour is so long that McPherson preferred the term "drawl." It is especially important before t, p, k, f, th, ch, and sh.

Exaggeration is a third direction he recommended. He claimed that "punching" "blowing" and "drawling" to an *exaggerated* degree on the part of the informant usually brought students somewhere close to the norm when they thought they were exaggerating.

A few more techniques that I have found useful:

For those having trouble with L, bite the tongue, (gently, of course), and try to make a sound.

Intonation marks on the blackboard aid pronunciation immensely for some students but I have never found textbooks filled with large dots and small dots of any efficient use. Many visual systems adopted by textbook publishers are too complicated.

A problem pronunciation pair for many students is *an eraser* and *a razor*. I have explained and described these two from every angle. Articles, syllables, /s/ vs. /z/. Students listen and nod in wonderful comprehension. But when I hold up a picture of a razor, I am likely to hear 80% of the class speak of the eraser behind me. A couple semesters ago I wrote ⌣ ⌣ / ⌣ for an eraser, and ⌣ / ⌣ for a razor. To my pleasure, the percent of success was just about reversed.

Another benefit of an easy direction is that students sometimes practice it by themselves. After stressing lip-rounding for R, I have noticed students at break practicing by themselves. With ⌣ ⌣ / ⌣ in their notebooks, I have seen students tapping their pens on the desk while looking at the notes they have just taken.

Student initiative is an essential ingredient for moving these isolated successful productions into the stream of speech. Student-operated tape recorders are another method of helping students take charge of their own pronunciation efforts. The opportunity to listen to himself while free of the burden of getting his thoughts together is valuable. Students who begin listening to their own English are often more critical than anyone else about what they hear.

Comparison with a native speaker can be helpful for some students. I have recently suggested that teachers might tape a short news announcement or commercial on the radio. Transcribe that short announcement and give it to the students in its written form. Let them practice changing the written form to spoken English and when they are ready, have them record themselves. After students have recorded themselves, play the recording of the radio announcer that you originally made. Let the students make whatever comparisons that are important to them.

One minimal contrast may be enough. I recently asked Florence Baskoff of NYU what works in her classes. Since she has written a book on guided composition, I expected to hear about a technique for teaching writing. Much to my surprise, she came up with a pronunciation technique. And it is simple. Everyone in her class gets a name of a famous person. The name contains the problem sound of the student. For example, Baskoff suggests that a person having trouble with /ch/ might be "Charlie Chaplin" in English class. I've already decided that my Japanese girl who is having trouble with both initial and final l is going to be Lauren Bacall. Baskoff claims that as the semester moves along, there is a carry over to other pronunciation activities, other oral occasions, from this practice of just one name.

This reminds me of another experience I've had which seemed to work. It comes from an early lesson with a junk box containing a number of things which put minimal pairs into reality— a pin and a pen, a net and a knot—in which students had to ask for something, i.e. "Give me a pen." The impact of being given a pin when one thought one was asking for a pen seems to be a profound experience regarding the importance of those two sounds in English. Student care and attention to those two sounds following such an experience long outlasts any results from the repetition of 100 minimal differences.

Some teachers are afraid to move students toward normal speed and intonation in their oral production, fearing that such speech habits will hinder writing habits. "If I encourage him to drawl the vowel and slight the t in *hot*, for example, he'll forget to write the t when writing," is a common reaction in some circles. It points to the necessity of addressing ourselves often, both in ESL classes and in teacher education programs, to the difference between speech and writing. One is not a careful

representation of the other and we do our students an injustice to lead them to believe that the two go together smoothly.

One of the best exercises to re-emphasize this important difference is dictation. I use it early and give students three possibilities from which to choose. Their papers may read:

   1. It is a bathroom.
     It is a bedroom.
     It is a bad room. but

I will pronounce only one of these at normal speed and intonation. They have to circle what they hear.

Later, they have to fill in parts of the utterance. Their papers may show: It _____ bedroom. And I'll pronounce, "It's a bedroom," at normal speed and intonation. Or, their paper may have: Fork___ _____ spoon_____ table. And I will pronounce, "Forks 'n spoons 're on the table."

Mary Hines has devised a format for this type of slotted dictation exercise which will provide students with immediate comparison of speech and writing. If Hines were preparing an exercise of the utterance just mentioned, her paper would look like this:

Fork___ _____ spoon _____ table.
    s and   s are on the

Students would be instructed to fold the bottom of their papers up to the top until all they could see would be the first utterance. (One has to plan things that will fit across one line.) After listening to the pronunciation, students attempt to write the written form of the speech they just heard, then slide their paper down to see what the intended answer was.

None of these techniques contains any magic. One technique may be useful for three students, another for two, and a third may help two more. Then, the fact that those seven students are improving their English will influence three more. (Some learn from their peers exactly what their peers learned from the teacher the day before.) Then ten students have moved closer to their goals. But there are several more students in the classroom. Every teacher has effective techniques. What additional suggestions can you add? Send them to the *Newsletter* for future additions to this column.   *TN 11/78*

asked to read one sentence of a story written on a strip of paper without the rest of a story, and to memorize it. When each student has memorized his single sentence, the strips of paper are collected and the students are charged with the task of getting the story put together again, orally.

Evidently teachers of non-readers have pointed out to Gibson that his good idea won't work for their students because it assumes that the students can read. One wonders if every good idea has to be good for all students at every step of their language development. But Gibson accepted the challenge and has come up with an excellent plan for groups of students whose age or proficiency covers a wide range. He elaborates as follows:

Given a situation where a group of younger and older ESOL students can be brought together, they can be paired off, one young nonreader with one older reader. Each pair of students would get one strip and the older one would read it to the younger one, both perhaps working together to memorize the sentence on the strip. After both had memorized their sentence, then all the older students would form a group to put the story back together in the usual fashion while all the younger students would form a different group to reconstruct the story.

It appears to me that this sort of cooperation between older and younger students would be good for both groups. It may enhance the older students' self confidence since they will discover that they have a skill that someone else needs. Sometimes the level of English language for recent immigrant students is similar regardless of age, although older students may have already learned to read while the younger ones have not. This cooperative approach would make use of their similarities and their differences in a positive way.

A second adaptation of the Strip Story for nonreaders involves either a Language Master machine or a cassette tape recorder. The sentences of the Strip Story can be recorded on Language Master cards, with or without illustrations or sentences printed on them. Then the cards can be given to the students who will spend time at the machine listening and practicing their sentences independently until they are memorized. The rest of the procedure follows the usual sequence for the Strip Story. If a Language Master is not available, each student could receive a prerecorded sentence on a cassette which could be used to learn the sentence independently.

TN 4/77

STRIP STORIES

Edited by Darlene Larson
New York University

We're grateful to two more teachers for sharing classroom ideas with us which have been successful with their students. Robert Gibson of the University of Hawaii has a follow-up to his article on the "Strip Story" which

originally appeared in the TESOL QUARTERLY in June of 1975, Vol. 9, No. 2.

You will recall that Gibson's technique is the one in which students are

RADIO NEWS

By Karen O'Neill
Palto Alto, California

While listening comprehension is usually the first skill to be acquired in any language learning situation, intermediate and advanced learners often remain frustrated with their level of listening comprehension. Personal conversations and communications which can be predicted from common knowledge and non-linguistic clues may be easily understood, but radio broadcasts, public announcements, and lectures may be unintelligible to even the more advanced students. Most students recognize the importance of understanding completely such things as announcements made over public address systems, as well as news broadcasts and lectures. It is in these situations, however, that the language learner has only one pass at the information, there is no opportunity to ask for a slower repetition or the explanation of a particular idiom. The typical response by the learner to these situations would be to "tune out" completely rather than listen to a seemingly meaningless barrage. In an advanced class (mixed language backgrounds) of listening comprehension we used songs, taped lectures, and problem solving—but the most successful were the news broadcast exercises.

I have found even advanced students to be frustrated with their attempts to listen to radio broadcasts, and very appreciative of the opportunity to sharpen their skills in this type of listening. These are students who can understand normal American speech, but yet report that their comprehension of public speeches or broadcasts is only 30-40%. In one four-week intensive program we worked specifically on understanding radio news programs with successful results in improved listening comprehension as well as impressive increases in vocabulary development, cultural understanding, and up-to-the-minute idiomatic usage.

The class met in the early afternoon three days a week. I recorded the morning news, weather, and sometimes feature announcements from a local radio station on a cassette before class. By recording the programs daily I insured that the material would be timely and fresh, and new to the students. I also gave the students a weekly radio schedule and encouraged them to tune in on their free time. Most radio stations have a set format and present the news in a regular sequence. For example, one station may always start with the time, go on to the local weather, have a commercial, then give the news before moving on to editorials, book reviews, traffic reports, movie critiques, etc. Knowing what type of information to expect in a

news program and the possible sequencing is important in decoding the fast-talking D.J. I recorded the news from the same station several different times so that students would become accustomed to the format of a particular program. We also discussed introductory and transitional phrases which are commonly used on the radio to switch from one topic to another. "What's in store for us over the weekend, Jack?", for example, is a rather typical introduction to a weather prediction report.

One of the greatest difficulties the students had was in determining when one news item ended and the next began. Most stations give a preview of the news to be included in the program in the form of "headlines" before the actual news presentation begins. Preparing students to hear about weather, commuter traffic conditions, sports, and news helped divide the departments, and "tuning in" to the headlines guided the item by item breakdown of the news itself. To help students further recognize each different news item I passed out outlines of the news as we listened to the tape. For the first few sessions with the recorded radio broadcasts the outlines noted the sequence of items and listed key words to center their listening on important facts. I stopped the tape several times during the ten-minute program to make sure that everyone was following the outline and understanding major points. Comprehension questions each time we stopped allowed students to fill in details that were not included in my outline. The outline also included commercials, which were the most difficult for the students to understand. After we had listened to and discussed each item, we listened to the tape again without stopping.

The first outlines were rather complete. Later, the outlines were in the form of basic topics with guiding questions which asked students to listen for who, what, when, where, and why. In this way, even while there were new idioms to be discussed, the first listening focused on the informative facts. Questions on commercials asked for the names of the product and the sponsor and the function of the product. Students complete these outlines by filling in short answers to the "wh" questions. In the final exercises with the recorded broadcasts, students wrote their own outlines and then referred to them in our discussion. The earlier practice in listening for who, what, when, where, and why shaped their outlines while allowing them to fill in details as they could. After the first listening with the

students taking their own notes we reviewed together what they had gleaned before listening again for more details. The use of outlines was central to the listening comprehension exercises while giving the bonus of familiarity with outline form and practice in quick note-taking.

The radio broadcasts were particularly valuable in providing meaningful material for subjects other than listening comprehension. The vocabulary lessons which grew from these exercises gave students new idioms, acronyms, and recently coined words. "The dark horse candidate" who "threw his hat in the ring" produced puzzled looks throughout the room and presented new idioms to even the most advanced student in the class. The news was also filled with newly coined phrases such as "teach-in" and introduced the manner in which the not-too-old "sit-in" had spawned a fresh variety of noun. Acronyms such as P.T.A. which are part of plain English to any native speaker were eagerly noted. The radio programs were a great way to pump contemporary American life into classroom lessons.

The commercials provided not only the most unusual vocabulary additions, but also many cultural comments. Everything from traveler's checks to pet vitamins were advertised in our sessions giving students a diverse look at product promotion. Students reported that the ads were the most difficult to understand, but provided the most useful information since knowing the brand name of a product made shopping more convenient. A greater understanding of national current events also helped ease the students into the American cultural setting. While most of our time was spent on news and weather, we also listened to editorials, book reviews, movie critiques, and feature stories. The editorials often tied in with the news providing ready examples of linguistic differences between reporting facts and expressing opinions. Book and movie reviews were also fine examples of expressing opinions, enthusiasm, and polite rejection. Feature stories expanded on topics of general human interest—often reflecting a current trend in social styles, medicine, or business. Jogging was one of the features which launched a group discussion of a recent American mania. The features usually include a few moments of taped interview which add another register to the typical radio narration.

Near the end of the course one of the students asked if I were playing the radio broadcasts at a slower speed. She couldn't believe how much she was able to understand. All students commented that the news exercises were the most useful and helpful part of the class. On the last day of the intensive program students presented skits. The group that had had this radio listening practice surprised me by producing a fifteen-minute comic news radio program complete with weather, traffic reports, interviews, and a toilet paper commercial!

I found the radio news to be a great resource for listening comprehension practice, for cultural interchanges, and for vocabulary additions for advanced students. The students were delighted with the ease with which they came to understand radio broadcasts and with the opportunity this developed skill gave them to understand more of American culture and issues. They also became adept at listening for important facts and taking notes in outline form. Whats' more, we all enjoyed it!

TN 2/79

USING NEWS BROADCASTS

Edited by Cathy Day
Eastern Michigan University

An "It Works" suggestion for vocabulary acquisition for advanced ESL learners used by Wilhelmina Juhlin, in ESL classes at Parsippany-Troy Hills School District, New Jersey, combines the use of news broadcasts and the cloze procedure. She suggests taping one complete news item from one of the all-news broadcasting stations. Ten to 15 minutes of news might have to be taped in order to obtain one item (250-300 words long) that is appropriate or appealing to your students. Newscasts are filled with relevant vocabulary and many idioms. They also provide a common base in current events and/or controversial issues for follow-up in a lively class discussion. The use of high quality tape equipment is recommended as newscasters speak rapidly and distortion of sound can complicate the learner's task. Once students get used to news broadcasts they may feel that the newscasters have slowed down.

After choosing the news item, transcribe it completely. This won't take as much time as one might think, as it should not be more than one page of double-spaced text. Point out unfamiliar vocabulary to your students. Make a second transcription with these words deleted (but do not delete less than every fifth word). A total of 20-25 words will provide more than enough material to challenge the student.

In the classroom, introduce the subject of the news item briefly. Then proceed as follows:

1. Present the unfamiliar vocabulary to the class. Discuss the words and put them on the board. At a future time, when students are familiar with the technique, this step can be eliminated, allowing students to discover word meanings on their own.

2. Listen to the tape.
3. Ask the students three to four basic questions to determine comprehension.
4. Listen to the tape again.
5. Ask the same three to four questions to clarify what the students have heard.
6. Hand out the completed transcription and listen to the tape again with the students reading along. At this point further discussion can be held about the news item itself and questions about the new vocabulary items can be answered.
7. Next, hand out the cloze transcription for the students to complete *without* the tape. The first transcription, of course, should be temporarily tucked away.
8. Listen to the tape for a final time while students self-correct. If they have used synonyms instead of the actual word, so much the better but it is important to discuss the reason why.

Any number of follow-up activities can be done using the new vocabulary items: they can be used as spelling words, for use in writing sentences, creating crossword puzzles, finding synonyms/antonyms, etc. For additional variations of the cloze transcription, try one with all the prepositions deleted or all the articles deleted.

This variation of the cloze procedure has been most successful in Ms. Juhlin's advanced ESL classes. She reports: "It provides a nice change of pace for the students and keeps their level of interest high as they view it as kind of a puzzle. It is a valuable tool for increasing their adeptness at using context clues and is a great way to improve listening comprehension. More importantly, it provides the students with the kind of vocabulary they will encounter out in the real world." *TN 12/83*

the country. A synopsis of the soap opera for a day was posted 2–3 days before. It listed the characters to appear and the general line of the story.

In addition to the soap opera itself, there were also an opening 5-minute news report, a 1-minute weather report, and advertisements. Particular students were assigned beforehand and it was up to them to prepare their own material.

The ½ hour presentation was divided as follows: 5-minute News, 1-minute Weather, 1-minute Advertisement, 10-minute Soap Opera (part 1), 1-minute Advertisement, 1-minute Advertisement, 10-minute Soap Opera (part 2)."

Mary's comments on the strengths of this lesson include the fact that the topics chosen can be current issues such as parent-child relations, the generation-gap, abortion, women's rights, drugs, etc. News articles concerning the topics were cut out and posted on a bulletin board for students to consult.

Just exactly what would be announced, reported and advertised was not plotted out and memorized in advance, just as the characters in the "Soap Opera" did not put their lines into a script before the presentation. As a result, students had to listen carefully to each other in order to determine what was being said and to respond in an appropriate manner.

Salvatore J. Sinatra has written to share a few ideas for use with groups. The first one he mentions is Robert Gibson's *Strip Story*, (TESOL-Q, Vol. 9, No. 2, June, 1975), probably the most *practical* article found in the *Quarterly* in the last several issues.

Additional contributions from Sinatra include an adaptation he has made from an original idea called *Murder Mystery*, devised by David and Frank Johnson, and found in a group dynamics text: *Joining Together*, Prentice-Hall, 1975, pp 121-122. Adapted for ESOL, Sinatra's challenge to each discussion group is to answer the questions:

Who was the killer?
Which weapon did he use?
What time did the murder occur?
Where was the victim killed?
Why was he killed?

Clues needed to solve the murder are prepared in advance by the teacher. Each clue is written on a separate card and distributed randomly to group members. The process involves assembly of all information, evaluation, and discussion so that the solution can be reached.

This adaptation includes the ingredient which is surely the key to the success of Gibson's *Strip Story* as well. That is, each member of the group is the sole possessor of one

SOAP OPERA, MURDER MYSTERY, OR HOME TOWN LORE

by Darlene Larson
New York University

The *TESOL NEWSLETTER* is happy to have received contributions from members for our second column of practical lesson ideas. Several having to do with oral group work are outlined below.

Mary E. Sarawit of the Srinakharinwirot University in Pitsanulok, Thailand, writes of the success she and her colleagues have had with a lesson she calls "Soap Opera." She writes:

"To begin with, each of the three teachers chose a theme for their class and assigned 18 characters. For example, one class's theme was about life in a city hospital. Another was a family situation complicated by having five daughters, and the third about life in

small piece of information which, in turn, is absolutely necessary to the completion of the task of putting the pieces together.

I'd like to encourage all of us to carry this successful technique into the students' wealth of experience and knowledge. All of our students arrive in the classroom as the sole possessors of lots of facts. We have the challenge of designing group tasks which will elicit from individuals the information that each one brings.

In university and adult classes, the students often come from a variety of home towns. Home towns usually contain town halls, town squares, historic places of interest. Groups might be given the task of preparing a report on town squares, municipal buildings and/or tourist attractions in the combined home towns of the members of the group. Each member would be responsible for providing the information about his home town. The report could be given orally on an assigned day, later written for display on a bulletin board. A list of guiding questions might get the group started . . . to be answered if pertinent, skipped if not. It might include questions on the size and location of the places, their history or origin, their present use and/or condition. More advanced groups might be assigned the task without any guiding questions to get them started.

One has to remember that in real life, every individual in every group does not arrive with a fact of his own which parallels the comparable facts of every other individual. Language texts have long contained bland paragraphs of information, or pages of pictures, which, when given a second look, fit perfectly clean, parallel language matrices of the sort that strike joy into the hearts of applied linguists. Rarely does the information possessed by a real, live class contain such symmetry. Go ahead and use it anyway. Venture into the real information of the students' experience. Express comparable facts with structural similarity if that's what they need. Teach them how to use *except for, however, on the other hand,* for those facts which differ. Some individuals might bring such differing listening backgrounds that their information wouldn't fit into the report. Perhaps such persons could play the role of group recorder and organizer of the written report, master of ceremonies of the oral report.

In other situations, individuals may become possessors of important bits of information as part of the task. One might ask a group to draw a floor plan of the first floor of the school library. The first step would be to send them off in pairs with measuring tapes and note pads, each pair to obtain the necessary data of a particular area of the floor.

Design a group task. Try it with your class. Write and tell us how it worked.

Other group activities have been outlined in "Practicum," in the MAT-SOL Newsletter, Vol. 4, No. 1, and in "Lessons that Work," in the IDIOM of NYS ESOL BEA, Vol. 6, No. 1.

TN 4/76

OVERCOMING THE FEAR OF A FOREIGN LANGUAGE PHONE CONVERSATION

by Donald Montalto
International Institute of Boston

One of the most difficult situations to master in a foreign language is a telephone conversation. There are no hand signals or gestures to help in understanding a strange word or phrase. The person at the other end of the line can't see the blank expression on the student's face and doesn't always realize that not much is being understood. The quality of the sound is often such that the student only hears the accented syllables and the general intonation, leaving even an advanced learner of the language hopelessly lost. Most students will admit that they have been afraid to answer their own phones because they didn't think they would be able to understand anything. Such fears are even expressed by fairly fluent students.

A common technique used in foreign language teaching to help students overcome their fear of phone conversations is to have them work in pairs, each student with his back to his partner. Since the students are sitting back-to-back, they cannot pick up any hand signals or facial gestures. Back-to-back pairing is a good step towards helping students function well in a foreign language phone conversation. But like many teaching techniques, it lacks reality.

One excellent method for practicing real phone calls in the classroom is to attach a speaker to a phone so that everyone in the room can hear both sides of the conversation. Such speakers are readily available at low cost (Radio Shack #43-231, $9.95) and can be easily attached and detached to a phone receiver by means of a suction-cup microphone. The phone conversation should also be recorded for follow-up exercises. The important advantage of such a set-up is that there is a real live native speaker at the other end of the line and not another student. This advantage is well worth the trouble of arranging to have the class meet in a room with a phone.

A good way to make both the teacher and the students familiar with the set-up is first to call recorded announcements such as time/temperature, weather reports, movie theaters, and road reports. Large cities often have hundreds of listed phone recordings ranging from "Dial-a-Joke" (New York 976-3838) to "The Why and How of Flossing Your Teeth" (Bufflao 855-3555, tape 301). As a follow-up exercise, the teacher might then ask straight-forward listening comprehension questions. For example, after calling a movie theater recording, the teacher might ask, "What is the name of the movie playing next week? . . . What's playing at the _____ Theater today? What time does the movie begin?"

Additional follow-up exercises can be done using the tape made in class of the phone recording. For example, dialing the weather forecast might yield something like the following in rapid blurred speech: "The Boston area forecast calls for sunny skies today and tomorrow with a 10% chance of rain through Tuesday night." Having recorded the forecast in class, the teacher can then replay the first phrase and ask the students to repeat what they have just heard. It will be difficult to do, but as each student contributes his or her knowledge, the group will eventually be able to recreate most of the recorded weather report. Even in advanced classes, there will usually be a word or phrase which no one in the class can decipher despite several repetitions of the tape. The teacher can then explain the word or phrase. Once everyone in the class understands the sentence, the teacher can have the students write it in the form of a dictation exercise. Such follow-up exercises help the students develop their ability to guess the meaning of distorted and difficult sentences. Students can be trained to understand most of a phone conversation even if only half of the individual words and phrases are decipherable, the rest being sheer guesswork.

After the students feel comfortable with the amplification and recording devices, they can try a real conversation. A safe phone call for a beginner might be to ask how late a store stays open. (Cultural note: Many foreign students come from countries where business hours are strictly regulated by law. If these students are recent arrivals, they may not be aware of the fact that not all American businesses open and close simultaneously and they may think such a phone inquiry is ridiculous.) Another non-anxiety-producing call is to the post office to find out about the postage on a letter to a foreign country. Students will be very reluctant at first to come forward and carry on a phone conversation for fear they will make fools of themselves in front of their classmates. It is therefore a good idea to begin with the most aggressive member of the class.

Intermediate and advanced students can practice more involved types of phone calls where the conversation might take on any imaginable direction, such as calling an airline, bus terminal, or AMTRAK for fares and scheduling information. Calls about jobs, apartments, or used cars advertised in the paper can be made, as well as calls to banks to inquire about a loan or checking account. If one of the students in the class needs to make an appointment, he or she might be invited to do so by phone in front of his classmates. In short, any kind of call which has to be made as a part of everyday life can be practiced in an ESL class.

With many types of calls, it is impossible to prepare students for all of the unfamiliar words and phrases which they might encounter. They should be ready with a phrase like, "I'm sorry. I don't understand you. Can you speak more slowly?" Upon hearing this phrase, most people at the other end of the line will begin to speak even more slowly than most ESL teachers do. The vocabulary and syntax often remain, however, just as baffling to the student, so that it may become necessary for the teacher to intervene. For example, a student calling about an ad for an apartment heard the following at lightning speed: "The brokers are all tied up at the moment. Can I put you on hold?" She asked to have the mumbled blur repeated, but she still couldn't understand "broken", "tied up", and "put on hold", all new vocabulary to her. At this point it became necessary for the teacher to bail her out and write on the board, "Can you wait?" Her face lit up and she replied, "No, that's O.K. I'll call later." After she hung up, her classmates applauded and cheered, as often happens after the tension of a foreign language phone call. The aforementioned follow-up exercises were then done, based on the tape recording of the conversation.

Live phone conversations practiced in class are a useful way to break up the potential monotony of a language class. Such conversations help the students learn the vocabulary necessary for survival in the new country by bringing the real world into the classroom.

TN 12/81

WHERE DO I PUT IT?

Mary Ann Christison
Snow College
Sharron Bassano
Santa Cruz Adult School

Understanding directions and space relationships are often exceedingly difficult parts of language learning. The meaning of many phrases is relative, not absolute, making aural comprehension difficult. In addition, instant understanding is essential, placing even more demands on the second language learner. If students are going to succeed in meeting these demands, they need practice in developing these skills. The challenge is in finding ways to provide sufficient communicative practice in the language classroom.

Most workbooks for improving listening comprehension provide numerous activities for students to practice following directions in response to teacher directed dictation exercises. They do not, however, suggest ways in which these activities may be adapted for students to direct the activities and interact with each other. What follows is a description of a method which makes this possible. It requires very little preparation for the teacher and can be used in understanding directions and in practicing space relationships and selected vocabulary items. It provides students with opportunities to use the language both receptively and productively.

Procedure

Divide students into pairs and seat them back-to-back. Give all the students a piece of paper and have them fold it into nine squares which open out to form a gameboard. Then give both of the partners an identical set of nine picture cards similar to the ones below.

Tell the students they must place the pictures on the gameboards in exactly the same positions, but they must not look at each other's boards or pieces. Have one student be the speaker, the other, the listener. The speaker describes the pictures, tells the listener where to place them, and places his or her own in the same spot. When all the pieces are in place, students compare, discuss, and then switch roles. Changing partners is a good idea before trying the activity again.

This lesson gives practice with the idea of horizontal rows (the top, the second from the top, etc.), vertical columns (the far left, the second from the left, etc.), and flat positions (upper left, lower right, etc.). Students could fold their papers to practice vertical columns and horizontal rows first before putting both concepts together for the flat positions.

Other variations are also possible. Have the students fold their papers into fifteen squares. This provides practice in using a different method to describe the flat positions. With the nine-square gameboard, each square has a specific name, i.e., lower right, middle right, upper right, etc. For the fifteen-square gameboard, instructions must be given in rows and columns. For example, fifteen squares with three rows and five columns might require this direction: the top row, the far left column. Fifteen squares with five rows and three columns might require this direction: the second row from the top, middle column.

Pictures are fun to begin with, but other items can be used. It is a great way to learn the names of punctuation marks, mathematical signs, shapes and numbers (Morley 1972). Simply write the symbols on a piece of paper (?, +, #, %, *, etc.) and give an identical set to each pair, or, write fifteen symbols or shapes randomly on a paper and give it to the speaker. Have the speaker tell where to place them and then mark them on his/her own gameboard for reference. This requires virtually no preparation for the teacher.

It is a good idea to use known items like basic colors when students are just beginning to work with the flat positions, horizontal rows, and vertical columns. As soon as they become more proficient in placing the items, introduce more challenging vocabulary and concepts.

This technique has been used over and over with great success. The back-to-back method encourages the students to have fun and enjoy their language learning experience. The classroom is also full of language and very little of it is generated by the teacher. In addition, most activities can be done with approximately five minutes of teacher preparation time. That should make any teacher smile!

Editor's Note: When TESOL specialists first rejected the mechanical emphasis of the audio-lingual method it was because they were concerned about their students developing communicative competence. The now popular term hadn't been heard often, but sensitive teachers knew that only the extremely efficient language learner could bridge the gap between classroom drills and real conversation, and they began devising classroom exercises which called for less teacher direction and more student initiative.

Many of us continue searching for task oriented classroom activities in which students interact with each other. Mistakes make a difference in the same way they make a difference in life. They hinder one from reaching a goal or completing a task,

as opposed to mistakes which say, "You missed two out of five." IT WORKS is happy to print this suggestion from Christison and Bassano. Despite the references to listening comprehension, the technique is just what is needed to develop both comprehension and production skills, ultimately leading to that elusive goal: communicative competence.

Teachers interested in such exercises will recall Richard Yorkey's "Paired Practice" suggestions found in this column in Volume XV, No. 6, December, 1981. Less recently

published but still available are Judy E. Winn-Bell Olsen's "Communication Starters" in ON TESOL '75, pp. 229-239, edited by Burt and Dulay. And an old favorite by Linda Kunz and Bob Viscount has recently been reprinted in NYS ESOL BEA's new volume, IDIOMATICALLY SPEAKING, pp. 63-67, edited by McConochie, Block-Brookes and Gonzales. **Darlene Larson**

Morley, Joan. *Improving Aural Comprehension.* Ann Arbor, Michigan: The University of Michigan Press, 1972.

TN 4/82

TIME OUT FOR CLASSROOM IDEAS AT TESOL '77

Edited by Darlene Larson
New York University

Between 3:00 and 4:30 p.m. on Thursday of convention week, after a long day of presentations, speeches, committee meetings, exhibits and panels, eleven panel members and over seventy-five convention-goers yielded not to the lure of the sun and sand and met to share ideas from the classroom. At Joan Morley's invitation, the first IT WORKS panel chalked off "more solid classroom suggestions in those 90 minutes" than some convention participants were able to collect in three days, according to some convention participants! Suggestions from three panelists are summarized below.

Penelope M. Alatis
Francis C. Hammond High School

Four topics covered by Ms. Alatis were puzzles, use of overhead projectors, using students' names, and magazine pictures. She feels that the overhead projector is an attention-getter. When the lights go out, students muster up a new effort to pay attention. Teacher-made transparencies enable her to create new material or use reproductions of newspapers and other sources. She can direct students' attention to specific points all at one time, and finds that the transparencies can be kept for another class, thus giving this spontaneous method some permanence. Turning on the overhead also eliminates excessive use of the blackboard and the need to write on the board during class.

Both crossword puzzles and "seek and find" puzzles are valuable activities for students who can work on them independently or in groups or with partners.

Substituting students' names in exercises, puzzles, tests, worksheets is a habit that adds humor and interest to many lessons. One result is a few chuckles. Another is that the practice becomes contagious, and students write or talk about themselves and their classmates quite readily.

Ms. Alatis's final recommendation had to do with the use of magazine

pictures. She brings many of her personal magazines to class and lets students select a picture they want to use for a lesson. Tasks assigned vary among the following: giving a title to a picture, making statements about a picture, asking questions about a picture, giving their opinions about the subjects in the picture, writing a dialog for the subjects in the picture, and many more.

All of these can be done individually or in groups or pairs. Many of these magazines which are common in the United States are unfamiliar to our students. Thus, the lesson is novel, interesting and pleasant for the students. Ms. Alatis has found these half-free, half-structured lessons most useful in moving students from controlled use of the language to free. She recommends that the teacher review each students' magazine work on a one-to-one basis to help him or her find alternatives to his first try.

Joyce Gilmour Zuck
English Language Institute
University of Michigan

An underlying concept for the remarks about reading which were given by Ms. Zuck might be stated as follows: People read because they want access to information that is *not* shared by all of their associates. When teachers ask students to read, and they ask all of the students to read the same thing, there really isn't much reason for everybody to hurry and read it. After doing so, there isn't much to talk about except, "What is the meaning of this word or that sentence?" We don't really have anything to ask anyone else who has just read the same thing we have just read. With this in mind, Ms. Zuck recommends the following.

Students at different proficiency levels in English can read a number of different articles at varying levels of difficulty if they're all on the same topic. Begin by thinking of a fairly broad topic, like "jobs" or "school" and start collecting articles on that

topic. Some may be written especially for second language students, and some may be from newspapers, journals, and magazines. Collect the articles in a folder. When it is time to work on that topic, let students select articles from your folder that they want to read.

According to Ms. Zuck, someone's easy article is the article about which he knows something. Students are the best judges. If you have a fat folder of articles that approach the broad topic from many different points of view, many different levels, you'll have something for everyone. (If you don't feel comfortable with that, try Haskell's recommendation to judge the difficulty of a reading selection by making a short cloze exercise taken from the selection and letting the student try to complete it. Then distribute articles on the basis of the students' abilities to perform the cloze selections for the articles.)

The exciting part of this technique is in getting a group of people together *of any age* who have some basic, sure knowledge about the topic because they have just read something about it, yet have genuine questions for their classmates about what they've read on the same topic. In other words, each student arrives with something to offer and something to ask.

A variation on the theme of not having everybody read the same thing is not having everybody read. The *National Geographic World* includes large posters which appeal to younger learners. Ms. Zuck assigns one or two children to read the article from *National Geographic World* which accompanies the poster. Their job is then to stand in the front of the room and answer the questions that the other children ask about the poster. Very quickly, they have to learn how to respond when they don't have the information sought. In that very real speech-act situation, discourse is started right away and you have a natural setting for the exchange of information. Other students have been motivated by the very large and stimulating poster and their information-seeking is relevant to their interests.

This concept applies to listening, as well. Ms. Zuck discusses these awkward times when students may give speeches but their classmates don't listen. The classmates need a reason to listen. She recommends that the speaker write a test to give his classmates about his speech. His speech will be graded on the basis of his classmates scores on his test.

A teacher in the audience offered his technique for getting listeners involved in what their classmates are saying. In a university class, this teacher asks students to take notes while their classmates are talking. The following day, the teacher gives a quiz on the previous day's talk. The students may refer to their notes while trying to answer the quiz.

Palmer Acheson
TESL Centre
Concordia University

Acheson shared more ideas for using magazine pictures, even small ones, crediting Don Byrne for some of his inspiration. At the very early stages when many texts recommend the learning of occupations and professions vocabulary in order to practice "to be", teachers can ask their students to find pictures of working people and bring them to class. Put the pictures on a card and let the students keep the pictures with them. When it is his or her turn, the student will answer questions about his or her picture. Classmates will ask after being given a minimal amount of information to get started. Acheson got the audience started with, "I have a picture of a man. He's standing outside." Audience: Is he in a uniform? Is he holding equipment? Is he holding anything? Is he in a business suit? The student holding the picture can see it and answers appropriately. (The small picture follows Zuck's theme. Since the other students can't see the picture, they really do have a reason to ask questions about it.)

The same routine can be followed with pictures of people from many countries of the world, this time practicing the vocabulary of nationalities. Starter from Acheson: I have a picture of a man. You are to try to discover his nationality. Audience: Is his hair black? PA: No, it's gray. Audience: Is he wearing Western clothing? PA: No, he's not. It's Western clothing, but it isn't typical Western clothing. Audience: Is he from Europe? PA: Yes, he is. Audience: Is he Irish? PA: No, he's not. Audience: Is he Scottish? PA: Yes, he is, and disclosed a man in a kilt, etc.

A large piece of tag board had a picture on one side, introduced as a secretary who has just had a big raise from her boss and is going to buy a number of things. What do you think she's going to buy? As the students ask questions about the things she's going to buy, the one holding the picture has no trouble answering because the reverse side of the tag board was covered with pictures of objects that the secretary would buy. A ring, a radio, etc. Changing the introduction to the fact that she's bought some of the things already changes the question to, "Has she bought a . . .?" instead of "Is she going to buy a . . .?"

My thanks to all of the teachers who were willing to participate in the panel as well as to share their ideas on the pages of the *Newsletter*. Let's hear ideas from you, our readers, and also hear from those of you who'd like to participate in the panel at TESOL '78.   *TN 9/77*

TESOL '77 (IT WORKS)

Edited by **Darlene Larson**
New York University

It is a pleasure to share two more teaching strategies with readers which were discussed by IT WORKS panel members at TESOL '77, plus a related idea or two from my own teaching.

John Dumicich
LaGuardia Community College
New York City

John Dumicich of LaGuardia Community College in New York City asked the audience to participate as students. He showed them a picture and asked them to give words that came to their minds when they looked at the picture. Dumicich wrote them on a blackboard as the audience gave them. After a good list, his second instruction was, "Now make sentences using at least three of these words." He accepted whatever sentences the participants gave him, simple and complex, pointing out that the sentences gathered were examples of sentences at the level of the students'

language development.

A third direction was for the audience to write five sentences of those that had been given or of additional ones. When they were read, they were read in a logical order.

One point that Dumicich emphasized was that we had begun with nonsense, yet had ended with the essential elements of composition. Words had been put into sentences and those sentences had been arranged in order. We had made sense out of the random calling out of words with which we started.

Mary E. Hines
LaGuardia Community College
New York City

A few speakers later, Mary Hines, also from LaGuardia Community College, referred to psychological vs. logical order. By encouraging what she calls a layman's version of free association, Hines throws out a word or name like, "New York City." Students are encouraged to mention the first thing that comes to their minds and to continue adding whatever thoughts they have about the original word or about other thoughts that are mentioned.

First, Hines is convinced that allowing all ideas to come forth and be recognized is an essential step toward getting complex ideas formed later. She believes that if one rejects words or bits of ideas when setting out to write, the more complex notions will never get expressed clearly.

Second, she feels that this strategy emphasizes the role of transitional expressions. When students look at lists of statements side by side like: New York is dangerous, New York is wonderful, it is clear that one cannot leave those two in parallel constructions without an explanation. A fairly early awareness develops as to the fact that one *can* say, "Although New York is _____, it is a _____ place to live." She also reminds the students that readers of writing are not readers of minds. One cannot assume that the reader is going to make the same associations as the writer. And it is through the use of transitional expressions that writers can express just how they relate all of the bits and pieces to the major topic.

Finally, Hines mentions that for students who feel they have nothing to say, this exercise reveals to them that, in fact, there are quite a few things on their minds and in their minds. She urges students to get these notions out in any order. After an array of bits of information is in front of students, they can then apply an examination process to find out what might be their thesis, which ideas would support it, and which could be examples.

Related Strategies

These lesson strategies are related to some I used with a group of intermediate students. Although their hour with me had an oral focus, I knew that a great deal of the rest of their program emphasized writing. With organization on my mind as a key to writing, I decided to find some oral tasks that were essentially organizing tasks.

On one day, I gave groups of four or five students files full of pictures that I use in other classes. I told them that the files were all mixed up, that I didn't care how they were organized, but I much wanted some kind of organization established. Several students set about first in taking inventory of what they had. In some groups, however, certain members started organizing as the inventory was just getting under way. That made other members in some groups quite happy and the group made a category decision about each picture as they came to it. As some became more thoroughly acquainted with the contents of the picture file, they went back and revised the category piles that they had started. It reminded me of the theories of setting expectations when one begins reading, then reading on to find out if everything one meets fits with one's earlier expectations. Other groups had some strong leaders who insisted on taking a survey of everything before they made any organizing moves.

On another occasion, I put seemingly unrelated pictures into an envelope—use 6 or 7 pictures of sun, snow, outside, inside, people, scenery . . .—and gave an envelope to groups of three. Their task was to make a story that involved all of the pictures in some way. They did not have to involve all pictures equally, but something had to be used from each one.

Not only did I enjoy the enthusiasm students showed while participating in the tasks, but the results were entertaining and thorough. The categorizing task resulted for one group in a major division, indoors and out, with subdivisions in each. Indoors was divided into kinds of interiors: office, school, home, and business, while outdoors had climate or weather divisions. Things for the home were divided further into different rooms of the house. The stories in the other lesson showed entertaining imaginations. Some combined the contrasting settings in a story about a family who lived in a cold climate but took a winter vacation in the tropics. Later in the year, I recommended this to another teacher who added, as homework, that the students write the story that their group created visually and orally in class. She was pleased with the following day's written work.

Wading

It occurs to me that none of us, neither Dumicich nor Hines nor I were prescribing anything to the students about the order that they had to make. Students don't need to be instructed that "wonderful" and "dangerous" don't fit together. In a sense, we were wading into the water with the students. Once human beings are immersed in what appears to be a chaotic hodge-podge of unrelated bits of information, relationships, or possible avenues of organization seem to come forth without much effort. Some begin to organize or categorize before they are ankle deep. Once in the water, students don't need teachers to tell them which water is deeper, which is colder, which has a stronger current. Perhaps it is only when one keeps the students on a bluff above the stream that one needs to instruct further about what the water is like.

TN 11/77

ONE LUMP OR TWO?

Edited by Darlene Larson
New York University

With our current awareness of how alienating the teacher/student, knower/learner roles can be, our realization that the classroom is an "unreal reality," and our ever-present goal of overcoming these major drawbacks to effective language learning, I'd like to begin this first classroom ideas column in the TESOL NEWSLETTER by encouraging teachers of adults to include refreshments in class from time to time. They may be as elaborate as Wilga Rivers Punch or Virginia Allen Dip, or they may be as simple as apple cider and Ritz crackers. They can be planned in advance or can appear unannounced. Students can be involved in planning a spread that covers all nations (and all of the table space in the room), or the event can be completely teacher-planned and initiated. Another class can be invited, or the fun can be confined to the usual group of students.

In other words, there's no formula as to just how it's supposed to work. The point is that if you're after student-initiated conversation, students involved in real communication, language practice in real situations, and student-directed lesson segments, including refreshments in adult classes every so often enables me to reach these goals.

An old favorite lesson of mine includes a recipe for Banana Nut Bread, the loaf pan, a measuring cup and spoons, and a sifter. I used to try to coordinate baking the bread at home, teaching the lesson in class and serving the bread after the lesson. But such coordination really isn't necessary. The bread can arrive in class by surprise a few weeks after the lesson. Students recall the ingredients and the directions for baking and talk about them naturally while they are tasting. Pronouncing measurements like "three-fourths of a cup" and "one-and-a-half teaspoons" is always difficult at first. A few weeks after the lesson students recall the parts that were difficult for them (sometimes different parts than I would select) and initiate attempts to try again.

Another student-initiated follow-up is when they begin to share recipes of their favorite dishes with one another. It's a short step from the lessons described above—and almost always takes place. They have the format of ingredients plus directions and that is enough to get them off to a usually successful attempt.

But it's not only recipes that we talk about when refreshments are served. A certain atmosphere develops that I relate to a party mood. We've often spent a good bit of time talking about what people do at parties. I make a careful effort not to ask adults to play games that they don't want to play. I'm just asking them to *talk about* party games . . . But as a rule, before much time goes by, they want to demonstrate as they talk. And that's just one step removed from playing the game—which, of course, is not at all ruled out if it's student-initiated.

If this kind of classroom discussion takes place a few times, it's quite easy to suggest that we plan a real party and invite the students and teacher from the next class. At an actual, planned event, we do, of course, ask people to participate in games and activities. Certain students are responsible for organizing the group to do something that they suggested a couple weeks earlier.

And once the "class next door" has been invited, we have host/guest roles (which can be extremely alienating in the real world but seem to bridge personality gaps in the classroom world.) It rarely fails that some adult who plays the student role with shyness and hesitancy can be found distributing paper cups and napkins before I had intended to serve refreshments! (The mind boggles at the thought of turning sociolinguists and cultural anthropologists loose at explaining this phenomenon. I have a few theories, but I'd prefer simply to share the idea and let someone else explain it.) Of course, if it's a first time, only time event, none of my guarantees hold. But if the group has participated in classes with refreshments now and then, I predict great success when adding "guests," too.

One final suggestion is to get the teacher next door involved, too. A colleague of mine at NYU prepared her students with all of the comments that fall off the tongues of guests when they enter New York apartments . . . "What a lovely place! Did you find it through an agent?" And the hosts were quite full of things like: "Oh, yes, I can never find anything by myself. Do you want his address?"

We also add the cultural information that New Yorkers always comment on how lovely the place is—even if it's as drab as an NYU classroom—and polite hostesses never let guests leave without protesting that they remain "just a little longer."

We used "Hello Dolly" as background music for a demonstration of Musical Chairs. Words were distributed for the asking, which they did, so we did. Lo and behold, there're things like, "It's so nice to have you back," and "You're lookin' swell," which students noted and used at a subsequent class with me when I entered the room.

When the time was up, we had to vacate the room in order that another class could come in. I consider it a measure of the effectiveness of the lesson that I found myself horribly uncomfortable with stepping back into my teacher role to announce that the time was up when one of my hostesses said, "Oh, please have another glass of punch. Call your husband and tell him you'll be a little late."

TN 4/76

SHUFFLED COMICS

by Richard Yorkey
St. Michael's College

Many teachers have used strip stories[1] to practice communication among students by means of a problem-solving approach that requires what Rivers calls "autonomous interaction."[2] An extension of this technique is comic strip stories, or what I call Shuffled Comics. The activity is a kind of visual version of a strip story, but rather than memorize sentences in order to reconstruct a story, students must describe a scene and report the dialog.

Not all comics are equally useful for this activity. So far I have found that the comic strip of *Blondie* is the most consistently useful, primarily because it deals with everyday domestic situations that relate to English-speaking customs and culture. (This comic strip is also fun for some students because it is already familiar to them as Dagbert in French or Lorenzo and Pepita in Spanish.) Occasionally *The Wizard of Id*, *B.C.*, or *Peanuts* can be used, but each of them has its own kind of humor and cultural references that may need to be explained.

The preparation for Shuffled Comics is easy. Simply cut out each panel of the comic strip and paste it on a 3x5-inch card. I have found that fewer than six or seven panels do not present enough challenge to make the interaction either interesting or helpful. And more than a dozen panels make the activity unwieldly and too much of a clerical task.

The following twelve (randomly arranged) panels from *Blondie* are an effective example of the technique. After cutting and pasting, I shuffle the cards and distribute one to each student. (If you are fortunate to have fewer than twelve, some students can have two cards. If you have many more than twelve, perhaps two groups can practice communication with Shuffled Comics simultaneously.)

Each student is asked to tell what the characters are doing and saying. A lot of present continuous tense is usually elicited (for example, *Dagwood and Blondie are standing outside their house*), occasionally other tenses (*Dagwood has just closed the door*), and frequent, natural use of the present tense with reported speech (*Blondie asks Dagwood if he has his wallet*, or *Dagwood tells her that he has it in his pocket*.)

This particular comic strip happens to have many examples of Yes-No questions: *Do you have your wallet? Did you remember. . . ? Are you sure you didn't forget anything?* Students in my class were fascinated by the different ways in which the affirmative reply can be spoken: *Yes, Sure did, Positive, Of course*—or even what is especially common in Vermont, *Yep*.

Because students cannot see each other's part of the comic strip, they must rely solely on their accuracy of verbal communication and comprehension in order to reassemble the pictures into their original order. After my students discussed possible sequences and their reasons, and then finally agreed on an appropriate order, they gathered around the desk and physically placed each picture in its proper place. As a conclusion, several couples read the parts of Dagwood and Blondie as a kind of dialog. (With an especially good class, a narrator can be assigned to describe each scene before the dialog is spoken.) The dialog reviewed and reinforced the question patterns. Students also, incidentally, enjoyed referring to each other as *honey* or *dear*! One student also experimented with different intonations to indicate the increasing irritation of Dagwood—and then a humiliated tone when he discovers he has forgotten the tickets.

At the end of this activity, two other points came up. One girl asked about the appropriateness of the prepositional phrase at the end of the punch line (*That's what I left the ticket on top of*). Some previous teacher had probably taught her never to end a sentence with

Copyright 1979 King Features, Syndicate, Inc.

a preposition, and her question led to a valuable discussion about grammar rules, styles, and the distinction between speaking and writing. I myself drew attention to one aspect of the humor which non-native-speakers of English could not be expected to appreciate. The idiom, *everything but the kitchen sink*, was unfamiliar to everyone in class, but they were amused to learn the expression and volunteered various translations in their language. Students were also pleasantly surprised to discover that the idiom is included in the *Longman Dictionary of Contemporary English*. (It is not listed in *Oxford Advanced Learner's Dictionary of Current English* or in any of the standard American desk dictionaries.)

This kind of activity is quick and easy to prepare and not too time-consuming in class. Most of all, it is a pleasant, purposeful way to practice recognition of visual and grammatical sequence signals and to reinforce oral communication and aural comprehension. *TN 10/81*

NOTES

[1] Robert E. Gibson, "The Strip Story: A Catalyst for Communication," *TESOL Quarterly*, IX.2 (June 1975), 149-154.

[2] Wilga M. Rivers and Mary S. Temperley, *A Practical Guide to the Teaching of English as a Second or Foreign Language* (New York: Oxford University Press, 1978), 47-61.

PAIRED PRACTICE

by Richard Yorkey
St. Michael's College

One enjoyable way to get intermediate ESL students to interact with each other is to challenge them with art! There are two interaction activities of this kind that I have found particularly useful.

Picture That!

Materials for this kind of oral language practice are very simple to prepare and easy to retrieve from your files whenever there is time for this "structured interaction."

Students work in pairs. Student A is given a picture such as the following:

Stick figures or stylized drawings of an unusual scene are best. There should be enough detail to elicit a reasonable stretch of descriptive language but not too much so that the drawing is cluttered or the communication takes too long. The picture can be pasted inside a manila folder so that Student A can easily see the picture while describing it, but Student B cannot see it. Student A is given the following directions with the picture:

Your task is to describe this picture to your partner. Your description must be accurate enough so that he or she can draw a similar picture. Your partner must not look at the picture! He or she can only listen, ask for clarification, and draw what you describe. After your partner has drawn the picture from your description, compare the two pictures and discuss any differences.

Student B is given a paper on which is a blank box, the same size as A's picture, and the following directions:

Your partner has a picture with stick figures which he or she will describe to you. You must not look at the picture! Just listen, and as your partner describes each detail, recreate the picture by drawing it in the frame below. If your partner's directions do not seem clear, ask for clarification. Your purpose is to make your picture as similar as possible to the one being described to you. When you have finished, look at the original picture. Compare the two pictures and discuss any differences with your partner.

The beauty of this activity, aside from its ease and speed of preparation, is that students get immediate feedback. The accuracy of the communication or comprehension is quickly verified simply by comparing the drawing with the original picture. In addition to this pedagogical advantage, there is the great amusement that students enjoy when they compare all the art work of the class.

Picture Differences

In this language interaction, each one of a pair of students is given a picture that is similar but not exactly alike. Their task is to discover in what ways the pictures are the same and different. For example, each student is given one of the pictures below and the following directions:

You and your partner have pictures that are similar but not exactly alike. Describe your picture to each other in order to discover their differences. Do not look at each other's picture! Discover verbally, not visually, at least a dozen ways in which the pictures are different.

For teachers who do not have the time or the talent to draw pictures, duplicate illustrations might be cut from two magazines and then, with typewriter correction fluid, certain things be blocked out and slight differences added. Again, the accuracy of the communication or comprehension can be immediately verified when the two pictures are compared.

For this interaction activity, students are given the task but no guidance on how to proceed. Most of them start at some specific point (the bus or the signs in the shop, for example, or they start at the left and work towards the right—although several of my Arab students reversed this direction). Some students, however, begin with a more global approach. In the case of one pair, when a student started this way ("I have a street scene with a bus on the right and buildings on the left"), his partner interrupted her to say, "No, no—think by think." When this failed to communicate his meaning, he reprocessed the message and said, "Only one think at a time." Somehow his partner understood this and so she started with the windows at the upper left—and there they quickly discovered the first difference.

Activities of this kind, which include common everyday words, often reveal surprising and serious gaps in vocabulary. These students (at a high intermediate level) had just been reading about deductive logic and had learned such words as *deduction*, *ambiguity*, *premise*, and *inference*. But they were not sure of the word for curtains (and in fact at first used their native language word, *cortinas*). Not familiar with the word *pole*, they resorted to calling it a *flag stick*.

Picture differences can sometimes be especially designed to test lexical or phonological problems caused by interferences of the native language—for example, *library* for *bookstore*, or as in this particular picture, the pronunciation contrast of *Hal* and *Al*.

Incidentally, for paired practice of this kind, a language lab can be useful. In most current language laboratories, it is possible to connect two students together so that they can converse with each other as if they were speaking on a telephone. A simple patch cord between the two inputs on the control console allows the two students to communicate without interfering with others in the lab. Furthermore, the teacher or lab monitor can listen in, or even record the conversation. Students enjoy listening to themselves afterward, and many of the error analysis studies that my graduate students conduct are based on the recorded data.　　　*TN 12/81*

intersection? Maybe a sketch on the board would help. Identify a crosswalk, sidewalk, traffic, traffic lights, window shoppers...whatever. But don't discuss personalities.

Then she groups students — maybe two or three perspective policemen, a few window-shoppers, a couple taxi passengers, drivers, etc. Each group studies the information on its own card. As the teacher moves from group to group, guiding questions might be asked like: What's over-time? How do you feel at the end of a day's work? ...and, regarding the other side, Is that something that would start a conversation? or would it be a response to someone else? Would a policeman say that particular line sharply or calmly? On what occasion — or to whom — do you think someone would say the next line? In other words, this period of time is meant to help the students anticipate the kinds of conversational occurrences that might arise, but they don't know when they'll be said nor by whom.

When each group seems to have an understanding of its role, the teacher asks for a volunteer to be first to play the role. Of course, after the first try, a great deal more information about the interaction of the personalities is known by all. But, since there are a couple other people who are prepared to play each part — and since each has a different personality and style — each short scene comes out differently. There are always a few surprises, and a lot of realistic oral experience.

We use both procedures. The Paulston discussion method is certainly preferable when the setting requires new cultural understanding. It is also a good way to get groups accustomed to role play activities. But the Hines method adds an element of reality which pushes the students to anticipate what might happen and to revise and adjust their conversational choices according to what does happen.

TN 5/75

LESSONS THAT WORK

Edited by Darlene Larson
New York University

Some "lessons that work" are currently available from TESOL. I'm referring to the Paulston article, **DEVELOPING COMMUNICATIVE COMPETENCE: GOALS, PROCEDURES AND TECHNIQUES — A Talk About Language Teaching**. It was delivered at the Lackland Air Force Base, English Language Branch of the Defense Language Institute by Christina Bratt Paulston of the University of Pittsburgh. Copies are well worth your dollar. Send to TESOL, 455 Nevils, Georgetown University, Washington, D.C. 20007.

Paulston mentions four basic types of activities for developing communicative competence and gives specific examples of each one. Her categories are: social formulas and dialogues, community-oriented tasks, problem-solving activities, and role play. Two of these lessons that worked well when tried in New York were the problem-solving activity about planning for a camping trip, and the role play about buying a house. I'd like to add to her comments about role play.

Role play consists of three parts: the situation, the roles, and useful expressions. It is crucial to set conditions for a potential conflict, as well. She describes a procedure which might span a week of class time in discussing the situation, perhaps including some background knowledge, explaining some of the sociolinguistic information in the expressions, explaining and assigning roles, and finally performing.

An alternative procedure for role play has been developed and shared by Mary Hines. In order to bring the lesson closer to reality and to add an increasing step of difficulty, Hines recommends that the exact nature of each character **not** be discussed in advance by the **entire** class. After all, when you meet in conversation someone with a personality quirk or problem, it isn't announced in advance.

They don't wear a banner which announces, "I find fault with everything," or, "I've just lost my job and my wife is sick and I'm not in a very good mood."

Hines recommends three supporting devices in preparation for the role play: lines to choose from; a description of the role; and a few minutes to consider how and when this personality might employ some of the suggested lines. Before class it is necessary to type on 5 x 8 cards the personality characteristics and the useful expressions that one has in mind. In other words, if there is a policeman, Hines would prepare a card, one side of which would tell the student that he is a policeman, he's been working all night and he's in his second over-time hour, he's worried about his promotion, and suddenly he gets a call to go to X. The other side of the card would have lines to choose from. Some would be answers, some questions, some comments. They'd be in no particular order and no one else's lines would be there.

Once the class begins, the first step is a brief discussion of the setting. Where are they? What's an

"GETTING TO KNOW YOU" THROUGH QUESTIONNAIRES

by **Ruth Shernoff**
LaGuardia Community College, CUNY

Many teachers have used questionnaires the first day of class to get a profile of their students, but this activity need not stop there. Questionnaires can be taken one step further.

Students have a natural curiosity about each other but often are afraid to ask questions or do not know *how* to ask for information. Questionnaires are a way to get students to interact, to see how they are alike or different from each other, to give opinions, or to tell their life stories. For each questionnaire, students read directions, fill out the questionnaire, and add a few questions of their own (following the examples). They can work in pairs, exchange papers with another student to sometimes combine their partner's answers with their own into *one* sentence, and at other times to simply report about their partner to the whole class or in small groups. Here are some possibilities:

Questionnaire I: Tell Me About You (tenses/modals/yes-no questions) Make a list of yes no questions: for example, "Do you like classical music?" "Can you type?"

Students check yes or no, exchange papers and report: "I like classical music but X doesn't." "X can't type, but I can." (Consider how many other ways this information can be combined.)

Questionnaire II: What Do You Think? (should/because clauses/passive). Make a list of questions beginning with **should**: for example, "Should junk food be sold in schools?" "Should over-the-counter drugs be sold behind the counter?" Students check **yes** or **no** and add a **because** or **because of** clause, exchange papers, compare answers and report: "Junk food shouldn't be sold in schools because it isn't healthy." "Over-the-counter drugs should be sold behind the counter because of the recent poisonings."

Questionnaire III: How Do You Respond to Situations? (conditional). Give the structures: What will/would/you do/have done if. . . + time marker. List some situations: for example win lottery/ meet (famous person). Ask the students to use their imagination and write sentences, exchange papers and report: "If X wins the lottery, he will fly home tomorrow."

Questionnaire IV: Are You Like Me? Set up a few categories such as: (1) special interests, (2) special foods (3) pet peeves.

Under each category list items: for example, (1) disco dancing (2) chocolate (3) compositions. Students place a check mark next to items that reveal their inclinations, exchange papers, compare and report.

Questionnaire V: Ask About Me (information questions). Make a list of parts of embedded statements: for example, Ask me: Where I was born. . . Who my parents were. Students write the questions, ask a partner the questions and report to the class.

Questionnaires set the stage for conversation and get students connected. They provide a format for all students to speak; the communication is real, the context is functional and the laughter is generally lively. The teaching of grammar is not an isolated activity. The students reveal who they are and exchange this information in a light-handed way. Questionnaires can also be a springboard for students to write their own questions.

This is one way to unify a class and talk about things of common interest. The questionnaires can be on a simple, personal level or on varying degrees of complexity, dealing with issues and opinions.

TN 4/83

THE FLUENCY WORKSHOP

by Keith Maurice
Center for Intensive English Studies
Florida State University

This technique was designed to help intermediate and advanced students improve their abilities to speak more fluently in the target language. The basic idea is to have each student speak on one topic three times to three different partners. The length of each "speech" changes with each partner; first, it's four minutes, then it's three minutes, and finally it's two minutes.

The reasoning behind the technique can be broken down into three elements.

1. Same topic/three times
2. Speaking to different partners
3. Shrinking time frames

Same topic/three times. All speakers, whether they are native speakers or non-native speakers, tend to make many pauses, stops and starts and to inundate their speech with utterances like "uh," "ya know," and so on. This is especially the case when we talk about a specific topic for the first time. As we get warmed up or after we've talked about a topic many times, these utterances and pauses tend to decrease.

Speaking to different partners. In a classroom situation, to talk about one topic to the same

partner three times would make the exercise seem like a meaningless drill, both for the speaker and for the one forced to listen to it. Changing partners enables each speaker to talk about his/her topic in a meaningful way to someone new. For the listeners, each person hears about the same topic from three different perspectives.

Shrinking time frame. This 4-/3-/2-minute sequence is used for several reasons. The first four-minute time frame allows the student time to think about the topic while struggling with the language. This time is usually filled with many pauses. When a student speaks for the second time, he/she already knows generally what he/she wants to say and should be able to condense the four minutes of pauses and backtracking into a more organized way of speaking. To be sure, there are still uncertainties in the speech, but the speakers are more comfortable with the topic. The last time frame, two minutes, is meant to push the students into speaking as fluently and naturally as they can. Because of their previous practice, they should be able to focus on the key elements of their speech and

communicate those thoughts in a clear, concise manner without hesitation.

HOW TO DO IT

First, have the students pair up. One person in each pair is an "A" and the other person is a "B." Then, announce the topics, one for the "As" and another one for the "Bs."

Next, explain what the exercise is about (to improve fluency by having each person speak about one topic three times to different partners for decreasing amounts of time and work on listening and reporting skills). Drawing a chart on the board can help the students to understand it better. (See illustration below.)

TOPICS IN 4-/3-/2-MINUTE SEQUENCES

		Partner #1	Partner #2	Partner #3
People with	TOPIC A	4 minutes	3 minutes	2 Minutes
People with	TOPIC B	4 minutes	3 minutes	2 minutes

Each "A" speaks for four minutes, then each "B" speaks for four minutes. Then they change partners. For simplicity's sake, and so that the students don't become a tangled mass of bodies in the classroom, I usually instruct the "As" to remain seated throughout the whole exercise. The "Bs" should get up when it's time to change partners and move to the next "A" on the right.

During the exercise, go among the students and listen, both for errors and for content (things that can be used to spur discussion later). When it's time to change partners, clap your hands loudly and say one or two words (such as "O.K. Change partners!"). This is also a good time discretely to take note of important, recurring errors and for whatever counseling work you might want to do with the students.

The listeners can be asked to do any number of things: concentrate on key points from each speech for later reporting (either spoken or written); jot down occasional questions for later discussion; think of ways to disagree with the speaker's opinion and so on.

The time needed to complete one exercise is about 30 minutes. That's five to ten minutes for initial explanations and 20 minutes for the actual exercise. During this period, each student speaks nine minutes. As such, there is a real intensity in this activity as each person speaks approximately 30% of the time (nine minutes out of 30).

Other activities. "The Fluency Workshop" can be very useful as a preparatory activity to public speaking practice. By practicing the speech, or parts of it, in the 4-/3-/2-format, the more formal speeches seem to come out better. It can also flow into other activities such as 1) a question and answer discussion session, 2) an argumentative discussion (where the listeners must respond to points made with contrary arguments, and 3) a reporting session (where listeners compare the contents of the speeches they've heard).

To sum up, this activity for intermediate and advanced students can be used in a variety of contexts. It can be made a part of lessons concentrating on structural points or situations or functions of the language. In the words of an old ad pitchman on TV: "Try it; you'll like it."

Note: "The Fluency Workshop" is reprinted from the the *TESOL Secondary Interest Section Newsletter*, Winter 1983.

TN 8/83

BOOK REVIEWS

NO HOT WATER TONIGHT

(Jean Bodman and Michael Lanzano,
Collier Macmillan, 1975, $3.95)

Carol Taylor and Dick Litwack
GTE Sylvania, Wenham, Mass.

No Hot Water Tonight, an ESL reading text for elementary-level adults, is an exciting book from many points of view. Foremost among these is its cultural realism and subsequent relevance to the lives and needs of students living in a large city. The topics of the reading passages revolve around a cast of characters which includes a lonely widow, a grasping landlord, an unruly teenager, his anxious mother, an immigrant superintendent, his daughter, two single working women and a young married couple, all of whom live in a lower-middle-class Manhattan tenement. In the twenty-five reading "episodes," the daily living problems and emotional conflicts that these people experience consistently hold the attention of reader (student and teacher!).

The book is superbly illustrated with a series of black and white drawings which serve several purposes: they provide a context for each passage, facilitate comprehension and reinforce the treatment of the survival challenge that an immigrant faces in a metropolitan area. The text also contains non-pictorial material which serves a practical function; that is, the life problem posed in a given episode is deliberately tied to the readers' lives by the inclusion of such things as clothing ads, application forms, anecdotes of consumer fraud, retail installment credit agreements, and computer dating forms. Items of this nature lend authenticity by aiding the assimilation/coping process, and this give greater relevance to the ESL class.

Superimposed onto the serially developed dramatic progression is a carefully constructed sequence in tasks engaging the students personally. They vary greatly in level and appropriateness because, as the authors point out in their preface, they're intended to serve the heterogeneity of most reading classes. To encourage fluent reading, free readings are included at the end of many chapters and additional structural points are dealt with in the supplementary exercises at the end. These tasks facilitate nonteacher-directed, individual and small group work.

There has been a need for a reader for beginning ESL students which resolves the issue of structural control versus motivating content. *No Hot Water Tonight* fills that gap in an original and thorough way. More important, a controlled grammatical sequence lets students experience success in reading; creative exercises allow them to acquire reading skills independently; and high interest material makes students want to continue the reading process. These factors are crucial if students are to become fluent readers in the second language. terms of both structure and readability. While following the grammatical development of any number of ESL texts, the authors have managed to minimize the evidence of structural control by maintaining the patterns of "real language." Again, we're back to realism. The outstanding feature of this book is its thematic and linguistic accuracy.

The numerous exercises following each passage typically fall into the broad categories of comprehension (with inference stressed from the beginning), vocabulary development, structural manipulation and creative

TN 12/75

ACTIVE ENGLISH

By Patricia A. Porter and Allen W. Sharp (Prentice-Hall, Inc., Englewood Cliffs, N.J., 1977).

Reviewed by David Eskey
American Language Institute
University of Southern California

These three books form the core of the larger ACTIVE ENGLISH program, which also includes *Active English: Pronunciation and Speech,* by Alis R. Bens, and *Active English: Listening Comprehension Materials,* a set of thirty tapes or cassettes with an accompanying *Student Workbook.* There are also teacher's manuals to accompany both the Bens text and this three-volume series.

For anyone interested in the development of ESL as a teaching profession, this series provides a fascinating contrast with the series of ten or fifteen years ago. Although the approach is still audio-lingual in many crucial respects, the authors have made major modifications in the interest of teaching what everyone is now attempting to teach—that is, communicative competence. Thus there are drills but there are three types of drills, the second and third types moving further and further from what language teachers used to think of as a drill—a simple manipulation of some part of the structure of the target language intended to contribute to the student's acquisition of new language habits. Learning a second language meant acquiring these new habits, and nothing more; but for Porter and Sharp, the whole purpose of the mechanical "1-drills" is to establish a base, as soon as possible, for the meaningful "2-drills," and even these are, in the long run, mere preparation for the communicative "3-drills," "the most important part of the cycle" and one that is meant to "take a significant amount of class time." Similarly, the reading and writing exercises are not described, as they once would have been, as providing "reinforcement" but rather as providing "further contextualization" of new patterns.

At the same time, there is much of the old in these texts. The *content* of each cycle remains a series of structures —more or less the same structures that, for example, the old Michigan texts attempted to teach, albeit in a more mechanical manner. The 1 and 2-drills employ such familiar devices as repetition, substitution, conversion, and short answers. And explanation is largely limited to a simple laying out of patterns in boxes, again reminiscent of the Michigan series. The texts are thus in a sense quite conservative, but they do incorporate current thinking in the field in the form of many classroom activities designed to generate meaningful communication. There are of course scholars today who would argue that no materials as teacher-controlled as these, or as carefully structured, can ever lead to real human communication. But to say that is to open the Great Question of the times, and there are no obvious answers to it yet.

One major virtue of this series is a very clear statement of the kind of audience and the kind of teaching program for whom and for which these books are intended. On the first page of the Preface, we are told that they are meant

for beginning students of English from all language backgrounds on the secondary and adult levels. The three books provide material for a one-semester course of two hours per day or a two-semester sequence of one hour per day. Accompanying language laboratory materials and pronunciation exercises make it possible to plan a four-hour-per-day intensive program. These materials have been used in the American Language Institute at San Francisco State University with students whose average entering T.O.E.F.L. score was 308. The range of entering scores for these students was 210 to 348.

Since good materials for beginners are in very short supply, the series and the remaining parts of *ACTIVE ENGLISH* may go a long way toward filling a very real need for the instructor in search of a modern approach who still remains unconvinced by more radical departures from audio-lingual methodology.

The books are handsomely packaged, with plenty of white space and attractive line drawings, and each of the thirty lessons includes, in addition to the drills and reading/writing exercises, a model dialogue and lists of new vocabulary and patterns. There are finally appendices to each volume listing first and last names used in the text and the new vocabulary arranged within a system of semantic categories.   4/78

(Reprinted from the CATESOL *Newsletter, November 1977)*

LISTENING IN AND SPEAKING OUT

(by Gary James, Charles G. Whitley, and Sharon Bode. Longman Inc., 1980)

Reviewed by Harvey M. Taylor
Beijing, China

The stated aims of *Listening In and Speaking Out, Intermediate* and it's accompanying tape are "1) to provide opportunities for students to talk; 2) to provide a classroom environment that is student, rather than teacher, oriented; 3) to provide students with the confidence, motivation and ideas for on-going self-teaching." After using these materials for one 12-week term, this author and his fellow teachers have found that the first two aims have been achieved; in line with the third aim, the students did demonstrate gains in confidence and motivation in speaking English to each other for as much as two hours at a stretch. Gains vis-à-vis attitudes towards self-teaching are not as yet known. For use at least, these materials have lived up to most of their stated aims—a laudable accomplishment for any text.

The Introduction gives the teacher sufficient suggestions for getting each sub-part of each of the 12 units off the ground. As the teacher gets better acquainted with the text, s/he may wish to modify these suggested procedures. Each unit is built around two recorded segments, one a monolog and the other a free-wheeling discussion among four native speakers.

A unit begins with "Getting Set," a four-sentence recorded dictation exercise; the Introduction gives some useful hints on how to handle the dictation. We save class time by having the students do this dictation as homework before class, since they have access to a tape and player. This exercise introduces the topic of the "Monolog," which is heard later. As the Introduction states, the rate of speech is normal (=fast) for even this introductory dictation section. Therefore, even though the vocabulary is generally familiar to even our low-intermediate students (TOEFL 400) and the sentences are also short (mostly 6-9 words), the normal characteristics of fast-speech English which occur here have provided sufficient challenge for even our best intermediate students (TOEFL 500).

The next sub-section is "Tuning In," a listing with English glosses of some of the words and phrases which occur in the Monolog section. A helpful innovation is the marking of those items in this list which have meanings in addition to the one provided to fit this context. Unfortunately, a number of unlisted items posed problems for our students (e.g., Unit 10: air pocket,

ground pilot). The teacher will do well to add to the list in each Tuning In section.

After the Tuning In section, the student listens to the Monolog, which is generally conversational and at normal speed. The monolog is often a re-worked humorous anecdote with a well-placed punch line. (It was gratifying week by week for us to hear laughter from more and more students when they heard the punch line for the first time.)

Three exercises provide a check on listening comprehension for the Monolog— "Summing Up" (multiple-choice sentence-completion), "Retelling" (guided restatement of the story), and "Filling In" (a dicto-cloze practice with every fifth word deleted). The Summing Up and Filling In exercises can also be done by the students outside of class time, provided they study the vocabulary in Tuning In beforehand. The Retelling provides the first speaking activity of the unit. In our course, we found it best to have the Retelling follow rather than precede the Filling In dicto-cloze activity, since by doing the Filling In, the students worked through the Monolog enough times so that remembering the details for the Retelling was not the problem it had been previously. (Although they had understood the tape, they hadn't remembered enough of the details from one or two hearings to retell the story.)

The "Pairing Up" exercise is sometimes related to the taped Monolog, sometimes to the taped "Discussion," and sometimes only a take-off on an idea found in either of them. For students who are not used to speaking freely in English, this a good beginning exercise in real communication— only the speaker knows the information, so it is truly a case of telling something new to the listener. However, when compared with the two later speaking activities, this more structured activity eventually lost its appeal to our students as their speaking improved throughout the term.

As with the Monolog, there are also Tuning In, Summing Up, Retelling, and Filling In sub-sections to provide listening and some speaking practice based on the taped Discussions. The Retelling was much more difficult for the Discussion than for the Monolog, since the Discussion is a recording of part of a natural four-way conversation, with the normal disorganization of true conversation. Our students

found this Retelling to be less useful than the one for the Monolog. Some even tried to memorize the Discussion in order to do the Retelling correctly. We eventually eliminated this to save class time for what came next.

By far the most innovative speaking activity in this text is the one called "Drawing Out." Five statements are given which require the student to make inferences from what has been said during the Discussion. The task is to decide whether the statement is "possible" or "not probable," and to support the conclusion drawn, e.g. "Sharon's children will probably have their own rooms" (p. 70). We divided the class into 5 discussion groups; each decided on the answer to one statement. Then a spokesperson from each group rotated through the other groups arguing for his/her own point of view. The statements are so well chosen that up to 10 minutes was easily spent by each group on each question, with lots of (sometimes heated) arguing.

One other speaking exercise concludes each unit—"Speaking Out." We paired up students and assigned each person in each pair to give his/her opinion on each of the (usually five) topics. For all but units two and three (which unfortunately have only three topics), the students talked non-stop for a full 50 minutes, and often continued as they left the classroom. Knowing that our students were all Chinese, were from different areas and employment positions throughout the country, and were generally reticent to discuss personal opinions with other Chinese, I went to the first class armed with some alternative (but unneeded) topics that would require less revelation of personal feelings and opinions. I was surprised at the gusto with which they volunteered very personal opinions and experiences—e.g., "Do you sometimes feel dumb? What makes you feel dumb? Are there times when 'playing dumb' is a good thing to do? Why?" (p. 48).

The authors are to be commended for their use of natural speech and speed in their taped segments. However, we have found it useful to make a study tape into which we have inserted pauses to allow time for students to write. On that tape we have also included enough repeats of the dictation sentences so the student (or teacher) doesn't have to rewind the tape and go back too far in the process.

The authors have focused on providing real listening materials, but it seems that given the great success we have had with their speaking activities, the publisher should at least give equal time to promoting the speaking component of the text. If it has worked so successfully for us (with one native speaker and two non-native speakers as the teachers of separate classes and with only Chinese students), it should be even more useful with students from different cultures and languages—the information exchanged then during the speaking activities should be even more interesting.

The topics covered by the 12 units are refreshingly out of the ordinary—and definitely adult. Implicit in each is some aspect of American culture, which the teacher may wish to explain, but which can be ignored without reducing the usefulness of the activities. Our non-native speakers were able to handle the course without this cultural knowledge beforehand.

Problems could develop in using this text if the students are not truly intermediate (c. 425-450 TOEFL). Also at the beginning students may feel uncomfortable because of the passive role of the teacher; the teacher is only a facilitator for the student's self-study of the listening portions, and just starts the speaking activities before taking on an observer's role.

Our students did not seem to enjoy attempts to get them to discuss/interpret the large drawings that go with various units —they found it hard to identify the characters and the activities shown. Additional speaking activities could have been devised to build on the illustrations if they had been more carefully integrated into the units. As it is, the illustrations may end up being primarily decorative.

The layout of the individual units is somewhat confusing in that "Monolog" appears as part of the unit title in a different and smaller type than "Discussion" does later on; yet the topics of both the Monolog and Discussion appear as the Unit title. Also the title "Discussion," though in huge letters, does not appear to tie the illustration to the discussion as clearly as it should. If the discussion topic could be stated with the title "Discussion," this confusion might be avoided.

The text comes with both an "Answer Key" and "Tapescript." One typo (the only one noticed) caused students trouble on page 81, where the Getting Set blanks indicate that 8 words are needed for sentence 2, and 7 words for sentence 3; however, sentence 2 has only 7 words while sentence 3 has 8.

All in all, this text does most of what it says it will for listening practice, and in addition it can be used very successfully for stimulating real-life spoken communication. If the announced sequel (for "advanced" students) follows the same imaginative route this intermediate text has taken, it should take the students on a profitable language learning trip.   TN 10/81

A FOREIGN STUDENT'S GUIDE TO DANGEROUS ENGLISH

(Elizabeth Claire. Rochelle Park, N.J.: Eardley Publications, 1980, 86 pp.)

Reviewed by Lise Winer
Université de Montréal

When one of your students—usually male —comes up to you in front of the class and innocently (?) asks, "Miss, what means /fock/?", you can: turn red and mumble something incoherent, tell him to look it up in the dictionary, tell him to ask another student, ask whether he doesn't have anything better to do, give a totally deadpan clinical definition with notes on sociolinguistic usage, or correct his pronunciation. Now, since the publication of *Dangerous English*, you can hand him the book and tell him to check page 27.

It is true that some socially taboo words can be found in some dictionaries, although usually not in those our students use. But many "dangerous" words are not included. Furthermore, even if you do find a dangerous word, it may be followed by a list of alternatives with no indication as to which choice would be appropriate for your purposes.

There are two basic considerations in the place of taboo words in language classes: recognition and usage. Students have to know how to recognize dangerous words. If someone says, "Fuck you," does that mean he is angry? How angry? Joking? If the student goes to a doctor, he should understand "(urine) specimen" or "echantillon de pip," or whatever native speakers say. There is, unfortunately, no clear way to recognize ahead of time which words are dangerous and which are not. In English, most taboo words concern the body, particularly excretion and sexual parts and functions, but it is not always easy to associate such phrases as *to fall off the roof* (to commence menstruation), or *to see a man about a horse* (to go to the bathroom, i.e., toilet, i.e. to defecate) with taboo areas. Although some English taboo words deal with religion, e.g. *damn*, this would not prepare an English speaker learning French for the danger in words like *hostie* (sacramental host, communion wafer). Some taboo words, even if partially overlapping in meaning, are not equivalent in usage: for example, the French *merde* has a somewhat wider range of acceptability than the English *shit*, but less syntactic flexibility, and is also the equivalent of the English theatrical *break a leg*. Faux amis can also present problems. To be *constipated* (blocked bowels) in English requires different medicine than to be *constipé* (us. blocked nose) in French. And while to be *indisposed* in English means "not feeling well," albeit coy, *être indisposée* in French almost always means "to have one's menstrual period." How can one distinguish dangerous idioms: *to make out* on an exam and *to make out* with someone? *To be cursed* and *to have the curse*? Why, in French, should *se pogner le cul* be no worse than *to waste time* or *to twiddle one's thumbs*, but *se pogner les fesses*, "to grab ass," be vulgar? Finally, we owe our students some protection; reprehensible as it is, some native speakers find it amusing to teach learners "fuck you very much" as an appropriate grateful response.

Many native English speakers use dangerous, taboo words frequently. Even ESL teachers have been known to use them—off-duty, of course. Our students hear taboo words all the time. But they do not always notice *who* uses *which* words, *when, how,* and under *what circumstances*. Of course, we do not want to teach our students to use dangerous words indiscriminately, or as much as they may hear peers using them. But if we do not tell them the limits of general acceptability, it is all too probable that no one else will—the very nature of the objection making correction difficult. People usually assume that the speaker knows what he is saying and simply judge a learner's use of language by the same criteria as a native speaker's. Thus, the first part of teaching "usage" is teaching what *not* to say, and when *not* to say it. Too often, learners find out dangerous words by making an embarrassing and unintentional double *entendre*; students appreciate knowing some of the more obvious pitfalls in advance. It can be helpful to know, for example, that French *engin* can refer to "penis", and that embarrassing moments can be engendered by mistaking *la manche* (sleeve) and *le manche* (penis). (One of the more public examples of dangerous French occurred recently when an Anglophone member of the provincial assembly complained that his constituents were fed up with their taxes "jusqu'au cul" (up to their ass), when he meant to say "jusqu'au cou" (up to their necks), making a case for some selective phoneme practice.)

I must emphasize here that I am *not* advocating a wholesale adoption of lessons based on taboo words, nor that they should be dealt with formally in class at all. It is easy to be embarrassed by this aspect of language as a classroom teacher. It is easy to disapprove, to be shocked or dismayed. But often this attitude leaves our students at the mercy of their own limited experience, and leaves them open to ridicule or being thought rude. There is a need for addressing this area of language because our students need it: they have medical or sexual problems—either theirs or their children's—that they have to talk about with counsellors and doctors; they go to movies, read novels and magazines and comics; watch television; take their pets to the vet; make friends among English speakers; hear and sometimes use language we don't use in the classroom; who want to understand jokes—in short, become competent users of the language.

Therefore, this book can fulfill a real need for learners of English as a second language (and not a few native speakers as well!) Even native speaking friends will find it difficult to sit down and give a learner a list of words to be careful of, hence the advantage of this book. The book is basically clear and well done, although I have some minor cavils. For example, part of the information for "defecate" includes: formal —*defecate*, general use—*have a bowel movement*, euphemism—*go to the bathroom*, children's—*make ka ka*, slang—*go to the can*, vulgar—*shit*. Although this method of presentation is very useful, it is not complete, in a sociolinguistic sense: *copulate* and *fornicate*, for example, both listed under formal expressions, do not convey the same legal-moral nuances. Also not indicated is that quite a few words are generally used more by or about one sex than the other. However, the information is certainly complete enough for students to learn which general or euphemistic phrases to use, and which slang or vulgar words to avoid. A variety of regional terms is included, so this book should be a good reference anywhere in North America. The pictures that accompany the definitions are clear, if somewhat male-oriented. Some of the pictures illustrating embarrassing moments resulting from "mistakes" are a bit cutesy, but clear.

Some taboo topics, including sex and bodily functions, are difficult, inadvisable, or impossible to discuss with particular classes. However, I have found at least recognition of formal terms very welcome, especially privately, or in small (monosexual) groups. Students have also appreciated being told that certain words they have "picked up" may be considered objectionable by some . This book can definitely help you help your students avoid fucking up their English.   TN 6/82

"SHUCK LOVES CHIRLEY": A NON-TECHNICAL TEACHING AID FOR TEACHERS OF BILINGUAL CHILDREN

Leonard Olguin, California,
Golden West College, 1968. 97 pp.

Reviewed by Teresa Delgadillo-Bevington
Northeastern Illinois University

For those new teachers of English to Spanish-dominant children, and for those experienced teachers who may have missed this most useful text the first time around, we recommend that you look at it now. Leonard Olguin approaches the subject of identifying areas of interference to English language learning. Olguin addresses himself to separating the many-phased problems encountered by the language learner and concentrates on corrective techniques based on the central concept that "a child cannot read what he/she cannot hear."

After discussing how sounds of Spanish might interfere with and impede the acquisition of the target language, English, Olguin suggests diagnostic tests to identify problem areas for individual children. He then presents suggested lessons for the individual sounds. The lessons include techniques for showing children how to articulate the new sounds, for ex-ample, the schwa. He points out that the "uh sound, is used more than any other sound in English. The lessons are filled with poems, jingles and rhymes giving children ample practice in hearing, then saying, the target sound in context. In closing comments Olguin says, "If a bilingual child can learn to hear and speak the general American dialect, I firmly believe that a great, great number of reading problems will never develop."

Additional helpful aspects of this book are a most readable Table of Contents, a contrastive analysis of Spanish-English sounds along with error predictability, and, as previously mentioned, diagnostic tests. The vocabulary is non-technical and glossed where terms might be unfamiliar to the teacher.

Olguin's direct approach will be welcome to teachers inundated with theory and insecure in practice.

TN 9/76

SOUNDS INTRIGUING

By Alan Maley and Alan Duff. Cambridge University Press, 1979.

Reviewed by Debra Denzer
University of Miami

Conversation or Spoken English teachers (whatever our labels) are always on the lookout for new ways to stimulate discussion among ESL students. There are often difficulties in doing so: one is finding interesting materials that provide the students with a real reason to speak English; another is the inhibition that some students suffer when attention is focused directly on *their* speaking English. Alan Maley and Alan Duff assist us in relieving these classroom maladies by providing us with an activity in which English is not the object of the lesson, but the means of communication.

Sounds Intriguing includes a book and a tape of sound sequences which are indeed intriguing. The object of using the sound sequences is to provide the students with a stimulus to get them talking. With attention not centered on correct usage and pronunciation, the students are free just to express their ideas. Because there is no right or wrong interpretation of the sounds, the students do not have to fear giving a wrong answer. This creates a more relaxed atmosphere in which they can express themselves in English. The activity encourages fluency.

The book is for the teacher's reference: the students do not have a text. They simply listen to the tape and then try to interpret the sounds they have heard. There are twenty-one sound sequences which pique the curiosity and stimulate the imagination of the listener. The following are samples of sound sequences:

> water (lapping) — humming — water (gushing) — pause — humming — silence — water lapping — sudden shout

Each sequence only lasts about a minute and contains little, if any, speech. While the occasional exclamations have a distinct British accent, these materials are far too innovative and interesting for this to deter anyone from using them in American English classrooms.

The tape is accompanied by a teacher's text which suggests ways to use the tape. Each sequence is transcribed in the book. In addition, there are suggested questions to get the students thinking. For example, "Is this taking place indoors or out;" "How many people are involved?" There are also suggestions for written and/or oral work, pertinent vocabulary with examples, and finally, possible interpretations of the sequences. For the first sequence transcribed above the authors have suggested several interpretations: (1) a man doing a crossword puzzle in the tub and finding the answer to a difficult clue; (2) a spy developing film and finding a photo he wanted has turned out; (3) an explorer recently returned from an expedition, upon taking his first bath, discovers that he has contracted a skin disease. Some of the suggested interpretations are quite outrageous and one wonders how they were imagined, but the students come to understand that they really are only possibilities, and so they want to become even more creative.

The main part of the text is followed by two appendices. One is a useful list of words for different sounds indexed by the maker of the sound—sounds made by humans, sounds made by birds, sounds made by water, etc.; the second appendix gives examples of written assignments based on the sequences. The writing suggestions seem less useful for a conversation class, but the other activities are particularly effective at getting the students involved and talking.

The authors do not presume to offer *Sounds Intriguing* as major work for a course, rather as an exercise to supplement those materials used to develop other conversation skills. It provides a pleasant break from more structured activities, much as occasionally using songs in class does. *Sounds Intriguing* works well at the beginning of a new term as an ice-breaker and works equally well during the times later in the term when the students begin to get restless, weary, or just plain bored. As such, I have found it very successful.

While Maley and Duff suggest that *Sounds Intriguing* can be used at any level, at the University of Miami's Intensive English Program, we have used it in Intermediate and Advanced Conversation classes. Following the directions of the authors, I divide my class into small groups, usually fours, and let the students listen to the sequence several times. They then discuss among themselves their interpretations of the sounds. After group discussion, we share interpretations as a class. There are usually several differing ideas and often rather excited discussion. Students comment on one another's interpretations, sometimes changing their own minds, sometimes disagreeing strongly. They are usually quick to point out if someone has not accounted for every sound.

Duff and Maley seem to have accomplished what they set out to do—provide an interesting, fluency-provoking exercise. The sound sequences work very well at getting the students involved in a discussion. While some of the text's suggestions seem less useful for a conversation (particularly the written exercises), the activities of listening, interpreting, and discussing are crucial, and *Sounds Intriguing* provides an exciting starting point. Sound intriguing? It is.
(Reprint from *The Gulf TESOL Newsletter*, Vol. I, No. 3, Winter 1981)

TN 10/81

DIALOGUES AND DRILLS: IDIOMATIC ENGLISH

William B. White. 3 vols. Tokyo: Warwick Press, 1978.

Reviewed by John Boylan
Toyo University, Tokyo

In the last few years I must have seen dozens of run-of-the-mill, impossible-to-teach collections of dialogues for ESL/EFL students. After seeing so many mediocre texts of this nature, I was delighted to find *Dialogs and Drills in Idiomatic English*—a series that not only avoids the pitfalls that plague most dialogue collections, but provides some really effective classroom teaching material. I'm sure you've come across some of the same faults I've found in many texts: silly, trite dialogues; stilted, stuffy conversations in "school book English;" items that are too long to be good for anything; dialogues that could never be applied to any real-life situation; scenes that sacrifice naturalness in order to cram in chosen grammatical patterns; dialogues that are wasted by being read once and then forgotten—unfortunately, the list goes on and on!

Somehow *Dialogs and Drills* has managed to avoid these difficulties. On first looking through a copy about a year ago I was impressed by the well-organized, easy-to-teach format, the clever cartoon illustrations and, most importantly, the dialogues themselves. In using the book since then in numerous classes, my original favorable impression has been confirmed, and I've even made some new discoveries: Mr. White has faithfully stuck to his stated purpose of actually teaching students living English —not old-fashioned, not "slangy," but solid, idiomatic English—the kind real people use. The dialogues are short, compact and self-contained, covering a wide range of real-life situations. Each conversation is followed by a wide range of direct and indirect comprehension questions—not the paltry half-dozen questions which often accompany dialogue materials, but really full sets of questions which allow the teacher to check comprehension while practicing structural transformations and vocabulary items in a fast-paced and highly entertaining drill session. I've found the "ask somebody . . ." questions have been especially valuable in getting students to begin to communicate with each other.

Although managing to retain a surprisingly natural flavor, the lessons in Volume III are packed with idioms. Some students at this level have become temporarily intimidated by the wealth of new material presented. I've found, however, that especially thorough introductions to each lesson eliminate any possible comprehension problems that might develop.

If I sound enthusiastic, I confess that I am! I strongly recommend that you try this book for yourself if you're looking for some really useful and "teachable" dialogue materials.

(Reprinted from the *JALT Newsletter*, 1 March 1979)

TN 6/79

GAMBITS

by Eric Keller
Language Bureau, Public Service Commission, Ottawa, Ontario

Gambits are conversational tools for introducing what we're about to say. We use them every day and in a variety of situations. For instance, when we want to state an opinion, we can say, "I think that . . ." or, "In my opinion. . . ." When we want to introduce something unsavory, we can say, "Whether we like it or not. . . .", and when we want to bow out of a conversation, we can try, "Well, it was nice talking to you." If our conversational partner couldn't take the hint, we can also hammer it home with, "Sorry, I've really got to go now."

There are more than 500 such gambits. For the skillful speaker of the language, they gain him an entry into the conversation, give him some breathing space as he thinks of what to say next, and provide a clear indication of what's to come. They give him all the verbal control over the conversation that he would want. And yet, we don't generally teach gambits in our ESL classes.

Consider interrupting openers, for instance. If you know the phrase "excuse me for interrupting, but. . .", or any equivalent phrase, you can break into nearly any conversation with reasonable aplomb. However, the ESL learner without a ready store of such expressions often finds himself frustrated. He is frequently excluded from conversations because he misses the small pauses during which he could break into the conversation. Instead of taking the lead, he's busy arranging in his head what he wants to say. As a result, the conversation goes on without him.

Our three-part series GAMBITS was written to give the student an opportunity to exercise such conversational skills. The emphasis is on "exercise." Words like "excuse," "for," or "interrupt" are very likely familiar to intermediate or advanced students. Therefore, they wont have to *learn* such gambits. They will already know most of them passively. But to make these expressions part of their active store, the students must exercise them in language situations that unequivocally call for certain types of gambits. For this reason, our series of modules provides a large and realistic set of language situations in which such expressions can be applied. The object was to recreate, as closely as possible, the type of language situations that the ESL learner would meet again outside the classroom. The situations range from telephone inquiries to dealing with fellows on the make at a party, from the serious to the facetious.

All exercises in this series are aimed at a *more or less advanced level*. It is assumed that the students who can profit most directly from these activities are those that can already manipulate basic and intermediate structures of the language.

The "advanced" words chosen for the series are quite varied. There are such handy items as "tax-deductible," "grumpy," "balaclava" and "correcting fluid," words that reach into many different linguistic situations. This is a natural consequence of the many different linguistic situations. This is a natural consequence of the many different types of gambits that introduce a rich diversity of language situations.

In fact, *variety* is one of the key principles of the series. Not only are language situations and activities varied in nature, even the *language modalities* and the *size of the groups* required for the activities are varied. Some exercises call for speaking, some for writing, some for role-playing and yet others are games. Some involve the whole class, while others are directed at small groups or even at individuals. Indeed, the use of the series itself should remain under the banner of variety. Not more than half an hour a day should be devoted to GAMBITS. Most exercises are designed to take only between 10 and 20 minutes. The rest of the teaching day should ideally be filled with many other varied learning activities.

The full series will inclalude a complete index of all gambits introduced, and the total number of activities will run to about 100. The booklets will probably be available through Information Canada bookstores, but if you'd like to have more publication information, write to Howard B. Woods, Language Bureau, Public Service Commission, Room 711, Killeany Building, 460 O'Connor Street, Ottawa, Ontario K1A 0M7.

TN 4/77

CONNECTIONS

John and Mary Ann Boyd. (New York: Regents, 1981), 147 pp.

Reviewd by Donna Bunch
Western Kentucky U.

This is a conversation I'd like you to complete orally with me now.
Me: There's a new listening and speaking text out.
You: ?
Me: *Connections.*
You: ?
Me: John and Mary Ann Boyd.
You: ?
Me: Regents.
You: ?
Me: Yes, and I think you will too.
You: ?
Me: Well, it contains 20 functionally-based one-sided phone conversations. The students listen to a speaker's communication and then actually become involved in the conversation by making appropriate responses.
You: ?
Me: Intermediate or low-advanced at the secondary, college, or adult level. *Connections* not only gives the student an opportunity to participate in a common communication process, but it also teaches the importance of listening to voice intonation and how a response depends upon the other speaker's intent and tone.
You: ?
Me: Let's see. Besides the real communication exchange in *Connections*, the Boyds have carefully prepared each short unit to include a student comprehension check. There's also a section in each unit for the students who may need more structure.
You: ?
Me: Yes, there is, and I think it's one of the most useful I've seen recently. The Teacher's Text has both speakers' parts in the dialogs. A veteran can readily use it, and a new ESL teacher won't be reluctant to do so. The Student's Text requires one to listen and respond spontaneously, listen and choose the correct response to read, or listen and mark a correct response. The student cannot rely on reading the other speaker's part; he must rely on and develop his own listening abilities to make the Connections.

(Reprint from *The Kentucky TESOL Newsletter*, September, 1981.)   TN 4/82

WHADDAYA SAY? GUIDED PRACTICE IN RELAXED SPOKEN ENGLISH

by Nina Weinstein. 1982. ELS Publications, 5761 Buckingham Parkway, Culver City, California 90230 (68 pp., $2.95).

Reviewed by Arlene Malinowski
North Carolina State University

Among the large selection of supplementary ESL materials currently available, there is one in particular that deserves the attention of foreign language educators. *Whaddaya Say? Guided Practice in Relaxed Spoken English* offers a unique perspective on the teaching and learning of conversational spoken English. As the author aptly points out in her prefatory remarks: "The careful, clearly articulated (and often slower) language typically heard in class and the 'relaxed speech' so commonly heard outside it do not quite match. When students encounter this phenomenon, therefore, a communications breakdown usually occurs: what they expect to hear and what they actually hear are not the same thing" (p. viii). The aim of this text is to introduce non-native speakers of English to the relaxed language patterns that characterize spoken American English today.

Concatenations 'n Contractions

In the twenty relatively brief lessons that comprise the text, such common concatenations and contractions as *wanna* (want to), *gonna* (going to), *hafta* (have to), and *whacha* (what do you) are presented in context for listening practice. In the first part of each lesson, the relaxed pronunciation is contrasted with the corresponding careful pronunciation of a speech segment. The aural portions of each lesson are recorded on accompanying cassette tapes; students are requested to listen to the relaxed patterns and to repeat and actively reproduce careful speech. Although some aspects of the manual appear to be a bit advanced for the mere beginner, the text is adaptable to almost any instructional level, and its use would certainly serve to accelerate and enhance the development of listening comprehension in the large majority of ESL learning situations.

It is frequently said that the methods and materials employed in the teaching of English as a Second Language are in general more advanced than those used in foreign language courses (for the teaching of, for example, Spanish and French). Weinstein's contributions to the ESL curriculum is a good illustration of this point. For the proper comprehension of "real world language," whatever the target language may be, an understanding and analysis of the relaxed speech patterns of that language are essential. Lest we allow an unhealthy preoccupation with purism to obstruct our efforts to prepare our students adequately, we ought to, at every opportunity, make use of the kind of material that Weinstein's text contains. It would not, moreover, be in the least undesirable or inappropriate if writers of elementary and intermediate textbooks intended for other target languages were to follow Weinstein's example and provide us with similar supplementary materials for use in the foreign language classroom.

TN 6/83

GETTING INTO IT...AN UNFINISHED BOOK

Dave Blot and Phyllis Berman Sher, Language Innovations, 1978

Reviewed by Jean McConochie
Pace University

The Counseling-Learning/Community Language Learning approach holds that trust and self-awareness, even if arrived at through confusion and discomfort, are crucial elements in adult language learning. *Getting Into It* exemplifies that premise in thirteen brief (400-500 word) first-person narratives which recount conflicts accompanying adult learning.

Pierre, for example, can't get started on his writing assignments; Lee Fong finds herself an alien in both American and Chinese culture; Nelson is hurt and angry when his wife returns to school. The trilogy of Berta's, Selina's and Leslie's stories offers the reader the exhiliration of expanding perception as the same incident is recounted from three different points of view.

Some of the discussion questions following each story call for inference ("What relationship can you see between Selina's feeling of aloneness and the way she acts with this group of people?" p. 15); some ask students to discuss their own feelings ("How do you feel about Benita's revealing such a personal story in front of a class?" p. 40). Writing assignments offer a choice between emotionally neutral topics (e.g. pretending to be someone else) and highly charged ones (describing a personal conflict similar to the one in the story).

While the book can easily be used as a supplementary text for intermediate and advanced students in reading and writing classes, it is not primarily intended to teach either of those skills. Its purpose, rather, is "to facilitate self-understanding and ultimately to encourage learning" (Teacher's Manual, p. 2).

Does a teacher need C-L/CLL training in order to use the book effectively? Those who have such training will find that the stories provide a context in which to practice the skill of "understanding". Those who are interested in ESL classroom applications of the C-L/CLL approach will find procedures clearly outlined in the Teacher's Manual. Anyone could profitably use *Getting Into It* to stimulate discussion of problems which confront all language teachers and learners.

The authors' concern and respect for both students and colleagues shine throughout the book. Although written for and about students in the U.S., the problems are universal in nature. For students of English abroad, it also illustrates conflicts which arise when a language learner is surrounded by native speakers.

Those who think of stories that haven't been included are encouraged to write them. The book won't be finished until you have added *your* story...
. . . .

(Copies may be ordered from LINC, 2112 Broadway, New York, NY 10023; student book, $2.50; Teacher's Manual, $0.50.)   TN 2/79

Section 11. Linguistics and Grammar

I am always surprised that the *TN* never started a column on points of grammar as the *CATESOL Newsletter* and so many others have. There have been few articles in the *TN* over the years which have dealt with grammar problems or with the presentation of interesting grammar ideas. This certainly says something about our profession—or about teachers, at least. We have not even received any letters on the subject. We did receive a letter, though, criticizing the language of the *TN*, the typos, especially because articles from the *Newsletter* were being used to teach English. (See the article from the August 1980 *TN* entitled "Why Is My Newsletter Always Late?")

This section begins with an article from 9/77 which describes sector analysis or x-word grammar vis-a-vis a review of *Working Sentences* authored by the creator of sector analysis, Robert L. Allen. It is followed by a short *It Works* column by Greg Larkin (10/79), "Role Playing Grammar," which uses sector analysis in a role playing technique.

The topic of sector analysis is discussed in two additional selections in section 13: an article by Sloane and Frörup "Teaching Written English Through Sector Analysis" (4/76) and a book review of Fred Malkemes and Debra Singer's *Looking at English* (10/81) reviewed by Helen Truax.

The next article in this section by Gregg Singer "Colorless Green Ideas" (12/81), considers the notion of "correctness" in the ESL classroom. The succeeding article by Gary Bevington, "On Being a Negative ESL Teacher" (4/79) presents the use of the negative in question and answer techniques and contains two charts from a paper by M. Akiyama which show how English and Japanese differ in handling negative questions. "On Being a Questionable English Teacher" (10/79) by Alendort was written in response to the Bevington article.

In "Definite Article" (12/80), Garry Molhot examines the importance of techniques for teaching the definite article. "The Importance of Melody" by Shakti Datta (4/81) explains why stress and rhythm patterns of a language are important in conveying meaning and, therefore, are crucial to successful communication. In her short article, "Conversation: Saying Hello and Goodbye" (2/79), Patricia Sullivan presents her attempt to determine what native speakers actually say, as opposed to what the textbooks tell us. It is an interesting bit of ad hoc research which any teacher or student might find useful as a model

for discovering the appropriateness of items being taught (or learned). Sullivan's article seems just a few steps ahead of the notional-functional trend which has lit up the 1980's. "Idioms and Auxiliaries," an *It Works* column by Darlene Larson (11/76), presents some new ideas on how to teach these difficult vocabulary items to ESL students. Suzanne Griffin's article "Teaching Structures in Situational Contexts" (4/76), provides a schema for situations in which various grammar points can most naturally and realistically be taught.

The article by Patrick Kameen, "The Passive Voice, It Must Be Spoken For" (6/80), like its companion article in section 4 by Patricia Byrd, stresses the importance of teaching the passive. Blau, Gonzales and Green present techniques to help "Students Sort Out Phrasal Verbs" (4/83).

The book reviews in this section reflect the *TN's* area of strength in the area of grammar teaching. The three grammar texts reviewed are representative of the types of grammar texts currently on the market and range from Paul Roberts' review of *A Communication Grammar of English* by Leech and Svartvik (6/78), to Tatsuroh Yamazaki's excellent and thorough examination of the Thomson and Martinet series *A Practical English Grammar* (4/81), to Robert Van Trieste's review of *Understanding and Using English Grammar* (6/82) by Betty Azar.

Donald Nilsen and Alleen Nilsen's wonderful introductory linguistics text, *Language Play*, is reviewed by Carol Qazi (6/78). The final review is by Paul Roberts, who looks at *What's the Difference? An American/British-British/American Dictionary* by Norman Moss (2/77).

Other grammar related articles worth noting here are James Herbolick's "Survey of Negation in Beginning ESL Teaching" (4/79), which complements the Bevington, Alendort and Sullivan articles. Paul Roberts, who like Audrey Reynolds, Jean McConochie and Mary Hines, has been a steadily contributing book reviewer for the *TN*, also contributed the short article on "Anaphora and Cataphora—Strong Medicine for Some Students" (9/77). J. Peter Maher in "A Strategy for Teaching Articles to Speakers of Languages Without Them" (2/82) and James F. Doubleday's "Expectation: A Case of Documentation" (8/81), about overgeneralizing grammar rules, also deal with grammar areas which cause teachers and students more than occasional distress.

SECTOR ANALYSIS AND *WORKING SENTENCES*

by Lynn E. Henrichsen
BYU, Laie, Hawaii

Sector analysis, as embodied in the textbook *Working Sentences,* is rapidly gaining widespread prominence as an effective way of teaching writing skills.

Not a recent development, sector analysis dates back to the time when Kenneth Pike was developing Tagmemics—slot-and-filler grammar. Not until 1975, however, was *Working Sentences* by Robert L. Allen, Doris Allen and Rita Pompian. (N.Y.: Thomas Y. Crowell, 1975), the first widely-used textbook based on sector analysis, published.

Unlike transformational grammar or other grammars intended to describe or generate the entire language, sector analysis is a specialized grammar designed by Robert L. Allen of Teachers College, Columbia University as a teaching grammar of "edited" English, the English used in mature writing. As the book's foreword to the instructor explains, "Sector analysis differs from most other grammars in two important ways: it is construction-oriented, not word-oriented; and it is a grammar of written English rather than of spoken English." The underlying premise of both the grammar and the text is that "in English, as in many modern languages, writing is a separate system—related to, but different from, the system of the spoken language.

Often called x-word grammar, sector analysis uses a number of modal auxiliaries called x-words to make yes-no questions, locate subjects, carry time, and much more. The manipulation of these x-words is the first step in dividing sentences into various units. In analyzing writing, language "chunks" are seen as being just as important as individual words, and student attention is focused on the large constructions that make up a sentence.

Intentionally ambiguous, the book's title, *Working Sentences,* indicates the book's dual purpose. The introduction explains, "*Working* sentences are obviously sentences that are productive and businesslike—sentences that do their job. But there is also another meaning for *working:* potters work clay into pots and vases, and glass-blowers work glass into different shapes for different purposes. *Work,* in this sense, means 'to shape' or 'to form' for a special purpose." After learning what *Working Sentences* teaches, students should be able to produce sentences that exhibit signs of care and reflection; sentences that

are more interesting, more effective, and more tightly knit together; sentences that have been loaded to their meaningful capacity; sentences that make up what is called "edited" English.

The first thing that many people see when they examine *Working Sentences* is a barrage of new and unfamiliar terms. *Shifters, includers, predicatids, trunks, half sentences, roving linkers,* and more confront the casual inspector of the book. Unfortunately, English teachers schooled in the Latin grammarians' tradition of eight parts of speech and the like are usually the least able to tolerate such a variety of new descriptive terms, and they are often the first to close the book in combined derision and bewilderment. This is unfortunate, because many of the new terms are more "logical," or at least more descriptive, than the traditional ones. A good example of this is found in the new names given to verb forms. Even staunch defenders of the traditional term "past participle" are hard pressed to define what "participle" really means. And besides, *past* participles don't always indicate past time (*Tomorrow I will have started.*). In sector analysis the same form is called the *D-T-N* form simply because it most often ends in the letter *d, t,* or *n.* Following the same line of reasoning, sector analysis presents the *ING,* the *S,* and the *No-S* forms of the English verb. Rounding out the picture are the *base* form and the *past* form.

There is more, however, to sector analysis than just a new set of names, and to really understand this new grammar one should study the entire book. An example or two, however, may help to make the point here. The above mentioned forms of the verb are divided into two categories: time oriented (*S, No-S,* and *past*) and time-less (*base, DTN,* and *ING*). Since they carry time, x-words can only be used alone or in connection with a timeless verb form, and they cannot be combined with time-oriented forms. Once students understand this, sentences such as *He working.* (no time) or *He doesn't works.* (time twice) are eliminated.

Sector analysis in *Working Sentences* gives some particularly lucid explanations of the grammar of written English. Perhaps the most valuable of these is the treatment of time-relationships in clauses. A simple diagram in the book does much to clear up stu-

dent confusion in this important area.

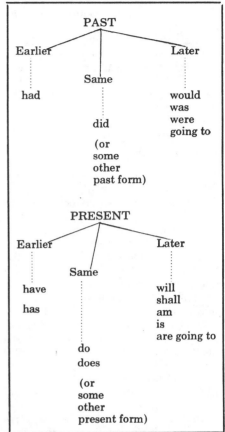

As the diagram indicates, certain x-words are used only in certain time slots. A sentence with past time orientation uses past throughout: *Tom said* (past orientation) *that his car had* (earlier) *broken down, that he was* (same time) *trying to fix it, and he would* (later) *be here as soon as possible.* Even though some of the events have already occurred (i.e. the breaking down of the car) the same sentence with present orientation uses present forms: *Tom says* (present orientation) *that his car has* (earlier) *broken down, that he is* (same time) *trying to fix it, and that he will* (later) *be here as soon as possible.* Any teacher who has struggled trying to explain this complex relationship to students will realize the great value of this simple-to-understand explanation of time in clauses.

Along with the new approach to sentence construction, time, and verb forms, *Working Sentences* displays good pedagogical sense. The book is very teachable with understandable explanations of the new grammar and very workable exercises for student practice.

The book itself is divided into fifteen units. The first five provide a foundation in sector analysis and, at the same time, a good review of some basic grammar concepts such as agreement, subjects and predicates, and pronouns, but approached from a different angle than traditionally. Just because it offers this new viewpoint, sector analysis' way of explaining the same old English is often helpful to students who have studied traditional grammar for a long time but never really understood it. After understanding the points presented in these first units, students will be able to write correct sentence *trunks* and continue on with the remaining ten chapters which explain the construction of more complex sentences and how additional information is added onto or "packed" into the basic sentence trunk.

Just as valuable as the new concepts and their explanations are the many good exercises which the book provides. Each unit has two or three "practices" interspersed through the unit and four "tasks" at the end which allow the student to use what he has learned. Whenever possible, a context is provided to make these challenging exercises more meaningful. For example, Task A of unit four, "Writing about Past Time" does not simply direct, "Change the following sentences to past tense." Instead, it explains, "The following is a transcript of notes made by a private detective shadowing a suspect. The detective recorded his notes on a miniature tape recorder in his pocket. He intended to type them up later on. In doing so, he intended to change all of the present forms to past forms, leaving the rest of his sentences pretty much as

he had recorded them, but you are asked to help him out by making the changes for him." This contextualization and humanization of exercises is appreciated by students and teachers alike.

For foreign ESL students, one drawback to the exercises is what may be called their "cultural difficulty." Interesting sentences about Andrew Wyeth or knock-knock jokes are not so interesting to ESL students who have never heard of the artist or the jokes. In some cases this extra cultural content may be an extra burden for the struggling student to bear.

A lot has been said about what *Working Sentences* does. Perhaps it would be in order to also mention what it does *not* do. After all, the book is not meant to be a complete English language teaching program.

First of all, it does not teach many basic grammatical points. Count and non-count nouns, proper use of articles, order of noun modifiers, and many other important points are not explained. It is assumed that the student has already learned such things through a thorough study of the spoken language. When students do not have a sound understanding of basic grammar, supplementary exercises must be provided.

A number of other assumptions are made. The explanations of how to use such things as includers ("*Because* he did not study, he failed.") are very good. But knowing how to construct such a sentence is only half the battle. Besides knowing how to make constructions using words such as *because, since, whether, if, in case,* or *although,* ESL students need to

know *which* includer to use for the desired meaning or relationship and *when* to use it. Especially when their native language does not have similar terms, students will need explanations and practice in the appropriate use of such constructions and the proper choice of includers, coordinators, and linkers showing contrast, reason, condition, etc.

The proper use of a number of constructions is left to the intuition of the writing student. The book explains that a certain construction (the half sentence, for example) "does not always 'feel' quite right" in a certain position. Native speakers working to improve their writing may know when something "feels" right. ESL speakers with a good deal of experience and exposure to the language might also have developed some sort of "feel" for the language. Many ESL students who do not have this "feel," however, will need some explanation in addition to that provided by the book.

In summary, the title of the book, *Working Sentences,* provides a good clue to what it does and does not do. The book is *not* called *Working Paragraphs* or *Working Essays,* because it does not pretend to teach organizational skills, thought development, stylistic conventions, or many of the other things requisite to good, formal writing. Properly used, it provides an essential interlude between standard instruction in basic grammar and later instruction in logical and coherent paragraph and essay writing.

[Reprinted from the *TESL Reporter,* Vol. 10, No. 3, Spring 1977]   TN 9/77

ROLE PLAYING GRAMMAR

By Greg Larkin
Brigham Young University

Many English teachers have regularly used role playing in literature classes, having the students act out the various characters and scenes they are reading about. In basic composition classes, role playing is often effectively used to illustrate rhetorical modes such as comparison-contrast, process, classification, etc. But in adult level ESL classes, where all too often students tend to find the content of the materials they are using somewhat less than interesting to start with, severe boredom may have set in by midterm, or even sometimes by mid-week. In such situations the judicious use of role playing can involve the students directly in the generation and analysis of various grammatical and non-grammatical forms.

For instance, role playing can increase recognition of sentence parts, such as dependent clauses. In my own ESL writ-

ing class, which uses Robert L. Allen's *Working Sentences,* I have used role playing to help students identify and use shifters and half sentences. (Essentially, "shifters" and "half sentences" are Allen's terms for certain types of dependent clauses.) I invite two students, a boy and a girl, to come to the front of the class, while I retire to the rear of the class, out of sight. Being a non-sexist teacher, I tell the two students that one of them is going to ask the other one for a date to the dance Friday night, but that they themselves must decide who will do the asking and who the responding. The only stipulation is that the asker must use a shifter in each sentence and the responder must use a half sentence in each response. This never fails to generate lively participation from every student in the class. Here is a transcription of a tape of one such session made this

semester.

Asker: (Using Shifter)	*Since you're a popular boy,* I'd like to ask you to the dance. Friday night.
Responder: (Using Half Sentence)	*Already having a date,* I must decline.
Asker: (Using Shifter)	*If you really want to go with me,* you could get rid of the other girl.
Responder: (Using Half Sentence)	*Fearing her father's wrath,* I must go with her Friday night.
Asker: (Using Shifter)	*Because you're such a coward,* I'll invite someone else to go with me.

As you can easily imagine, the dialogs

rapidly get much more exciting than this. But the critical point is not how "good" the dialog is, but that the students are creating their own text, which is the key to their increased involvement in it.

Many variations of the basic role playing format are possible. For instance, about halfway through a dialog the teacher can request the students to switch grammatical patterns, or both. As another variation, a third student can be chosen to direct the selection of roles and grammatical patterns. To involve the entire class, teams can be chosen, with each member in turn responsible to add a sentence to the dialog.

When students tire of the dialog, many new situations can be invented, using the same format as explained above. Some I've found popular with my students are:

1. Two political candidates arguing a hot question, such as drug laws, abortion, or ERA.
2. A teacher and a student discussing a grade on the last paper or test.
3. A mother and daughter discussing the daughter's newest boyfriend.

As a final variation, groups of students can prepare skits or plays based on any grammatical structures that the teacher thinks would be beneficial to the class members. With the aid of a tape recorder all these role playing creations can be transferred to a written form for later analysis and study by the students and/ or the teacher. Thus, because they have created it, the students become directly involved in their text.   TN 10/79

COLORLESS GREEN IDEAS

by Gregg Singer
Ohio University

What Means Ungrammatical?

I. *It was a Pomeranian I think, but I don't think so.*
       Malloy, Samuel Beckett
II. *This is one of those things which sounds harder to play than it sounds.*
       NPRC disc jockey
III. *Keep shampoo out of eyes. If it does, wash out with water.*
       Shampoo label
VI. *With the radio blaring, she goes driving just as fast as she can now; She forgot all about the library she told her old man, now.*
       Fun, Fun, Fun, The Beach Boys
V. *—You suppose that I could walk across the bay at low tide?*
   —You might could.

Save during the Structuralist hiatus, the problem of 'correctness' has always been a bugaboo for serious students of language. In a sense, post-Chomskyan linguistics has brought us full circle to the prescriptivists of the 18th century; again, linguistic principles are to be un-earthed by discriminating well- from ill-formed pieces of language.

Unfortunately though, grammaticality as a concept seems unwilling to stand still. The current tendency is to regard 'deviant' words, sentences, or discourses as performance errors—that is, errors which occur somewhere between the brain's ideal language capacity and the mouth. I would submit, though, that all of the above sentences are clearly 'deviant' in some sense, but none are the result of performance errors. In fact, none of them are even 'mistakes' in the sense that Zwicky, Fromkin, and others have used the word.

The simplest form of deviance to account for is dialectal variance as in V. There exists apparently a rule in North Carolina English which permits the substitution of 'could' for 'be able to'. In SAE, two modals can never come back to back except in abutting sentences, e.g., 'I can, can I?'

The other examples are more difficult to account for, though. Do the Beach Boys have a rule stating: 'About' can never occur twice in the same sentence, especially if it interferes with rhyme and meter? I doubt it; yet few can de-tect the deviance of this sentence without prompting.

Is Beckett, in I., unaware of the ordinary implications of doubling negation? Does advertising copy have its own grammar such that III. is an 'acceptable' sentence pair? Or does a radio announcer dialect exist which regularizes semantic tangles like II.? I think not.

What the widespread acceptance of sentences such as these seems to suggest is that the actual standard we, as users of language, apply to language is one of intelligibility. The only sentences which actually slow us down are those in which deviance ambiguates (vulgar verb!) the speaker's intent. I'm certain that those shampoo directions were written by a native speaker and passed the muster of countless advertising ex-ecutives. III. is only ungrammatical if grammaticality is defined as 'those ut-terances which a trained linguist will accept after reflection'.

(Reprinted from *Ohio TESOL News.* V. 2 Spring 1981).   TN 12/81

ON BEING A NEGATIVE ESL TEACHER

By Gary Bevington
Northeastern Illinois University

Negation in English is a topic of enormous importance to the ESL teacher and learner. We can support this statement first by pointing to its frequency of usage both in spoken and written forms of the language. Further-more, we can observe that negation is a probably linguistic universal or nearly so, which is to say that every language has a system of positive and negative statements and a set of rules for relating them. While negation may be a uni-versal of language, it is clear that the system of positive and negative state-ments and the set of rules relating them are not and the range of variation in negation among natural languages is quite broad. The significance of these observations for the ESL teacher is that negation is a subject that should be dealt with early on in ESL instruction and that the ESL learner comes to the task of learning English with an im-plicit system of knowledge and beliefs about negation from his native language language that must be dealt with di-rectly or indirectly by the ESL teacher.

The question arises as to what knowl-edge and skills the ESL teacher should acquire to make him successful in deal-ing with English negation. Minimally, he must have a basic grasp of the way negation works in English. It will also be useful for him to have some knowl-edge of common types of negation sys-tems in other languages; that is, it may be useful to be aware of what the stu-dent might bring with him from his native language, both as a way of guess-ing where there may be areas of dif-ficulty and as a diagnostic tool after problems have arisen. Finally, the teacher should have a strategy for pre-senting the material to the student.

In this brief report it is, of course, impossible to come to serious grips with even one of the three issues just mentioned. Any one of them is clearly worthy of a monograph, but unfortu-nately suitable treatments for the ESL teacher are not available. Instead, we must content ourselves here with a few largely anecdotal illustrations of the problems involved and a few references to the woefully inadequate literature which may be consulted.

Turning first to the question of English negation, we can refer the reader to the article in this area by Edward Klima "Negation in English" (in J. Fodor & J. Katz *The Structure of Language* (Prentice-Hall, 1964) pp. 246-323). Unfortunately, it is difficult reading even for a person with considerable background in theoretical linguistics and all but inaccessible to anyone else. An excellent brief and very readable summary of Klima's analysis is presented at the beginning of a theoretical article on negation by R. Jackendoff "An Interpretative Theory of Negation" in *Foundations of Language* 5(1969)218-241. A word of warning is necessary, however, don't go beyond the first section (pp. 218-222) unless you're really into negation and theoretical linguistics. A presentation of negation available to those with minimal linguistic training is Quirk *et al*, *A Grammar of Contemporary English*, pp. 374-385.

Klima's fundamental insight is that negation was basically something that happens to sentences. I think that this observation has a great deal of significance for the ESL teacher. The most effective way of dealing with negation is to talk about it as something that happens to *sentences* and not, say, *verbs* as one might assume. Consider sentence (1):

(1) John had some money once.

An ESL student taught that negation is something you do to verbs might reasonably come up with (2).

(2) John didn't have some money once.

For the native speaker of English, at least two negative versions of this sentence are immediately apparent.

(3) John never had any money.
(4) John didn't ever have any money.

Other possibilities exist:

(5) John didn't have any money ever.
(6) John had no money ever.

What can we reasonably expect from an ESL learner? I think that we would all agree that for his active use of the language, we would hope for sufficient mastery of the language to avoid (2) and be able to produce one of the versions (3) through (6), probably (3) as our first choice. Even this will be no mean accomplishment for learner and teacher.

It is useful for the teacher to have some idea of what the ESL student may bring to task of mastering English negation from his native language. In other words, some general information on the typology of negation in human language is an important topic. But it is almost shocking how little is available to the reader on this important topic. In fact, the only significant study I have been able to find goes back to Otto Jespersen's article "Negation in English and Other Languages" written in 1917 and reprinted in *Selected Writings of Otto Jespersen*.

The most important thing that ESL teacher should keep in mind is that as systems of negation go in natural languages English is almost "weird". A couple of simple examples will illustrate this. First, multiple negation, e.g. "Nobody didn't never say nothing nowhere to nobody." is really the most common and reasonable way for a language to carry out sentence negation. That it is reasonable I think is amply illustrated by the fact that the deviant example given above is perfectly comprehensible to English speakers and we all understand it in exactly the same way, as simple sentence negation not as an accretion of negative operators operating on one another as one might expect given the old school-grammar saw about two negatives making a positive. This latter interpretation would, absurdly, make the above statement equivalent to a positive statement since it contains an even number of negative operators (six) which would in effect wipe each other out. This of course then represents a common kind of interference problem in negation confronting the ESL teacher. To compound the problem is the fact that there are dialects of English with multiple negation and the ESL learner is quite likely to come in contact with speakers of these dialects which will reinforce his use of such a system in English. The heart of the problem here is the value that English-speaking bourgeois society places on the use of multiple negation. Somehow this must be explained in a human and non-condescending way to ESL students, even though they come from a milieu where this is the norm for spoken English.

Another example is what might be called after a popular song of the 1940's the "Yes-we-have-no bananas" syndrome. Consider the following sentences:

(7) John has five dollars.
(8) John doesn't have five dollars.

The statements are contradictory; one or the other is true but not both. Consider now the yes/no question forms of (7) and (8):

(9) Does John have five dollars?
(10) Doesn't John have five dollars?

Both (9) and (10) have two appropriate answers: affirmative (yes) and negative (no). Answering (9) affirmatively asserts the truth of (7) and the falsity of (8); answering it negatively asserts the truth of (8) and the falsity of (7). Consider the answers to (10). It would be "reasonable" to assume that things would be reversed, i.e. an affirmative answer would assert the truth of (8) and the falsity of (7). While this is "reasonable", for English it is simply not accurate; affirmative and negative answers to (9) and (10) make exactly the same assertions of truth and falsity with regard to (7) and (8). That this "unreasonable" state of affairs in English is not the case in other languages

Table 1. The two dimensions of the yes-no question-answering system in 16th century English, Modern English, and Japanese *

	Agreement to the statement of a question	Disagreement to the statement of a question	
	16th century English		Modern English
Positive: no negation in the highest clause in an answer	(Are you going?) Yes.	(Aren't you going?) Yes.	Are you going? Aren't you going? Yes, I am going.
Negative: negation in the highest clause in an answer	(Aren't you going?) No.	(Are you going?) Nay.	Aren't you going? Are you going? No, I am not going.
	Japanese		
	Are you going? Yes, I am going.	Aren't you going? No, I am going.	
	Aren't you going? Yes, I am not going.	Are you going? No, I am not going.	

* From M. Akiyama. "Negative Questions in Young Children," Child Language Acquisition Forum, Stanford, 1976.   *TN 4/79*

is mirrored in the obvious non-native reply in the old song. When these facts about English are pointed out to even fairly advanced ESL students, one very often gets reactions ranging from surprise to bewilderment to moral outrage.

The general point we are trying to make about interference in teaching negation is that it does play a significant role. But the ESL teacher can anticipate a number of problems based on general observations about cross-linguistic negative typology without the necessity of understanding the details of the mechanics of negation in the individual native languages of one's ESL students.

To conclude this discussion we wish to make a few observations about pedagogical strategy in teaching negation. First, it should be emphasized that the solution is not "a lesson" or "a unit" or "a chapter" on negation. The problem is simply too complex for that. Instead, a systematic "layering-on" approach must be taken. By this we mean that the topic of negation must be divided in managable-sized "packages" which are then prioritized and integrated into other material the student is being taught. The core elements of negation are to be presented very early to the student and added on to at regular intervals throughout the student's training even to very advanced levels. The most basic or "core" elements center around the mechanics of verbal negation. At a slightly more advanced level one would be concerned with such things as affectives (some/any, etc.), and basic variations and equivalencies among negated sentences. At an advanced level topics relating to in-

Table 2. Analysis of negative questions, answers to them, and the underlying intention in speakers of different languages*

Language of Speaker	Negative question	Answer	Underlying Intention
English speaker	Aren't you going? (negative)	Yes, (positive)	I am going. (positive)
	Aren't you going? (negative)	No, (negative)	I am not going. (negative)
Japanese speaker	Aren't you going? (negative)	No, (negative)	I am going. (positive)
	Aren't you going? (negative)	Yes, (positive)	I am not going. (negative)
English-Japanese bilingual speaker	Aren't you going? (negative)	Yes, (positive) No, (negative)	I am going. (positive)
	Aren't you going? (negative)	No, (negative) Yes, (positive)	I am not going. (negative)

* From M. Akiyama. "Negative Questions in Young Children," Child Language Acquisition Forum, Stanford, 1976.

TN 4/79

terclausal negation such as raising (cf. *I think he hasn't left.=I don't think he has left.* BUT *I know that he hasn't left.≠I don't know that he has left.*) and multiple negation (which *does* exist in standard English, e.g. *I didn't say nobody won.*) It is also important to stress the efficacy of pattern drills, particulary oral ones, in developing proficiency with negation in ESL students. While an understanding of the mechanisms of negation may be helpful, particularly for adult ESL learners, the only thing that really counts in the ability to produce correct negatives and correctly understand those produced by native speakers. In most situations, ESL learners do not enjoy the luxury of being able to intellectualize about this. Instead, they must perform rapidly, and this kind of performance is most easily achieved by oral pattern drills.

It should be clear that the foregoing remarks have only scratched the surface of the problem of negation in ESL. Hopefully, others may see the virtue of dealing with some of the topics touched on here in the detail which they deserve. *TN 4/79*

ON BEING A QUESTIONABLE ESL TEACHER

By Marilyn Aledort
Adelphi University

Gary Bevington's article "On Being a Negative ESL Teacher," in the TESOL Newsletter of April, 1979, provoked a lot of thought. Two of the most intriguing topics for theoretical linguists and ESL teachers have been (1) language universals—that is, those grammatical and semantic categories many or most natural languages have in common, and (2) language anomalies—those structures that appear to be idiosyncratic and unique to a language and which not only defy word-by-word translation but are elusive to reasoned analysis as well. They simply are, and as such they must be taught and they must be learned. Indeed, anomalous forms often express the richest part of a language and the spirit and imagination of those born into its linguistic community.

We need not linger here over language universals, although they will no doubt continue to be the subject of countless journal articles to come. Cognate forms, whatever their nature, serve to facilitate and expedite our work as language teachers and learners. It is the vexed and vexing questions (in this case, negative questions) of how to find strategies for teaching negation, especially when it is combined with interrogation, that demand our energy and attention. The problem is complex, not because negation is "almost 'weird' " in English, but because it works both a structural and semantic hardship on the learner when it is combined, as it so often is, with interrogation. And this is true even when the ESL learner has a parallel form in his own tongue.

If one examines two of the most familiar and closely related languages of the Indo-European group heard and spoken in the United States, for example French and Spanish, is not each of these unique in its system of negation? Each requires a specific order and number of negative elements and each shifts in its own unique way to formulate questions. Where English may be a species of linguistic odd-man-out is in its system of auxiliary verbs, without which the ESL student can frame neither negative statements nor questions.

Experience in the ESL classroom over a long period of time leads me to contend that it is negative interrogation, not negation in itself, that constitutes a major problem for teacher and learner. To frame a yes/no question, the evolution of the English language has fixed the auxiliary verbs (is, are, was, were, do, does, did, can etc.) right up front in initial position, a structural requirement difficult to master for most English learners. Having to change the auxiliary into its negative form (using another English peculiarity, the contraction) seems to compound the difficulty. Furthermore, negative questions are most often negative in the grammatical sense only; semantically they cover a very wide range of meanings. Consider the following: (1) Isn't she beautiful? (2) Aren't they here yet? (3) Aren't you going to the game? (4) Won't you have a little more wine? (5) Can't you stay a little longer? (6) Wouldn't you consider marrying him?

Even allowing for various interpretations, each of the sentences is uniquely loaded as to message and purpose. Sentence (1) is not only not negative, it is not even a question. It is what we say when we need to express enthusiastic approval and admiration. (2) and (3) could very well indicate 'negative' emotions such as disappointment, frustrated expectation, annoyance, or even anxiety, but not necessarily so. (3) could signify mild surprise or idle curiosity. (4) expresses hospitality or politeness (unless, of course, the motive is ulterior), and (5) is an out-an-out plea. (6) appears to seek confirmation or corroboration of an idea in the questioner's mind, a common function of negative questions.

Bevington suggests that negation is so complex in English that the topic "must be divided into manageable-sized 'packages' . . . and integrated into other material the student is being taught." I see no fault with the "systematic 'layering-on' approach" he outlines in his article, but I would attempt to assemble interrogative 'packages' made up of sentences like the above, and others that present special communicative difficulties, both structurally and semantically. These would probably have to be reserved for intermediate or even advanced level students, to whom it would be possible and profitable to indicate the various psycholinguistic purposes and exigencies they serve.

It is also true, as Bevington points out, citing Akiyama (1976) that in Japanese (and in other modern languages as well) the answer to the negative question "Aren't you going?" would be either "No, I am going," indicating disagreement with the questioner, or "Yes, I am not going," indicating agreement with the negative

idea in the questioner's mind. As complicated as this is in terms of comparative linguistics (psycho-linguistics really), it could also be interpreted as a translation problem. The question could be translated into English as "Do you mean you're *not* going?" Then the answer would offer the same possibilities in English as it does in Japanese: No (you're wrong), I *am* going. or Yes (you're correct), I'm *not* going.

The pattern of Japanese addresses itself to the truth or falsity of the questioner's assumption, rather than to the fact or proposition that someone either is or is not going somewhere, or planning to do something. This is sometimes the case in English too but, in general, regardless of the pattern of the student's own language, he or she must learn that the English question "Aren't you going?" follows the pattern of all other yes/no questions; that is to say, it demands either an affirmative "Yes, I am." or a negative "No, I'm not.", addressing the truth about the respondent's future behavior, not reflecting on the questioner's state of mind.

As professional teachers we are constrained to separate for our students those segments of language that can be learned or memorized by the application of a rule or paradigm, e.g. word order of statements and questions, possessive case, the negative/affirmative switch on statements using tag questions, etc. Unfortunately, for the learner at least, discourse makes copious use of those vast areas of language (idioms for instance) which must be learned and mastered by dint of every strategy the learner can summon—ears, wits, humor and creative imagination. We owe it to our students to help them make semantic 'rules' and categories and then offer them ample opportunity for application and practice. Our aim should be to make effective as well as competent communicators of them.

On the question of another English anomaly, the double negative, I suggest that we stick to our guns, academically if not socially, and teach negation as rule-governed: that is, one negative element to a clause when the verb is negative. Of course, there are exceptions, arising from previous discourse and semantic clarification, but these are relatively rare. "I didn't say nobody won" is the example Bevington chooses to

demonstrate how we break our own taboos. But this sentence actually has two clause elements and could be uttered or written as "I didn't say that nobody won." or "I didn't say, 'Nobody won'." We do not respond to this kind of sentence, or to the "Not ony did he not . . ." variety of compounded negation, as we do to "I didn't hear nothing" or "Don't give me no back talk." or "He ain't got no job", even though, clearly, we understand their meanings and even accept the fact that although they are considered non-standard, they are ubiquitously used.

It can be pointed out to advanced students that not all native speakers use grammatical English, a phenomenon not unheard of in their own speech communities, and that responses to semantically governed categories may also vary widely. A common example of a troublesome form is the locution "Would you mind. . . . (closing the window)". Grammatically, the appropriate response should take a negative form. However, many native American children, and some adults as well, either do not know the appropriate response or do not feel comfortable answering negatively. As a result, one hears "Yes, of course." or "Certainly." or "Okay." It is entirely possible that, over time, the affirmative answer might win out. Nevertheless, just as we teach foreign students that the expression "Would you mind . . ." takes the gerund form in the verb that follows, it is our responsibility to instruct them in the polite and appropriate response, even though native speakers may break the rules.

As Bevington suggests, these discussions (and even those in our best ESL texts) only scratch the surface. If we are to enlighten ourselves and our students, encouraging them to try out new modes of thought and expression, we must stress the idea that language is a product of human creativity and imagination, more varied and various than any of the arts or sciences dependent upon language for information and elucidation.

Editor's Note: The tables by M. Akiyjama referred to above from the paper "Negative Questions in Young Children" printed along with the Bevington article in the April 1979 issue of the TN were added by the editor.   TN 10/79

CONTRIBUTIONS OF THE DEFINITE ARTICLE TO THE COHERENCE OF DISCOURSE

by Garry Molhot
University of Riyadh

Though our teaching materials include necessary information about the function of the definite article, the difficulty we have in teaching its proper use provides extensive evidence that our materials are

not sufficient. By increasing the number of relevant categories, it is possible to formulate a more generalized concept of the function of *the*. *The* contributes to the coherence of discourse by indicating

the presence of a referential relation.

Referential relation is used here to mean the type of semantic intersection obtaining between any two nouns in a discourse. Any N1 may have the same, different, or partial reference to any N2. For a discourse to be coherent, we must know these referential relations, as explained below.

I. Introduction, Subsequent Mention, and Reintroduction.

There is a problem with analysing the use of the articles in the following sequence as examples of *introduction* and *subsequent mention.*

1. Joy threw *a ball.*
2. *The ball* went into *a window.*

Subsequent mention implies that *the* will be used for all further instances of the lexical item *ball* in this discourse. There are, however, two important cases when this is not true. First, it is possible that there will be reference to *a different ball,* which would require *ball* to be introduced again, along with an appropriate adjective indicating the difference. The second case is more complex. If the perspective of the discourse is shifted from that of the speaker/writer to a participant, *ball* could be reintroduced, as in (3) in sequence with (1) and (2):

3. When George saw that Joy threw *a ball* through *a window,* he laughed.

Here, *a ball* follows *the ball,* and a *window* (in (2) above.) According to the general concept of subsequent mention, we would expect *ball* and *window* in (3) to be preceded by *the.* Thus, the concept of subsequent mention, though useful, should be altered to include the notion of continued perspective. With a shift of perspective, subsequent mention does not necessarily imply that *the* is appropriate.

When different lexical items are used with the same reference, as in the following sequence:

4. *A woman* in a red dress came into church.

5. Mr. Jones greeted   *the lady*   with a smile.   *the trollop*

the situation becomes more complex. We do not always agree on which lexical items are suitable for renaming. One man's *saint* might be another man's *sinner,* etc., etc. For this reason, within the framework of traditional transformational generative grammar, as explained by Thomas Bever and John Ross in their unpublished paper *Meaning Postulates* (1967 MIT Department of Linguistics), this type of perceptual problem has been shifted from the discipline of linguistics to psychology even though there is an overt linguistic marker, *the,* manifesting the presence of a referential relation. Rather than shift this to psychology, however, we should be able to discuss it in terms of intended relations. That is, if someone wants to imply a relation between N1 and N2 in a discourse, we should know what structures are available to facilitate that intention. This allows us to include a valid concept in linguistics without the necessity of writing an encyclopedic component in the grammar, as Bever and Ross insist we would have to if we did not "sweep this under the rug" of psychology. Of course we cannot write a grammar which includes all possible relations, especially since we maintain that language is creative, reflecting an ever changing world.

II. Enumeration

Consider the sequence:

6. I went to a *baseball game* in St. Louis.
    The teams played well.
    The hot dogs tasted great.
    The fans were a lot of fun.
    Also, they have *a new score board* there which shoots fireworks.

Teams, hot dogs, and *fans* are preceded by *the,* meaning that there is an intended relation between them, and in this case, *a baseball game.* These are well understood components of a baseball game. However, in this sequence, the type of scoreboard is perceived as special, not an ordinary part of most games, so it is preceded by *a* to emphasize this.

Again, this involves perception. If someone intends to portray a relationship as ordinary or as special, there are overt linguistic markers to facilitate this, even if the relationship seems improbable, as in:

7. I bought *a new house,* but *the launching pad* is broken.

Here we understand that the speaker/writer intends for us to accept the idea that a *launching* pad is a normal part of a *house,* but, for most of us, this would result in a polite question regarding the sense of the statement.

Consider the enumeration of abstract concepts such as *love* in:

8. *The love* corporal ———— showed for his country is exemplified by his actions. He did X, Y, and Z. ————

in which X, Y, and Z are intended to enumerate the concept of *love,* involves actions as well as nouns, and is also subject to perceptual differences. Since this construction is a special (cataphoric) construction (the "subsequently mentioned" item occurs first and is followed by an explanation) it really belongs in the next section, Combination.

III. Combination

Combination also occurs with abstract and concrete concepts. After enumerating several nouns, their combined total may be subsequently mentioned with one cover term, as in:

9. On the stage we saw *a chair, a couch, a lamp,* and *an old trunk. The furniture* was arranged neatly.

where *furniture* stands for the total. Of course, any of the items could be reintroduced from a different perspective. Perception plays a part, especially with abstract concepts, as in:

10. Tim was shouting at Grace, and Grace was shouting at Tim. *The argument* lasted for ten minutes.

or

11. Ralph, the banker, took all the bank's money and bet it on the winning horse. *The stroke of genius* saved the town.

In (10) *argument* is an acceptable cover term, but in (11), *stroke of genius* might raise objections in favor of *folly, risk, crime* or some similar term. Whichever term is perceived as appropriate, the definite article *the* is used to show that there is an intended relation.

IV. Conclusion

The is one of the most frequently occurring words in English. From the examples given above, it is clear that we need a better definition of its function than to say it is used for subsequent mention, unique entities, or nouns which have "undergone" definitization. The definition should neither be misleading, incomplete, nor vacuous.

The common characteristic of the function of *the* in the above examples is that it indicates the presence of an intended referential relation, whether or not that relation is between the same or different lexical items, and whether or not it is within one sentence or between different sentences. Without the relation, coherence is severely damaged. We would not know what is being referred to. Yet, with several of these occurring in the same discourse, sometimes overlapping each other, we have no way of determining whether the concepts refer to each other or not unless we have already processed the semantic information. In the sequence:

12. A noun. . . . a noun. . . . the noun. . . . a noun. . . . the noun. . . . the noun. . . . a noun. . . . a noun. . . . the noun. . . .

we are lost if we want to decide which nouns are related, until we semantically decode the nouns. Then we are able to process the information provided by the *a*'s and *the*'s.

Thus, this feature of the language suggests that a semantic based discourse grammar is needed to account for the coherence of texts.

As for *the* itself, it is one of the cues used to inform the *reader/listener* that the following information should be familiar, either through the linguistic or cultural context of the discourse. It is also an invitation to the *reader/listener* to question the reference intended.

TN 12/80

THE IMPORTANCE OF TEACHING THE MELODY OF A LANGUAGE

by Shakti Datta
Educational Solutions Inc.

Words and their correct sequence are essential components of a language. Their appropriate use allows one to express one's thoughts, feelings and perceptions. The proper use of another essential component—the melody of the language—enables one to be "expressive" in that language.

This insight must, in a non-verbal and a non-intellectual form, have been actively present in all of us at the time we taught ourselves our mother tongue. We must also have known, intuitively, that we needed to work with precision on our vocal apparatus in order to "embellish" our voice with the melody of the language of our environment. We must have known that our early attempts were no measure of whether or not we could acquire the right melody. It must have been—in an empirical sense—a part of our awareness that improved articulation is the result of persistent attempts at approximation.

That is why we neither felt frustration nor gave up, but kept on trying. We worked diligently yet effortlessly. We made mistakes and remained nonjudgmental towards ourselves. We allowed ourselves time to correct our mistakes and to practice so that we could function spontaneously in areas not yet mastered by us. All of us, all over the world, own the melody of our mother tongue as an integral part of our speech. We must have done the "right things" in teaching ourselves—and in learning—our first language.

Implications for Teaching

The implications of these observations are of significance in language teaching. The following are some of the ways in which my approach to teaching a second language has been affected by them:

1. I consider those who come to me to learn a language as being equipped with the capacity to work on themselves and therefore as capable of learning the melody of a language which is new to them.

2. It is my responsibility to bring learners into contact with their own functionings so that, along with acquiring new words, they learn to give their utterances a new melody by making the required changes in their functionings.

3. It would be a mistake on my part to expect perfection from the start, but it is equally wrong to conclude that the melody of the target language is beyond the grasp of learners and that teaching it may therefore be left aside.

4. A sensitivity for the new melody is best developed when:

(a) teaching helps learners become aware of what to do with themselves to produce utterances which carry the right melody;

(b) learners are given ample practice so that they gain facility and can become spontaneously right;

(c) learners' mistakes are utilized for enhancing their learning;

(d) each learner is given the opportunity to discover and internalize the criteria for the right melody.

Working with students on the melody of the target language, in terms of sensitivity, allows the students to feel the reality of the new language in their flesh, for it is indeed quite literally in their flesh that they make the changes that are necessary in order to sense and own the new melody.

Components of "Melody"

Melody includes pronunciation, intonation, stresses, pauses and ups and downs of the voice. Learning these various facets of the new melody means being intimately in contact with the muscle tone of one's lips, one's tongue, one's vocal cords, and so on. It requires knowing how much energy to place in one's breath, and at what points in one's speech, in order to produce the desired results. It requires sensing when to run the words together and when to pause, when to let the voice rise and when to let it fall. In essence, making the melody of a new language a part of one's sensitivity is equivalent to learning to create new patterns of sounds through the distribution of one's energy. This can be a very exciting activity if played as a subtle game of energy distribution over the "somatic instrument" one owns. It is rewarding too, because the melody of a language—an objective reality—when transformed into the quality of one's voice, undoubtedly adds elegance to one's self-expression and helps to convey meaning better.

Non-native speakers may not be able to sound exactly like natives. But the speech of non-natives can certainly express their awareness of the melody of the language and their best attempt at respecting this vital aspect of the language, as they use it. This can be achieved by incorporating in one's teaching precise techniques designed to facilitate learning of the melody of the target language creatively.

TN 4/81

REFERENCES

Gattegno, Caleb, *The Common Sense of Teaching Foreign Languages* (New York: Educational Solutions, 1976), *The Universe of Babies* (New York: Educational Solutions, 1973), and *Teaching Foreign Languages in Schools: The Silent Way* (New York: Educational Solutions; 1963).

From *Idiom*, February 1979

CONVERSATION: SAYING HELLO AND GOODBYE

By Patricia Sullivan
University of Hawaii

A: Hello, Ann. How are you?
B: I'm fine, thank you. And you?
A: Fine, thanks.

———————

A: Goodbye.
B: Goodbye.

What words are used in American conversations? Does the above dialogue represent American speech? Do dialogues in language textbooks accurately reflect the way language is used? Do we, as language teachers, teach what is actually said in conversation? Students who want to communicate need to know not only what is grammatically correct, but also what is appropriate. In an attempt to find out what expressions are locally used, and to find answers to questions such as the above. I studied greetings and farewells in Honolulu, Hawaii. The study consisted of recording and analyzing greetings and farewells spontaneously uttered, collecting data from native speakers about what they think they say, and comparing the collected data to a sampling of dialogues from ESL textbooks. For the purposes of this study, expressions of greetings and farewells were analyzed as isolated occurrences. They were tabulated according to frequency of use, sex of speaker, and place spoken; and were collected from such varied places as beauty parlors, elevators, office buildings, airports, stores, and television. The responses were collected from people between the ages of approximately 18 and 45.

It will not be surprising to most native speakers to hear that the word "hi" was overwhelmingly the preferred greeting. What is surprising is the almost exclusive use of "hi" by females. Of the 46 greetings heard from females, 31 said "hi." The other 15 greetings were divided into seven different categories. Males, on the other hand, used "hi" in 7 of the 19 collected greetings. The second most common greeting by males was "hello."

The results of farewells heard may be more surprising. Out of the 60 farewells, the word "goodbye" was heard only once, and that was spoken in anger. The most often-heard expressions were "I'll (we'll) see ya," "ba-bye," and "bye." Again there is a difference depending on the sex of the speaker. Males overwhelmingly used the expressions "I'll (we'll) see ya," whereas females most often said "ba-bye" or "bye."

Thirteen native speakers, randomly selected, were asked about their most often used expressions of greetings and farewells. For greetings, the responses matched those heard in spontaneous speech; that is, most speakers said that they use the word "hi" most often as a greeting. The polled answers for farewells, however, did not match the spontaneously-heard data. The word "ba-bye," which was one of the most frequently heard in spontaneous speech, was never given as a possible farewell by any of the thirteen native speakers.

In the sampling of textbooks, the dialogues did not match the collected data of spontaneous speech. In the seven textbooks sampled, the most commonly used greeting in dialogues was "How are you?," whereas in the collected data, "How are you?" was heard only once in 65 greetings. In the textbooks sampled, "bye" and 'ba-bye" were never used in dialogues. The expressions "See you later (tomorrow)" were occasionally used. From this sample, it appears that many textbook dialogues do not represent spontaneously-spoken American greetings or farewells.

One question that we as teachers need to answer is what style of conversation we should teach. From my experience, students in the U.S. rarely have any difficulty in picking up local and often-used expressions, such as "hi," 'ba-bye," or "see ya." Need such expressions, then, be written in textbooks? Should they be taught in the classroom? I am not advocating that textbooks drop all formal English dialogues and adopt only informal usage. When using a dialogue, however, a teacher should certainly discuss questions such as: Who says these words? When? In what other ways can the same ideas be expressed?

Does the dialogue given at the beginning of this article accurately represent spontaneous speech? Probably not. This study, of course, may show only speech patterns local to Hawaii. It is up to each teacher to listen discriminatingly to local speech, and to determine what words are actually spoken in the local community. As we learned from this study, many ESL textbooks do not accurately represent parts of American conversation. There is a difference between what we say, what we think we say, and what the textbooks say we say. An English language teacher should certainly be aware of these differences.

TN 2/79

THE PASSIVE VOICE: IT MUST BE SPOKEN FOR

by Patrick Kameen
University of Louisville

Although most ESL instructors readily agree that they do not follow a prescriptive approach to language teaching, this is unfortunately not true in terms of the way many teach, or do not teach, the passive voice. In spite of very clear empirical evidence in support of a new approach to teaching the passive, prejudice against the passive continues to flourish, fueled by those ESL texts and rhetoric handbooks that either warn students against its use, or list only a very few of the many contexts in which the passive may be used appropriately.

Quickly summaried, the research highlights are these: First, at least three studies contradict the common claim that increased use of the passive detracts from overall writing quality. In fact, in all three studies, higher incidence of passive voice correlated with better overall writing. Second, two studies have shown that even "piled-up" passives do not make a passage more difficult to read when compared to the readability of the same passage with all active verbs. Third, various studies have revealed that passives are used much more frequently in speaking and writing than has been believed. On average, one of every eight verbs in speaking and writing appears in the passive, with this ratio increasing to one of three in informative, scientific writing.

Since many of our students pursue careers in which they will have to read a great deal of passive-laden scientific writing, and produce in their lab reports and research papers a large number of passives, it is especially important that we teach our students how to use the passive. It is with this goal in mind that I have compiled the following list of contexts in which the passive is used appropriately.

1. Use the passive to place a short object and verb before a long subject, thus avoiding front-heavy sentences.
   Ex. *The IRS has been cheated* by otherwise honest individuals who feel too large a percentage of their salaries goes for taxes and who believe that the government is wasting their tax dollars.

2. Use the passive to avoid misplacing modifiers, especially participial phrases and relative clauses.
   Ex. After having provided evidence that led to an important arrest, *the witness was repeatedly threatened* (by the criminal).

3. Use the agentless "passive of non-responsibility" to avoid placing blame.
   Ex. The decision to ask you to retire *has been made*, and it *cannot be reconsidered.*

4. Use the "it" or "second passive" form to sound objective or to indicate that there is no absolute proof for the statement.
   Ex. It is *reported/said/known/felt/ assumed/thought/believed* that the governor is a high-stakes gambler.
   Ex. The governor is *reported/ . . . / believed* to be a high-stakes gambler.

5. The passive is almost always used with *to be composed of, known for,* and *noted for;* and is frequently used with *to be connected, converted, deduced, attributed to, activated, conducted, examined, measured, recorded, based on, classified, distributed, made up of, comprised of,* and *derived from.*
   Ex. Einstein *is noted for* his formulation of the theory of relativity.

6. Use the agentless passive when the agent is well known, unknown, or unimportant.
   Ex. Cars *are manufactured* in Detroit.

7. Use the agentless passive to describe technical processes and to report research procedures and results.
   Ex. Hydrogen and chlorine *were combined*, and the resulting chemical reaction *was observed.*

8. Use the passive with the *by*-agent phrase when referring to historically or socially significant works—works in which the result of the action is at least as well known as the performer.
   Ex. *Gone With the Wind was written* by Margaret Mitchell.

9. Use the passive to keep similar parts of clauses or sentences parallel, especially when an element in the first clause or sentence is co-referential to an element in second clause or sentence.
   Ex. In the past few years, the inner city has undergone a massive *rejuvenation.* (*This rejuvenation has been*) *aided* by the sharp increase in property values in the suburbs and the availability of low-interest loans.

TN

IDIOMS AND AUXILIARIES

Edited by Darlene Larson
New York University

We are grateful to Phyllis Van Horn of the University of Idaho in Moscow and Virginia Heringer of the University of Southern California in Los Angeles for sharing with us some classroom practices that they have found successful. Write and let us know how well they work for you, and what adaptations you made to make them fit your class.

Phyllis was looking for a way around the problem of providing a situation that would allow students free practice of idioms they had been learning and at the same time allow the teacher some possibility of evaluating usage and comprehension. Sources of idioms are:

Idiom Drills, George McCallum (Thomas Y. Crowell, 1970)

Idioms in Action, George Reeves (Newbury House, 1974)

The Key to English: Two-Word Verbs (Collier-Macmillan, 1964)

Essential Idioms in English, Robert J. Dixson (Regents Publishing Co., 1972),

Handbook of American Idioms and Idiomatic Usage, Harold C. Whitford and Robert J. Dixson (Regents Publishing Co., 1973).

First, a technique to see if students have an understanding of how the idiom should be used. Make a series of sentences, each of which contains one idiom used correctly or incorrectly. Read it aloud and have the students indicate whether the idiom is correct or not by marking an "X" for incorrect or a "C" for correct. Test items might include:

1. Can you go to the store with me *just as soon*?*

2. It's windy, so I have to *brush up on** my hair.

3. Jean's staying with her sister *for the time being*.

Phyllis recommends that the test items be grammatically correct with only the meaning of the idiom in question. Each sentence is graded on a scale of one point per item.

Her second suggestion assesses whether or not the students can produce the idiom correctly when assisted with both meaning and a key word. The teacher first reads a sentence containing the definition of an idiom, then isolates the definition and reads a key word from the idiom. The key word is usually the one which receives the primary stress in normal spoken usage. The student writes only the complete idiom, changing number, person or tense to agree with the content of the sentence. All of the sentences are related contextually. Ex:

1. I decided to use the good weather for my benefit and go for a walk. Use for my benefit . . . advantage. (The students would then write, "take advantage of.")

2. My roommate disapproved of my idea. Disapproved of . . . view. (The students would write, "took a dim view of.")

These items may be graded on a three-point scale: one point for the accuracy of the idiom, one for agreement of tense, number and person, and one for the correct inclusion of articles and particles.

Her third technique assesses the oral production of the idioms being studied. She recommends taping a conversation in which the student is given cards with six unrelated idioms written in the root form. The student's card might read:

> sooner or later
> go too far
> have someone over
> make sense
> as for
> find out

The teacher presents questions in conversational style and the student responds, including one of the idioms in his answer. The teacher might say, "Jack's been in school for two years with no vacation. Now he wants to take a course during the winter break. What about that?"

Replies could be, "Sooner or later he'll have a vacation," or "He's going too far!" or "I'll have him over during the break," or "That makes sense. He'll be able to graduate sooner."

The teacher has six questions or statements similar to the example, and the student is free to use any one of the six idioms on his card in his answer. Evaluation of the student's tape is made in a private auditing session using three scales of five points each: usage of the idiom, pronunciation of the idiom, and the appropriateness of the response to the question. She suggests the desirability of having two people audit this part, rate it independently, and average the scores.

(This last technique of giving partial information on cards reminds me of the Hines strategy in role playing— reported in the *IDIOM* of NYS ESOL BEA, Vol. 5, No. 2, page 3, "Lessons that Work," and reprinted in the *TESOL NEWSLETTER*, Vol. IX, No. 3, p. 9.—It would be interesting to incorporate previously studied idioms into "Lines to Choose From" role play cards and see whether students select them or not.)

* * *

Virginia is outlining a technique she uses in which she insists on the use of modals, but believes the exercise is much closer to conversational practices that could take place in reality than other exercises suggested in texts and grammars. Since students can express possibility and probability well with adverbial constructions, it is necessary to ask them to eliminate the adverbs this time around and use, instead, the modals of possibility and probability, *can, could, may, might,* and *must.*

The exercise is essentially a set of puzzles in which students speculate on the possible occupation of a person, basing their guesses on clues given by the teacher. The clues are arranged in such a way that the students come closer to the correct answer as they progress through them, finally arriving at the one that *must be* correct. Preparation for the exercise means arranging sets of clues from general to specific. This progression also provides a clue to the modal to choose for the response, matching the modals that indicate more certainty with "guesses" that are based on more specifics.

The teacher, or another student, reads three clues one at a time. After each clue students are asked to guess what kind of work the person does, forming their guesses not into questions, but into statements containing one of the modals of possibility or probability.

EXAMPLE A

Clue 1: Mr. Smith usually sits at a desk while he is working.

Response: He might be a teacher/ an executive/a manager/an accountant.

Clue 2: He uses pencils and straight-edges and large sheets of paper.

Response: He could be an engineer/ an architect/a designer/a draftsman.

Clue 3: Occasionally he visits construction sites where bridges and roads are being built.

Response: He must be an engineer.

Virginia comments that *Example B* usually brings up some discussion of sex-typing in jobs. I would think that lots of discussion could be generated about similarities and differences in job training and education requirements, conditions, and performance. She also mentions that students are sure to give answers using adverbs instead of modals and this provides a good opportunity to discuss the similarity in meaning.

If students are really "into" discussing the pros and cons of one guess over another, I believe Virginia's follow-up suggestion should be a winner. She mentions that after clue #2, the conditional and negatives are appropriate. A possible response in Example A: Mr. Smith couldn't be an accountant. If he were, he might use pencils and big sheets of paper, but he wouldn't need straight edges. And in B: Mary couldn't be a butcher. If she were, she might wear a white coat, but she wouldn't need to attend school for many years learning how to do her job.

Once you've built up a file of clues and the students are well-versed in vocabulary and details of many occupations, this should be an excellent small group activity. Virginia suggests that advanced students can probably make up puzzles themselves to give to each other.

Teachers of beginning classes are probably wondering how they'll ever get their students to the point where they could participate in these suggestions. I've found that an important first step into modals is a contrast with *to be*. Put an item in the gag and close the bag (before class), or select an object whose use or identification *isn't* immediately discernable. Ask: What is it? Require a response like: I don't know, but it could be/might be a _____. Or,

Have one student hide something. He's the only one who knows where it is. 1.) Other students suggest to each other (not to the knower) that the object might be/could be under the _____, in the _____, on the _____. 2.) As they discuss among themselves where it might be or could be, they check from time to time with the person who knows. When addressing the knower, switch to the question form and *be*, i.e., Is it under the _____? Is it behind the _____? 3.) After a few alternatives have been eliminated and they're beginning to predict with more certainty, switch to: It must be in the _____.

Thanks again to Phyllis Van Horn and Virginia Heringer for sharing their ideas that work.   *TN 11/76*

TEACHING GRAMMATICAL STRUCTURES IN SITUATIONAL CONTEXTS

Suzanne Griffin
EL Center, U of S.F.

Below is a list used as a reference point from which to write lesson plans for usage and grammar classes. Many of the ideas lend themselves well to skits and role-playing. It was first presented at rap session at TESOL 1975, then revised and presented at the CATESOL Convention in 1975. It is presented here in its revised form.

GRAMMAR POINT	SITUATION
Imperative verb forms Present continuous tense	Make a cake using a boxed cake mix.
Locative prepositions Imperative verb forms Present tense Non-referential *it*	Direct another person to some part of the city using a map.
Future tense	Discuss plans for a trip, vacation, the weekend, etc.
Simple past tense *(What did you do ----?)*	Discuss a past vacation, weekend, etc.
any, some, one(s) indirect obj.	Role play a shopping trip to buy gifts.
any, some, one(s), *another, the other*	Role play shopping in a supermarket.
be (present tense) possessive adjectives	Answer information questions: name, address, etc.
be - locative prepositions	Tell someone where to find things in your kitchen.
have/has - possessive adjectives	Tell other students about your family.
Present perfect tense	Fill out a medical history form (adapted)
Present perfect progressive	Role play a medical interview—particularly on a visit to a new doctor.
Non-referential *it*	Make a daily weather report.
Habitual present *at, between, from - to*	Report daily schedules (of people in the class, buses in the city, airlines, trains, etc.)
Non-referential *it* clauses subordinated by *because*	Relate clothes to weather in a role playing situation (i.e. mother and child on a rainy day).
like + Noun/like to + Verb want + Noun/want to + Verb too + adjective/adjective + enough	Role play a shopping trip to buy clothes.
want to - have to - to - *need to* - Verb	Mail a package at the post office—insure it.
would like - Object - Verb (sentence and question patterns)	Invite someone to a party—make a phone call or write an invitation.
can, must, should, ought to	Explain rules and regulations to someone—i.e. school rules, doctor's instructions to a sick patient.
about to - Verb (- Noun)	Describe a sports event in progress. Point out an airplane about to land.
have to (in conditional clauses) if .... Subject *will have to* ...	Give a new customer the information he needs to establish his account with Gas Co. or Bell Telephone.
Past conditional and past perfect tenses	Report a historical event and discuss the conditions under which a different outcome *might have resulted*.
Present Perfect tense - Active and Passive Voice in contrast	React to the burglary of your apartment—in the presence of another person upon initial discovery (Active Voice) —in making a police report (Passive Voice)
still, already, yet	1. Call someone who has placed a classified ad to advertise a job or something for sale (i.e. a car or furniture). 2. Report on the progress of your shopping trip to a companion.
used to	Interview someone about— a. Past employment b. Cuisine and dining customs in their country.

Reprinted From The *CATESOL Newsletter* Vol. 7, No. 4, Jan. 76   *TN 4/76*

HELPING STUDENTS SORT OUT PHRASAL VERBS

by Eileen K. Blau, Joan B. Gonzales and John M. Green
University of Puerto Rico at Mayaguez

English has hundreds of phrasal verbs and the capacity to produce many more. In the modern world we are all too often **ripped off, burned out, put down, freaked out,** and occasionally we **luck out.** Not only is the number of phrasal verbs increasing, but verb-particle combinations seem to be forming tighter units. We sense, for instance, that the decline in such utterances as **For what are you looking?** shows a growing tendency among speakers of English to consider prepositions as somehow glued to the verbs they follow, rather than as movable units of meaning. The cementing is complete in nominalized forms like **printout** and **handout.**

These admittedly speculative ideas suggest that the ESL student's need to understand this already troublesome feature of English will only increase in the future. What follows is not so much a classroom recipe for teaching phrasal verbs as a useful road map that we can easily pass on to our students. This road map works in conjunction with the *Longman Dictionary of Contemporary English (LDOCE),* and we feel that the student who has learned to use this approach will face considerably less difficulty in dealing with phrasal verbs.

Students' problems with phrasal verbs fall into two broad categories: lexicosemantic (vocabulary problems) and syntactic (word order problems). Students often fail to think of the two- or three-word verb as a semantic unit with a special meaning. This is especially true if phrasal verbs do not exist in the student's own language, and, with the exception of Germanic languages, such is usually the case. When a single word conveys the meaning in their native language, students find it hard to see the importance of the particle, or final word, of the English phrasal verb. (Contrast colums 1 and 2 in the chart below.)

As a result, they produce sentences like:

    *Turn the stove.
    *Pick the laundry.
instead of:
    Turn on the stove.
    Pick up the laundry.

They also confuse phrasal verbs like **take off** and **take out** where the only difference is a couple of letters in that extraneous (they think) second word.

The second major problem, the syntactic one, involves the placement of objects in relation to particles, and it is here that teachers and textbooks sometimes tend to create more confusion than is necessary. Students are led to believe that they need to memorize a "separable" or "non-separable" label for every phrasal verb they learn in order to avoid such errors as:

    *Pick up it.
    *Throw away them.
    *I heard them from.

Of course, if the object can be expressed as a noun, the student has an escape hatch. Even though other syntactic options may also be available, placing the noun object after the particle will always be correct.

    Pick up the laundry.
    Throw away the papers.
    I heard from my parents.

Knowing this can be especially useful in conversation when it is impossible to stop and check an authority.

Although our students should be aware of this escape hatch, they should not let it become their only way of handling the situation. They still must work toward native-like usage, which does, indeed, involve separation in some cases.

All phrasal verbs fall into one of four categories. First, if a two-word verb is composed of a verb and a preposition (**call on, run into, go over, hear from** —see Row A in the chart), the pre-position, as

its name suggests, must precede any object, and therefore these combinations are non-separable. In the *LDOCE* these are labelled **v prep.** Second, all three-word verbs (Row B in the chart) are also non-separable, as the third word is always a preposition, and therefore must precede its object. The *LDOCE* labels these **v adv prep.** Third, all transitive two-word verbs that are not verb + preposition combinations are separable (Row C of the chart). The *LDOCE* labels these **v adv (T).** Finally, all intransitive two-word verbs (Row D in the chart), whether they are **v prep** or **v adv,** are by definition non-separable. Clearly, if a verb takes no object, there is no need for a student to memorize whether or not it is separable by an object. Such phrasal verbs are labelled (1) in the *LDOCE.* It should be noted that some **v adv** phrasal verbs may be either transitive or intransitive:

    My mother gets me up at seven
        every morning.
    I get up at seven every morning.

The dictionary clearly identifies both uses. But of course, the phrasal verb is separable only when transitive.

Students can thus confront the syntactic (word order) problem presented by two-word phrasal verbs with pronoun objects by referring to the *LDOCE* to see whether a given phrasal verb is **v adv** or **v prep** and remembering that separation is obligatory in the first case but not permitted in the second. No object means no problem. Nor is there a problem if the phrasal verb has three words. As the chart shows, only one out of four categories requires separation with pronoun objects. Any memorization of separable/non-separable outside of this category is counter-productive. A student who is unsure whether or not a verb is transitive can consult the dictionary.

As for the vocabulary problem, ESL/EFL students should realize that this is where most of their attention should be focused: on learning the meanings of these semantic units and, then, using them when the communicative situation arises. The fact that most phrasal verbs have separable entries in the *LDOCE* is certainly a help, as are this dictionary's exceptionally clear definitions.

What seemed like utter confusion has thus been **cut down** to four categories which easily **tie in** with the labels of the *LDOCE.* All the non-native speaker needs, then, is the knowledge of how to use the *Longman Dictionary* and a willingness to **pick up** new vocabulary.

SORTING OUT PHRASAL VERBS—with help from the Longman Dictionary of Contemporary English

	Column 1*	Column 2	Column 3
Row A	Míralo. Búscalo.	Look at it. Look for it.	verb + preposition combinations marked **v prep** in *LDOCE*
Row B	Sopórtalo. Repaso el francés.	Put up with it. I'm brushing up on French.	three-word verbs marked **v adv prep** in *LDOCE*
Row C	Recógelo. Bótalo. Préndelo. Apágalo.	Pick it up. Throw it away. Turn it on. Turn it off.	transitive two-word verbs marked **v adv (T)** in *LDOCE*
Row D	Me levanté. Regresé. La lluvia disminuyó.	I got up. I came back. The rain let up.	Intransitive two-word verbs marked (I) in *LDOCE* (may be **v adv** or **v prep**)

*Spanish is used for illustrative purposes only.

BOOK REVIEWS

A COMMUNICATIVE GRAMMAR OF ENGLISH

By Geoffrey Leech and Jan Svartvik,
London, Longman's, 1975

Reviewed by Paul D. Roberts,
Free University of Berlin

Leech & Svartvik have written a noteworthy book for those teachers of grammar in ESL/EFL who are interested in using the "communicative" or "notional" approach. It is especially valuable to those of us who require a published reference book of English grammar but write our own exercises.

The book is divided into four parts dealing with the varieties of English, intonation, grammar in use and a grammatical compendium completes the last third of the book. In the first rather brief part of the book dealing with the varieties of English there is a treatment of such matters as geographical variety, written and spoken English and levels of usage. In the second part dealing with intonation there is a five page discussion of that area as it relates to grammar. In part three a number of pertinent points are taken up. First of all, grammatical concepts such as duration, frequency, place, manner, cause, etc. are presented. Next, information, reality and belief; mood, emotion and attitude; and meanings in connected discourse are discussed in detail. The fourth section, the grammatical compendium, serves as a grammatical index for the student, much in the manner of the various handbooks put out by publishers in the United States for freshman English courses.

While this is a British book, the authors have taken great care in including the American grammatical forms where they differ from that of "received standard". As a grammar reference for students who are studying the American variety of English, it is quite satisfactory in that respect. It must, however, be remembered that this is indeed a reference text and does not include any exercises although it does include a large number of examples to illustrate the grammatical points which are covered.

The authors state in the preface that the book is based on another work, A Grammar of Contemporary English (Longman's, 1972) which is, no doubt, familiar to most teachers of English grammar. Part four, the Grammatical Compendium, is cross-referenced to this monumental work.

The authors also recommend that the book be used with advanced foreign students such as those who are in their first year of college or university. It is designed for those students who have had a previous course in English and have received a foundation of the grammar of the language.

It is indeed a suitable book for use with students who have several years of "school English" and a certain mastery of basic structure. While the book presents English grammar as it functions, it does not exclude the necessary structural frame which students must have in order to "communicate" in the language beyond a basic level. With well-written exercises to practice the functions presented by the book and the teacher, a great deal of success can be expected in a grammar course which is intended to teach students how to "use" the grammar of the language rather than simply internalize its grammatical structures.

TN 6/78

UNDERSTANDING AND USING ENGLISH GRAMMAR

(Betty S. Azar, Englewood Cliffs, New
Jersey: Prentice-Hall, Inc., 1981. 400 pp.)

Reviewed by Robert F. Van Trieste
*Inter American University
of Puerto Rico*

Ms. Azar states that her book is intended for "intermediate through advanced students of English as a second language" (p. xiii). However, after having used the book with graduate students at New York University's Puerto Rico Residence Center, I have come to the conclusion that this book is best suited for advanced ESL or ESL refresher courses. I think that a description of Parts I and III of Chapter 3 will support my conclusion. First, there are two and one half pages of questions about the past such as "Did you cut your finger?" Then there are four and one half pages containing a list of the simple, past and past par-

On the other hand, Ms. Azar occasionally gives inaccurate information that would probably confuse students. For example, the author states, "A pronoun is used in place of a noun. It refers to a noun which comes before it. The noun it refers to is called the antecedent. Example: I read the *book*. *It* was good. The noun *book* is the antecedent for it" (p. 385). Ms. Azar's example contains another pronoun, *I*, which is not "used in place of a noun" and which does not "refer to a noun which comes before it." Many times the pronouns *I* and *you* do not have antecedents, at least not in the usual sense of the word.

Another inaccuracy, which is more serious and more confusing than the above exticiple forms of 120 irregular verbs. Next there is a page on "troublesome verbs." A page on the pronounciation of -*ed*, a section on spelling -*ing* and -*ed* forms, and four short exercises requiring the correct spelling of -*ing* and -*ed* forms end the first part of this chapter. All of this is presented before any explanation of the uses of any of the tenses is given. Part III of the third chapter explains, illustrates and drills all of the verb tenses within forty-two pages. Certainly, anyone who has taught intermediate ESL students will realize that such a pace is definitely beyond the intermediate level. However, such a pace is not beyond the level of advanced students or students who have been exposed to all or most of the material before. This book is especially appropriate for a quick and intensive review. ample, is the author's presentation of Possessive Pronouns and, although not identified, Possessive Adjectives.

The author presents these in the following manner.

"POSSESSIVE my, mine   our, ours
PRONOUNS your, yours your, yours
              his, her-hers, its their, theirs
Examples of possessive
pronoun usage:
It is my book. It is mine.
This is your coat.
This is yours." (p. 385)

Such a presentation is bound to cause problems.

Despite these flaws, I found the book to be basically sound and very appropriate for the refresher course that I taught, and I intend to use this book the next time that I teach the course.

The author's explanations, usually in the form of charts, are usually accurate and sometimes offer useful information about informal spoken English. For example, after giving the example sentence "There is a pen and a piece of paper on the desk.", the author writes, "Sometimes in informal English a singular verb is used after *there* when the first of two subjects connected by *and* is singular" (p. 32). Another example of exposure to informal speech is an exercise on page 13 which contains incomplete sentences. In a footnote to the exercise, the author notes, "These incomplete sentences are representative of spoken, not written, English." This is the sort of information that advanced students need to know in order to comprehend much spoken American English.   *TN 6/82*

185

LANGUAGE PLAY

By Donald L. F. Nilsen and Alleen Pace Nilsen, Newbury House Publishers.

Reviewed by Carol Qazi, Arizona State University

"Language play is the newest frontier of American English," state the authors of *Language Play*, and students, as readers of this fascinating book, become frontiersmen and women as they follow the authors' orderly and insightful new approach to linguistics: they become language players.

The Nilsens have become well-known for their efforts in making basic linguistics accessible and relevant to students who would otherwise not find it so, and *Language Play* is their finest book to date. Students learn that the "mystery" behind everyday slang, CB jargon, advertising techniques, graffiti, etc., is no mystery at all, but is the result of the interaction of phonology, morphology, and semantics. Students are led to this discovery chapter-by-chapter as the Nilsens discuss language play in a highly readable and conversational style which is sure to capture every student's attention. Moreover, at the end of each chapter, there are production and analysis exercises which require students to find examples of language play on their own. *Language Play*, therefore, becomes perhaps one of the most vital and germane books available for use in either an introductory linguistics class or a freshman composition class.

As the title indicates, this book covers all areas of basic linguistics. The Nilsens begin with a general discussion about the nature of language (paralanguage, phonetics, etc.), and a discussion of "What exactly is language play?" It is the "creative and unusual" use of language, students are told; this creative use is expressed in metaphors, graffiti, exaggeration, citizen-band radio jargon (this section of chapter four is especially delightful with its run-down on all the CB terms used for highway patrolmen), euphemisms, logos, etc. Students are given specific, often amusing, examples of where these types of language play are used in the real world, familiar to all of them. For example, bumper stickers often feature instances of the expression of the driver's individuality: "I'm not a dirty old man, I'm a sexy senior citizen!" Rock groups often choose two word names for themselves that are contradictory and are therefore fascinating: for example, "Iron Butterfly". Advertisers depend on advertising effectiveness by using pure and simple language play. The advertisements used by the various pantyhose companies are the best examples of this, say the Nilsens, who refer to pantyhose ads as "The great cover-up of the 1970's". *L'eggs*, for example, plays on the word *legs* (obviously, legs are where women use *L'eggs*) by turning it into *L'eggs*, and marketing the stockings in a plastic egg.

Many students reading *Language Play* will be aware of these phenomena before they read the Nilsen's book. But certainly few of them will have appreciated the extent to which their native language, the most taken-for-granted tool at their disposal, not only works for them but amuses them as well.

TN 6/78

There are some advantages of *PEG*. Among them is the quality and clarity of its grammar explanations. Its description of tenses is very detailed with the help of diagrams. For example, the past perfect can be use "for an action which began before the time of speaking in the past, and (1) was still continuing at that time, (2) stopped at that time or just before it, or (3) stopped some time before the time of speaking" (p. 162). These respective structures are shown in diagram below (the line AB is action in the past perfect, and ^T_S for the time of speaking in the past).

(1) A——————T——S——————B

(2) A——————————————B ——T——S

(3) A——————————B ———— T——S

The authors give a sentence of each type.

(1) *Bill was in uniform when I met him. He had been a soldier for ten years/since he was seventeen, and planned to stay in the army till he was thirty.*

(2) *The old oak tree, which had stood in the churchyard for 300 years/since before the church was built, suddenly crashed to the ground.*

(3) *He had served in the army for ten years; then he had retired and married. His children were now at school* (p. 162).

Secondly, by means of comparison of tense aspects the book is even able to explain subtle connotations of certain structures. For instance, the past continuous tense is compared with the simple past "to indicate a more casual, less deliberate action" (p. 151). According to the authors, the first sentence, below, "gives the impression that the action was in no way unusual or remarkable. It also tends to remove responsibility from the subject" (p. 151). On the other hand, sentence (2), below, could be rephrased as *I took the initiative of the conversation.*

(1) *I was talking to Tom the other day.*
(2) *I talked to Tom.*

As the authors intend, another positive feature of *PEG* is its preference for conversational style over written forms for illustration of structures. Conversations between two speakers give examples of typical conversational exchanges and proper wording. For example, *would care* is not normally used in the affirmative, so *would like* replaces it in the affirmative response to the following question.

A: *Would you care to come?*
B: *Yes, I'd like to very much.* (p. 201)

In some of *PEG's* chapters serial numbers or letters are marked with a box (.e.g., 210 B, 279) to show that the explanations under them are a little too detailed or not exactly major points for the first reading. This provides valuable guidance for the student using this book, since it helps the new

---

A PRACTICAL ENGLISH GRAMMAR

A Practical English Grammar (third edition). A. J. Thomson and A. V. Martinet. Oxford, England: Oxford University Press, 1980, pp. 369.
A Practical English Grammar Exercises 1 (second edition). A. J. Thomson and A. V. Martinet. Oxford, England: Oxford University Press, 1980, pp. 176.

A Practical English Grammar Exercises 2 (second edition). A. J. Thomson and A. V. Martinet. Oxford, England: Oxford University Press, 1980, pp. 205. $5.50
(There are also *A Practical English Grammar: Structure Drill 1* and 2 accompanying tapes or cassettes.)

Reviewed by Tatsuroh Yamazaki
Northeastern Illinois University

A Practical English Grammar (henceforth, *PEG*) is designed, according to its authors, mainly for intermediate and advanced students in the higher forms of schools. Also this book is intended as reference for ESL teachers.

This book is "a comprehensive survey of grammar written in simple modern English with numerous examples . . ." (preface). A special feature of *PEG* is its careful and detailed explanations about the use of tenses and auxiliary verbs which are considered to give particular difficulty to students. Another feature, according to the authors, is its emphasis on conversational forms which give the student the concrete examples of how a particular grammatical structure can be used in conversation. In the explanations of most of the structures, examples of short conversations between two people can be found.

learner to focus on the main concept or usage of the words of phrases described and guides the advanced user to learn more about the subtleties and nuances of the language.

An additional positive feature of *PEG* is that the index is very detailed and provides concrete illustrations and word use. Under the heading, *grammatical aspects, examples of key sentences of use* are listed with a paragraph number and/or a section letter so that the reader can locate the exact reference in the book.

However, some of the shortcomings of *PEG* must be mentioned. British English (BE) expressions and usage which may confuse American English (AE) speakers are not annotated. Although this book was published in England (Oxford Univ. Press), it also presumes use among ESL students in the U.S. This requires that the authors be aware of the current differences in usage between these countries and either avoid these cases as much as possible or give equivalent American expressions where British ones are used. This is not, however, the case with *PEG* and its companion volumes. For example, the words *learn* and *study* while interchangeable in BE, are not so in AE. Consequently, *"How long have you learnt English?"* (p. 159) is regarded as incorrect in American usage. In fact the word *learnt* does not exist in Standard American English, the word *learned* being similar in form but not having the same usage as the British form.

Another example of this problem can be seen in the "List of irregular verbs" (pp. 290-294). Many forms listed here are not used in AE, but there is no indiction which verb forms are used in BE and which in AE, even where two separate forms are given. Therefore, the reader may believe that the verb forms "learn, learned/learnt, learned/learnt" (p. 292) can be interchangeably used in both types of English. And, to complicate the problem, for some verbs the AE usage is given first (i.e., before a slash) (see the example of *learn* above), and for others, BE first (e.g., wake, waked/woke, waked/woken p. 294). Also the placement of pronunciation symbols in this list is misleading. The simple past and the past participle of *lean* is illustrated as follows:

leaned/leant
(/lent/)

This format suggests that the former word should be pronounced as /lent/, which is obviously wrong.

Also the list neglects to give *gotten* as the alternate past participle form of *get*, an unfortunate omission for students of AE, which uses the two forms equally.

As a further disadvantage to the student, *PEG* uses highly technical terms or expressions in many places. Therefore, intermediate students may not be able to figure out the grammatical terminology or operations indicated in this book without a teacher's help. For example, question formation using the present perfect tense is described thus: "The interrogative is formed by inverting the auxiliary and subject" (p. 152). *Interrogative* is an unnecessarily technical word and *to invert* could also be rephrased in a simpler way for the less advanced student. A student working independently would doubtless find the jargon difficult to under-

stand. The teacher would probably also have to replace such words with more familiar ones or supply more explanations when presenting this material for the first time in class.

This book, as a whole, is quite organized, easy to use, and rich in conversational English. It is useful for giving handy and concise information about grammar. On the other hand, British expressions and usage may confuse AE students, particularly intermediate students and those working independently, to whom the book is directed. This book would probably be more appropriate for use in Britain although it could be a useful reference handbook for the ESL teacher in U.S.

Exercises 1 and *2* are probably best used by the ESL teacher for student's (homework) assignments, using those exercises without answers, of course. Each of the 185 exercises contains on the average 36 problems on a particular grammatical structure. Many of the exercises contrast two or more grammatical structures which students easily confuse. This helps the student to distinguish between the particular usage of two somewhat similar forms such as the present perfect and the simple past, the simple past and past perfect (simple and continuous), *a* and *the* (articles), etc. Such exercises, particularly ones of this length, are difficult to find elsewhere.

These books are also good for independent student work because the student can practice and check what he has learned in *PEG* with the help of answers in back.

There are, however, some disadvantages as well. Since these books deal with transformations so often (e.g., tense, positive to negative, statement to question change etc.), that is, contain essentially structural exer-

cises, these books are not suitably designed to build up communicative competence. In other words, despite the stated objective of the books "to encourage students to speak the language as it is spoken by native speakers today" the books actually only train the student to manipulate forms grammatically rather than to communicate or use the forms to perform practical daily life functions. No place in the book do students use meaningful statements or ask questions relevant to themselves; they do not say things about themselves or others they know or relate what is going on around them.

Also most exercises have 36 problems requiring the same structural change. It is quite boring and unnatural to repeat the same type of practice 36 times and of doubtful value in improving one's communicative competence. The structural approach of these exercise books may be useful or valuable for an EFL student, who is merely studying English as a discipline or a student wanting a rapid review of grammatical functions or structures before the TOEFL test. But for most ESL students in this country, who want to learn *how to communicate* rather than how to manipulate grammatical patterns for their own sake, the approach of *Exercises 1* and *2* would be very boring, at best, and not very useful for improving their language production.

To summarize, this writer feels that *Exercises 1* and *2* could be useful as a source of homework drills for ESL students and might also prove valuable for an advanced student needing a quick review of structural patterns, as in preparation for the TOEFL test. But, as explained above, these books are of limited value as a class text or to significantly improve students' communicative competence. *TN 4/81*

WHAT'S THE DIFFERENCE? AN AMERICAN/BRITISH-BRITISH/AMERICAN DICTIONARY

Norman Moss. London:
Hutchinson & Co., Ltd. 1973

Review by
Paul D. Roberts
Free University of Berlin

Norman Ross has written a highly useful and, at the same time, highly entertaining little reference book which can be of great help to English language teachers. It is of particular value to those of us who have British colleagues and/or students who have received most of their English language training in the British form.

Moss states within his introduction that the criterion for inclusion is whether a word or expression is familiar to most people in one country or the other, not whether it is listed in some dictionary. He also explains that the word, "British" in the title is used to refer to the predominant language spoken in the British Isles, as distinguished from that which is spoken in the other parts of the English-speaking world. By virtue of his above mentioned criterion for inclusion, Moss has necessarily put into his book a cross section of different types of usage ranging from formal to slang,

young to old, as well as certain regional and dialectal items.

The book is organized into four parts: a rather witty and informative introduction; the American/British section; the British/American section; and two very useful subject lists divided into such topics as accommodation, household, food, etc.

A few sample entries from the text will serve to illustrate both the tone and usefulness of this dictionary:

Alsatian, n–German shepherd dog.
Bank holiday, n–public holiday.
Public school, n–a private school.
Oatmeal, n–porridge.
Tick off, v (col)–to tell off.
Twit, n–a spectacular fool.

In addition to such entries as the above, there is also included a number of socially unacceptable words and expressions which are quite amusing to compare. *TN 2/77*

Section 12. Reading and Vocabulary

Even though they only partially cover the topic of reading, the articles included in this section are among the more interesting contributions from the *TN* on the subject. They begin with the unusual title of Eric Nadelstern's article "Is Frank Smith Frightening?" (8/81). The article reports on Smith's presentation at the 1981 New York State TESOL annual meeting in which he challenged many current practices in ESL teaching.

Stephen Krashen makes a case for specializing the content of the student's reading in "A Case for Narrow Reading" (12/81). In another article, Haskell encourages teachers to try the "Language Experience Approach" (11/78) to teach reading to adults in ESL or in adult literacy classes.

The controversial practice of having students read aloud is dealt with by Donald Knapp in his article on "The Utility of Oral Reading" (6/78) and in a report on one of his speeches by Anna Maria Malkoç (6/68). One of the more interesting proposals for teachers, which encourages reading and the development and evaluation of comprehension skills, is put forth by Donald Adamson in his article "Prediction and Explanation" (9/77). Adamson suggests we take a new look at two "tried and true" techniques which help the students guess at what the content of a paragraph might be after having read the preceding one. Darlene Larson's *It Works* column titled "Reading Up To Expectations" (4/79), takes a similar approach to improving reading comprehension. Haskell's "Using Cloze to Select Reading Material" (4/79) was the first article to evaluate various deletion rates and scoring procedures for the cloze test of readability used with ESL students. He suggests easy and economical ways to use this procedure when determining readability or choosing reading material for ESL students.

Chris Broadhurst (4/79) in an article reprinted from the *TEAM Bulletin* of the University of Petroleum and Minerals, takes up the arguments and decisions made regarding the use of bilingual versus monolingual dictionaries by ESL students. Inez Marquez, in her 12/80 article "The Meaning of 'Blurp': Teaching Dictionary Use," talks about the use of guessing as a means of improving vocabulary.

Mary Ann Christison's *It Works* article, "Using Poetry in ESL," is one of several good articles which have appeared in the *TN* on the use of poetry in the ESL classroom. "An Approach to Teaching Reading to Literate Adults" (10/82) by Joanne Kalnitz and Kathy Reyen Judd is a shortened version of an excellent article discussing a number of ideas that can be used with literate students. Caroline Dobbs' article "Freire and Literacy" (4/82) presents Paolo Friere's philosophy of education as it began in his Brazilian literacy program and which he has since taken to other third world countries. (Note Wallerstein's article on Freire in section 9.)

It was hard to pick reviews of reading materials but the ones included here are among the most interesting texts on the market today. Amy Sonka's *Skillful Reading* (12/81), for example, presents graded reading material and innovative comprehension exercises within each modular unit of reading. Each unit takes a topic and discusses it first in simple terms and then moves to more complicated related aspects of the subject. Carlos Yorio's *Who Done It?* which he wrote with Canadian detective novelist L.A. Morse (4/82), contains original stories in a genre that adults love to read. The Yorkey volumes, *Reply Requested* (8/82), a take off on advice-to-the-lovelorn columns such as those of Ann Landers, *Checklist for Vocabulary*, which teaches about word formation as a means to learning vocabulary, and *The English Notebook*, which he subtitles, "Exercises for Mastering the Essential Structures," are as instructive to the teacher as they are useful to the student. Fraida Dubin and Elite Olshtain's book, *Reading By All Means*, reviewed by Liz Hamp-Lyons, is a collection of reading material that also provides the student with a variety of topics and formats in writing. In *What's the Story?*, reviewed by Robert Oprandy (2/83), Linda Markstein and Dorien Grunbaum provide sequential photographs for language practice. *Focus on Reading* by Nell McCutchen, reviewed by Susan Hill (12/80), is an unusual reading text because it begins with pre-reading developmental reading exercises.

In section 13, you may also want to look at Mary Ruetten Hank's "Using Short Stories in the Advanced ESL Composition Class" which provides ways of complementing the teaching of reading and composition.

Other articles dealing with reading or vocabulary abound in the *TN*. Among the more interesting to consider reading are Karen O'Neill and Carol Qazi's "ESL Reading Objectives: Using Semantic, Syntactic and Discourse Cues" (12/81) and Christine de Alvarado and David Chiquizu's article on the use of metaphor as a means of helping students improve reading comprehension titled "The Use of Extended Meaning Cues" (6/82). Irma Gaudreau wrote on "Teaching Reading Comprehension Skills" (9/77) and JoAnn Crandall reported on Virginia French Allen's speech in which Allen talked about the "Importance of Vocabulary in Reading" (4/79). The Laubach Society's approach to teaching reading was presented in a "Report on National Affiliation for Literacy Advance" (4/80). Don Henderson discussed "Teaching the Short Story to ESL Students Entering College" (8/83) and Marilyn Funk wrote about "Teaching Literal and Figurative Meaning Using Food Vocabulary" (4/78). Last, but not least, is an amusing article by Leslie Leavitt, "Animals in Our Language—A Whale of a Tale" (2/82), in which he talks about the many expressions in English which use animal names metaphorically.

IS FRANK SMITH FRIGHTENING?

by Eric Nadelstern
New York City Board of Education

"Frank Smith is an alarmist! He is frightening! So begins a review by Louise Matteoni, member of the New York State Board of Regents, of Professor Smith's last book, *Reading Without Nonsense*, published in 1979 by Teachers College Press. This review, which appeared in the January 13, 1980 issue of the *New York Teacher*, came to mind as I sat in the front row of Horace Mann Auditorium at Teachers College, waiting for Smith, a keynote speaker at the Tenth Annual Conference of New York State English to Speakers of Other Languages and Bilingual Educators Association, last October 26th.

I didn't expect talons or oversized incisors, nor did I expect that Smith would be the dapper Richard Dawson look-alike who finally stepped up to the podium. His announcement that his talk would center on spelling drew laughter from the audience and dispelled what little was left of the image of a frightening individual created by Matteoni's review.

The focus of Smith's presentation was not spelling. It was learning, and more specifically, learning to read. His insights into spelling began with an estimate that each one of us knows how to spell at least 50,000 words which we have had to memorize since the rules governing English spellings prove useless in light of the many exceptions. He continued by pointing out that most of us are aware of the 1000 words or so that we cannot spell. Our problem is not that we don't know the correct spelling of these words, but that we have also learned an incorrect spelling. Each time we try to spell one of these words, both the correct and the incorrect one come to mind. No matter how often we refer to a dictionary, we will be presented with the same problem the next time we have occasion to spell the word. Unintentionally, we have learned too much. And, as language teachers know all too well, it is ex-

tremely difficult to unlearn something.

Smith went on to discuss language in broader terms. He indicated that language offers no choices. There is a convention for each and every verbal and written interaction, as well as for non-verbal aspects of communication. There is nothing logical about a convention so it cannot be predicted. What matters is that the convention exists and that everyone agrees upon it. Since all language conventions are arbitrary, they have to be learned separately (or is it seperately?) and independently.

We are able to learn language in all its complexity because our brains learn all the time. This state of affairs enables us to memorize the spellings of more than 50,000 words and to learn a complex system of conventions which governs all linguistic interactions between speakers of the same language. Furthermore, many of us have learned all this in more than one language, and given the fact that we have learned so many other things at the same time, the wonder is that our brains do not let us down more often.

All people have trouble learning some things. Some people have not been able to learn how to swim. Others have had great difficulty in acquiring the skills necessary to drive a car. And there are those who cannot read. In explaining this lapse in the function of the brain, Smith delineated three aspects of learning: demonstration, engagement, and sensitivity.

Learning takes place in the presence of demonstrations and what is learned is that which has been demonstrated. The world is full of demonstrations and the brain is a learning machine which soaks it all in. The most important demonstration we can make as language teachers is that language works. That is, how we use and feel about language has a significant effect upon our students' abilities to learn.

Engagement is the next aspect of

learning. It is the interaction of the brain with demonstrations. Through this process, we test our hypotheses by engaging in learning trials.

Smith defines sensitivity, the final aspect of learning, as the absence of the belief that one will not learn. Engagement will take place if there is sensitivity and will not take place if there is no sensitivity. In other words, we learn when we believe that we can be successful at it.

Although children are capable of effortlessly learning things as complex as reading, many fail to master the reading process because they lack the requisite sensitivity. As teachers, we have succeeded in demonstrating, unconsciously more often than not, that reading is difficult and that many of our students, particularly certain groups of them, will not learn this important skill. Having successfully convinced them that they will not learn how to read, we reinforce this belief by labeling them in need of remedial instruction or minimally brain damaged, further preventing their brains from engaging with the demonstrations we provide.

Frank Smith is no more of an alarmist than the good citizen who notifies the fire department of the existence of a four-alarm blaze. Yet he is frightening. He is frightening to all those who would see the role of teacher reduced from educator to program follower. He is frightening to those with a vested interest in convincing us that educational technology and not the warmth and understanding of an enlightened teacher holds the key to the literacy problem. And worst of all, he is frightening to educational leaders who, in recent years, have attempted to make up budget deficits through an infusion of special federal and state funds which are based on the failure of large numbers of students to acquire basic reading skills and are earmarked for remediation technology. *TN 8/81*

THE CASE FOR NARROW READING

by Stephen D. Krashen
University of Southern California[1]

Our tendency in both second language and foreign language teaching has been to supply students with input on a variety of topics. "Readers", for example, typically include several different sorts of articles and stories, and introductory courses in literature usually give the student only one (short) example of each author's work. These practices derive from the premise that exposure to different styles and genres is

beneficial.

The purpose of this note is to suggest that narrow reading, and perhaps narrow input in general, is more efficient for second language acquisition. I am suggesting, in other words, *early* rather than late specialization in the second language acquisition career of acquirers, encouraging reading on only one topic, and several books by the same author in early and intermediate stages.

The case for narrow reading is based on the idea that the acquisition of both structure and vocabulary comes from *many* exposures in a comprehensible context: we acquire new structures and words when we understand the messages, many messages, they encode.[2] Narrow reading facilitates this process in several ways. First, since each writer has favorite expressions and a distinctive style, and since each topic has its own vocabulary and discourse as well, narrow reading provides built-in review. Second, familiarity with context is a tremendous facilitator of comprehension, and thus a facilitator of language acquisition. The more one reads in one area, the more one learns about the area, and the easier one finds subsequent reading in the area.

An example of this can be termed the "first few pages" effect.[3] Intermediate students, reading a novel in a second language, often report that they find the first few pages of a new author's work hard going. After this initial difficulty, the rest of the book goes much easier. This is due to the fact that the context, the story, was new, and, in addition, the reader had not adjusted to the author's style. Providing only short and varied selections never allows our students to get beyond this stage. Instead, it forces them to move from frustration to frustration.[4]

It may be argued that narrow reading produces only the ability to read in just one area. This is not true. First of all, deep reading in any topic will provide exposure to a tremendous amount of syntax and vocabulary that is used in other domains. Any technical field, for example, will utilize subtechnical vocabulary, words such as *function, inference, isolate, relation,* etc. (Cowen, 1974). Second, we do not expect the

student to read only in one area for the rest of his or her second language career. The best way to expand might be a gradual movement from closely related field to related field, taking advantage of the overlap in context and language.

The clearest advantage of narrow reading, however, is that it is potentially very motivating. In any anthology, it is certain that most topics are not of great interest to many members of the class. The combination of new vocabulary, unfamiliar style, the lack of context, and uninterest in the subject matter insures that much reading remains an exercise in deliberate decoding. On the other hand, narrow reading in a topic of real interest has a chance of resulting in students' reading *for the message,* for meaning, in very early stages, a phenomenon considered to be essential for real language acquisition.[5]

Here are some suggestions. Within the framework of the regular class, narrow reading can be encouraged by literature courses (e.g. for the third year foreign language student) that deal with the work of a single author (we usually delay these until at least the senior year). In second language acquisition situations, a course could focus on a single topic, such as current events (with regular reading of the daily newspaper), history of the new country, etc.

At the University of Ottawa, experimentation is now taking place in which second language students do entire courses in subject matter. In such courses, students are tested on content and not language. To help insure comprehensible input, native speakers are excluded. This "adult immersion" (see e.g. Cohen and Swain, 1976) is the logical extension of the narrow reading idea, since students focus on one area for an entire semester (see Krashen, in press, for further discussion). □

FOOTNOTES

1. This paper was written while the author was a visiting professor at the Centre for Second Language Learning, University of Ottawa (fall, 1981).
2. See e.g. Krashen, 1981.
3. I thank Mari Wesche for pointing this out.
4. But see Hauptman (1981) for a discussion of ways of alleviating this problem by preparing students for new material.
5. Philip Hauptman has pointed out to me that narrow reading could have a negative effect if the topic the acquirer is forced to read in is in an area the acquirer dislikes!

BIBLIOGRAPHY

Cohen, A. and Swain, M. 1976. Bilingual education: the "immersion" model in the North American context. *TESOL Quarterly* 10: 45-53.

Cowen, R. 1974. Lexical and syntactic research for the design of EFL reading materials. *TESOL Quarterly* 8: 389-399.

Hauptman, P. 1981. L'application d'une théorie cognitive à la lecture en langue seconde. *Champs Éducatifs* 3.

Krashen, S. 1981. *Second Language Acquisition and Second Language Learning.* Oxford: Pergamon Press.

Krashen, S. *Principles and Practice in Second Language Acquisition.* New York: Pergamon Press, in press.

TN 12/81

TEACHING BEGINNING READING IN ESL, BILINGUAL AND ADULT LITERACY CLASSES THROUGH LANGUAGE EXPERIENCE

By John F. Haskell
Northeastern Illinois University

Like so many good ideas from other fields, the Language Experience Approach (LEA) for teaching beginning reading, which comes from the elementary language arts area, lies virtually unused and untried by most ESL, bilingual and literacy teachers. When I bring up the idea to a group of ESL teachers (in my best Moses-from-the-mountain manner), the immediate, and unfortunately, often sustained, response is either (a) if they are elementary school trained, "Oh, I already know about that." (though it is still unused in their classes), or (b) "You see, it proves that oral reading is valid after all." (obviously missing the point both of LEA and the criticisms of oral reading).

The Language Experience Approach was first suggested by Roach Van Allen, in part, as a means of teaching reading (decoding) skills to native English speaking children. It has been discussed at various TESOL meetings by such ESL and Reading specialists as Stanley Levenson and Pat Rigg (see bibliography below). According to Van Allen, Language Experience is based on the following:

A. What a student can/does think about, he can talk about;

B. What a student says can be written (or dictated to the teacher);

C. What has been thus written can be read.

The Language Experience Approach, when used by classroom teachers with second language learners, child and adult, has been extremely successful because it provides a way for the student to acquire the basic skills of reading, whether he is literate (able to read) in his first language or not, with comfortable, familiar and non-threatening material . . . his own.

It is an admirable approach, not only because of its simplicity but also because it allows for manageable individualization and utilizes the student's knowledge and interests. Best of all, it virtually eliminates the need for readability formulae, word frequency counts, and testing—where measurement is

often inadequate and inappropriate if not impossible.

Essentially, the procedure includes the following elements, though there is no strict sequence of procedure and flexibility is the by-word.

I

The student's "experience" may be a drawing, something he brings to class such as a picture, a souvenir, a recording or the like; or participation in an experience such as a trip or visit, a film or party, etc., planned by the teacher. Or it may simply be a discussion of some topic or event that the student relates to. The need for and the kind of stimulus will depend upon the level of the student (age) and the kind of lesson (individual or group).

II

The student is then asked to tell about his experience. The student may be telling the teacher, another student, a group of students or the whole class, depending upon the student's ability to communicate, the kind of follow-up exercise planned, and the reading need of the student. The goal is to get the student to talk about something he wants to talk about and for him to use his own words.

III

The student then dictates his "story" or "experience" to the teacher (or to another student), using his own words. The writer copies down the story just as it is told—errors and all. The teacher or fellow student may help the one dictating to find words, but *it is crucial that the dictation be written down just as the student says it*, that the student's (*not* the teacher's) words, phrasing, syntax be written down. Remember, you are teaching reading—how to decode the relationships between the spoken and written language—not grammar. At this stage the student will not learn incorrect language because he sees it in his reading materials: he doesn't *see* it. He is much too concerned with the experience and the process. Rigg points out that the greatest incidence of teacher failure occurs at this point, when teachers, to be helpful (i.e. to "teach"), edit and repair the student's story as it is being put onto paper, rather than copying it down exactly as the student tells it.

IV

The teacher then reads the story back to the student while the student reads along. In the very beginning the teacher may want to read the dictation back at the end of each sentence, helping the student to make immediate connection between his spoken words and their written forms. It also gives the student a chance to edit his dictation for the first time.

When the student is ready, he may want to read the story aloud to the teacher or to another student. Of course, he may read it silently to himself at any time. The more re-reading he does, the better. The teacher may help the student, pronouncing words or rereading the story with him. The student knows the words and understands the story; he is, at this point, learning to identify the written symbols of the words he has already spoken.

V

The student may also want to try writing the story himself. Students will gradually begin correcting and changing their own stories as they begin to recognize errors and as their vocabulary increases. As a normal process, second and third readings often result in self-editing.

Stories that the student has told and dictated or re-written can be made into individual readers. With children, the "readers" may include their own drawings thus becoming their own illustrated library, one they can share with other students, their families and friends. For adults they may become notebooks of "stories" which they can use to practice with or share. These notebooks then become a measure for the students (and the teacher) of their progress in language and writing as well as reading.

VI

When the basic skill of decoding has been achieved, teacher-prepared or commercial materials may be introduced. For children, these may be basal readers, storybooks and other activity materials. For adults, the materials might be application forms, driver's test materials, grocery store flyers and labels. Letter writing or diary keeping might be good transitional and on-going activities in view of their built-in experience or story-telling nature.

The Language Experience Approach can be used as a class, small group or individual activity. Rigg suggests, in her discussion of ideas for whole class presentation, the use of wordless picture books to initiate the "experience" telling.

Language experience takes advantage of student interests and knowledge rather than relying on the arbitrary selection of topics and materials that, though they may be interesting to some, are seldom motivating for all. It can be a step towards the understanding and use of vocabulary and materials in other areas of the student's life, helping him along in other courses or a job, rather than focusing solely on literature or culture. As Van Allen puts it,

> the basis of children's oral and written expression is their sensitivity to their environment, especially their language environment, both within the classroom and in the world at large. The continuing responsibility of the teacher is to help (the student) at all levels of ability become increasingly aware of the world in which they live—to 'talk' about . . . and to relate their observations and impressions to their own experiences.

In a bilingual program, the LEA allows students to begin with reading and writing in their first language almost immediately, as well as providing a means of moving gradually into the second language. (Although this may result in the students using both languages on occasion, the admonition that what the student says is what should be put to paper, still holds.) In adult literacy or ESL classes, where the students may be illiterate in their first language, Language Experience provides a simple way of moving the student into the process of decoding, just as it does for the child.

In all cases, since the approach is individualized and ungraded, it avoids the problems of "ability" grouping. Students can begin when they are able to express themselves; "readiness" becomes a matter of the student having something to say. Students learn to recognize the regularities and irregularities of spelling. Van Allen believes that this is because Language Experience makes no distinction between the development of reading skills and the development of listening, speaking, spelling, and writing skills. All are essential provide reciprocal reinforcement. All facets of language are used as experience related to the construction of printed materials. All the student's experiences which he can express, especially in oral language, are included as the raw material out of which reading refinement grows.

Unlike most commercially prepared materials, the Language Experience materials that the student reads tend to be "culture-fair" and meaningful to him because they are his words and his experience. Almost equally important, the student is not placed at a disadvantage because his oral skills are unequal to the material he is asked to read. As Levenson states it, Language Experience "values the language of each (student), faulty as it may be, as a beginning point for further development." In so doing it puts the thinking of each (student) at the heart of the teaching learning process.

Although I have emphasized Language Experience as a means of acquiring the decoding skill (so essential in the initial stages of the reading process), in order to establish a limit to oral reading practice, Language Experience is, in truth, a rationale for the entire language learning/using experience. The student's entire knowledge, his every experience is the catalyst, the stimulus, the impetus for communication, whether in reading, writing, listening or speaking; whether in the classroom or at home, on the job or on the street. It is his need and his thoughts that will lead him, take him to successful language acquisition. It is the teacher who must be ready, prepared to navigate.

TN 11/78

For further reading:

Levenson, Stanley. "The LEA (Teaching Beginning Reading to Speakers of Other Languages: The Language Experience Approach)." Paper given at TESOL Convention, Chicago, March 7, 1969. (ED 032 519)

Rigg, Pat. "Beginning to Read in English the LEA way", *SPEAQ Journal*, Vol. 1, No. 3, Autumn, 1977.

Van Allen, Roach and Claryce Allen. *Language Experience Activities*, Boston: Houghton-Mifflin, 1976.

TN 11/78

THE UTILITY OF ORAL READING IN TEACHING ESL

By Donald Knapp
Temple University

Should we use Oral Reading to teach "reading" to our ESL students? It is an interesting question to consider, since oral reading is an area in which the recommendations of specialists (in reading, psychology and TESL) clash with the wide concensus of teaching practice.

Most teachers in early or intermediate level ESL classes use oral reading, students reading out loud to the teacher or other students, as a major technique for teaching reading. Almost all primary grade teachers use oral reading in their ESL or bilingual-ESL classes to teach reading. But most specialists oppose oral reading as a practice to teach reading in elementary school or in beginning and intermediate levels of ESL. They approve of the teacher reading aloud and the students following along in their books, but they feel it is a bad teaching practice to have students read aloud to the class, bad for them to read aloud at all, except in a few special situations.

There are many reasons why teachers use oral reading, some good, some not so good;

(1) It gives the student an opportunity to have immediate feedback from the teacher.
(2) It involves everyone in the same activity (perhaps more useful for those moments when everything is going to pieces).
(3) It supplies the teacher with an identifiable role, how s/he can be helpful, it gives a basis for praise or criticism.
(4) It can give the student a basis for a feeling of confidence, offering the shy, reticent student a task that can be performed with self-assurance.
(5) It allows the student to "show off" his accomplishments, encouraging practice at home, even though it may be a false sense of reading ability.
(6) It can be used as a diagnostic test, a basis for error (miscue) analysis, and inferentially used to evaluate comprehension.
(7) Is a way to "share" the printed content (disseminate information, enjoy the essence of a passage, appreciate a play, a dialogue, or a poem, to "tell" a story to children or someone otherwise unable to read to himself).
(8) And, admittedly, teachers do use oral reading on occasion to "impress visitors" and "because everyone else does it", and because, in most instances, students expect it and enjoy it.

What is Reading

But what students think reading is and what teachers think reading is are not necessarily the same. Word-calling is *not* reading. *Reading is a meaning-gathering activity.* Sophisticated readers do not read every word, but they comprehend the meaning of the passage. Three processes are involved in reading; (1) making a correspondence between symbol and sound, (2) getting meaning from the context, and (3) getting meaning from the sentence structure.

In oral reading, every word must be read. In oral reading, intonation, pitch, stress, juncture, and expression are important. At worst, the oral reader must look at each letter and sound out the word. The oral reader often becomes so preoccupied with and frustrated by these mechanics that the meaning of the passage is lost. The reading deteriorates to word-calling and the reading rate grinds to a halt . . . not to mention the boredom and suffering of classmates who must follow along.

In proficient silent reading, written symbols are put directly into meaning. Only absolute beginners decode written symbols to oral symbols and then, only when necessary for special purposes, to meaning. Good readers should decode written symbols to meaning and then to oral symbols. The essence of the reading process is deriving meaning from *written* language, not from the oral counterpart of the written language.

Making Predictions

The reader is directly involved in making predictions while reading. S/he makes guesses that may, or may not, be confirmed. For example, "The cowboy got down from his horse and led his _____." What comes next? Did he lead his 'horse to the barn'? That is the answer that one might have predicted. But the sentence actually reads "The cowboy got down from his horse and led his girlfriend to the bar", the unconfirmed guess would cause the reader to do a 'double-take', to regress, to go back a few words. Good readers do regress in silent reading as they make large-scale guesses, based on context: lexical, syntactical, informational. However, good readers regress less and correct better than poor readers. In the special circumstances of a student reading to a teacher trained in miscue analysis, a student's "mistakes" and his/her very awareness that he needs to make correction are important in helping him improve his reading skills. Ordinary teacher correction doesn't help the student learn the reading process; it just pushes the student along. The self correcting of miscues is associated with

superior readers. Silent reading gives practice in making guesses and in self-correction when necessary.

Decoding and Performance

True reading is actually silent reading. Oral reading is a school exercise that emphasizes word calling to the detriment of meaning. Students say just what is on the page rather than what the passage means. Oral reading emphasizes the application of the mechanical aspects of reading and is, therefore, *not* a good teaching practice, generally speaking. Reading experts accept the fact that at the very early decoding stage, the transference of oral skills to visual symbol, oral reading is a good check of the process. They agree that on an *individual* basis, (the student reading alone with the teacher), oral reading may be used for diagnosis (miscue analysis) and they suggest that *oral reading otherwise is best reserved for performance.* It is hard to think of a reason, other than performance, that a person would have to read aloud.

There is no reason to ignore performance, especially when students enjoy it. But it requires special skills, "story telling", acting, or declamatory skills, if you will. And it is best done with a great deal of practice, repeatedly reading the same piece. Often the pronunciation, since it is symbol oriented, is different from normal conversational pronunciation.

Reading Skills

But the skills one wants a student to acquire in 'reading' are silent skills; skimming, reading for information, reading to understand, reading that requires the ability to take large chunks (rather than individual words) and process them internally. Reading is a process that allows for regressions and hypothesizing.

Oral reading is not a skill that is often used by students outside the classroom. Oral reading in the classroom may be a conventional practice and may even be enjoyable to the students for a variety of reasons including the students occasional pleasure in performing. But the teacher must be cautioned that oral reading is not usually a useful goal in the ESL class; it may actually be harmful to the development of good reading habits. Students and teachers should not equate students ability to read orally with the real objectives of reading instruction: reading efficiently for understanding and meaning. *TN 6/78*

NOTES FROM DONALD KNAPP'S TALK ON READING

By Anna Maria Malkoç

I. Problems in the Teaching of Reading

1. Uncertainties and misconceptions concerning reading comprehension.

Meaning. We are not clear on what we mean by "comprehension" and how we can measure it. Do we mean the ability to answer comprehension questions? Can a person who reads answer questions so that others can understand the answers? *The problem here is that most of these questions measure recall, not comprehension.* We can, for example, recall what we don't understand, and vice versa. Can we measure any kind of questions? Does this indicate comprehension? No, it shows we don't have a firm idea of "comprehension".

Writer's intent. Do we approach reading comprehension by looking for the exact understanding of what the writer intended? This allows the reader to separate main points from extraneous points, filter off the points that are not central. The problem here, however, is: What is the writer's intention? This makes scoring for comprehension difficult because it is subjective.

Reader's intent. Putting more emphasis and greater attention on the reader, we can ask: What was the reader's intention or purpose when he or she began the reading, and are these expectations fulfilled?

Even here, though, we must consider that perhaps the reader's feelings, purpose or intention may change during the reading. Any account of comprehension must consider that we are not all in agreement when we say: I read that with medium comprehension. So many interpretations of "comprehension" are possible: there is no really clear conception of reading or its testing.

2. Inadequate classroom techniques for teaching reading.

We are becoming more concerned with the development of reading material than developing the student's reading skill. We assign reading tasks and then ask questions to test comprehension. Does this really develop reading skills? Students may learn to read anyway, but are we really *teaching* reading skills? This is more like a kind of exposure with very little focused teaching.

3. Reading teachers and students have little understanding of the psychology of reading skills.

Students may be able to read strings of words, but this is *not* reading. Teachers may teach phonics, but this also is not a suitable approach to use with our students.

II. Some Solutions to Reading Problems

There are some revolutionary thinkers in reading field, Frank Smith and Kenneth Goodman, to name two outstanding people. Their articles appear in such publications as the *Reading Teacher* and *Reading Research Quarterly*.

1. The process of reading involves deriving meaning from the written language.

Only in the earlist stages does the reader first recognize individual words, then decode them into meaning. Very early on, the reader learns to decode directly; he doesn't have time to make phonic forms, but puts it back into phonic, oral, form after decoding. At this point the reader is reading with comprehension.

2. Cultural relevance in reading and comprehension:

What governs a reader's comprehension? Personal experience, feelings, expectations. A key factor in reading comprehension is *hypothesis formation*.

Good comprehension comes from the fact that most materials are well-written and that most readers are good hypothesizers. All of this is based on *culture*. To illustrate: a speaker (or writer) introduces the phrase "southern woman descends the staircase." The audience (or reader) may immediately picture how she is dressed—in a long white dress, and what kind of staircase it is—carved wooden spiral, etc. Or given the phrase "a boy walking down a country road," we probably picture a boy dressed in blue jeans or overalls, wearing a straw hat, accompanied by a dog, and so on.

As we read along, we have expectations and we continually create literally thousands of hypotheses, confirming them or making new ones. Someone from another culture, however, reading the same material would not be creating these same hypotheses; they are all culturebound. We are influenced in our reading by our cultural pre-conceptions.

3. Some suggested activities to develop hypotheses formation:

A. **Bread-and-Butter.** Select a number of pairs of words in common usage that are usually thought of as "pairs". Give the first word in the pair and ask the class to supply the second word.

B. **Reading and stopping.** Choose a reading passage designed to stimulate the students' interest. Read a portion (or have the class read it silently), stopping at critical points to ask: What would happen next in the story if this were taking place in your country?

C. **Children's stories.** Select stories that are based on redundant elements: "Chicken Little," "The Gingerbread Man", "The Little Red Hen," are some. Such stories are often used very successfully to develop reading skills because of their repetitive features.

III. Questions from the Audience

1. What can students do to help themselves?

Get them to read in English about their own culture. In so doing, their hypotheses are being confirmed as they read along, and they understand everything but the words. Culture shock sets in when the student's or newcomer's hypotheses, expectations, are *not* confirmed, especially when this happens over and over again to the point of not being able to cope. Therefore, the reading material for new readers should not be too full of strange words and concepts.

2. What about using a "dictionary"?

If a dictionary is being used too much the material is too difficult. Not that *all* words have to be understood—we read in English (that is, in our own language), and don't understand every word always. But the students need to make a "psychological jump" to gain self confidence in order to read along on their own in their new language.

3. What about "redundancy" in English?

Adding redundant features is helpful. If a sentence is too difficult, we tend to add synonyms or to cut the sentence shorter. But using paraphrasing and apposition is a much better tactic. This semantic redundancy helps in gathering and expanding meaning.

4. How useful is "oral reading" for students?

Only for diagnostic purposes or for declamatory reading—for recitation or memorization of the Declaration of Independence, for example. Or if the *teacher* reads orally, this can be useful for modeling pronunciation and phrasing. But there are many reasons *not* to have the students read orally: First, it forces students to read every word. Whereas, to be good readers, they must learn not to do this but to read in much larger chunks.

Listening to fellow students reading is boring.

Oral reading is much more difficult than silent reading.

The British approach, as at Summerhill School, is good, very successful. On the elementary level, the teacher reads to pupils and they sit around and listen, then talk.

5. What about "culture block" in heterogeneous classes using scientific/technical materials?

The students need to be *interested*. To help them develop their reading skills, select materials that have content they are already familiar with, a basic text in their own field, for example. *TN 6/78*

PREDICTION AND EXPLANATION

by Donald Adamson
Kuwait University

In the Science Faculty of Kuwait University we are experimenting with new types of exercises for use with our highest level course, which is offered as an option for students who have already completed two terms of English. One set of exercises attempts to deal with skills which are so fundamental that it seems surprising that EST (English for Science and Technology) courses have tended to ignore them. Since the exercises are proving successful with these highly-motivated students we may introduce them at lower levels.

Research on reading comprehension tends to bring out the role of *prediction* in efficient reading: the reader is considered as one who is constantly forming and updating hypotheses about the content of a text. And it is clear that in forming these hypotheses the reader is using the totality of his own knowledge—knowledge of the world, knowledge of the subject he is reading about, and knowledge gained from the stretch of text already studied. Unfortunately, many exercises on comprehension discourage the student from applying his own knowledge; the student is asked to 'stick to the passage.' Yet it would seem that in reading scientific text-books this is precisely what the student cannot afford to do: hence our inclusion of exercises involving also *explanation* which will encourage the student to use the knowledge he has.

The use of such exercises may also help to overcome a fundamental problem in ESP (English for Specific Purposes). Obviously, students are expected to master science at levels beyond the scientific competence of most English teachers. It is sometimes said that this is not really a problem, since getting students to explain obscure points is valid teaching technique. In practice, however, one may find that the students' scientific knowledge—and certainly their explanations—are imprecise. It is a real advantage if one can isolate points which require explanation and reach decisions on whether the obscurity lies with the author, the student's knowledge, the student's explanation or the gaps in the teacher's scientific knowledge.

A unit on prediction and explanation may consist of four or five pages of text and exercise material, and one page which reproduces the diagrams relevant to the text. Students are encouraged to study the diagrams before working through any of the text. The text itself is 'authentic'; the only doctoring it receives is in the manner of spreading it out over a number of pages with exercises on each paragraph or section, and in the omission of sentences to be re-inserted by the student (as will be explained below).

Introductory Letter of Explanation to the Students

We would like to tell you something about the course units dealing with PREDICTION and EXPLANATION. Each unit will consist of five or six pages. There will usually be one page of diagrams which you can look at before starting to read. The unit will contain a passage of several paragraphs from a genuine science book. The pages of the unit will not be in the correct order (except for the first page). This is because we want you to predict what is coming before you actually read what is coming. Of course, if you want to practice reading quickly through all the pages of the unit before you answer, we have no objection.

Sometimes we will ask you to predict the sentence that is coming. Sometimes we will ask you to predict the 'idea' that is coming.

The other part of the unit will be on EXPLANATION. When a non-scientist (like your English teacher) reads a scientific passage, he may get ideas from it that are false, or only half-true. We will be asking you to comment on these ideas from your own scientific knowledge, in other words to explain the true facts fully, if you can. We hope there will be things you can explain, whether you are a biologist, chemist, mathematician, etc.

Read the passage below and answer the questions which follow:

In the synthesis described so far, we have assumed that carbon atoms were essential for life. Is carbon the only basis for life? Organic matter is made up chiefly of carbon, hydrogen, nitrogen and oxygen. Phosphorus and sulphur participate to a limited extent. There are also the monatomic ions of the elements—sodium, potassium, magnesium, calcium and chlorine. Iron manganese, cobalt, copper and zinc are also found as trace metals, binding metallo-organic complexes.

We might include a few comprehension questions designed to bring out certain key concepts in the texts before going on to the first question on explanation; the statements below are made from the standpoint of one who is scientifically not-quite-ignorant, at least to the extent of realizing that there is a difference between an atom and a molecule, and that there must be a relationship between atoms, ions and electrons:

Question: *From your own knowledge, mark the following suppositions of a non-scientist as TRUE, PARTLY TRUE or FALSE. Be ready to expand them into more accurate statements if necessary.*

a) *The ions of Na, K, Mg, Ca and Cl have only one atom.*

b) *Ions can consist of more than one atom.*

c) *Na, K, Mg, Ca and Cl exist in living organisms in the form of ions, whereas C, H, N and O exist in some other form.*

The following exercise contains work on prediction. The student has to decide on the content of the next paragraph, but—and this is important—he cannot do this simply by looking at the beginning of page 2, *since the paragraphs belonging to the text have been randomized over subsequent pages* (although we have no objection if he skims over *all* the subsequent pages in order to reach a decision, since practice in skimming is in itself valuable).

Question: *The following paragraph is likely to be about:*

a) *A relationship between the elements mentioned, their atomic structure, and their suitability for use in living organisms.*

b) *Certain elements which are not used in living organisms.*

c) *The structure of the protein molecule.*

Next, the student may be invited to make a prediction at sentence level. Once again, the student cannot find the answer by simply looking through subsequent pages, since each 'first sentence' has been deleted:

Question: *The next sentence will be:*

a) *We might summarize the reasons for the suitability of carbon as follows:*

b) *Many molecules exhibit mobility in the composition of their chemical bonds.*

c) *We might pose the question, why hydrogen, oxygen, nitrogen and carbon?*

The student is then invited to re-assess his predictions, and is finally told which page he should move on to.

The format of the following pages is similar, except for the page containing the last page of the text. At this point, it seems useful to gather together various strands of the total text with work on summary or outlining, or more extended work on explanation (e.g., *Choose any of the statements you have marked as TRUE, PARTLY TRUE, or FALSE, and write a paragraph explaining the facts in detail*).

The format described above is by no means rigidly fixed for all units. Sometimes we ask for completion of the sentence or idea at the *end* of a stretch of text; or we may ask students to form questions which a subsequent paragraph would answer. An example of such a variation is given below. It comes half-way through a unit with a meteorological emphasis, dealing with the constituents of the lower atmosphere:

Fairly high concentrations of ozone often occur in the lowest few hundred meters of the atmosphere, especially over urban areas. Ozone, which is a corrosive, toxic gas, is an important constituent of the so-called photochemical 'smog' that afflicts some large cities. The atomic oxygen required for the reaction described above is formed in smog principally through the action of solar radiation on nitrogen dioxide.

Question: *What question does the paragraph immediately above answer?* (Note: Students have already been asked to anticipate the paragraph above by forming questions which a subsequent paragraph might answer).

Question: *The last words in the passage above are:*

a)—*the formula of which is NO².*

b)—*a product of combustion.*

c)—*a toxic gas.*

d)—*which reacts with water to form nitric acid.*

Question: *How many sources of solid particles in the atmosphere can you think of? Check your own ideas with the paragraph which follows, on page ————.*

Whatever the precise format (and many other variations are possible) the main thing is that we regard a text as an ongoing stretch of language and comprehension of a text as an organic self-monitoring process involving factors within and outside the text. Viewed in this way one's approach to constructing reading comprehension material naturally changes; while it may be valid to present a text as a finished artifact, with questions on it for *testing* purposes, if we are in the business of practicing the actual reading strategies which a student requires, we must tackle the text from the point of view of one who *is reading* as distinct from *has read*. This seems to be the approach which is most likely to lead to concrete results in the long term.

TN 9/77

READING UP TO EXPECTATIONS

By Darlene Larson
New York University

Experts tell us that what a reader brings to a page—his or her experience, knowledge, opinions, and language proficiency—is every bit as important as what the page brings to the reader. We "size up" a piece of writing. We approach it with an attitude of, "I'll bet I know what this is about." In short, we set expectations. Then we read to confirm those expectations.

You and I, language teachers, are challenged with the task of getting students to tackle things they don't know, to realize that they probably know more than they think they do, and to persuade them to see if the piece of writing is anything like what they supposed. This is no easy step in a second language because it is no easy step in a first language. Have a native speaker look at "read" and pronounce it. Nobody is sure if it is read or read. But when students approach a piece of writing in a second language, they want to be absolutely certain of every letter as they meet it. This is impossible, and we have to give them the confidence to make a guess at something, go right on to the next part, and if things don't "hang together", to come back later.

The device which I have been working with is the format of the cloze test. This is the technique in which a piece of writing is rewritten with every fifth word deleted. Then, by asking students to reconstruct the original, and scoring their success in doing so, researchers have found it a handy method for placement tests, for grouping of students, for determining readability of material, and

for measuring language proficiency. I am not concerned with these objectives at this time. I am interested in this format because it is so easy to prepare, and because on looking at it, there clearly are words that the students don't know—because they aren't there. Thus, one takes a matter-of-fact kind of attitude that says, "Of course you don't know every word on the page. You never do. But you can figure out what they mean, anyway."

I don't want this exercise to be a test. Thus, I encourage students to work in pairs or in groups of three and to help each other. (By the way, when you divide into partners for a cooperative task like this one, give each set of partners only one piece of paper. Time after time, no matter what you say in your directions, if you divide into partners and give each partner a sheet to work on, you'll get two people seated together but working independently. Two people and one sheet result in more cooperative efforts.) Tell them to make guesses and go on to the next word. If they can think of two or three possibilities, put them *all* down and come back later to decide.

One good thing about the random deletion of every fifth word in the cloze format is that some blanks will be vocabulary items and others will be function words of the language. Expectations for one will be set by the content, the story, the situation. Expectations for the other will be set by grammatical information. And so it is in the act of reading. Not only do we have expecta-

tions about the ideas expressed and the thesis of the article, but we make hypotheses about the letters, words, and phrases as well. Students draw on all of their knowledge in order to complete this task, just as they do when reading.

One last word about the cloze format. As I am putting an exercise together and come to a fifth word that is a person's name, the first time that person is mentioned I usually leave the name and take out the sixth word and go on from there. There are certain content words which no one can guess. Whether the lady's name is Gertrude or Agnes or Blanche is not terribly important and it doesn't do much good to have students spend a lot of time on what her name might be.

Let us suppose that your students have been divided into partners and have been given a single sheet with a cloze passage on it, and enough time has passed that they have gotten started and are doing the task cooperatively. *Now* give the other partner a sheet so that each student has a copy, making it easier for them to work and making certain each student will have a copy for his or her notebook. It will take a few minutes now for them to go back over what they have done in order to get both partners' sheets up-to-date. They often notice things that they missed the first time through. After a few more minutes have the partner on the left stand up, and move to the next couple, or, in other words, change partners. When the new partners get together, there will be more reason to discuss and review what each one has and to see where they agree and disagree. Change partners several times according to the length and difficulty of the passage.

With the realization that it is important for readers to bring information to the written page, it seems to me that we should give second language students reading practice on selections about topics they know and that interest them. I suggest a paragraph or two about the history of the town in which you teach. High school students are often anxious to get a driver's license. A cloze passage about the procedure for getting a license, or a description of the location of the testing office would be good. Passages about the countries included in the social studies syllabus, about the plants and animals in the biology course, about city and state government or political parties at the time of elections ought to be safe bets that they would not be strange and remote from the students' experience.

The Bobst Library is a place with which my NYU students need to become acquainted. I have prepared Form A and Form B of a passage which includes the library hours, information about the smoking areas of the library, rules about eating and drinking there, and the location of drinking fountains and pencil sharpeners. A follow-up passage explains the computerized circulation system of the library—zebra labels and all. Students need to become acquainted with cafeteria regulations, campus organizations, transportation systems and the like. All students who have found their way to a classroom know something about all of these phases of students and city life. Thus, they'll be bringing personal knowledge to the printed page, but they'll be interested in learning more.

One form is enough. You don't have to have two. But how will students find out what the original said? There are several ways. One, if the passage is easy enough, the students should be able to construct the original, or a close version of it, after they have changed partners a few times. Although I give credit for any synonyms or variations that mean about the same thing, students are often curious to know exactly what the passage said before they worked on it.

Option 1. After changing partners several times, give a copy of the passage as it was before you put it into cloze.

Option 2. Record the passage on tape. After students have changed partners several times and have figured out just about all they can, turn on the tape recorder and let them listen and read to themselves. Let the students operate the recorder, stopping it where they wish, rewinding and playing again the parts that they didn't catch. When you record, try to keep conversational speed and intonation. Don't use your announcer voice. Use your conversational voice and pretend you are saying these passages to a friend of yours. With all of the reductions and contractions of normal speech, students have trouble catching a lot of words *even after they have worked with the passage.* When you record, wait a minute and record a second time. That will save some rewinding.

Option 3. Record the passage on tape. Play the tape as a listening activity when students arrive in the room. Later, divide into partners and distribute the passage in cloze format. Proceed as in #1 or #2.

Option 4. Make two forms of the passage, Form A and Form B, but don't tell the students that they have different ones. When you divide into partners the first time, make an aisle down the middle of your classroom. Give Form A to all the partners on one side, and Form B to the other. Whenever you change partners that day make sure that nobody crosses the aisle. Finally, on the last change of partners, tell everyone to get a new partner from across the aisle. Then, when they start working with their pages and comparing their work they will find that they can recreate the original by putting their forms together.

Whether I use Option 1, 2, 3, or 4, I always finish by giving each student a copy of the original as it was in paragraph form. The written, single-spaced paragraph form is what they usually meet and can't handle. Here it is again, only this time they know what to expect. Conscientious students often sit right down and read from beginning to end this "original" copy when they receive it at the end. One would think that they would know it forwards and backwards and that putting it back into paragraph form would be a waste of paper. But that's the beast that usually conquers them. There are certain kinds of language learners who take great pleasure in meeting that written word and knowing what it is talking about. I hope you have a classroom full of them.

TN 4/79

USING CLOZE TO SELECT READING MATERIAL

By John F. Haskell
University of Puerto Rico

How can I choose a story that is not too difficult for my students to read? How can I be sure that they will be able to read enough of it so that we can discuss it together?

Many teachers have a limited selection of books from which they can choose reading material. With first language speakers these books are usually selected for a certain grade level of student. But for second language learners we have no way of determining what the "level" of the student in reading is. We still have the same books. How can we use them most effectively? Can we SELECT materials from them that are both interesting and READABLE?

The Cloze Test is a simple way to determine whether or not reading material is too difficult for students to read—with success. Note that the key word here is SUCCESS. We should be trying to choose materials that will be appropriate for ALL of our students and easy enough to read so that we can provide growth in knowledge and greater skill in reading.

The Cloze testing device is easily made and easily scored.

1. The first step is to find a story that you think will be generally interesting to the students or that you want to use for some specific grammar or reading skills building exercises. . . hopefully interesting as well.

2. Take the first 200 or so words and delete every fifth word, putting a blank in its place. (For easy scoring fifty blanks is most easily converted to a percentage score, but it is not necessary to have that may blanks). This amount can be easily typed or written on one side of a single sheet of paper and duplicated.

3. Give only this much of the selected passage to your students to read. Ask them to fill in the blanks as they read by guessing what should be there. You may want to have numbered the blanks for easier scoring, also. This will allow you to re-use the test sheets if you have students write the words on a separate numbered piece of paper.

Students should be given as much time as possible though it will take very little time as they become familiar with the Cloze procedure. They are asked to fill in each blank with a single word only (though contractions are permissible). The student can read and reread the passage as many times as he needs and in fact, will find it necessary to do so.

4. When the students are finished you are ready to score the papers.

Remember—your are NOT grading students and the students should be told that. You are trying to determine whether or not all the students in your class will have success in reading the whole story.

The cloze passage may also be used to initiate a motivating-learner experience by discussing it with the students after they have finished filling in the blanks. This should be done even though you may find, after scoring the papers, that the passage is too difficult to use any further. Both content and especially grammar choices can be discussed with the students.

The simplest and most effective scoring procedure is to match each student's response with the list of words you deleted. Accept ONLY those words, even though you may find synonyms or other appropriate words being used by the students. Synonyms and "other" words will tell you much about the individual student's knowledge of English but *will not be necessary* for you to decide whether the reading election is appropriate for the WHOLE CLASS. For this decision you will find the more objective general score more suitable.

5. If you have fifty blanks, the conversion to percentage scores will be easy—multiply by two. If not, changing the score to percentage figures will take a little more time.

Once you have these scores for the whole class you will be able to determine the readability of the materials—for that class.

Remember that in general, second language students will not be able to fill in accurately more than sixty or seventy percent of the blanks of even easy reading material. They should be told this from the beginning. Both the teacher and the student should be aware that (a) the student will not always pick the original word and yet may have understood correctly what he is reading. And (b), the student will be able to read and understand a good deal of the passage even though he may not know all the words—we all do it occasionally in our reading.

If students get above 53 per cent they can probably read the story on their own. The teacher will know that this is a story which can be assigned as extra reading or to be read at home.

If the students get below 43 per cent then the material is too difficult for them to read—even with the help of the teacher in the classroom. It will indicate that there are just too many grammatical and lexical roadblocks in the way of the student for him to be able to read the story successfully and without frustration.

What the teacher is looking for is a set of scores for ALL students in the class that will be above 43 per cent (and for the most part below 53 per cent).

An that's it! If a large number of students are below 43 per cent— DON'T use the story. . .at least not with those students. Try again with another selection instead. If it seems impossible to find a story to use for the whole class from the material (books) you have then you will know that you must do one of two things. . . or both. You must find some reading material that is more appropriate for your students, that you can use with them in the classroom, that they will have success with, and that will take them ahead that one little step in grammar knowledge and reading skill, and towards new experience or information. You may also find that it is time to consider breaking up your classroom into two or more reading groups.

These scoring areas, frustrational (below 43 percent), instructional (43 to 53 percent) and independent reading (above 53 percent), are general areas and the teacher may find that they need to be adjusted somewhat. They are not absolute percentages. But the cloze procedure works, it will tell you a lot about your reading material.

Try it! Experiment! Use it!

TN 4/79

REFERENCES

Anderson. Jonathon "Selecting a Suitable Reader: Procedures for Teachers to Assess Language Differences." *SELC Journal II* (December, 1971) 34-42.

Haskell. John F. "Refining the Cloze Procedures for English as a Second Language." *English Record XXV* (Winter, 1973) 77-82.

"Refining Cloze Testing and Scoring Procedure for Use With ESL Students." (Dissertation. Teachers College. Columbia University. April. 1973).

"Putting Cloze Into the Classroom." *English Record XXVI* (Spring, 1975) pg. 83-90.

Krashen, Stephen D., Zelinti, Stanley J., and Jones, Carl M. "Report On A Cloze Test" *Idiom* IV (Summer, 1974)

Oller, John Jr. "Level of Difficulty and Scoring Methods for Cloze Tests of English as a Second Language Proficiency." *Language Teaching IIV* (April 1971) 254-59.

Pack, Alice C. "Cloze Testing and Procedure" *TESL Reporter* VI (Winter, 1973) 1-2

DICTIONARY BLOWOUT

By Chris Broadhurst
University of Petroleum & Minerals
Dhahran, Saudi Arabia

The big question was, "Shall we continue to issue English/English dictionaries to our students or shall we take a gargantuan step and hand out English/Arabic dictionaries?"

The English/English case states,

1. "We need to get our students out of the translation rut."

2. "We want the students to use English, not Arabic."

3. "We do not want extra interference from the native language."

4. "Pictures can be used to explain concrete objects."

5. "Students benefit more from explanations in English of abstract words. Let's use the language we are teaching!"

6. "Students will use their English/Arabic dictionaries as crutches, looking up every word they do not know."

The big steppers came back strong:

1. "Our faculty is not bilingual in the students' native language."

2. "A quick word in Arabic is the only way to explain abstract words."

3. "A protracted explanation of an abstract word in English is a good way to turn a reading lesson, a lab session, a structure drill or grammatical explanation into a vocabulary lesson."

4. "From an English/English dictionary explanation the students will proceed to guess at translations and whisper their guess to each other. Do we want to play guessing games?"

5. "Our students seldom voluntarily use the English/English dictionaries we give out every year."

6. "Many of our students do not have the dictionary habit and cannot look up a word in an Arabic/Arabic dictionary with facility. Once they are taught how to use an English/Arabic dictionary they will use them on their own."

7. "The students who buy dictionaries with their own money seldom buy English/English dictionaries."

8. "The students do not use English /Arabic dictionaries as a crutch."

9. "In an English/English dictionary you can end up looking up words to explain words to explain words. . . .'"

Let us pretend that you are learning Arabic, a non-Western language, and are at the beginning or intermediate stage. Would you use an Arabic/Arabic dictionary? If the answer is "no", then why should your students be expected to do just the opposite: use an English/English dictionary. Or is your answer "yes?"

Almost all of us in second foreign language teaching approach the dictionary with fear and trembling. We have seen our students rely on the dictionary when they should be guessing from context. At the same time we often have to rely on a dictionary ourselves when a word cannot be deciphered from context. A dictionary hovers between a curse and blessing. It is hoped that the program outlined below will help make the dictionary a blessing rather than a curse. Students hopefully will develop essential dictionary skills one step at a time and not be overloaded with skills they cannot use meaningfully.

When our students arrive at the ELC they usually do not have much in the way of dictionary skills. Often they lack that most basic of dictionary skills: alphabetization. The use of the English/ Arabic dictionary should develop those skills. Certainly it is all the dictionary they will need for their basic program.

As the English proficiency of students increases and their need for more use of a dictionary increases teachers will be free to issue a learner's dictionary. The teachers that do so will have to teach some basic dictionary skills so that the dictionary will not be merely an ornament.

Once the student gets to the UEP and more advanced reading and writing a real university level dictionary becomes useful and thus will be issued. Students in the sophomore courses will probably find use for a bilingual technical dictionary appropriate to their fields of major interest.

(Reprinted from *Team*, No. 26, Dec. 1978)

TN 4/79

THE MEANING OF "BLURP": TEACHING DICTIONARY USE

by Inez Marquez
University of Florida

A "hand" is that part of the human anatomy attached at the wrist to the lower arm and having four fingers and a thumb. Right? Well, think again as you read these sentences:

1. *Hand* me the salt, please.
2. I finally have a winning *hand*!
3. The audience gave her a big *hand*.
4. Joe needs a new hired *hand*.
5. The children are in good *hands*.
6. Can I lend you a *hand*?
7. Mom keeps some extra money on *hand*.

Obviously the above definition is inappropriate for these sentences. A look at the *Longman Dictionary of Contemporary English* reveals fifty-four definitions under the entry "hand." It is not surprising, therefore, that the learner of English as a foreign language finds dictionary definitions confusing and the English language capricious.

Rather than banning the dictionary from the classroom, the teacher of English as a foreign language should guide students in its proper use. The dictionary can become a valuable aid for self-instruction. The following steps have proven successful with my students and may be useful in your own classroom.

First, don't assume your students know the alphabet. It must be taught. Even when the students' native writing system is similar to that of English. Moreover, students should distinguish between the "name" of a letter and its "sound." Before introducing the alphabet the teacher should be sure the students understand its usefulness. This awareness can be fostered by having students name instances in which knowledge of the alphabet is useful, such as spelling your name over the telephone or finding a name in the telephone directory.

Second, give students practice in alphabetizing words by their first letter, as in "busy, clean, delicate, elegant," to alphabetizing by the fourth or fifth letter, as in "immature, immediate, immigrant, immoral."

Third, create awareness of the multiple meanings of words. Have students go through the dictionary to find the number of definitions entered under such words as "hand," "head," and "light." Students may also look at a dictionary of their native language to note how words in their own language also have multiple meanings.

Fourth, create awareness of the multiple grammatical functions a word can play. The use of a nonsense word in sentences such as the following will help students understand these differences:

1. Mrs. Elbers is a famous *blurp*.
2. Mrs. Elbers will *blurp* in the opera.
3. Mrs. Elbers has a *blurp* in her apartment window.
4. The *blurp* drink helped me go to sleep.
5. The mother *blurped* the baby to sleep by telling him a story.
6. The *unblurply* sound of the train is heard in the distance.

The teacher should help students note the context clues and affix clues which indicate the grammatical function of the nonsense word.

Fifth, once students are conscious of the multiple grammatical functions of a word, direct students to find the appropriate meaning of words. To do this they must first identify the word's grammatical function in a sentence and then find the most appropriate meaning in the given context. Thus for the nonsense word "blurp" the teacher may provide the following definitions:

blurp n. 1. a tropical song bird of the South Pacific
2. the song of this bird
3. a person who sings with great ability
v. 4. to sing beautifully
5. to calm a person with one's voice
adj. 6. musical
7. having a calming effect

In the first sentence, "Mrs. Elbers is a famous *blurp*," since "blurp" is a noun, definitions four through seven can be disregarded. Of the first three definitions, number three is the most appropriate for this context. The teacher continues with this procedure with each of the remaining examples. Additional practice should be given with other nonsense words before students use the dictionary to find the meaning of English words. Students may then proceed to find the meaning of words in sentences such as those presented for the word "hand."

TN 12/80

USING POETRY IN ESL

by Mary Ann Christison
Snow College

For the past few years I have been using poetry in my ESL classes with great success—success exemplified not only in terms of how I feel as a teacher but also in terms of how enthusiastic and accepting my students have been about the poetry and the activities the poetry has prompted. The following outlines some criteria for selecting poetry for ESL classes and offers suggestions for developing activities for the classroom.

Criteria for Selection (Christison, 1981)

1. High student interest. Choose poetry which reflects the everyday world of the students. Since the quality of their experience will be determined by the kind of poems which are offered to them, the teacher should select poems students can identify with.

2. Short and Simple. Poetry which is simple, direct, and to the point makes it easy to remember and hard to forget. This is an essential quality in the language classroom. The poetry should not have excessive idioms or unusual vocabulary. These will all have to be taught and discussed. Two or three items make it fun, but many more make it too difficult and students lose interest.

3. Fun-filled and rhythmic. Experience in language classes has taught us that language learners enjoy easy rhymes, alliteration, quick action and the humor much

poetry contains. Poems which capitalize on this naturally give students a feel for the rhythm and flow of English that they otherwise wouldn't get.

Activities for the Classroom

Once you have selected a poem which meets the criteria presented above, what do you do with the poem? As an example of the many possibilities for activities with poetry, consider the following poem entitled "Street Song" by Myra Cohn Livingston.

O, I have been walking
with a bag of potato chips
me and potato chips
munching along.

Walking along
eating potato chips
big old potato chips
crunching along.

Walking along
munching potato chips
me and potato chips
lunching along.

Tell students you are going to read a poem about potato chips. Find out how many students eat potato chips. (Bring some small bags to class if you wish.) Read the poem (remember to practice it first). After two readings, ask students how they would "crunch," "lunch," and "munch." Have them "mime" it for you.

The next time you read the poem, have them "crunch," "munch" or "lunch" everytime they hear the words. Next, pick the word *walking*. Everytime you say the word *walking*, they all stand up and walk. So the second time they must listen for *crunching, munching, lunching* and *walking*. Lastly, I add *potato chips*. When they hear this word, I have them hold a bag of potato chips in the air. (This could be real or otherwise.)

An activity of this type does several things for the students. It breaks down their inhibitions and it prepares them for additional activities later on. Of course, I never force anyone to participate. I just do it first. When I do this and approach the task with fun and enthusiasm, I have never had anyone sit for very long!

This activity can be used with a variety of poems on a variety of subjects. "Street Song" was selected because at the time my students were talking about food and the poem reinforced the content of the lesson. A poem should be used to enhance the material and topics already being introduced. For example, after the mime activity, I broke my students into small groups and had them generate answers to these questions about snacking customs.

Questions for small group discussion

1. What is a snack?
2. When do people snack?
3. What other foods besides (instead of) potato chips do you have for snacks?
4. What's your favorite snack?
5. Why do people snack?
6. What snacks have you seen people eat which you find strange?

These questions prompted a whole discussion on snacking, eating customs and habits. We also talked about tastes, sounds, how snacks are made, and when people eat them. Many students brought snacks to class the next day and we all shared, talked, and asked questions, (e.g., "What does this taste like?" "What's this made from?") Their enthusiasm for the whole lesson was, in part, a result of the attitude that was established with the first.

There are poems about almost everything imaginable—money, colors, numbers, weather, clothes, cars, cities, animals . . . and the list goes on and on. With such a wide variety of poems to choose from, there is no excuse for bringing poetry into the class which does not meet the needs of your students.

Non-academic adults have enjoyed "Money" by Richard Armour:

Workers earn it,
Spendthrifts burn it,
Bankers lend it,

We all spend it,
Forgers fake it,
Taxes take it,
Dying leave it,
Heirs receive it,
Thrifty save it,
Misers crave it,
Robbers seize it,
Rich increase it,
Gamblers lose it
I could use it.

Following an introduction of this poem, talk about money. Moreover, bring real money to class. What money you use, of course, depends on the kind of currency the students need to learn. For example, refugees in the United States would have to become familiar with U. S. currency while foreign students studying in Britain would have a different need. Give students practice in shopping and buying things by bringing empty packages to class such as cereal boxes and coffee cans. Using money, the students should find various items on a list, pay for them, and make change.

You might also try an activity called "strip poetry." Richard Armour's poem above works well because it's in couplets and the couplets can be arranged in a number of ways and still make sense. Write the poem on a large chart. Use the chart to introduce the poem and to have the group practice orally. On a second chart, copy the poem and cut it into strips. Pass the poetry strips out to the students. Have them memorize the strips and take them away. Then have the class put the poem back together orally in the correct order without looking at a copy of the poem!

Discover it for yourself: using poetry in TESL teaching is fun and exciting.

REFERENCES

Armour, Richard. *An Armoury of Light Verse.* Bruce Humphries.

Christison, Mary Ann. 1981. *English Through Poetry.* San Francisco: The Alemany Press, Ltd.

Livingston, Myra Cohn. 1974. *The Way Things Are and Other Poems.* New York: Atheneum Publishers.

TN 10/82

FREIRE AND LITERACY

by Caroline Dobbs
William Raney Harper College

The illiteracy problem in the United States is growing. Our illiterate population includes both native and non-native speakers of English and both adolescents and adults. Richard Orem, president of Illinois TESOL/BE, has pointed out that:

"Our country has failed in any attempt to this day to reverse the trend toward a more and more illiterate society. The pressure placed on our public school systems by growing numbers of illiterate refugee populations is more than simply an educational problem. It is also a political, social, and economic problem." (1)

In these two sentences, Orem has suggested several aspects of the problem. One is that the incoming refugees present several different types of illiteracy.

There are those who are literate in their native languages for whom literacy in English is essentially a matter of transferring skills. A second group is comprised of those who are totally or mostly illiterate in their first languages but who come from literate societies and are therefore aware of the world of print although they themselves have been excluded from it. A third group is comprised of those from non-literate societies, such as the Hmong who have essentially no written tradition as their language has only recently been put into written form. These have not been excluded from their society because of an inability to read and write; they have been fully functioning members of it.

One approach to the problem of literacy was that used by Paulo Freire in

Brazil. In 1959, Freire was coordinator of an adult education program at the University of Recife, Brazil. In an effort to bring education to as many people as possible, Freire developed what he called 'Circles of Culture' which were used for what is now called consciousness-raising. These circles were discussion groups, conducted in the villages, where people exchanged ideas with the educators on such topics as nationalism, democracy, and illiteracy. In the course of this, Freire discovered that many of the illiterate groups would not engage in these discussions. They believed that their condition in life was God's will and were therefore resistant to the idea that they could change their lives. Freire, a Christian Marxist, believes that literacy is a political tool. He views the illiterate as disenfranchised members of a literate society existing in a 'culture of silence' in which

> ". . . the masses are 'mute,' that is, they are prohibited in taking part in the transformation of their society and therefore prohibited from being." (2)

In order to overcome the passivity of the Brazilian illiterate population, Freire chose to work with the anthropological concept of culture, which differentiates nature from culture. For Freire, this included the distinction between man and animal and the use of oral and written language. To this end, he commissioned an artist friend to paint a series of ten tightly-structured pictures. To Freire, pictures embody the concept of *codification*, and projection of a picture, or codification of an existential situation, on a wall promulgates the first step in the act of knowing—it enables the learner to gain distance from the knowable object and, therefore, to reflect on it.

The first picture in the series shows a farmer, a tree, a pig, a well, and a house. It is used to teach the learners to distinguish that which is manmade from that which is not. Questions such as 'Who made the well?' and 'Why did he do it?' as opposed to 'Who made the pig?' and 'Who made the tree?' enable the participants to see that they are cultured because they use natural materials to create things for their own purposes. Gradually further distinctions are made: relationships between people can be that of equals; culture is transmitted from one generation to the next, but for those who cannot read and write, it must be done orally; some machines are too complex to make without reading written instructions, and too expensive to buy for those who are illiterate; the impact of education on technology; man's ability to exert control over his methods of obtaining food; clay pots made by a peasant are as much culture as the work of a great sculpture; songs with only an oral tradition can be put into writing; up to the final picture of a Circle of Culture in action, which allows the participants to reflect on their own activity. This is a very simplified overview of what takes place in these discussions, but the ultimate result is that the participants discover that even though they are illiterate, they are capable of complex thoughts and that by becoming literate, they can become subjects of their existence, rather than objects.

Freire felt that the consciousness-raising effected by these discussions would motivate people to learn to read and would release great energy directed toward this learning. After about six months of conducting these circles with enormous success, Freire realized that the same method might be just as successful in the actual teaching of literacy. Freire believed that education can do one of two things—it can teach people to be critical thinkers or it can teach them to accept the status quo. In order to achieve the first goal, Freire felt that literacy had to be taught as a part of conciousness-raising. The first step that he and his colleagues took was to develop literacy materials containing words that were familiar and meaningful to the adults in any given community. He posited that it was possible to select a brief list of words that would contain all the phonemes in Portuguese, so that the learners would then be able to sound out other words in Portuguese by means of this brief list. He and his colleagues discovered that seventeen words are enough to teach adults to begin to read and write both in Portuguese and in Spanish. The words selected for these lists were called generative

> ". . . in the double sense that the words would generate among non-literates impassioned discussions of the social and political realities of their lives . . . and by breaking the 17 words into syllables and rearranging the syllables non-literates could generate other words and transcribe their own words." (3)

In order to create a list of generative words for a given community, the educators would initially spend some time in that community investigating its culture. After explaining why they had come, they would enlist the aid of members of the community, and with their aid they would analyze the community's activities. From this, they would develop a list of words that were capable of provoking discussion in that community and that also contained all the phonemes in Portuguese. These words were then arranged in a careful sequence. The first word on the list always consisted of three syllables, and each syllable consisted of one consonant and one vowel. The rest of the words were arranged according to their phonetic complexity, moving from the concrete to the more abstract in meaning. The next step was to prepare pictures for the situations represented by each word. Freire believed that the ideas represented by the words should be discussed before beginning to teach literacy skills. After this, the first, trisyllabic, word would be presented. This word was then broken down into syllables. The coordinator would present the first syllable and then combine the consonant of this syllable with all the other vowel sounds in Portuguese. On one list, the first word is *tijolo* (brick). The coordinator would introduce *ti* and then *ta, te, ti, to, tu.* Then the next syllable was introduced in the same manner, and finally the third. At this point the learners would begin to combine other syllables together to produce other words that they knew. Learners would begin by writing lists of their own recombinations of syllables,

and before very long, many started writing longer sentences. Meetings were held every weeknight for an hour for a period of six to eight weeks. By the end of the literacy course, some 30 to 45 hours, those who had completed it could read and write simple texts, could get some understanding of the local newspapers, and could discuss Brazilian problems.

The idea that dominated Freire's literacy courses was that the learners were participants actively engaged in their own learning rather than empty vessels waiting to be filled up with someone else's learning and pedagogy. The whole point of the discussions by the Circles of Culture invoked by the first ten paintings was to bring the illiterate populations to a belief in their own abilities to reflect on and express ideas about the issues of their lives and to a realization that their thoughts and opinions were valid. For this reason, Freire opposed the use of outside primers. He believed that by writing their own ideas, the learners were accepting the validity of their own ideas about their own existential situations.

Some of Freire's concepts and methodology are already a part of TESL. His reasons for not using a primer but, instead, having the students read their own writings in the early stage of acquiring basic literacy skills are obviously embodied in the Language Experience Approach to literacy. It is certainly a tenet of ESL teaching that the student is a person worthy of respect, that s/he comes to class a whole person with his or her own experiences and thoughts, and with his/her own culture, and that all of these are to be treated with respect by the teacher. The LEA is one way of reinforcing these concepts.

Classroom discussion before writing is a technique used in many English composition classes, and the use of pictures to provoke discussion is a technique used to great benefit in ESL classes. The idea that the student is a worthy person and that his/her thoughts (and the oral and written expression of those thoughts) have validity enables the students to set their own goals, to see that they need not be limited to survival skills if they don't want to be. An approach to the teaching of literacy based on these concepts and methods should develop a type of literacy awareness in the students that alleviates the problem of the teacher, consciously or unconsciously, setting inappropriate goals for them. □

TN 4/82

1 Orem, Richard. (1981). 'Entering the 80's—some professional perspectives.' *Illinois TESOL/BE Newsletter.* 9:1.

2 Freire, Paulo. (1970). 'The adult literacy process as cultural action for freedom.' *Harvard Educational Review.* 40:2, p. 213.

3 Brown, Cynthia. 'Literacy in 30 hours: Paulo Freire's Process.' *Urban Review.* 7 (July) p. 252.

AN APPROACH TO TEACHING ESL READING TO LITERATE ADULTS

by Joanne Kalnitz
and Kathy Reyen Judd
Truman College, Chicago

We have found that despite the fact that our students may be fluent readers in their native languages, they often cannot transfer these skills to reading in English. They are focused on the word rather than on the entire text, are tied to their dictionaries, read slowly and word by word, and have unreasonable expectations about how much they should be able to understand. We have to help our students learn how to relax with reading. We have to teach them how to guess meanings by using signal words and context clues. Our students need to be aware of the rhetorical patterns of English so that they can identify main ideas, distinguish generalizations from specifics, and read critically. We have to be aware of the underlying cultural assumptions in readings we assign and we need to promote cultural awareness in the classroom. Most importantly, our students need to be able to determine their purpose for reading and to be able to choose appropriate strategies to achieve their goals.

By asking our students, we learned that they need to read a variety of different things in English: textbooks, newspapers, business reports and letters, menus, signs, etc. As we examined the skills of successful reading, we found that there is a lot of overlap between the skills needed to read the various materials that our students confront. For example, students may skim a newspaper as well as the phone book. Context clues can be used to determine the meaning of an unfamiliar word in a textbook as well as in a novel.

We begin with some assumptions about reading based on Kenneth Goodman and other readings. Goodman says that reading is a "psycholinguistic guessing game" (1972), involving the reader actively in the process of receiving the message that the writer has put on the page. Another way to say this is that reading consists of an interaction between the knowledge the reader has and the message (information) the writer has communicated. Reading is not just putting sounds together; native speakers decode directly from the text to the meaning without recourse to sound. The goal for second-language readers, of course, is to approximate as closely as possible the skills of native speakers. Reading is not just word recognition. For example: *saw this is one I the—* is a collection of words, but it has no meaning at all. Rearranged, "This is the one I saw," it still has very little meaning without a context. Is *one* a movie, a dog, a person, a house? Reading is ideas, and anything less than that is not really reading but word-calling. There

must be interaction between the reader and the writer (via the message). The reader must be an active participant in the communicative process, bringing ideas and expectations to the text and integrating the author's ideas into what s/he knows of the world. In summary, reading is getting meaning, always in context.

How do our students approach reading in English, and how does their approach inhibit them from becoming fluent readers? Perhaps one of the misconceptions about reading is that adults who are fluent readers in their native language will automatically be able to transfer these reading skills to a second language once they have learned enough of the language to be able to read it. Our own experience reading in the languages we studied in college shows us that such is not the case. We found ourselves frustrated and unsuccessful despite the fact that we are fluent readers in English. We all have also had numerous students who were well-educated in their native countries who are, nevertheless, extremely handicapped when attempting to read in English.

Why is this the case? Our students, because they are reading in a language that is not their own, tend to focus on the word as the unit of meaning instead of looking beyond the word to the sentence, paragraph and the entire text. As a result, they find themselves immensely frustrated since they may encounter several words in a single sentence whose meaning they are unsure of. They stop at each unfamiliar word, afraid to go on for fear of missing something. They are tied to their dictionaries, relying on translation to understand word meanings. They end up spending more time looking up words than they do reading the text.

Other strategies also inhibit our students when they read in English. For one, our students tend to have unrealistic expectations of how much they should be able to understand. They feel frustrated and dissatisfied if they have less than 100% comprehension. In addition, our students generally read everything the same way, regardless of the type of text; they read newspapers, stories and textbooks in the same manner. Finally, many of our students read aloud or subvocalize which slows them down and may inhibit comprehension.

How Can We Help Students to Change Their Strategies?

First of all, we need to help our students relax with reading and to reconsider the strategies they use. We like to begin our reading classes each semester

by discussing with our students how they read in English, what they think is the best way to read, and the problems they have in reading. This is usually a lively and thought-provoking discussion for our students because it gets to the heart of their frustrations with reading in a language not their own. Although this is only the first step in our campaign to help our students change their reading strategies, some of our students exhibit a visible sense of relief as they are introduced to the idea that they are not expected to understand 100% of what they read, that they don't have to look up every word, and that they can and should read faster.

Of course, we have not won over our students to our side with this initial discussion. Some may concede that our approach has validity, while others may remain unconvinced. Therefore, we like to spend the first week or two of the semester doing classroom exercises that focus on what our students know rather than what they don't know. They are only too aware of what they don't know. Our goal is to convince them that in many cases, they already possess the tools to understand what they are reading.

We can use exercises that help students realize that they don't need to understand every word in order to understand the general idea of what they are reading—and that understanding the general idea is all they can expect from themselves until they are fluent in English. One way to do this is by having the students read a passage with words missing. Students discover that they are still able to understand the meaning of the passage. Another kind of exercise that can accomplish this same purpose is a recall exercise. Students read a passage without the help of a dictionary, then close their books and either recall orally or write down everything they remember. We have done this exercise, first asking students what percent of the passage they understand, and have gotten low estimates like 40-50%. However, when asked to recall, students covered all the main ideas of the passage. They were surprised when it was pointed out to them that they had understood everything that was important, and that they had only missed some of the details. Students tend to base their percentages on the number of words they don't recognize rather than on whether or not they got the idea. These kinds of exercises help to change their concept of what is important in reading.

In addition, we can also present exercises that convince them that when they need to know words, they can often figure out the meanings by themselves. We can do this by presenting exercises where the contexts are so obvious that students can't fail to understand the meaning of a new word. For example: It was *hazy* outside, so I could not see clearly.

Once we have gotten our students to think differently about their approach to reading, we can begin to teach additional skills in the reading class. For the sake of convenience, we have divided these skills into two areas— language-related skills and text-related skills, though this is an artificial division, and they overlap one another.

Language Skills

After we have proven to the students that they don't have to depend on the dictionary each time they come across an unfamiliar word, we have to teach them skills that will help them to guess the general meaning of the word. Guessing cannot be exact, nor is the exact meaning necessary. This needs to be pointed out to our students. The skills we have to teach fall into three categories:

1. determining the part of speech of the unknown word
2. using context clues to guess the meaning of the word
3. using morphological clues to guess meaning.

Our students need to be aware of clues that will help them to determine the part of speech of the unknown word as this will help them to limit the range of their guessing. If the word could be any part of speech, the student has nowhere to start from in trying to guess. We have found this to be a problem with our ESL students, who need to be taught a sensitivity to the clues that are present. However, these clues are not infallible. Students must also be taught to look not only at the word itself, not only at the surrounding words, but at the entire sentence, paragraph and text for clues.

There are two types of clues that can help students determine the part of speech of an unknown word. These are grammatical markers and syntactic clues. The parts of speech identified by these clues are nouns, verbs, adjectives and adverbs.

Students can be sensitized to these clues by using worksheets that focus on the clues. For example, a sample worksheet focusing on syntactic clues would contain sentences with words missing, but with the signal word present. Students would be asked to determine the part of speech of the missing word and to identify the signal they used. The exercise is good to help students use more than one signal, and to show them that

no signal works 100% of the time. For example:

In order to be eligible for financial aid at Truman College a ——— must be a citizen or permanent resident of the U.S.

Students should be able to identify *a* as a signal for a noun. However, an article can also be followed by an adjective or an adverb, so students must look beyond to see that a modal follows the blank and therefore, the missing word is a noun. The exercise can be carried one step further by asking students to supply any noun that fits the meaning of the sentence.

A similar worksheet can be devised for grammatical markers. Students can be given sentences where one word is unknown, and they should be able to use grammatical markers and any other clues present to determine the part of speech. For example:

The school *determines* who is eligible for the work-study program, how much they will earn, and where they will work.

The students should be able to identify the *s* as a grammatical marker. The *s* by itself isn't enough, however, to signal a verb, as it is also the plural marker for nouns. Students must also use syntactic clues here.

After doing exercises with isolated sentences, students can then be asked to do the same thing when reading an entire text. This kind of skill can be reinforced throughout the semester.

After students know how to determine the part of speech of the unknown word, they can also be taught to use the clues within the text, both before and after the unknown word, to narrow the meaning of the word. Again, students should not be aiming for an exact definition. After looking at a large number of reading texts which list varying kinds of context clues, we have come up with six comprehensive categories. Except for the last category, each has signal words that are clues to meaning. However, these kinds of contexts can exist without the signals. The exercises we do in the classroom are used to heighten students' awareness and to increase their sensitivity to the signal words and the contexts in which they occur.

Again, once exercises like these have been done at the sentence level, students can be asked to apply the same skills when reading an entire text.

The third element in word attack skills is the morphological analysis of words. We can teach them the most common prefixes, suffixes and stems and show them how these combine and how this can aid in understanding words within a context. In class, we can give students worksheets in which they have

to match meanings once they know the meaning of a particular prefix, suffix, or stem. We can also have them create words with a particular meaning. Again, context is a must as some prefixes and suffixes have more than one meaning. For example, -en can mean *made of* as in *wooden*, *cause to be* as in *sharpen*, and *put into* as in *encircle*. Or, there may be different stems with similar meanings where only context will help. For example, -dis and -un both can mean *not* or *opposite of*, so that only context will help our students understand the difference in meaning between *dislike* and *unlike* or *discover* and *uncover*.

The other language area that interferes with our students' understanding of a text is substitutions and deletions. A breakdown in understanding a text, particularly a complex one, may occur when words are substituted or deleted and students are unaware of what the substitutions stand for or what the deleted words are. We used *A Concise Grammar of Contemporary English* by Quirk and Greenbaum (1975) to aid us in our compilation of the kinds of substitutions and deletions that occur in English. We have eliminated some of them, and recombined and reorganized others with pedagogical considerations in mind. We have listed two kinds of substitutions and three kinds of deletions that should be taught in the ESL reading class.

In the classroom, one effective way to sensitize students to substitutions is to take a text, such as an article in a student newspaper, circle all the pro forms, and have students identify what they refer to. Students can also be asked to do substitution exercises themselves, where they actually supply the pro forms.

To sensitize students to deletions, students can work with the same text, and can be asked to supply what has been deleted. They can also be asked to create deletions themselves.

Text-related Skills

One important rhetorical device of English is the use of generalizations supported by examples in expository prose. Like everything else that seems clear and straightforward to native speakers, this concept is one which ESL students need to be made aware of. They need to know how to recognize and identify generalizations and distinguish them from examples. We introduce the concepts of generalization and example and teach the vocabulary peculiar to each (*in general, on the whole, always/never* vs. *for example, for instance*). First, we ask students to identify the generalization in a paragraph, noting its location, and then we ask them to identify the examples, noting the proportion of examples to generalizations. We provide other paragraphs or longer writings for students to examine as well. A more sophisticated skill is determining whether or not the examples given actually support the generalization. These are skills of critical reading. After teaching generalizations and examples early in the semester, we continue identifying them throughout the semester, making sure that students know what to look for and how to spot them. Students can then make use of the concept as a means of identifying the main idea, in skimming, and in locating topic sentences. They need to be able to distinguish examples in scanning for specific information and evaluating arguments.

Not all cultures and languages organize information in the same way; as a result the rhetorical conventions of expository prose differ from one language to another. Kaplan (1966) points out the circular pattern of exposition in Oriental writing vs. linearity in English vs. the greater latitude of digression permitted in Semitic writing. Our students need to be exposed to the styles of English rhetoric so that they can make use of them in understanding what they read in English. If successful reading depends upon accurate prediction of what is to follow, as in Goodman's guessing game, then knowing the rhetorical structures and how they function will enhance fluent reading by increasing the likelihood of successful prediction.

In English, the concept of generalization and example leads to the structure of main idea and details. Many reading texts ask questions about the main idea of a reading selection, but usually there are far more questions about the details. Since the main idea is the most important one, it seems logical that more attention in reading class should be devoted to finding it, being sure all students understand it, and clarifying how the details are subordinate. The ratio of detail to main idea questions in most reading texts, however, is just the opposite of this, leading students to focus on minute details while running the risk of missing the main point.

Just as students should be exposed to the vocabulary of generalizations and examples, they should be taught the clues that English rhetoric provides for identifying the main idea, such as topic sentences, conclusions, and phrases (*most important*, etc.). Ideas that support the main idea are generally identified by *for example, in addition, moreover*, etc. Students also need to know how to identify and evaluate ideas which are in opposition to the main idea. These may be introduced by phrases like *on the other hand, some say, however*, and others. In a text, we expect to find fewer of these than supporting ideas.

If the reader understands the main idea of a piece, this is often sufficient. Many of our students believe that they must understand every small detail of what they read. ESL reading texts may give far more comprehension questions than a passage warrants. The questions often focus on minute, nonessential details. If that's what texts do, teachers may follow, even though it goes against their common sense. We do our students a disservice, however, if we insist they read everything that we give them to find all the little insignificant details. This practice only reinforces their (fallacious) idea that every word on the page is equally important and deserving of attention.

Two of the tools students need for maximally efficient reading are skimming and scanning. Skimming is quick reading for the general idea(s) of a passage. Preview skimming is used to decide whether or not to read something more thoroughly, while overview skimming is used when there is no time for a more complete reading. Scanning is looking quickly for specific information using textual clues plus graphic information. We scan to find information in a dictionary or telephone book as well as to find the answer to a specific question in prose.

If preview skimming and other reading exercises are to be meaningful, there must be time for reading of student-selected materials in class. Only by having students spend time in class reading can the instructor ensure 1) that they read the assignment and 2) that they read quickly, without their bilingual dictionaries. A reading lab with a large selection of materials at different levels and on different subjects is best suited for this; another possibility is to collect articles from newspapers and magazines (choosing those which will not be out of date next week) and to provide a file of these for students to choose from for in-class reading. The follow-up exercises can include explaining the article's idea or story's plot to another student who has not read it, answering questions the teacher has prepared, or—nothing. Sometimes just reading is enough. In real life, we often read either for pleasure or to pass the time. Students sometimes need to read things for which they are not held accountable.

An essential idea in all of this is the concept of determining purpose for reading and then suiting reading strategy to meet that purpose. Students need to be flexible both in speed of reading and in choice of strategy; as teachers, our goal is to teach students to determine their own purpose and to adopt the needed strategies (Clarke & Silberstein 1979: 50). We find that our students tend to approach everything to be read in English as if it had to be studied, but we try to teach them a variety of techniques and show them how different ones are appropriate in different situations. Among the various techniques students should be able to employ are skimming and scanning, as mentioned above, as well as study techniques such as SQ3R (Survey, Question, Read, Recite, Review) of S.R.A. fame. ESL students need to increase their reading rate, but they must also know when to slow down for specific tasks.

In prereading activities, ESL teachers are familiar with the technique of previewing unfamiliar vocabulary or syntax likely to present problems in comprehension for students. Selekman and Kleinmann (1978) argue that we should not neglect previewing unfamiliar sociocultural concepts as part of prereading. Based on their examples, we have used previewing of cultural concepts in our classes with good results.

Selekman and Kleinmann maintain that students' active involvement in a simulation focusing on the cultural concept is the best way to ensure students' understanding of, as well as involvement in, the reading. We have found that identifying the underlying cultural assumptions is in itself a worthwhile project for the instructor, who is forced to examine American culture somewhat from the viewpoint of the non-native student. The result of this can be increased awareness on the part of the instructor that there are indeed assumptions which are not shared—or even recognized—by students from other cultures.

Conclusion

The approaches to reading instruction described here can be incorporated into reading classes for literate adults at various levels of ESL study. Beginning with the deliberate modifications of their reading strategies and continuing throughout the course to add flexibility by means of increasing the repertoire of skills students have to draw upon, we hope to produce independent second-language readers who can set their own reasonable goals and then accomplish them with success and confidence. □

REFERENCES

Goodman, Kenneth S. 1972. "Reading: A Psycholinguistic Guessing Game," in Larry A. Harris and Carl B. Smith (eds.) *Individualizing Reading Instruction: A Reader*. New York: Holt, Rinehart, and Winston.

Kaplan, Robert B. 1966. "Cultural Thought Patterns in Inter-Cultural Education." *Language Learning* 16. 1-20.

Quirk, Randolph and Sidney Greenbaum. 1975. *A Concise Grammar of Contemporary English*. New York: Harcourt Brace Jovanovich.

Selekman, Howard R. and Howard H. Kleinmann. 1978. "Aiding Second Language Reading Comprehension." In Charles H. Blatchford and Jacqueline Schacter (eds.) *On TESOL '78 EFL Policies, Programs, Practices*. Washington, D.C.: TESOL. 165-175.

Editor's Note: This article is excerpted from a longer paper given at the 1st Midwest TESOL Meeting/9th Illinois TESOL Meeting held in Champaign, Illinois, April 2-4 1981. It appears in full in the Collected Papers of that meeting.

BOOK REVIEWS

SKILLFUL READING

(Amy Sonka, Englewood Cliffs, New Jersey: Prentice Hall, Inc., 1980)

Reviewed by Anita Reiner
University of Massachusetts, Boston

Amy Sonka's *Skillful Reading* might well be subtitled "The Compleat Reader." Its purpose is to prepare intermediate students to read well for academic courses. Its language and content reflect that commonly found in high school and college texts. Its approach to the task of reading is one of building the parts into the whole, and the whole is structured around particular rhetorical forms.

Before students get to the main reading in each of the nine chapters, they are given five warm-up exercises. These require "gathering thoughts" about the reading topic, learning five or six essential words, and reading rapidly for eye movement and comprehension. The rapid reading exercise includes material that the students will encounter in the main reading of the chapter. As the author says, "The rapid reading exercise is intended to have students let go of the need to cling to each word and to enable students to recognize key sentences later." Using short paragraphs, the students practice techniques in identifying and understanding the main rhetorical pattern that they will encounter in the long reading—chronological order or contrast, for example. The final pre-reading exercise is to have students anticipate the overall organization of the main reading by counting the number of paragraphs it includes, looking for key words, and identifying topic sentences to anticipate where specific information is presented.

The main reading selection itself is long enough (930 to 1640 words) to require cumulative comprehension. A major problem with many reading texts at any level is their shot-gun approach to subject matter —too many directions, all too short. In Sonka's book the readings are long enough to give students a guided experience in the reality of reading a textbook in English.

Having read the main passage, students are not immediately asked the usual comprehension and vocabulary questions. Instead, they are invited to talk and write about the reading at their own levels of these skills. They are guided in making outlines, taking notes, using notes in a "semi-controlled framework for expressing the information in the chapter orally and in writing." The use of notes involves dyads and small group discussion. It includes students quizzing each other and writing paragraphs from their notes.

Next students are given an examination practice. They are asked to write short answers based on the reading; for example, "Illustrate the effect of color on people." This provides experience with the sometimes puzzling language of examination questions, and opportunity for developing strategies for writing answers to such questions. A specific reading skill follows, for example, scanning, skimming, or understanding pronoun usage. There are vocabulary practices using both the context expected from the reading and multiple contexts.

In case someone is still looking for something to do, a variety of interesting projects are provided for independent work. Finally, the supplementary reading practice in each chapter enables students to use their reading, speaking, and listening skills on new material related to the topic of the chapter.

Each of the nine chapters has one main topic. These topics include color, architecture, nutrition, language, memory, economics, electronics, and pollution—a good range. As all of us know, however, each class must include a student who says that he is only interested in—. Here such a student should be easily sold on the variety of activities and the look of a real textbook in the main reading selections.

The language of the readings is controlled in the first five chapters to present tense, active and passive. Past tense is used in and after chapter five. The author has avoided the obvious abnormal redundancy of usage sometimes found in intermediate material. The style is clear and readable, better than many academic textbooks foisted on college students.

The author describes her book as directed toward the intermediate student, but it can and has been used at higher levels as well. Her intention is to guide students in reading fairly long, substantive passages.. The students are challenged but not frustrated because they quickly recognize in the main reading some material they have already encountered in the pre-reading exercises. Then they are given the opportunity to talk about the material, hear about it, and take notes on it at their individual language levels. Although the readings are at a relatively high level for the intermediate student, they are appropriate for the receptive skill of reading, especially with the guidance given.

Skillful Reading not only prepares students to read a challenging piece successfully, but it also gives them the techniques to crack open and use the contents. The one question asked the author by those who know her is "Are you sure you wrote it, Amy? It's so serious!" *Skillful Reading* is a serious, effective text, interesting and substantive in subject matter, exercises, and activities. It reflects the author's skillful teaching. *TN 12/81*

high school to college. *Who Done Did It?* encourages students to read for enjoyment while it forces them to focus on word meanings in order to understand all the intricate details of mysteries. Because mysteries have a universal appeal, this book will most definitely be a "hit" with all students.

The text is divided into eight separate short stories of approximately 10 pages each. There is an introductory chapter which explains some of the history and traditions surrounding mystery stories. Familiar literary names such as Edgar Allen Poe, Sir Arthur Conan Doyle, and Agatha Christie are mentioned in the introduction so that the reader will be able to place subsequent short stories in their proper literary tradition and understand allusions to famous detectives. Acquainting students with other mystery writers also serves to direct them to additional sources of reading. The introduction prepares students for the more academic type of reading they will encounter later on in literature and history classes. The expository style of this chapter and the short glossary of terms at the end help students analyze and comprehend this literary genre.

Each story is an entity unto itself and can be adequately covered in one class session. Subsequent classes can be devoted to completing the variety of exercises which accompany each chapter. Exercises include tests of comprehension and vocabulary usage, cloze passages, questions for oral discussion, and suggestions for compositions. Unfortunately, the text does not include an answer key either at the end of each chapter or at the end of the book. Such an addition, if only consisting of answers for the comprehension and vocabulary exercises, would enable the text to be used for individual instruction and allow for self-testing. Students would also profit from the immediate feedback that an answer key provides.

The book is most enjoyable and will serve students in many ways. A number of common, everyday expressions are used (e.g., "spend money to make money," p. 45), and these terms may stimulate class discussions of "truisms." Also included are expressions (such as "Peter Stone's the name and detection's the game," p. 84) that will no doubt further the foreign students' understanding of American humor. The names of characters are cleverly chosen (e.g., "Violet Cornichon"—*cornichon* in French is a pickle), and their reappearance in other stories helps to form a connecting thread.

Because of its format and comprehensive coverage of all types of crime stories, the book prepares students well for the next step—reading a mystery novel. Upon completion of *Who Done Did It?*, students will have the lexical and literary competence to undertake the reading of an entire novel.

Who Done Did It? is most successful in fulfilling one of its goals—making language fun. Although the authors state that *Who Done Did It?* is not primarily a writing textbook, it teaches good writing by example. The paragraphs and stories are well written and well organized. The text will undoubtedly provide teachers and students alike with many fine hours of reading and discussion. *TN 4/82*

WHO DONE IT?

(Carlos A. Yorio and L. A. Morse. Englewood Cliffs, N.J.: Prentice Hall, 1981.)

Reviewed by Janice Dowd
Teaneck Board of Education

Who Done Did It?, a delightful collection of crime stories, is a welcomed addition to the present assortment of ESL readers. The book is designed for advanced ESL classes or remedial English classes and can be used on a variety of levels from

REPLY REQUESTED

(by Richard Yorkey. Reading, Massachusetts: Addison Wesley Publishing Company. 1981)

CHECKLIST FOR VOCABULARY

(by Richard Yorkey. New York City: Longman Inc. 1981)

THE ENGLISH NOTEBOOK

(by Richard Yorkey. Minerva. 1981)

Reviewed by John Haskell
Northeastern Illinois University

If Dick Yorkey had written only his *Study Skills for Students of English as a Second Language* (McGraw-Hill: 1970, revised 1981) he would have provided a seminal volume in the field. Add to it, however, the *InterCom (International Communication) Series* (American Book Company; 1978) and you can see the breadth of the creativity his writings represent. Last year, in a blitzkrieg of publications, Yorkey produced, yet again, three very useful volumes, each as different as they are practical.

Reply Requested, is certainly one of the most thought provoking sets of materials on the market today. Those teachers who want language and culture in a format that is current and immediate, will be pleased to see the innovative ways in which Yorkey presents Ann Landers' columns. There are few more "American" cultural stereotypes than the 'advice to the lovelorn' column. These columns have moved from the realm of 'should I accept the proposal from Johnny or Jimmy?' columns to questions (and intelligent answers) on topics as diverse as herpes and wedding invitations. In *Reply Requested,* Yorkey has selected thirty Landers columns on such typical American (or universal?) problems as a newlywed husband watching TV in bed, dieting diners, feeding the babysitter, married children living at home, parent's opinions of children's choices for friends, lovers, spouses, and the like, and the myriad of other social disasters and successes which at times seem to engulf us—or frustrate us, anyway.

Each 'letter' is accompanied by a vocabulary list, a set of straightforward factual questions which help to insure at least surface comprehension, and Notes on Language Use special items in the letter which might benefit by some further explication. In one chapter, for example, the term 'white lie' is explained and the question is asked: "What is a white lie called in your language?" Each lesson (letter) is also accompanied by a set of discussion questions which lead to the Language in Life section. This section asks the students to take the notion or idea discussed in the letter and relate it to events in their own lives. In the "white lie" lesson, for example, the idea of a white lie is discussed first in terms of its form (the structure, the kind of questions asked and the reply), some possible situations or requests are offered to which a white lie might be an appropriate or expected response, and then the students are asked to suggest what kinds of white lies they might use in response. In this lesson a set of 'role plays' are also presented for the students to enact and this is followed by a Letter Writing exercise in which the

students are asked to write an answer to the letter (the problem) which they have been discussing. Finally, each lesson includes Ann Landers' reply and the students are asked to discuss how they feel about her reply.

If you have ever had trouble thinking of ways to get your students actively participating in conversations on topics that would interest them, on which they could express their own opinions, without fear, this volume is perfect. Students can discover and relate to the similarities and differences between their cultures and those of the US through a look at very personal, very real—social problems. I believe that secondary school age students and most adult groups (and teachers) would find this volume to their liking. You will certainly find out a lot about your students' attitudes about the US and American culture by offering them the opportunity to discuss the topics in this book. The lessons, by the way, need not be done in any order; it is not a syllabus. The various letters can be selected for currency or appropriateness or interest as the teacher or the students' wish.

There are a number of 'vocabulary' type texts on the market at present, and while I might have wished for a different, less crowded set-up for each page, the content of Yorkey's book *Checklist for Vocabulary Study,* is the very best. If I could only give my students the information in the preface 'To the Student,' I would have given them more than most students ever get in an understanding of how words in English are 'put together.' It suggests to the student how English uses prefixes and suffixes, how these elements determine or signal the class or list into which the word is placed (noun, verb, adjective, and adverb) and to what extent meaning is also given, adjusted, expanded, etc. The book is to be used in conjunction with a dictionary and students will find that their dictionary skills will increase with each exercise. One of the most difficult tasks a student has in using a dictionary is finding the right meaning and then selecting the right form of the word for his use. This book is divided into Checklists, units which deal with one particular suffix or group of words with similar suffixes Checklist 4, for example, deals with -tion and its various forms. Words are presented in a list which shows the noun, verb, adjective and adverb forms (if they exist) and in this case, separates the words into smaller units depending upon the spelling convention that dictates the form of -tion ending the words take (ie., words that end in the 'silent -e', words that end in '-fy', etc.) The Checklist is then followed by a

number of different kinds of 'fill-in-the-blank' (or choose-the-right-word and form-of-the-word) sentences (exercises). In some cases the word is given and in some exercises the student is asked to select the right word and the right form from the words in the Checklist. At the end of each group of four Checklists there are two Crossword Puzzles for the student to do, using words from the preceding four Checklists. The clues are given in the same type of 'fill-in-the-blank' sentences that make up the exercises which accompany each Checklist. (If you have any doubts about answers, as I always do in texts that offer puzzles and 'meaningful' exercises, you will be grateful for the answers found at the end of the book for all the exercises and puzzles.)

The Checklists themselves are also interesting in that while all of them are made of fairly common words (drawn from the word lists of either Praninskis or West), and most of the Checklists contain words, many of which have all four forms, there are other kinds of Checklists. One, for example, contains a set of words, none of which have a verb form, another which lists words which have only a noun form, and another which lists words which have only adverb and adjective forms. (I learned a lot myself.) At the end of the book there are four Review Quizzes which can be used to check students' progress. Guessing is certainly one of the most important skills that ESL students need to master if they are ever to be able to be creative and to read with speed (and pleasure) in English. The vocabulary exercises in this book will go a long way in helping the student to acquire the kind of 'how to psych out a word' skills that are requisite to being able to read and write (and understand what people say) in English. I think that any intermediate or advanced ESL student, particularly at the secondary or adult level will find this book useful.

The English Notebook is subtitled Exercises for Mastering the Essential Structures, and the preface states that the 88 exercises which it contains are "created to help intermediate-level students of English as a Second/Foreign Language practice and reinforce some of the basic grammatical forms and sentence patterns of English." The book has an intriguing cover, that black speckled cover of one of the more common types of note-taking book, a picture of "the class" on the inside cover, including the teacher (Yorkey, himself), and what at first glance seems like a boring inside. But once over the hump of cheap (but easy to write on) paper and a fairly colorless page after page of exercises, a more careful look will turn up a typically Yorkeyan presentation that is clear, clean, packed with good exercises (and examples) and not a little information both in the form of "notes on usage," notes on form, and such incidental information as the adjective forms for various countries and the nouns used to describe the language of that country.

All in all it is an excellent review text for any student (and many a teacher). other Yorkey Books, I learned a lot myself from using this one. I bet you and your students will too.

TN 8/82

ENGLISH THROUGH POETRY

by Mary Ann Christison. 1982. Alemany Press,
P.O. Box 5265, San Francisco, CA 94101.
(150 pages; paperback only, $6.95.)

Reviewed by Corless Smith
University of California, Berkeley

One of the magical properties of poetry is its ability to revitalize familiar words by placing them in new contexts or slightly altering their meanings. In this respect ESL students are natural poets, producing easily and inadvertently novelties which native-speaking poets cannot evolve because of their knowledge of the language. Some errors, which teachers are obliged to correct, are, nonetheless, highly expressive. Statements such as "We are enjoyed by automatic things" or simple misspellings such as "wishcraft" for "witchcraft" can be powerfully evocative.

Many of the activities in *English Through Poetry* are designed to stimulate poetry writing, but Christison's primary goal is to promote language use in general. Her book is divided into sections devoted to verse-related exercises, choral readings, readers' theater, and a short anthology of verse for use in the classroom.

Christison argues that poetry should be incorporated in the ESL class because this is an "excellent way to improve reading skills, develop more vocabulary and nurture a love of words and sounds in adults and children. . . [and it] provides a firm foundation on which to build more advanced language skills later on."

The book is a very useful compendium of verse-related classroom activities most suitable for children and adult learners at beginning stages. For example, Christison presents an onomatopoetic piece about potato chips and suggests that the teacher distribute potato chips with which the students could learn experientially the meaning of "crunching" and "munching." She offers 38 such activities of greater and lesser sophistication, all of which use verse to promote language use and classroom verve.

Likewise, Christison's bibliography is a good source of further activities and places where one can pursue topics she introduces, often in a provocative way, her treatment of *haiku* for example. Her exercises on similes are excellent,

and she gives several good fill-in-the-blank exercises to stimulate students to write their own poems.

Actually, however, the book is misnamed. It could more accurately be called *English Through Verse*, for it conveys little sense of the special power of poetic discourse to provide access to a world of knowledge otherwise unavailable. To Christison, poetry is (apparently) distinguished by its typographical arrangement on the page, its use of similes and certain units of composition, such as *haiku* or couplets, and its existence as an arena in which to consider thoughts and feelings in more meditative ways than expository writing allows.

All these are certainly elements of poetry, but if they were the substance of it, we might wonder why poetry has been so important to the human spirit for thousands of years. Christison's selections for her short anthology make most obvious the limitations of her approach. Most of the poems are doggerel, such as "Ignore dull days; forget the showers; keep count of only shining hours." Only two poems, "The Road Not Taken" by Robert Frost and "This Is Just to Say" by William Carlos Williams, have sufficient magnitude to be considered great poems: they evoke and address significant and profound thoughts and emotions.

Even Christison's shortcomings are useful though, for they point out directions others may take. She has illuminated more clearly the task of those who want to present their advanced students more serious works of literature. Not only is the need for a better anthology apparent, but we are also led to consider pedagogical strategies for opening the great literary texts in English to nonnative speakers. If doggerel promotes love for the language, surely masterpieces, the "best that has been thought and said," can also be accessible and have even greater effect.

—from *CATESOL NEWS*, December 1982.

TN 8/83

WHAT'S THE STORY?

by Linda Markstein and Dorien Grunbaum. 1981. Longman, Inc.: 19 West 44th Street, New York, NY 10036.

Reviewed by Robert Oprandy
Teachers College, Columbia University
New York, New York

What's the Story? Sequential Photographs for Language Practice is a four-book series that revolves around twelve sets of four sequential photos of real people embroiled in seemingly true circumstances. The materials, beautifully put together by co-authors Linda Markstein and Dorien Grunbaum (who did all the photography as well), are a must for any program concerned with the promotion of communicative competence and looking for excellent stimuli towards that end.

Professionally photographed, the pictures provide foci for a number of carefully designed activities that help students work on all four basic language skills. Students can progress from Book 1's carefully controlled vocabulary and structures to Book 4's emphasis on composition skills.

The dozen units of each book correspond to the twelve sets of photos, which remain constant for all four student books. If a language program

decided to use all four stages of *What's the Story?*, a student who spent more than a term or two with the series would most likely master a good deal of language but perhaps tire of the same story lines.

However, if the 18" x 24" spiral-bound sets of photographs—or the small copies found at the back of each book—are used in the numerous ways suggested in the Teacher's Guide, a good deal of creative storytelling will yield new versions or twists to each story. The stories, as written in the student books, are already quite creative. They portray a wide range of people involved in engaging, believable experiences. Three-year-old Carolita experiences the painful arrival of a new sibling into *her* household. A ball-playing boy picks up a $20 bill dropped by a woman as she pays a taxi driver, and the youngster is left to decide how to handle his values conflict. Senior citizens share pictures on a park bench.

Unlike the lifeless "people" found in the sketches of so many ESL texts and previous progressive picture pads and books, Markstein and Grunbaum's characters show a panoply of emotions—nervousness, disappointment, anger, frustration, jealousy, failure, sympathy, indecisiveness and joy. The characters and their stories lend themselves to lots of discussion for their own sake as well as creating contexts for students to share their own life experiences and the emotions surrounding them. Some stories are amusing with their clever twists at the end; all are engaging and well designed as stimuli for classroom interaction, including role-playing.

The 44-page *Teacher's Guide* for the entire series contains a concise, thorough collection of suggestions for how to use the photo charts. It also supplements the wide range of activities in the texts. Security is provided for inexperienced teachers through the clarity of the suggestions, and challenges await experienced teachers who may have a limited repertoire in using sequential pictures. The authors declare some of their beliefs about learning by offering suggestions aimed at providing students with choices and with opportunities to use their imaginations without fear of being "wrong" as they reproduce verbally what the photos present visually.

The *Teacher's Guide*, the best I've read, also offers several ideas for written work, for making new vocabulary come alive, and for utilizing the passport-sized pictures in the back of the students' books in ways the spiral-bound picture pads cannot be used.

Also in the *Guide*, the writers share their research in testing out their materials. They go over the story line that most students came up with for each set of pictures and relate a few unexpected plots. They summarize language activities they have found particularly useful and list grammar and vocabulary items that logically flow from each story, clustering the latter into semantic sets they label "environment," "clothing," and "miscellaneous." Cloze dictations are also provided for use with Books 3 and 4.

The writers' intention to make *What's the Story?* a challenging series of language practice activities comes across clearly in the *Guide*. They expect students not to be able to understand everything immediately but to work hard for a little more than they currently control. Even in Book 1, no one's intelligence is questioned or insulted. The natural use of English begins with the title and is found throughout all the books; it is assumed by Book 4 that the readers have been exposed to lots of idiomatic language use.

The layout, editing and 6¾" x 10" size of the books, which range in length from 44 to 66 pages, are excellent. The pads, however, would stand up more easily on narrow chalk trays if they had a slightly stiffer cardboard backing. Also, the inclusion of the small photos at the back of each book may rob classes of the spontaneity a teacher would hope to have upon introducing a new set of photos. Most curious students, upon examining their new books at the beginning of a term, would certainly take a look at the photos long before the lessons dealing with them. This could be an advantage, however, if students begin to hypothesize in English about possible versions of the stories.

Much more could be said about this rich new set of materials. If you enjoyed using previous sets of progressive pictures, you will love the possibilities Markstein and Grunbaum's photos and accompanying texts provide.

TN 2/83

READING BY ALL MEANS

Fraida Dubin and Elite Olshtain. 1981. Addison-Wesley, Reading Massachusetts 01867.

Reviewed by Liz Hamp-Lyons
University of Edinburgh

Dubin and Olshtain's book declares itself to be "a self-instructional text," although a plan for its use by a teacher with a class is also included. One of the most exciting things about this book is that it contains many readings, each of which is only used for one or two activities/exercises, rather than the much more common approach of having a small number of readings followed (and/or preceded) by a large number of activities/exercises. The obvious advantages of Dubin and Olshtain's approach are that the students get a much greater exposure to a variety of texts, and they are less likely to become bored due to over-utilization of a text.

The organization of the text moves from reading narratives, to reading general information, to reading specialized information, and one assumes that the authors saw some difficulty or skill progression here. I suspect, however, that many young adult foreign students would have more trouble with the concepts in Bronowski's "A Moral for Any Age" or Markandaya's "Remembering" than with those in later selections such as Gwenda Blair's "Why Dick Can't Stop Smoking" or "All About That Baby" (*Newsweek*) which are much more factual and written in a much more literal (as opposed to literary) style. I also find it difficult to distinguish between some of the readings used in the "reading for general information" section and those in the "reading for specialized information" section in terms of the reading skills needed to gain comprehension from them. What is more important, however, is that the authors have clearly thought out what it is they want the student to learn from this book and have then sought out reading passages which will fulfill their objectives, rather than the other way around, which I suspect is the more common approach. The "Guide for Locating the Strategies" in the front of the book is not only a useful guide to the teacher or the self-study student; it is a clear indication that the authors have thought through their views about the strategies involved in reading and have set out to introduce students to these strategies and offer them opportunities for practice, while avoiding lengthy metalinguistic explanations. One may well wish that certain reading strategies had been presented more frequently (for example, topic sentence activities only occur twice; reference words rate three exercises and there are only four

scanning activities) and that activities/exercises were more precisely headed (for example, Unit 17, C: "Analyzing the Supporting Ideas in Each Paragraph" is, in fact, a cohesion exercise which includes reference items; it would more correctly have been titled "Discourse Threads," according to the Guide). But such criticisms cannot detract from the major achievement of this book: it teaches advanced reading skills. Where *Reading By All Means* has led the way, other books will surely follow, and one hopes that these will avoid the weaknesses and consolidate the strengths it contains.

The introduction to the book does not indicate the level at which it is aimed, but my own feeling is that it is quite advanced. In general, the readings tend to be more difficult than the activities which relate to them. I find this to be a sensible approach, but the inexperienced teacher might find it difficult to handle, and I cannot help having reservations about how the self-study student would handle it alone.

The best feature of this book is that it really is a *reading* text. It teaches and practices reading skills, it draws upon the students' own background experiences and responses to support their reading comprehension, and it aims to operate on the students and make them react to text at the personal, critical level; it acknowledges that reading comprehension cannot take place in a vacuum. I feel that the only time the authors get diverted from the central issue here is in the written summarizing exercises. Summarizing is a high level writing skill which, although related to reading, does not depend entirely on reading comprehension. Unlike oral summarizing, written summarizing makes very stringent demands on a person's grammatical, structural and stylistic abilities, and its use tempts both teacher and student to lose sight of the goal, which is reading comprehension. I would prefer to see the summary exercises in the book used only for oral summary, perhaps as group work. The summary "answers" in the back of the book are by no means the only correct responses.

In conclusion, however, I want to reemphasize that *Reading By All Means* is much more than another reading instruction text. It represents a step, not perfect, but rich with promise, into a new generation in ESL reading instruction at the advanced level. *TN 10/82*

FOCUS ON READING

Nell McCutchan (Prentice-Hall, Inc., 1980)

by Susan S. Hill
University of Florida

Reading is a complex process that combines the use of a number of different skills to arrive at comprehension. In her introduction to *Focus on Reading* Nell McCutchan explains:

> The reading process is like driving a car. When you drive you need to know not only how to use the gas pedal, gear shift, and brakes but also when to use them. When you read, it is necessary for you to make the same kind of decisions. At times you will read about a subject with which

you are already familiar, and your eyes will move quickly across the page. At other times you will read about a subject that is new to you. Then you may need to slow down to consider the spelling and sound of individual words. Occasionally you will have to put on the brakes and stop to use your dictionary.

To extend McCutchan's analogy, *Focus on Reading* is an excellent book for getting your car started and backed out of the driveway. That is, it is a good book

for building and strengthening beginning reading skills such as word analysis, structural analysis, dictionary use, and meanings from context. It would be most appropriate for advanced-beginner or low intermediate ESL college students or adult ESL learners who already have some background in English. The book uses a "workbook" format of explanation followed by exercises. Its goal is to increase students' reading ability through an understanding of English orthography and an awareness of the syntactic and semantic information in the text.

The book is divided into five parts which include: I. The Sound System, II. The Dictionary, III. The Spelling System, IV. Word Formation, and V. Reading for Meaning. Part I begins with an introduction to English sounds and Dictionary symbols. Direct application of these skills is provided in Part II ("Dictionary Use"). Part III is a long section which consists of consonant and vowel spelling units in which each vowel is presented in an individual unit. Part IV ("Word Formation") is divided into two sections. The first section (Chapter 11 "Making Predictions from Context") demonstrates how to make predictions by the use of syntactic and semantic clues in the context.

The general approach used in *Focus on Reading* differs considerably from most other ESL reading materials. It begins with "pre-reading" skills and follows a developmental reading approach commonly used with beginning readers, whereas most ESL materials provide reading selections and exercises but little developmental instruction. For this reason, the book is not appropriate for more advanced ESL students since the emphasis is on developing beginning reading skills and critical and evaluative reading skills are not dealt with.

Although reading passages are included in the last section they are not numerous enough nor varied enough for this book to be used alone. In addition, the comprehension questions and exercises focus on the factual level and do not ask for inferential or evaluative responses. The teacher would need to provide some higher level questioning as well as some overall comprehension exercises such as summaries or reading reconstructions. McCutchan suggests that a reader be used to supplement the workbook.

Overall the book is well organized, with explanations that are simple and easily understood by students and teachers. With its developmental approach and emphasis on "pre-reading" skills it could be a very useful book in the low level ESL reading class. *TN 12/80*

(from *Gulf Area TESOL Newsletter,* Summer 1980)

Section 13. Composition and Writing

The largest category of articles on a single topic to appear in the *TN* has been in the area of teaching composition and writing. Perhaps, as with reading, this reflects the paucity of good books on the subject of teaching composition or the rise in importance of these skills as we move from audio-lingual dogma. Of the articles included in this section, many may be described as innovative or unusual, but most are just good ideas.

The first article in this section, "Teaching Written English Through Sector Analysis" by Eleanor Frörup and David Sloane (4/76), is based on the ideas and techniques developed by Robert Allen.

The second article is Gerald Dykstra's "Toward Interactive Modes in Graded Composition" (9/77), an edited version of a longer article which first appeared in the *TESL Reporter*. It presents, for the first time in the *TN*, the basic principles behind Dykstra's original notions of guided or controlled composition which became so popular in the 1970's through the texts of Christina Paulston (*Guided Exercises in Controlled Composition*) and Linda Kunz (*10 Steps* and *26 Steps*). Lynn Henrichsen's *It Works* contribution, "Cradnid Gringling: An Exercise in Controlled Creativity" (1-2/77), is another example of using control as a writing technique.

Andrew Cohen's "Reformulating Compositions" (12/83) presents a new, and already much talked about, approach to assisting students edit and rewrite compositions. The "Spelling Flow Chart" (2/83) by Eric Nelson, from an *It Works* column edited by Cathy Day, is a short and cleverly drawn idea that can be easily reproduced for students. William Myers' article, "Community Language and the Teaching of Composition in ESL" (6/82), looks at counseling-learning techniques and Peter Elbow's views of counseling strategies as used in the teaching of writing. Mary Hines writes about "A New Theme on an Old Angle" in an early *It Works* column (9/76). This classic technique uses the student's knowledge of mathematical theorems to present the basic format underlying the organization of a simple composition. It works.

Lise Winer's "Quiet: People Communicating" (2/78) and Ruth Schneider's "Try a Diary . . ." (9/78) suggest two writing techniques that encourage writing for communication on topics and in areas of writing students need and want to write on. Sandra McKay's article, "Using Film as a Pre-Writing Activity" (11/81), and Mary Ruetten Hank's "Using Short Stories in an Advanced ESL Composition Class" (4/80) represent two of the numerous ideas for using one medium or set of materials to trigger basic writing activities.

The reviews included in this section on teaching composition reflect the large number which have appeared in the *TN*. They were selected in part because they complement the articles which are included in this section. For example, the Carol Fraser review of Vivian Horn's *Composition Steps* and the Mary Hines review of Linda Kunz's *26 Steps* look at texts which were developed along with or out of Dykstra's ideas on controlled composition. The Helen Truax review of the Fred Malkemes and Deborah Singer book *Looking at Englishh* and the Jeffrey Butler review of the Alice Pack and Lynn Henrichsen book, *Writing and Combining Standard English Sentences*, are of texts based in some part on the x-word grammar of Robert Allen's sector analysis.

Basic Writing by Mina Shaughnessy (2/78) is a classic text for teaching writing in ESL or developmental writing classes. *Write Away*, by Gloria Gallingame and Donald Byrd (4/78), and *Paragraph Development*, by Mary Barnett and Martin Arnaudet (8/81), are new looks at specific writing techniques. *Send Me a Letter*, by Sol Gonshack and Joanna McKenzie, provides another practical idea for teaching useful writing skills, such as those of Winer and Schneider above. *The Process of Composition* by Joy Reid, reviewed by Mary Ann Olivier (8/83), is simply that, a text that takes us through the step by step process of writing.

Other articles on composition which appear elsewhere in this volume are "Teaching Technical Writing Courses for Foreign Students in U.S. Colleges and Universities" by Pat Byrd and Gregory West (4/81) and Byrd's "Chemistry and the Agentless Passive Sentences," both of which appear in section 4.

Among other articles worth looking up from past *TNs* are "ESL and Composition: A Report" by Bill Powell (6/80), which looks at current techniques and controversies in composition teaching; "Writing From an Experiential Base" by Janet Fuller (1-2/77), which suggests the development of writing based on real life experiences that classes can have as a group; and "A Guided Writing Technique for Advanced ESL Learners" by Bob Weiseberg (6/78). "Changing Speed" by Thelma Borodkin (10/80) and "Glue: A Useful Concept for Eliminating Fragments and Run-Ons" by Helaine Marshall (2/82) are *It Works* columns. "Memo Writing and Silence in the ESL Writing Class" by Pat Byrd, Moira Derrick, Eileen Blau and Sharon McKinley (2/77) describes techniques similar to those found in the Winder article included in this section.

Another article relating to writing is "The Role of Handwriting in TESOL" by Hector Nevarez, Virginia Berk and Curtis Hayes (2/79). It generated more response than any other article to appear in the *TN*. You might also want to look at some of those responses which appeared in the *Letters* column of succeeding issues as well. "Library Search Strategies" by Barbara Broch and Peter Archer (4/80) is a useful article to consider, especially for teachers of students in higher education programs. It addresses those skills necessary for gathering information to be used in writing papers. Note, too, the review of Dean Memerings's book on research in section 8. Susan Lewis English wrote an unusual *It Works* column (8/82) titled "Paraphrase or Plagiarism" in which she discusses one of the ever-present problems faced by teachers of writing. Perhaps one of the most interesting to look at the writing needs of students comes from an article by Alice Myers Roy (6/82), "What They Know About Writing," which discusses the observations students make about what *they* think they should be learning.

TEACHING WRITTEN ENGLISH THROUGH SECTOR ANALYSIS

by David E. E. Sloane and Eleanor Frörup, Medgar Evers College, CUNY

Teachers have needed for sometime a vehicle for systematic attempts at focusing student interest on sentence structure. In some places, transformational grammar has filled the vacuum in writing instruction left by the collapse of confidence in the old fashioned Reed and Kellogg sentence diagramming. Typically, teachers of English as a second language have been more pragmatic than both conventional and transformational schools, working heavily with language markers and positional relationships. Sector Analysis should prove a valuable tool in this area. Developed originally to teach English sentence structure to twelve-year-olds in Turkey, it has proved adaptable to ESL as well as to remedial language instruction in writing in the open enrollment situation; a number of instructors in C.U.N.Y. institutions have reported success with it, and controlled experiments are soon to be set in motion in Ontario and Baltimore County, Maryland. Nevertheless, with one or two major exceptions, Sector Analysis as a potential tool for teachers of "edited" American English remains a well-kept secret. Robert L. Allen, of Columbia Teachers College in New York City, developed Sector Analysis at about the same time that Kenneth Pike established Tagmemics—slot-and-filler grammar—as a system of linguistic analysis. Since the two systems are similar, this may account for the relative obscurity of Sector Analysis. With the publication of a work-text, *Working Sentences*, Thomas Y. Crowell Co., 1975 (with which this article is chiefly concerned), Sector Analysis now becomes generally available for teaching written English and its popularity should increase.

Sector Analysis is called "X-Word Grammar" by many of its users because of its emphasis on the function of twenty or so modal auxiliaries which are used in the formation of question and answer patterns in English. English, and particularly written English, is approached from a linguistic perspective as a slot-and-filler or position-and-construction language. Sector Analysis is defined, therefore, as a practical linguistically-oriented grammar which describes the "edited" American English sentence as a sequence of positions (subject, predicate, adverbials, etc.) which may be filled by various construction types (noun clusters, clauses, phrases, half-sentences, etc.) One of the most useful aspects of this grammar is that the

regularity with which certain constructions fill certain positions in English opens the way for pattern acquisition, drill, diagrammatic analysis, and even advanced stylistic studies through a wide range of instructional programs in language development; identification of determiners, language ties between subjects and verbs, and related pattern keys can be advantageous to both the ESL, FL, and remedial learner.

Dr. Allen's approach actually emphasizes a consciousness of language patterns that is best used as a form of editing. Traditional grammar tends to obscure the lines between spoken English and the standards of "edited" American English; Sector Analysis depends on patterns acquired through the spoken-language experience of learners, but its orientation fosters an awareness of the slightly different conventions governing *written* English. Both the "Preface" to *Working Sentences* and the accompanying teacher's guide stress the use of students' editing ability through the recognition of units of language anticipated by native speakers in expository writing (as opposed to drama or other forms of transcribed speech). Language "chunking," the ability to recognize constructions and word clusters as conveyors of meaning, is as important as individual word recognition. Consequently, students who have some vocabulary problems may still advance rapidly in the recognition of meaningful word units. One of the techniques in remedial instruction has been to offer sentences composed of nonsense words for analysis through structural markers and positions; students become remarkably adept at such drills in a few weeks and seem to expand their own use of language structures. A language instruction program based on Sector Analysis may be more concept-oriented than word-oriented, a boon to teachers who have never felt that Reed and Kellogg diagramming adequately explains such language choices as plural and singular agreement for "Half of the apples *are* . . ." but "Half of the pie *is* . . ."— a choice made relatively simple to understand through the treatment of subjects as noun clusters, language chunks, rather than as single words independently related to a verb. The checking of such patterns using X-Word Grammar "tools" represents the editing ability mentioned above.

A close examination of the work-text, *Working Sentences*, by Robert L.

Allen, Rita Pompian, and Doris A. Allen, indicates a variety of uses to which the grammar can be put in helping the student to consciously identify his own grammatical patterns and employ this knowledge. The fifteen "Units" into which the book is divided focus on major areas of reference, modification, and predication. Particular attention is paid to the basic trunk pattern and its relationship to the functions of the twenty most common X-Words and to the packing process by which trunks can be expanded and given variety in writing. The yes-no question-answer pattern *(Is John here?/ John is here.)* is the basis of Sector Analysis. Twenty X-Words which begin such question patterns *(am/is/are/was/were/ /do/ does/did/ /have/has/had/ /shall/ will/could/would/should/ /may/ might/must/can)* send information merely by position. When these X-Words introduce a sentence, they indicate a question just as clearly as does the inverted question mark in written Spanish; in the middle of a sentence they identify a statement. One of Dr. Allen's chief contentions is that the ability to formulate these language patterns is rapidly acquired, and classroom experience indicates that students can use the patterns with very high success in one or two weeks of instruction. The movement of the X-Word serves to identify the subject sector (regardless of whether it is filled by a single word or *x* number of words which together function as a nominal construction) and the predicate in the basic English trunk—the first five units of the text cover this material. The linguistic ties governing subject-verb agreement in number and verb tense formation, crucial prestige features of English, are dealt with in units three and four. Unit five introduces the basic positions of the predicate and establishes the groundwork for the following eight units, which deal with various techniques for embedding information and for packing sentence trunks with additional information. In later units, the student is introduced to optional sentence sectors through a few simple terms, such as "shifter" and "insert," which identify their most obvious characteristics. Included clauses and half-sentences (one of Dr. Allen's most useful concepts for teachers working with secondary predications and substitutions of verbal phrases) are identified as important construction types. Charts covering (1) X-

Word/verb combinations for verb phrases, (2) forms of irregular verbs, (3) includers—the words which signal the beginning of included clauses, or subordinate clauses in traditional grammar, and (4) the twenty X-Words, appear at the end of the text for student reference.

The format of the text is particularly worthy of note. *Working Sentences* employs brief sub-sections composed of explanations followed by examples. A practice exercise follows each subsection and calls for diagramming or closing to complete a structural requirement. Units are concluded by controlled tasks using the new techniques to encourage the student to manipulate sentence parts and finally generate his own sentences on a given topic. Brief concluding essay assignments call for the constructions and sentence patterns of the unit. Because of this approach, punctuation is subordinated to the developmnet of structure, and as the student masters the repertoire of sentence sectors and appropriate construction fillers, he discovers that punctuation rules are reduced to a minimum. We have felt that this subordination of marking conventions to structural logic is a major advantage of Sector Analysis.

The *Instructor's Manual to Working Sentences* is helpful to the teacher who has not taken formal courses in Sector Analysis. Explanatory notes take up the conventions of written English and offer more detailed explications of the theory than would have been appropriate in the work-text itself. Suggestions are given for dealing with specific student questions likely to occur as well as for the development of additional practice exercises. "A Final Word to the Instructor" makes the mind-set of the authors particularly clear—focus on the lesson and ignore peripheral areas, do not inhibit with excessive red penciling, use the book as a tool for the student to develop his own writing rather than as an end in itself.

The chief application of Sector Analysis for the purposes of this commentary are seen to lie in the area of remediation, particularly in the first semester college freshman in the CUNY open admission environment. Initial writing samples show fragments to be one of the most persistent problems in this area. Usually, the student has been told that he has a major problem, and *"fr.,"* or "fragment" is well-known to him as an identification of his error, but the student has no concept of what fragment means and no tangible way to identify or correct it. Sector Analysis offers such means: first, after working with yes-no questions to identify subjects and predicates, the student

learns how to identify the omission of verbs, X-Words, or subject sectors; second, as the student goes deeper into Sector Analysis, learning to identify construction types such as clauses or half-sentences, and learning the optional sectors (e.g., front and end positions for secondary predications, which if filled are often filled with clauses), he learns why a clause punctuated as a sentence is a fragment, and moreover, how to incorporate this clause into the preceding or following sentence. Even before the student covers this step, if he applies the yes-no question strategy—and tries to turn his clause into a yes-no question—he can identify the fragment because the question sentence cannot be formed.

Editing is very important in this process; simply learning sectors and construction types may not be enough. Students often need coaxing to actually test the interchange. One successful exercise uses a student writing sample which is reasonably connected discourse with all the errors, except fragments, corrected. Students are told how many fragments appear and are asked to find them one by one, rewriting the passages and comparing the two writing samples as they proceed. Numbering the sentences in the exercise prevents the student from being overwhelmed and helps him to limit his focus; word groups punctuated as sentences can be treated one at a time. The rewriting practice is beneficial by itself, and the comparison of the two samples clearly delineates sectors and constructions, completing the lesson. This structured approach to editing prepares the student for longer assignments. Similar techniques also teach the identification and correction of run-ons, comma splices, and subject-verb ties.

Another important application of Sector Analysis is in the development of sentence variety. One of our colleagues at Hunter College, teaching bilinguals and native speakers, uses color-coded algebricks, identifying a different construction type with each color, with one color for single words; varying colors are used to build sentences. Students learn to construct sentences by visual dictation. Sophistication and clarity both increase. Even in cases of the Black English language population, analysis of constructions indicates that new areas of the sentence are used and there is an increase of correct constructions which is striking—and these changes begin taking place even before the casual reader (and sometimes casual grader) is aware of writing improvement. Still, the teacher is cautioned that practice

and time are essential; they may well be lags in affective growth and we do not yet know to what extent regression occurs with this approach.

The behavioral effects of a program based on Sector Analysis are worthy of special note. Self-confidence is radically expanded through experience with the system of X-Word Grammar. In one graduate program for minorities, instructors who were educational psychologists made special note of the growth in volume of writing, increased personal self-confidence, and of some students' use of sentence diagrams in their actual log-writing. The same educational psychologists noted a second significant feature of X-Word Grammar; it allows teacher and student to focus writing instruction on the needs of the reader—his expectations for conventional sentence patterns and the inability of many readers to resolve departures from those types. Refocusing instruction toward reader needs makes the learning environment less threatening to the student.

Sector Analysis, because it offers a systematic language structure perhaps, seems to be a much freer body of material in the classroom. Dr. Allen spends time with his own students on "Boinguage," which uses the word "boing" in place of content words—nouns, verbs, and adjectives, with "boingly" in place of -*ly* adverbs. A sample sentence might be "Boing can boing the boing." With such sentences, students can be introduced rapidly to the common markers in English and be convinced of their importance; and even without technical knowledge, most readers will admit that they can identify the subject sector of such a sentence, the object (a noun cluster), and the predicate. It is even possible to demand of students: "Don't think!", thereby stressing the positions and patterns which they already recognize unconsciously if native speakers of the language. Soon students can neither be defeated by Boinguage, other nonsense sentences, or English sentences in which the vocabulary is foreign to their experience; reading and writing skills are both developed in this case. There is a distinct advantage to the teacher in separating closed lists of structure words, which can be memorized, from the unending list of content words which frequently confuse the grammar lesson.

The use of Sector Analysis in the teaching of reading is of major importance and teaching across the entire spectrum of the English curriculum may respond positively to the potential which Sector Analysis holds.

TN 4/76

TOWARD INTERACTIVE MODES IN GUIDED COMPOSITION

by Gerald Dykstra
University of Hawaii

Guided composition is a tool now widely used by teachers to elicit relatively large amounts of substantially correct and acceptable writing while simultaneously calling on each writer to contribute at a level commensurate with his or her ability.

It is worth emphasizing that guided composition arose out of the traditional school goal of composition writing and that the two still resemble each other very much.

I want first to propose a manner of relating guided composition to much of current thought in linguistics and psycholinguistics, then propose some still little-used but promising learner interactions that can contribute added variation, vitality, and relevance to composition and the teaching of composition.

Society's insistence on "the three R's" has given an important place to writing in our school systems. Our school systems, in interpreting the writing mandate, have included composition. Composition thereafter evolved as a need within our educational institutions. The extent to which it actually functions for all people in life outside of our educational institutions has been and may continue for some time to be a question subject to varying answers and points of view. We need not insist on the answer here, but it is useful to recognize doubts about its efficacy and relevance.

Very clearly, however, students in schools are asked to write. Composition writing is highly relevant to school life. Furthermore, student writing is not expected to reflect a highly personal style. It must, rather, reflect common standards of form and style to a considerable extent. Teachers giving writing assignments usually assume these standards. The results have not always been encouraging. The student products resulting from writing assignments have, for the most part, been less than fully acceptable to teachers. Guided and controlled composition in a wide range of forms came in response to the evident needs. They have been suggested as one approach to support all the early stages of learning to write. There is an attempt in guided composition to break down the writing assignment from the broad "write a composition" to ever smaller components until we come to the assignment that the learner can handle readily. The learner can then move up the scale until we finally reach once again, the assignment "write a composition."

The basic format of controlled and guided composition is a series of models, one or more paragraphs long. The learner uses the model as a guide and follows the explicit directions of a step which varies according to the learner's ability. If the learner is relatively unsophisticated, she/he follows the directions of a beginning step which will call for minimal learner contributions. If the learner is relatively advanced, she/he follows the directions of a step that calls for more extensive, or even maximum learner contribution. In this framework, the length and sophistication of the model remain stable throughout the course and students at varying levels of ability produce final writing products that look approximately equally sophisticated and that are very regularly acceptable in form and style.

Where is guided composition in relation to some of the current rationalist outlook in linguistics and psycho-linguistics? This may be of interest inasmuch as some followers of transformationalist theories have uniformly condemned efforts to introduce control into the acquisition of any ability related to language.

I think we can show such condemnations to be misdirected and counter to the rationalist view itself. In the first place, at least one major variety of guided composition (that variety which is the principal concern of this article), rests "heavily upon transformation, albeit less to explain grammar than to elicit actualizations of it in performance. More important, the condemnation rests upon the obviously erroneous assumption that writing a composition is a species specific behavior on a par with learning to speak a language. The rationalist framework suggests that universal species specific behaviors are acquired without reference to training or structural programs. It does not imply that other behaviors are so acquired. Quite the contrary. Still more important, students with guided composition are demonstrating learning that was not equally achieved without this structure. Just as we might presumably have a lesser number of successful physicists or engineers if we relied wholly upon "natural" situations without educational institutions or programs it seems we would have fewer and less acceptable compositions without appropriately developed programs. One might be happy with such a situation, but that relates to the question of out-of-school relevance which we cannot consider here.

None of the above should suggest that we have reached a plateau in progress. It only suggests that we now have an alternative that is superior to the simple instruction "write a composition." That simple instruction commonly had to be combined with the hope that writing a composition would be intuitively learned by all students in a way exactly parallel to the way that oral language had been learned.

Assuming for the present that learning to write compositions is a less predetermined learning category than learning to speak, and assuming that composition writing is nevertheless a desired goal, we may accept the legitimacy of environmental adjustment in the form of (1) programming from easier to harder for the learner and also, (2) providing contingencies of reward in the form of making the tasks more varied and vital, and putting them in richer and more relevant social contexts.

Since composition is not as universally learned as oral language, since its relevance or extent of function outside the classroom is not immediately clear to all, since it is nevertheless required of almost all of our young people, and since we have been able to put considerable structure and sequence into the assignment "write a composition," to the point where success is more readily achieved by a larger number under more favorable conditions for both teacher and student, we might now gain a further step by adding oral language and other interactive modes to our guided composition programs.

We will present two simple interactive modes here (I and II) with variations on each and with an indication of how they may be combined (III). Essentially all of the possibilities mentioned here have been validated in a range of learning environments, though all have not been validated with the guided composition programs referred to in this article. Finally, we will mention an interactive mode that highlights evaluation and suggests possible future developments toward getting the writing of compositions to tie in more closely with life's needs and possibly having it become more naturally learnable like oral language though possibly with less relevance for composition programs as we now know them.

I. Interactive variations in producing the composition.

At the most advanced stage of normal use of guided composition the learner always knows the appropriate step to work on. She/he locates this step number on a chart and selects one or several models on which that step can be worked. The learner can then proceed with the task and usually does so successfully. Ordinarily the writer works alone.

A minor variation which adds a new dimension is to have two "writers" (whom we shall here call A and B) work together in any of the following slightly variant ways.

1. A dictates what is to be written, B writes it from that dictation.

2. A and B discuss what is to be written and produce a joint project.

3. A writes while B watches the process and comments wherever B thinks improvement is possible or has a question. A is free to ask for advice at any point, but the product is A's.

II. Interactive variations in checking or reading the composition.

In the normal classroom, laboratory or programmed use of guided composition, the teacher can quickly spot check the learners' compositions. Little time is needed for traditional correction work. Learner papers are all substantially correct and yet each is working at approximately his or her maximum level of contribution within the current framework of prepared programs in guided composition, within the constraints that are given.

Yet, the teacher is still ordinarily the ultimate target—the one for whom the composition is written. The teacher is the only guaranteed reader or checker—the one who determines whether the learner advances to the next step. This is true to the traditions from which guided composition sprang.

A minor variation on the teachers serving as the only reader consists of having one or more learners serve as readers too, in any of the following slightly variant ways.

Learner A writes, learner B proofreads before initialing the work and passing it on to the teacher. (Further variations are possible here inasmuch as B's proofreading, and any resultant notations, may be passed directly on to the teacher or may be used by A to make corrections on the original version or to write a corrected version.)

III. Combinations of interactions.

Although the variations presented above are minor enough so that they can be initiated without necessarily changing the procedures of a guided composition classroom in any drastic way, it will be noted that highly detailed procedures are not given. In II, above, for example, a loose arrangement may be set up wherein each writer is required to submit any completed composition to a proofreader and all other members of the class constitute qualified proofreaders. Alternatively, learners are paired and serve as proofreaders for each other only. Alternatively, again, the proofreading task may be considered a de-sirable introduction to a step that must subsequently be achieved. In this case qualified proofreaders consist only, or mostly, of those who have not yet reached a given step but who are next in line to reach that step. Alternatively, once more, the proofreading task may be considered the determining factor in deciding whether the learner is to proceed to the next higher step. In this case qualified proofreaders consist of those who have just successfully completed a given step, etc.

It is also probable that the reading and correcting roles of the teacher could and should be diminished or eliminated for most purposes.

REFERENCES

1. Dykstra, Gerald. "Eliciting Language Practice in Writing," in *English Language Teaching*, London, 1963.
2. Dykstra, Gerald. "Breaking Down Your Writing Goals," in *English for American Indians*, Curriculum Bulletin No. 4, Selections from the first three issues. Washington, D.C.: Bureau of Indian Affairs, 1968, 9.
3. Dykstra, Gerald, Richard Port, and Antonette Port. *Ananse Tales: Course in Controlled Composition.* New York: Teachers College Press, Columbia University, 1966.
4. Paulston, Christina Bratt, and Gerald Dykstra. Controlled Composition in English as a Second Language. New York: Regents, 1973.
5. Dykstra, Gerald, Richard Port, Antonette Port, Jan Prins, Carol Jankowski, Lois Morton, Hafiz Baghban, and Alice Pack. *Composition: Guided Free.* New York: Teachers College Press, Columbia University, 1974 and in press.

[Excerpted from the *TESL Reporter*, Vol. 10, No. 3, Spring 1977] TN 9/77

REFORMULATING COMPOSITIONS

by Andrew D. Cohen
The Hebrew University of Jerusalem

Second-language teachers typically have a stack of essays to correct at one time. To do just a thorough edit—not a rewrite—of every paper would be a monumental task. So, teachers usually content themselves with being selective—singling out a few of the more conspicuous rhetorical, lexical, and grammatical problems. It is probably fair to say that teachers rarely write entire sentences over, but rather provide comments here or there. Thus, in reality students are only getting partial feedback as to what would make their writing more native-like on any given draft of an essay.[1] For example, many language teachers do not have or do not take the time to suggest alternatives for even a few of the student's inappropriate lexical choices. For one thing, imprecise vocabulary may sound acceptable in the context of other imprecise vocabulary. Students are then often en-couraged to rewrite these partially-corrected essays at home, incorporating the suggested changes.

The question that comes to my mind is whether a student essay, even after multiple edits incorporating a configuration of teacher and peer feedback, would constitute the way that such an essay would look if a native were to write it. Perhaps we do not envision mastery as a realistic goal for nonnative writers, and so our approaches to feedback on written work have reflected more modest goals. Yet it may be healthy, nonetheless, to consider techniques for bringing our students—particularly the more advanced ones—closer to mastery.

In one study that I undertook a few years ago (Cohen and Robbins 1976), I was struck by how unsystematic my feedback to students was on written work over a ten-week university-level ESL course. I had, in fact, been using a detailed framework for written work. All the same, when I lined up 15 samples of English writing from three Chinese speakers in the class, I realized that I had been inconsistent—sometimes catching conspicuous errors, sometimes not. And I had also been inconsistent in my diagnosis of what the source of the problem was.

In light of these considerations, it seemed to me that something was missing regarding feedback on written work. It was then that my colleague at the Hebrew University, Eddie Levenston, put me on to the "reformulation" technique as an important complement to the typical form of error analysis that characterizes the feedback learners usually receive with respect to their written work (Levenston 1978).

Levenston took an essay written in English by an eleventh-grade Israeli student, and demonstrated how, even after surface errors were eliminated, the essay was still in need of correction of the kind often provided by teachers of native-language composition—correction regarding problems such as lexical inadequacy, syntactic

---

[1] It is true that in feedback systems which put emphasis on the process of writing (see Zamel 1982), students may eventually receive comprehensive feedback—possibly through meetings with the teacher or with a peer tutor.

213

blending (two separate ideas in one syntactic construction), conceptual confusion, rhetorical deviance, and ambiguity. Levenston proposed that we distinguish a first stage aimed at removing "goofs," from a further stage of *reformulation* aimed at improving the style and clarity of thought. But he stopped short of proposing that such a technique be utilized in the second-language classroom. He asked, ". . . what second-language teacher has time for such detailed treatment, much of which should be handled in the first-language classroom?" (Levenston 1978:11).

My students and I responded to Levenston's challenge and took his idea out into the second-language classroom. In this article, I will describe the technique as I have adapted it from Levenston, suggest possible applications, give an example of what the technique actually looks like, and then discuss some of its limitations.

Reformulation

This is how the reformulation technique works. First, the learners write a relatively short composition (say, 300-400 words in length). Then, the teachers provide feedback on one or more drafts of the writing so that it better approximates the target language. Ideally they do this without the learners' input as to what they meant to write. Teachers are asked to provide feedback in their usual way—whether by simply indicating the presence or specific location of errors or by giving clues or examples of how students could correct their errors (see Hendrickson 1980).

Then the learners are requested to submit a revised draft of the essay to a native speaker to be *reformulated*. What this means is that the native speaker is to rewrite the very same essay without changing content, but to reformulate it from beginning to end so that it sounds as native-like as possible. In other words, the natives do not simply rewrite a sentence or two, but actually rethink the essay so that it reflects their style—their approach to expressing those ideas. Sometimes the reformulator is the classroom teacher, but usually the learners are requested to find their own reformulator from among their circle of friends and acquaintances.

The reason for having natives reformulate what the nonnatives write rather than writing about their own ideas is that in this way the nonnatives are able to feel that the essay is still *theirs*, even though it is reformulated. Consequently, the nonnatives' motivation to analyze the way in which the natives write up their same ideas will probably be greater than, say, their motivation to analyze the way a published source might write about the same topic. This motivation may be even greater if the reformulation comes from a native-speaking *peer* (e.g., a fellow student) rather than from a teacher.

Once the reformulation has been completed or perhaps while it is going on, the nonnatives compare their carefully revised version with this reformulation. Ideally, the reformulator or another native provides assistance in this task. The way I suggest conducting this comparison is by making several passes through the essay, each time focussing on a different aspect of the writing. Separate passes could be made for each of the following:

1. *Selection of vocabulary*—How does the native's and the nonnative's choice of lexical items and phrases compare? For example, does the native use more precise words, more concise phrases, and more/less formal words?

2. *Choice and ordering of syntactic structures*—For example, does the native alter or replace syntactic structures, and if so, what is used in place of them? When does the native use more complex or less complex sentences to convey the same meaning?

3. *Markers of cohesion*—In what ways does the native writer link together the different ideas to form a text (i.e., within sentences, and across sentences and paragraphs)? Such links are established by means of grammatical forms such as conjunctions (for combining ideas, contrasting them, and for indicating causality), pronouns (personal and demonstrative), and lexical items (e.g., repetition of the same word or use of synonyms).

4. *Discourse functions*—If the essay includes functions such as categorizing, defining, hypothesizing, or questioning, does the native realize these discourse functions in a different way from the nonnative?

Applications

While on sabbatical leave at the University of California, Los Angeles, in Fall 1980, I had foreign students in the advanced ESL writing class (English 106J) that I taught compare the revised version of an essay that each one wrote with a reformulated version. The students then had to produce a list of differences. Their response to the technique was quite positive.

My experience with this classroom activity suggested that the payoff to nonnative students could be substantial. Rather than just dealing with successive revisions of their writing, they now had the opportunity to see where they were in relation to where they would be if they wrote natively. The value is not just in seeing the distinction between themselves and mastery, but also in determining areas which they may wish to focus on. My experience also showed, however, that the majority of nonnatives may wish to do the composition analysis with the assistance of a native. Whereas some learners have the motivation and "monitoring" ability to do the comparison on their own, others need more guidance.

The reformulation approach may dramatically call into focus areas that the nonnative was unaware of. For example, when a UCLA native-speaking graduate student provided feedback on a friendly letter written by a Chinese ESL student, the letter appeared basically quite acceptable. Yet a systematic comparison of the revised version and the reformulation revealed that this nonnative was transferring discourse functions (e.g., opening, closing, apology, and invitation) from business English. Such functions were consistent with her work experience with business English, but incompatible with the nature of the friendly letter that she was writing (Dally 1981). Thus, we see that reformulation may point up major deviations from native-like writing in the writing of nonnative students—deviations which if overlooked, could well lead to significant fossilization.

An Example

Let us now take a look at one excerpt that has been revised and then reformulated. The following are the opening lines of an essay written by one of my students in the advanced ESL writing class at UCLA:

> If the time ever comes when a woman is elected to the presidency of the United States, how well will she perform? Will she be able to rule better than our male presidents have? Will she be able to handle the problems of running a country? In this essay, I'm going to answer these questions by analyzing the women who have ruled in other countries.
>
> One woman is Cleopatra. She became ruler of Egypt at the age of eighteen. Even at that young age she had a strong thrust for power . . .

I was the instructor in the course and made no changes in the opening paragraph when I corrected this essay. In the second paragraph I suggested changing the first sentence from "One woman is Cleopatra" to "One such woman leader is Cleopatra," and wrote the word "cohesion" in the margin. I also changed "thrust" to "lust" in the second sentence of that paragraph, while the student probably meant "thirst."

The reformulation of this excerpt, written by a friend of the student, was as follows:

> How well will a woman perform if she is ever elected president of the United States? Will she execute the duties of her office better than males? Will she be able to handle our country's problems? In this essay I will explore these questions by analyzing women rulers of other countries.
>
> One such woman is Cleopatra. At the tender age of eighteen she ascended Egypt's highest office. Even at such an early age she had a strong compulsion for power . . .

Let us compare the slightly revised version to the reformulated one. In terms of selection of vocabulary, we see that the native writer replaced or modified a number of the lexical phrases just in these few lines. For example, "able to rule" was replaced by "execute the duties of her office," "answer these questions" by "explore these questions," "become ruler of Egypt" by "ascended Egypt's highest office," "the age of eighteen" by "the tender age of eighteen," "young age" by "early age," and "lust for power" by "compulsion for power." We also note that the native writer replaced the informal "I'm going to (answer)" with "I will (explore)." It would also appear that the native supplied several questionable forms—e.g., "males" (line 3) instead of "men" or "a man," in contrast to "woman"; and "office" instead of perhaps "throne."

With respect to syntax, the native chose not to begin the essay with the "if" clause, but rather to reverse the order. In the second sentence of the second paragraph, the native fronted the adverbial clause. Otherwise the nonnative's syntactic patterns were preserved. The native also introduced a grammatical error in using "ascended" (line 8) instead of "ascended to." With respect to cohesion, the native switched the pronominal referent "our" from reference to "our male presidents" to "our country's problems." Finally, with respect to discourse functions, the native chose to focus immediately on the rhetorical question introduced by "how," rather than leading with the "if" clause.

Discussion

We are just beginning to exercise this idea more extensively in teaching, but it seems to have potential. Following the UCLA study, I conducted a study in which my own writing in Hebrew as a second language was reformulated, as well as a small-scale study involving the reformulation of university-level EFL and Hebrew-second-language essays (Cohen 1983b). The findings from these two studies were consistent with the earlier experiences reported here. A subsequent study involving 53 advanced college-level Hebrew-second-language writers compared the reformulation technique to one of discussing the teacher's suggested revisions. In this study, the reformulation technique did not fare as well as discussion of the teacher's suggested revisions, although for some students the reformulation approach provided

major breakthroughs.

The results of the most recent study would suggest that the reformulation technique be reserved for some students some of the time (Cohen 1983a). All the studies seem to underscore the advisability of utilizing this technique with students at the intermediate levels and above. In fact, it may have its greatest impact among advanced students who really are trying to perfect their second-language writing skills, particularly in some area of language for special purposes.

As with any technique, there are problems. For instance, what if the nonnatives are weak writers in their native language? This factor may prevent them from deriving full benefit from such a technique. Also, does it matter if the reformulators are not good writers? It could be argued that their being native writers at least gives the nonnatives exposure to one of the ways a native could do it. After all, nonnatives learn to *speak* by associating with and receiving spoken input from all kinds of native speakers. Why not have them learn to write by associating with all kinds of native writers? All the same, it may be advisable for the nonnative to have several natives rewrite the essay—when feasible. (In the reformulating of my Hebrew writing (Cohen 1983b) I had three reformulators.) Especially in countries where the target language is taught as a foreign language and where native speakers are few in number, it may take some effort to find reformulators for all the students in a class, but it may well be worth the effort.

Furthermore, there is a clear advantage in having the nonnative engage the reformulator or the teacher/tutor in a dialogue regarding the comparison between the revised version and the reformulation. There will surely be instances in which the nonnative will want to explain or justify the use of forms that were replaced in the reformulation. There will also be instances in which attention might be called to forms in the *native* version which are actually inappropriate (as in the case described above)—though our experience is that there are not very many of these cases. It may be that

discussion could be conducted in class in small groups of nonnative students, with the occasional assistance of the teacher.

In addition, can we really expect nonnatives to gain mastery of, say, lexical phrasing so that they could come up with the turns of phrase found in the reformulation presented above? Perhaps we cannot expect this of even the most advanced nonnative writers, but we can at least provide them with an opportunity to see what mastery might look like. Then they can make the choice concerning the extent to which they wish to approximate such models.

In conclusion, I see exposure to the reformulation technique as only one modest means of achieving greater mastery of writing in a second language. There is no doubt that nonnative learners can also benefit greatly from exposure to the written work of natives writing about their own ideas—with regard to both the *form* of the message as well as its *content*. In fact, one method of teaching ESL composition to adults calls for learners to first analyze native writings by means of criteria that they later use to analyze and edit their own writings (Anderson 1981). The reason that this reformulation technique is attractive to me is that it has the potential for dramatic results—for stirring up some real interest in native-like writing among nonnative writers. 🔴

Note: My thanks to Bill Gaskill, Marianne Celce-Murcia, Jackie Schachter, Frances Hinofotis, Evelyn Hatch, Ann Raimes, and an anonymous reviewer for their comments on earlier versions of this paper.

REFERENCES

Anderson, P.L. 1981. The use of editing to teach composition to adults. Honolulu: Department of English as a Second Language, University of Hawaii.
Cohen, A.D. 1983a. Reformulating second-language compositions: A potential source of input for the learner. Jerusalem: School of Education, Hebrew University.
Cohen, A.D. 1983b. Writing like a native. The process of reformulation. ERIC ED 224 338.
Cohen, A.D. and Robbins, M. 1976. Toward assessing interlanguage performance: The relationship between selected errors, learners' characteristics, and the learners' explanations. *Language Learning,* 26 (1), 45-66.
Dally, Patrice. 1981. Contrastive analysis of Chinese letter writing in English as a second language: With special attention to discourse function. Los Angeles: English as a Second Language, University of California.
Hendrickson, J.M. 1980. The treatment of error in written work. *Modern Language Journal,* 64 (2), 216-221.
Levenston, E.A. Error analysis of free composition: The theory and the practice. *Indian Journal of Applied Linguistics,* 4 (1), 1-11.
Zamel, V. 1982. Writing: The process of discovering meaning. *TESOL Quarterly,* 16 (2), 195-210.

TRY A DIARY IN YOUR SECOND LANGUAGE

by Ruth M. Schneider
Catholic University, Ponce, P.R.

One of the best ways I know to individualize instruction and to lay the groundwork for future writing assignments is to have students keep a diary. Although keeping a diary, or a journal, is common practice in many writing classes and even in some literature classes, it is not a technique generally found in the ESL classroom. I suggest that diaries are an excellent way for students to become comfortable with their new language.

For one thing, a diary can help provide each of twenty-five to thirty students in a classroom with a vocabulary tailored to his or her personal interests. Oh, don't think I haven't given out those vocabulary sheets. My students have learned, perhaps in meaningful segments, about "The Supermarket," or "The Drugstore," until almost anyone can ask cheerily, "How much is it?" and can even understand the answer. But what if he or she wants to discuss a

film, religion, nuclear disarmament, or environmental pollution? It is my responsibility as a language teacher to help the student feel adequately prepared to talk in the area of his special interest. *No adult learning a new language should find himself caught discussing the price of cars or coffee in his second language in a situation where he would be discussing politics or romance in his first. And nothing assures me that the vocabulary sheet I give is what the* student needs or wants in order to talk about the same things in his new language that he does in his native tongue. By correcting his diary, however, I can quickly ascertain these needs and give him the words he wants with a slip of my pen.

How does it work? Simple. On the first day of class I tell students that they are to buy a small notebook and keep a diary in English. I explain that I only want them to write a few sentences each day about what they have done, or what they are thinking. Nothing fancy, just a few sentences. The next day I ask everyone to read what they have written, and sometimes I even read the diary I am writing in Spanish to show them that mistakes are acceptable (look how many *she* makes!), to build rapport, and to demonstrate that anyone can do it. I spend only a short part of the period doing this, perhaps fifteen minutes. My focus is totally on content. Occasionally I ask a question or two, "What did you buy at the store?" I *never* comment on the use of the language. Then each day thereafter I have at least two or three people read their diaries, and I remind everyone to keep writing.

On the day of their first in-class writing assignment, worksheet, or quiz, I pick up as many diaries as I can read during their working time, and quickly correct them. From then on, whenever my students are busy in the classroom, I read diaries. It is necessary to keep in mind that I am merely correcting, not criticizing, and not explaining the corrections to any extent. Therefore, the reading goes very quickly. In the beginning I can read through four or five diaries in a class hour. Occasionally I will chat with a student about his/her diary while I am reading, and perhaps I will point out a consistent misuse of a tense or a structure. Now and then, in order to show that they've communicated, I draw a face, or I say "I agree!" or "Yes!"

Which brings me to a warning. You must not be judgmental when you read a student's diary. Don't be picky. Give information, give vocabulary, give correct structures (I simply put the correct word or phrase above the incorrect one). Diaries must always work *for* a student, never against him. I grade with an Ok, Ok+, Ok−, and occasionally a +.

After I have read everyone's diary once (which usually takes the first three or four weeks of class, since my reading time is so spread out), I suggest certain developments in writing style. Initially students tell me the most elemental things about their lives: "I get up. I go to class. I study. I come home. At night I watch T.V." After a few days in class, and a reminder about the past tense (not necessarily related to their diary writing) I often read, "During the weekend I went to church. I studied my lessons. I visited my friend yesterday afternoon, I read some newspapers last night." At this point I suggest that they write more about their thoughts, and that they try ordering their ideas in some sort of logical form. By the end of the semester, I have read all of the diaries at least three times, and I begin to look for paragraph structure. By this time I am apt to read, "This was a beautiful day. The birds sang and the flowers smiled. My boyfriend writes from New York that he loves me and I am very happy."

My students are pleased with the personal attention their diaries receive, and they like having a place to try out language structures of which they are uncertain, knowing that no penalities are attached. I seldom have to have a class on sentence structure, and my students are comfortable writing sentences or short paragraphs on tests because they have been communicating with me in writing every day. We've got a nice thing going.

Reprinted from the *TESOL-GRAM*, Spring 1978.   TN 9/78

CRANDID GRINGLING: AN EXERCISE IN CONTROLLED CREATIVITY

by Lynn E. Henrichsen
Department of Education
Pago Pago, Samoa

When your class is getting dreary,
  and you don't know what to do,
Try gringling a cradnid
  or fringling a gnu.

If all of this sounds like nonsense, then you've got the right idea. Nonsense words are what make this classroom activity work. The original inspiration came from a short poem entitled "I Fringled a Gnu" by Grover Haynes. Here is the poem and what was done to make it into a very successful ESL classroom activity; one that really works!

*I Fringled a Gnu**

As I was gringling creadnids
  among the hollyfudds,
I spied a moisha springle
  with fiddies in her tud.
She skiddled 'round so fordly
  I couldn't help but watch.
I craned my rink to frappish,
  and sure enough was true.
She took off her mendashie
  and fringled with a gnu!

* Grover Haynes, "I Fringled a Gnu" (Studio City, California: Three Penny Press, 1959).

I. Write short answers to the following questions:
1. What was I doing to the cradnids?
2. When did I spy a moisha?
3. What did I do to my rink?
4. Who took off her mendashie?
5. Where did the moisha have fiddies?
6. What did she do so fordly?
7. What was I doing among the hollyfuds?
8. Did I watch?
9. When did she fringle?
10. Why did I crane my rink?

II. Many of the words in this poem are unusual or imaginary. Rewrite this poem bytaking out all of these unusual or imaginary words and putting in words which are familiar to you. Make sure that the words which you choose fit grammatically. Be prepared to read your new poem aloud to the class.

Henrichsen points out that Part II restricts students' efforts structurally yet allows them semantic freedom. In order to succeed, he feels that students must develop a sound understanding of which types of words fit into which environments. He elaborates: The verb chosen to replace *gringling* must be able to take a plural object; *coming* will not do. And verb forms are as important as verb choices. Substituting *watch* for *gringling* is not acceptable; it has to be *watching*. If a non-feminine noun is chosen to replace *moisha* in line three, *her* in line four must be changed appropriately.

Additional reasons why Henrichsen recommends this activity:

A. It's entertaining. B. It weans some students away from the dictionary. C. Students gain an appreciation of the power of structure words. D. Verb forms and pronoun relationships take on a new importance. E. It's confidence-building to realize that one can answer all sorts of questions correctly without knowing the exact meaning of every word. F. The fantastic range of possible lexical substitutions provides a challenge to venture into the language.

COMMUNITY LEARNING AND THE TEACHING OF COMPOSITION IN ESL

by William F. Myers
College of DuPage

This article will look at Peter Elbow's approach to a community writing environment in light of some theories and practice regarding Community Language Learning (CLL) as we observe it at present in the teaching of ESL. I have used Earl Stevick's book *A Way and Ways*[1] and the textbook *Getting into It: An Unfinished Book*, by David Blot and Phyllis Berinan Sher,[2] to give perspective to Elbow's books, viz. *Writing without Teachers* and *Writing with Power*.[3]

Much of Stevick's purpose in *A Way and Ways* is to find a broader application of some highly specialized approaches to learning language, among them CLL. In his helpful way he defines the "community" setting to mean simply that power is "more evenly distributed between knower and learner in the classroom." Furthermore, the relationship between learner and knower cannot be defined by fixed roles, but rather, rests lightly on a "constantly shifting equilibrium." Far from abdicating responsibility, the teacher-counselor-knower can and should lend as much structure "as the learner needs"; he is further obligated, as a member of the community, not to let the learner's reality (i.e., the correspondence between what he is doing and what he thinks he is doing) become distorted. At any time the knower-teacher may find himself in the learner's role and some other element in the class may be providing the teacher-functions indicated above.

This community setting is incorporated into the use of the Blot/Sher composition textbook *Getting into It*. Here are thirteen "stories" all written in the first person apparently by advanced ESL students; each character writes his story (or has someone else tell his story) about 'making it' in an alien culture and with a second language. All stories are followed by a set of group-discussion questions and some individual writing assignments; suggestions for group roleplaying projects follow some stories. The questions ask the group to state their perceptions—non-judgmentally if possible—of the people in the story. Since these are *perceptions*, there is little chance of 'right' or 'wrong' on the resultant shared opinions. The individual writing assignments always provide at least one invitation to the student to write about himself, though usually there is the chance to write about the character or situation in the story, or about similar people and situations the learner has encountered elsewhere.

Most of the above format fits Stevik's criterion of what is beneficial in CLL; i.e., the strategies are designed to engage "the whole learner." Group feeling and support among learners should develop as classmates shift their primary focus from the life struggles in the textbook stories to the mutual confrontation of their own 'present reality,' in their writing. At the same time the learner's sense of security is cushioned in various ways; for one thing, he knows that no writing assignment will demand that he directly expose himself, as he is always given other options.

Peter Elbow comes close to the counselor-teacher role himself in the very presentations of his books. In *Writing with Power* in particular he addresses himself directly to a would-be writer—and thereby makes no real distinction in his audience between students and teachers of writing. Like Stevick, he writes clearly and can present sophisticated learning theories in simple terms. But where Stevick attracts his readers to himself, with his experiences and opinions, and even with his own fascination at how his own mind works, Elbow manages to keep his audience interested in its own thought processes and responses—in how it probably functions as a writer, and how it might find support, criticism and audience from others. Elbow is supporting the writer, as it were, from behind the would-be writer's own chair something like the classic counselor-learner, who stands outside and behind his learning—group.

Elbow's community classroom, though it did not originate in the so-called Chicago school of counseling-learning, does have interesting parallels to CLL. An important part of Elbow's community structure consists of a form of what Stevic calls *reflection*: in Elbow's plan the class members read and listen to what one of their group has written and then summarize what the writer has shown them, and/or restate his purpose, and/or speculate on what kinds of motivation they imagine the writer to be operating from if they were to draw inferences from this piece of work alone. No attempt at group agreement is to be forced. If different class members summarize a paper differently, for example, the writer takes this to mean merely that his paper communicated in different ways. No one's interpretation of or reaction to a paper is ever to be pointed out as wrong, though of course a commentator may well hear ensuing comments that clearly differ from his own. Even more interesting, the writer is not permitted to speak or in any other way explain his work while his class members discuss it. Far from creating insecurity, this ground rule, Elbow believes, *relieves* the writer from having to defend his work from what he hears about it, and in turn frees his energy for *listening*.

Writers in Elbow's community may be given *suggestions* for writing (In fact, he provides numerous pointers for the person who feels he is afflicted with writers' block.), but the writer is not assigned a specific topic nor a mode for organizing it. Instead, he is left free either to play it safe or take the risk that comes with 1) the attempt at new forms, 2) presenting untested views, or 3) self-exposure. A 'teacher,' if he chooses to be present in the community, is there on the same premise that Elbow suggests for the other participants. Beyond that, the teacher may find no special function for himself besides that of umpire, an enforcer of ground rules, until another member of the class, or the class as a whole, becomes strong enough to take care of them.

Stevic points out that the originators of CLL—most of whom are therapists or graduate students in counseling—considered the actual language learning as secondary—a by-product, if you will, of the goal of forming a tight group knit through deeper self and interpersonal understanding. Likewise the individual and group activity suggested in the Blot/Sher book is designed to create a safe arena for self exploration. Elbow's books alter that focus by implicitly asking every participant to assume a role—*not* that of someone learning a language, or passing tests, or going to school, or struggling with a culture—but that of a *writer*, someone who differs from other writers, great or obscure, in degree only, never in kind. And while most of Stevick's criteria for reaching the whole learner are still maintained, the knower-teacher's role is now switched from being less of a counselor-facilitator to being more of a writing coach or even friend. The goal of language learning is ascendant again.

Elbow was not writing his books with the ESL student particularly in mind. But neither Elbow nor Stevick, nor Blot gives consideration to a final question which must inevitably arise: i.e., given the modification of the teaching role in the/a community setting, how does that change the way the composition teacher treats those characteristic ESL problems he always faces—grammar, syntax, vocabulary, idiom? That question is worth a paper in itself.   *TN 6/82*

1 Newbury House Publishers, Inc., 1980. Stevick provides an initial description of CLL in his earlier book *Memory, Meaning and Method* (1976).

2 Language Innovations, Inc., 1978.

3 Oxford University Press, 1973 and 1981 respectively.

A SPELLING FLOW CHART

Edited by Cathy Day
Eastern Michigan University

As most ESL teachers will testify, learning to spell correctly in English can be extremely difficult and frustrating for many students. This "It Works" suggestion is aimed at simplifying the learning task through the use of a flow-chart. Eric Nelson, from the University of Minnesota, reports that his students enjoy using this flow-chart, that they prefer it to the usual "formidable-looking traditional presentation of the rules," and he hopes that other ESL students might enjoy it as well. (For students who are interested in business, it's a good way to learn about flow-charts at the same time.)

The flow-chart is aimed at making it "as easy as possible for students to avoid errors in spelling -*ing* forms, -*ed* forms, and -*s* forms," according to Nelson. The student is guided through a series of yes or no questions to the correct form. The student starts at the appropriate point—the -*ing* circle, the -*ed* circle, or the -*s* circle—and proceeds down the chart by answering questions about the base form of the verb. The student is instructed to make whatever stem changes are necessary (doubling a consonant or changing *y* to *ie* for example) and ends by adding the suffix. The chart limitations are:

1. It does not include a rule to produce *does* and *goes* rather than *dos and *gos. Those forms could have been dealt with in the chart, but are instead included in a note outside the chart.

2. The chart does not include the *ck* rule that applies in, for example, *panicking*. Again, this rule could easily be integrated into the chart, but is instead mentioned it in a note.

3. The chart does not include the exceptional-*s* form *has*.

4. The chart does not point out that consonant doubling applies in words such as *sidestepping* even though the stress is on the first syllable (as in *offering*) rather than on the second syllable (as in *referring*). (Or, to put it another way: that a word such as *step* requires consonant doubling when it occurs as the second element of a compound, regardless of stress.)

TN 2/83

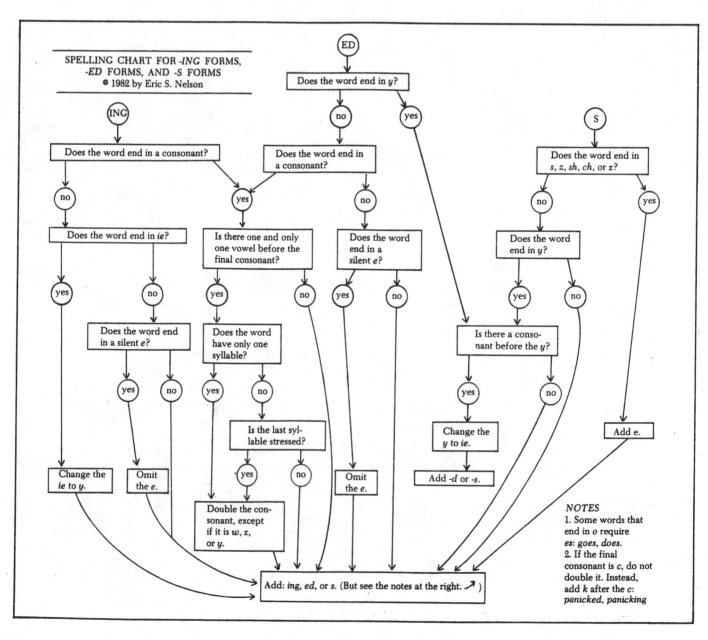

A NEW THEME ON AN OLD ANGLE

Edited by Darlene Larson
New York University

Have you ever had a group of students in your composition class who all too willingly informed you, "I can't write in Korean, either," or asked, "What do you mean by a topic sentence," or stated, "What do you mean by support? There's nothing more to say. What I've said is clear." Well, Mary Hines has . . . both at LaGuardia Community College and previously at New York University. She has found that the following technique makes sense—or gets through—to a number of these students, and is willing to share it with us because it works.

Mary Recommends the Socratic approach to eliciting from students the statement and proof of a geometric theorem. Once the proof has been established by students, it is an easy move to demonstrate that the order and support of their evidence is the simplest outline of a paragraph having a thesis sentence, support, and a conclusion. Thus, the demonstration of a theorem plus transitional expression and prose equals a well-organized, clear paragraph.

Mary provides the following proof and resulting paragraph as a model:

• • •

I would expect a good geometry book, perhaps the same one your students are using in math class, to provide other proofs and thus allow students practice in supplying transitional expressions and the prose needed to change the given to a paragraph. Of course, an advanced group could begin by developing their own proofs right from the start.

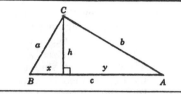

Given: Right triangle ABC with legs a and b and hypotenuse c
Prove: $c^2 = a^2 + b^2$
Analysis: Use Theorem 66 to find the values of a^2 and b^2 and add the results.

STATEMENTS	REASONS
1. Right $\triangle ABC$ with legs a, b, and hypotenuse c	1. Given.
2. Draw the altitude from the vertex C to side c. Let x be the projection of a on c, and y the projection of b on c.	2. A perpendicular to a line can be constructed from a point outside the line.
3. Then $a^2 = cx$	3. The square of a leg of a right triangle is equal to the product of the hypotenuse and the projection of this leg on the hypotenuse.
4. $b^2 = cy$	4. Same as 3.
5. $a^2 + b^2 = cx + cy = c(x + y)$	5. If equal numbers are added to equal numbers, the sums are equal.
6. $x + y = c$	6. A set of points lying between the endpoints of a line segment divides the segment into a set of consecutive segments the sum of whose lengths equal the length of the given segment.
7. $\therefore a^2 + b^2 = c^2$	7. Any number may be substituted for its equal in any expression.

Theorem 67—The square of the hypotenuse of a right triangle is equal to the sum of the squares of the legs.

The square of the hypotenuse of a right triangle is equal to the sum of the squares of the legs. Given a right triangle, *ABC*, with legs *a, b,* and *c,* we draw the altitude from the vertex *C* to side *c.* Let *x* be the projection of *a* on *c* and *y* the projection of *b* on *c* because a perpendicular to a line can be constructed from a point outside the line. *a²* equals *cx* because the square of a leg of a right triangle is equal to the product of the hypotenuse and the projection of this leg on the hypotenuse. For the same reason, *b²* equals *cy.* If equal numbers are added to equal numbers, the sums are equal so *a² + b²* equals *cx* and *cy* equals *c(x + y).* In addition, we can say *x + y* equals *c* because a set of points lying between the endpoints of a line divides the segment into a set of consecutive segments the sum of whose lengths equals the length of the given segment. *Therefore, a² + b² equals c² because any number may be substituted for its equal in any expression.*

TN 9/76

QUIET: PEOPLE COMMUNICATING

by Lise Winer
Concordia University, Montreal

Do your students hate writing? Do they view it as a useless painful exercise necessary only for exams? If so, help is a pen in the hand. Silent writing can help not only to improve writing itself, but also to help the student develop effective communication skills.

As Michael Sharwood-Smith has pointed out (1976: 18), the great disadvantage of the speaking situation is that much of the information a non-native speaker wants to communicate can be understood from non-linguistic cues such as facial expression, gestures, and general context. It only takes one unusual question or comment to show that the learner's command of the language is not as good as it appears. In a situation in which only writing is permitted, however, the learner is forced to perfect his/her communicative skills in the target language itself.

The idea of the "silent class" was developed by Lavonne Mueller, a high school English teacher in Illinois, for a 9-week remedial English course (1975). No talking of any sort was permitted, and all communication was carried out by written "memos". Specific problems were dealt with individually in writing, or on posters for the whole class. The immediacy and high degree of individualism this entailed encouraged the students tremendously, Mueller reports. Although it seemed very demanding—even impossible—at first, students became both more consciously aware of errors and more able to deal with them.

In adapting this approach for intermediate ESL classes, I have made silent memos a regular part of classroom activity. Not only are memos good for days when you just don't feel like talking, they also help to teach students to read and follow directions, to depend on themselves and other students instead of just the teacher for help, to pay attention to their own work and that of others, and to realize that writing can indeed be an effective and even enjoyable form of communication.

If you'd like to try it, here are some ideas. When I use memos in class, I usually write the assignment on the board under a "No Talking, Please" heading. I add that anyone who has a question can ask me in writing. This technique may, at the beginning, make students laugh or become panic-stricken. Refuse to speak, and don't let them speak either. Then wait it out—students usually get the idea in two to three minutes.

During the writing, you can add written information to the board, or call their attention to something already written there by tapping on the board and pointing to the appropriate spot.

Memos can be short or long, simple or very complex. They may or may not be directly related to another class assignment. They may involve writing between students only, between students and teacher, or both. (It should be made very clear that memos between students are absolutely private and will never be seen by the teacher.)

Sample Assignments

The following are some examples of simple memos.

1. Give another student in the class directions on how to get to your house. (Find out first where she/he will be coming from.)

2. Ask another student, in writing, for suggestions about a good restaurant. What kind of food does it serve? How much does it cost?

3. Ask another student for help with a problem (e.g. I've lost a library book/my boy-(girl) friend/my job).

These questions may, of course, be posed directly by the teacher, for example, "I'd like to take my 16-year-old sister to a movie for her birthday. What do you recommend and why?"

The recipient of a question, either a student or the teacher, can then ask, in writing, for clarification (including "I can't read this!") or further information ("Does your sister like spy movies?"). This may involve quite a lot of note-passing back and forth; students who regularly pass notes in their other classes may be delighted to utilize this talent, previously unappreciated by the teacher.

Other memos involve two steps: usually a student-to-student task first, and then a report from one or both students to the teacher. The teacher does not see the first step, only its reported result.

One such memo I use at the beginning of the term is a useful variation of "Tell us about yourself." The first part of the assignment is: "Introduce yourself, in writing, to another student in the class."

The student who receives this introduction must then write down at least three questions requesting further information; these questions are then answered, also silently, by the first student. When the second student feels s/he has enough information, s/he then writes a memo to the teacher, introducing his/her new friend (the first student). The teacher can then ask the "interviewer" further questions about the first student. The answers must be obtained from the first student by the interviewer; the information is then incorporated into the written introduction.

The usual problem with this type of "interview" conversation is that students give a minimal reply and then stop (e.g.

An Advanced Memo Assignment

Similar but more advanced and complex memo exercises can also be devised. The trick is to find a plausible urgent situation in which writing is the only means of communication. Such situations might include rescue attempts for people stranded as a result of floods or plane crashes, instructions to someone looking for a hidden treasure (a raider of the lost ark?), a newspaper reporter in a war zone, members of a mountain-climbing expedition, a kidnaper holding a jewel for ransom. Messages can be transmitted in writing via carrier pigeons, helicopters, spies, catapults and bottles, in addition to the post. One note of caution: almost any subject, particularly those relating to terrorism, can be potentially upsetting to your students, although I have generally found that they are enthusiastic.

In one example, students found the following instructions on the board when they came into the classroom. Part I: Work in pairs. One person is a hijacker, and the other is a negotiator. All phone lines between you have been cut, so *all* your communication will haave to be done in writing. The negotiations you undertake are top secret!

A. Hijackers. Make your demands and threats. Establish your sitution. (Whom do you represent? What resources do you have? What do you have to bargain with?) Try to make the negotiator give you what you want.

B. Negotiators. Establish your situation. (Whom do you represent? What resources do you have? How firm are the hijacker's demands? How much can you compromise?) Try to convince the hijacker to give up or to make concessions. Try to negotiate a settlement with as little damage as possible.

Part II: Newspaper Report

After the problem with the hijacker has been resolved, the editor of the local newspaper will need a report on the incident. One report should be submitted by each team. Include relevant information such as the identity and aims of the hijacker, what happened during the negoiations, and the final outcome of the situation.

One day, when there was an uneven number of students, I got to be a hijacker in Part I. I can testify personally that the assignment required a great deal of involvement! Students constantly looked up words in their dictionaries and referred to their past writings. Meanings obviously had to be precise, since "countless lives" depended on a lack of misunderstanding. Students became very inventive, planning strategies furiously. My own negoiator, in fact, started a whole series of stage directions, in parentheses, so that I would know how to play along and fall into her trap! The reports from Part II were remarkably clear and well organized, in addition to being realistic and exciting.

In addition to putting up assignments and other serious business on the board, I often write little notes and comments to my students. During the baseball season especially, students are apt to find a large "Way to go, Expos!" or "Bad beginnings make good endings." on the board. Even if they respond with a groan, the message and the medium have been responded to!

References:

Byrd, Patricia, et al, 1977 "Memo Writing and Silence in the ESL Composition Class." *TESOL Newsletter* 22:2.

Mueller, Lavonne, 1975. "The Silent Class." *Illinois English Bulletin* 63:2.

Sharwood-Smith, Michael, 1976. "A Note on 'Writing versus Speech'." *English Language Teaching Journal*, 31:1.

(Excerpted from the *TESOL Communique* Fall 1977.)

TN 2/78

USING SHORT STORIES IN THE ADVANCED ESL COMPOSITION CLASS

Mary Ruetten Hank
University of New Orleans

The use of literature in the ESL classroom fell into disfavor at the heyday of the audio-lingual method, perhaps as a reaction to the earlier grammar translation method which concentrated on translating literature, and has not been seriously considered since. Having been thoroughly schooled in the notion that literature has no place in ESL, I looked with skepticism at a collection of short stories I was given to accompany an ex-

pository composition text in an advanced freshman composition class for international students. At the outset of the class, I thought I would have preferred a prose reader on relevant modern topics. However, my skepticism turned to pleasant surprise when I found that the short stories provided excellent material for class discussions and compositions in which different rhetorical techniques could be practiced.

The objection to using literature in ESL has been summed up by Donald M. Topping (1968:95): "literature has no legitimate place in a second-language program whose purpose is to teach language skills to a cross section of students who are preparing for studies or work in a variety of disciplines." Even the use of literature to familiarize second language learners with English or American culture has been rejected by Topping (1968:99) on the grounds that literature reflects "tradition, a past stage in the evolution of American culture." Furthermore, the problem Gatbonton and Tucker (1971) refer to as "cultural filtering," the judging of a work of literature from a different cultural perspective and hence misreading the intent of the author, can be persistent. Certainly my own experience teaching English in Peace Corps Swaziland bore this out. A poem (Thomas 1966) which decried the takeover of man by machine could only be perceived as a glorification of machines in that developing third-world country. The problems connected with the use of literature in ESL—relevance, cultural filtering, simplification—have seemed so persistent and so overwhelming that I had never seriously considered using any literature in ESL until I was given a short story text as a *fait accompli*.

I found, to my surprise, that at least in one ESL situation, short stories can work very well. I would agree that the use of literature is probably out of place at elementary and intermediate levels of ESL instruction where students are still mastering the basic syntactic patterns of the language and have a fairly limited vocabulary. I would also question its use in some English-as-a-foreign-language situations. My form III (tenth grade) students in Swaziland simply did not have either the language facility or cross-cultural sophistication to understand the intent of the poem mentioned above. However, on the college freshman level, we are generally dealing with students who have had years of English study and who have obtained quite a high degree of proficiency in the language. According to Zamel (1976), the language skills being taught in an ESL freshman composition class are essentially the same as the skills American students are learning. This is true, she says, because second language learners by this time have developed the competence necessary to communicate through composition. Furthermore, many of our students have already spent several years in the United States, where they have been in constant contact with American culture. As a result, they have developed a certain degree of understanding of our culture and of cross-cultural sophistication. Cultural filtering should not present a significant problem. Also, these students are generally older, more studious, and more mature than their American freshman counterparts. They have already formulated ideas about the world and consider their ideas important. These students, I believe, can profit from reading short stories and writing about them.

In most freshman composition courses, the main focus is on development of writing skills using different rhetorical techniques such as cause/effect, example, definition, and comparison/contrast. The freshman composition class which I taught used Robert G. Bander's second edition of *American English Rhetoric* (1978) as its basic text. The Bander text gives short passages as examples of the rhetorical techniques being studied. However, it does not have longer passages which would prompt class discussions or composition topics. The classic problem for the composition teacher is to devise composition topics which both interest and challenge all the students and of which they all have knowledge. In most freshman composition courses, some sort of prose reader, often containing quasi-professional or popular articles on current topics like pollution or population control, is used for this purpose (e.g. Jacobus 1978, Baumwoll and Saitz 1965, Hirasawa and Markstein 1974). Instead of this type of reader, I used Jean A. McConochie's *20th Century American Short Stories* (1975), which contains nine modern American short stories, to accompany Bander. McConochie (1975:xi) did not simplify the short stories but chose them "on the criteria of recognized literary quality, brevity, and cultural and linguistic accessibility to non-native speakers of American English." I found that this collection of short stories worked well to provide composition topics while allowing practice in different rhetorical techniques.

The short stories were beneficial for several reasons. First, since literature has the quality of being universal, the short stories allowed us to deal with *human* problems. In our class discussions we explored questions about the essential nature of human beings, what is common to all of us. In the American university system, many international students feel cut off from and misunderstood by Americans. Class discussions allowed students to voice some of these feelings, focus on them, and perhaps gain some perspective on them. For example, in Jesse Stuart's story "Love," the father kills a beneficial snake on his farm just because he hates all snakes. This led to a discussion of prejudice, war, hate and love. This helped students in my class to understand, at least philosophically, some of the adverse reactions which Americans displayed toward them and which they had about Americans.

Then, in the writing assignments, a student can take an essentially human problem and analyze his own feelings and attitudes. Since he is drawing from his own experience, the problem of not having knowledge about the subject, as might occur on a topic about pollution, does not come up. Further, because he is expressing his own personal feelings about an issue, the student tends to see the topic as important, gets involved in it, and will spend a good deal of time on it. According to Zamel (1976:74), "The act of composing should become the result of a genuine need to express one's personal feeling, experience, or reaction." Although writing about American students, Fenstermaker (1977:35) makes the same point when he says "The literature based course offers students excellent practice in writing about subjects of real substance from the perspective afforded by genuine involvement." I found that the topics which required students to draw from their own personal attitudes and philosophy were perceived as "real," mature, worthy of their time and effort, while the topics assigned out of the text, on say comparing two universities or two cities, were perceived as mere exercises. The opportunity to write about personal values and beliefs, especially when so many ESL students are otherwise studying science and engineering, affords them a useful release mechanism.

The danger in writing about personal values and feelings is producing a theme which is a string of generalizations and familiar platitudes. Because we had read the short stories, the students had something specific to react to. I could assign topics which needed specific support from the stories or which made students deal concretely with the ideas in the stories. In this process, we could also practice the different rhetorical techniques we were studying. For example, Jesse Stuart's "Love" and John Collier's "The Chaser" both deal with love. Students can compare and/or contrast the two authors' concepts of love or compare and contrast them with their own ideas on love. Because they had something to compare to, this assignment made students try to define their own concept of love quite carefully and in relation to love as shown in the stories. Further, Stuart's story contains several different kinds of love, that is, parent/child love, male/female love, and love of nature. In another assignment, students can be asked to classify and explain the different types. Some of my students wrote excellent argumentative papers on Shirley Jackson's "The Lottery" in which they asserted that the lottery in the story was either a superstition or a religious practice according to definitions of those terms and then supported their assertion with evidence from the story. Also, an interesting cause/effect assignment could be worked out on "The Secret Life of Walter Mitty." The story contains detailed, concrete objects and incidents that touch off Mitty's daydreams. There is also the larger question of what causes Mitty to escape into his daydreams. Or, in the Walter Mitty story one could compare what is considered heroic, both cross-culturally and personally. These are just some of the possible writing assignments springing from the short stories that require concrete, specific development.

I would not like to suggest that ESL instructors adopt short stories wholesale for use in composition classes. In order for short stories to both spark discussions and provide worthwhile composition topics, some care must be taken in selection. For instance, in McConochie's text, I could not find a use for "The Use of Force" by William Carlos Williams, so I omitted it. I also feel that the kinds of topics which are discussed in most prose readers, such as pollution and population control, are important and relevant. They allow students to deal more impersonally with issues that are crucial in our modern world. Perhaps an ideal situation in the freshman ESL composition class would be the incorporation of both short stories, to deal with human problems, and prose readings, to point up practical/technical problems. After all, a truly educated person should have the composing facility to deal with both.

REFERENCES

Bander, Robert G. 1978. *American English Rhetoric* (2nd ed.). New York: Holt, Rinehart and Winston.

Baumwoll, D. and Saitz, R. L. 1965. *Advanced reading and writing: Exercises in English as a second language.* New York: Holt, Rinehart and Winston.

Fenstermaker, John J. 1977. Literature in the Composition Class. *College Composition and Communication* 28, 34-37.

Gatbonton, Elizabeth C. and Tucker, G. Richard. 1971. Cultural Orientation and the Study of Foreign Literature. *TESOL Quarterly* 5, 137-142.

Hirasawa, Louise and Markstein, Linda. 1974. *Developing Reading Skills, Advanced.* Rowley, Massachusetts: Newbury House Publishers, Inc.

Jacobus, Lee A. 1978. *Improving College Reading* (3rd ed.). New York: Harcourt, Brace Jovanovich, Inc.

McConochie, Jean A. 1975. *20th Century American Short Stories.* New York: Collier Macmillian International, Inc.

Thomas, R. S. 1966. Cynddylan on a Tractor. In Ian V. Hansen, ed., *One Voice.* London: Edward Arnold LTD., 27.

Topping, Donald M. 1968. Linguistics or Literature: An Approach to Language. *TESOL Quarterly* 2, 95-100.

Zamel, Vivian. 1976. Teaching Composition in the ESL Classroom: What we Can Learn from Research in the Teaching of English. *TESOL Quarterly* 10, 67-76.

TN 4/80

USING FILMS AS A PRE-WRITING ACTIVITY

by Sandra McKay
San Francisco State University

Composing involves the dual task of deciding what to say and how to say it. Perhaps due to the concern of ESL classes with accuracy, the emphasis in teaching composition has often been on how to say it. Many writing texts provide ESL students with a topic, or else assume they already have something to say and thus, immediately proceed to the how of a composition. While this aspect of the writing process certainly must be dealt with, if equal attention is not given to the question of what to say, we as composition teachers will likely fail to promote effective writing.

Shaughnessy (1978: 81-82) contends that implicit in the art of writing is the following sequence: first, getting the thought; second, getting the thought down; and third, readying the written statement for other eyes. She maintains that although students have difficulty with each of these steps, the most difficult is getting the thought. Many strategies have been suggested to aid students in this initial task, dating from Aristotle's classical *topoi* to more recent theories like the Pike, Becker and Young's particle, wave and field approach. However, one effective method for invention that has not received the attention it should is the use of short unnarrated films.

Films have several advantages in helping students find something to say. First, they provide students with a concrete context in which to explore their own feelings and experiences. According to Langer (1953:412) film "is 'like' a dream in the mode of its presentation: it creates a virtual present, an order of direct apparition. . . . The most noteworthy formal characteristic of dream is that the dreamer is always at the center of it." Clearly, it is the immediacy of the experience, the "virtual present," that makes film a valuable tool for generating writing ideas.

Secondly, films share with literature a potential for not only drawing forth personal experiences, but also ordering those experiences. According to Rosenblatt (1978: 11), a literary text serves two functions: "First, a text is a stimulus, activating elements of the reader's past experience. . . . Second, the text serves as a blueprint, a guide for the selecting, rejecting and ordering of what is being called forth." Certainly, films offer these same benefits, with one additional advantage. While the linguistic difficulty of a literary selection may impede a non-native speaker's own aesthetic experience, unnarrated films avoid this problem. Films, of course, like literature, will elicit very different reactions, some perhaps due to cultural differences. Yet, in this way, they provide a context in which to explore cultural differences. The viewing of a film, like the reading of a literary text, involves an interplay between the culture of the text and the culture of the viewer. Rosenblatt's (1978: 56) description of a reader is certainly applicable to the viewer of a film: "The reader draws on his own internalized culture in order to elicit from the text this world which may differ from his own in many respects. . . . The literary transaction may thus embody, and probably to some degree always embodies, an interplay between at least two sets of values."

Films, then, in so far as they activate and order personal experience, can be of benefit in getting a writer started. The challenge of a composition class, however, is to bridge the gap between getting the thought and discovering a creative and effective way to express this thought. It is at this point in the writing process that students need the most help. As Selfe and Rodi (1980: 169) put it,

As teachers of composition and rhetoric, most of us have come to realize the necessity and benefits of involving students in the initial process of invention—that process which actively engages students both in examining their experiences for that which they find interesting and valuable, and in determining or discovering the most effective way to write about these experiences for the composing task at hand. And yet many of us have also come to recognize the reluctance and sometimes the inability of students to undertake autonomously this dual task.

While the viewing of a film can aid students with the first task, that of examining their experiences, they are still faced with the second task of discovering the most effective way to write about them. What the students need are some heuristic devices to help them in ordering their thoughts for the composition. The following is an example of two such heuristic devices designed for use with a specific film.

The film is *Le Haricot* (*The String Bean*), a short unnarrated film (seventeen minutes) by the French photographer, Edmond Sechan. The film is a portrait of an old woman who carefully guards a potted bean plant from birth to death. She plants the seed in her apartment, watches it develop, replants it in a nearby park, and finally witnesses it being discarded by the park gardener. However, before it is thrown away, she is able to salvage some seeds, take them home, and begin anew the task of nurturing a string bean. The film is thus not only a vignette of an old woman, but a commentary on man's relationship with his environment.

In order to explore the various themes of the film, the following heuristic devices could be used. The first chart requires students to focus on the actions of the old woman, and to then use these actions to make inferences about her character.

Directions: While you watch the film write down all the actions of the old woman. After viewing the film, indicate what you believe each action demonstrates about her personality. The first one is done for you.

ACTION

1. The old woman finishes her sewing for the day, puts the thread and scissors in the drawer, and closes the sewing machine.

INFERENCE

1. The fact that she carefully returns each item to a designated spot suggests that she is neat and orderly.

ACTION

2. She takes out the cooking pot, fills it with water, and puts in some bean seeds.

After completing this sheet, an important follow-up would be for the students to share their findings. Undoubtedly each student will note different actions in the film, and draw quite varied conclusions about these actions. The fact that some students may attribute the putting away of the sewing items to neatness, while others see it as complusiveness will illustrate the uniqueness of their inferences. By completing the chart, the students will have made some progress toward what Shaughnessy terms "getting the thought down." In the essay itself then they might explore the character of the old woman. The reaction sheet will no doubt be valuable in forming generalizations about the old woman's personality and substantiating them with relevant examples. An alternate assignment might entail having the students observe the actions of a stranger, and draw inferences about these actions as the basis for a character sketch.

A second reaction sheet that could be used with the same film draws on the theme of man's relationship with his environment. Selfe and Rodi (1980: 170) describe a heuristic device to help students arrive at a fuller definition of self. This is done by asking students to view themselves from three different perspectives as they evolve over time. Each frame in their structure can be expanded on with additional questions. For example, an exploration of self in the past might involve questions such as, "What did I like/dislike about myself five years ago?"

SELF-DEFINITION

PAST   What was I like at 5 years of age?

PRESENT   What kind of person am I today?

FUTURE   What kind of person will I be in 5 years?

SOCIAL-DEFINITION

PAST   How did others see me physically as a child?

PRESENT   How do others see me physically today?

FUTURE   How might others see me in the future?

ENVIRONMENTAL DEFINITION

PAST   What "things" helped me reach goals 10 years ago?

PRESENT   What "things" do I utilize to reach my present goals?

FUTURE   What "things" might I use to reach my future goals?

Le Haricot is a film which explores an individual largely from the environment perspective. The following device is designed to help students define the old woman in terms of her relationship with the plant as it develops over time.

Directions: List the various things that the old woman does with the plant. Then indicate how you think she felt about the plant at each stage. In order to describe how she felt, it will be particularly useful to carefully observe her facial expressions.

ACTIONS

1. The old woman boils the seeds in order to plant them.
2. She goes to the market to find some soil to plant the seed.

FEELINGS

How do you think the woman felt about the plant . . .
when she first planted it?
when the rain watered the plant?
when she planted it in the garden outside?
when the gardener picked the plant?
when she headed home with the dead plant?
when she boiled the seeds from the dead plant?
when she planted the new seeds?
when the new plant began to grow?

Once students compare their ideas about the old woman's feelings toward the plant, they could then proceed to write an essay in which they discuss the old woman's relationship with the plant. In an alternate assignment they might examine their own relationship with something in the environment (an object or place), and its development over time. The following is a student essay written in response to such an assignment.

The Porcelain Bell

I have a brown porcelain bell on a shelf in my house. It is very important to me because it helped me a lot several years ago. I got it at a small temple in Japan when I was very unhappy. I visited the temple to beg Buddha to give me a baby because I had just lost my first baby before, and also I was told by a doctor that there was no hope for me to have a baby again.

I met a Buddhist priest who taught me to wait for a baby spirit's coming from heaven. He said, "Buddha might send you a baby spirit someday when you are ready, but you have to clean your mind and not to forget to thank him for what he does every day for you. This bell will remind you to pray and to thank Buddha, and Buddha will hear your bell and be reminded to think about you too. But remember that the more you clean your mind, the more beautiful sound you make with this bell." Then he gave me the small bell. After I came home, I kept ringing the bell because I wanted to have a baby so much. I rang the bell twice a day and prayed, and eight months later, I began to recognize a different sound. I was crazy about making and creating a beautiful sound and I almost forgot why I was ringing the bell. And soon I noticed a baby spirit inside of me. Now I have two children, one husband and the bell.

As this essay illustrates, films can be valuable in getting the students started to write. Clearly, viewing the film is not sufficient. What is essential is that the teacher provide some type of heuristic device to help students order their reactions to the film. Once the students have in Shaughnessy's terms "gotten the thought" and begun to "get the thought down," they can proceed to the final step, the usual focus of composition classes, "readying the statement for other eyes." Each step is equally important and warrants attention in the ESL composition class. Clearly, film is one way we as composition teachers can help students in the most difficult part of the composing process, finding something to say.

TN 11/81

REFERENCES

Rosenblatt, L. 1978. *The Reader, The Text, The Poem: The Transaction Theory of the Literary Work.* Carbondale, Illinois: Southern Illinois University Press.
Sechan, Edmond. 1964. *Le Haricot.* (16 mm color film). A contemporary film distributed by McGraw-Hill.
Selfe, C. and Rodi, S. 1980. "An Invention Heuristic for Expressive Writing." *College Composition and Communication.* 31: 169-174.
Shaughnessy, Mina. 1977. *Errors and Expectations.* New York: Oxford University Press.
Young, R. E., A. L. Becker and K. L. Pike. 1970. *Rhetoric: Discovery and Change.* New York: Harcourt, Brace and World.   □

BOOK REVIEWS

COMPOSITION STEPS

By Vivian Horn, edited and annotated by
Esther Rosman (Rowley, Mass.: Newbury
House Publishers, Inc., 1977) $6.05,
Teacher's Manual $2.65.

**Reviewed by Carol Fraser,
Concordia University, Montreal**

For years as a CEGEP, Continuing
Education, and now university ESL
instructor, I have felt the need for a
beginning adult composition text. In
business or at school, our students need to
write using a basic expository form;
writing grammar exercises hasn't
necessarily helped them to do this.
Composition Steps, by the late Vivian
Horn, goes a long way toward answering
this need.

Composition Steps aims to introduce
low intermediate students to the principles
of expository writing. In the belief that
composition begins when sentences are
put together to communicate an idea,
students are presented rhetorical ideas
that extend beyond single sentences. For
example, in Unit 3 students are introduced
to the idea of topic sentence and in Unit 5
to coherence or the logical order of
sentences in a paragraph.

However, unlike most ESL rhetoric
texts, *Composition Steps* does not assume
that students using it can already write
correct sentences. Using the text, students
practice writing correct sentences at the
same time that they are learning to write
short paragraphs.

Learning composition skills is a long,
slow process and should begin as
early as possible. It should not be
delayed so that it follows grammar,

for that will not allow sufficient time
for development of the composition
skills. Besides, the teaching of
grammar never really ends.
(*Teacher's Manual*, p. 1.)

Students prepare for the paragraph
writing exercises through a series of
grammar review exercises covering
irregular verbs, personal pronouns,
possessive adjectives and the position of
adverbs. The language used (both
vocabulary and syntax) is simple and
should be well within the range of the low
intermediate ESL student.

The nicest thing about *Composition
Steps* is the wide variety of exercises for
students. Explanations and rules are kept
to a minimum. Here is a sampling of the
wide range of writing exercises:

  copying
  copy reading (looking for errors)
  spelling
  paragraph completion
  alphabetizing
  scrambled paragraphs
  dictation
  paragraph writing by answering
    questions
  following directions
  free writing

This text certainly exemplifies the belief
that students learn by doing. *TN 2/78*

ERRORS AND EXPECTATIONS: A GUIDE FOR THE TEACHER OF BASIC WRITING

by Mina P. Shaughnessy
(Oxford University Press, 1977)

**Reviewed by Audrey Reynolds,
Northeastern Illinois University.**

Those who teach writing to
remedial/developmental students have
long been aware of the need for a book
which would describe the writing
problems their students are likely to have
and would provide practical suggestions
for those who wish to help these students
improve their writing. Mina P.
Shaughnessy's *Errors and Expectations: A
Guide for the Teacher of Basic Writing*
is designed to meet that need.

An understanding of the implications of
the title is essential to an understanding of
the work itself, for the word "error," as it
is used in this book, has a significance
which is different from that which English
teachers customarily associate with the
word. "Writing errors," for Ms.
Shaughnessy, are not merely chaotic and
random, as standard writing handbooks
might lead one to believe; nor are they

simply the result of interference between
standard and nonstandard English, as
some sociolinguists might argue. Instead,
"errors" are seen as systematic deviations
from the code of formal academic
English.

The word "systematic" is an important
one, for it reflects Ms. Shaughnessy's
acknowledged debt to current
psycholinguistic investigations of
language acquisition. Like the
psycholinguist who studies first or second
language acquisition, she assumes that
language is systematic, rule-governed
behavior; that one who examines the
errors produced by students who are
learning/acquiring a language will
discover regular patterns; and finally, that
one who analyzes the patterns will be able
to discover 'why' the particular errors are
made. Her treatment of 'comma splices'

provides an excellent example of her
methodology at work. In examining the
data produced by the students, she
discovers that some sentences exhibit
'comma splices,' while other sentences
don't. The obvious question is "Why?"
Her answer? Comma splices occur when a
student senses that there is a close
relationship between the independent
clauses, but is unaware of syntactic
processes like embedding which would
make the relationship explicit. As soon as
one knows the causes for the error, one
can address one's attention to appropriate
exercises, in this case to work on
embedding constructions and sentence
combining instead of telling the student to
throw in a semi-colon as a way of
cosmetically camouflaging the error.

Thus, Ms. Shaughnessy is not content
with merely identifying or cataloging
writing errors. She looks for underlying
explanations for the errors and then
provides suggestions which the teacher
can use in order to help the students
eliminate the errors.

The word "Expectations" is equally
important to an understanding of this
book, for Ms. Shaughnessy does believe
that "Basic Writing" students can learn
how to write. Her ten years of experience,
first with students enrolled in the SEEK
program designed for poverty-area youth
and then with the Open Admissions policy
at City College of the City University of
New York, have given her ample
opportunity to discover that underprepared students are educable.

Finally, her choice of the term "Basic
Writing", rather than Remedial Writing or
Developmental Writing, is significant; for
she believes that many of her students are
in fact "beginners" when it comes to
writing. To students educated in schools
where little or no writing was required,
writing itself, not to speak of formal
academic writing, is an alien activity.
Therefore, she is not 'remediating'
students who failed to learn what they
were taught; nor is she 'developing' a
partially-mastered skill. She is teaching
"Basic Writing."

With a sense of the general philosophy
of the book, we can turn to a discussion of
the content. While it is impossible in a
review of this scope to discuss specifics, a
survey of the topics covered will give one
an idea of the range of the work. The
errors are organized into six categories,
with a chapter devoted to each: (1)
Handwriting and Punctuation, in which
Ms. Shaughnessy not only discusses
'typical' problems with which all writing
teachers are familiar; e.g., fragments and
run-on sentences, but also offers astute
observations on why writing, including
the physical process of writing by hand, is
so difficult for underprepared students; (2)
Syntax; i.e., the kinds of syntactic
difficulties (using *syntactic* in the linguistic
sense of putting words together to form
grammatical sentences) which

underprepared students encounter when they try to write in an alien academic style; (3) Common Errors; i.e., 'inflectional' problems with subject-verb agreement, noun plurals, etc.; (4) Spelling; (5) Vocabulary; and (6) Beyond the Sentence—paragraph and essay organization. Thus, the author attempts to address all the general types of problems which appear in the papers of Basic Writing students.

How adequate is her discussion of the topics? Although Ms. Shaughnessy would be the first to admit that the book does not provide everything one would like to know about both the problems and the solutions, the book, in my opinion, provides a pioneering contribution to a field which, prior to this book, was virtually non-existent; namely, descriptions of the language actually produced by Basic Writing students. Writing teachers, experienced as well as inexperienced, will find much to learn about "Error." Problems which are familiar to anyone who has read standard handbooks on writing, like fragments, subject-verb agreement, or spelling, are treated from a novel perspective: that of "Error Analysis." Moreover, when Ms. Shaughnessy analyzes specific errors, she brings to the task a sensitivity to the complexity of the 'linguistic rules' which students are expected to master. As a result, teachers who have wondered why their students 'still' have difficulty with something as 'simple' as subject-verb agreement will discover that subject-verb agreement is actually a very complex phenomenon. In addition, Ms. Shaughnessy provides insights into errors whose existence seems to be unknown to writers of standard handbooks; e.g., those discussed in the chapter on syntax and those discussed in the chapter on vocabulary.

While the book is 'linguistically' interesting, it is also 'pedagogically' interesting because the author *does* provide practical suggestions in each chapter for the teacher who wants to help students improve their writing. The word 'suggestions' is an important one, for Ms. Shaughnessy does not pretend that she has all the answers. She knows how little psycholinguists know about first and second language acquisition, how little they know about teaching language skills. As a result, the book is refreshingly free of dogmatic prescriptions and panaceas.

The book will also be useful pedagogically to one who masters the analytic technique exemplified in the book. "Error Analysis" is a technique which has proved to be quite valuable for those who teach English as a second language; and as Ms. Shaughnessy's book demonstrates, it promises to be equally valuable for those who are teaching students "Written English" as a second language.

In conclusion, this lucidly written book will be a useful addition to the library of any English composition teacher. Those who have questioned whether "Basic Writing" students are educable will learn that the answer is "Yes." Those who believe the students are educable but feel inadequate themselves when faced with severe writing difficulties of a kind they have never encountered before, will receive "a" way to approach those difficulties. Those who have had some success teaching Basic Writing students but want to learn more will find a great deal to learn in *Errors and Expectations*, the best book on the topic which has appeared to date.

TN 2/78

(*Reprinted from the* NARDPSE Newsletter *November 1977, Vol. 1, No. 2.*)

feels more of the same kind of work has to be done, the student can repeat the exercise with a *new* passage.

A major virtue of the book is this: repetition of a type of exercise in a new situation. Students who need to re-do an exercise do not work with the same content but repeat the very same step whether it be copying or working with subordinate clauses with new, refreshing content. The psychological dangers of feeling an assignment is punitive or boring because of repetition are minimized.

There is one limitation to *26 Steps*: paragraphs do not resemble in substance the paragraphs most teachers cry for. The author in fact makes a strong disclaimer in the *Teacher Manual* that controlled composition cannot help the student "organize his thoughts, express himself clearly, or develop concepts such as thesis, topic sentence, illustration, definition, conclusion." Nevertheless, it is these, especially illustrations or examples, that teachers have so much difficulty getting students to produce. It may be a fine point and a debatable one ("I want to focus on one thing at a time.") But the sheer size of the paragraphs, one and two sentences in length at times, lead students to believe that this is exactly what a paragraph looks like.

The problem is the same we run into when we choose a contemporary news article to stimulate reading and discussion among students. The articles serve that purpose, but by their nature, they are brief and also, courtesy of journalese style, one and two sentences long. Having read and worked with a number of them, students fail to see the difference when they write their own paragraphs loaded (or limp) with one, two or three statements without any support for what they are saying.

On the other hand, the author assumes that the content of students' original papers will be developed through other lessons in writing. The *Teacher Manual,* for that matter, is not only a guide to using these particular exercises. It offers further valuable suggestions for controlled composition use. With that in mind *26 Steps* is a *good* supplementary text helping students to work on form with as much guarantee for success as possible.

Ms. Kunz's passages are humorous and mature (junior high school teachers take note) centering around adult and, primarily, city problems. It will be the rare student who won't enjoy manipulating sentence structures within the given context. *TN 2/76*

26 STEPS

26 Steps, a course in controlled composition for intermediate and advanced ESL students by Linda Ann Kunz (New York Language Innovations, Inc., 1972. $2.95)

by Mary E. Hines
LaGuardia Community College, CUNY

Is a text dealing with the mechanics of writing through graded exercises. With 51 original passages about a variety of contemporary subjects (modern living, astrology, family life, simple anecdotes—categories which are noted in each chapter so that a teacher can also direct students to topics they are interested in), the book provides practice in a variety of skills: copy and substitution, gender and number changes, tense changes, sequence of tenses, direct speech, voice change, negation, vocabulary and combining clauses.

In any one class, students can work with individual problems. At the end of one passage, for example, one student may be assigned exercise 1 (copy the entire passage); a second student may be assigned exercise 5 (gender and number changes); a third may work with exercise 7 (tense changes). With an awareness of the need for proof reading as one goal of the text, students can self-correct lapses indicated by the teacher—a teacher task which can be done quickly given the nature of the assignments. If frequency of errors is so great that a teacher

WRITE AWAY, BOOK ONE

By Gloria Gallingane and Donald Byrd
(Collier Macmillan, 1977)

**Reviewed by Ellen Shaw,
American Language Institute,
New York University**

Flexibility is the key to Gallingane and Byrd's gem of a text, *Write Away, Book One*. Designed for beginning to low-intermediate students, Book One provides writing practice with a variety of transformation operations. Rewriting model paragraphs with inflectional changes enhances the student's insight into the grammatical system of English while the sentence-combining units give him the opportunity to discover the many choices he, as a writer, has.

Transformation operations include pluralization, negation, question formation, verb-tense changes and others. In the sentence combining units, clusters of sentences are combined through co-ordination and subordination operations. Vocabulary is controlled, with particularly difficult words asterisked and defined at the end of the unit. Suggestions for free writing follow the controlled operations, and these are suitable for group discussion. The topics relate to the student, his world and his beliefs. For example, accompanying "The House Husband," the suggeston is "Write your own ideas about the man's role in a marriage." Or following "An Irish Story," a suspenseful tale of a leprechaun and a hunter, the student is asked, "Do you know a folk story from your country? White about it." These suggested topics are supplementary, however, and the instructor may omit them if he wishes.

In using the model paragraphs, the teacher might choose to concentrate on just one rewrite operation, or capitalize on all the possible transformations, which exploit the model to the fullest but do not produce stilted English. For example, "High Blood Pressure" describes what Mr. Morales does each day to combat this condition. Three of the operations are: (1) Mr. Morales' wife also has hypertension. Write about her; (2) Now write about Mr. and Mrs. Morales; (3) Now Mr. Morales' blood pressure is down and he is better. Write about it (past tense). The structures here are basic, but the content is not childish. The sentence combining activities lead the student to discover an assortment of surface structures representing the same kernel sentences. The student and teacher are advised that the

answer key, very useful for independent work, is not the last word; other choices exist. Again, flexibility is the key.

Having used experimental versions of the materials with beginning and intermediate students of various language backgrounds over the last two years, I can testify to the book's effectiveness, both in terms of students' performance and enthusiasm. These materials involve the learner in more than just a linguistic exercise. The adult themes are relevant, contemporary and humorous . . . and God knows, we could use some more humor in ESL classes! The passages deal with a broad range of topics, in which the use of racial, national and sexual stereotypes is avoided, producing a contemporarily balanced text. I use the word *balanced* because no one role for men or women is championed. We encounter male and female nurses, athletes, radio announcers, circus performers and factory workers as well as women studying police work and engineering, traditional housewives and a house husband. Furthermore, minorities are not depicted as "starting from the bottom" where they are often forced to remain.

While it is not the primary purpose of the book to set the stage for classroom debate, certainly many of the situations could spark discussion, even healthy controversy. "A house husband? Never!" "A woman detective? Why not?" Indeed, why not allow beginning students of English to express their attitudes about all kinds of topics? The student is learning on many levels, and the affective is not to be ignored.

A minor flaw is that the table of contents supplies only the titles of the fifty units, providing no information about grammatical content, although the index, primarily for teachers, is adequate. A table of contents with complete listing of structures would be helpful in the forthcoming books of the series.

Happily, the authors advocate no particular methodology. Rather, they start with the premise that learning comes through doing, especially when the doing is meaningful. We look forward to the release of Books Two and Three right away!   4/78

reviews which may postulate potential effects of a book in the classroom.

Writing and Combining Standard English Sentences is a grammar workbook used in the final preparatory courses before students enter our freshman English class. All students using the text come from one of two tracts: advanced ESL students taught in our English Language Institute, or nonforeign students who require a basic grammar review before entering freshman English. These students come from over 30 different countries and are speakers of about half that many languages. Further, the teachers who instruct them through use of the text are both ESL and non-ESL trained in academic preparation.

The grammatical approach for much of this text is sector analysis, a grammar which is construction, rather than word, oriented. It also concerns itself with written, not spoken, English.

One purpose in emphasizing constructions (phrases, clauses, sentences) rather than more traditional word grammars is to help students recognize large syntactic units initially which they can later combine into sophisticated sentences. Such a grammatical approach rests on the assumption that a student ought not to be expected to combine sentences effectively until he knows the constructions that characterize them and how these constructions may be put together. Thus, the first half of the book is concerned with teaching how to write simple correct English sentences, while the second half presents numerous transforming and combining techniques designed to produce complexity and variety in sentence structure. Paragraph construction, the traditional starting point of freshman English, is taught indirectly through contextually connected exercises. Thus, individual sentences do not stand alone, but are part of a contextual whole.

For teachers and students, *Writing and Combining Standard English Sentences* has four primary strengths.

First, the choice of grammatical labels has been descriptive rather than traditional. The authors have selected their grammatical terms according to how they best characterize the concepts being explained. For example, adverbs and adverbial clauses which may be moved to different positions within a sentence without significantly altering the basic meaning are called "shifters." ("Shifters" is Robert L. Allen's term, used in *Working Sentences*.) Such terms reinforce learning by combining labels and the concepts they represent.

Second, the presentation of English verbs is particularly effective. Using the English tense-aspect system (earlier-

WRITING AND COMBINING STANDARD ENGLISH SENTENCES

By Alice Pack and Lynn Henrichsen.

Reviewed by Jeffrey Butler

We have been using *Writing and Combining Standard English Sentences* at BYU—Hawaii Campus for the past year, and I will refer from time to time

to our experiences with it throughout this review. I do so simply to offer an evaluation of the text which is based on teaching with it, as opposed to some

same-later time in both present and past tenses), the authors have presented an understandable method through which verbs can be learned by speakers of other languages. This system also gives formal reasons why pidgin and creole verb patterns often cannot fit edited written English. While the authors do not claim their verb system to be the only one acceptable in written English, they do provide a scheme which would be consistently functional for formalized writing.

Third, grammatical explanations are brief throughout the book. This brevity and directness are in marked contrast to many grammar books on the market today. An important result of these brief explanations is evident: learning takes place primarily through exercises rather than through explanations. Thus inductive, rather than deductive, learning predominates, and in writing this means that retention of skills is high.

Fourth, the exercises which comprise the heart of the book are imaginitive and contextual. That is, they provide a variety of learning experiences within limits of the principles being taught. Following each grammatical point are three sets of exercises. These allow the instructor to use as many or as few of them as he feels necessary for learning purposes. Exercises usually follow a sequence of (1) recognition of a grammatical concept/construction, (2) limited guided production of the concept/construction, (3) original writing which integrates the new concept/construction with previously developed language patterns. Through these steps students are led along the familiar linguistic path from recognition to hesitant command to fluent command.

A few qualifications about the use of this text seem necessary, however, at this point.

Writing and Combining Standard English Sentences is not appropriate for beginning ESL students. It presumes intermediate to advanced ESL grammatical preparation, and its exercises frequently require significant depth of thought, even for native English speakers. Occasionally the complexity of ex-

ercises may be a little uneven. Within a few pages assignments may range in difficulty from simple to extremely complex. This unevenness is, no doubt, a reflection of both the skills required and the generous number of exercises in the book.

In addition, the vocabulary used in the exercises is not always in keeping with ESP (English for Special Purposes) guidelines for college ESL students. However, one reason for this discrepancy is that the variety of topics which were specifically created to maximize student interest requires a correspondingly varied vocabulary.

A final notation concerns the brevity of language characterizing much of the instructional material. Such clipped explanations sometimes result in a chart or diagram being only partially clarified through examples. That is, the visual aid is assumed to be self-evident when, occasionally, further explanation would be helpful.

On balance, *Writing and Combining Standard English Sentences* has shown itself to be the most effective tool we've used for these two courses at BYU—HC. Two concrete results of its use demonstrate the book's effectiveness: Last year, in spite of the problems invariably associated with using a new text, ten percent more students were evaluated at the end of their courses as being prepared for freshman English than the year before. Further, a high percentage of repeaters, students who had failed these courses one or more times, finally passed last year. This meant that several students understood concepts and gained skills which they had once given up being able to learn. In short, the book worked.

As with most new texts, *Writing and Combining Standard English Sentences* is undergoing minor polishing in light of what we find out about it in the classroom. To this point, however, all of the changes have been small, with no significant rewriting seen in the future.

Writing and Combining Standard English Sentences, in two volumes, will be published by Newbury House in the Fall.   *TN 2/80*

understanding of the structure of a five-paragraph composition.

The major rhetorical techniques focused on are those needed in all expository writing, but particularly in the technical fields. The book therefore helps fulfill the needs of the majority of the foreign university students now studying in the United States.

In the English for International Students program at George Washington University, the text is used in the two high-intermediate levels, where its greatest value has been that it teaches not only organization, but also the grammatical and structural forms used to develop and express each rhetorical technique. Earlier ESL writing texts too often assumed that students had mastered the grammatical structures and needed only to be presented with the types of organization. (What instructor has not had problems when students were told that "although," "however," and "contrary to" showed contrast only to find that the students had no idea that these expressions could not be substituted one for another?)

Visually, the text is highly effective. Important points (key phrases, words, structures) are clearly separated from explanatory material. Charts, illustrations and graphs clarify relationships, while clear, direct language makes the concepts easy to grasp. Large type and adequate spacing between lines and sections make it easy for students to follow, and ample space is provided for the students to complete the exercises in the book.

The varied subject matter of the sample paragraphs ranges from "survival" topics (finding an apartment or changing a tire) to those with a cultural focus (the distances Americans use when speaking to each other or the stages of adjustment to a new culture) to more technical subjects still of general interest (the benefits of vitamins or two types of sleep).

The quantity of examples and exercises affords the instructor great flexibility and eliminates the need for preparation of supplementary materials. The ample practice work permits individualization of instruction. Quicker students can proceed to the final exercises while others work through as many exercises as are needed to master the concepts and techniques.

What the book intends to do, that is, teach students how to develop effective paragraphs, it does exceptionally well. In a composition course, however, the book must be supplemented. At this level, students move quickly, and in our program they are asked to write compositions for other university courses. Work on moving from paragraph to composition is especially needed for the chapters on comparison and contrast,

---

PARAGRAPH DEVELOPMENT

Mary Ellen Barrett and Martin Arnaudet (Prentice-Hall, Inc., 1981)

**Reviewed by Patricia Johnson
and Shirley Thompson**
George Washington University

This writing workbook/textbook guides students from an understanding of what a paragraph is, through ways to limit a topic, to means of fully developing paragraphs of classification, cause and effect,

process, comparison, contrast and definition, by using details, examples, anecdotes, facts and statistics. The final chapter, "From Paragraph to Composition," demonstrates how to expand one's

extended definition, and cause and effect, since the very nature of these organizational patterns often involves fuller development than can be achieved at the paragraph level. However, with the solid grounding students receive in paragraph development, it is relatively easy for the instructor to help them make the transition to compositions.

Paragraph Development is a clearly written, interesting and effective text. Its appearance has made a major contribution to the teaching of writing in ESL programs.

Reprinted from the *WATESOL Newsletter* II. 3, March 1981.   *TN 8/81*

LOOKING AT ENGLISH: ESL TEXT-WORKBOOK FOR BEGINNERS

Fred Malkemes and Deborah Singer Pires; Prentice-Hall, New York, 1981.

Reviewed by Helen Truax
LaGuardia Community College

Looking At English is a text-workbook which provides teachers and beginning ESL/EFL students with materials for an intensive course in English. I've used it in several courses over the past two years and can vouch for its organized and comprehensive content, and clarity and ease of implementation. There are many other course texts on the market that possess the same qualities. What's distinctive about Malkemes' and Pires' work is that these qualities are not imposed. Rather, they emerge from a content which reflects extensive and experienced knowledge of teaching and the language learning process. The cumulative result is that teachers as well as students benefit from involvement with the text.

Based on my own observations of teachers, I've noted that two problems are recurrent. 1) The oral mode is the most prevalent medium of communication, often to the exclusion of other mediums. And 2), while classes are teacher controlled, they are teacher dominated.

Malkemes and Pires provide teachers with materials that present each item through a variety of mediums. If a student can't grasp the item through the aural mode, then *Looking At English* has materials that the teacher can use to re-present the item graphically thus giving the student another chance to succeed. This redundancy is evidenced in visuals throughout the text, reiterating John Carroll's conclusions on studies of learning—'Materials presented visually facilitate acquisition and retention.' In sum, the presentation of language, in *Looking At English*, from a variety of perspectives nurtures security in the language learner because it gives him many opportunities to learn. It nurtures security in the teacher because it provides him with many opportunities to teach to individual needs.

X-word grammar, too, communicates security to the language learner and teacher. It is part of a larger grammatical description called Sector Analysis, developed by Robert Allen at Teachers College, Columbia University. Malkemes and Pires incorporate X-word grammar in their text thus providing students and teachers with a simple and logical system for perceiving and manipulating the language. It's amazing how the problems of question formation are minimized when students can locate the X-word and know to signal the question by shifting it to the beginning of the sentence.

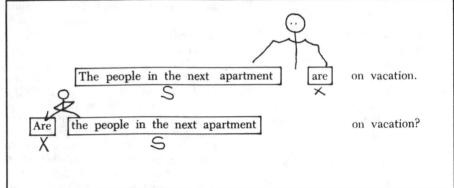

The rule is tangible and no longer abstract. And it works!

One reason it works in *Looking At English* is that Malkemes and Pires are careful at this beginning level to make the distinction between spoken English and written English. Besides a number of pronunciation activities that deal with reductions, the authors contrast this well in the dictation format suggested.

"My brother's going to watch T.V."

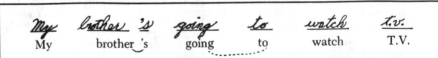

Students cover the answer and hear '*My brother's "gonna" watch T.V.*' then they fill in the blank. When they uncover the answer they can immediately see the relationship between what they heard and what is written.

Security is provided by giving students and teachers an opportunity to learn and teach through a variety of mediums. It is also achieved by engaging students in activities that move from a controlled—less demanding task to a less controlled—more demanding one. For example, it is easier to read aloud, with little room for error, '*Pedro is from Venezuela.*' than it is to read aloud '*Pedro _____ from Venezuela.*' The task becomes more difficult if a student is asked to present the same information orally with no visual support. The advantage to this variety of activities is that, given the controls, the dynamics of the classroom can also vary from teacher-centered to include pair practice and group work. One reason teachers persist in dominating the class is that they aren't aware that they can control the activities as Malkemes and Pires do through the materials. *Looking At English* demonstrates that a teacher-controlled class can be a student dominated one, too.

The materials in the text are clear and tightly organized so that students can easily advance as can the teacher advance in his understanding of teaching. Because the text-workbook provides the teacher with handouts, visual aids, and assignments, many of which the students can correct themselves with the appendix, the teacher has time to explore other areas of language teaching and design materials to supplement the course. I think a teacher will want to do this as *Looking At English* does not ostensibly address the functions of the content presented nor does it ostensibly incorporate language about students' own experience. Motivation to learn can be enhanced if students perceive that language can do something (ex. '*I can't see you tonight because I'm going to the movies with my mother.*') and if students are invested in what is being learned. Though Malkemes and Pires don't ignore function and students' life experiences, these aren't their primary focus here and therefore need to be brought in. Given the demonstration in teaching and language learning that Malkemes and Pires have provided, teachers should be able to do this confidently and effectively.   □

TN 10/81

SEND ME A LETTER! A BASIC GUIDE TO LETTER WRITING

(Sol Gonshack and Joanna McKenzie: Prentice-Hall, Inc., 1982, 245 pages.)

Reviewed by
Susan G. McAlister
University of Houston
Language & Culture Center

Send Me a Letter is a text intended for high intermediate and advanced students of ESL as well as for native speakers. The stated aims are to help students increase their knowledge of colloquial, informal, and idiomatic English and to teach the essentials of letter writing for everyday situations.

The book is divided into three parts—"An Overview of Letters," "Business Letters," and "Writing Notes"; the second part is further subdivided into sections on various types of (personal) business letters—letters pertaining to complaints, information, goods and services, reservations, jobs, and finances. Eight dialogues, which take place in a hypothetical letter-writing class, serve to introduce the various types of letters and to link the sections of the book. Each dialogue includes a model letter and is followed by questions for discussion. While the information contained in the dialogues is generally well thought out and complete, the dialogues themselves are often quite contrived and may detract from rather than aid the learning process. This information might be more effectively presented through ordinary prose passages or included in the suggestions to the teacher at the front of the book.

What follows each dialogue is one of the stronger aspects of the book—a series of short, original stories, each presenting a situation in which the need to write a letter might occur. For example, the section on complaint letters includes "The Case of the Faulty Refrigerator," "The Case of the Big Squeak," "The Case of the Unfinished Swimming Pool," and so on. The stories, twenty-eight in all, are generally entertaining and present a great deal of current vocabulary as well as cultural information. The accompanying illustrations are also amusing and could by themselves provoke some good class discussion. New words and expressions are glossed in the margins. Unfortunately, there is no comprehensive glossary at the end of the book—a useful addition should the book be revised. Also, many of the definitions given would not, I feel, elucidate the meaning for an ESL student. For example, *unconditionally guaranteed* is defined as "absolutely pledged to meet stated specifications" (p. 15)!

Four types of exercises follow each story—vocabulary, analysis, extension, and writing. The vocabulary reinforcement exercises vary among scrambled words and matching, fill in the blank, and multiple choice. A possible improvement here might be to increase the number of items in each exercise as, in most cases, only five or six out of twenty or more words and expressions glossed are practiced. In the analysis exercises, students working in pairs read a statement which expresses a notion ("Bea was delighted . . ." p. 202) and match it with a statement from the story ("How wonderful!" p. 100). The authors also suggest that the students role play the statements and discuss other vocabulary and expressions related to the notion. The idea is an interesting one, and while the exercise format is

not at all varied from one section to the next, it should provide a vehicle by which students can focus on the precise meanings of words and expressions and increase their command of colloquial English. The extension assignments include role plays based on the stories and some shorter writing activities (writing summaries, answering questions, making lists). These exercises are varied and appear quite usable and useful. The final part of each story section includes a model letter followed by a writing assignment—always a letter, often a response to the model. The assignments are clear and complete and should give ESL students adequate guidance and practice in letter writing to cope with living in our society.

My main criticisms of *Send Me a Letter* include the occasional peculiarities in word choice (The word *spouse* is used to the total exclusion of "husband" or "wife." And, for the first time, I encountered the expression "weather caster"), and the frequent artificiality of language—a strange blend of formal and informal—in dialogues purported to represent colloquial, informal English. (Perhaps the pomposity and sarcasm of Ms. Carpenter, the teacher of the hypothetical class, is intended as humorous; if so, it might be mentioned in the teacher's guide.) Also, while the stories are amusing, some are literally and unnaturally *packed* with idioms, and some events try the imagination to say the least. In "The Case of the Wrong Car," a character discovers that his new car is red, and not white, *after* driving it home! Finally, the brevity of the section on social letters makes me wonder why it was included at all. Perhaps it could be expanded or combined with the section on writing notes at the end of the book.

Although I doubt native speakers (as the authors claim) would be willing to wade through the more than two hundred pages of stories, vocabulary reinforcement exercises, etc., to get to the model letters, upper intermediate and advanced ESL students living in the United States should find this a useful book. *Send Me a Letter* should be appropriate not only for instructors teaching classes in letter writing and survival skills but also for those teaching general adult ESL classes who are looking for a change of pace from the standard ESL text.

TN 6/82

THE PROCESS OF COMPOSITION

by Joy M. Reid. 1982. Prentice-Hall, Inc., Englewood Cliffs, NJ 07632 (xii + 206 pp., $10.95).

Reviewed by Maryann O'Brien
University of Houston

The key concept of this advanced ESL writing text is found in the title: it is a *process* by which foreign students can learn to produce the kinds of writing they will need in their university work.

Because of her experience in both foreign and native-speaker writing programs, Ms. Reid has been able to write a text that helps students make the transition from the ESL writing class to the composition courses required by most American universities. Another important consideration of the book is that it is as useful for prospective graduate students as it is for undergraduates.

The first few chapters review basic paragraph structure, techniques of support, and the methods of development common to university writing. The middle section deals with the expository and argumentative essay, and the final section, particularly useful for students in technology and the sciences, covers advanced library research, which includes abstracting and indexing journals, review periodicals, and bibliographies. There is also valuable material on how to write summaries, abstracts, and resumes, and a chapter of grammatical explanations and

exercises dealing with recurring problems in student prose. Samples of foreign student writing ranging in topics from botulism to Turkish coffee houses, are included for their weaknesses as well as for their strengths. One section, essential for graduate students, is an exercise on the format of American masters' theses.

The greatest strength of the text is that it does prepare students for university writing. Straightforward linear development and adequate support of the topic are the goals. Rhetorical terminology is explained and used throughout. This is not a book from which the inexperienced teacher can easily select exercises and writing assignments, but after a semester's thorough use, students will write acceptable, well-organized university prose.

I have used this book in manuscript for four semesters and many students have come back to tell me how well-prepared they were—the undergraduates for their freshman composition courses, and the graduates for their thesis writing. There can be no higher praise for a text than that which comes from students who have actually benefited from it.

Section 14. Classroom Materials and Techniques

While there are, in fact, many different kinds of ESL materials, tests and realia described in other articles and reviews in this volume, they are, in large part, tied to the topics of their respective sections. The following articles and reviews are of sufficient interest in and of themselves to be placed in this section.

This section begins with the article by Bryce Van Syoc, "Some Suggested Changes for the Order of Presenting Materials in ESL Textbooks" (4/78), in which he takes a look at ESL texts and the organization or sequencing of materials, which has changed little since *English for Today*, and offers some alternatives to the presentation of some of the elements in the general textbook syllabus.

Alice Pack and Deborah Dillon discuss "Peer Tutoring Activities for the ESL Classroom" (6/80), suggesting numerous ideas for group work, particularly the use of dyads. In "The Role Play Comes Alive Through a Technological Twist," Jeffra Flaitz (12/83) presents a classroom technique which combines the role playing ideas of Christina Paulston, the "skits" of Mary Hines and the tape recorder of counseling-learning. Helen Fragiadakis, in an *It Works* column "A Notional Approach to *Frankenstein*" (4/81), discusses the use of plays in the ESL classroom. In "A New Look at Pictures" (4/77), John Boyd and Mary Ann Boyd present a number of innovative ways to use this standard teacher resource that are communicative and natural. The Larry Cisar article, "Hot Rods" (11/78), and the Karen Czarnecki article, "Cattle Crossing" (6/76), have titles that are not self-explanatory. Cisar is discussing cuisinaire rods which are part of Silent Way materials, while Czarnecki looks at the need to teach the meaning and use of street and highway signs to limited English speakers. Jerry Steinberg writes about "Games ESL People Play" (8/81) in their ESL classrooms to promote communicative competence.

The next two articles deal with a part of the audio-lingual baby presumed to have been thrown out with the bath water. Wayne Dickerson discusses how teachers can "Improve Production of Teacher Made Tapes" (4/76). He provides the reader with a simple, easy to follow set of steps to make classroom or laboratory materials sound better. Gerry Strei writes about "Reviving the Language Lab" (4/77). His article is a call for using rather than abandoning those laboratories that still exist, often unused or used for other purposes. (Computer assisted instruction proponents might take a healthy look at the lessons to be drawn from the language laboratory bandwagon of the 1960's and the problems which accrued when over-zealous believers filled those rooms with tape recording machines only to be faced with a lack of good material to accompany them.)

David Wyatt, in "Computer Assisted Instruction Comes of Age" (6/83) from the *On Line* column, presents a clear and critical look at what we can expect, now and in the future, from computer assisted instruction. The last article

in this section is a look at what the experts suggest is a basic or "Bare-Bones" teaching library. Given the number of texts published in ESL since this 1979 article was first published, it is perhaps time to consider updating it. Nevertheless, the remarks of the authors are still timely and useful.

This section ends with a set of reviews on a variety of topics ranging from *Developing Communicative Competence Through Interaction Activities in ESL* by Judith Kettering and *Roleplays in ESL* by Paulston, Brunetti, Britten and Hoover, reviewed by Mary E. Hines (2/77) to *Skits in ESL* by Mary Hines (6/80), *English in Three Acts* by Richard Via and *Six Stories for Acting* by George McCallum, reviewed in 9/77 by Paul Roberts, Ruth Shernoff and Donald L. F. Nilson. *The Minds Eye* by Alan Maley, Alan Duff and Francoise Grellet is reviewed by Ann Raimes (8/81) and two songbooks, *If You Feel Like Singing* by Alice Osman and Jean McConochie, reviewed by Robert King, and *English: Sing It* by Millie Greenough, reviewed by Alice Osman, present musical ways to present language. *Visual Aids for the Classroom* by Susan Holden (6/80), which supplements John Boyd and Mary Ann Boyd's article above, is reviewed by Joyce Zuck, and two classic volumes in ESL teaching, *Caring and Sharing* by Gertrude Moskowitz, reviewed by Audrey Reynolds (10/79), and *What To Do Until the Books Arrive . . . and After*, by Jean Maculatis and Mona Scheraga, conclude this section.

A number of other interesting articles which describe or develop special ESL materials have appeared in past *TNs*. Among them are: "Everyday, Everywhere Materials for Your Classroom" by Sadae Iwataki (9/78); Michael Dobbyn's "English Language Newspapers Overseas: Materials for Extensive Reading" (11/78) and George Raney's "Using the *National Observer* in the ESOL Classroom" (4/76); "For Your International Smorgasbord: Or Culture and Communication Through Cooking" by Alice Osman (4/76); "Opening the Language Hub" by Courtney Chadwell (4/76) and "Changing Speech to Writing in the Language Lab" by Thelmsa Borodkin (8/80). Lee Jaffe wrote "Using Music to Teach English" (11-12/76), which was accompanied by a chart by Alice Osman and Laurie Wellman from their "Music and ESL Workshop" (11-12/76), showing various popular songs and the structures which could be taught by using them. "Computers and TESOL: Three Alternatives" by Richard Schreck (4/79) appeared long before the *On Line* column, which Schreck edits, appeared in the *TN*. Other computer assisted instruction articles to look up are "Adding Sight and Sound to CAI: Interactive Video" by Kearney Reitman (12/81); "The Computer as a Communicative Environment" by Richard Schreck and John Higgens (12/83); and any of the articles which appear in the *On Line* column.

SOME SUGGESTED CHANGES FOR THE ORDER OF PRESENTING MATERIALS IN ESL TEXTBOOKS

By Bryce Van Syoc
Southern Illinois University

In recent years those of us in the business of second language teaching have been bombarded with new theories in our field and presented with updated and refined statements of older theories. For example, there are the different statements relative to the cognitive learning theory as opposed to the behavioral learning theory, which was so popular not too long ago. We have been confronted with statements that language competence and language performance are paired, but that they are quite different in nature. We have been advised that both language competence and language performance can be better achieved through student-centered, individualized instructions. It has been helpful to be reminded by new theorists that, although language is rule based and rule governed, it must be considered chiefly as a creative process.

The effect of the newer statements regarding theories of language and of language acquisition has, in the main, been healthy. They have forced us to again rethink our instructional techniques to see if there is some way these newer concepts can help us improve our teaching. However, one has only to teach English composition to a class of foreign students to perceive that many, if not most, of them have failed to acquire adequate language skills on either the competence or the performance level. Even students who have made good scores on the various English proficiency examinations required for the issuing of student visas or for university admission have often failed to master, on the performance level, such basic features of English as the singular-plural number system. Others have not mastered, either at the competence or performance level, the English modal system or the English verb auxiliaries. Many are poor at pronouncing important syntactic morphemes. A large percentage of them can read English with good comprehension and moderate speed only with great difficulty. In many cases the writing level of these same students parallels the low level of performance in the other areas just described.

There could be, of course, myriad causes for such low levels of performance still prevailing after several decades of stating and refining our various linguistic theories and of trying hard to improve classroom techniques. It seems to the writer of this paper that such a deplorable state of affairs may result in part from the poor ordering of materials in the textbooks which we are using for ESL today, textbooks which frequently do not reflect adequately what is known about the nature of language and of language acquisition.

In examining the rather large number of beginning and advanced ESL textbooks which have come to my attention during the past ten years or so, there appears to me to be a surprising lack of originality in the ordering of the instructional materials.

The purpose of this paper is to suggest some changes in ordering of materials which would, I believe, enhance the possibilities of taking advantage of cognitive learning theories and recent linguistic theories.

The first suggestion in syntax ordering would be the use of modal words such as "can" or "must" in the beginning sentence patterns, these modal words to be followed, of course, by the non-finite or simple form of a verb which the text writer feels would be useful for the students to learn. So, rather than start with a sentence pattern such as "This is a desk" or "This is a pencil" the following frame could well be used:

I can see

    hear

    talk

    walk

Or, using a transitive situation, the sentence could be, "Bill will meet Mary," etc.

Starting instruction with modals in the verb phrase may seem strange but it has many advantages. One of these is that most languages have within their verb phrase system something akin to the modals of English; that is, a modal-like word, possibly even a verb, which carries the semantic notions found in English modals, followed by a verb in either its root form or its infinitive form. In English texts, by introducing verbs in connection with modals, the root form of the verb can be used, thus reducing the number of problems confronting the learner at one time and making it easier for him to begin to communicate quickly in the target language on a creative rather than a mimic-and-memorize basis.

Another advantage of starting with modals followed by the simple form of the verb is that it should help to lessen the widespread and perennial use of the "to" infinitive in such sentences as "I can to swim." and "I must to read a book."

This common mistake suggests that students should not be introduced to the "to" infinitive forms until after they have mastered the use of the simple forms of verbs following a modal. By introducing new verbs in their simple form rather than in their "to" form, or one of the inflected forms, it is easier to teach questions, the imperative mood, and what is left of the subjunctive mood. By starting in this way, the introduction of "to" infinitives can be delayed and introduced in a more appropriate place with the nominals and the adjectivals.

By the imaginative use of dramatization and visual materials, for example illustrations within the text, or a separate set of charts, a textbook writer can lead students to produce creatively action type sentences from the start, thus giving more variety and interest to the lesson. The possibilities are almost endless but the following are examples:

You may open your book.

    read your letter.

    buy one pencil.

    go to the door.

Another advantage of starting with modals is that the subjects and objects of the sentences can be either singular or plural without demanding a change in the verb phrase. Also, the subject can be in first, second, or third person without requiring a change in the verb construction as is the case in starting with a finite form of a verb. Of course, students of English must eventually learn all about the required agreement between the subject of a sentence and finite verb forms, but by starting with modals, problems of agreement which seem difficult for students of English as a second language to master, can be delayed until they can be more conveniently handled, bearing always in mind that the student must develop in a cognitive way both competence and performance in the target language.

The use of modals makes a convenient means of introducing variety in sentence patterns. It is easy to introduce compound sentences and certain types of complex ones, being able to concentrate on the process of compounding and embedding rather than having also to watch for subject-verb agreement, as when the lessons start with other types of verb phrases. Negation can be taught easily with modals, and once that is mastered tag sentences and questions are easily managed by students. This procedure should help to avoid such sentences as "You can go downtown today, isn't it?" which one hears with frequency in so many parts of the world where English is the second language. Tag sentences are not difficult with modals. The learning load is much lighter in a sentence like "Bill will eat fish, but the girls won't" than it is in the sentence, "Bill is tall, but the girls aren't."

One seeming disadvantage in starting instruction with modals is that verb tense and person of nouns must be delayed until finite verbs are introduced. But this is not really a disadvantage, in my opinion. On the contrary, it can be advantageous and even more efficient, in terms of cognitive learning, to delay these two grammatical categories a little. Both tense and person are relatively easy to learn in English if they are taught one by one, and not all together, as is the case when a text starts with finite verbs.

As to a second change in ordering of syntax, it would seem wise, soon after modals have been presented, for the textbook writer to begin a systematic and extended, but vigorous, attack on the complicated set and subsets of noun determiners used in English. As a rule, authors who start with finite verbs also tend to introduce the article determiners before the other types. Many languages have articles in noun phrase construction, of course, but certainly not all do, and those that have them often use them differently from the way English does. On the other hand, the use of numbers as noun determiners is a very common language phenomenon, as is the use of possessive determiners. It would seem wise then to consider introducing the set of determiners with sentences such as "Bill must read two books," or "He must finish his lesson." This could easily be followed by a more generalized possessive determiner as in "Sue's brother will ride Bill's bicycle." After the definite article has been introduced, many common noun possessives would be available for use as noun determiners.

The determiner system of English is so involved, including as it does the predeterminers and the post determiners with all their ramifications, that instruction dealing with it will probably be stretched out through at least the upper intermediate level of instruction. But starting with numbers, possessives, and zero determiners rather than with articles makes considerable sense. If by changing the order of introducing determiners we can prevent students from coming out with "I must buy one book," when they mean "I must buy a book," the change in order would have been worth-

while. It might also be of use to teach "some" as the plural of "a" rather than along with the other indefinite determiners, as is usually done. It might help in resolving the problem of the difference between "a" and "one" in English. Thus, the instruction on this point could begin with sentences of this type:

The girls might need some books.
Sue should have a notebook that she
   can carry.
I will buy the book that my friends
   must read.

A third change of order in syntax presentation which might be helpful is related to the teaching of the direction of modification. English, like most other languages of the world, has both progressive and regressive modification. It is true that English has a much more full-blown pre-nominal system of modification than some languages, but it also has a plentiful number of types of post-nominal modifiers as well. My suggestion would be to introduce the post-nominal modifiers first, then the single adjectives and other single-word modifiers which in general occur before nominals in English sentences. For example, locative prepositional phrases, relative clauses, and even complex participial constructions, and infinitive constructions tend to present few problems to ESL students, occurring as they do in a manner quite similar to many other languages. If single-word pre-nominal modifiers of noun phrases were delayed awhile, perhaps they would present fewer problems.

Another change of syntax ordering should prove helpful in teaching those prepositions or particles which have a penchant for attaching themselves semantically to the verbs preceding them, such as "turn in," "try on," "look over," "run down," "talk to," "dream of," etc. Since one researcher discovered fifteen hundred of these semantic units in modern English, it would seem that students of ESL ought to master a sizable number of them. Presently textbook writers tend to introduce them at the intermediate level, and as a verb plus a preposition or adverb which by some rather mystical process become united. It would seem wiser to start the use of these combinations in the very early lessons, not getting involved with the analysis of the makeup of the combinations, as interesting as that may be at the competence level of learning.

If modals are used in the first part of a beginning text, it would not be a difficult problem to start teaching these semantic units almost from the very first, using such sentences as "I will turn in my notes," "We must turn on the lights," and "Bill should look over his lesson again." Even more complicated units,

such as "put up with," or "get along with" could be introduced relatively early rather than delaying them for a more analytical treatment later.

Prepositions in general do not seem easy for foreign students to master, especially in their distribution with certain case uses of nouns in English. At present the instructional procedures used in textbooks, regardless of what order is used, do not lead to mastery of them for good performance in the use of English. Perhaps some day the theories of case grammar will make clear what the ordering of prepositions used to introduce noun constructions should be. There must be a better way to teach prepositions, and perhaps a change in the order of presentation is the answer.

Making one change as radical as starting a text with sentences using modals implies delaying the presentation of many other items. Several have been mentioned, such as the delay of tense, number, and person. Others which might be profitably delayed are the use of the auxiliaries: be, have, and do. This would also force the delay of progressive and perfect forms and all questions which are not formed with a modal.

Teaching questions first with modals is especially attractive as in this way the students learn in a very simple form the underlying ingredient of English questions—the reversal in position of the subject and the first word of the verb phrase. The large number of questions starting with a form of "do" stem from an exception to the general rule for questions, and certainly should be delayed until the students have mastered the basic rules for creating questions.

Also to support the syntax, it might be well to teach important final consonants and clusters before some of the initial consonants are taught. For example, it might be much more productive for the student to learn to say "owns" before he learns to say its homophonous mirror, "snow"; or to say "treats" before he is taught to say "street".

Some text writers ignore stress and intonation patterns almost completely until the end of the elementary lessons, if they treat them at all. A few books, however, encourage students to learn the intonation contours of sentences, and the stress patterns of polysyllabic words right from the start, and it would seem well for the sake of both receptive and productive performance to do more of this.

It should be stressed that the innovations recommended in this paper are not just for the mere sake of change, or as an effort to break loose from tradition. Rather, they are made with the hope of improving students' performance in the English language.   4/78

PEER-TUTORING ACTIVITIES FOR THE ESL CLASSROOM

By Alice C. Pack and Deborah Dillon
Brigham Young University, Hawaii Campus

Certain frustrations are shared by nearly all classroom teachers as they try to meet the individual needs of their students. In addition to unwieldy class size, the difficulties posed by student inattention, dissimilar needs and capacities, and lack of motivation constitute all-too-familiar obstacles to effective learning. Peer-tutoring techniques were developed in response to these concerns and, we believe, can be of great help in dealing with them. Student response to a variety of peer-tutoring activities has been encouraging in terms of both sustained interest and improved performance. In this article we will explain why these techniques work and present examples of peer-tutoring activities we have used.

Peer tutoring typically involves a pair of students (ideally of different language backgrounds) who alternately assume the roles of tutor and learner. Interaction is more or less structured according to student needs and the nature of the materials being used. Paired students work at their own speed and rely on one another for constant feedback. Peer tutoring thereby implies a new role for the classroom teacher—one in which the principal function is that of a consultant, and in which contact with students is brief, but frequent and individual.

The effectiveness of peer tutoring depends on numerous factors. The constant involvement of all the students in the class requires that they be alert and thinking at all times. The fact that students are paired gives each more personal attention and feedback than a single teacher could ever provide. Moreover, it permits a teacher to match students of similar levels and complementary capabilities. In this way, the variety of strengths and weaknesses which students bring with them to a class can facilitate rather than impede learning. As students realize that they know things which can be of use to others, a close camaraderie develops among members of the class. An increased sense of common purpose and the habit of responsible participation in the learning process are developed at the same time. This, in turn, encourages individual initiative and reduces the danger of unproductive dependence on the teacher.

Two sets of materials to be used specifically for peer tutoring have been developed at the Hawaii campus of Brigham Young University. We rely heavily on both in our English Language Institute program. One is a set of three books (*Dyads: Prepositions, Dyads: Pronouns and Determiners* and *Dyads: Verb Choices and Verb Forms*) written by Alice C. Pack (Newbury House, 1977). The other is a set of pronunciation cards by Lynn E. Henrichsen (to be published). Each of these sets of materials is discussed below.

DYADS

An analysis of errors drawn from ESL students' compositions led to the identification of three broad types of grammatical difficulty. Each of these categories is treated in a separate volume of the Dyad series, whose purpose is to help students internalize grammatical structures through repeated exposure to sentences requiring clozure.

Texts have two components—one without answers ("student" copy) and one with answers ("tutor" copy)—and students work in pairs. The steps consist of a series of unconnected sentences with fifteen clozure blanks in each section. For each blank, students select one from a group of two to six potentially confusing items. (Review sections have unlimited choices.) The "student" (or respondent) reads each sentence aloud, indicating clozure by filling the blank or blanks with the correct word or words indicated by the context of the sentence. The "tutor," whose book has the correct clozure items listed, reinforces the respondent's clozure selection when the sentence is read by saying "mmhmm" with rising intonation if the item is correct, and "mm-mm" with falling intonation if the item is incorrect. If the clozure item is incorrect, the respondent again reads the sentence with another selected clozure item. Students alternate as respondent and tutor in each dyad after a respondent has read all of the sentences in one section.

Because the answers present little or no ambiguity and the program is highly structured, the *Dyads* work equally well in classrooms and in situations where a teacher is not present, such as in a language lab. These texts are very effective for teaching discrete grammar points and are particularly well suited to speaking and writing classes. Teachers can also use the dyad model in constructing additional exercises to meet the specific needs of their own students.

PRONUNCIATION CARDS

The peer-tutoring approach was also used in an activity designed to allow students to focus on individual pronunciation problems which might not be shared by the rest of the class. The activity, in a game format, uses sets of cards, each set containing two yellow cards and twenty orange cards. Each set presents two members of a targeted minimal pair distinction (e.g. pill/bill) in a sentence content. On each of the cards is a pictorial representation of one of the minimal pair sentences. The sentences on the two yellow cards differ only in the substitution of one minimal pair member for the other.

Students work in pairs (of different language backgrounds whenever possible) and proceed as outlined below: (S = speaker, L = listener)

preparation:

—students sit facing one another
—S holds shuffled orange cards so S can see them but L cannot
—L puts yellow cards on table so both S and L can see them

method:

—S reads sentence which corresponds to picture on top orange card
—L points to yellow card which illustrates the sentence he heard
—if L points to correct card S gives L the top orange card
—if L points to incorrect card, S puts top orange card back into pile

Students continue until all cards are gone, change roles and record completed sets on a chart. While students are working the teacher circulates among them, monitoring progress and giving individual help.

In working with the pronunciation cards students often discover that they really do have problems with speaking and hearing specific sounds. They develop an awareness of the importance of individual sounds in effective communication. The game requires accuracy on the part of both listener and speaker, for a mistake made by either can halt progress. When two students cannot agree if a mistake was the listener's or the speaker's, the teacher is called upon to arbitrate. The use of these cards invariably generates a great deal of energy and enthusiasm as students help each other produce and recognize phonemic distinctions. Here, too, it is possible for teachers to make their own cards (with or without pictures) depending on their students' needs. For a more detailed discussion of the cards see Henrichsen (1978).

Materials specifically designed for peer tutoring have been discussed up to this point. The peer-tutoring approach can also be successfully applied to already familiar activities, e.g. checking reading exercises, editing homework, proofreading essays, and giving speeches. Examples of each follow.

CHECKING READING HOMEWORK

Since reading is a silent activity, it is sometimes difficult for a teacher to determine whether any thinking is actually taking place while a student is reading. For this reason, most textbooks designed to teach reading provide a set of comprehension questions to ensure that students have actually understood the passage. Unfortunately, however, such questions can often be answered correctly with little or no thought.

A peer-tutoring reading check helps students think while they read. After students have answered comprehension questions they gather in groups of two or three and compare their responses. When answers to any given question differ, each student must defend his own choice. As the students work, the teacher circulates among them, helping them find ways to support their arguments.

The reading check stimulates mental activity during and after reading. Students often give more careful thought to answers which they know they must later defend. As they learn to ask and answer their own questions while reading, they become more critical readers.

EDITING HOMEWORK

The moment a student hands in a homework assignment, motivation is at its peak. Having committed himself to certain answers, he is eager to find out if they are correct. In the traditional classroom situation, the teacher collects homework, checks it and returns it the following day, at best. By then, however, the student is concentrating on something else, so he barely glances at the corrections and he then proceeds to make the same errors on the next similar assignment. A very precious moment has been wasted and, as a result, the student continues to make the same errors and the teacher continues to correct them.

A peer-tutoring homework check is very simple. The procedures are similar to those in a reading check. In groups of two or three, students compare answers to written homework assignments and defend their own when differences are found. Again, the teacher circulates among the students, answering specific questions and mediating unresolved disputes.

The homework check takes advantage of the fact that a student's interest in an assignment is greatest at the time he hands it in to be corrected. It is at that point that he wants most to know whether or not his answers are correct. Students find that a few minutes' consultation with a peer provides them with the opportunity to check areas about which they are uncertain. Editing homework helps students and teacher break the vicious circle of repeated errors and corrections.

PROOFREADING ESSAYS

Most native speakers proofread their grammar as they write, and most good writers proofread a series of drafts before they are satisfied with the finished product. ESL teachers, however, often encourage proofreading only by reminding students to write a rough draft and then correct mistakes. Yet error correction in a second language can be a monumental task. In teaching proofreading we have learned two very important things from our students: 1) it is extremely difficult for them to find their own errors and 2) they cannot check everything at once. Therefore, until students have learned some techniques of proofreading, it does little good to ask them to correct their errors.

The first time students proofread they should look for only one or two types of errors. As they gain experience, knowledge and confidence, they can handle many more. When peer tutoring is used to help teach proofreading in one of our intermediate level classes (where verbs, prepositions, and word forms have already been studied) the following procedure is used:

1) One student reads his paragraph slowly to his partner.
2) Both students look for mistakes in spelling and punctuation.
3) Either student stops reading any time he thinks he spots an error. The error is discussed, a mutual decision is reached (perhaps to save the question for the teacher) and the students continue reading.
4) Students repeat steps 1-3 looking for verb errors (S-V agreement, verb time agreement, forms).
5) Students repeat steps 1-3 looking at prepositions.
6) Students repeat steps 1-3 looking at word forms.

7) Students repeat steps 1-3 looking at anything else that does not look or sound correct.

We find that teaching students to recognize and correct the errors in their own and their classmates' essays encourages them to avoid such mistakes in all their writing.

GIVING SPEECHES

Assigning students to give speeches in front of a class is a familiar activity in speaking classes. While a student nervously stumbles through his speech, his classmates often have their minds elsewhere. They are worrying about their own speeches or perhaps wondering what they will have for lunch. The teacher gives the student a grade and the student returns to his seat. Little, if any, communication has taken place between the speaker and his audience.

A peer-tutoring approach to such speeches provides for constant interaction between speaker and audience. The promise of a quiz on the following day gives the audience an immediate reason for being attentive. When they do not understand something the speaker has said, they are encouraged to interrupt and ask for repetition or clarification.

This more informal approach to giving speeches in the classroom benefits the speaker in that continual feedback from his fellow students permits him to know exactly when he is and when he is not communicating. Thus, he can monitor his own performance and regulate his behavior accordingly. This approach is equally valuable to students in the audience, who soon learn that listening is not a passive activity. By taking notes they learn to extract and organize important information in a speech, and at the same time overcome their reluctance to ask questions the answers to which are necessary to their understanding. Both speakers and audience come to know the considerable confusion that can be caused by inaccurate pronunciation or inappropriate grammatical construction. Indeed, students seem more apt to learn from one another than from a teacher the crucial value of making themselves intelligible.

The possibilities for using peer tutoring are endless and we have found it to be adaptable to nearly any class setting, and subject and any set of materials. There is ample evidence in journals and other publications that many other teachers are discovering and enjoying the many benefits of peer-tutoring procedures in teaching reading (Dykstra 1970; Ford 1977), writing (Kohn and Vajda 1975; Witbeck 1976) and in speaking and listening activities such as map-reading (Winn-Bell Olsen 1977) and strip stories (Gibson 1975;

Rutherford 1975).

In using peer-tutoring activities teachers should be aware that it, like any other teaching method, is not fail-safe. It cannot be used to replace the teacher in a classroom. Except in the *Dyads*, the teacher plays an important, irreplaceable role in the learning process. Also, peer tutoring can fail if it is overused—variety in the classroom is essential and students will tire of a strict diet of peer tutoring as surely as they will of anything else. Peer tutoring will also fail if activities are loosely structured before students are familiar with the procedures.

The classroom situation imposes certain limitations on how learning can take place. Peer tutoring is, of course, not a panacea, but we have found that its techniques provide useful alternatives in tackling many of the problems caused by these limitations. By actively involving students in the learning process, peer tutoring can be of tremendous value to the classroom teacher.

REFERENCES

Dykstra, Gerald and Shiho S. Nunes. 1970. The language skills program of the English project. *Educational Perspectives* 9: 283-289.
Ford, James E. 1977. Improving reading comprehension through peer persuasion and competition. *TESL Reporter* 11, 1:3.
Gibson, Robert E. 1975. The strip story: a catalyst for communication. *TESOL Quarterly* 9, 2: 149-154.
Henrichsen, Lynn E. 1978. Peer-tutoring pronunciation contrasts. *English Teaching Forum*. April 1978: 18-22.
Kohn, James J. and Peter G. Vajda. 1975. Peer-mediated instruction and small-group interaction in the ESL classroom. *TESOL Quarterly* 9, 4: 379-390.
Pack, Alice C. 1977. *Dyads Learning Program: Prepositions/Pronouns and Determiners/Verb Choices and Verb Forms* (three books). Rowley, Massachusetts: Newbury House Publishers, Inc.
Rutherford, William E. 1975. *Modern English*, vol. 1 teacher's guide. San Francisco: Harcourt Brace Jovanovich, Inc.
Winn-Bell Olsen, Judy E. 1977. *Communication Starters and Other Activities for the ESL Classroom*. San Francisco: The Alemany Press.
Witbeck, Michael C. 1976. Peer correction procedures for intermediate and advanced ESL composition lessons. *TESOL Quarterly* 10, 3: 321-326.

TN 6/80

THE ROLE PLAY COMES ALIVE THROUGH A TECHNOLOGICAL TWIST

by Jeffra Flaitz
Intensive English Language Institute SUNY/Buffalo

Unless skillfully orchestrated, a role play in a foreign language classroom can produce what one might call, much to Stephen Krashen's distaste, "INcomprehensible OUTput." A role play's success depends perhaps as much upon how it is treated *upon completion* as upon the pre-exercise preparation, the trusting and warm ambiance of the classroom, and the relevance of the topic. Christina Bratt Paulston's cryptic advice to do a "friendly postmortem" on the role play actually provides little direction for how to handle potentially the most valuable learning/teaching aspect of the entire exercise.

Often, without much guidance on how to implement this relatively new technique, a teacher will allow the role play to proceed without interruption, all the while making mental or written notes of gross errors in the students' speech. It is at this point, I would argue, that role plays are irreversibly compromised for the primary reason that so much speech is lost and opportunities for language practice wasted. A fitting analogy may be that of a carefully aged bottle of champagne, the contents of which bubble over the lips so energetically when uncorked that precious little is left to savour. So, too, is the richness of a role play sacrificed to the element of time and fate. Often problems that arise during the performance fall into a hierarchy of gravity with lesser, (yet still problematic), language errors either given a minimum of attention or passed over altogether in the postperformance critique for the sake of time. Consequently, students may be left either to repeat their uncorrected mistakes, thus reinforcing them, or to fail to develop confidence in their linguistic abilities due to what they sense are unattended errors or deficiencies. Without a commitment to devote a good deal of time to the entire role play exercise as well as a means to recall word for word the script of the play, many of those involved in the language learning/teaching experience would agree that this kind of communicative exercise becomes a rather frustrating endeavor in

its disappointingly partial realization.

For those teachers who have a tape recorder at their disposal and who, once a week, are in a position to rearrange their syllabi to give one hour exclusively to the role play exercise, a promising solution is at hand. What follows is one teacher's suggestion for enhancing the value and possibilities of the role play technique. It owes its development to three points of personal interest and concern: 1) the genius of the general role play idea, 2) frustrations with role play exercises of the type described above, and 3) a brief exposure to the way in which the tape recorder is used in Curran's Counseling-Learning/Community Language Learning.

The advantage of using a tape recorder, of course, is that total recall of the script is a simple matter of buttonpushing. In the same sense, the use of a tape recorder in acting out and critiquing role plays provides a perfect and contemporaneous solution to the problem of wasting language practice opportunity. However, to minimize the mechanical effect projected by the use of the tape recorder in C-L/CLL, it should not be switched on and off as students struggle to communicate. As in the most exemplary role play as described by Paulston, the activity should be one of meaningful and uninhibited communication based on the prescribed topic, integrating the useful expressions and register specifications discussed beforehand. In effect, students should attempt to forget the presence of the recorder—it should not intrude—and proceed as they would for acting out role plays as before.

Normally at this point, the role play exercise suffers a decline of interest because the actual performance is over and the exercise seems essentially finished. Despite valiant attempts on the part of the teacher to engage the students in a communal critique, a combination of flagging interest, memory limitations, and even unwillingness to criticize the speech of peers can impede the development of the critique into the genuinely valuable learning

experience it can be. The use of a tape recorder, however, allows the class to relive the event by providing a word-for-word script of the performance. It encourages students to take responsibility for correcting the script by identifying their own speeches and making or soliciting alterations. As with the C-L/CLL technique, the tape recorder may be rewound to the beginning of the role play and then replayed, pausing after each statement or speech for the purpose of clarifying these. Problematic utterances can be written on the board or on a large piece of newsprint with students given the opportunity to offer corrections themselves and ask questions. Utterances of particular difficulty or interest should be transferred to the students' notebooks for use in whatever spin-off exercises the teacher devises, for personal reference, or for study purposes. This type of critique also allows the teacher the opportunity to point out register differences or social rules that may have been overlooked in preparation of the role play, appropriate idioms, and variations of a single speech. Later, students may be asked to write dialogs of their own incorporating the new idioms, expressions, or troublesome grammar points that surfaced during the exercise. The teacher, too, having an accurate record to work from, may create drills or other exercises drawn from the students' own authentic speech to reinforce learning.

This approach to the role play exercise obviously demands an extra time commitment as it requires a more thorough perusal of the performance than was heretofore possible. But even a seasoned ESL teacher with faculties sharpened by years of experience can benefit from the convenience and increased versatility made possible by technology. Two great inventions—the tape recorder and the role play—in the hands of a dedicated teacher can add a new dimension of precision, thoroughness, and relevance to language learning. 🌐

REFERENCE
Curran, Charles A. 1972. Counseling-Learning: A Whole-Person Model for Education. New York: Grune and Stratton.

TN 12/83

A NOTIONAL APPROACH TO *FRANKENSTEIN*

by Helen Fragiadakis
U.C. Berkeley Extension

When I first planned to use drama in an intermediate Listening/Speaking class, my major goals were to introduce new vocabulary and to provide a context in which pronunciation could be practiced. My focus, though, changed after I read the play "Frankenstein" from *Six Stories for Acting from American and English Literature* (ELS International Inc., Portland, Oregon, 1976).

As I read the play, I realized that it provided an excellent context for describing what was transpiring among the speakers in terms not only of information, but of emotions, disbelief, shock, impatience, support, etc. For example, "I have been able to . . . though I wish now that I never had" could be interpreted as 'regret'; "But that's impossible" could be interpreted as an expression of 'disbelief'; and "Victor, what is it? Have you seen a ghost?" could be interpreted as an expression of shock and concern. I then checked D. A. Wilkins' *Notional Syllabuses* and found such expressions as regret, disbelief, etc. listed as "categories of communicative function." According to Wilkins, "The categories are based on the meaning that arises from the fundamental distinction, very important for language teaching, between what we *do* through language and what we report by means of language" (p. 41). I thought that it would be exciting to change my original goals and use the play only as a tool which would provide examples of these categories, which I called "messages".

But then I was struck by one particular sentence of Wilkins' regarding the category of personal emotions: "It need perhaps only be pointed out that to know the word 'anger' is not to know how to express anger" (p. 54). At this point I had to define my objectives for myself, and decided that I wanted my students to learn to identify and label some of the categories of communicative function expressed in the play, and to learn and use various expressions (not necessarily from the play) that serve to communicate these messages. (Wilkins' categories of communicative function are listed and defined on pages 41-54.)

In class we first read the play and discussed the new vocabulary. As the students got the feeling of the drama, they were able to describe what was being expressed ("messages") in their own words. We then labeled the messages: impatience, regret, disbelief, anger, etc. Next, I gave the students two handouts, one which listed expressions from the play next to the messages. For example:

impatience: "Ssh! Let him continue."

support: "Please go on. . ."

guilt: "I've neglected everyone."

impatience: I can't wait!
Hurry up!
Put a move on!

The other handout listed common expressions (not necessarily from the play) used by native speakers to express the messages. For example:

shock, surprise, disbelief:

What's going on!
Oh my God!
I can't believe my eyes (ears)!
It can't be!

It was pointed out that these expressions often had overlapping messages. For instance, a person who is impatient might also be angry, depending on the situation.

The students were then given a list of situations for dialogues to be written in pairs, which were to include some of the new expressions from both handouts. For example: (1) A flying saucer has landed. Two people express *disbelief*. (2) A student has been rejected by a university. S/he expresses *disappointment* to a friend who expresses *concern* and *support*. (3) A child begs for a new toy and mother or father expresses *impatience*, and then gives in (*concedes*). (4) The driver of a car feels it is *urgent* to drive fast. The passenger expresses *caution*. This activity was extremely successful and enjoyable. Students commented on each other's effectiveness in communicating particular messages, and they had practice in listening to and using the new expressions in different contexts.

I did not expected or want the students to learn all the vocabulary from the three handouts. The students were always given choices when writing dialogues, and through their own use of some expressions and in listening to other dialogues, some of the expressions were retained, even if only for

recognition. I did, however, expect the students to learn the labels for "messages", and throughout the quarter, when any situation arose which expressed messages we studied, I asked the students, "What is this person expressing? How does he feel?"; in other words, this work can be easily and quite naturally reviewed. For example, every day at five minutes to twelve one of my students packed up his books and sat on the edge of his seat. He claimed that he was hungry. He became known as "impatient Eduardo".

A third handout contained a list of the most useful idioms used in the play. Students were asked to write dialogues using some of the idioms, again in pairs. After the dialogues were performed in class, the audience was asked to point out which messages had been expressed.

For the midterm I asked myself how I could possibly test the students on such work. It occurred to me that pictures would be very effective, and I cut out pictures from magazines. Next to each I wrote a few lines which expressed particular messages. For instance, next to a melancholy Woody Allen, I wrote: "Stop laughing at me! You're going to make me go mad (an expression from "Frankenstein"). Just leave me alone, O.K.!!!" The students were asked to write in the message expressed: anger. In another section of the exam I had cartoons which showed various situations where our messages were being expressed. In one, a man in a strange flying contraption tipped his hat to a man looking at him from a window in a skyscraper. The students were told: "The man in the window can't believe what he sees. Write a dialogue between the two men." Student responses were extremely humorous and contained expressions studied in class.

The play, "Frankenstein", played an essential, yet secondary role in our class activities. Any play (or even dialogue) can provide a context upon which a "notional approach" can be built. My original goals, to introduce new vocabulary and to practice pronunciation were still achieved in this way, while the students learned to define what had been actually communicated in the play. As an added and most important prize, they themselves experienced communicating some of these messages too.

TN 4/81

A NEW LOOK AT PICTURES

by John Boyd and Mary Ann Boyd
University High School, Illinois State University

Pictures have traditionally played an important role in the ESL classroom. Nevertheless there has always been a need to improve their effectiveness especially with intermediate and advanced students. Too often the communication generated through pictures at these levels turns out to be mostly teacher talk, or if the students do converse about the picture, the ensuing conversation takes place outside of a framework in which errors can be recognized and eliminated. Students thus tend to remain at their level of proficiency and the benefits of the picture as a teaching tool are seriously diminished.

After much trial and error, we believe that we have devised a very workable technique that combines and encourages communication based on pictures but retains elements of structured control through which language growth can occur. Behind our method lie two philosophical attitudes nurtured through our exposure to the Silent Way. Caleb Gattegno states that the teacher's role is to concentrate on the student while the student concentrates on the language. Secondly, he stresses that teacher silence can lead to student talk. With these philosophical underpinnings, we have developed a technique utilizing pictures to teach, practice and communicate using structures at varying levels of difficulty.

A part of each class session for us involves showing one or more pictures, carefully selected for their size, clarity and content relationship to the structures we wish to emphasize. For example, in a lesson contrasting verb tenses we might choose a picture of a young boy standing by a broken vase being confronted by his mother. If we are working with low level students we may stress only one feature of a picture (i.e., one action using the present continuous tense). With a more advanced group of students we may use the same picture to elicit more complex interchanges.

At whatever level, the teacher's role is that of a facilitator and a guide and is basically non-verbal from the outset of the exercise. The students' first task is to identify vocabulary from the picture. With one student at the blackboard as the recorder and with the teacher pointing to items in the picture, the students name vocabulary words as they are pointed out. The teacher is not here concerned with "teaching" vocabulary. We have discovered that there are very few words that are unknown to all the students in the class; therefore, the teacher allows the students to interact and elicit from each other the English vocabulary and spellings. After a few minutes, a fairly comprehensive list of words—identified under appropriate "noun", "verb", "adjective", etc. labels —has been written on the board.

Then the heart of the lesson begins— a lesson that will combine structured control with student freedom of choice in framing meaningful sentences based on the picture. The teacher, without having to speak, points to several words on the board and then asks a student to make a sentence incorporating these words. Since the essential words for a correct English sentence have been given, the student has a framework within which to make any number of statements. However, because verbs are written in their base form only and determiners, connectors and prepositions, etc. are not listed, the student must generate a sentence without all of the props that a more conventional drill exercise employs. It is precisely these small elements of structure that so often prove the stumbling blocks to communication in real-life situations. The same student who can say, "Only one of the three archers is aiming at the target." In a tightly controlled drill may have great difficulty in making such a statement outside of the controlled atmosphere of the classroom. Our technique, unlike the traditional exercise, in supplying the more exotic vocabulary items, frees the student to concentrate on that which has not been provided—i.e., essential elements of structure.

The teacher's guidance, although primarily unspoken, remains throughout the lesson, giving the students a sense of security and providing focus for the exercise. By choosing the words and therefore the complexity of the sentences to be spoken, the teacher can accommodate the varying levels of student language facility that always exist within a class. Even a beginning student within a more advanced class can feel included if a simple sentence pattern is presented to him. For example, the teacher points to the words *man, carry, suitcase,* and the student produces the sentence, "The man is carrying a suitcase." To another student he points to the words *man, carry, suitcase, hand,* and that student responds with "The man is carrying a suitcase in his left hand." Turning to a third student, the teacher then points to *man, shirt, blue, carry, suitcase, hand,* and the student replies, "The man in the blue shirt is carrying a suitcase in his left hand." And so on. A question mark can expand the scope significantly and students can question and answer each other with the teacher acting merely as guide and coordinator.

If practice in writing is desired, the teacher can give a dictation from the board, again pointing out to the students a sentence framework in which they must supply the details.

We feel that there are three important byproducts from this method. First, pictures are fun or interesting or both and the prospect of a different picture can make repeated practice on the same structure more enjoyable. Second, since the pictures and their corresponding vocabulary are at the front of the class, the students are looking up—at the board and at each other—there is no opportunity to bury one's nose in a book. At the same time, oral work is being reinforced by the written, often a needed reinforcement for students conditioned from earliest experiences to learn through written stimuli. Finally, the class is working as a group with lively interaction and an awareness of the direction of the lesson. Information and exchanges take place between students instead of between student and teacher. Errors can also handled through student-teacher interchange if the teacher is content to be silent and chooses to create an environment wherein the students feel that error detection and correction are their responsibilities.

The more we use this technique the more satisfied we are with its possibilities and rewards. We recommend it for use with students in any teaching situation as we have seen it work successfully with adults and with children, in small tutorial settings and with fairly large classes, and for a wide variety of instructional purposes at various levels of complexity. *TN 4/79*

"CATTLE CROSSING"

by Karen E. Czarnecki

Cultural orientation for the foreign student should always be of primary importance in the ESL classroom. Yet it is an area often neglected or shunted to the when-and-if-we-have-time portion of the instructor's teaching schedule. Frequently it is taught as an entity in itself, which is better than nothing, but with a little pre-planning, structural and/or lexical items and culture can be melded into a dynamic blend. A happy corollary of this is the fact that since the cultural items are of more immediacy to the student and interest in them is high, the perhaps less interesting accompanying grammatical structures have a better chance of being internalized: this may be due to their initial connection with the more engrossing cultural item.

The type and amount of traffic signs bear some scrutiny if we are to use them successfully in day-to-day class activities. There are two major classifications: the traditional signs which have printed instruction in English, and the new international signs which use pictures only. Of the former there are four sub-groups: road directionals ("One Way"), road instructionals ("Form Two Lanes"), parking instructionals ("2 Hour Metered Parking"), and traffic instructionals ("Cross on Walk Signal Only"). A typical person living in an urban area of the U.S. confronts on an average at least 30 signs daily, most of which are still non-pictorial. Some of these are confusing even to native Americans: for example, ("1 Hour Metered Parking/ 8 AM-4 PM/Tues., Wed., Fri., Sat./ 8 AM-4 PM & 6 PM-9 PM Mon. & Thurs."), and some marginally grammatical ("No Stopping or Standing"). Yet traffic signs are an indigenous part of the American scene and are expected to be adhered to no matter what. And we might reflect that it is preferable for the foreign student to learn at least some of the "no matter what's" in the security of his classroom rather than the hard way.

With the above in mind, let us look more closely at the utilization of traffic signs. Even a cursory glance at those most frequently encountered will reveal that many of them are in the present continuous tense. Possibilities either for initial presentation or reinforcement of grammatical understandings, in addition to survival skills, begin to emerge.

Hard-to-learn prepositions of place may take on a new interest in view of everyone's need to cope with "No Parking From Here to Corner." or similarly, "No Parking Between Signs." Building on this same item can lead to valuable speaking, listening, and coping skills as well. For example, the instructor can create and encourage the students to develop a conversation situation in which one student acts out the part of a policeman who has just found another student parked in a "No Parking" zone.

The enterprising instructor can utilize traffic sign diction for linguistic drill as well. For example, the final "ng" in "standing" and "stopping" is frequently mispronounced "k" by certain foreign language speakers and can be practiced for reduction of this error. Further, students can sharpen composition skills by helping each other write out the conversations they created around a specific traffic situation as suggested above.

Commonly used abbreviations such as "JCT" or "ALT" need exploration and expansion, as do elliptical forms found in such instructions as "Delayed Green Wait." The latter example might be suitable for a more advanced class which is also working with the same construction found in newspaper headlines. This level class will also find reinforcement for participle study in signs such as "Merging Traffic." A beginning class, working with time concepts, will find added stimulus in typical urban instructions for "2 Hour Parking/8 AM to 6 PM."

The activities outlined above by no means exhaust the possibilities inherent in this approach. Further, each locale offers traffic signs relevant to its own area (e.g. "Cattle Crossing") in addition to the standard ones. Such signs become even more valuable to the ESL class because of their specific relevance to the immediate environment and culture.

Probably the single most effective way of presenting such information to students is through the use of color slides snapped by the instructor. Close-ups are usually more effective, but an occasional shot of a busy intersection with a half dozen signs all vying for attention, brings the real-life situation into the classroom with dramatic immediacy. In short, possibilities for combining culture and content, even through traffic signs, are limitless.

TN 6/76

HOT RODS

By Larry Cisar
Tokyo, Japan

A lot of teachers have been buying Cuisinaire rods to teach grammar. The Silent Way has made them very popular for this. But a lot of us have other types of classes. Can the rods be used in them? At Athénée Francais I have taught several speech/conversation classes. I have had fairly good success using the rods in them. I have been using them in several different ways. Following are six different techniques that I use in class to promote conversation. They are not the only techniques that I use but they are some of the more effective ones.

Before getting into how to use them, there are two important points to keep in mind. First, rods are tools. As tools they are not perfect. They do not solve all the problems of conversation classes. Some students will not like working with rods. Others will get bored with them after a short time. The teacher must be aware of this. The second point is that the specific technique is not as important as the language experience. If students start altering your carefully laid out rules, do not panic. Unless you have a specific reason for that rule, let them change it. Being familiar with Community Language Learning will help you to keep these points in mind and to work effectively with them.

As to the techniques themselves, the first one is called Islamabad. A good demonstration of this was given by Betsy Bedell at the KALT meeting in March of this year. One student takes the rods and builds a place that the others have not seen. The student describes it to them. The others ask questions, add commentary and redescribe it. The teacher acts as a language counsellor. His or her role is to provide unknown vocabulary or structures. If the target language for some idea is not available it can be glossed over. One or two minor points do not destroy a language experience. My students like it. They usually do something simple the first time. After that, they get more complex as they build their confidence.

My students came up with three variations of this which they like. The first was to have one of them build the area around his house. He would describe the neighborhood telling what stores, buildings, and other features there were and where they were. The others would listen carefully and freely ask questions. They needed to find out and remember as much as they possibly could about the neighborhood. After the students understood the map, the first student would give directions on how to find his house. The others had to follow the directions and locate the house. Afterwards, they discussed why they had/hadn't had trouble locating the house. Again the teacher was there primarily to offer the language.

The second variation was to build a map of a well-known area and talk about it. Although it was familiar to all of them, there were a lot of disagreements. They found that there were different ideas as to what was where. They became so involved in what they were doing that they did not realize how involved their language had become.

The third variation was to design a model city. The group decided what they would like to see in the perfect city and where they would want to live. They set the limit of only what was possible with modern technology. They did not want to try to use future developments. As they went along, they had to compromise as to what was to be included and excluded. They made themselves justify what they did to the city. When they located their home in the city, they had to explain why they wanted to be in that neighborhood. All of this was organized by them.

Islamabad and the variations presented here are good activities for students who are using Morley's *Improving Aural Comprehension*. Once they have done the unit on spatial relationships, they are ready to work with their own ideas and concepts.

I find that the above work best with upper level students. The lower level students tend to be overawed by them. The second technique is also for use by upper level students. This activity is often used on native speakers of a language to show how imprecise they are when talking. I use it to show students that they need to be precise when trying to convey ideas.

The actual procedure is really very simple. You have two students sitting at desks facing each other. Between them you put a barrier that they cannot see over or around. Each has the same number and color rods. Student A starts to build something and tells B what he is doing. B tries to duplicate exactly what A is building. I provide limits as to the type of conversation that can take place between the two. Four simple limitations are 1.) B cannot say anything. 2.) A can ask yes/no questions and B can answer only using *yes* or *no*, 3.) A can ask "WH" questions and B can answer them, and 4.) B can ask the questions and A can answer. There are more variations that can be used. During this exercise the teacher must establish how much vocabulary he will give. To check survival ability, give no vocabulary. To encourage more information exchange, give a lot of vocabulary. The important thing is to decide the limitations at the beginning, announce them to the students and stick to them.

This exercise is more difficult than it at first seems and can easily lead to frustration. I usually put a ten-minute time limit on each team. With a really weak student, five minutes is a good maximum.

The third technique works best with low intermediate students. You have them sit in a group (a circle around a small table works nicely.) One person spells out a word with the blocks and then tells how it relates to him. One example, a student spelled out the word "mountain" and then told the group about her trip to Mt. Akegi the day before. The group asked her about visiting mountains. The discussion that followed resulted in several students talking about the word.

The fourth technique is closely related to the third. Instead of a word, the student makes a symbol and tells

how it relates to him. The activity becomes more personal as symbols often do not mean much to others. One student made a peace symbol. It was something personal, out of his life, that he wanted to share. The conversation centered around his ideas and did not expand into others' ideas as technique three did. This was done in a low intermediate class.

The fifth technique builds up from the previous two. Here the discussion is established without the rods. The rods are used to help illustrate a point, show a position or just give a picture of what they mean. The rods are used as moveable drawing tools. The students are not using them to initiate the exchange. The exchanges are initiating the use of the rods. If the students can use the rods well in this type of exercise, they are ready to use the first two techniques mentioned in this article.

The last technique I will present can be used with almost any level. A value is placed on each color. For example, black might mean present perfect and yellow personal pronoun. A student picks up the colors that he wants to use and makes a story using them. The first few times the student should be allowed to choose what he wants. Once the student is good at it, he can be given a blind draw. With the blind draw the student needs more time to think over his story. Also he should not be limited to only what he draws. The important point is to get him to use them correctly in his story. The blind draw should be limited to five so it does not get too complicated.

This technique can also be used for group work. The group writes the story or dialogue using the rods drawn. The number of variations to this simple technique is unlimited.

These are only some of the ways that rods can be used in conversation classes. A little thinking and you can probably come up with more. The best source for these are your students. They have shown me more about using rods than I have shown them. One important thing I have found is to let the students do the activity. Let them talk and use the language. If the teacher takes over, interest dies. Moreover, the students do not get to express themselves. Language is expressing yourself. Freedom to work with the rods is vital.   *TN 11/78*

(Reprinted from *The Kanto* (Japan) *Assoc. of Language Teachers Newsletter*, Vol. 1, No. 8, Aug. 1978.
TN 11/78

GAMES ESL PEOPLE PLAY

by Jerry Steinberg
St. Jean, Quebec

I don't wait for the closing minutes of the period or day to play a game with my students. You can "catch" me playing games with my students at *any time* of the day—yes, even at the very start of the day's lessons. And I never feel that I'm "slacking off" when we play.

Games have many "raisons d'être", seven of which I'll outline for you. (Memorize them and you can defend yourself if you ever have to justify playing games with your students.)

I use games to *reinforce* newly-acquired material. For example: You've just taught the cardinal numbers and you want to give your students an opportunity to use them in a meaningful context. So, you play "Ninety-eight", a card game which requires the players to orally add card values to a maximum of 98.

A second justification for games is *review*. Suppose it's been a while since you taught the simple past of irregular verbs and you want to check and refresh your students' memories. One of my favorites is "Tic-Tac-Toe" (or "Xs and Os"). The class is divided into two teams, namely; Team X and Team O. One member of Team X chooses a position on the grid and must use the verb

occupying that position in a sentence in the simple past. If the sentence is correct, Team X gains that position. If wrong, the turn is lost and a member of Team O can try for any vacant position which will help his team. The first team to occupy three positions in a row (vertically, horizontally or diagonally) wins the match. New verbs replace used ones for each successive match.

If your class has been working hard for a long time in their seats, a game would be an enjoyable and profitable form of *relaxation*. A popular game with my students is "Rhyme Mime". One player thinks of two rhyming words (such as "ship" and "trip" or "hot" and "pot") and acts them out in mime. The student who guesses one word wins two points, the second word is worth one point, and if both words are guessed by the same person, he/she wins 5 points.

If there is a task ahead, for which neither you nor your students can muster much enthusiasm, a game can

be offered as a future *reward* to encourage co-operation. Or, if your class has performed exceptionally well during a certain activity, such as an oral drill or independent reading, a game provides an immediate *reward* for good behaviour. One of our most preferred games is "Password". The students are paired off and one partner of each team is shown the "Password" (example: "cup") and, in turn, says one word which will, he hopes, prompt his partner to guess the "Password". Words such as "coffee", or "glass", or "handle" or "saucer" are good clues. I allow my students to refer to their dictionaries or thesauruses when it isn't their turn to speak, but I advise them to avoid choosing words which their partners won't understand.

To make the game more challenging, I stipulate that clues cannot contain or be contained by the "Password", so that if the "Password" is "blackboard", "black" and "board" cannot be given as clues to elicit the "Password". I also insist that clues cannot be proper nouns. This prevents students from insulting each other, should the "Password" be a word such as "fat", or "ugly" or "stupid".

Games tend to *reduce inhibition,*

especially if the competitive element is diminished or eliminated. The shy or linguistically weak student will feel more at ease and will participate freely if the object is just to have fun, and not to score points and win or lose. Although competition often adds excitement and increases participation, it can just as often increase the pressure to perform well and exclude the timid student or the one who is less sure of his facility with the language.

Should a lull occur in the interest ex-

hibited toward the lesson being taught, a short game would *raise attentiveness* so that the lesson could be resumed for the benefit of all.

If you've been having trouble with rowdy students, a game can *restrain rebellion*. Class clowns don't have to "clown around" to get attention, and who would risk irritating the teacher, thereby bringing a premature end to a fun activity.

Each and every game in my collec-

tion of over 150 games utilizes a linguistic structure and develops at least one linguistic skill (if not all four). Therefore, none of them can be labelled a waste of time.

So whether a game is used as a warm-up or a cool-down activity, it can be beneficial to language students, both linguistically and behaviourally. And I can vouch for the fact that teachers enjoy games, too.

Who says learning (and teaching) can't be enjoyable! *TN 8/81*

REVIVING THE LANGUAGE LAB

by Gerry Strei
Director of Lab Services Concordia University, Montreal

In language learning situations where audio-lingual drills of the stimulus-response pattern practice type no longer serve the needs of our ESL students, what can we use instead? This question is of vital importance if we are to "revive" the language laboratory. Here are some practical ideas about preparing lab materials which may serve as alternatives or supplements to traditional lab drills.

Dictation Tapes

Although dictation has been around for a long time, its usefulness in a laboratory setting is sometimes overlooked. The language content for dictation tapes can range from the simple dictation of numbers and alphabet letters to dialogs containing complex sentence structures. Unless used for testing purposes or limited to a single playback source, tapes of this type should be made available on individual play-back machines which allow students to pace themselves and to go over material as many times as necessary.

"Cloze" Tapes

The cloze procedure, wherein every fifth to tenth word in a text is deleted, can easily be used with an audio format. For example, a brief conversation between two persons is constructed with certain words masked with white noise or distorted in some fashion so as to make them imperceptible. The student listens to the entire conversation twice, the second time writing down or speaking (recording) the missing words. Finally, students check their answers by listening to the conversation in its unmasked form. In order to achieve a more "real life" effect, a conversation can be recorded on a noisy street corner. Then a student lab script is prepared with blanks for imperceptible words and phrases. Students can check their answers as above and correct items and supply missing ones by listening to the final version as a dictation.

Picture Elicited Speech

Students are asked to pretend they

are talking to someone who can't see them (a blind person, someone at the other end of the telephone). They are asked to describe, react to, or answer particular questions about a picture they have been given. Pictures can be carefully chosen to elicit specific vocabulary or sentence structures (Ex. "In my picture *there is/there are*. . . It *is* sitt*ing*. . . It *is* eat*ing*. . ."). Both the choice of the picture and the instructions or questions the students are given can help to control the responses to some extent, allowing for some type of comparison or correction during playback. For example, after the student has recorded his description, reaction, or answers, he can be given a list of vocabulary items and sentences which would probably be used in relation to his picture.

Instruction and Direction Giving

Students are told to prepare a tape of instructions which could be used to guide someone in their absence. Any process or instructions—"How to Build a Campfire" or "How to Get from School to My House"—can be used. As a guide, and to elicit specific vocabulary and structures, a very skeletal outline on paper can be given students before they begin to record. For some titles, model tapes can be prepared for students to listen to and compare with their own. To test for communicative content, student tapes can be played back in class to see if the instructions or directions can be understood in a real life situation—to see if others can perform the task or follow the directions (Ex. "How to Tie a Shoe").

Word Associations

Taped exercises, sometimes in the form of games, can be made to help students develop and maintain vocabulary through word association bonds. Some excellent ideas for exercises of this type appear in a recent article by Wilga Rivers and Mary Temperley (English Teaching Forum 15,1). Although most of their examples are of written tasks for use in the classroom,

many can be made into taped exercises requiring either oral or written responses. Here are some samples:
"Write down (say) as many words as you can think of which have a natural association with *tree*:
(Sample responses) grass, lawn, garden, flower. . .

Write down (say) all the words you know which have a similar meaning to *house*:

home, apartment/flat, cottage, villa. . .
Make as may words as you can from the letters in the sentence given. No letter may be used more times than it appears in the sentence: *That's a tree.* that, a tree, hat, tar, rat, tat, three, area. . . ."

Newscasts and Lectures

Real life language material is available all around us in a variety of discourse formats which can be recorded on audio or video tape and used in a variety of ways. For advanced ESL groups at Concordia, newscasts and university lectures have been videotaped for comprehension exercises. Several different exercise formats can be used with such tapes—audio or written comprehension questions requiring oral or written responses, cloze exercises (oral or written responses), and dictations.

These are only a few ideas for preparation of language laboratory materials which can be used to replace repetitive, mechanical, audio lingual-type drills. However, it is important to bear in mind that it is not only intelligent, carefully prepared courseware which makes a lab program work, but also the coordination of these language materials (on the part of the language departments concerned) to fit the particular objectives of a given course. According to one educator, Arthur Gionet (NAALD Journal 9,3), ". . . the use of the language laboratory can never fully reach its potential without the active involvement of the whole faculty in cooperation with the laboratory director and his associates."

IMPROVING TEACHER–MADE LANGUAGE TAPES

by Wayne B. Dickerson
University of Illinois

Many teachers have discovered the advantages of making rather than purchasing language laboratory recordings. In general, teachers can achieve a better match between supplemental lab work and classroom instruction by using their own tapes instead of commercial tapes. In particular, tapes can be made to exactly the right length, to cover the most appropriate topics, to provide the desired emphasis with the best selection of exercises, and to accommodate innovation and individualization. These important advantages, however, may be lost if the materials are not expertly recorded. One of the major problems which mars many otherwise superb teacher-made tapes is that of *incorrect recording volume*. A few pointers in this area may help teachers get more satisfying results from their tape making.

In order to appreciate the importance of correct recording volume, it is necessary to understand what is meant by incorrect volume. Incorrect recording volume may be volume that it too high. This typically results in the distortion of words so that they are hard to understand. Incorrect recording volume may also be volume that is too low. The recordist's voice is not recorded loudly enough to cover the hissing noise that is inherent in every tape and in every recorder. Correct volume, then, is volume that is high enough to hide the hiss but low enough not to distort the sound.

The importance of staying within the safe recording zone lies ultimately in our concern for our students and their ability to learn from our recorded materials. If, on the one hand, the volume is too high, the tape will provide an irritation to the student. In self-defense, the student will tune out the content. If, on the other hand, the volume is too low, not only will it be difficult for the student to hear with

ease, but the background hiss will induce listener fatigue which works against learning.

How can we be certain we are using the correct recording volume every time we record? Unfortunately, for nonprofessional machines, recorder manuals are not very explicit on this point. Because there is so much individual variation among recordists, manufacturers find it difficult to state explicitly how to use record-level meters. Some manufacturers try to solve the problem with an automatic volume control. The automatic volume control feature has its uses, but recording language drills is *not* among them. The recording mechanism is designed to turn up the record volume automatically when there is little or no incoming sound. When this happens, as during a silence left on the tape for student participation, the wide open volume puts a large amount of hiss on the tape—exactly what the recordist is trying to avoid. For language recording purposes, a manual volume control is far superior to the automatic volume control. With the manual volume control, any teacher can arrive at the correct recording level on any recorder by using a simple two-minute trial-run procedure.

The aim of the trial-run procedure is to record your voice at normal conversational loudness so that on one-third playback volume your recorded voice will sound as loud as your voice was when recording. To find the record-volume setting which will achieve this aim, the following steps should be followed.

Trial-Run Procedure

1. Position the microphone about 4–6 inches from your mouth. Set the record level to 1/2 full volume, then say into the mike what record setting you are using. For example, record:

"I am recording at 1/2 full record level. Then record 10-15 seconds of material at normal conversational loudness.

2. Change the record-level setting to 2/3 full volume and record on the tape what volume you are using. Record an additional 10–15 seconds of material at normal conversational loudness.

3. Change the record-level setting to 3/4 full volume and announce what setting you are using. Record 10–15 seconds of material as before.

4. Rewind the tape to the beginning and set the playback volume to 1/3 full volume. Play the tape and note which setting yields the best volume, that is, the volume which is most like your normal conversational loudness.

5. If no setting gives satisfactory results, that is, not sufficiently loud volume, either bring the microphone closer to your mouth or change the microphone distance and speak somewhat louder (without straining). Then repeat the above steps.

6. When recording, use your trial-run findings: the record-level setting best suited to your voice loudness and mouth-microphone distance.

In summary, teacher-made tapes can surpass commercial tape in matching the growing and changing needs of an ESL program. Furthermore, the recording quality of such tapes can compete favorably with professionally-produced tapes, provided a few pointers are followed.*

* (For more information on recorders, microphones, tape, and techniques for recording language materials, see the forthcoming paperback book, *Tips on Taping, Language Recording in the Social Sciences,* by Wayne and Lonna Dickerson, published by William Carey Library, 305 Pasadena Avenue, South Pasadena, California 91030).

TN 4/76

COMPUTER–ASSISTED LANGUAGE LEARNING COMES OF AGE

by David H. Wyatt
Georgetown University

It surprises many language teachers to hear that computers have been in routine use for language learning since the mid-1970's. The reason for the general lack of awareness is easily understood: very few institutions were able to afford the expensive mainframe or minicomputer systems which were previously necessary to provide computer-aided lessons. Thus, computer-assisted language learning (CALL) has had little impact on our profession until now.

However, the 1983 TESOL Conference served as a dramatic demonstration that this situation is changing completely. Low-cost microcomputers, or personal computers, have become available as an affordable means of implementing CALL in any language teaching institution. Through both the academic presentations and the commercial exhibits, it became obvious that a small but rapidly-growing section of the profession is working on the development and use of microcomputer-based

learning materials. The attendance at the many computer-related presentations—not even standing room was generally available—demonstrated that large numbers of ESL teachers are now interested in using CALL in their classrooms.

What impact is CALL likely to have on TESOL, and what materials are available at the moment? Let us briefly consider some main aspects of language instruction in turn.

● **Reading/Vocabulary** Computer-assisted learning techniques are likely to have a major impact on the teaching of reading. Indeed, recent textbooks using the 'reading skills' approach lend themselves so well to CALL that they might almost have been written for this purpose. Similarly, 'reading laboratory' materials can be directly transferred to the microcomputer, with considerable gains in terms of individualization, interaction, and motivation. At present, no microcomputer-based reading skills materials are available for ESL, although increasing amounts of courseware are being published for native speakers. Aids to vocabulary learning for ESL students are already on the market.

● **Writing** Microcomputers are expected to have a strong impact on the teaching of writing. Here, however, the computer will chiefly be used as a 'tool' in the writing process, operating in the role of word processor. (It should be noted that the same microcomputer can function in many different roles. It is the particular software in use at the moment—usually supplied in the form of diskettes—which determines whether the computer will operate as a learning aid, word processor, checkbook balancer, etc.)

As a word processor, the computer provides an ideal solution to the problem of getting students to incorporate and learn from the corrections you make to their assignments. Major and minor errors can very easily be corrected; if you feel that entire paragraphs should be moved around to produce a more logical structure, the student can achieve this on the word processor with just a few keystrokes before printing out a perfect final copy. If you wish, a complete spelling check can be made by computer and errors corrected even before you see the first draft. At the moment, although hundreds of word processors are available, none is adapted specifically for use with foreign learners.

● **Grammar** There is the area which has generated the most controversy so far, partly because most of the available material employs a structuralist approach. However, there is no reason *a priori* that courseware employing a notional-functional or communicative approach could not be developed. It seems likely that opinions will remain very much divided on this aspect of computer-aided instruction. Teachers who see a place in the curriculum for grammar-oriented materials will probably welcome the computer-based drill and tutorial as freeing class time for more communicative activities. Other teachers may reject this type of CALL in its entirety. Ironically, this is the type of courseware which is most widely available at the moment.

● **Listening/Speaking** Listening skills are one of the areas in which computer-aided learning holds most promise. The potential of a listening skills course based partly on videodiscs under microcomputer control is exciting, particularly for those methodologists who have recently been proposing introductory periods of listening and meaningful language input before requiring any extensive production by the student. Recent developments suggest that videodiscs and videodisc players will soon become standard, affordable educational equipment, but at present there is very little courseware available for language teaching.

On the other hand, speaking is an area in which CALL probably has very little contribution to make in the foreseeable future. Computers may be of help in limited roles such as in the analysis and correction of pronunciation problems. Work along these lines is already in progress, but there appears to be no usable ESL courseware as yet.

● **Testing** As far as objective tests are concerned, the computer is an ideal administrator, collator, and calculator of results and statistics. Computers are also potentially capable of more efficient and accurate testing through their ability to adapt interactively to the ability of the student during the testing process. Thus, although few interactive or traditional objective tests are yet available in computerized form, this state of affairs is likely to change very soon.

It is important to recognize that the situation with regard to availability of courseware is far from satisfactory. In some of the areas indicated above, the problem of *quantity*—simple lack of ready-to-use to use materials—will probably be solved within the next twelve months. However, the question of the *quality* of the courseware is also a critical problem, and it is here that we will increasingly need to focus our attention. *TN 6/83*

A BARE-BONES BIBLIOGRAPHY FOR TEACHERS OF ESL

by John F. Haskell
Northeastern Illinois University

Last Spring I asked a number of teachers and teacher trainers to speculate on a basic library for an ESL teacher. They were asked to provide a list of ten books which they thought would be a practical beginning collection (with the provision that they might add up to five additional books as future choices and any supplemental articles they might think important). The selections, listed below reflect the diversity of our field, not surprisingly the personal tastes and preferences of the listers, and by their comments (and the number who could not stick to ten) the difficulty producing such a list entailed. The lists are reprinted as received, tidied up where necessary, with annotation when included and with some of the appropriate comments that accompanied them. Publication information was not otherwise added as it was felt that author and title were sufficient information needed to find any book listed.

The lists are all excellent and unique and will perhaps in their reading suggest individual volumes which may be suitable to your need. I couldn't resist adding my own list, in large part because, as Virginia Allen said of her list, it contains books no one else mentioned.

* Title borrowed from Dick Yorkey's list.

RICHARD YORKEY

**A Bare-Bones Bibliography For
Teachers Of English To Speakers
Of Other Languages**

In selecting and rejecting ideas for this very limited, highly personal bibliography, I have had in mind an ESL teacher who at one time or another will undoubtedly have to adapt material from a prescribed text, prepare original material, answer questions from students in class and who will occasionally want to satisfy his or her professional interest in theoretical ideas and technical facts about language learning and the English language.

I have assumed that every ESL teacher already has a good, up-to-date desk dictionary of the English language, if not the unabridged Webster III and/or the Shorter Oxford.

Where fools rush in, I suppose the only way to answer the question of "Why this book and not that one?" is to counter with an equally unanswerable question, "Why that book and not this one?" For what it is worth then, here is my list of basic resources that every professional ESL teacher ought to have. Note that there is no particular significance to the order in which I have listed the books.

1. The best, and most complete and current, grammar of English is Randolph Quirk *et al.*, *A Grammar of Contemporary English* (London: Longman, 1972). It is also the most expensive. A reasonable abridgement, by Randolph Quirk and Sydney Greenbaum, is *A University Grammar of English* (London: Longman, 1973) and the American edition, *A Concise Grammar of Contemporary English* (New York: Harcourt Brace Jovanovich, 1973). A new kind of grammar with a different orientation, but also based on *A Grammar of Contemporary English*, is Geoffrey Leech and Jan Svartvik, *A Communicative Grammar of English* (London: Longman, 1975). After making distinctions between formal and informal, written and spoken, British and American uses of English, and a brief description of English in-

242

tonation, the authors present the facts of English grammar according to the uses and communicative purposes of grammar rather than the traditional organization by structure. The final part is an alphabetically arranged guide to English morphology and syntax, with definitions and examples of grammatical terms. Any one of these grammars would be a useful professional resource.

2. A. S. Hornby, *Guide to Patterns and Usage in English* (London: Oxford University Press, second edition, 1975). This little reference book is an authoritative, conveniently organized guide to British and American syntax. It is divided into five parts: (1) Verbs and verb patterns, including 80 tables of 25 basic sentence patterns with numerous examples of each and detailed notes of explanation. (The numbered patterns correspond with those in Hornby's *Oxford Advanced Learner's Dictionary of Current English*); (2) Time and Tense, which is 30 pages of clear descriptions and examples of tense forms and meanings; (3) Nouns, Determiners, and Adjectives; (4) Adverbials; and (5) Various concepts and ways in which they are expressed. (Long before notions were fashionable, Hornby explored the grammatical forms and phrases to express such notions as requests, instructions, permission, probability, possibility, intention, refusals, purpose, concession, etc.)

3. *Longman Dictionary of Contemporary English* (London: Longman, 1978.) Although this and the *Oxford Advanced Learner's Dictionary of Current English* are both excellent for ESL purposes, and either one should be on any teacher's professional shelf, I prefer the Longman dictionary. The defining vocabulary is limited to the words in the *General Service List* and listed in the appendix. There are more defining sentences that are better contextualized for meaning. Usage notes are realistic recognition of the needs of ESL students (and a useful guide for ESL teachers). It includes more current slang and informal usage, particularly of American English. The grammar and syntax of entries are coded with reference to introductory explanations and examples, based on *A Grammar of Contemporary English*.

4. Donn Byrne, *Teaching Oral English* (London: Longman 1976). This book is a distillation of Bryne's many years of practical experience in teaching ESL in the artificial environment of the classroom. His theoretical statements are always followed by practical application and examples for teaching oral communication, listening comprehension, and a methodology that follows a careful progression from the presentation stage, through the practice stage, to the production stage. Final chapters include ideas about language games, oral composition, play reading, and audio-visual aids.

5. Christina Bratt Paulston and Mary Bruder, *From Substitution to Substance: A Handbook of Structural Pattern Drills* (Rowley, Mass.: Newbury House, 1975). Since teachers will inevitably use some kind of pattern drills, they could profit from the theoretical considerations here and the distinction between mechanical, meaningful, and communicative drills. The Index of Patterns is an inventory of grammatical and syntactic structures that are included, with

suggested frames for pattern practice and situational contexts for communicative practice.

6. A teacher should have a reference that gives a clear presentation of the theoretical aspects of phonology and practical suggestions and examples for teaching pronunciation. A good choice is between J. Donald Bowen, *Patterns of English Pronunciation* (Rowley Mass.: Newbury House, 1975) and Clifford J. Prator and Betty Wallace Robinett, *Manual of American English Pronunciation* (New York: Holt Rinehart and Winston, third edition, 1972).

7. Fe R. Dacanay, *Techniques and Procedures in Second-Language Teaching* (Quezon City: Phoenix Press, 1963; reprinted and distributed by Oceana Press, Dobbs Ferry, New York). Despite its age, references to Tagalog and teaching ESL in the Philippines, this book remains one of the most complete and useful resources for ESL teachers. It is especially valuable for practical ideas for presenting English structure (Chapter 1) and for lists and examples of major and minor spelling patterns (Chapter 6). Chapters on the teaching of pronunciation, reading and writing, and on testing are also filled with practical ideas for the elementary and secondary levels, but which could easily be adapted to adult levels and intensive programs.

8. J. B. Heaton, *Writing English Language Tests* (London: Longman, 1975). This is a practical guide to the construction of English tests intended primarily for the classroom teacher. Following introductory chapters about language testing in general and objective testing in particular, chapters include information and examples of tests of grammar, vocabulary, listening comprehension, oral production, reading and writing skills. Final chapters include a discussion of criteria and types of tests and interpreting test scores.

9. J. A. van Ek, *The Threshold Level for Modern Language Learning in Schools* (London: Longman, 1977). Based on *The Threshold Level in a European Unit/Credit System for Modern Language Learning by Adults* (Strasbourg: Council of Europe, 1975), this adaptation considers the functional-notional syllabus for high school students. Much theoretical and explanatory information is included in the first thirty pages. Its chief value as a resource, however, is the detailed listing of objectives for topic-related language behavior, the index of language functions and general notions, and the content specifications with exponents for English. Of particular value for teachers are the lexical and structural inventories.

10. W. R. Lee, *Language Teaching Games and Contests* (London: Oxford University Press, 1965). To add interest and variety in a class, games are useful, especially for those unplanned few minutes in class. This book is a good collection of games for spelling, reading and writing, pronunciation, and oral English practice.

CHRISTINA BRATT PAULSTON

Ten Volumes That A New Teacher Might Find Useful

Teachers are constantly told, by me as well, that there is nothing as practical as

good theory. Maybe that is true, but it strikes me forcefully on finishing up a course on theories of language acquisition how very little we know about language learning on a theoretical level. Therefore, it seems to me that it makes little sense to stuff an unwilling teacher with speculative theories, and so my list is primarily concerned with matters of the class room; in short, a survival list. Allen and Corder's (1975) *Papers in Applied Linguistics Vol 2* will suffice for theoretical issues.

A major weakness of many beginning teachers, native speakers as well as non-native, is a lack of knowledge of English grammar. The teacher needs a reference grammar as well as a pedagogically oriented work and my choices are Quirk and Greenbaum (1973) and Crowell's *Index to Modern English* (1964). A dictionary is also a necessity, and my one splurge recommendation is for the big hardcover college edition of *The American Heritage Dictionary of the English Language* with its fine introductory essays as an extra perq. Another weakness tends to be in testing, and every teacher can use at least one handbook on testing, such as Harris' *Testing English as a Second Language* (1969).

What most teachers perceive as their major need, and I frankly think they are right, is a source for methods and techniques. In alphabetical order here are three: Allen and Valette, *Modern Language Classroom Techniques*, (1972); Rivers and Temperley, *A Practical Guide to the Teaching of English* (1978); and Robinett, *Teaching English to Speakers of Other Languages* (1978).

An ESL teacher often ends up in bilingual education programs or as consultant to elementary school teachers, and for such situations Saville-Troike's *Foundations for Teaching English as a Second Language* (1976) will come in handy. Finally ESL teachers need to realize that they are part of a professional body as well as to keep up with recent developments, and to that purpose for a tenth volume I would recommend membership in TESOL and its subscriptions to the *TESOL Quarterly* and the *TESOL Newsletter*. And just so that they would really feel with it, add to the list of ten volumes an article each on (in no particular order) The Silent Way, Suggestopedia, Community Counseling Learning, and Notional-Functional Syllabuses.

For the five additional books, what I would really do, whether for a hypothetical teacher or for myself going abroad to teach ESL, is to pick five "best" textbooks in ESL from which I could augment the lessons of the no doubt bad texts I would end up teaching from. But since I don't suppose that was the intention of this exercise, here are five more:

Bright and McGregor, *Teaching English as a Second Language* (1970)
Chastain, *Developing Second Language Skills* (1976)
Fries, *Teaching and Learning English as a Foreign Language* (1945)
Jesperson, *How to Teach a Foreign Language* (1904)
Kelly, *25 Centuries of Language Teaching* (1969)
Lado, *Linguistics Across Cultures* (1957)

VIRGINIA FRENCH ALLEN

Good luck on your bibliography project. I'll be interested in the outcome, as my mind rebelled against specifying the *10 most useful*. I found myself reasoning, "Maybe no one else will mention this really good item, so I'd better put it in"— thus leaving out some equally valuable stuff. I deliberately included a few "oldie but goodie" books, as I think we should combat the tendency to rule out everything published more than five years ago.

In your article you may want to put asterisks on items that were suggested by most of your consultants, but make it clear that the fact someone omitted it might simply mean it was *too* obvious a choice (as implied in my first paragraph).

Benardo, Leo U. and Dora F. Pantell. *English: Your New Language.* Morristown, N.J.: Silver Burdett, 1966. With accompanying Teacher's Edition, Book I serves as an interesting first text for adults and high-school age students, Book II for more advanced levels of English proficiency; attractively illustrated, most suitable for "survival" courses rather than college prep.

Dale, Edgar and Joseph O'Rourke. *The Living Word Vocabulary: The Words We Know.* Elgin, IL: Dome Press, 1976. Not for the teacher's personal library because of its cost, but useful for the district's curriculum library, as it lists 40,000 words (with separate senses indicated) and shows at which grade each word is known by most American students. For those who are helping students prepare to compete with native speakers at various grade levels.

Danielson, Dorothy and Rebecca Hayden. *Using English, Your Second Language.* Englewood Cliffs, N.J.: Prentice-Hall, 1973. One of the meatiest of the exercise/activity texts for upper level students, for grammar, reading, composition, punctuation.

Fries, Charles C. *Teaching and Learning English as a Foreign Language.* Ann Arbor: Univ. of Michigan Press, 1945. Chapter IV and V of this classic Methods text still have much to say to teachers about vocabulary learning. Even portions of the book which make currently disputed claims ought to be read by professionals in TESOL.

Guide for the Volunteer English Teacher. Washington, D.C.: National Association for Foreign Student Affairs, 1973. A bird's eye view of the field in about 25 pages, for real novices, with brief bibliography.

Johnson, Francis C. *English as a Second Language: An Individualized Approach.* Brisbane, Australia: Jacaranda Press, 1973. How to get students to teach other students, by one who has successfully done it.

MET (Modern English Teacher): A Magazine of Practical Suggestions for Teaching English as a Foreign Language. Subscriptions Dept.: 8 Hainton Avenue, Grimsby DN32 9BB, South Humberside, England. Published four times a year, full of interesting things for students, and ideas for teachers; very useful illustrations.

Neustadt, Bertha C. *Speaking of the U.S.A.: A Reader for Discussion.* N.Y.: Harper & Row, 1975. Fairly comprehen-sive coverage of American institutions (government, libraries, media, arts, education, etc.) for courses designed to orient advanced students to the American scene.

Nida, Eugene A. *Customs and Cultures.* N.Y.: Harper, 1954. Comments by a missionary who had to learn to communicate with many different cultures, richly illustrating the influence of culture on language, full of enlightening details.

Phillips, Nina. *Conversational English for the Non-English Speaking Child.* N.Y.: Teachers College Press, 1967. Unlike most Methods books, this focuses on the really young learner and practical classroom activities for that age group. Designed for untrained volunteers, better for low-income pupils than for more affluent children; urban teachers often recommend it.

Prator, Clifford H. and Betty W. Robinett. *A Manual of American English Pronunciation.* For teacher reference and also classroom exercises on intonation, stress, and other aspects of the sound system.

Thonis, Eleanor Wall. *Teaching Reading to Non-English Speakers.* N.Y.: Macmillan, 1970. Detailed suggestion's on teaching reading at all levels of instruction, with a balanced discussion of contributions of different approaches.

Yorkey, Richard C. *Study Skills for Students of English as a Second Language.* N.Y.: McGraw-Hill, 1970. Basically a Freshman Composition text for speakers of other languages, dealing with library skills, use of dictionary, outlining, note-taking, examination strategies. For academically oriented adolescents and college students.

JAYNE HARDER

My emphasis is on information about the English language rather than on methodology or materials—though I have not completely excluded these. In no particular order, my choices follow.

(1) Allen, Harold B. and Russell N. Campbell, eds. *Teaching English as a Second Language.* New York: McGraw-Hill, 1972.

(2) Close, R. A. *English as a Foreign Language,* 2d edition. London: George Allen & Unwin Ltd., 1977.

(3) Quirk, Randolph and Sidney Greenbaum. *A Concise Grammar of Contemporary English.* New York: Harcourt Brace Jovanovich Inc., 1976.

(4) Nilsen, Donald and Aleen Pace Nilsen. *Pronunciation Contrasts in English.* New York: Regents, 1973.

(5) A good phonetics book which has clear articulatory descriptions, such as Thomas, Charles K. *An Introduction to the Phonetics of American English.* New York: The Ronald Press Co., 1958.

(6) Halliday, M. A. K., Angus McIntosh, and Peter Strevens. *The Linguistic Sciences and Language Teaching.* London: Longmans, Green, 1964.

(7) Kelly, L. G. *25 Centuries of Language Teaching.* Rowley, Mass.: Newbury House, 1969.

(8) Allen, J. P. B. and S. Pit Corder, eds. *Techniques in Applied Linguistics,* Vol. 3 of The Edinburgh Course in Applied Linguistics. London: Oxford University Press, 1974.

(9) Finocchiaro, Mary. *English as a Second Language: From Theory to Practice.* New York: Regents, 1974.

(10) Diller, Karl Conrad. *The Language Teaching Controversy.* Rowley, Mass.: Newbury House, 1978.

In addition to the basic ten, I would suggest expanding the collection with the following:

(11) Guth, Hans P. *English Today and Tomorrow.* Englewood Cliffs, N.J.: Prentice-Hall, 1964. [I don't know his newer books, but this one continues to have much merit.]

(12) Wilkins, D. A. *Linguistics in Language Teaching.* Cambridge Mass.: The M. I. T. Press, 1972.

(13) Palmer, Leslie and Bernard Spolsky, eds. *Papers on Language Testing 1967-1974.* Washington, D.C.: TESOL, 1975.

(14) Lado, Robert. *Linguistics Across Cultures.* Ann Arbor, Mich.: University of Michigan Press, 1957.

I hope we can assume that an ESL teacher (no matter how new) will own a well-worn good dictionary, such as *Webster's New Collegiate,* latest edition. A very useful second dictionary which I would recommend is A. S. Hornby's *Oxford Advanced Learners' Dictionary of Current English* (London: Oxford University Press, 1974). I like it because, among other good things, it shows differences between American and British usage.

J. DONALD BOWEN

I'll list categories, with several items in them; since you want my opinion for a single identification, my choice will be the first listed. But you'll see that I select arbitrarily, usually the book I've worked on or the one I know best. So out the window with impartiality. [I'll mention books by author(s) or titles only; I assume you don't need formal entries.]

1. A substantial monolingual dictionary: *Webster's New World, Funk & Wagnall's Standard College, Webster's Collegiate,* etc.
2. A student dictionary: Hornby et al.'s *Advanced Learner's Dictionary of Current English.* (This dictionary has a lot of very useful grammatical information. I might settle for it alone if it were not limited to British English.)
3. A pronunciation textbook: Bowen's *Patterns of English Pronunciation,* Prator's *Manual of American English Pronunciation.*
4. A pronunciation reference: Kenyon and Knott, *A Pronouncing Dictionary of American English.*
5. A standard methodology: Dacanay, Rivers, Chastain, Finocchiaro, Robinett, Dubin & Olshtain, Paulston & Bruder.
6. A good anthology: Allen & Campbell, Croft, Celce Murcia & McIntosh (actually I think maybe because of dating, I'd put this volume first on my list), Oller & Richards, Schumann & Stenson, Lugton, Light and Osman.
7. A good pedagogical grammar: Rutherford, Frank, Praninskas, Danielson & Hayden, etc.
8. A reference grammar: Quirk et al. (*A Grammar of Contemporary English*— not the cut down version) Jesperson, Kruisinga, Poutsma.

9. Spiritual nourishment: Stevick (*Memory, Meaning & Method*)

10. Perspective: Kelly *25 Centuries of Language Teaching*; Mouton, *Ling & Language Teaching*.

But now that I'm started I can't stop: When the dam breaks and we can have more than ten books (or categories of books), I'd want to make some additions.

11. Vocabulary: Roget's *Thesaurus* (if I could teach how to use it).

12. Vocabulary teaching: Thorndike and Lorge, *Teacher's Word Book of 30,000 Words*.

All these, and I haven't touched culture, specific texts for written language skills, language analysis (grammatical, error, contrastive), second-language acquisition (which I feel sure I'd be much interested in if I only knew something about it), bilingualism, bilingual education, pidgins and pidginization, language testing, linguistic theory (or maybe 'history'), such as Bolinger's *Aspects of Language*.

That's probably enough from me. I won't count the volumes. I think it may be easier to establish the categories than the individual volumes, and anyway there is often not so much difference between, say, methodologies, pedagogical grammars, etc. Everyone will likely have preferences, if only based on his experience using one or another volume. And if he has been an author, there's no chance to escape.

One comment I failed to make above: there's no preference in order after the first item on a list. I haven't consulted even my preferences in that much detail.

MARY FINOCCHIARO

Bowen, J. D., *Patterns of English Pronunciation*, Rowley Mass Newbury, 1975.

Dobson, Julia, *Effective Techniques for English Conversation Groups*, Rowley Mass, Newbury, 1974.

Dorry, Gertrude, *Games for Second Language Learning*, New York, McGraw-Hill, 1966.

Finocchiaro M. and M. Bonomo, *The Forreign Language Learner: A Guide for Teachers*, Regents, 1973.

Finocchiaro, M. and S. Sako, *Foreign Language Testing*, Regents, 1979.

Harris, D., *Testing English as a Second Language*, New York, McGraw-Hill, 1969.

Madson, H. and J. Bowen, *Adaptation in Language Teaching*, Rowley Mass., Newbury, 1978.

Newton, Anne (ed.), *The Art of TESOL*, Newbury, 1978.

Nilsen, D. & A. Nilsen, *Pronunciation Contrasts in English*, Regents, 1973.

Paulston, C. & M. Bruder, *Teaching English as a Second Language*, Winthrop, 1976.

Prator, C. & B. Robinett, *A Manual of American English Pronunciation* (rev'd ed), New York, Holt, Reinhart.

Rivers, W. & M. Temperley, *A Practical Guide to the Teaching of English as a Second or Foreign Language*, Oxford, 1978.

Robinett, B., *Teaching English to Speakers of Other Languages: Substance and Technique*, McGraw-Hill, 1978.

Saville-Troike, M., *Foundations for Teaching English as a Second Language: Theory and Method of Multicultural Education*, Prentice-Hall, 1976.

Also

Leech, Svartvik, et al. *A Communicative Grammar of English*, Longmans.

April 1979 Issue of *English Teaching Forum*—"The Functional Notional Syllabus".

JEAN BODMAN

Here is my list of books I'd take with me if I were heading back to Afghanistan.

1. Rivers, Wilga. *Teaching foreign language skills*. University of Chicago.

2. Curran, Charles. *Counseling-learning in second languages*. Apple River Press.

3. Gattegno, Caleb. *The common sense of teaching foreign languages*. Educational Solutions, Inc.

4. Lozanov, Georgi. *Suggestology and outlines of suggestopedy*. Gordon & Breach.

5. van Ek, J.A. *The threshold level for modern language learning in schools*. Longman.

6. Leech, Geoffrey and Jan Svartvik. *A communicative grammar of English*. Longman.

7. Hall, Edward T. *The Silent Language*. Doubleday.

8. Rosten, Leo. *The Education of Hyman Kaplan*. Harper & Row.

9. *Bibliography of Handouts*. Available from the Adult Education Resource Center, Jersey City State College, Jersey City, N.J. 07305.

10. Smith, Frank. *Understanding reading*. Holt, Rinehart and Winston.

I would also add (for new teachers) one complete textbook series of their own choice. And, if they can manage 1 book from the following authors: Lawrence, Morley, Raimes, Markstein & Hirasawa, Bodman & Lanzano (if I may be so bold), Alexander, and Hines. Another interesting book for ABE teachers is: Pope, Lilly. *Guidelines to Teaching Remedial Reading*. Book Lab, Inc. Two more books that could be added to an ABE teacher's library are: Kohl, Herbert. *Reading, How To* and Carver & Fotinos. *A Conversation Book: English in Everyday Life*. Prentice Hall.

I guess what I really want to say here is if the ESL teacher is inexperienced, then s/he should first acquire actual teaching texts. If they have had a formal ESL background, they should have the basic texts on the major teaching methods, some good grammar reference books and then gradually add research materials such as work by Lambert, Carroll, Chomsky, Hymes, Coulthard, Jakobovits, etc.

One other thing that I forgot to mention! If going abroad, I'd bring at least one copy of a test (Michigan, CELT, The John Test).

Needless to say, if the teacher really wants to be a good teacher of ESL, s/he should also have a box of rods, a big picture file and a sturdy canvas bag.

I could go on, but I'll be merciful and stop. I hope you find this interesting. Stevick would have an interesting list if you would like to include him on your survey.

JACK RICHARDS

List I (alphabetical) 10 volumes for the teacher's desk/library

1. Allen, Harold and Russell N. Campbell. *Teaching English as a Second Language*. 1972. McGraw Hill, N.Y.

2. Broughton, Geoffrey et al. 1978. *Teaching English as a Foreign Language*. Routledge and Kegan Paul, London.

3. Close, R. A. *A Reference Grammar for Students of English*. 1975. Longman, London.

4. Close, R. A. *English as a Foreign Language*. 1962. Allen and Unwin.

5. Corder, S. P. and J. P. B. Allen. *The Edinburgh Course in Applied Linguistics, Vol. 3, Techniques in Applied Linguistics*. 1974. Oxford University Press, London.

6. Heaton, J. B. *Writing English Language Tests*. 1975. Longman, London.

7. *Longman Dictionary of Contemporary English*. Longman, London. 1978.

8. Joiner, Elizabeth, and Patricia Westphal. *Developing Communication Skills*. 1978. Newbury House, Rowley.

9. Newton, Anne (compiler). *The Art of TESOL, Parts 1 and 2*. 1978. Newbury House, Rowley, Mass.

10. Rogers, John. 1978. *Group Activities for Language Learning*. RELC, Singapore.

List II. 5 additional books as a later addition.

1. Corder, S. P. and J. P. B. Allen. 1974. *The Edinburgh Course in Applied Linguistics Vol. 2, Papers in Applied Linguistics*. Oxford University Press, London.

2. Rivers, Wilga. *Teaching Foreign Language Skills*. 1968. University of Chicago, Chicago.

3. Stevick, Earl. *Memory, Meaning and Method*. 1976. Newbury House, Rowley, MA.

4. Widdowson, H. G. *Teaching Language as Communication*. 1978. Oxford University Press, London.

5. Wilkins, David. *Notional Syllabuses*, 1976. Oxford University Press, London.

List III. Articles

1. Allen, Patrick. Structural and Functional Models in Language Teaching. *TESL Talk* Vol 8, No. I, Jan. 1977. p. 5-15.

2. Clark, Mark and Sandra Silberstein. Towards a Realization of Psycholinguistic Principles in the ESL Reading Class. *Language Learning*. Vol. 27/I, June 1977, 135-154.

3. Hendrickson, James. Error Correction in Foreign Language Teaching. *Modern Language Journal*, Dec. '78. 387-398.

4. Holmes, Janet and Dorothy F. Brown. Developing Sociolinguistic Competence in a Second Language. *TESOL Quarterly*. 10/4, 1974. 423-432.

5. Krashen, Stephen D. The Monitor Model for Adult Second Language Performance. In *Viewpoints on English as a Second Language*. Marina Burt, Heidi Dulay and Mary Finocchiaro (editors). Regents, NY, 1972. 152-161.

6. Stratton, Florence. Putting the Communicative Syllabus in its Place. *TESOL Quarterly*, 11/2 1977. 131-142.

BERNARD SUSSER

I. Textbook

(1) Chastain, Kenneth. *Developing Second-Language Skills: Theory to Practice.* Chicago: Rand McNally, second edition, 1976.

Part One of this book is an excellent introduction to the discipline of foreign language teaching; Part Two should be used in conjunction with a cookbook.

II. Cookbooks

(2) Paulston, Christina Bratt and Mary Newton Bruder. *Teaching English as a Second Language, Techniques and Procedures.* Cambridge: Winthrop Publishers, 1976.

(3) Rivers, Wilga M. and Mary S. Temperley. *A Practical Guide to the Teaching of English as a Second or Foreign Language.* New York: Oxford University Press, 1978.

Despite the similarity of their tables of contents, these books are quite different. It is not just that R & T are more subtle than P & B, or that they are fonder of jargon. P & B are writing from the point of view of the teacher, or more strictly speaking, of the lesson plan, while R & T are looking at what happens in the classroom in terms of what is supposedly taking place inside the student's head. (Compare, e.g., their treatments of multiple choice questions for testing listening comprehension: P & B, p. 140ff; R & T, p. 95ff.)

III. Collections

(4) Allen, Harold B. and Russell N. Campbell. *Teaching English as a Second Language, A Book of Readings.* New York: McGraw-Hill, second edition, 1972.

(5) Croft, Kenneth, ed. *Readings on English as a Second Language.* Cambridge: Winthrop Publishers, 1972.

IV. Grammar

(6) Stageberg, Norman C. *An Introductory English Grammar.* New York: Holt, Rinehart and Winston, second edition, 1971.

Any standard reference grammar of American English will do here.

V. Pronunciation/Phonetics

(7) Bowen, J. Donald. *Patterns of English Pronunciation.* Rowley: Newbury House Publishers, 1975.

Or any other standard study of American English pronunciation.

VI. Horse's Mouth

[TESOL students/teachers need an introduction to some of the important new trends in foreign language teaching. Since these have not been particularly well served by summaries in secondary works, I recommend going straight to the horse's mouth (although some may assign these works to another portion of the horse's anatomy).]

(8) Gattegno, Caleb. *Teaching Foreign Languages in Schools the Silent Way.* New York: Educational Solutions, second edition, 1972.

It grieves me to recommend a book whose incomprehensibility seems to be a point of pride with the author, but the ideas are important if only for their shock value, and no secondary description can be trusted. (For example, Robinett's *Teaching*

English to Speakers of Other Languages ((University of Minnesota Press and McGraw Hill, 1978) has a whole chapter on "trends and issues in language teaching" but devotes only six lines (p. 167) to the silent way, and these six lines are not based on any study of or even familiarity with Gattegno's work but are taken from Stevick, a man who himself pleads physical inability for hard thinking (*Memory, Meaning and Method,* p. 106) and admits that his description of the Silent Way is "fragmentary and in no sense authoritative." (ibid., p. 135))

(9) Curran, Charles A. *Counseling-Learning in Second Languages.* Apple River Press, 1976.

(10) Asher, James J. and C. Adamski. *Learning Another Language Through Actions: The Complete Teacher's Guidebook.* Los Gatos: Sky Oak Productions, 1977.

I have chosen these three because they are important but any number of other works might be substituted here. The important thing is that a course in TESOL teacher training should devote considerable time to study and discussion of books and articles presenting new ideas or written from unusual standpoints. The reason for this is that once these students graduate and begin teaching, they will have no trouble getting through the books on teaching methods for TESOL that are emerging from the publishers in a steady stream like a substitution drill from a tape recorder, but they will have trouble with original material unless they are taught how to analyse it. (In short, I am saying that a course on TESOL methodology must do what every course in the humanities and social sciences must do, teach students how to read. And this applies to native speakers as well as non-natives.)

VII. TESOL students and beginning teachers also need to know about:

a. Professional organizations: 1) in their own countries; 2) IATEFL, TESOL and other "international" organizations

b. Sources of information about textbooks and other teaching materials

c. Bibliography: 1) Items such as those mentioned in my *JALT Newsletter* article; 2) ERIC; 3) Croft, Kenneth. *A Composite Bibliography for ESOL Teacher Training.* Washington: TESOL, 1974.

RUTH CRYMES

Making book lists seems to be in the air. Did you know that the RELC Journal was doing something along these lines? Some time ago I got a request to list books for various areas and then later I got a questionnaire with several pages of titles listed which I was asked to rate. I don't know when they plan to publish the results.

Also last fall I was asking myself what books and readings in our field would constitute a kind of core reading list that would define our field and I asked our faculty to list titles—but I didn't have much luck getting responses from them. I keep thinking that there must be some kind of basic list of titles that any specialist in the field would be familiar with. But that's different from what you are trying to do.

Enclosed is my effort to list ten titles that I would recommend for a beginning ESL teacher's library. I limited it to books —I wouldn't know where to begin or stop if I listed articles.

Recommended Titles For An ESL Teacher's Library

Cazden, Courtney B., Vera P. John and Dell Hymes, eds. 1972. *Functions of language in the classroom.* New York, Teachers College Press.

Coulthard, Malcolm. 1977. *An introduction to discourse analysis.* London, Longman.

Diller, Karl. 1978. *The language teaching controversy.* Rowley, Mass., Newbury House.

Jespersen, Otto. 1904. *How to teach a foreign language.* London, George Allen and Unwin.

Madsen, Harold S. and J. Donald Bowen. 1978. *Adaptation in language teaching.* Rowley, Mass., Newbury House.

Quirk, Randolph et al. 1972. *A grammar of contemporary English.* London, Longman. Or Randolph Quirk and Sidney Greenbaum. 1973. *A concise grammar of contemporary English.* New York, Harcourt Brace Jovanovich. and, possibly Geoffrey Leech and Jan Svartvik. 1975. *A communicative grammar of English.* London, Longman.

Rivers, Wilga M. and Mary Temperley. 1978. *A practical guide to the teaching of English as a second or foreign language.* New York, Oxford University Press.

Stevick, Earl W. 1976. *Memory, meaning and method.* Rowley, Mass., Newbury House.

Via, Richard A. 1976. *English in three acts.* Honolulu, University Press of Hawaii.

Widdowson, Henry G. 1978. *Teaching language as communication.* London, Oxford University Press.

DONALD KNAPP

1. Fries, Charles C. *Teaching and Learning English as a Foreign Language.* U. of Michigan Press, 1945.

2. Stevick, Earl J. *Adapting and Writing Language Lessons.* Foreign Service Institute, 1971.

3. Leavitt, Leslie W. *Practical Help in Teaching English as a Foreign Language.* Beirut: American Univ., 1964.

4. Robinett, Betty. *Teaching English to Speakers of Other Languages: Substance and Technique.* McGraw-Hill, 1978.

5. Rivers, Wilga and Mary Temperley *A Practical Guide to Teaching English as a Second Language.* Oxford, 1978.

6. Harris, David. *Testing English as a Second Language.* McGraw-Hill, 1969.

7. Pauston, Christina and Mary Bruder. *Teaching English as a Second Language: Techniques and Procedures.* Winthrop, 1976.

8. Gallwey, Timothy. *The Inner Game of Tennis.* Random House, 1974.

9. Smith, Frank. *Understanding Reading, Second Edition.* Holt Rinehart Winston, 1971.

10. Van Ek, J. A. *The Threshold Level of Modern Language Teaching in Schools.* Longmans, 1978.

TED PLAISTER

Enclosed is THE LIST. Needless to say this is a [explitive deleted] to compile.

I wonder how many people will list Fries. I'm just old-fashioned enough to think that a little history is good for everybody, plus his ideas on vocabulary ain't all that bad. Ken Jackson is in the process of putting together a book (so he tells me) on the history of language teaching—sort of Kelly brought up-to-date. If it is any good, it should be on the list. But it isn't anywhere near completion, so let's just forget that. There are things I don't like about Bernard's [Spolsky] book, but it is still an important overview—I think.

1. Alexander, L. G., W. Stannard Allen, R. A. Close, and R. J. O'Neill. 1970. *English grammatical structure: A general syllabus for teachers.* London: Longman Group Limited.

2. Fries, Charles C. 1945. *Teaching and learning English as a foreign language.* Ann Arbor: The University of Michigan Press.

3. Madsen, Harold S. and J. Donald Bowen. 1978. *Adaptation in language teaching.* Rowley, Mass.: Newbury House Publishers, Inc.

4. Munby, John. 1978. *Communicative syllabus design: A socio-linguistic model for defining the content of purpose-specific language programmes.* London: Cambridge University Press.

5. Rivers, Wilga M. and Mary S. Temperley. 1978. *A practical guide to the teaching of English as a second or foreign language.* New York: Oxford University Press.

6. Smith, Frank. 1978. *Understanding reading. 2d ed.* New York: Holt, Rinehart and Winston.

7. Spolsky, Bernard. 1978. *Educational linguistics.* Rowley, Mass.: Newbury House Publishers, Inc.

8. Stevick, Earl W. 1976. *Memory, meaning, and method: Some psychological perspectives on language learning.* Rowley, Mass.: Newbury House Publishers, Inc.

9. Valette, Rebecca M. 1977. *Modern language testing. 2d ed.* New York: Harcourt Brace Jovanovich, Inc.

10. Via, Richard A. 1976. *English in three acts.* Honolulu: The University Press of Hawaii.

Four additional books.

1. Coulthard, Malcolm. 1977. *An introduction to discourse analysis.* London: Longman Group Ltd.

2. Foss, Donald J. and David T. Hakes. 1978. *Psycholinguistics: An introduction to the psychology of language.* Englewood Cliffs, N.J.: Prentice-Hall, Inc.

3. Fromkin, Victoria and Robert Rodman. 1974. *An introduction to language.* New York: Holt, Rinehart and Winston, Inc.

4. Halliday, M. A. K. 1973. *Explorations in the functions of language.* London: Edward Arnold (Publishers) Ltd.

DARLENE LARSON

After the extensive work that you have done in preparing a bibliography for your methods students, you are well aware of how impossible it is to choose ten books.

But I have found it a "fun thing" to do, anyway. I'm dying to hear what others selected. For me, I'd recommend the following:

1. A grammar written for ESL students: Lorenz, Praninskas, Crowell, Frank . . .
2. A dictionary
3. Edward T. Hall's *The Hidden Dimension*
4. Timothy Gallwey's *The Inner Game of Tennis*
5. Earl Stevick's *Memory, Meaning, and Method*
6. Frank Smith's *Comprehension and Learning*
7. Dave Harris's *Testing English as a Second Language*
8. Nilson and Nilson's *Pronunciation Contrasts*
9. Dykstra, Port and Port's *Ananse Tales*
10. Martin Joos' *The Five Clocks*

Instead of articles or five more books to add later, I'm going to recommend the following as essential resources for a teacher who is going to work with beginning or intermediate students.

1. An atlas of the world (National Geographic's is excellent.)
2. *The Farmer's Almanac*
3. Road maps of the State and information about state parks.
4. Tourist guides of the city in which you teach.
5. A list of government agencies and community services in your city.
6. A picture file.
   a. some of isolated objects
   b. some of single subjects doing something or going somewhere
   c. some of active groups
   d. some "busy" pics—crowds, composites, etc.

THOMAS BUCKINGHAM

1. Michael West's *Teaching English Under Difficult Circumstances.* On my list because it was the first book that ever gave me help in teaching English—and because it still seems to me the best available in teaching English in a non-English speaking country, even though one of the oldest.

2. Stevick, Earl. *Adapting and Writing Language Lessons.* My own limited language experience keeps me from making much use of the appendices but the first three chapters are so full of insights on what makes material work that after years of using the book I am still "discovering" it.

3. Wilga Rivers and Mary Temperley. *A Practical Guide to Teaching English as a Second Language.*

4. William F. Mackey. *Language Teaching Analysis.* Out of date, unfortunately, but still the Sears Roebuck catalog of ESL/EFL.

5. Robinett, Betty Wallace. *Teaching English to Speakers of Other Languages.* The most balanced presentation of basics available.

6. Richards, Jack and John Oller. *Focus on the Learner.* Covers the current issues of interest.

7. Finocchiaro, Mary. *Teaching English as a Second Language From Theory to Practice.* The first, little book, not the later expanded one, because it is a good, clear,

simply presented statement of what to do for the untrained, inexperienced.

8. Widdowson, Henry. *Teaching Language as Communication.* An inspired book—cuts through the nonsense and gets at what we should be thinking about.

9. *The Art of TESOL. Vols. I and II.* Good things not available elsewhere.

10. Heaton, J. B. *Language Testing.*

W. R. LEE

Here are the titles of ten books that a 'new' teacher of TEFL or TESL might find useful. I have borne in mind that such a teacher might find himself or herself, in due course, teaching at any age-level or level of achievement in any part of the world; thus this is not a book-list for any kind of specialized training; nor is it a list, therefore, that will be equally suitable for 'new' teachers anywhere. It is a difficult problem you have set and I have tried to solve it by omitting books on linguistics and applied linguistics, on the English language itself, and on specific aspects of language learning and teaching (e.g. games, dramatization, songs, writing and reading skills, etc.), omissions on which I would normally regard as inexcusable. What remains is a list of 'broad' and general books, which include or touch on matters that every 'new' teacher should think about. Even so, the choice is arbitrary and some titles are missing that really should be there.

1. F. L. Billows: *The Techniques of Foreign Language Teaching* (Longman)
2. J. A. Bright and G. P. McGregor: *Teaching English as a Second Language* (Longman)
3. G. Broughton, C. Brumfit, R. Flavell, P. Hill, A. Pincas: *Teaching English as a Foreign Language* (Routledge and Kegan Paul)
4. Mary Finocchiaro: *Teaching English as a Second Language* (Harper and Row)
5. A. S. Hornby: *The Teaching of Structural Words and Sentence Patterns* (O.U.P.)
6. W. F. Mackey: *Language Teaching Analysis* (Longman)
7. Wilga M. Rivers and Mary S. Temperley: *A Practical Guide to the Teaching of English as a Second or Foreign Language* (O.U.P.)
8. P. Strevens: *New Orientations in the Teaching of English* (O.U.P.)
9. H. G. Widdowson: *Teaching Language as Communication* (O.U.P.)
10. D. Wilkins: *Second-Language Learning and Teaching* (Arnold)

As for an additional four or five, I find it impossible to keep to that number, and suggest at least the following:

I. Dunlop: *Practical Techniques in the Teaching of Oral English* (Almquist and Wiksell, Stockholm)

R. Lado: *Language Teaching—A Scientific Approach* (McGraw-Hill)

H. E. Palmer: *The Principles of Language Study* (O.U.P.)

F. C. Johnson: *English as a Second Language—an Individualized Approach* (Murray)

P. Gurrey: *Teaching English as a Foreign Language* (Longman)

L. G. Kelly: *Twenty-Five Centuries of Language Teaching* (Newbury House)

Betty W. Robinett: *Teaching English to Speakers of Other Languages* (McGraw-Hill and University of Minnesota Press)

But really, wouldn't it be best for teachers in training to find a quiet corner in a good library to read *in* these books and other books? None of it will mean much, anyway, until they have done some teaching, quite a bit of teaching. So perhaps it would be better to *possess* a few practical books about drawing on the chalkboard (e.g. '*Draw It, Magistern*', by A. Hermansson and B. Astrom—Svenska Bokforlaget, Sweden); games and dramatisation (e.g. L. A. Hill's '*English Language Teaching Games for Adult Students*', Evans; and '*Drama Techniques in Language Learning*' by A. Maley and A. Duff, C.U.P.). But again, what the 'new' teacher really needs is to browse over a number of such books and select what he or she requires and is interested in at the time.

In listing *articles* one is forced to be even more arbitrary. Herewith a small number of fairly 'general' articles that 'new' teachers might find interesting:

R. A. Close, 'Banners and Bandwaggons', *ELT Journal*, 31, 3, 1977.

D. Girard, 'Motivation: the Responsibility of the Teacher' *ELT Journal*, 31, 2, 1977.

A. H. King, 'Notes on remedial English at higher-education level', *ELT Journal*, 27, 3, 1973.

P. Mugglestone, 'The Primary Curiosity Motive', *ELTJ*, 31, 2, 1977.

J. Forrester, 'Demonstration lessons', *ELTJ*, 29, 1, 1974.

L. Greer, 'Teacher Training Projects', *ELTJ*, 31, 2, 1977.

P. Wingard, 'Teaching practice,' *ELTJ*, 29, 1, 1974.

B. Pattison, 'Research priorities', *ELTJ*, 25, 1, 1970.

I. Schmidt-Mackey, 'Repetition within a context', *ELTJ*, 21, 3, 1967.

W. R. Lee, 'For and against an early start', *Foreign Language Annuals*, 10, 3, 1977.

——, 'Syllabus Construction for Foreign-Language Teaching: Reconciling the Approaches', *ELT Documents*, London.

J. L. Trim, 'Modern languages in education, with special reference to a projected European unit? credit system', Council of Europe *EES Symposium* 57, 3, 1973.

M. Macmillan, 'In defence of English', *ELTJ*, 27, 3, 1973.

A. L. W. Rees, 'Getting questions asked', *ELTJ*, 30, 4, 1946.

Christina B. Paulston, 'The sequencing of structural pattern drills, *TESOL Quarterly*, 5, 1971.

R. L. Allen, 'Using Drills Creatively, *English Teaching Forum*, 10, 6, 1972.

Florence Stratton, 'Putting the Communicative Syllabus in its Place,' *TESOL Quarterly* 11, 2, 1977.

R. V. White, 'Telling What Happened,' *TESOL Quarterly*, 11, 3, 1977.

However, once again, it would be best for the teacher in training, or 'new' teacher, to consult back issues of *English Teaching Forum*, *TESOL Quarterly*, *ELT Journal*, *Modern English Teacher*, etc., in pursuit of his or her own needs, lines of interest, etc.

EARL STEVICK

Thanks for your invitation to make sug-

gestion for a "basic" library for new ESL/EFL teachers. As you said in your letter, it's hard to know where to stop in such a list. I will therefore attach great weight to your two words: a *basic* library for *new* teachers. On that ground I have eliminated much that I consider to be merely "excellent," "invaluable" and "indispensable" for the fully formed teacher.

I would begin, as I have said several times in the past, with a book which sets out what a teacher or a learner may (and may not) reasonably try to do, and which does so without distracting the reader's attention from essentials by talking about language classes: W. Timothy Gallwey's *The Inner Game of Tennis*.

Second, I would move to a book written by a gifted language teacher, but written long enough ago so that it would not immediately draw the reader into present-day issues and controversies: Otto Jespersen's *How to Teach a Foreign Language*.

Third, I would go to something which is more recent, but which is old enough to give a longish perspective on what we are doing now: Wilga Rivers' *The Psychologist and the Foreign Language Teacher*. The issues that Rivers deals with in this book are no longer the focus of attention in the profession as they were when she wrote, but they will always be with us, and the clarity of her treatment is exemplary.

Fourth, I would ask a new teacher to read the introduction to Maley and Duff's *Drama Techniques in Language Learning*. These few pages are unmatched, as far as I know, for brevity and clarity in sketching what there is to be taught and learned besides sounds, words and grammar.

By now, I think the reader would be ready for a book which describes one good solid method, and describes it with both clarity and conviction. One such book is Paulston and Bruder's *Teaching English as a Second Language: Techniques and Procedures*.

Then a sampling of what can be done with live and lively bits of communication by and for native speakers: the *Student's Book* written by Abbs and Sexton for the *Challenges* course published by Longman.

About here, the reader-teacher ought to look at something by Krashen that draws a distinction between adult "learning" and adult "acquisition" of a second language, and lists some of the characteristics of "acquisition": probably his *Language Acquisition and Second Language Teaching*.°

This would be a good time for the new teacher to go on and sample the multiple techniques which make up the bulk of the Maley and Duff book.

Then s/he might look at a clear and clarifying treatment of theory: Diller *On the Language Teaching Controversy*;

and at her/himself in relation to teaching, through Jersild's *When Teachers Look at Themselves*;

and last, at teachers and learners as human beings, through Martin Buber's essays "On Education" and "On the Education of Character" (in *Between Man and Man*).

As I said in the first paragraph, I have taken you literally and concentrated on "basics" that have been of help to me. From these, the new teacher may go on to

books that provide an introduction to such essentials as phonetics, grammatical analysis, and testing.

I need hardly point out that these books are "basic" only for people who would like to become the kind of teacher that I would like to become.

°John—I'm not sure whether this has actually been published.

JOHN F. HASKELL

These may not be the best, they certainly are not the only books one might choose, but they are basic, practical, and provide a well-rounded library to begin with.

1. Robinett, Betty W. *Teaching ESOL: Substance and Technique*. The first books since Nida to spell out what elements of English need to be known by and taught by the teacher; syntax, pronunciation, and word formation—*and* how to do it.

2. Pauston, Christina, and Mary Bruder. *Teaching ESL: Techniques and Procedures*. A good practical cook book that says things no one else says.

3. Crowell, Thomas L. *Index to Modern English*. Of all the grammars this is the easiest to use for a new teacher.

4. Valette, Rebecca. *Modern Language Testing*. I like Heaton a lot, too, but this is so easy to get into.

5. Stevick, Earl. *Adapting and Writing Language Lessons*. I like all of Stevick's works beginning with *Helping People Learn English*. Next to Virginia Allen he makes the most sense to me as a speaker to teachers. This particular book is so full that it is never old, and no one provides a better measure against which to judge materials than Stevick does in this book.

6. *TESOL Quarterly* and *TESOL Newsletter*. I think the best way to keep current in the field is to be a member of a professional organization that provides the kinds of publications that TESOL (or NCTE) provide.

7. Brown, H. Douglas. *Principles of Language Learning and Teaching*. (Prentice-Hall, 1979). Sure to be on everyones list, next year, this book is very up-to-date and readable.

8. Illyin, Donna, and Thomas Tragardh. *Classroom Practices in Adult ESL*. A really good cookbook, the Fe Dacany or Mary Finocchiaro book of the 70's.

9. Hall, Edward. *The Silent Language* (and/or *The Hidden Dimension*) and/or *ESL in Bilingual Education* by Alatis and Twaddell. I had a hard time, here. Fortunately, Hall is a 'drugstore' paperback so maybe both are affordable. Everyone should read it. But my U.S. ESL teachers need to understand B1/BC, too and the Alatis and Twaddell book is a beginning.

10. Valette, Rebecca and Renee Disick. *Modern Language Performance Objectives*. Add this to Stevick as a basic 'teacher' book. Most teachers are desperate to know how to prepare a lesson, a unit, an exercise. This book helps a lot. Only Finocchiaro's *ESL: Theory to Practice* (old edition) comes close.

My additional books are added here basically because they seem to supplement best the above books (and did not occur on anyone else's list). Again, they are books I have used and continue to find useful.

Burt, Dulay and Finocchairo. *Viewpoints on ESL.* Regents, 1977.

Gordon and Wong. *A Manual for Speech Improvement.* Prentice-Hall, 1961.

Dixon, Robert J. *Regents English Workbooks* (Vol. 1 & 2), 1956.

And, if I could find them, the works of Virginia French Allen and those of Robert L. Allen.

SUMMARY

The intent of requesting these lists was to provide, hopefully, some general agreement as to what would be, say ten books that anyone could recommend to the beginning teacher. But there were no more than two dozen books which appeared on more than three lists, and over one third of the books listed fall generally into the classification of methods texts. Using Don Bowen's general format, I have subjectively and arbitrarily divided the entries into ten categories (and a few subcategories), because frequency alone would have left me with seven methods texts and a tie of fifteen books for eighth place. I have included in the categories below, the author, title, publisher, and date of publication of those two dozen books which were mentioned on more than three lists.

1. **General Methods Books.** Every list includes at least one method book, most of them two or more. Two texts were mentioned most often, in fact more often than any other books in any category; Betty Robinett's *Teaching English to Speakers of Other Languages: Substance and Technique* (McGraw-Hill 1978) and Rivers and Temperley's *A Practical Guide to the Teaching of English as Second or Foreign Language* (Oxford 1978). Paulston and Bruder's *Teaching English as a Second Language: Techniques and Procedures* (Winthrop 1976) and Henry Widdowson's *Teaching Language as Communication* (Oxford 1978) were also mentioned on a number of lists.

Interestingly, five books, all of which might, at this point, be called Classic Audio-Lingual texts were also mentioned on a number of lists; Charles Fries' *Teaching and Learning English as a Foreign Language* (U of Michigan Press 1945), Mary Finocchiaro's *English as a Second Language: From Theory to Practice* (Regents 1964, rev. 1974), Fe Dacanay's *Techniques and Procedures in Second Language Teaching* (Oceana Press 1963), and two collections of articles, Allen and Campbell's *Teaching English as a Second Language: A Book of Readings* (McGraw-Hill, 2nd Ed. 1972), and Anne Newton's collection of articles from the *English Teaching Forum* entitled *The Art of TESOL* (Newbury House 1978).

2. **Topical Methods Books.** Methods books could easily be divided into a number of subcategories subsuming even some of the arbitrarily established categories below such as Language and Culture, or Testing. Generally, one might say they were extensions of chapters from a General Methods text, such as those above, on Reading, Composition, etc. One such book mentioned on a number of lists was Frank Smith's *Understanding Reading* (Holt Rinehart Winston 1971).

Curiously, even with the lack of favor

that the teaching of pronunciation, per se, seems to presently find itself with, and the inclusion in every methods book of at least one chapter on the teaching of pronunciation, most lists included an additional book on some area of pronunciation. Two books, both teaching texts, were mentioned most frequently; Prator and Robinett's *A Manual of American English Pronunciation* (1972) and Don Bowen's *Pattern of English Pronunciation* (Newbury House 1975). Nilson and Nilson's *Pronunciation Contrasts in English* (Simon and Schuster 1971) also appeared on a number of lists.

Another kind of subcategory for topical methods texts might be those which promote a particular method or approach to language teaching/acquisition. Although a number of such books were mentioned only once, Van Ek's *The Threshold Level for Modern Language Learning in Schools* (Longmans 1978) appeared on more than three lists.

3. **Grammar and Linguistics.** Bowen divides Grammar into pedagogical (or teaching) grammars and reference grammars, and I have added a third subcategory, linguistics books. While none of the volumes which might be called teaching grammars such as Crowell, Praninskis or Hornby were mentioned more than twice, almost all lists include one of these and/or one of two short versions of Quirk, Greenbaum, Leech and Svartvik's *Grammar of Contemporary English;* Quirk and Greenbaum's, *A Concise Grammar of Contemporary English* (Harcourt Brace Jovanovich 1972) or Leech and Svartvik's, *A Communication Grammar of English* (Longman 1975).

Some lists suggested a general linguistics reference for the basic library, such as Bolinger, but no general consensus could be made.

4. **Testing.** While most methods or collections contain chapters on testing, many lists contained at least one volume in addition, either a reference volume or a collection of current trends. The two books most frequently mentioned were David Harris' *Testing English as a Second Language* (McGraw-Hill 1969) and J. B. Heaton's *Writing English Language Tests: A Practical Guide for Teachers of English as a Second or Foreign Language* (Longman 1975).

5. **Current Trends.** While there were a number of current collections of articles mentioned the single book in this category that was most often mentioned was Earl Stevick's *Memory, Meaning and Method* (Newbury House 1978). A number of lists suggested the *TESOL Quarterly* and the *TESOL Newsletter,* as sources of current information.

6. **Materials.** It was hard to justify this category, but the two books included here occurred on so many lists that it was selected as a separate category. Also the topic did not seem to be a regular chapter in the methods books. Other books were also mentioned but two were most often listed; Earl Stevick's *Adapting and Writing Language Lessons* (Foreign Service Institute 1971) and Madsen and Bowen's *Adaptation in Language Teaching* (Newbury House 1978).

7. **Teacher Reference.** This was for al-

most all lists, dictionary, though almanac and atlas, even grammar might also fit here. No American English monolingual dictionary was a particular favorite, nor any particular pronunciation or idiom dictionary. Both the Oxford and Longmans (British English) dictionaries were mentioned on a number of lists as ESL dictionaries.

8. **Language and Culture.** There were no books mentioned frequently enough in this category to list here. In fact, I found books on bilingual education, sociolinguistics, or language and culture curiously missing from most lists. Edward Hall's books were most often mentioned.

9. **Supplementary Materials.** Games, songs, activities, etc. Here, again, no one book seemed to stand out even though some such volume was suggested on a large number of lists.

10. **Miscellaneous.** Other categories come to mind: Methodologies, texts on specific methods; English for Special Purposes; Textbook series, etc. I called the 10th category miscellaneous because there was one book mentioned by a number of lists that did not seem to fit into any of the other categories or sub-categories and that was Kelly's *25 Centuries of Language Teaching* (a boring book). There is no intention, I might add, of suggesting in these ten categories that one book should be selected from each one, so in summary:

(1) **General methods** (choose at least one, preferably one of the more current volumes. Add as many others as you can as part of your first ten or supplemental to it. Be sure to include (or at least read) somewhere along the line, one of the 'classic' audio-lingual texts or collections. (2) **Topical Methods.** Choose at least one book from this category, one that will best supplement category 1. (3) **Grammar and Linguistics.** Choose at least one good reference book on grammar either from the teaching type or general reference. Pick one from the other subcategory of grammar later on. Somewhere along the line, either take a course in linguistics or get a readable general linguistics text. (4) **Testing.** Choose one book either as a general reference on types of tests or as a supplement to your methods books, on current trends in testing. (5) **Current Events.** Choose at least one current volume in this area. (Join TESOL and get the *Quarterly* and the *Newsletter* annually). (6) **Materials.** Choose one book that tells you how to make materials. (7) **Teacher Reference.** Have a good dictionary and learn how to use it. Add other reference volumes as you can. (8) **Language and Culture.** Find at least one good book in language and culture, bilingual education, kinesics, or some such subtopic in this category. (9) **Supplementary Materials.** Find some volume that can supplement your textbook; games, activities, skits, exercises, etc. (10) **Miscellaneous.** Skip this category in favor of adding another book from one of the preceding nine categories. (Unless you want to choose something like Gallwey or Rosten.) It is perhaps redundant to note here that at least one volume each by Robinett, Bowen and Stevick seems to be generally a good bet. *TN 12/79*

BOOK REVIEWS

DEVELOPING COMMUNICATIVE COMPETENCE: INTERACTION ACTIVITIES IN ESL

Judith Kettering
U. of Pittsburgh Press, 1975

ROLEPLAYS IN ESL.

Christina Bratt Paulston, Barry Brunetti, Dale Britton, and John Hoover; University of Pittsburgh Press, 1975.

Reviewed by Mary E. Hines
LaGuardia Community College, CUNY

Everyone wants to ensure "communicative competence" among students in addition to, and better, *while,* teaching English. Yet teachers discover again and again the problems inherent in having students act in class, primarily that of students producing so much original language that is so often agrammatical. Teachers wonder when and how to correct, whether their corrections have any meaning or whether, in fact, they should impede free language at all. In the last year, three texts which enhance free conversation to varying degrees have appeared.

In *Developing Communicative Competence: Interaction Activities in English as a Second Language* (University of Pittsburgh), Judith Carl Kettering ranges from controlled dialogues to situations calling for original language. Her dialogues, developing "social realtions skills through conversations" are bland by nature but they do introduce students to cultural stances by noting the distinction between formal and informal language and which expressions are appropriate for given situations. The situations themselves are in turn structured, semi-structured, and unstructured (the last calling for language beyond what participants in the dialogues could provide). The likelihood that students assigned to role B are not going to meet A's expressions outside of class exists but it is assumed a given class would find its own range. There is, too, a section called "Problem Solving and Compromising" which establishes roles and conflicts quickly but calls for a wide range of structures and vocabulary. Their use will help students explore and enjoy English but it is

likely to lead to language breakdown rather quickly and teachers will again wonder about the when, how, and whether to correct problems. The best section of the book deals with "Community Oriented Projects" which assigns field tasks to students, getting them out of the class into the community to explore the supermarket, ways of looking for an apartment, and coping with the post office or bank. Precise questions regarding information students are to seek are provided and the tasks are an excellent guide to newly arrived foreign students. The section is a stimulus to get into the community.

Useful, too, with a class of foreign students, is another book in the Pittsburgh series, *Roleplays in English as a Second Language* (Paulston, Brunetti, Britton and Hoover) which moves from bland interview to murder and marijuana scenes, always providing the situation, role assignments, useful expressions and vocabulary. The text is a good source of idiomatic English, and of imaginitive scenes which teachers will happily turn to on a Friday afternoon. They will have the correction problem, but students enjoy participating in the situations and any exercise which immerses students so quickly and happily plays a role in the EFL class. The "Unhappy Student" allows for students to argue the correct way to learn a language and at the same time resolve attitudes toward language learning. "The T.V. Commercial" calls for students to compose an ad which will attract the American buyer and lends itself to nuances of American culture. The reader wishes there were more assignments similar to the last two. *TN 2/77*

ENGLISH IN THREE ACTS

By Richard Via (U. of Hawaii Press, 1976)

Reviewed by Ruth Shernoff
Queens College

Richard Via knows what drama is all about. He has written one-act plays, been an actor, stage manager and director. Under a Fulbright scholarship, he traveled to Japan to bring western theatre to student ac-

tors. The problems he encountered there were similar to that of the classroom ESL teacher. And so he virtually became a teacher of English as a second language. However, his methodology incorporated all the techniques used in acting classes and in Broadway rehearsals.

English in Three Acts emphasizes drama as a natural way to communicate effectively inasmuch as it is a good model of the way we talk. (It is not for absolute beginners). Act I takes the reader step by step through preliminary activities which are so valuable in themselves that one need not even get to the play itself to reap benefits. For example, there are breathing and voice exercises, suggestions for body talk and improvisation. (Are you having trouble hearing your students? Tell them to kick an imaginary soccer ball hard and then use that kind of energy to push out their voice, or practice the sounds that initiate the martial arts. Out with inhibitions.)

The singularly most important exercise in the book is the Talk and Listen method for dialogues. Students never read but maintain eye-to-eye contact when speaking and listening. It's talk, listen, talk, etc. Students speak from cards with only their lines on it, or they might have cards with a choice of responses to ensure more careful listening. Added to this, Mr. Via suggests speaking the lines in different speeds and tone (change the situation) to show how language can be changed in meaning and feeling. Mr. Via gets angry with those who feel that conversation means *speaking* only. He calls such speakers "robots roaming the world ready to pounce upon some innocent native speaker." He wishes someone would give them a punch in the nose and shout, "Listen!"

Act II presents seven of the author's one-act plays for the classroom. However, these are too long for a 50 minute class. (Mr. Via recently explained to this writer that a book with shorter plays would be forthcoming.) The plays in the book are all lively with natural dialogues using popular idioms and colloquial expressions. *Never on Wednesday* dramatizes a humorous family situation with a communication gap not only between parents and children but parents and grandparents as well. *Garage Sale* is an informal social event; meeting neighbors, picking up inexpensive items that have been cleaned out. At the end of the play there is a vocabulary list defining the popular expressions.

Act III helps the teacher stage a play for an audience. The Epilogue answers teachers' questions (they might be yours) and lists some one- and three-act plays by notable playwrights.

Mr. Via reassures us that we do not have to know about theatre and acting. The purpose of the book is not to develop actors, but to learn natural conversational English by *using* it in a natural context. He also reminds us that the sense of community in the team effort is supportive and self-motivating.

The author makes a particularly strong point of encouraging the students to express and add their *own* selves through the characters, drawing on their *own* experiences and perceptions. He never models a line for a student. He only corrects pronunciation and diction. He feels that real security comes when a student finds out how to say it correctly himself.

A healthy classroom needs people who can be authentic. Students learning a language do tighten up and restrict the expressive flow of their true selves. How to release the energy is challenging. There may be more than one way. It is this reviewer's opinion that Mr. Via has made a worthy contribution to a possible solution to the problem.   TN 9/77

SKITS IN ENGLISH

Skits in English (New Edition) by Mary Elizabeth Hines: Regents Publishing Company, Inc., 1980, 121 pages.

Reviewed by Paul D. Roberts
Free University of Berlin

Learning English can be stimulating as well as instructive and, above all, fun. This is the message which comes through time and again in Mary Hines' new book. It is designed to fulfill the needs of the teacher who is both concerned with the "nuts and bolts" of the language i.e., basic structures, and with what people really say.

While originally intended for adults at the beginning level, the skits have great potential for students at higher levels; particularly, in the realms of stress, intonation and the non-verbal aspects of English.

The rationale behind the skits, given by the author in the introduction, is especially important: and that is, that students are provided with what might be called "an ego shield" by assuming the persona of another individual within the role-playing activity. Experienced teachers of the initial level will immediately recognize the value of any technique which encourages students to reduce their inhibitions and self-con-

sciousness.

The book is arranged into thirty skits, each with a title and a statement of the notion(s) and structure(s) to be practiced therein. At the end of each skit are two types of exercises: the first intended for comprehension confirmation and the second suggesting improvisational activities. These improvisations are mostly of two varieties: one for the purpose of follow-up reinforcement and the other for more imaginative experimentation.

The format is much improved by the new, more mature illustrations and the elimination of certain stereotypic sex roles.

All in all, this is a fine little book, cleverly written and imaginatively arranged, which provides the learner with ample opportunities for developing those crucial strategies of dealing with the unpredictable. It is to be certain that student and teacher alike will derive many hours of pleasure from its use in addition to quite valuable instruction.
    TN 9/77

SIX STORIES FOR ACTING

By George R. McCallum (Portland, Ore.: ELS International, 1976)

Reviewed by Donald L. F. Nilsen
Arizona State University

My wife, Alleen Pace Nilsen, teaches children's and adolescent literature at ASU; in the past she has taught English as a Foreign Language at various universities, and whenever she does, she combines these two methods, for she believes as I do, that one of the best ways of teaching EFL is through the use of children's and adolescent literature. I feel that the selections and the adaptations made by George McCallum were appropriate and effective to reach the upper-intermediate level he was aming at. The fact that he chose excerpts from both British and American liter-

ature enhances the quality of the book, and it is a very convenient and pedagogically sound fact that there are tape recordings of the selections read by readers speaking the same dialect (British or American) as did the original author. The materials are also pedagogically sound in that unlike many other materials of a literary nature, they involve the students very actively in their performance (even to the point of costuming and plots if desired). The questions at the ends of the selections are generally good, especially the open ended ones having students conjecture on what would

have happened if. . . The only difficulty I found was that the materials were so condensed that there was an occasional flashback, aside or other transition that was a bit difficult to manage, without being forced to re-read the passage to get matters straight.

The six adapted excerpts were taken from "Frankenstein" by Mary Shelley, "The Cop and the Anthem" by O. Henry, "A Mad Tea-Party" by Lewis Carroll, "Washington Square" by Henry James, "Dick Spindler's Family Christmas" by Bret Harte, and "Dinner for David" by Charles Dickens. The three primary criteria for these choices were characterization, suspense, and humor, and these three criteria are very well met. David Copperfield, Dick Spindler, and the characters in "Washington Square" are especially well developed. Irony was used very effectively to build suspense. Frankenstein's monster had convinced Frankenstein that he would be perfectly peaceful if only he had a wife, and Frankenstein began to create a monster wife, until he considered the possibility that the monster wife may reject the original monster, or that together they might create monster children that would cause all kinds of problems. The ending is also suspenseful: "Perhaps he (the monster) is nearer than we think—and listening to what we are saying."

"The Cop and the Anthem" is even more ironic. In order to get arrested and sent to a nice warm jail with warm food, Soapy broke a plate glass window, didn't pay for a large meal, tried to molest a girl, and took someone's umbrella. The cop didn't believe he broke the window; he had to wash dishes for the meal; the girl didn't mind being molested, and the umbrella he took had already been stolen from someone else. Finally he went to a chapel where he heard a hymn that made him want to change his ways, and it was then that a cop saw him and decided after all that he had been the one who had broken the window.

When Dick Spindler struck gold and decided to break with the tradition of throwing a drunken brawl, and invite his relatives to a family Christmas followed by an open house, instead, his friends wanted to get even with him for spoiling their fun. They were going to drop firecrackers down the chimney, until they met one of the relatives—Kate—who they decided was even more fun than the drunken brawl would have been. I'm sure EFL students would enjoy watching (or role playing) David Copperfield's getting duped in the restaurant.

251

William first tells David that the beer is poison, but in order to keep it from going to waste he'll drink it, since he does it all the time and is therefore immune to its effects. Then he eats some of David's beef, saying that it will reduce the harmful effects of the beer. After that he has a pie-eating contest with David, and, of course, wins. Finally, he tells David such a sob story that David gives him an additional shilling, adding a nice ironic twist.

The stories are also humorous. Most of the irony mentioned above not only builds suspense, but adds to the humor as well. In addition our expectations are often violated in a number of humorous ways. In "A Mad Tea-Party," the Hare asks "Why is a raven like a writing desk?" but never bothers to answer the riddle. The Mad Hatter recites a poem with which we are all familiar, but somehow it doesn't come out exactly right:

Twinkle, twinkle, little bat!
How I wonder what you're at!
Up above the world you fly,
Like a tea-tray in the sky.

And Alice has a strange dialogue with the Hare and the Hatter when they ask her to have some more tea. Alice says, "More? I haven't had any tea yet, so I can't have more," to which the Hatter replies "You mean you can't have less. It's very easy to have more when you haven't had any." So let me conclude this review by saying that the book is better. Don't be like the Mad Hatter and ask me" . . . than what?"

TN 9/77

THE MIND'S EYE

Alan Maley, Alan Duff and Francoise Grellet. Cambridge: Cambridge University Press, 1980. Student's Book, 96 pp. Paperback, $5.95. Teacher's Book, 42 pp. Paperback, $6.95.

Reviewed by Ann Raimes
Hunter College, CUNY

The Mind's Eye catches the reader's eye immediately. On the cover is a color reproduction of Magritte's *Le Faux Miroir*, a close-up of, at first glance, a regular eye—but wait, aren't those clouds in the blue of the iris? A quick flip through the 96 pages of the student's book intrigues the reader even more: mysterious, striking or amusing pictures, Escher, more Magritte, more color, picture sequences, cartoons and doodles. This doesn't look like an ESL book. There's no mention of books, homework, teacher, John and Mary, no line drawings of short-skirted secretaries with wide eyes, pert bosoms and rounded buttocks, no pictures of foreign students smiling with glee at the latest pattern practice, no photographs of tourist landmarks. Sighs of relief all round. But it is a book "intended for language learners—mother tongue and foreign language alike—who need, and want, language practice." And it does provide a great deal of practice in speaking and writing in situations that will engage the eyes and the minds of both students and teachers.

The Student's Book is divided into fifteen sections: Portraits, Objects, Mystery, Collages, Split Cartoons and the like. Each section contains a full-page picture, a set of exercises, more pictures of the same category with exercises, and a double-page spread of pictures to use in any communicative situations that the book, teachers or students suggest. The exercises are designed so that students work in pairs or small groups and then communicate what they produce to the rest of the class. Throughout, the aim of the exercises is to get students freely associating, thinking, speaking and writing in English, and listening and responding to each other as language users. The only controls are those provided by the pictures and the limits of the exercises. There are no sentence rules or paragraph patterns for students to follow. And that is a virtue, for the students are encouraged to attempt to express their ideas without being locked into a grammatical or rhetorical cage. Many of the exercises are inferential: not just, "Describe the picture," but questions like, "What is outside the frame of the picture?" "If you had to give a one-word title to this picture, what would it be?" and "How does the picture make you feel?"

What is most appealing about this book is its adult, stimulating material, which, without being condescending, is useful at all levels of language learning. As the authors point out, with non-verbal material the level is "determined by the user, not by the material." The following tasks, based on a picture of two men sitting back to back on a train, have no inherent level of difficulty in them that restricts them to elementary, intermediate or advanced levels of language learning: Where are these two men? Who are they? What do they do? What exactly is each of them doing right now? Where are they going? Imagine these two men keep a diary. What does each of them write for that day? Learners use their own powers of observation and inference and the language at their disposal to respond.

To help teachers adapt the pictures to all student levels and to use other pictures in an equally creative way to stimulate communication in the classroom, the 42-page Teacher's Book is a treasure trove. Teachers looking for right answers to the exercises in the student's book won't find them here. This teacher's book doesn't give answers. It does something far more valuable. It suggests sixteen techniques that teachers can use with different types of pictures, techniques that get students to remember, record, imagine, question each other, and argue. Detailed instructions are given on how to organize the class so that students will work in groups, then move on to another group and share information, and then report to the class as a whole. The principle at work here is that of creating an "information gap" in the classroom with pictures that not all the students see, or simply with the ideas that some of the students have and communicate to others. The last fourteen pages of the Teacher's Book are more traditional in that they deal with the material in the Student's Book, chapter by chapter. Comments are suggestive, not prescriptive: ideas for other pictures to use, other techniques, other questions.

At the heart of these books is attention to meaning, to real usage, and to real people using real language. In Earl Stevick's basic ESL bibliography (in *A Way and Ways*, Newbury House, 1980), he recommends the introduction to *Drama Techniques in Language Learning* by two of the authors of *The Mind's Eye*, Alan Maley and Alan Duff (Cambridge University Press, 1978). Eminently readable and full of common sense, this introduction emphasizes the need for language classes to recognize meaning, intention, role, shared knowledge, and feeling and to include real communication in place of those endless discussions with "faceless citizens with conveniently pronounceable name like Brown and Grey, who rarely state anything but the obvious." *The Mind's Eye* develops this idea and provides teachers with a wealth of communicative activities that will find a place in any syllabus where the concern is to engage the students in as much language activity as possible, talking and listening to each other in groups, taking risks, and developing fluency. □

TN 8/81

ENGLISH: SING IT!

Millie Grenough
(McGraw-Hill, Inc., 1976)
Pupil's Edition, $3; Teacher's Edition,
$4.64; 2 tape cassettes, $20

Reviewed by Alice H. Osman
Adult Learning Center
LaGuardia Community College

For those ESL teachers who have already used singing in English as supplemnetary activity in their classrooms, and for those who have wanted to and haven't quite dared, *English: Sing It!* is a most welcome event. Two cassettes and a 56-page, 8½" × 11" soft-cover volume complete the "kit" which will surely help make superb song leaders of even those souls who feel they "can't sing a note." The slim volume slips quite nicely into those handy pockets featured on the inside covers of students' ring binders making it easily retrievable at "song time" in the classroom.

Sing It! contains 39 traditional, folk, and popular songs ranging from "Clementine" and "Oh, Susanna" to selections from Woody Guthrie, Pete Seeger, and Carole King—to mention only a few. The collection is quite clearly aimed at adults (from the teens and upwards) although a few children's songs are included as well. Many of the songs have repeated lines so that less advanced students can easily join in and feel themselves part of the singing group without immediately learning *all* of the words.

The sub-title of this collection is "A structured presentation of spoken English through the use of songs." We all know, however, that it is rather difficult to find traditional songs that follow the normal word order of spoken English. What is one to do? Exercise a bit of poetic license and change a few items (a practice long advocated by this reviewer)! This has, in fact, been done by the author so that in numerous songs, lexical or structural changes have been made. One song familiar to us all is "Clementine" and in the *Sing It!* version, it goes like this:

In a cavern, in a canyon, excavating
    for a mine,
Lived a miner, forty-niner and his
    daughter, Clementine.
She was light and like a fairy, and
    her shoes were number nine,
Herring boxes without topses were
    sandals for Clementine. (etc.)

And it works! For the most part, the structural and lexical changes made in most of the songs are quite acceptable. However, I did find some changes a bit jarring: "Dem Bones" changed to "Those Bones" seems to jolt me out of my seat altogether and I find the *Sing It!* version of "Go, Tell It on the

Mountain" *totally* altered from the two versions known to me.

An attempt has been made to group the songs in the table of contents by their main grammatical structures. Sometimes this works and sometimes it doesn't. "Michael, Row the Boat Ashore" does very well in being classified under "imperatives" while "Rock My Soul" (with new verses by the author) misses the boat altogether except for the repeated title line. I feel that it might better have been classified under simple present tense.

Other special features worth noting include: eminently practical teaching tips (several pages in the teacher's edition); brief explanations of the songs establishing their places on the American scene; and the index of grammatical features. Generous illustrations add greatly to the happy tone of the collection, although it is a bit disappointing that the drawings do not convey more character and cultural information than they do.

The tape cassettes are pure listening pleasure! The male and female vocalists perform in an unpretentious manner, and their diction is almost impeccable. The accompaniments are beguiling in their simplicity, artistry, sweetness and innocence (dare one use these words in the times we live in?) and at the same time, bounce and verve. The tempi of several selections are deliberately slowed down to accommodate the listener's being able to "get" the sounds of the language. If there is any criticism of the tapes, it is that a few (and only a very few) of the songs are pitched too high for average untrained singing voices.

In conclusion, one can sense that the project that led to *Sing It!* has been a labor of love and joy, not only for the author, but for those who assisted her (staff and students of the Institute de Estudio Norteamericanos in Barcelona as well as members of her own family).

Sing It! the volume itself but especially the accompanying cassettes—will be a definite asset in many an ESL/EFL classroom in the U.S. and abroad.   *TN 4/77*

IF YOU FEEL LIKE SINGING

Alice H. Osman and Jean McConochie.
New York: Longman, Inc., 1979. 92 pgs.

Reviewed by Robert King
Miami-Dade Community College

Introduction. The situation is a familiar one. You have just finished the chapter on the present perfect and as you are leaving the classroom, you can't help but notice the hard glaze in your students' eyes. You remember that the same students who, only the day before, were guffawing even at your worst jokes, today were unable to distinguish between a funny story and a set of directions for an exercise. No doubt about it, they need a break, but the weekend is still three days away. You look at your syllabus: no help there; you've got the passive and past perfect coming up. What can you do with a group that is afflicted with a disease that the French have described so well—*ennui?* You can sing the blues— or you can just plain sing. This, at least, is the advice of Osman and McConochie in their latest book *If You Feel Like Singing.* While many of us in ESL have long been using song in the classroom, there may remain some skeptics of the pedagogical usefulness of singing. I would first, then, like to review some reasons for classroom singing.

Rationale. In the first place, singing can be fun. It takes the students away from a direct involvement with language study and, as Widdowson has pointed out, the direct approach may not always be the best one. Songs can also be used

to reinforce recently taught structures. In addition, singing and listening to songs can serve as practice for both pronunciation and aural comprehension. (This is especially true when "talking through" a song.)

One point that may be overlooked when teaching songs is the possibility of enculturation (which is in no way synonymous with indoctrination!) It can be persuasively argued that singing is at the heart of every culture. Learn the traditional songs of a country and you gain a subtle kinship with that culture and its psyche.

The Book. Strong words, some may say, but it's easy for those who can play an instrument and/or sing. What about the closet (or more precisely water closet) singers? Singing in the shower is fine, but the classroom?! With the help of *If You Feel Like Singing,* the answer is *yes.* Osman and McConochie have chosen, for the most part, traditional favorites that all Americans should know: songs of youth and love ("You Are My Sunshine"), work and play ("I've Been Workin' On The Railroad"), war and protest ("The Hammer Song"), gospel songs and spirituals ("Rock-a-My-Soul"), and western songs ("Home on the Range").

This well-designed ESL songbook,

however, is not "all play and no work." Each song is a three-part presentation. The first part is a brief description of the song: its creation and its role in American culture and music. This part also includes a short section on words and phrases the students may not recognize. The second part is the song itself with the notes for singing and the chords for playing the guitar. (There are even diagrams of the chords for beginning guitarists.) This section also includes singing tips, which are generally interesting. The third and last part is a set of three exercises, graded according to difficulty.

Besides this tripartite arrangement, the authors have added two sections that make this good ESL songbook an excellent one. The first "appendix" is a series of tips for teaching the songs (or any song). These are extremely helpful, even for veteran ESL songmakers. The second "appendix" is even more helpful for doing language work in addition to having fun. The authors have made an excellent chart ("Songs At a Glance") that lists each song, its page number, major grammatical structures in the song as well as selected pronunciation features, and finally, the activities suggested for each song.

Besides this, lest anyone begin to think, "Well, that's fine for singers and guitarists, but I can't sing," the authors have nipped that objection in the bud. They have provided a tape with all the songs, including some interesting new arrangements of old favorites.

In spite of the general excellence of this book, there are some problems. First of all, the choice of some songs is questionable. While it is clear that lack of space precludes longer songs (such as choosing "Oh! Susanna" instead of "Old Folks at Home"), there are still some songs that, in my opinion, are not traditional classics, e.g., "Go Tell Aunt Rhody," "All the Pretty Little Horses," and "Pat on the Railway." Interestingly enough, the first and last of these examples are two of the longest songs in the book. Also, I was not particularly enamored of (and this is admittedly subjective) singing about "poor little lambie" with "the bees and butterflies peckin' out its eyes."

Besides the song selection, there is a problem, I believe, with the suggested activities. Although the songs can be taught to all levels, the activities are usually aimed at low to low-intermediate ESL students. This is unfortunate in such a fine book, but these activities might well suggest others more appropriate to each teacher's specific classroom situation.

Finally, and this is a minor complaint, the tape is not as good as the book. The voices on the tape, except for one, are weak and sometimes off-key. Accompanying such a fine book, this tape was a disappointment for me.

In conclusion, while there are a few problems with this book, it nonetheless stands out as an excellent pedagogical tool to soften that glaze in the students' eyes. In a directed manner, Osman and McConochie have given us an effective alternative to throwing in the towel on "Oh-hell-it's Monday" days. Next time it happens, make it a "Thank-God-it's-Friday" day—with a song.

Reprinted from *Gulf TESOL Newsletter*, Winter, 1980

TN 4/80

VISUAL AIDS FOR CLASSROOM INTERACTION

Susan Holden, editor. 1978. London: Modern English Publications, Ltd.

Reviewed by Joyce Gilmour Zuck
The University of Michigan

Visual Aids for Classroom Interaction is a thoughtful little book which most people will never pick up. Unfortunately, "visual aids" usually refer to a very narrow range of pictorial classroom materials which have developed strong advocates and equally strong opponents. Furthermore, the range of activities associated with the more traditional visual aids has been more limited than the aids themselves. Therefore, my reaction to this book might have been indifference had I not been first introduced to the second half of the title, namely, "Classroom Interaction."

I think we have neglected too long the small numbers of speakers of other languages who find themselves scattered throughout the monolingual classrooms in our school systems. The one or two limited English speakers have been sent out of the room to practice with an adult tutor or to the back of the room to practice (!) with a language master. Not only are we failing to improve the English of these limited English speakers at any significant rate but we are also failing to expand the linguistic and cultural horizons of the monolingual Anglo children in our classes. This little book suggests to my mind a new direction for classroom activities in two or more languages; but it also does much more.

Holden indicates in the preface that the collection of twelve articles falls into three main sections: a survey of visual aids in language teaching, followed by specific examples; communication games; and, finally, the use of the overhead projector in developing and presenting visual aids. However, I would like to organize my comments around just two topics: the functions of visual aids including the role of ambiguity in those functions and the range of courses in which visuals are useful. These two topics appear in one form or another in almost all the articles.

An understanding of the function of visuals in language practice and everyday life is central to their exploitation. In spite of the many changes in language teaching methodology in the last few years, Bryne still sees the dialogue as an important bridge for the language practice activities that occur between presentation and free use. Bryne notes two functions of visuals in such practice: "to serve as a context for language and, significantly, to convey those dimensions of meaning which cannot at this level be conveyed by language alone" (p. 10). In contrast, Shaw and Taylor note that 'real life' pictures in newspapers, magazines, and textbooks differ in purpose in that they are "generally used to illustrate information rather than convey it" (p. 18). Corder has noted that in every day life pictures are the *object* of the activity rather than an accessory. Corder further observed that talk about pictures occurs *"after* rather than *while* we are 'using' them and our discussions are critical rather than descriptive" (Corder 1966; quoted by Byrne, p. 10).

Perhaps the lack of agreement on the function of visuals has led naturally to a lack of agreement on the form of the visuals. Although Holden does not see the articles as contradictory (preface), there is an apparent lack of agreement on the desirability of ambiguity in visuals. The views expressed range from avoid it, tolerate it, build it in, to you can't avoid it. The reasoning behind the views is equally provocative. Brims is very explicit: "It is fairly obvious that pictorial ambiguity should generally be avoided" (p. 60). Though citing Richards' (English Language Journal 20) argument that the ambiguity of pictures adds to their value, Brims maintains that students bring their various cultural experiences into play to find multiple interpretation of even stick figures. I agree that a teacher should not allow his personal interpretation of a picture to be any more influential (correct) than anyone else's. However, I have had excellent results by asking students to substantiate their personal interpretations and to discuss and rank the relative possibility, probability, or necessity of the conclusions reached, by the members of the class. In my experience, interpretations based on "insufficient evidence" amount only to guesses. In this situation, any guess (including the teacher's) is as possible as anyone else's and doesn't lead to very responsible or even very interesting language use.

In what may have been intended as reassurance to the insecure artist in all of us, Shaw and Taylor encourage teachers and students to make their own visuals and not to worry about clarity; however, they use an unfortunate example. They comment that it is an advantage for a graph not to be clear because this lack of clarity leads to discussion and gives the students reasons to have gotten incorrect answers (p. 18). However, I disagree with this illustration; while good pictures can be unclear, it is not in the nature of good graphs to be unclear.

Kerr also encourages limited ambiguity. "Although most of the pictures should be immediately identifiable, there are advantages in including a number which are not altogether easy to recognize, particularly for more advanced students. This will enable them to practice language expressing uncertainty or caution.

For Bryne, "no picture is ever complete." The potential ambiguity of a piece of visual material is easily exploited because the language learner will bring his own experience to the interpretation. He provides a simple illustration of a woman looking out a window and a complex one of a busy city. I have found that most students agree that any picture worth a second glance in real life has its own built-in ambiguity. The obvious exception is the complexity rather than ambiguity which is prevalent in technical and scientific illustrations and graphics.

From these differing points of view on the single issue of ambiguity, it should be obvious that this collection is not just a set of pat exercises for a routine set of visuals; rather it is a thought-stretching excursion into the use of a variety of visual materials in new settings.

Throughout the book there is an emphasis on activities that a person might enjoy in his own language. Let me illustrate two activities which could be used to supplement a grammatically based syllabus. Wright suggests that slight changes make all the difference:

In teaching prepositions many teachers have, traditionally, placed a pen on a book and asked, 'Where's the pen?' They have meant, 'What is the English sentence. . . .' However, if the teacher asks the pupil to look at and try to remember the positions of a *variety of objects* and then to turn away, the question, 'Where's the pen?' becomes meaningful. The pupil, now having turned his back on the objects, must try to remember. His mind is filled wth the idea of 'where' and the object's position rather than with the English sentence for an obvious fact. (p. 20)

Another example which could be used for imperatives or prepositions (or a variety of other speech patterns) is Cripwell's Leggo man (p. 51). One student has access to a model and either describes it to the others or responds to

their questions in an attempt to help them build a similar complicated figure out of Leggo pieces.

Kerr suggests cue cards as a means of organizing pair work. Five examples of activity types are given and four sets of pictures which can be made into cards are appended to the book. The activities are notable because the pairs are given 'sufficiently interesting tasks' and a clear understanding of instructions with a minimum of teacher control/help/intervention. To practice "making, granting and refusing requests" (a common task in a notional/functional syllabus), students use 10-12 cards (in this case, household objects) and a dice. They are given the following instructions:

A. 1. Pick up a card.
   2. Ask B to lend you the object pictured. Give a reason why you need it.

B. 1. Throw the dice.
      2a. If the dice is *even*, agree to A's request but make a condition.
      or
      2b. If the dice is *odd*, refuse A's request and give a suitable reason.

A. 1. Make a comment (of thanks or complaint) about what B says.
   2. Replace the card.
      (Instructions abridged from p. 45)

Kerr then gives some illustrative realizations of the activity. The activity promotes creativity, encourages anticipation of possible responses, and provides for variation in proficiency level.

Visuals for adult language practice are presented. Byrne's 'Let's Go Together' (p. 50) can be used as is or varied for any age group of socially motivated language learners. This activity seems to encourage language use related to its task but not required by it. Furthermore, the activity is interesting enough in its own right to be an ice-breaking party game among native speakers of the same language. For the technically motivated adult, 'How to change the wheel of a car' (p. 28) is an excellent example of Harrison's technique of "moveable aids." Using a sticky, reusable clay, called Blutack, he has developed a system of layering of visual material that provides

both flexibility and a three-dimensional quality that seems to appeal to adults. His aids encourage technical discussion of alternative procedures and can even include conversational negotiations and expressions of feelings. Harrison makes the interesting observation that "it is easier to pull an aid to pieces than to try to reassemble it" (p. 28). Most visual aids are designed to be assembled in the classroom rather than disassembled. (Further attraction to this method lies in the neat storage of the pieces in 9x12 envelopes.)

Additional examples of unusual uses of visual material such as wall charts and non-pictorial aids could be given. However, there is one article that alone makes the book worth reading. In "Communicative Games-2", Geddes and McAlpine describe and illustrate four types of games which provide clear student directions, maximum student involvement, natural language use, and suggestions for developing similar activities (pp. 54-57). The same principles are involved for all four types of games:

Since the games require students to transfer information, and the results are visible, these language functions will be practiced by the students as they interact, by trial and error, to achieve successful transfer of information. It is, therefore, by encouraging linguistic resourcefulness through genuine interaction that these games can develop oral communcation skills. (pp. 56-57)

In addition to encouraging natural use of language, the best ideas in this book have another feature in common: Simplicity. Harrison has frequently told me, "Teachers like simple aids." This statement could be the put down of all time for teachers. Or it could be a recognition of something that kids have known for a long time but toy manufacturers and ESL publishers have ignored: Simple things have the flexibility to adapt to multiple uses and are, therefore, worth playing with and talking about.

I encourage you to look for this book in spite of its title. Holden has collected many simple ideas into a small, readable handbook which just might make language classes the scene of "classroom interaction" by using visual materials in essentially real-life ways.

TN 6/80

CARING AND SHARING IN THE FOREIGN LANGUAGE CLASS

By Gertrude Moskowitz
(Newbury House: Rowley, Mass., 1978)

Reviewed by Audrey Reynolds
Northeastern Illinois University

ESOL teachers who wish to encourage real communication in the classroom will be interested in Gertrude Moskowitz's *Caring and Sharing in the Foreign Language Class,* for the book is designed to help language teachers become aware

of the insights which humanistic educational theory provides and learn how to apply such insights in order to foster real communication in the classroom.

Three of the five chapters (the first two and the last) introduce Ms. Mosknowitz's humanistic approach to language teaching, which emphasizes that teachers need to make educational experience relate to students' personal lives and that teachers should engage in affective education by helping students develop positive self-concepts. In these chapters, Ms. Moskowitz makes it clear that humanistic teaching in the foreign language class should focus on having students discuss positive experiences and emotions rather than negative ones. Although this emphasis on the positive may strike some readers as unrelentingly sweet, Ms. Moskowitz justifies her decision by explaining that she accentuates the positive because most students are already familiar with the negative in their lives and, perhaps equally important, because few language teachers have the training in clinical psychology which one needs if one is to help students handle negative experiences and emotions.

The third and fourth chapters provide the "heart" of the book. The third chapter presents 100 communication exercises which are designed to give students an opportunity for both affective and linguistic development, as well as real communication about themselves and their experiences. The fourth chapter, which provides 20 additional exercises, is designed to help teachers learn how to create their own humanistic exercises.

Although it is impossible in a review of this scope to give an indication of all the topics which Ms. Moskowitz chooses for classroom discussion, a sampling will indicate the range. Topics vary from having students discuss their values to their fantasies, from their memories to their relationships with others. As a result, the exercises have a universal appeal which makes most of them useable in most ESL classrooms.

The outstanding feature of the exercises is that they are presented with the kind of practical information that language teachers need. For instance, in addition to stating the affective purpose of each exercise (e.g., to encourage students to verbalize positive feelings about themselves or one another), Ms. Moskowitz states its linguistic purpose (e.g., to practice questions or particular verb tenses or particular vocabulary) and linguistic level (beginning, intermediate, etc.) which students need in order to participate in the exercise. In addition, there is an appendix which provides a cross-reference index where teachers can discover which exercises are particularly useful for particular linguistic constructions, along with two appendices which provide vocabulary supplements of words which students will need to express their feelings about themselves and one another.

Thus, the book is a useable source of ideas for almost any ESL teacher, for in spite of the foreign language emphasis of the book, most of the exercises could be used in ESL programs. In addition, those who work in teacher-training programs might find the book useful for students who need to learn more than purely linguistic approaches to ESL teaching.   *TN 10/79*

Bank; Welcome Handbooks: An Easy Bilingual Project; Planning Successful Field Trips; Using the Telephone and Directory With Ease; and others devoted to career discussions and consumer education. There is even a section on successful fund-raising projects as vocabulary-builders and money-makers. Most examples are drawn from high school and adult populations, but the underlying strategies are adaptable for younger ESL groups.

The most practical aspect of this exciting handbook lies in the appendices. These tell you about duplicating masters, appropriate selection of textbooks, workbooks, and criteria for choosing worthwhile teaching aids. As an added bonus the authors have provided an up-to-date professional bibliography, consisting of approximately 140 entries, each of which is classified according to genre. The categories are: article; game; handbook; reference book; textbook and workbook.

There are two minor criticism which I believe detract from the excellent caliber of this book. One is the authors' inability to resist the use of catchy titles in some of the chapter subheadings (i.e., "The ESL Teacher: Resourcefulness Is Our Middle Name" "They've Got Your Number—Using the Telephone;" You Can Really Go a *Long Distance* With A Great Deal of Free Material and Imagination;" etc.) Cute, but too contrived for a book of this professional quality.

The other comment reflects this reviewer's structuralist training. I bridled at the absence of accent marks (which are orthographic markers influencing meaning) in the printed versions of the Spanish Welcome Books written by the students of Passaic High School. Hardcore prescriptivism gives way before the spoken language, but, for me, the printed language is still sacred. These minor points fade into oblivion, however, when held against the treasures in store for those who choose this book.

The most impressive feature of *What To Do* is the overall philosophy that permeates its every page. Section II embodies the authors' credo: "Empathy, Sensitivity, Learning: *Who** We Are Teaching Comes First." (*I warned you—the style is conversational.) It is in this section that Scheraga and Maculaitis really get to the heart of the matter—the need for the teacher to understand and emphatize with the culture and values of the students who are studying English as their second language. The advice offered to ESL teachers is worth sharing with *all* teachers who are attempting to reach students of different backgrounds.

What to do after reading this review? Get a copy of this excellent new book!

TN 12/81

WHAT TO DO UNTIL THE BOOKS ARRIVE...AND AFTER

(Jean D'Arcy Maculaitis and Mona Scheraga
—Alemany Press, 1981)

by **Gladys Nussenbaum**
William Paterson College of New Jersey

From the very first page of *What To Do Until The Books Arrive . . . And After* (here after referred to as: What To Do), the reader is impressed by the warm, caring style of these two successful ESL teachers who, as authors, want to share what they have learned with others in the profession. The Dedication, Acknowledgements and Preface by Jean Maculaitis and Mona Scheraga are notes from loving parents, when compared to the usual perfunctory tributes paid by most textbook writers. Here is a 161 page handbook for *all* ESL teachers—the seasoned as well as the unseasoned. It is written in the informal register; living proof that effective prose should be lively and pleasant to *hear*.

What To Do's format is straight-forward, with twelve helpful chapters, including: Setting Up the ESL Classroom; The Language

Appendix A: Authors List

Appendix B: Bibliography of Articles by Issue

TESOL Newsletter No. 1 (*Edited by Harold Allen*) June 1966 (6 pg) (Includes insert on the TESOL Constitution and the TESOL Constitution, 4 pg)

Alfred Aarons, Editor 1967-1970

Volume 1.

Number 1, April 1967 (24 pg)

Allen, Harold B. (From the TESOL President)

Anderson, Theodore. The Bilingual in the Southwest (Reprinted from the Spring 1967 *Florida FL Reporter*)

Malmstrom, Jean. Dialects (Reprinted from the Winter 1966-7 *Florida FL Reporter*)

Finocchiaro, Mary. Random Thoughts on Teaching English as a Second Language (Reprinted from January 1965 *Florida FL Reporter*)

Aarons, Alfred C. TESOL Bibliography

Bowen, J. Donald. The Teaching of English to Speakers of Other Languages (Abridged from the January 1965 *Florida FL Reporter*)

Bell, Paul. The Other Side of the Coin (From the Spring 1967 *Florida FL Reporter*)

Volume II

Numbers 1 and 2, January-March 1968 (40 pg)

(San Antonio Convention Issue)

Anthony, Edward M. (From the TESOL President)

Cervenka, Edward J. TESOL-The State of the Art Today

Stevick, Earl W. UHF and Microwaves in Transmitting Language Skills

Marquwardt, William F. The Tenth International Congress of Linguists: Implications for Teaching English as a Second Language.

Bowen, J. Donald. Terminal Behavior in Language Teaching

Gaarder, A. Bruce. Statement before the Special Subcommittee on Bilingual Education of the Committee on Labor and Public Welfare of the United States Senate, May 18, 1967.

Croft, Kenneth. Some Implications of the Phrase "As Everybody Knows"

Alatis, James E. The First Annual Convention of TESOL, Miami Beach 1967

Aarons, Alfred C. TESOL Materials Bibliography

Aarons, Alfred C. Quote and Unqote

Number 3, May 1968 (8 pg)

Bell, Paul W. (From the TESOL President)

Howe, Harold, II. Cowboys, Indians and American Education

Number 4, November 1968 (16 pg)

Bell, Paul W. "A Letter from the TESOL President"

Wissot, Jay. The Teacher, His Roles and the Cuban Student

Aarons, Alfred C. ESL/EFL Materials Bibliography

Inclan, Rosa. Visuals to the Rescue of the ESL Teacher

Volume III

Number 1, February 1969 (16 pg)

(Chicago Convention Issue)

Kaplan, Robert B. 1968 Summer ESOL Institute at USC

Northwest Newsletter, October 1968. Alaska Readers for First Graders.

Volume IV

Number 1, February 1970 (28 pg)

(San Francisco Convention Issue)

Wardhaugh, Ronald. Teaching English to Speakers of Other Languages: The State of the Art.

TESL and Bilingual Education Urged (From the *Gallup, New Mexico Independent*, January 27, 1970)

Richard Light, Editor 1970-1971

Numbers 2 and 3, September-December 1970 (32 pg)

Harris, David P. 1970 TESOL Presidential Report to the Membership

Marckwardt, Albert. Statements of Qualifications and Guidelines for Preparation of Teachers of English to Speakers of Other Languages.

Spolsky, Bernard. Getting Down to the Grass Roots: Affiliate Affairs

Position Paper by the Committee on Sociopolitical Concerns of Minority Groups in TESOL, Feb. 1, 1970

Kaplan, Robert B. Up from the Grass Roots (with Muddy Feet): or, The Race Against Obsolence

Volume V

Number 1, February 1971 (20 pg)

(New Orleans Convention Issue)

Spolsky, Bernard. Attitudinal Aspects of Second Language Learning

Number 2, June 1971 (16 pg)

Finocchiaro, Mary. TESOL Presidential Report to the Membership, 1971

Volume V Cont'd.

Numbers 3 and 4, September-December 1971 (36 pg)

(Washington Convention Issue)

Shugrue, Michael F. The Price of Accountability in English

Shuy, Roger W. Social Dialects and Second Language Learning: A Case of Territorial Overlap

Fasold, Ralph W. What Can an English Teacher Do About Non-standard Dialect?

Bell, Paul W. Bilingual Education—A Second Look.

Ruth Wineberg, Editor 1972-1975

Volume VI

Number 1, May 1972 (8 pg)

Washington Convention Report

Harris, David P. Current Issues in ESL

Krear, Serafina. The Forum: Thinking and Feeling in Two Cultures.

Number 2, November 1972 (8 pg)

(San Juan Convention Issue)

Taschler, Kathrine and Richard Hitt. Teacher-Training in ESL For Adults: New Jersey Suggests a Model

Seward, Bernard. Cross-Cultural Study at the University of Colorado.

(Volume VII)*

Number 3, April 1973 (8 pg)

Viñas de Vasquez, Paquita. The Teaching of English in Puerto Rico

Number 4, July 1973 (16 pg)

("Informal Issue")

Robinett, Betty Wallace. From the President

Book Reviews

TESOL Constitution

Number 5, September 1973 (8 pg)

Adlam, Raymond. TESOL Convention 1973

Number 6, November 1973 (8 pg)

Blatchford, Charles. TESOL Membership

Book Reviews

Volume VIII

Numbers 1 and 2, January-March 1974 (8 pg)

(Denver Convention Issue)

Number 3, May 1974 (16 pg)

Saville-Troike, Muriel. Message from the President

Robinett, Betty Wallace. TESOL: Can it be All Things to All Members?

Number 4, July 1974 (8 pg)

(From the Central Office)

Numbers 5 and 6, September-November 1974 (12 pg)

Saville-Troike, Muriel. Message from the President

Mullins, Robert. Choosing Your Overseas Job

Volume IX

Number 1, January 1975 (12 pg)

(Los Angeles Convention Issue.)

New Editor Named

John Haskell, Editor 1975-1983

Number 2, March 1975 (16 pg)

Galvan, Mary. TESOL Conference Roundup: Directions for TESOL 1975-7.

Excerpts from the Convention Program

Book Reviews: Books, Journals and Newsletters

Number 3, May 1975 (12 pg)

Gomes de Matos, Francisco. Humo(u)r: A Neglected Feature in Foreign Language Teaching

Anger, Larry. Some Priorities for a Good ESL Class.

Excerpts from the Convention Program

Larson, Darlene. Lessons That Work

Number 4, July 1975 (12 pg)

Excerpts from Convention Program

Number 5, October 1975 (16 pg)

Llado, Nitza. Report on Bilingual Conference in Chicago

LeClair, Carol. Meeting the TESOL Office Staff

Convention Abstracts

Book Reviews

Report on WATESOL Workshops

Number 6, December 1975 (20 pg)

Troike, Rudolph. ESL Not Appropriate (from the *Linguistics Reporter*, October 1975)

New York Conference Report

Czarnecki, Karen and Joseph Ramos. Counseling-Learning: A Wholistic View of the Learner.

Galvan, Mary. ESL *Is* Appropriate.

Haskell, John. Our Vietnamese

Van Naerssen, Margaret. Tourist ESL

Carlovich, Ann and Ernestine Hazuka. What is Bilingual Education and What Makes Bilingual Programs Work?

Alatis, James E. On Acronyms, Part I.

Book Reviews:

Using English: Your Second Language by Dorothy Danielson and Rebecca Hayden (Carletta Hartsough)

No Hot Water Tonight by Jean Bodman and Michael Lanzano (Carol Taylor and Dick Litwak).

Volume X

Volume XV

Volume XVII Cont'd.

Number 5, October 1983 (32 pg)

Larson, Penny. TESOL in Texas

Mettler, Sally. Exercising Language Options: Speech into Writing—and Back

Humak, Barbara. Cultural Aspects of Prevocational ESL

Day, Cathy and Carol Svendsen. *It Works*: Understanding on the Job

Handscombe, Richard. TESOL Summer Meeting: Toronto 1983 Evaluation in ESL Programs

Schreck, Richard and William Mead. *On Line*: A Course in CALL for an MA Program in TESL

Reviews:

On TESOL 82: Pacific Perspectives on Language Learning and Teaching by Mark A. Clarke and Jean Handscombe (Jim Nattinger)

Fitting In by Margaret Pogemiller Coffey (Ada P. Snyder)

The Third Language by Alan Duff (Phyllis Ryan and Brigitte Chavez)

Kreidler, Carol and Linda Tobash. *The Standard Bearer*: A Report: Collective Bargaining in a Period of Retrenchment

Wallerstein, Nina. Problem-posing Can Help Students Learn

Gage, Julia L. ESL Program in Southeast Asia Refugee Camps

Number 6, December 1983 (32 pg)

Cohen, Andrew D. Reformulating Compositions

Houston Oiling Up for TESOL Convention

Day, Cathy and Richard Hughes. *It Works*: Using the Soaps

Contrasting Commentaries on *It Works*: What do you Mean, 'It Works'? by Karl Krahnke; Neither an Elixir or a Philosophy but 'It Works' by Darlene Larson

Flaitz, Jeffra. The Role Play Comes Alive Through a Technological Twist

Schreck, Richard and John Higgins. *On Line*: The Computer as a Communicative Environment

Reviews: .

Functions of American English by Leo Jones and C. von Baeyer (Jim T. Nibungco)

A Poet's Mind by James Emanuel (Howard Sage)

Absence of Decision by Crawford Goodwin and Michael Nacht (Joel Bloch)

Kreidler, Carol J. *The Standard Bearer*: Some Ups and Some Downs

Gerould, Kim and Lisa Pred. Language Instruction in Cuba

*Volume VII was actually labeled Volume VI